LONGMAN-PENGUIN PUTNAM INC.
VALUE PACKAGES IN EDUCATION

Add these classics to your course for a few dollars more!

Ideal as further reading for any Education course, these Penguin Putnam Inc. titles give students the opportunity to explore contemporary and classic topics in depth. To bundle Penguin Putnam Inc. titles with a Longman Education text, please contact your local Addison Wesley Longman sales representative for ISBN information.

◎ Dahl, *James and the Giant Peach*
◎ Grahame, *The Wind in the Willows*
◎ Taylor, *Roll of Thunder, Hear My Cry*
◎ Toussaint, *Great Books for African American Children*

See overleaf for more Penguin Putnam Inc. titles.

0321076184

Literature for Today's Young Adults

Literature for Today's Young Adults

SIXTH EDITION

Alleen Pace Nilsen
Arizona State University

Kenneth L. Donelson
Arizona State University

Longman

New York   Boston   San Francisco
London   Toronto   Sydney   Tokyo   Singapore   Madrid
Mexico City   Munich   Paris   Cape Town   Hong Kong   Montreal

Publisher: Priscilla McGeehon
Acquisitions Editor: Aurora Martinez-Ramos
Print Supplements Editor: Jennifer Ackerman
Media Supplements Editor: Mark Toews
Full Service Production Manager: Mark Naccarelli
Project Coordination, Text Design, and Electronic Page Makeup: Nesbitt Graphics, Inc.
Design Manager: Wendy Ann Fredericks
Cover Design: Kay Petronio
Cover Photo: Arnold Katz
Print Buyer: Al Dorsey
Printer and Binder: Quebecor World—Taunton
Cover Printer: Coral Graphic Services, Inc.

For permission to use copyrighted material, grateful acknowledgment is made to the copyright holders on pp. 461–462, which are hereby made part of this copyright page.

Library of Congress Cataloging-in-Publication Data
Nilsen, Alleen Pace.
    Literature for today's young adults / Alleen Pace Nilsen, Kenneth L. Donelson.—6th ed.
        p.   cm.
    Includes indexes.
    ISBN 0–321–03788–X
        1. Teenagers—United States—Books and reading. 2. Young adult literature,
English—History and criticism. 3. Young adult fiction, English—History and criticism.
4. Young adult literature, English—Bibliography. 5. Young adult fiction,
English—Bibliography. I. Donelson, Kenneth L. II. Title.

Z1037.A1.N55 2000
028.5'5—dc21   00–021608
                                                                CIP

Please visit our website at http://www.awl.com

ISBN 0–321–03788–X

1 2 3 4 5 6 7 8 9 10—RNT—03 02 01 00

Dedication

To Bob Carlsen from Ken and Alleen,
our beloved teacher, critic, and friend, who never
tired of telling his classes, "Good books people our lives,"
and who never stopped living that truth.

And to our grandchildren who are already
finding some of these books.

From Alleen to Taryn, Britton, Kami,
David, Lauren, Michael, Jim, and Luke

From Ken to Jason, Devon, Valerie, Amanda,
JoJo, Jackie, and Jacob

CONTENTS

PART TWO
Modern Young Adult Reading   111

Chapter Four
The New Realism: Of Life and Problems   113

Chapter Five
The Old Romanticism: Of Wishing and Winning   144

Chapter Six
Adventure, Mysteries, the Supernatural, and Humor From Goose Bumps to Giggles   175

PART THREE

Adults and the Literature of Young Adults   311

Chapter Ten
Evaluating, Promoting, and Using Young Adult Books   313

Chapter Eleven
Literature in the English Class: Short Stories, Novels, Creative Writing, Film, and Thematic Units   357

Chapter Twelve
Censorship: Of Worrying and Wondering   390

SPECIALIZED CONTENTS

Author Statements

Tables and Charts

PREFACE

As we said in the preface to the fifth edition of *Literature for Today's Young Adults*, doing another version is both an obligation and an opportunity because the field of young adult books, along with what it means to be a young adult, is always changing.

Since the first edition, defining the nature of the literary canon has further confused our lives, but determining the "true" canon is no closer than it was twenty years ago or last month. And even a dozen years back, who could have foreseen the emphasis on computers in schools and homes? Or who would have predicted the kinds of violence we have witnessed in the past few years and the ties that some people have made between violence and media—including the music teenagers listen to, the books and Internet messages they read, and the television and movies they view. Because of such changes and the varying opinions that are being expressed, we wrote a new Chapter Three on relationships between teenagers and popular culture. To make room for this chapter, we moved much of Chapter Two (the literary terms illustrated through young adult literature) into Appendix A. Several previous users of the text advised this change because they said by the time they meet their students most of them have had introduction to literature classes. If this is not the case, then the teacher should probably spend some time working with the concepts in Appendix A. But some things are eternal challenges or opportunities for all of us—namely getting the best books out to kids and helping kids learn about the joy of reading.

Young adult literature continues to gain respectability and commercial viability. Even MTV entered the book publishing business this year, and Amazon.com has a large young adult section. Outside of cyberspace, we've been pleased to see more bookstores establishing young adult sections as distinct from children's. The best proof, however, is the continued excellence of authors as good as Robert Cormier, Louis Sachar, Jacqueline Woodson, M. E. Kerr, Robert Lipsyte, Katherine Paterson, Brock Cole, James Bennett, Lois Lowry, Peter Dickinson, Berlie Doherty, Gary Paulsen, Francesca Lia Block, and Philip Pullman.

In this revision, we've tried to take into account all these changes and balance them with the latest books that kids will want to read and to include the best in the field, no matter what the copyright date. We've continued to add many titles and brief descriptions of recommended books, movies, and magazines. While Alleen wrote most of the new Chapter Three on Young Adults and the Media, Ken made a whole new set of Film Boxes. We expanded our use of both Film Boxes and Focus Boxes for new books because adults told us these worked well to photocopy and distribute to young readers.

In the fifth edition, we succumbed to people's requests to provide Focus Boxes containing books about particular ethnic groups. In this edition, we have resisted what seems to us to be an artificial kind of grouping. We made one Focus Box of books in which characters relate across cultures and we made a couple of focus boxes to help adults succeed in using multicultural materials, but in general we tried to move beyond the stage of color-coding books and work them into the main curriculum. Also, we hope to offer a Web site in which each year we can update the Honor List and present some of the Author Boxes deleted from previous editions for lack of space.

As we've said before, we have many reasons for continuing to work on this book, but chief among them is our belief that it is needed and worth doing. When in the late 1970s we surveyed teachers of young adult literature in library science, English, and education departments, an overwhelming majority expressed a need for a scholarly and readable book to provide history and background for the field. One teacher wrote that her major problem "in establishing and promoting the work of the course was the sometimes skeptical view of colleagues about the worth of this literature" and that she would welcome a text to educate professionals in related fields about the growing body of good young adult literature. We hope our book answers some of these needs, not just for academic classes in young adult literature but also for librarians, teachers, counselors, and others working with young people between the ages of 12 and 18.

For our purposes, we define *young adult literature* as any book freely chosen for reading by someone in this age group, which means that we do not make a distinction between books distributed by juvenile divisions and adult divisions of publishing houses. Young people read and enjoy both, and we share in the obvious goal of moving teenagers toward reading more and more adult books.

Throughout the text, we present criteria for evaluating various kinds of books, but these criteria are tentative starting places. Developing evaluation skills comes only with wide reading and practice in comparing books and matching them to particular needs. Similarly, our lists of recommended titles are only a beginning and should be supplemented by your own judgments and by current book-reviewing sources and annual lists of best books compiled by the Young Adult Library Services Association, the editors of *School Library Journal, Booklist,* the *ALAN Review,* the *New York Times, VOYA,* the *English Journal,* and other groups.

Although we know that paperbacks are far more widely read by young people than the original hardbound books, in our book lists we show the hardback publishers (where applicable). We do this to give credit to the companies who found the authors and did the initial editorial and promotion work. Also, by relying on the hardback publishers, we are able to be more consistent and accurate. The paperback publishing industry is fluid, and a title may be published and then go out of print within a few months. To find paperback editions of any of the books we have listed, consult the most recent issue of *Paperbound Books in Print* published annually (with periodic supplements) by R. R. Bowker Company and purchased by most libraries.

A comprehensive Instructor's Manual, written by Elizabeth Wahlquist of Brigham Young University, is being provided by the publisher to accompany the text. It includes such features as chapter summaries, activities, discussion questions, more information on literary terms, and reproducible handouts. A book specfic website is also available at http://www.awl.com/nilsen. This online course companion provides a wealth of resources for both students and instructors using *Literature for Today's Young Adults, Sixth Edition.* Students will find chapter summaries, review questions, annotated web links, periodic updates by the authors, and more. Instructors will have access to a list of useful teaching links and can also take advantage of Syllabus Builder, our comprehensive course management system.

For help in preparing this sixth edition, we acknowledge the support of the English Department at Arizona State University, particularly our secretary Mary Jones. We thank Chris Crowe from Brigham Young University for preparing a new list of Internet recommendations and Diane Tuccillo from the Mesa Public Library for preparing new recommendations for magazines with YA appeal. Our current doctoral students have taught us as much as we have taught them, and we thank Doreen Bardsley, Wendy Glenn, Marie Hardenbrook, Kate Harts, Beth Jones, Dirk Mattson, Susan Ourada, and Julie Robinson. We also thank all of our friends and colleagues who toil the fields of adolescent literature and make it more fruitful and far more fun. Their ideas and words have probably found their way into our pages more than we realize. In alphabetical order and in no particular order of importance, we salute Dick Abrahamson, Dorothy Broderick, Patty Campbell, Betty Carter, Mary K. Chelton, Leila Christenbury, Hazel Davis, Don Gallo, Ted Hipple, Paul Janecsko, Terry Ley, Maia Pank Mertz, Ginger Monseau, Beth and Ben Nelms, Bob Probst, Gary Salvner, John Simmons, Bob Small, Anne Webb, and Jerry Weiss.

Anyone who has read much in the history of English education will recognize how much we owe to the spirits of four great master teachers and writers, four people who were dedicated to reading and adolescent literature—Samuel Thurber, Dora V. Smith, Lou LaBrant, and Dwight Burton. Without them and their work, there never would have been a reason for a book like this.

We thank Nicolette Wickman for help with proofreading and indexing, and we thank critics of the fifth edition and the readers of our manuscript who saved us from more errors than we might have made otherwise: Betty Carter – Texas Women's University, Linda Miller Cleary – University of Minnesota at Duluth, Leila Christenbury – Virginia Commonwealth University, Steven Grubaugh – University of Nevada at Las Vegas, Robert Lamm – Arkansas State University at Jonesboro, Sandra Lott – Montevallo University, Janice Patten – San Jose State University, Peter Schiff – Northern Kentucky University, Elizabeth Wahlquist – Bringham Young University.

We also thank the young adult authors who contributed their statements. Lastly, we thank Ginny Blanford, Longman's Senior acquisitions editor, for supporting us on this edition.

More than a hundred years ago, Edward Salmon justified his work in children's literature by writing:

> It is no uncommon thing to hear children's literature condemned as wholly bad, and some people are good enough to commiserate with me on having waded through so much ephemeral matter. It may be my fault or my misfortune not to be able to see my loss. I have spent many pleasant and I may say not unprofitable hours in company with the printed thoughts of Mr. Kingston, Mr. Ballantyne, Mr. Henty, Jules Verne, Miss Alcott, Miss Mead, Miss Molesworth, Miss Doudney, Miss Younge, and a dozen others, and hope to spend as many more in the time to come as a busy life will permit.*

* Edward Salmon. "Should Children Have a Special Literature?" *The Parent's Review* 1 (June 1890): 399.

Today, it is heartening to consider how many talented people share Edward Salmon's feelings and, like us, feel joy in spending their lives working in a field of literature that is always changing, exciting, and alive.

Alleen Pace Nilsen
Kenneth L. Donelson

Literature for Today's Young Adults

Understanding Young Adults and Books

Young Adults and Their Reading

"Of all passages, coming of age, or reaching adolescence, is the purest, in that it is the loneliest. In birth one is not truly conscious; in marriage one has a partner; even death is faced with a life's experience by one's side," wrote David Van Biema for a special issue of *Life* magazine devoted to *The Journey of Our Lives*.

He went on to explain that going from boy or girl to man or woman is "a huge leap on the slimmest of information." The person who fails grows older without growing wiser and faces ostracism, insanity, or profound sorrow. Because such a debilitated or warped individual is a "drag on the community," the community bands together with the young person to see that the journey is accomplished.[1]

Life would go more smoothly if young people's aspirations were simply to step into the roles of their parents. The job of growing up, however, is more demanding because, at the same time that young people are trying to become adults, they are also trying to show that they are different from their parents. This leaves each generation scrambling to find its own way to be unique, which is one of the reasons that literature for young adults tends to be a contemporary medium. Each generation wants its own stories.

What Is Young Adult Literature?

We recently heard young adults defined as "those who think they're too old to be children but who others think are too young to be adults." In this book, we use the term to include students in junior high as well as those graduating from high school and still finding their way into adult life. By *young adult literature*, we mean anything that readers between the approximate ages of 12 and 18 choose to read (as opposed to what they may be coerced to read for class assignments). When we talk about *children's literature*, we refer to books released by the juvenile or junior division of a publisher and intended for children from prekindergarten to about sixth grade.

While not all libraries have special rooms for young adults, most libraries make an effort to show teenagers that they are no longer considered to be children.

While our definition of *children's literature* is fairly standard, we should caution that not all educators define young adults the same as we do. The Educational Resources Information Clearinghouse (ERIC), for example, defines young adults as those between the ages of 18 and 22, whereas the National Assessment of Educational Progress (NAEP), administered by the Educational Testing Service, refers to "young adults, ages 21 through 25."

We confess to feeling pretentious when referring to a 12- or 13-year-old as a *young adult,* but we shy away from using the term *adolescent literature* because as librarians have confided, "It has the ugly ring of pimples and puberty," and "It suggests *immature* in a derogatory sense." Still, most such college courses in English Departments are entitled *Adolescent Literature,* and, because of our English teaching backgrounds, we find ourselves using the term for variety, along with *teenage books, teen fiction,* and *YA* or *young adult literature.* The terms *juvenile literature, junior novel, teen novel,* and *juvie* have been used in the past, but they became so weighed down with negative connotations that they are seldom heard today. Even with the newer terms of *young adult* and *YA,* some teenagers feel condescended to, so librarians and teachers are looking for alternatives. David Spritz, writing in *Time* magazine in 1999, used the term *teen fiction* for the genre that he said "used to be called" *young-adult novels.*[2] While some librarians and bookstores have experimented with the term *popular literature,* at least in academic circles chances are that *young adult* is so firmly established that it will continue to be used for the near future even though it has the disadvantage of lumping 13-year-olds in with 18-year-olds. With adults, a five-year age difference may not affect choice of subject matter and intellectual and emotional response, but for teenagers even two or three years can make a tremendous difference.

It wasn't until the early 1930s that most publishers divided their offerings into adult and juvenile categories. Today it is sometimes little more than chance whether an adult or juvenile editor happens to get a manuscript. Robert Cormier had never thought of himself as a writer for young people, but when his agent submitted *The Chocolate War* to Pantheon, the editor convinced Cormier that, as good as the book was, it would be simply one more in a catalog of adult books. If it were published for teenagers, however, it might sell well, and it certainly would not be one more in a long string of available adolescent novels. The editor's predictions came true, and Cormier later acknowledged that although his initial reaction to becoming a "young adult" author was one of shock followed by a month-long writer's block, he is grateful for the editorial help, which led to considerable attention from reviewers as well as his first financial success as an author.

People who enjoy reading and talking about books need to feel comfortable in using literary terms efficiently and accurately. The main terms used in this textbook are defined in Appendix A. Before going on to the other chapters in this text, it would probably be a good idea to review those terms to ensure that your understanding of them matches the way they are used throughout this book. Some of you need only a quick review, but for those who have not recently had a literature class, you may want to read and reread the definitions and to work with other class members in finding new examples that test your understanding. This is important because being able to use literary terms:

- Gives you terminology and techniques to use in sharing your insights with young readers.
- Helps you to get insights into authors' working methods so that you get more out of your reading.
- Enables you to evaluate books and assist readers to move forward in developing literature appreciation skills.
- Helps you read reviews, articles, and critical analyses with greater understanding.

A Brief Unsettled Heritage

The decade of the mid-1970s through the mid-1980s may come to be known as the golden age of young adult literature. An editor in the 1980s told us that while he used to count on one hand the number of young adult authors who earned their living exclusively by writing (most were teachers or were partially supported by spouses), he could now name thirty authors writing for teenagers who could accurately be described as affluent because of the way their books were selling.

Contributing to the change was the need by television and movie producers for stories that would appeal to a youth-oriented society. Also, in many schools, teachers who had previously scorned teenage books found themselves facing students who simply could not, or would not, read the so-called classics. Taking a pragmatic approach, these teachers concluded that it was better to teach adolescent literature than no literature at all. This made schools and libraries a primary market for young adult books, especially paperbacks. When the book industry discovered that teenagers were willing to spend their own money for paperbacks, both financial and critical bases began to change.

Ever since the 1970s, educators' interest in young adult books has continued to increase as shown by the success of such publications as *VOYA* (Voice of Youth Advocates) and *The ALAN Review* (Assembly on Literature for Adolescents of NCTE), the numbers of teachers and librarians attending workshops on contemporary young adult books, the adoption of whole-language teaching methods, the inclusion in reading and literature textbooks of YA literature, the increased number of professional articles and books on the subject, and the honoring of such writers as Robert Cormier, Lois Duncan, S. E. Hinton, M. E. Kerr, Anne McCaffrey, Walter Dean Myers, Gary Paulsen, and Cynthia Voigt with the Margaret A. Edwards award. In spite of these positive signs, however, book lovers are worried by doom-and-gloom predictions about today's kids being unable or unwilling to read. They also worry that as independent publishing houses are purchased by conglomerates, the focus moves toward the margin of profit rather than toward developing individual authors and building up the genre of young adult literature. New authors find it harder to break into the field, while well-known authors are encouraged to move toward quantity rather than quality as when, for example, they write series books.

While independent bookstores have been willing to carry two or three copies of many moderately popular books published over the last several years, the chain bookstores find that their profits are greater when they carry many copies of a few current best-sellers. Such a reliance on mass appeal means that publishers are less likely to take chances on experimental subjects and styles. They produce fewer books and keep only the most popular in print. A downside is that teachers can no longer depend on having access to books they have found especially useful for in-class reading or thematic units. Authors complain that by the time they get a follow-up book or a sequel published, the original on which it is based has gone out of print. Some well-established writers are now working through small, independent publishers and marketing their own books after the copyrights have been returned by the major publishers.

Before we grow too discouraged over present conditions, we need to realize that the field as a whole is a relatively new area and that all literary scenes have their ups and downs. The domination of chain bookstores is already threatened by Amazon.com, which uses sophisticated computer programming to sell through the Internet (see Chapter 3 for a discussion).

Today's Authors

If we compare the total group of today's young adult authors with those of a generation ago, we have much for which to be thankful. Don Gallo's *Speaking for Ourselves: Autobiographical Sketches by Notable Authors of Books for Young Adults* and its sequel *Speaking for Ourselves, Too* have autobiographical statements from nearly 150 active and well-respected authors. As part of a Twentieth-Century Writers Series, the St. James Press features nearly 500 authors in its 1999 *St. James Guide to Young Adult Writers* edited by Tom Pendergast and Sara Pendergast. Charles Scribner's Sons gave fuller write-ups to the 125 authors featured in the three-volume set *Writers for Young Adults,* edited by Ted Hipple and published in 1996. Another 25 are included in a year 2000 supplement.

We should be encouraged not only by the numbers but also by the variety. Today's writers for young readers include men and women from all socioeconomic levels and from all over the world writing about life experiences of every possible kind (see Focus Box 1.1 for memoirs by some of these interesting individuals). Donna Jo Napoli (see her statement on p. 377) is chair of the linguistics program at Swarthmore College, while Joan Bauer (see her statement on p. 199) came to writing from the world of advertising. Berlie Doherty wrote her first YA book after interviewing young adults for her job as a BBC telejournalist. At a recent National Council of Teachers of English conference, it was fun to listen to Gary Paulsen, Will Hobbs, and Theodore Taylor swap stories about their childhoods spent in places as varied as the Panama Canal Zone, the Philippines, and Craddock, Virginia. Their adult jobs ranged from wilderness guide to merchant seaman and soldier and from roofer to truck driver and teacher. In the course of gathering the comments for our Author Boxes, we also learned that our American fantasy writer, Robin McKinley, is married to the British fantasy writer Peter Dickinson, and they really do have a garden filled with the beautiful roses that McKinley likes to write about.

Moving from this encouraging kaleidoscope of authors and going back to less happy interpretations, there have always been critics who questioned the value of books written for teenagers. In 1965, J. Donald Adams, editor of the "Speaking of Books" page in *The New York Times Book Review,* pointed to adolescent literature as a symptom of what is wrong with American education and American culture:

> The teen-age book, it seems to me, is a phenomenon which belongs properly only to a society of morons. I have nothing but respect for the writers of good books for children; they perform one of the most admirable functions of which a writer is capable. One proof of their value is the fact that the greatest books which children can enjoy are read with equal delight by their elders. But what person of mature years and reasonably mature understanding (for there is often a wide disparity) can read without impatience a book written for adolescents.[3]

In 1977, John Goldthwaite, writing in *Harper's,* gave as one of his nine suggestions for improving literature for young readers in particular and the world in general the termination of teenage fiction. His reasoning was that any literate 12-year-old could understand most science fiction and fantasy, and "As for all that novelized stuff about alienation, drugs, and pregnancy, the great bulk of it might be more enjoyable presented in comic books."[4] With the recent advent of graphic novels, Goldthwaite may have been some twenty years ahead of his time.

But even people who are known to be committed to the concept of adolescent literature (see Will Weaver's statement on p. 9) sometimes question its authenticity.

In a 1998 book promoting a multicultural approach to literature, we were surprised and disappointed to read as part of the summary to a forty-four-page chapter on African-American literature:

> Missing from this review are the writings of several African American authors who have tremendous appeal to young adults: Rosa Guy (*The Friends, Ruby, The Ups and Downs of Carl Davis III,* and *The Music of Summer*); Rita Williams-Garcia (*Blue Tights*); and Walter Dean Myers (*Scorpions, Glory Field*). Their writings are not part of the curriculum. The absence of their work in this

FOCUS BOX 1.1

Memoirs by Honor List Authors

The Abracadabra Kid: A Writer's Life by Sid Fleischman. Greenwillow, 1996. Fleischman was only 15-years-old when he and a friend embarked on a tour of northern California to present "A Glittering Array of Mysteries" from "The Mirthful Conjurers." The two aspiring magicians barely managed to break even, but the experience provided Fleischman a lifetime of golden ore from which he mined some forty books and screenplays, most famous of which are the McBroom tall tales.

All God's Children Need Traveling Shoes (1986) and **I Know Why the Caged Bird Sings** (1970), both Random House, by Maya Angelou. These lyrical and powerful autobiographies remain favorites of both adults and young readers. Angelou continues her story in *Gather Together in My Name, The Heart of a Woman,* and *Even the Stars Look Lonesome.*

Anonymously Yours by Richard Peck. Julian Messner, 1991. Readers can make interesting comparisons between the real-life events in *Anonymously Yours* and the fictional events that Peck writes about in his 1998 Newbery Honor Book, *A Long Way from Chicago.*

Black Ice by Lorene Cary. Knopf, 1991. While written for a general adult audience, this memoir is accessible to older high school students because the focus is on Cary's feelings of being an outsider when she moved as a scholarship student from the public schools of West Philadelphia to the prestigious St. Paul's prep school.

Frenchtown Summer by Robert Cormier. Delacorte, 1999. Although Cormier doesn't say this is an autobiography, the 30 narrative poems all in first person are told with such feeling that readers can't help but think they are Cormier's own story.

Knots in My Yo-Yo String by Jerry Spinelli. Knopf, 1998. Spinelli uses the lively style of his fiction to tell about the events he remembers from his first 16 years.

Looking Back: A Book of Memories by Lois Lowry. Walter Lorraine, 1998. "Why did it take a children's book author to think of this?" asked one reviewer, while another shuddered at the thought of less-skilled authors rummaging through their photos and trying to get similar publications. Lowry comments on and explains photos from four generations of her family.

ME, ME, ME, ME, ME, Not a Novel by M. E. Kerr. HarperCollins, 1983. Although this collection of eleven short stories is just as much fun to read as most of Kerr's novels, she says this one is a true account of the young life of Marijane Meaker, which is Kerr's real name.

My Life in Dog Years by Gary Paulsen. Delacorte, 1997. In this unusual approach to an autobiography, Paulsen recounts his experiences with ten different dogs. The dogs are different from the Iditarod dogs he tells about in his 1990 *Woodsong.*

No Pretty Pictures: A Child of War by Anita Lobel. Greenwillow, 1998. The title alludes to Lobel's career as an illustrator of children's books. She begins her Holocaust memories in Krakow, Poland, when she is 5 years old and her father disappears one night from her family's upscale apartment. The story ends when she arrives in New York City as a 16-year-old refugee.

Oddballs by William Sleator. Dutton, 1993. Kids who dream of getting even with family members by telling the world how strange they are can use Sleator's nine funny stories as a model.

The Pigman and Me by Paul Zindel. HarperCollins, 1992. Readers will both laugh and cry at this true account of a year in the teenage life of Paul Zindel when he was lucky enough to have Nonno Frankie (the model for Zindel's fictional Pigman) as a mentor.

Starting from Home: A Writer's Beginnings by Milton Meltzer. Viking, 1988. Meltzer has brought different periods of history alive for thousands of young readers, and now he does the same thing for the early 1900s, as he tells about his family and childhood.

A Way Out of No Way: Writing about Growing Up Black in America ed. by Jacqueline Woodson. Holt, 1996. Woodson writes about the hope and inspiration that she received from reading wonderful literature written by African-American authors. She includes pieces by Honor List authors James Baldwin, Ernest J. Gaines, Rosa Guy, and Ntozake Shange.

WILL WEAVER
Being a YA Author

For the last couple of years I've been misleading people—including myself. I've been traveling around, as authors do, rattling on about books, about why I write what I write. Truly, I tell people who ask, I'm an "adult" fiction writer. My first book, *Red Earth, White Earth,* was a big Midwestern novel eventually produced for CBS television. My second book, *A Gravestone Made of Wheat,* was a collection of short stories also for adults. True, my last three novels have been for young adults—but that's only because of my family life. I'm a husband and father with two teenagers: my mind (and heart) are taken by my kids and their concerns. That's why I've been writing for young adults. But this is temporary, I say. A literary detour. Something to keep my writing career alive until I can return to "adult" fiction.

But is this all true? Why do I so thoroughly enjoy writing young adult fiction? Why are the best parts of my two "adult" books the chapters and stories that deal with kids, with coming-of-age? Why is it that I can remember incidents from school days with photographic clarity, but as an adult can't remember to buy milk at the store?

Recently I bumped—literally—into a high school acquaintance whom I hadn't seen in 20 years. "Ricky," I said immediately, and he and I began to talk about school days, about ball-playing, about cars, about the night Danny Hawks died, about Mike and Nancy—what a golden couple they were. We talked as if the 3:00 P.M. school bell had just rung.

Afterward, I realized another personal truth. I have always felt that my teen years were unmatched in terms of their intensity, their wonder, their brutality. Our growing-up years encompass our highest highs, our lowest lows. In adult life, a big score on the stock market is small potatoes next to tipping in a winning basket in a tournament game. In adult life, the loss of a job promotion is nothing compared to having bad acne or being fat or skinny in eighth grade. Our school and teenage years make, break, and bend us; they forge our personalities, perhaps even our futures. That's why I keep coming back to young adult themes.

For some adults, William Faulkner wrote, "The past is not a diminishing road but a meadow which no winter ever touches." I include myself in this group, though would add (metaphorically) mosquitoes, rocks, and snakes to Faulkner's meadow. Writers must avoid romanticizing the past or sentimentalizing the present.

Writers also, it seems to me, should be as useful to other people as possible. Good fiction allows all of us—young adults in particular—to try on other people's lives, to compare meadows. For these reasons, I'm guessing I'll continue writing for young adults not out of necessity, but of choice. It just feels right.

Will Weaver's books include *Striking Out,* 1993; *Farm Team,* 1995; *Hard Ball,* 1998; and *Memory Boy,* 2000, all HarperCollins.

chapter is not because these authors' voices are unimportant but because their work has yet to enter the mainstream of young adult literature used in schools in grades 9–12.[5]

We were glad to see at least an after-the-fact acknowledgement of these young adult authors but were disappointed that while the writer of the chapter was brave enough to give information about and to recommend the teaching of dozens of different stories and novels that are not currently part of the curriculum, her courage failed when it came to these young adult authors. Perhaps she had never read their books and so felt more comfortable writing about works written for general adult audiences; or, perhaps she feels that it's hard enough to sell minority literature without also trying to sell young adult literature. Either way, her reluctance to recommend that young adult literature become part of the curriculum illustrates the mixed feelings that people have toward the genre.

Another illustration is the current argument in the American Library Association revolving around the Alex Award, which was established in 1998 to honor adult titles that are being recommended for teenagers. The award's stated purpose is "to help librarians encourage young adults ages 12–18 to read by introducing them to high quality books written for adults." The award is named for Margaret Alexander Edwards, who, for her work during the 1940s and 1950s at the Enoch Pratt Free Library in Baltimore, is generally credited with being the first YA librarian. Patty Campbell wrote in her "The Sand in the Oyster" column in *Horn Book* magazine that Edwards and her staff "combed the stacks for such cheerful goodies as *Cheaper by the Dozen* and *Mrs. Mike* and promoted them energetically to their young patrons." But, Campbell argues, the reason Margaret Edwards is considered a pioneer and that she had to work so hard to interest teens is because there was no young adult literature, as such. Edwards retired in 1962, five years before S. E. Hinton's *The Outsiders* launched modern YA fiction. For most of her career, Campbell says, Edwards had to play the game without a ball, and we are being regressive if we don't take advantage of "the magnificent body of literature for teens" that has developed over the past thirty years. Campbell thinks it's only between the ages of 11 and 16 that readers feel comfortable with young adult literature, so she asks:

> Why waste any of the precious opportunity by promoting less relevant adult titles? They'll move on soon enough, but let's not push that transition until they've had time to savor Chris Crutcher's wisdom, Francesca Lia Block's audacity, Robert Cormier's dark complexities, Richard Peck's wit. Once a young person begins to read adult fiction, I am convinced that they seldom look back, and the chance is gone forever.[6]

While we have grounds for rejecting the kinds of negative criticism quoted previously, we need to be aware that it exists. Such a pessimistic view of teenage books is an unfortunate literary heritage that may well influence the attitudes of school boards, library directors, parents, teachers, and anyone else who has had no particular reason to read and examine the best of the new young adult literature. Besides, so many new books for young readers appear each year (approximately 2000, with about one-fourth of these aimed at teenagers) that people who have already made up their minds about adolescent literature can probably find titles to support their beliefs no matter what they are. In an area as new as young adult literature, we can look at much of the disagreement and the conflicting views as inevitable—as signs of a lively and interesting field.

Characteristics of the Best Young Adult Literature

We did some research to come up with a selection of books that would be representative of what both young adults and professionals working in the field consider the best books. We should caution, however, that books are selected as "the best" on the basis of many different criteria, and one person's best is not necessarily yours or that of the young people with whom you work. We hope that you will read many books, so that you can recommend them not because you saw them on a list, but because you enjoyed them and believe they will appeal to a particular student.

In drawing up our list of "best books," we started with 1967 because this seemed to be a milestone year, when writers and publishers turned in new directions. We have compiled this list from several other "Best Book" lists, including yearly lists from the editors of *School Library Journal, Booklist, VOYA,* and *Horn Book* magazine and from such committees as those who choose the Newbery Awards and the Boston Globe-Horn Book Awards as well as the units of the American Library Association that put together such lists as "Best Books for Young Adults," "Recommended Books for the Reluctant Young Adult Reader," and "Notable Children's Books."

We have also used our own judgment and that of our colleagues and taken into consideration any special, retrospective lists that happen to appear. We have labeled the results of our research our Honor List, but we make no claim that it includes all the good books or even the best books published each year. We guarantee, however, that a number of knowledgeable people—professionals as well as young readers—were favorably impressed with each book that appears on the Honor List.

As the years have gone by, the number of books has made the list so unwieldy that for this edition we deleted some books that are out of print and moved the biographies and collections of poetry and short stories to Focus Boxes in appropriate chapters. Informative nonfiction seems to date more quickly than other books; books still in print and in use are worked into Chapter 9. Occasionally we add a book to the Honor List when it is growing in respect and popularity, as we did a few years ago with Robert Lipsyte's *The Contender* and are now doing with Sandra Cisneros's *The House on Mango Street.*

We used to identify books as coming from either the juvenile division or the adult division of a publishing house, but this no longer seems like crucial information because within the last 15 years virtually all the Honor books have been published by juvenile divisions. This is partly because the reviewing sources from which we take our list are slanted toward juvenile books, but a second reason is that today's publishers have a kind of freedom they did not have in 1975 when, for example, Bradbury created an "adult" division specifically to publish Judy Blume's *Forever.* They hoped to soften the controversy by having it come out as an "adult" rather than a "children's book." An asterisk indicates that a book has been made into a movie.

TABLE 1.1

HONOR LIST

Title and Author	Hardbound Publisher	Paperback Publisher	Genre	Protagonist Sex	Age	Number of Pages	Ethnic Group or Unusual Setting
1999							
Anna of Byzantium Tracy Barrett	Delacorte		Historical Fiction	F	Older teens	209	11th Century Byzantium
Frenchtown Summer Robert Cormier	Delacorte		Realistic Poetry	M	12	113	early 1920s
Hard Love Ellen Wittlinger	Simon & Schuster		Problem Quest	M/F	16	224	
Monster Walter Dean Myers	HarperCollins		Problem	M	16	240	
Never Trust a Dead Man Vivian Vande Velde	Harcourt		Mystery Supernatural	M	17	194	Medieval
Safe at Second Scott Johnson	Philomel		Sports Problem	M	17	224	
The Smugglers Iain Lawrence	Delacorte		Adventure	M	16	183	19th Century England
When Zachary Beaver Came to Town Kimberly Willis Holt	Henry Holt		Realistic	M	13	231	
1998							
Clockwork: Or All Wound Up Philip Pullman	Scholastic		Fantasy	M/F	Teens	112	
Go and Come Back Joan Abelove	DK Ink	Puffin	Realistic Historical	F	13	177	Peru
Holes Louis Sachar	FS&G	Dell	Fanciful Adventure	M	14	233	
The Killer's Cousin Nancy Werlin	Delacorte	Dell	Psychological Mystery	M	17	228	

Title and Author	Hardbound Publisher	Paperback Publisher	Genre	Protagonist Sex	Age	Number of Pages	Ethnic Group or Unusual Setting
Rules of the Road Joan Bauer	Putnam's	Puffin	Realistic	F	16	201	
Soldier's Heart Gary Paulsen	Delacorte		Historical	M	15	106	
Whirligig Paul Fleischman	Holt	Dell	Realistic	M	17	133	
The Wreckers Iain Lawrence	Delacorte	Bantam	Historical Adventure	M	14	191	
1997							
Blood and Chocolate Annette Curtis Klause	Delacorte	Dell	Supernatural	F	18	288	
Buried Onions Gary Soto	Harcourt Brace	Harper Collins	Realistic	M	18	149	Hispanic
Dancing on the Edge Han Nolan	Harcourt Brace	Puffin	Realistic	F	12	244	
Ella Enchanted Gale Carson Levine	HarperCollins	Harper Trophy	Cinderella Parody	F	12	232	
The Facts Speak for Themselves Brock Cole	Front Street	Puffin	Realistic Abuse	F	13	184	
Out of the Dust Karen Hesse	Scholastic	Scholastic	Narrative Poetry	F	13	227	Depression
When She Was Good Norma Fox Mazer	Scholastic	Scholastic	Realistic Mental Health	F	Early 20s	240	
Whistle Me Home Barbara Wersba	Holt		Realistic Homosexuality	M/F	17	108	
1996							
After the War Carol Matas	Simon & Schuster	Aladdin	Historical Realistic	F	15	116	Palestine

Title and Author	Hardbound Publisher	Paperback Publisher	Genre	Protagonist Sex	Age	Number of Pages	Ethnic Group or Unusual Setting
A Girl Named Disaster Nancy Garden	Orchard	Puffin	Realistic	F	14	306	Africa
The Golden Compass Philip Pullman	Knopf	Del Rey	Fantasy/ SciFi	F	14	396	
Jip: His Story Katherine Paterson	Lodestar	Puffin	Historical Realistic	M	11	181	African-American
Rats Saw God Rob Thomas	Simon & Schuster	Aladdin	Realistic	M	17	219	
1995							
The Eagle Kite Paula Fox	Orchard	Dell	Realistic Death	M	13	127	
Ironman Chris Crutcher	Greenwillow	Dell	Realistic Sports	M	16	181	
Like Sisters on the Homefront Rita Williams-Garcia	Lodestar/ Dutton	Puffin	Realistic	F	14	165	African-American
The Midwife's Apprentice Karen Cushman	Clarion	Harper Trophy	Historical	F	13	122	Medieval
The War of Jenkins' Ear Michael Morpurgo	Philomel	Paper Star	Realistic/ Religious	M	14	171	1951 England
1994							
Deliver Us from Evie M. E. Kerr	HarperCollins	Harper Trophy	Realistic Lesbianism	F	17	177	
Driver's Ed. Caroline Cooney	Delacorte	Bantam	Suspense	M/F	Teens	184	
Iceman Chris Lynch	HarperCollins	Harper Trophy	Realistic Sports	M	14	181	
Letters from the Inside John Marsden	Houghton Mifflin	Dell	Realistic	F	Teens	146	Australia

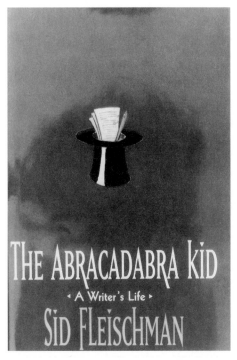 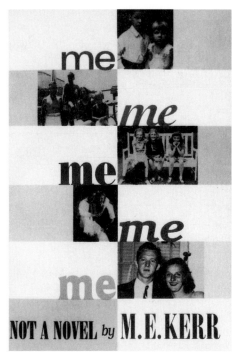

See Focus Box 1.1 for memoirs written by authors whose books are on the Honor List. Honor List biographies, poetry, and informative nonfiction have been worked into the appropriate chapters.

Title and Author	Hardbound Publisher	Paperback Publisher	Genre	Protagonist Sex	Age	Number of Pages	Ethnic Group or Unusual Setting
When She Hollers Cynthia Voigt	Scholastic	Scholastic	Realistic Abuse	F	17	177	
1993							
The Giver Lois Lowry	Houghton Mifflin	Dell Bantam	Science Fiction	M	Mixed	180	Futuristic Dystopia
Harris and Me Gary Paulsen	Harcourt Brace	Dell	Realistic Humorous	M	Young teens	157	Rural
Make Lemonade Virginia Euwer Wolff	Holt	Scholastic	Realistic Single parent	F	14/17	200	Inner City
Missing Angel Juan Francesca Lia Block	HarperCollins	Harper Trophy	Problem Occult	F	Teens	138	Los Angeles New York

Title and Author	Hardbound Publisher	Paperback Publisher	Genre	Protagonist Sex	Age	Number of Pages	Ethnic Group or Unusual Setting
Shadow Boxer Chris Lynch	HarperCollins	Harper Trophy	Realistic Sports	M	Young teens	215	
1992							
Dear Nobody Berlie Doherty	Orchard	Beech Tree Morrow	Realistic Pregnancy	M/F	Older teens	192	England
The Harmony Arms Ron Koertge		Little	Realistic Humorous	M	14	182	Los Angeles
Missing May Cynthia Rylant	Orchard	Dell	Realistic Death	M/F	Mixed	89	
Somewhere in the Darkness Walter Dean Myers	Scholastic	Scholastic	Realistic Family	M	14	224	African-American
1991							
The Brave Robert Lipsyte	HarperCollins	Harper Trophy	Realistic Sports	M	18	195	Native-American
Castle in the Air Diana Wynne Jones	Greenwillow		Fantasy	M/F	Teens	199	Middle East
Lyddie Katherine Paterson	Lodestar	Puffin	Historical mid-1800s	F	13	183	U.S. North-east
The Man from the Other Side Uri Orlev	Houghton Mifflin	Puffin	Historical	M	14	186	Poland WW II
Nothing But the Truth Avi	Orchard	Avon Flare	Realistic	M	14	177	
1990							
The Shining Company Rosemary Sutcliff	Farrar	Farrar	Historical 7th century	M	Mixed	296	England
The Silver Kiss Annette Curtis Klause	Bradbury	Dell	Occult Romance	F	Teens	198	
The True Confessions of Charlotte Doyle Avi	Orchard	Avon	Historical Adventure	F	13	215	1800s Trans-Atlantic

Title and Author	Hardbound Publisher	Paperback Publisher	Genre	Protagonist Sex	Age	Number of Pages	Ethnic Group or Unusual Setting
White Peak Farm Berlie Doherty	Orchard	Morrow	Realistic Family	F	Older teens	86	England
1989							
Blitzcat Robert Westall	Scholastic	Scholastic	Animal	M	—	230	England WW II
Celine Brock Cole	Farrar	Farrar	Realistic	F	16	216	
Eva Peter Dickinson	Delacorte	Dell	Science Fiction	F	13	219	Dystopian Future
No Kidding Bruce Brooks	HarperCollins		Science Fiction	M	14	207	Dystopian Future
Shabanu: Daughter of the Wind Suzanne Fisher Staples	Knopf		Realistic Problem	F	12	140	Pakistan Desert
Weetzie Bat Francesca Lia Block	HarperCollins		Realistic Spoof	M/F	Teens	88	Hollywood
1988							
Fade Robert Cormier	Delacorte	Dell	Occult	M/F	Mixed	320	
Fallen Angels Walter Dean Myers	Scholastic	Scholastic	Realistic	M	Older teens	309	Vietnam War/Ethnic Mix
A Kindness Cynthia Rylant	Orchard	Dell	Realistic Family	M	15	117	
Memory Margaret Mahy	Macmillan	Dell	Realistic Disability	M/F	19 80+	240	New Zealand
Probably Still Nick Swanson Virginia Euwer Wolff	Holt	Scholastic	Realistic Disability	M	Teens	144	
Scorpions Walter Dean Myers	HarperCollins		Realistic Crime	M	Teens	167	Ethnic Mix

Title and Author	Hardbound Publisher	Paperback Publisher	Genre	Protagonist Sex	Age	Number of Pages	Ethnic Group or Unusual Setting
Sex Education Jenny Davis	Orchard	Bantam	Realistic Death	F	Teens	150	
1987							
After the Rain Norma Fox Mazer	Morrow	Avon	Realistic Death	F	Mid-teens	290	
The Crazy Horse Electric Game Chris Crutcher	Greenwillow	Dell	Realistic Sports Disability	M	Teens	224	Ethnic Mix
The Goats Brock Cole	Farrar	Farrar	Realistic	M/F	Teens	184	
*Hatchet Gary Paulsen	Bradbury	Aladdin	Adventure Survival	M	12	195	
Permanent Connections Sue Ellen Bridgers	HarperCollins	Banks Channel	Realistic Family	M/F	Teens	164	
Sons from Afar Cynthia Voigt	Atheneum	Aladdin	Realistic	M	Mid-teens	224	
The Tricksters Margaret Mahy	Macmillan	Aladdin	Occult	F	17	266	New Zealand
1986							
Cat, Herself Mollie Hunter	HarperCollins		Historical	F	Teens	279	British Nomads
The Catalogue of the Universe Margaret Mahy	Macmillan		Realistic	F	17	185	New Zealand
Izzy, Willy-Nilly Cynthia Voigt	Atheneum	Aladdin	Realistic Disability	F	15	288	
Midnight Hour Encores Bruce Brooks	HarperCollins	Harper Trophy	Realistic	F	16	288	Mixed Ethnic
1985							
Beyond the Chocolate War Robert Cormier	Knopf	Dell	Realistic	M	17	234	

Title and Author	Hardbound Publisher	Paperback Publisher	Genre	Protagonist Sex	Age	Number of Pages	Ethnic Group or Unusual Setting
Dogsong Gary Paulsen	Bradbury	Aladdin	Adventure Occult	M	13	177	Alaska Inuit
Ender's Game Orson Scott Card	Tor	Tor	Science Fiction	M	Young teens	357	
In Country Bobbie Ann Mason	HarperCollins	Harper Perrenial	Realistic	F	Teens	247	
The Moonlight Man Paula Fox	Bradbury	Dell	Realistic Alcoholism	F	Teens	192	Nova Scotia
Remembering the Good Times Richard Peck	Delacorte	Dell	Realistic Suicide	M/F	Teens	192	
1984							
The Changeover: A Supernatural Romance Margaret Mahy	Macmillan	Puffin	Fantasy	M/F	Teens	214	New Zealand
Cold Sassy Tree Olive Ann Burns	Ticknor & Fields	Dell Delta	Realistic	M/F	Mixed	391	1906 Rural Georgia
Downtown Norma Fox Mazer	Morrow	Avon	Realistic	M/F	Young teens	216	
Interstellar Pig William Sleator	Dutton	Puffin	Science Fiction	M	16	197	
The Moves Make the Man Bruce Brooks	HarperCollins	Harper Trophy	Realistic	M	Young teens	280	Ethnic Mix
One-Eyed Cat Paula Fox	Bradbury	Dell	Realistic	M	Young teens	216	
1983							
Beyond the Divide Kathryn Lasky	Macmillan	Aladdin	Historical Fiction	F	Teens	254	1800s American West
The Bumblebee Flies Anyway Robert Cormier	Pantheon	Dell	Futuristic	M	Teens	211	

Title and Author	Hardbound Publisher	Paperback Publisher	Genre	Protagonist Sex	Age	Number of Pages	Ethnic Group or Unusual Setting
The House on Mango Street Sandra Cisneros	Arte Publico	Random	Realistic	F	Young teens	134	Hispanic
A Solitary Blue Cynthia Voigt	Atheneum	Scholastic	Realistic Family	M	Early teens	182	
1982							
Annie on My Mind Nancy Garden	Farrar	Farrar	Realistic Lesbianism	F	Teens	233	
The Blue Sword Robin McKinley	Greenwillow	Ace	Fantasy	F	Late teens	272	
A Formal Feeling Zibby Oneal	Viking		Realistic Death	F	Teens	162	
*A Midnight Clear William Wharton	Knopf	Newmarket	Realistic	M	Early 20s	241	World War II
Sweet Whispers, Brother Rush Virginia Hamilton	Philomel	Avon	Occult	F	Teens	224	African-American
1981							
Let the Circle Be Unbroken Mildred D. Taylor	Dial	Puffin	Historical U.S. South	F	Early teens	166	African-American
Notes for Another Life Sue Ellen Bridgers	Knopf	Replica	Realistic Family	M/F	Teens	252	
Rainbow Jordan Alice Childress	Coward McCann	Avon	Realistic	F	14	142	African-American
Stranger with My Face Lois Duncan	Little	Dell	Occult	F	17	250	
Tiger Eyes Judy Blume	Bradbury	Dell	Realistic	F	15	206	New Mexico Ethnic Mix

Title and Author	Hardbound Publisher	Paperback Publisher	Genre	Protagonist Sex	Age	Number of Pages	Ethnic Group or Unusual Setting
Westmark Lloyd Alexander	Dutton	Dell	Historical Fiction	M	16	184	England
1980							
The Beginning Place Ursula K. Le Guin	HarperCollins		Fantasy	M/F	Early 20s	183	
The Hitchhiker's Guide to the Galaxy Douglas Adams	Crown	Ballantine	Fantasy	M	Adults	224	
Jacob Have I Loved Katherine Paterson	Crowell	Harper-Trophy	Realistic Family	F	Teens	216	Chesapeake Bay WW II
1979							
After the First Death Robert Cormier	Pantheon	Dell	Realistic Suspense	M/F	Teens	233	
All Together Now Sue Ellen Bridgers	Knopf	Bantam	Realistic Family	M/F	Teens	238	
*Birdy William Wharton	Knopf Random	Vintage	Realistic Insanity	M	Early 20s	310	
The Last Mission Harry Mazer	Delacorte	Dell	Realistic	M	Late teens	182	World War II
*Tex S. E. Hinton	Delacorte	Dell	Realistic	M	Teens	194	
*Words by Heart Ouida Sebestyen	Little, Brown	Bantam Dell	Realistic 1920s West	F	Young teens	162	African-American
1978							
Beauty: A Retelling . . . Robin McKinley	HarperCollins	Harper Trophy	Fantasy	F	Teens	247	
The Book of the Dun Cow Walter Wangerin, Jr.	HarperCollins	Harper Trophy	Animal Fantasy Religion	—	—	255	
Gentlehands M. E. Kerr	HarperCollins	Harper Trophy	Realistic	M	Teens	283	

Title and Author	Hardbound Publisher	Paperback Publisher	Genre	Protagonist Sex	Age	Number of Pages	Ethnic Group or Unusual Setting
Killing Mr. Griffin Lois Duncan	Little, Brown	Dell	Realistic Suspense	M/F	Teens	166	
1977							
Dragonsinger Anne McCaffrey	Atheneum	Bantam	Fantasy	F	Teens	256	
**I Am the Cheese* Robert Cormier	Knopf	Dell	Realistic Suspense	M	Teens	233	
One Fat Summer Robin Lipsyte	HarperCollins	Harper Collins	Realistic	M	Teens	150	
Winning Robin Brancato	Knopf	Knopf	Realistic Disability	M	Teens	211	
1976							
**Are You in the House Alone?* Richard Peck	Viking	Dell	Realistic Rape	F	Teens	156	
Home Before Dark Sue Ellen Bridgers	Knopf	Replica	Realistic	F	Teens	176	Migrant Workers
**Ordinary People* Judith Guest	Viking	Penguin	Realistic Family	M	Teens	263	
1975							
Dragonwings Laurence Yep	HarperCollins	Harper Trophy	Historical Fiction	M	Toung teens	248	Chinese-American
Forever Judy Blume	Bradbury	Pocket Books	Realistic	F	17	216	
**Rumble Fish* S. E. Hinton	Delacorte	Dell	Realistic	M	Teens	122	
Z for Zachariah Robert C. O'Brien	Atheneum	Aladdin	Science Fiction	F	16	249	Postnuclear
1974							
**The Chocolate War* Robert Cormier	Pantheon	Dell	Realistic	M	14	253	

Title and Author	Hardbound Publisher	Paperback Publisher	Genre	Protagonist Sex	Age	Number of Pages	Ethnic Group or Unusual Setting
Carrie Stephen King	Doubleday	NAL Pocket Books	Occult	F	Preteen	199	
House of Stairs William Sleator	Dutton	Puffin	Science Fiction	M/F	Teens	166	
If Beale Street Could Talk James Baldwin	Dial	Dell	Realistic	F	19	197	African-American
M. C. Higgins, the Great Virginia Hamilton	Macmillan	Aladdin	Realistic	M	13	278	African-American
1973							
A Day No Pigs Would Die Robert Newton Peck	Knopf	Dell Random	Historical 1920s	M	13	159	Rural Vermont
The Friends Rosa Guy	Holt	Bantam	Realistic	F	Early teens	203	West Indians in New York
A Hero Ain't Nothin' But a Sandwich Alice Childress	Coward McCann	Avon	Realistic Drugs	M	Early teens	126	African-American
The Slave Dancer Paula Fox	Bradbury	Dell	Historical 1800s	M	13	176	Ethnic Mix
Summer of My German Soldier Bette Greene	Dial	Dell Puffin	Historical WW II	F	14	199	U.S. South Jewish
1972							
Deathwatch Robb White	Doubleday	Dell	Realistic Suspense	M	Early 20s	228	
Dinky Hocker Shoots Smack! M. E. Kerr	HarperCollins	Harper Trophy	Realistic Family	F	14	198	
The Man Without a Face Isabelle Holland	Lippincott	Harper Trophy	Realistic Homosexuality	M	16	248	

Title and Author	Hardbound Publisher	Paperback Publisher	Genre	Protagonist Sex	Age	Number of Pages	Ethnic Group or Unusual Setting
My Name Is Asher Lev Chaim Potok	Knopf	Ballantine	Realistic Family	M	Teens	369	Hasidic Jews
A Teacup Full of Roses Sharon Bell Mathis	Viking	Viking	Realistic Drugs	M	17	125	African-American
1971							
*The Autobiography of Miss Jane Pittman Ernest Gaines	Dial	Bantam	Historical U.S. South	F	Lifetime	245	African-American
*The Bell Jar Sylvia Plath	HarperCollins	Bantam	Realistic Suicide	F	19	196	
1970							
*Bless the Beasts and Children Glendon Swarthout	Doubleday	Pocket Books	Realistic	M	Early teens	205	American Southwest
1969							
My Darling, My Hamburger Paul Zindel	HarperCollins	Bantam	Realistic Abortion	M/F	17/18	168	
*Sounder William Armstrong	HarperCollins	Harper Collins	Historical U.S. South	M	14	116	African-American
Where the Lilies Bloom Vera and Bill Cleaver	Lippincott	Harper Trophy	Realistic	F	14	174	Rural Isolated
1968							
The Pigman Paul Zindel	HarperCollins	Bantam	Realistic Death	M/F	16	182	
*Red Sky at Morning Richard Bradford	Lippincott	Harper Perrenial	Realistic	M	17	256	New Mexico Ethnic Mix
1967							
*The Chosen Chaim Potok	Simon & Schuster	Fawcett	Realistic	M	Teen	284	Hasidic Jews

Title and Author	Hardbound Publisher	Paperback Publisher	Genre	Protagonist Sex	Age	Number of Pages	Ethnic Group or Unusual Setting
The Contender Robert Lipsyte	HarperCollins	Carousel	Realistic	M	17	167	African-American
Mr. and Mrs. Bo Jo Jones Ann Head	Putnam	NAL	Realistic Pregnancy	M/F	18	253	
The Outsiders S. E. Hinton	Viking	Dell Puffin	Realistic	M	14	156	

If a book is included on this Honor List, obviously it is outstanding in some way, but the reasons might differ considerably. One book may be here because of its originality, another for its popularity, and another for its literary quality. We should warn that just because a book has not found its way to this list, it should not be dismissed as mediocre. The list covers over thirty years during which there were many more outstanding books published than the ones included here. Whenever such lists are drawn up, a degree of chance is involved.

Many of these books are described in more detail in the following chapters. Here they are simply cited as evidence to illustrate the following generalizations about the best of modern young adult literature.

Characteristic 1: Young Adult Authors Write from the Viewpoint of Young People

A prerequisite to attracting young readers is to write through the eyes of a young person. One of the ways authors do this is to write in the first person. This brings an immediacy to such a beginning as the one in Norma Fox Mazer's *When She Was Good:*

> I didn't believe Pamela would ever die. She was too big, too mad, too furious for anything so shabby and easy as death. And for a few moments as she lay on the floor that day, I thought it was one of her jokes. The playing-dead joke. I thought that at any moment she would spring up, seize me by the hair, and drag me around the room. It wouldn't be the first time. . . .

Another technique is for authors to have a young narrator even when the story belongs to someone else. For example, Joan Abelove's *Go and Come Back* is the story of two anthropologists who are in their late 20s when they go for a two-year study visit to a mountain tribe in Peru. What readers learn about the anthropologists comes through the eyes of a young Peruvian girl, Alicia, who refers to the anthropologists as "old women." The tribe is fictionally named the Isabos, and Alicia's first-person observations are supplemented by the conversations she has with her friends, with the two "old women," and with her observant and sarcastic mother.

In *Fade*, Robert Cormier uses the technique of having the story told by the protagonist, Paul Moreaux, as long as he is in his youth. When the story gets to his adult years, however, Cormier changes the narrator to Moreaux's young female cousin, who aspires to follow in Moreaux's footsteps as a writer.

The most consistent characteristic of the books on the Honor List is the age of the protagonists. Teenagers like to read about other teenagers as shown by such books as Sandra Cisneros's *The House on Mango Street*, Orson Scott Card's *Ender's Game*, and Bobbie Ann Mason's *In Country*. In spite of being published and marketed to general adult audiences, these books found their way to teen readers because the protagonists were young. With other Honor List books published for adults, young people play important roles even if they aren't the main characters as with the grandson in Olive Ann Burns's *Cold Sassy Tree* and the surviving son in Judith Guest's *Ordinary People*. General adult books that do not include teenagers, for example, Douglas Adams's *The Hitchhiker's Guide to the Galaxy* and William Wharton's *A Midnight Clear* and *Birdy*, have protagonists who are only slightly older than teen readers and are involved in activities with which young people identify, such as beginning to live on one's own, finding someone to love, and deciding whether earning money is more important than doing what one wants to do.

The big dividing line—the final rite of passage—between childhood and adulthood used to be having children of one's own so that stories about parenting seldom, if ever, appeared in young adult fiction. With the public acknowledgment of a soaring birthrate to teenaged mothers, however, this is no longer true as shown by the success of Virginia Euwer Wolff's *Make Lemonade*, the story of 14-year-old Verna LaVaughn who answers a baby-sitting ad and is surprised to find that it was put up by Jolly, the teenaged mother of 2-year-old Jeremy and a younger "gooey baby" named Jilly. Rita Williams-Garcia's *Like Sisters on the Homefront* is the story of 14-year-old Gayle, whose mother forces her to have an abortion after she gets pregnant a second time and then sends Gayle and her seven-month-old baby boy from Jamaica, New York, to rural Georgia to live "with family."

Characteristic 2: "Please, Mother, I Want the Credit!"

With formula fiction for young readers, one of the first things an author does is to figure out how to get rid of the parents so that the young person is free to take credit for his or her own accomplishments. Although the Honor List is not made up of formula fiction, there is still evidence of the "Please, Mother, I want to get the credit" syndrome. For example, in *Whirligig*, Brent Bishop needs to atone for causing a fatal traffic accident, so author Paul Fleischman contrives to have him travel on a Greyhound bus to the four corners of the United States where he constructs a memorial in remembrance of the girl who was killed. Brent's wealthy father had brought his checkbook to the meeting with the grieving family, but the story is much better because for the first time in Brent's life he must make amends by himself.

Other Honor books in which young people are forced to come to terms with their problems without the help of their parents include Iain Lawrence's *The Wreckers*, Gary Soto's *Buried Onions*, Carol Matas's *After the War*, Nancy Garden's *A Girl Named Disaster*, Francesca Lia Block's *Weetzie Bat*, Chris Crutcher's *The Crazy Horse Electric Game*, and all of S. E. Hinton's books.

Perhaps because they are both on the edge of—close but not central to—the mainstream of power, young people seem able to relate more comfortably with elderly than with middle-aged adults. They are like Anne Fine (see her statement on p. 28), who learned to tell stories by listening to her grandmother. In Joan Bauer's *Rules of the Road,* 16-year-old Jenna Louise Boller is happy to leave behind her troublesome parents when she is offered the summer job of driving the "supremely aged" Mrs. Gladstone across country to inspect each of the 172 shoe stores that her company owns. In Han Nolan's *Dancing on the Edge,* Miracle McCloy is at the mercy of some truly bad adults, but at least she knows that her grandfather is there for her. See Focus Box 1.2 for other fine books in which main characters relate across generations.

In keeping with the variety that exists in the Honor List, other books lead young readers to look more realistically at themselves and at parent-child relationships. Among the books that feature at least one capable parent playing a strong, supportive role for a young protagonist are Louis Sachar's *Holes,* Joan Abelove's *Go and Come Back,* Berlie Doherty's *White Peak Farm,* Peter Dickinson's *Eva,* Virginia Euwer Wolff's *Probably Still Nick Swanson,* Alice Childress's *A Hero Ain't Nothin' But a Sandwich,* and Kathryn Lasky's *Beyond the Divide.* In Robert Newton Peck's *A Day No Pigs Would Die,* the boy desperately loves his father, and in Bobbie Ann Mason's *In Country* and Bruce Brooks's *Midnight Hour Encores,* the young protagonists place great importance on learning about an unknown parent.

Characteristic 3: Young Adult Literature Is Fast-Paced

In July of 1999, *Time* reporter David Spitz wrote that, "Teen fiction may, in fact, be the first literary genre born of the Internet. Its fast-paced narratives draw upon the target demographic's kinship with MTV . . . and with the Internet and kids' ease in processing information in unconventional formats."[7] In reality, what Spitz calls "edgy" teen fiction was around long before the Internet, but his point is well taken that many of the most popular books tell their stories at almost the same frantic pace and with the same emphasis on powerful images that viewers have come to expect from MTV. The impetus for Spitz's article was, in fact, a new partnership between MTV and Pocketbooks, which in February of 1999 published *The Perks of Being a Wallflower* by 29-year-old screenwriter Stephen Chbosky. Spitz said that thanks to the Internet, Chbosky's book was fast developing a cult following. Other writers whose books he mentioned as fitting into the the same dramatic schema are Louis Sachar, Brock Cole, Walter Dean Myers, Melvin Burgess, and Adam Rapp.

Postindustrial countries have become hurry-up societies, and people want their stories to be presented in the same fashion. Books from the Honor List that come close to being MTV stories because of their pace and their exaggerated and powerful images include Louis Sachar's *Holes,* Annette Curtis Klause's *The Silver Kiss* and *Blood and Chocolate,* and Francesca Lia Block's *Missing Angel Juan* and *Weetzie Bat.* The latter is only eighty-eight pages long. When it was published in 1989, it was a shocking book because people were so accustomed to reading realistic problem novels providing role models for teenagers, that they weren't ready for a fairytale spoof of Hollywood and for a writer who was less interested in presenting role models than in presenting vivid images and unforgettable characters.

Not all young adult books are going to have the disjointed punch of music videos or the randomness of the Internet, but there is a relationship because modern mass-media entertainers appeal to the same powerful emotions of adoles-

ANNE FINE
On "Where Do You Get Your Ideas?"

Authors get asked this all the time. But one of the things I like most about life is how vices, properly channelled into the right job, can so easily become virtues. "Now you're telling me stories!" is a criticism. But everyone loves the person whose most boring tale becomes so intricate, so convoluted, so absolutely *wonderful* in the telling that it leaves everyone entranced. So maybe we ought to ask the question a different way. "It's not *such* a brilliant idea. How come you managed to do all that with it?"

Some authors learn the art simply from reading—still and always the very best practice for becoming a writer. But you can learn a lot from listening to a storyteller. In my family, it was my grandmother. Sent up to wash our hands before the meal, we might catch the basis of the story, almost the plain, unvarnished truth. "I've just been to the store, and that Mrs. Leroy gave me a very odd look."

By the time the table was laid, the story would have taken root and sprouted its first shoots. "I just stuck my head round the door, no more than that, and the *look* she gave me. Really, that woman could crack *stone.* They ought to think of employing her down the quarry."

Over lunch, she'd fill in a little of the background and emotional development. "She's *always* hated me, of course. It's because of my Larry. Mind you, she can't be blamed. Stuck with that Harold of hers, what woman wouldn't go peculiar? There's something very *strange* about her Harold. . . ."

Dialogue would be added gradually. "So I said, 'Is there a problem, Mrs. Leroy?' She went red as a radish. I've never seen a body change color so fast. She was so scarlet, you could have flash fried these steaks on her, Mary, truly you could."

Through the long afternoon, we'd hear the story a dozen times or more. The short exchange would burgeon, gloriously and mysteriously into a fifteen- or twenty-minute tale of envy and bitterness, hostile challenges and viper-tongued replies. By suppertime, a whole supporting cast would have been added.

"So I turned to that Mr. Hearst from the library . . ."

"I thought you told us there was no one else there."

"I never said that. You can't have been listening properly. No, I turned to Mr. Hearst and said, really frostily . . ."

"Upstairs, you children. It's well past your bed time."

"But we're *listening.* We're listening to *Granny.*"

"You've heard it all before."

"But it was *different,* then."

"I don't care. Granny's telling your father now. Off you all go to bed."

And so my father got the best of it. The final, tirelessly crafted, beautifully polished, story. And it was wasted on him, wasted utterly, because the fact that it was not the *truth* (nothing like truth had been left standing several hours before) bothered him, and ruined his enjoyment of the story.

But at the bottom of the stairs, still contentedly eavesdropping, unwittingly learning her future trade, was the storyteller's apprentice. Me.

Anne Fine's books include *Alias Madame Doubtfire,* 1988; *Step by Wicked Step,* 1995; *The Tulip Touch,* 1997; *The Book of the Banshee,* 1992; and *Flour Babies,* 1994, all from Little Brown.

FOCUS BOX 1.2

Relating Across Generations

Alida's Song by Gary Paulsen. Delacorte, 1999. A grown man learns from a bundle of old letters that his grandmother's getting him a summer job on a farm when he was fourteen was only a small part of what she had done for him.

Belle Prater's Boy by Ruth White. Farrar, 1996. In this vivid portrayal of a 1950s small town in Virginia, cross-eyed Woodrow comes to live with his affluent grandparents, who fortunately live next door to Woodrow's 12-year-old cousin Gypsy.

Grams, Her Boyfriend, My Family, and Me by Pat Derby. Farrar, 1994. When a grandmother decides to marry, it's up to the grandchildren to help her because her son and his fiancée do not approve.

Like Sisters on the Homefront by Rita Williams-Garcia. Lodestar/Dutton, 1995. Against her wishes, 14-year-old Gayle and her 7-month-old baby are sent from her "homefront" in Jamaica, New York, to relatives in rural Georgia where she develops a surprising relationship with her dying grandmother.

Missing May by Cynthia Rylant. Orchard, 1992. Twelve-year-old Summer has lived with her beloved Aunt May and Uncle Ob since she was 6. When Aunt May dies, Uncle Ob is so devastated that Summer almost loses him too.

Phoenix Rising by Karen Hesse. Holt, 1994. Thirteen-year-old Nyle Sumner lives with her grandmother on a Vermont sheep farm that has been poisoned by an accident at a nearby nuclear power plant. As Nyle follows the example of her grandmother, she sees love and hope rise from death and destruction.

The Real Plato Jones by Nina Bawden. Clarion, 1993. Humor runs through this story of Plato's unravelling the story of his two grandfathers, one a famous World War II spy and the other a traitor.

A Sunburned Prayer by Marc Talbert. Simon & Schuster, 1995. Eleven-year-old Eloy walks seventeen miles across a New Mexico desert to the Santuario de Chimayo. It is Good Friday and Eloy hopes his efforts will bring a miraculous cure to his dying grandmother.

Tiger, Tiger, Burning Bright: A Novel by Ron Koertge. Orchard/Kroupa, 1994. The subject is grim but the approach humorous in this story of 13-year-old Jesse covering up for his cowboy grandfather's problems with symptoms of Alzheimer's disease.

Walk Two Moons by Sharon Creech. HarperCollins, 1994. In this unusual Newbery Award winner, 13-year-old Sal takes a car trip—a gift of genuine love—from Ohio to Idaho with her grandparents.

cence—love, romance, sex, horror, and fear—as do young adult authors. These strong emotions are best shown through a limited number of characters and narrative events and language that flow naturally while still presenting dramatic images. The shorter and more powerful books are among those that have been made into impressive movies; for example, William Armstrong's 1969 *Sounder* with only 116 pages, Alice Childress's 1973 *A Hero Ain't Nothin' But a Sandwich* with only 126 pages, and S. E. Hinton's 1975 *Rumble Fish* with only 122 pages, Richard Peck's 1976 *Are You in the House Alone?* with 156 pages, and Ouida Sebestyen's 1979 *Words by Heart* with 162 pages.

The assumption that publishers start with is that teenagers have shorter attention spans than adults and less ability to hold one strand of a plot in mind while reading about another strand. There is a tremendous difference, however, in the reading abilities of young people between the ages of 12 and 18. As students mature and become better readers, they are able to stick with longer, more complex books. Five of the nine books on the Honor List with more than 300 pages were published for general adult audiences. Even though most of the books published for teenagers are fairly short, many of them are complex. Not one of Robert Cormier's books is simple and straightforward. Philip Pullman's fantasies require careful reading and perseverance, and so do Annette Curtis Klause's modern stories of vampires and werewolves. Gary Paulsen's *Dogsong* blends the past and the future with the present, whereas with Ernest Gaines's *A Gathering of Old Men*, William Wharton's *Birdy*, and Alice Childress's *A Hero Ain't Nothin' But a Sandwich* readers must draw together and sort out alternating viewpoints and chronologies. It is obvious from reading Judith Guest's *Ordinary People*, Rosemary Sutcliff's *The Shining Company*, and James Baldwin's *If Beale Street Could Talk* that their appeal is based on something other than easy reading.

Characteristic 4: Young Adult Literature Includes a Variety of Genres and Subjects

Because the *raison d'être* for adolescent literature is to tell a story about making the passage from childhood to adulthood, some people assume that books for teenagers are all alike. People who say this are revealing more about their reading patterns than about the field of adolescent literature. The Honor List reveals a tremendous variety of subjects, themes, and genres. Although we have moved our Honor List poetry books to Chapter 9, short story collections to Chapter 11, and personal narratives and biographies to Chapter 8 with biographies, there is still plenty of variety. Examples of historical fiction on the Honor List include Gary Paulsen's Civil War *Soldier's Heart*, Carol Matas's World War II *After the War*, Katherine Paterson's pre–Civil War *Jip: His Story*, Olive Ann Burns's romantic *Cold Sassy Tree*, Kathryn Lasky's pioneer story *Beyond the Divide*, and Rosemary Sutcliff's *The Shining Company*, set in England in 600 A.D. Elements of fantasy and science fiction are as old as the oldest folktales (Gale Carson Levine's *Ella Enchanted* and Walter Wangerin's *The Book of the Dun Cow*) and as new as nuclear war and the latest board game (Robert C. O'Brien's *Z for Zachariah* and William Sleator's *Interstellar Pig*). Occult fiction is filled with romance (Annette Curtis Klause's *The Silver Kiss* and Virginia Hamilton's *Sweet Whispers, Brother Rush*), while futuristic stories thrive on high-tech intrigue (Peter Dickinson's *Eva* and Robert Cormier's *The Bumblebee Flies Anyway*).

Although about half the books are contemporary, realistic fiction, they range from tightly plotted suspense stories as in Nancy Werlin's *The Killer's Cousin* and John Marsden's *Letters from the Inside* to serious introspection as in Paula Fox's *One-Eyed Cat*. The theme of alienation and loneliness is seen in William Wharton's *Birdy*, whereas the need for a hero is seen in Robert Newton Peck's *A Day No Pigs Would Die* and Glendon Swarthout's *Bless the Beasts and Children*. Threats to the social order are explored in William Sleator's *House of Stairs* and *Interstellar Pig* and in Lois Lowry's *The Giver*. A search for values is shown in Richard Bradford's *Red Sky at Morning* and Chris Crutcher's *The Crazy Horse Electric Game*. What it means to care for others is examined in Han Nolan's *Dancing on the Edge*, Annette Curtis Klause's *The Silver Kiss*, Norma Fox Mazer's *Downtown*, Isabelle Holland's *The Man Without a Face*, Francesca Lia Block's *Missing Angel Juan*, and Gary Paulsen's *Harris and Me*.

Characteristic 5: The Body of Work Includes Stories About Characters from Many Different Ethnic and Cultural Groups

Forty years ago, the novels written specifically for teenagers and sold to schools and public libraries presented the same kind of middle-class, white, picket-fence neighborhoods as the one featured in the *Dick and Jane* readers from which most

American children were taught to read. But the mid-1960s witnessed a striking change in attitudes. One by one, taboos on profanity, divorce, sexuality, drinking, racial unrest, abortion, pregnancy, and drugs disappeared. With this change, writers were freed to set their stories in realistic rather than romanticized neighborhoods and to explore the experiences of characters whose stories had not been told before.

This freedom was a primary factor in the coming of age of adolescent literature. Probably because there was such a lack of good books about non–middle-class protagonists, and because this was where interesting things were happening, many writers during the late 1960s and the 1970s focused on minorities and on the kinds of kids that S. E. Hinton called *The Outsiders*. With the conservative swing that the United States took in the 1980s, not as much attention has been paid to minority experiences; nevertheless, several of the most appealing of the new books feature minority characters and will probably be read by large numbers of teenagers of all races. It's also encouraging that we are seeing books with main characters from different ethnic groups relating to each other. In Virginia Euwer Wolff's *Make Lemonade,* there is no overt mention of skin color, but as one reviewer stated, Jolly and LaVaughn are held together by "the race of poverty."

Although most schools and libraries are making a concerted effort to stock and teach books reflecting many different cultures, educators worry that publishers who are now marketing books directly to teenagers are not working as hard to include books about minority characters because less affluent kids, many of whom are from minorities, are not as likely to spend money on books as are white, middle-class teenagers. Also, as publishers try to attract readers by making their books more wishfulfilling, they tend to return to the romanticized beautiful-people view that was characteristic of the old adolescent literature.

Another fear is that, as with most television programming, everything is watered down to suit mass tastes. But there are some crucial differences, because one person at a time reads a book, while television is usually viewed by a group. Even with cable television, the number of channels from which a viewer can choose is limited, but books offer a vast choice. Moreover, advertisers pay for most television programs, while readers pay the production costs of books.

As more and more schools sponsor summer travel and exchange programs, and as the Internet and other mass media continue to shrink national boundaries, teenagers are becoming less parochial in their reading. Joan Abelove's *Go and Come Back* is set in 1970s Peru, Carol Matas's *After the War* is set in 1940s Poland and Palestine, while Nancy Garden's *A Girl Named Disaster* is set in 1980s Mozambique and Zimbabwe. *Shabanu: Daughter of the Wind,* set in present-day Pakistan, was written by Suzanne Fisher Staples, a UPI news correspondent. She uses the story of a young woman's betrothal to introduce English readers to a culture very different from their own. Mollie Hunter's *Cat, Herself* is a romantic story of a Scottish gypsy; Gary Paulsen's *Dogsong* is about a young Inuit; John Marsden's *Letters from the Inside* is set in Australia; Margaret Mahy's books *Memory* and *The Tricksters* are set in New Zealand; and Berlie Doherty's *White Peak Farm* grew out of her work preparing a BBC documentary in Sheffield, England.

Characteristic 6: Young Adult Books Are Basically Optimistic, with Characters Making Worthy Accomplishments

Ensuring that teenage characters are as smart as, or smarter than, their parents is only one of the devices that authors use to appeal to young readers. They also involve young characters in accomplishments that are challenging enough to earn the reader's respect. In the 1970s, when realism became the vogue and books were written with painful honesty about the frequently cruel world that teenagers face, some critics worried that modern young adult literature had become too pessimistic and cynical. However, even in so-called downer books, authors created characters that readers could admire for the way they faced up to their challenges.

A comparison of E. B. White's beloved *Charlotte's Web* and Robert Newton Peck's *A Day No Pigs Would Die* illustrates one of the differences between children's and adolescent literature. In White's classic children's book, a beloved but useless pig wins a ribbon at the County Fair and is allowed to live a long and happy life, whereas in Peck's young adult book a beloved but useless pig wins a ribbon at the County Fair but must be slaughtered anyway. Nevertheless, rather than being devastated by the death of the pig, readers identify with the boy and take pride in his ability to do what had to be done.

This kind of change and growth is the most common theme appearing in young adult literature, regardless of format. It suggests, either directly or symbolically, the gaining of maturity (i.e., the loss of innocence as part of the passage from childhood to adulthood). Such stories communicate a sense of time and change, a sense of becoming and catching glimpses of possibilities—some that are fearful and others that are awesome, odd, funny, perplexing, or wondrous.

One of the most popular ways to show change and growth is through a quest story (see Chapter 5 for a discussion and Focus Box 5.1 for examples). Avi's *The True Confessions of Charlotte Doyle* is an almost pure example of a quest story camouflaged as a rollicking historical adventure. The intrepid narrator explains on page 1:

> . . . before I begin relating what happened, you must know something about me as I was in the year 1832 when these events transpired. At the time my name *was* Charlotte Doyle. And though I have kept the name, I am not for reasons you will soon discover the *same* Charlotte Doyle.

This captures the psychologically satisfying essence of quest stories, which is that over the course of the story, the protagonist learns something and changes significantly as do the protagonists in Gary Soto's *Buried Onions,* Joan Bauer's *Rules of the Road,* Iain Lawrence's *The Wreckers,* Han Nolan's *Dancing on the Edge,* Norma Fox Mazer's *When She Was Good,* Chris Lynch's *Iceman* and *Shadow Boxer,* Cynthia Voigt's *Izzy, Willy-Nilly,* Katherine Paterson's *Lyddie* and *Jip: His Story,* Brock Cole's *The Goats* and *The Facts Speak for Themselves,* Bruce Brooks's *Midnight Hour Encores* and *No Kidding,* and Bobbie Ann Mason's *In Country.* Quest stories with varying degrees of fantasy include Peter Dickinson's *Eva,* Annette Curtis Klause's *The Silver Kiss,* Mollie Hunter's *Cat, Herself,* Lloyd Alexander's *Westmark,* and Robin McKinley's *The Blue Sword.*

Characteristic 7: Successful Young Adult Novels Deal with Emotions That Are Important to Young Adults

Often the difference in the life span between two books that are equally well written from a literary standpoint is that the ephemeral book fails to touch kids where they live, whereas the long-lasting book treats experiences that are psychologically important to young people. Good authors do not peruse psychology books searching for case histories or symptoms of teenage problems they can envision making into good stories. This would be as unlikely and as unproductive as it would be for a writer to study a book on literary devices and make a list: "First, I will use a metaphor and then a bit of alliteration and some imagery, followed by personification."

The psychological aspects of well-written novels are a natural part of the story as protagonists face the same kinds of challenges readers are experiencing, such as the developmental tasks outlined two generations ago by Robert J. Havighurst.

1. Acquiring more mature social skills.
2. Achieving a masculine or feminine sex role.
3. Accepting the changes in one's body, using the body effectively, and accepting one's physique.
4. Achieving emotional independence from parents and other adults.
5. Preparing for sex, marriage, and parenthood.
6. Selecting and preparing for an occupation.
7. Developing a personal ideology and ethical standards.
8. Assuming membership in the larger community. [8]

Some psychologists gather all developmental tasks under the umbrella heading of achieving an identity, which they describe as *the* task of adolescence, and some aspect of this is in practically any piece of teenage fiction, as well as in such other genres as poetry, drama, informative nonfiction, biographies, and self-help books.

Close connections exist between adolescent literature and adolescent psychology, with psychology providing the overall picture and adolescent literature providing individual portraits. Because space in this text is too limited to include more than a hint of what you need to know about adolescent psychology, we suggest that professionals working with young people would profit from reading one or more of the books listed in Focus Box 1.3 because teachers and librarians who understand the psychology of young people are better able to

- Judge the soundness of the books they read.
- Decide which ones are worthy of promotion.
- Predict which ones will last and which will be transitory.
- Make better recommendations to individuals.
- Discuss books with students from their viewpoints.
- Gain more understanding and pleasure from personal reading.

Stages of Literary Appreciation

In today's world the development of literary appreciation has as much to do with the commercialization of the popular culture and the mass media as it does with books. For example, clothes and furnishings for babies come decorated with such literary figures as Peter Rabbit, Winnie the Pooh, and Paddington Bear, and, as illustrated by a story in the *Journal of Nursing Jocularity,* clothes for toddlers are often decorated with television characters. An emergency room nurse, trying to get a

FOCUS BOX 1.3

Books to Help Adults Understand Teenagers

The Adolescent: Development, Relationships, and Culture, 9th ed., by F. Philip Rice. Allyn & Bacon, 1998. First published in 1975, Rice's text is comprehensive in presenting the contributions, strengths, and weaknesses of several different theories. Readers come away well informed about current scholarship as well as with an understanding of what being a teenager is like in today's world.

The Adolescent Years: Social Influences and Educational Challenges: 97th Yearbook of the National Society for the Study of Education, Kathryn Borman and Barbara Schneider, eds. National Society for the Study of Education, 1998. Contributors write about how changes in social contexts affect the two biggest tasks of adolescent: the establishment of identity and the search for autonomy.

All Grown Up and No Place to Go: Teenagers in Crisis, rev. ed., by David Elkind. Perseus Press, 1997. Elkind argues against the "hurried teens" and the pressure currently put on many teens to grow up quickly.

The Body Project: An Intimate History of American Girls by Joan Jacobs Blumburg. Random House, 1997. Young adult readers, as well as the professionals working with them, will gain perspective about society's focus on physical appearance and the pressure this puts on young women.

The Courage to Raise Good Men by Olga Silverstein and Beth Rashbaum. Viking, 1994. Silverstein, a family therapist, calls for mothers and fathers to quit "sanctioning the emotional shutdown" that American culture has deemed appropriate for boys. When one-fourth of boys live in households headed by a woman, she sensibly points out that we need to rethink the old adage that "only a father can make a boy a man."

The Culture of Adolescent Risk-Taking by Cynthia Lightfoot. Guilford Press, 1999. Lightfoot helps adults understand and deal with the pressures that contribute to teen attitudes of invincibility and daring.

The Decline of Males by Lionel Tiger. Golden Books, 1999. While not everyone will agree with Tiger's observations, they provide food for thought on social change and the many issues surrounding the education and treatment of males and females.

Early Adolescence: Understanding the 10 to 15 Year Old by Gail A. Caissy. Insight Books, 1994. Caissy writes directly about adolescent development and behavior showing how successful teaching and management relates to understanding adolescents' intellectual, physical, and social development.

Ophelia Speaks: Adolescent Girls Write about Their Search for Self by Sara Shandler. Harperperennial Library, 1999. Shandler sent out 7,000 letters asking junior and senior high school teachers to encourage young women to write their own stories as a rebuttal or a supplement to Mary Bray Pipher's *Reviving Ophelia.* Shandler created her well-received book from the 800 responses she received.

Promiscuities: The Secret Struggle for Womanhood by Naomi Wolf. Random House, 1997. As in her *The Beauty Myth: How Images of Beauty Are Used against Women* (Morrow, 1991), Wolf gives readers much to think about when contemplating the values that young men and women are likely to absorb from the society in which they live.

Reviving Ophelia: Saving the Selves of Adolescent Girls by Mary Bray Pipher. Putnam, 1994. Pipher is a clinical psychologist and wrote her book to focus attention on her observation that all is not well with the first generation of girls to grow up since the feminist movement. She offers concrete suggestions for helping girls build and maintain a strong sense of self.

A Tribe Apart: A Journey into the Heart of American Adolescence by Patricia Hersch. Fawcett/Ballantine, 1998. Over a three-year period, Hersch did a close study of eight teenagers in grades 7 to 12. About one of her chief findings (the absence of adults in the lives of teenagers), she tells what teachers and librarians can do for teens who are in need of adult connections.

chattering four-year-old girl to quit talking so she could listen to her heart, put her stethoscope on the girl's chest, and said, "Shh . . . I have to see if Barney is in here!" The girl gave her a withering look of condescension and declared, "Jesus is in my heart! Barney is on my underpants!"

Older children wear shirts decorated with comic book heroes, while the shirts of college students contain M. C. Escher drawings, rock band logos, funny one-liners, and literary quotes. In many high schools, T-shirt messages have grown so controversial that students are not allowed to wear imprinted clothing.

While clothing is the most visible manifestation of how the popular culture is connected to literary appreciation, it is only a tiny part of the overall picture. Students come to school already influenced by years of watching television, and, for most students, what they take from literature classes is applied more often to their mass-media experiences than to the "Literature with a capital L" that English teachers love.

Table 1.1, The Stages of Literary Appreciation, presents an approximation of how individuals develop the personal attitudes and the reading, watching, and listening skills that are a necessary part of literary appreciation. The table should be read from the bottom up because each level is built on the one below it. People do not go *through* these stages of development; instead they *add on* so that at each level they have all that they had before plus a new way to gain pleasure and understanding (see also the discussion of teaching literature in Chapter 11).

Thanks to commercialization and the mass media, children are introduced to literary characters long before they meet them in books.

TABLE 1.2

STAGES OF LITERARY APPRECIATION

Read this chart from the bottom up to trace the stages of development most commonly found in reading the autobiographies of adults who love to read.

Level	Optimal Age	Stage	Sample Literary Materials	Sample Actions
7	Adulthood to death	Aesthetic appreciation	Classics Significant contemporary books Drama Film	Reads constantly Dreams of writing the great American novel Enjoys literary and film criticism Reads 50 books a year Sees plays Revisits favorites
6	College	Reading widely	Best-sellers Acclaimed novels, poems, plays, films, magazines	Talks about books and films with friends Joins a book club Gathers books to take on vacation
5	High school	Venturing beyond self	Science fiction Social issues fiction Forbidden material "Different" stories	Begins buying own books Sees movies with friends Gets reading suggestions from friends Reads beyond school assignments
4	Junior high	Finding oneself in literature	Realistic fiction Contemporary problem novels Wish-fulfilling stories	Hides novels inside textbooks to read during classes Stays up at night reading Uses reading as an escape from social pressures
3	Late elementary	Losing oneself in literature	Series books Fantasies Animal stories Anything one can disappear into	Reads while doing chores Reads while traveling Makes friends with a librarian Checks books out regularly Gets "into" reading a particular genre or author
2	Primary grades	Learning to decode Developing an attention span	School reading texts Easy-to-read books Signs and other real-world messages	Takes pride in reading to parents or others Enjoys reading alone Has favorite authors
1	Birth to kindergarten	Understanding of pleasure and profit from printed words and from visual depictions	Nursery rhymes Folktales Picture books Television programs	Has favorite books for reading aloud "Reads" signs for certain restaurants and food Memorizes favorite stories and pretends to read Enjoys listening to adults read

Level 1: Understanding That Pleasure and Profit Come from Literature

Children are fortunate if they have loving adults who share songs and nursery rhymes and who talk with children about the television and the movies they see together. They are also lucky if they get to go to bookstores and libraries for buying and borrowing books and for participating in group story hours. Researchers in reading education are discovering the social nature of reading. Children who seem to get the most from their reading are those who have had opportunities for "talking story" and for having what Ralph Peterson and Maryann Eeds call "grand conversations" both with other children and with adults.[9]

If children are to put forth the intellectual energy required in learning to read, they need to be convinced that it is worthwhile—that pleasure awaits them—or that there are concrete benefits to be gained. In U.S. metropolitan areas, there's hardly a 4-year-old who doesn't recognize the golden arches of a McDonald's restaurant. Toddlers too young to walk around grocery stores reach out from their seats in grocery carts to grab favorite brands of cereal. We know one child who by the time he entered first grade had taught himself to read from *TV Guide*. While its format breaks almost every rule any good textbook writer would follow in designing a primer for clear and easy reading, it had one overpowering advantage. The child could get immediate feedback. If he made a correct guess, he was rewarded by getting to watch the program he wanted. If he made a mistake, he knew immediately that he had to return to the printed page to try again.

Level 2: Learning to Read

Learning to decode (i.e., to turn the squiggles on a page into meaningful sounds) is the second stage of development. It gets maximum attention during the primary grades, where as much as 70 percent of the school day is devoted to language arts. Developing literacy, however, is more than just decoding; it is a never-ending task for anyone who is intellectually active. Even at a mundane level, adults continue working to develop their reading skills. People tackling new computer programs or rereading tax guides in preparation for an audit exhibit the same symptoms of concentrated effort as do children first learning to read. They point with their fingers, move their lips, return to reread difficult parts, and in frustration slam the offending booklet to the floor. In each case, however, they are motivated by a vision of some benefit to be gained, so they increase their efforts.

Those of us who learned to read with ease may forget to help children who are struggling to find pleasure and enjoyment. Children who learn to read easily—the girl who sits in the backseat of the car and reads all through the family vacation and the boy who reads a book while delivering the neighborhood newspapers—find their own rewards for reading. For these children, the years between 7 and 12 are golden. They can read the great body of literature that the world has saved for them: *Charlotte's Web*, the Little House books, *The Borrowers*, *The Chronicles of Narnia*, *The Wizard of Oz*, *Where the Red Fern Grows*, and books by Beverly Cleary, William Steig, Dr. Seuss, and hundreds of other good writers.

At this stage, children are undemanding. They are in what Margaret Early has described as a stage of unconscious enjoyment.[10] With help, they may enjoy such classics as *Alice in Wonderland*, *The Wind in the Willows*, *Treasure Island*, and *Little*

Women, but by themselves they are far more likely to turn to less challenging material. Parents worry that their children are wasting time, but nearly 100 percent of our college students who say they love to read went through childhood stages of being addicted for months to one particular kind of book. Apparently, readers find comfort in knowing the characters in a book and what to expect, and this comfort helps them develop speed and skill.

Level 3: Losing Oneself in a Story

Children who read only during the time set aside in school and children who live in homes where the television set is constantly switched from channel to channel and where the exigencies of daily life leave little time for uninterrupted conversations and stories probably have a hard time losing themselves in a good story. There are exceptions, of course, such as Worm (short for bookworm), the 11-year-old in Rod Philbrick's *Max the Mighty,* who escapes the horrors of her everyday life by reading all the time. She even uses a miner's helmet and headlight to read in the dark.

Because of life's complications, many children do not lose themselves in a good story until much later than the third or fourth grades, which is typical of good readers, or it may not happen at all, especially with boys (see Robert Lipsyte's statement on facing page). In this segment quoted from *The Car Thief* by Theodore Weesner, Alex Housman, who is being kept in a detention home, is 17 years old when he first experiences losing himself in a story (i.e., finding what we refer to as "a good read"). Someone has donated a box of books to the detention home, and, because there's nothing else to do, Alex starts to read. He is intimidated by the words because he had never read anything before except school assignments, but because the book is straightforward and written in a style he can understand,

> He sat on the floor reading until he grew sleepy. When his eyelids began to slide down and his head began to cloud, he lay over on his side on the floor to sleep awhile, pulling up his knees, resting his head on his arm. When he woke he got up and carried the book with him to the bathroom . . . reading the book again, he became so involved in the story that his legs fell asleep. He kept reading, intending to get up at the end of this page, then at the end of this page, if only because he would feel more comfortable with his pants up and buttoned, but he read on. . . . Something was happening to him, something as pleasantly strange as the feeling he had had for Irene Scheaffer. By now, if he knew a way, he would prolong the book the distance his mind could see, and he rose again, quietly, to sustain the pleasant sensation, the escape he seemed already to have made from the scarred and unlighted corridor. Within this shadowed space there were now other things: war and food and worry over cigarettes and rations, leaving and returning, dying and escaping. The corridor itself, and his own life, was less present.[11]

Level 4: Finding Oneself in a Story

The more experience children have with literature, whether through words or pictures, the more discriminating they become. To receive pleasure they have to respect the story. In reminiscing about his childhood fondness for both *The Hardy Boys* and motorcycles, the late John Gardner remarked that his development as a

ROBERT LIPSYTE
On Books for Boys

Whenever I say that boys need more good books, people roll their eyes, "C'mon, boys got it all, even now." True. But what they've got is not necessarily in all our best interests. And books can be part of the problem in a society that conditions boys to grow up to be men who beat up smaller people, including women and children, boys who become men fearful of each other, who will fight back any attempt to socialize them out of violence.

I was lucky as a kid, although I certainly didn't think so at the time. I was very fat. I might as well have been a girl. Fat boys could read; we didn't matter.

But for normal boys, not your star athletes, just your everyday boys, reading was—is—a problem. Boys typically read about sports, about specific subjects and science, but rarely about the arts or social problems. Some experts claim this comes from the difference between the sexes: Boys want to master the world; girls want to understand it.

I think that boys don't read as much as we'd like them to because (1) current books tend not to deal with the real problems and fears of boys, and (2) there is a tendency to treat boys as a group—which is where males are at their absolute worst—instead of as individuals who have to be led into reading secretly and one at a time.

Boys are afraid of being humiliated, of being hurt, of being hit by the ball, of being made to look dumb or inadequate in front of other boys and in front of girls. Most of the sports books boys are force-fed reinforce those fears with the false values of winning as the only goal, bending mindlessly to authority, preserving the status quo, often at the cost of truth. I think I was very lucky not being a sports fan as a kid and hardly reading any sports books at all.

Boys need reassurance that their fears of violence and humiliation and competition are shared fears. Books can reassure them. But to be able to read a book properly, you have to be able to sink into a scene, to absorb characters, to care, to empathize. You have to be willing to make yourself vulnerable to a book as surely as you need to make yourself vulnerable to a person. This is not easy for a male in this society to do, particularly an adolescent male who is unsure of his own identity, his sexuality, his future.

So, you say, we have to change society first, and then boys will read good books. This is true. But if we can get just a few boys to read a few good books, we will have started the change. Cajole, *coerce,* do whatever needs to be done to get one book into one boy's hands, or back pocket. A book that he can make into a cave he can crawl into, roll around in, explore, for what's in there and what's in himself, find places of his own he never touched before, find out that a book is something you can do all by yourself, where no one can see you laughing or crying. It is the intellectual and emotional equivalent of safer sex.

Robert Lipsyte's books include *Michael Jordan: A Life above the Rim,* 1994; *Arnold Schwarzenegger: Hercules in America,* 1993; *The Chief,* 1993; *The Brave,* 1991; *One Fat Summer,* 1982, and *The Contender,* 1967; all from HarperCollins.

literary critic took a step forward when he lost patience with the leisurely conversations that the Hardy boys were supposed to have as they roared down country roads side by side on their motorcycles.

Good readers begin developing this critical sense in literature at about the same time they develop it in real life at the end of childhood and the beginning of their teen years. They move away from a simple interest in what happened in a story to ask *why*. They want logical development and are no longer satisfied with stereotypes. They want characters controlled by believable human motives because now their reading has a real purpose to it. They are reading to find out about themselves, not simply to escape into someone else's experiences for a few pleasurable hours. They may read dozens of contemporary teenage novels, looking for lives as much like their own as possible. They read about real people in biographies, personal essays, and journalistic stories. They are also curious about other sides of life, and so they seek out books that present lives totally different from their own. They look for anything bizarre, unbelievable, weird, or grotesque: stories of occult happenings, trivia books, and horror stories. And, of course, for their leisure-time reading and viewing they may revert to level 3 of escaping into a good story. When they are working at the highest level of their capability, however, their purpose is largely one of finding themselves and their places in society. Parents and teachers sometimes worry, as did Han Nolan (See her statement on p. 94), when children seem stuck at a particular level or with a particular kind of book. In most instances, as long as there are other choices available as well as time for reading, students sooner or later venture onward in a natural kind of progression.

Level 5: Venturing Beyond Themselves

The next stage in literary appreciation comes when people go beyond their egocentrism and look at the larger circle of society. Senior high school English teachers have some of their best teaching experiences with books and stories by such writers as Ernest Hemingway, John Steinbeck, Harper Lee, F. Scott Fitzgerald, Carson McCullers, William Faulkner, Arthur Miller, and Flannery O'Connor. Students respond to the way these books raise questions about conformity, social pressures, justice, and other aspects of human frailties and strengths. Book discussions at this level can have real meat to them because readers make different interpretations as they bring their own experiences into play against those in the books.

Obviously, getting to this level of literary appreciation is more than a matter of developing an advanced set of decoding skills. It is closely tied to intellectual, physical, and emotional development. Teenagers face the tremendous responsibility of assessing the world around them and deciding where they fit in. Reading at this level allows teenagers to focus on their own psychological needs in relation to society. The more directly they can do this, the more efficient they feel, which probably explains the popularity of contemporary problem novels featuring young protagonists, as in the books by Will Hobbs, Brock Cole, M. E. Kerr, Robert Cormier, Jacqueline Woodson, Paula Fox, Sue Ellen Bridgers, Richard Peck, and Virginia Euwer Wolff.

Although many people read fantasy and science fiction at the level of losing themselves in a good story, others may read such books as Neal Shusterman's *The Dark Side of Nowhere* and Philip Pullman's *The Subtle Knife* and *Clockwork—Or All Wound Up* at a higher level of reflection. Such readers come back from spending a few hours in the imagined society with new ideas about their own society.

Levels 6 and 7: Aesthetic Appreciation

When people have developed the skills and attitudes necessary to enjoy imaginative literary experiences at all the levels described so far, they are ready to embark on a lifetime of aesthetic appreciation. This is the level at which producers, playwrights, authors, critics, talented performers, and literary scholars concentrate their efforts. Even they don't work at this level all the time, however, because it is as demanding as it is rewarding. The professor who teaches Shakespeare goes home at night and relaxes by watching *The Simpsons* or scanning the Internet to see what might turn up on the Drudge Report or on various bulletin boards. The author who writes for hours in the morning might put herself to sleep at night by listening to a tape recording of Ayn Rand's *The Fountainhead,* while the producer of a new play may flip through magazines as a way of relaxing. Teenagers are much the same. Top students take a break from the seriousness of homework by watching *Dawson's Creek,* listening to music, or playing video games.

In summary, the important points to learn from this discussion of stages of literary appreciation are that teachers, librarians, and parents should meet young people where they are and help them feel comfortable at that stage before trying to move them on, and that we need to continue to provide for all the levels below the one on which we are focusing; for example, people at any stage need to experience pleasure and profit from their reading, viewing, and listening. This is especially true with reading, which requires an extra measure of intellectual effort. People who feel they are not being appropriately rewarded for their efforts may grow discouraged and join the millions of adults who no longer read for personal fulfillment and pleasure but only to get the factual information needed to manage the daily requirements of modern living.

Notes

[1] David Van Biema, "The Loneliest—and Purest—Rite of Passage: Adolescence and Initiation," *The Journey of Our Lives, Life* magazine (October 1991):31.

[2] David Spritz, "Reads Like Teen Spirit." *Time* magazine, July 19, 1999, p. 79.

[3] J. Donald Adams, *Speaking of Books and Life* (Holt, Rinehart and Winston, 1965), pp. 251–252.

[4] John Goldthwaite, "Notes on the Children's Book Trade," *Harper's* 254 (January 1977):84

[5] Arlette Ingraham Willis, "Celebrating African American Literary Achievements," *Teaching and Using Multicultural Literature in Grades 9–12: Going Beyond the Canon,* ed. by Arlette Willis. (Christopher-Gordon, 1998), p. 72.

[6] Patty Campbell, "The Sand in the Oyster: Don't Ask Alex." *Horn Book Magazine* 74 (September/October, 1998):633–634.

[7] David Spritz, "Reads Like Teen Spirit." *Time* magazine, July 19, 1999, p. 79.

[8] Robert Havighurst, *Developmental Tasks and Education* (McKay, 1972).

[9] Ralph Peterson and Maryann Eeds. *Grand Conversations: Literature Groups in Action* (Scholastic, 1990).

[10] Margaret Early, "Stages of Growth in Literary Appreciation," *English Journal* 49 (March 1960):163–66.

[11] First cited by G. Robert Carlsen in an article exploring stages of reading development, "Literature Is," *English Journal* 63 (February 1974):23–27.

Titles, Other than the Honor List, Mentioned in the Text of Chapter One

Chbosky, Stephen. *The Perks of Being a Wallflower.* MTV/Pocket Books, 1999.

Gilbreth, Frank B., Jr. *Cheaper by the Dozen.* Crowell, 1948.

Gallo, Donald R., ed. *Speaking for Ourselves: Autobiographical Sketches by Notable Authors of Books for Young Adults.* National Council of Teachers of English, 1990.

Gallo, Donald R., ed. *Speaking for Ourselves, Too: More Autobiographical Sketches by Notable Authors of Books for Young Adults.* National Council of Teachers of English, 1993.

Guy, Rosa. *The Music of Summer.* Delacorte, 1992.

Guy, Rosa. *Ruby.* Viking, 1976.

Guy, Rosa. *The Ups and Downs of Carl Davis III.* Delacorte, 1989.

Hipple, Ted, ed. *Writers for Young Adults* (four volumes). Charles Scribner's, 1996, 2000.

Myers, Walter Dean. *The Glory Field.* Scholastic, 1994.

Myers, Walter Dean. *Scorpions.* HarperCollins, 1988.

Pendergast, Tom and Sara Pendergast. *Twentieth-Century Young Adult Writers,* 2nd edition. St. James Press, 1999.

Philbrick, Rod. *Max the Mighty.* Scholastic/Blue Sky, 1998.

Pullman, Philip. *The Subtle Knife.* Knopf, 1997.

Rand, Ayn. *The Fountainhead.* Macmillan, 1968.

Schusterman, Neal. *The Dark Side of Nowhere.* Little, Brown, 1997.

Weesner, Theodore. *The Car Thief.* Random House, 1972.

Williams-Garcia, Rita. *Blue Tights.* Dutton, 1988.

Information on the availability of paperback editions of these titles is available online from such book sellers as Barnes & Noble and Amazon.com, and through *Books in Print* compiled by R. R. Bowker Company and available either in person or online from major libraries.

A Brief History of Adolescent Literature

Although we would not argue with teachers and librarians that the best way to know adolescent literature is to read widely in contemporary books, a case can be made that professionals ought to know the history of their own fields for at least three reasons. First, they ought to know not merely where they are but also how they got there, and far too many teachers and librarians are unaware of their history. We were, for too many of us, miraculously born from nothing as a profession the day before yesterday. More than just being aware of a mixture of fascinating historical tidbits, knowing our common backgrounds gives us a sense of the past and a way of knowing why and how certain kinds of books have consistently proven popular and where books today came from.

Second, for anyone who cares about the mores and morals of our time reflected in adolescent books, there is a fascination in knowing how they came to be. There is no better way to see what adults wanted young people to accept as good and noble at any point in history than to examine adolescent books of the time. The analysis may breed some cynicism as we detect the discrepancies between the lessons taught by a Felsen or an Alger or a Stratemeyer Syndicate author and the truth about the world of the time, but the lessons are nonetheless important and not necessarily less sincere.

Third, and this may be difficult to believe for those who have not dipped into books out of the past, many of the older books are surprisingly fun to read. We're not suggesting that many deserve to be reprinted and circulated among today's young adults, only that librarians and teachers may discover that books as different as Mabel Robinson's *Bright Island* (1937) or John Tunis's *Go, Team, Go!* (1954) or John Bennett's *Master Skylark* (1897) are fun, or that other books such as Ralph Henry Barbour's *The Crimson Sweater* (1906) or Susan Coolidge's *What Katy Did* (1872) or Mary Stolz's *Pray Love, Remember* (1954) are not without their charm.

For the convenience of readers, this chapter is divided into roughly equal parts: 1800–1900, 1900–1940, and 1940–1966, each affected by the conditions and technologies of the day (see Karen Hesse's statement on p. 44).

KAREN HESSE
On Technology

Books were once a new technology. They were handwritten on animal skins, stacked in unwieldy piles or rolled into awkward scrolls. They organized the world in a way it had never been organized before. But those books belonged only to the elite. Then, Gutenberg introduced a new technology and, with a sudden explosion, books reached the masses.

There are few technologies more satisfying than a book. It is portable, it needs no artificial power source to operate, nor does it take time to boot up. Access is instantaneous. You can rummage through a book, locating random bits of data by simply flipping pages. You can operate a book lying down, sitting up, swinging in a hammock, bent over a desk, cradled in the bough of a tree, rocking in the belly of a boat, reclining in a meadow, sunbathing at the beach, soaking in a fragrant tub, before, during, and after lift off and landing, or simply standing in the hall, waiting for your daughter to finish ballet class.

I cannot remember a time when I didn't love books. From the moment I learned to read I found friendship, understanding, excitement, mystery, adventure, laughter, and redemption in the pages of books. I opened my heart and my mind each time I opened a book; I let the book's reality enter inside me, let it move in and hook up with my own reality.

A young reader once told me, "Every now and then I wish that I could think like someone else or be someone else just to see what they feel like." Children can feel so alone, even under the best of circumstances. Embracing the reality of a book is one of the finest ways I've ever found to "feel like" someone else.

I think about evenings in this country. I think about our children tucked along rural roads, side by side in cities, sprawled along endless suburban avenues. I think about the extraordinary range of circumstances in which our children live, and then I think of the blue light of a television screen or a computer monitor, its glow reflected in those children's eyes. These new technologies may be opening the minds of our children, but are they opening their hearts?

Perhaps someday the technology of books will also be abandoned, replaced by a better technology. But until that technology arrives, a technology more engaging, more absorbing, more enriching than a book, until that technology arrives in a form which does not require compromise on our part to compensate for the limitations on the part of that technology, we must all take time, every now and then, to turn off the television, shut down the computer, and open ourselves to a book.

Karen Hesse's books include *Letters from Rifka*, Holt, 1992; *The Music of Dolphins*, Scholastic, 1996; *Phoenix Rising*, Holt, 1994; *Out of the Dust*, Scholastic, 1997; and *A Time of Angels*, Hyperion, 1995.

1800–1900: A Century of Purity with a Few Passions

Before 1800, literature read by children and young adults alike was largely religious. Such books as John Bunyan's *The Pilgrim's Progress* (1678) reminded young people that they were merely small adults who soon must face the wrath of God. In the 1800s, the attitude of adults toward the young gradually changed. The country expanded, we moved inevitably toward an urban society, medical knowledge rapidly developed, and young people no longer began working so early in their lives. The literature that emerged for young adults remained pious and sober, but it hinted at the possibility of humanity's experiencing a satisfying life here on earth. Books reflected adult values and fashions but of this world, not merely the next.

The American Sunday School Union

Largely forgotten, a spiritual and practical movement that began in 1817 in Philadelphia under the title of the Sunday and Adult School Union changed its title to the American Sunday School Union in 1824. By 1830, it had determined to change the course of American education by offering Sunday School lessons that taught religion at the same time they educated young people in mathematics and grammar and history and all sorts of practical, job-related skills.

For the next 40 years, the Union produced millions of books for use in Sunday Schools, which were open from 8:00 A.M. to 10:00 A.M. and from 4:00 P.M. to 6:00 P.M. All titles were approved by a board representing six major religions. Titles varied from *History of Patriarchs, Wild Flowers: or the May Day Walk, The Early Saxons, Curiosities of Egypt, Delaware and Iroquois Indians,* to *Kindness to Animals, or the Sin of Cruelty Exposed and Rebuked.*

The Union was best known, however, for its heavily moralistic fiction, rarely deviating from two basic formulas. A young child near death would remind readers of all his virtues, all that they must remember and practice, and then the child would die, to the relief of readers. On page 1 of E. P. Grey's *My Teacher's Present: A Select Biography of the Young,* the author wrote:

> You have in this little volume the biography of six Sunday school pupils, who were early called from this world. They were happy and beloved whilst they lived, and deeply lamented when they died.

Another formula portrayed good children who had temporarily forgotten duties to parents and siblings and who would soon get their comeuppance, for example, *Alfred Graham, or the Dangers of Disobedience, Hubert Lee, or How a Child May Do Good,* and *The Prize Garden.*

Most of the books were little more than sugar-coated sermons; the titles usually gave away the plot, and the writing was unbelievably mawkish. By the 1870s and 1880s, the Union books lost most of their readership to the almost equally badly written work of Horatio Alger, to the often brilliant prose of Louisa May Alcott, and to various writers of dime novels or domestic novels. At a time when few children had any chance of a formal education in schools, however, the American Sunday School Union books were widely read and did much to advance the cause of literacy in America.

Alcott and Alger

Louisa May Alcott and Horatio Alger, Jr., were the first writers for young adults to gain national attention, but the similarity between the two ends almost as it begins. Alcott wrote of happy family life. Alger wrote about broken homes. Alcott's novels were sometimes harsh but always honest. Alger's novels were romantic fantasies. Alcott's novels are still read for good reason. Alger's novels are rarely read save by the historian or the specialist.

The second daughter of visionary Amos Bronson Alcott, Louisa May Alcott lived her youth near Concord and Boston with a practical mother and a father who was brilliant, generous, improvident, and impractical. The reigning young adult writer of the time was Oliver Optic (the pen name of William T. Adams), and Boston publishers Roberts Brothers were eager to find a story for young adults that would compete with Optic. Thomas Niles, Roberts's representative, suggested in September 1866 that Louisa May Alcott write a girls' book, and in May 1868 he gently reminded her that she had agreed to try.

She sent a manuscript to Niles, who thought parts of it dull, but other readers at the publisher's office disagreed, and the first part of *Little Women: Meg, Jo, Beth, and Amy. The Story of Their Lives. A Girl's Book* was published September 30, 1868. With three illustrations and a frontispiece for $1.50 a copy, *Little Women* was favorably reviewed, and sales were good, here and in England. By early November 1868, Alcott had begun work on the second part, which was published on April 14, 1869.

Little Women has vitality and joy and real life devoid of the sentimentality common at the time, a wistful portrait of the life and world Alcott must have wished she could have lived. The Civil War background is subtle, expressing the loneliness and never-ending war far better than many adult war novels, for all their suffering, pain, and horror. Aimed at young adults, *Little Women* has maintained steady popularity with them and children. Adults reread it (sometimes repeatedly) to gain a sense of where they were when they were children.

If *Little Women* is Alcott's best-known book, most of the recent research and criticism on Alcott has been devoted to the thrillers she wrote anonymously to make money for the family. Madeleine Stern has edited several collections of these thrillers (e.g., *Behind A Mask: The Unknown Thrillers of Louisa May Alcott; Plots and Counterplots: More Unknown Thrillers of Louisa May Alcott;* and *The Lost Stories of Louisa May Alcott).* The most recent is edited by Kent Bicknell, *A Long Fatal Love Chase.*

Son of an unctuous Unitarian clergyman, Horatio Alger, Jr., graduated from Harvard at eighteen. Ordained a Unitarian minister in 1864, he served a Brewster, Massachusetts, church only to leave it two years later under a cloud of scandal and claims of sodomy, all hushed at the time. He moved to New York City and began writing full-time.

The same year, he sent *Ragged Dick; or, Street Life in New York* to Oliver Optic's magazine, *Student and Schoolmate,* a popular goody-goody magazine. Optic recognized salable pap when he spotted it, and he bought Alger's book for the January 1867 issue. Published in hardcover in 1867 or 1868, *Ragged Dick* was the first of

FOCUS BOX 2.1

Old Stories in New Dress

Ella Enchanted by Gale Carson Levine. HarperCollins, 1997. Levin's charming new telling of Cinderella was chosen as a Newbery Honor Book.

The Magic Flute retold by Anne Gatti, illustrated by Peter Malone. Chronicle, 1997. A multisensory feast is prepared for readers in this retelling of Mozart's operatic fairy tale, which comes with full-page paintings and a CD to match each page.

Othello: A Novel by Julius Lester. Scholastic, 1995. In giving it a starred review, *School Library Journal* praised Lester for "an incredibly skillful blend of his own words and Shakespeare's language into modern English."

Parzival: The Quest of the Grail Knight by Katherine Paterson. Lodestar, 1998. Parzival (or Percevel) is one of the lesser known of King Arthur's knights, which is fine with Paterson because it gave her more freedom to create an 800-year-old character who is both touching and humorous.

Robin of Sherwood by Michael Morpurgo, illustrated by Michael Foreman. Harcourt, 1996. The characters have the same names as in the classic tale, but they have distinguishing characteristics that makes them quite different. The story starts with a contemporary boy finding Robin's skull, fainting, and dreaming of Robin. The same team created *Arthur: High King of Britain* (Harcourt, 1995).

Shadow Spinner by Susan Fletcher. Simon & Schuster/Atheneum, 1998. A young crippled storyteller, Marjan, brings a new story to Queen Shahrazad, who has already been spinning stories for nearly 1000 nights. Complications ensue when Marjan can't remember the ending.

The Silver Treasure: Myths and Legends of the World by Geraldine McCaughrean, illustrated by Bee Willey. Simon & Schuster, 1997. Among the characters to whom McCaughrean gives new life are Rip Van Winkle, King Arthur, and Sir Patrick Spens.

Sirena by Donna Jo Napoli. Scholastic, 1998. Sirena is one of ten sirens (mermaids) intent on luring sailors to their island because of the belief that a man's love will give them immortality. Sirena does not participate in her sister's tricks but, as luck would have it, is the one to fall in love with a mortal when the injured Philocetes is abandoned by his shipmates.

Spider's Voice by Gloria Skurzynski. Simon & Schuster/Atheneum, 1999. Skurzynski retells the story of the twelfth century French lovers Abelard and (H)Eloise through the voice of a fictional servant nicknamed Spider. The plot is as tangled as a spider's web and the characters' lives as easily dismantled.

Zel by Donna Jo Napoli. Dutton, 1996. Napoli tells the old fairy tale about Rapunzel through exploring the psychology of the mother who keeps the beautiful girl locked in the tower. She treated a similar theme in her 1993 *The Magic Circle* (Dutton) which explores the witch who imprisons Hansel and Gretel.

---

many successes for Alger and his publishers, and it is still his most readable work, probably because it was the first from a mold that soon became predictably moldy.

The plot, as in most Alger books, consisted of semiconnected episodes illustrating a boy's first steps toward maturity, respectability, and affluence. Ragged Dick, a young bootblack, is grubby but not dirty, he smokes and gambles occasionally, but even the most casual reader recognizes his essential goodness. Through a series of increasingly difficult-to-believe chapters, Ragged Dick is transformed by the model of a young man and the trust of an older one into respectability. But where the sequence of events was hard to believe, Alger now makes events impossible to believe as he introduces the note that typified his later books. What pluck and hard work had brought to Dick is now cast aside as luck enters in—a little boy

Today's high school students are reading many of the same basic stories that teenagers read a hundred years ago. See Focus Box 2.1 Old Stories in New Dress.

falls overboard from a ferry, Dick saves the child, and a grateful father rewards Dick with new clothes and a better job. Some readers label Alger's books "rags to riches" stories, but the hero rarely achieves riches, although at the close of the book he is a rung or two higher on the ladder of success than he has any reason to deserve. "Rags to respectability" is a more accurate statement about Alger's work.

Other Series Writers

The Boston publishing firm of Lee and Shepard established *the* format for young adult series, and to the distress of teachers, librarians, and parents, series books became the method of publishing for many young adult novels, although the format would be far more sophisticated a few years later when Edward Stratemeyer became the king of series books. If sales were any index, readers delighted in Lee and Shepard's 440 authors and 900 books published in 1887 alone.

Four series writers were especially popular. Under the pen name of Harry Castlemon, Charles Austin Fosdick wrote his first novel, *Frank the Young Naturalist* (1864), while in the Navy. Castlemon's novels are close to unreadable today, but his books were popular well into the twentieth century. Oliver Optic, the pen name of William Taylor Adams, was a prolific writer of more than 100 books. *The Boat Club* (1885), his first book and the first of the six-book Boat Club series, ran through sixty editions.

Martha Finley (pen name of Martha Farquharson) wrote the amazingly popular Elsie Dinsmore series, twenty-eight volumes carrying Elsie from girlhood to grandmother. A favorite with young women who seemingly loved crying over every other page, Elsie is persistently and nauseatingly docile, pious, virtuous, sweet, humble, timid, ignorant, good, and lachrymose. Published in 1867 and running to an incredible number of editions after that, *Elsie Dinsmore* opened with the ever-virtuous and Christian Elsie awaiting the return of her cold father. His return proves again how unloving he is and how patient Elsie is. Elsie exhibits virtues no matter what happens to her, and much does, for she is no actor, but only a reactor.

Susan Coolidge (pen name of Sarah Chauncey Woolsey) wrote only a few books, but one series rivaled Alcott's books with many girls. *What Katy Did* (1872) featured tomboy Katy Carr, her widowed doctor father, her sisters and brothers, and an invalid aunt. Although too much of the book is concerned with retribution for Katy's obstinancy, Katy is prankish and fun and essentially good.

The Two Most Popular Types of Novels: Domestic and Dime Novels

In 1855, Nathaniel Hawthorne wrote his publisher bitterly lamenting the state of American literature:

> America is now wholly given over to a d—d mob of scribbling women, and I should have no chance of success while the public taste is occupied with their trash—and should be ashamed of myself if I did succeed. What is the mystery of these innumerable editions of *The Lamplighter,* and other books neither better nor worse?—worse they could not be, and better they need not be, when they sell by the 10,000?[1]

The trash was the domestic novel. Born out of the belief that humanity was redeemable, the domestic novel preached morality; woman's submission to man; the value of cultural, social, and political conservatism; a religion of the heart and the Bible; and the glories of suffering.

Most domestic novels concerned a young girl, orphaned and placed in the home of a relative or some benefactor, who meets a darkly handsome young man with shadows from his past, a man not to be trusted but worth redeeming and converting. Domestic novels promised some adventure amidst many moral lessons. The heroines differed more in names than characteristics. Uniformly submissive to—yet distrustful of—their betters and men generally, they were self-sacrificing and self-denying beyond belief or common sense and interested in the primacy of the family and marriage as the goal of all decent women. Domestic novels were products of the religious sentiment of the time, the espousal of traditional virtues, and the anxieties and frustrations of women trying to find a role in a changing society.

Writing under the pen name of Elizabeth Wetherell, Susan Warner wrote more than twenty novels and the first domestic novel, *The Wide, Wide World* (1850). As much as forty years later, the novel was said to be one of the four most widely read books in the United States, along with the Bible, *The Pilgrim's Progress,* and *Uncle Tom's Cabin.* An abridged edition was published in England in 1950 by the University of London Press, and the Feminist Press republished Warner's book in 1987.

The novel was rejected by several New York publishers. George Putnam was ready to return it but decided to ask his mother to read it. She did, she loved it, she urged her son to publish it, and the book was out in time for the Christmas trade. Sales slowly picked up, and the first edition sold out in four months. Translations into French, German, Swedish, and Italian followed, and by 1852, *The Wide, Wide World* was in its fourteenth printing.

The author's life paralleled that of her heroine, Ellen Montgomery. Warner's father was pathetically and persistently broke, and although the fictional world is not quite so ugly, Ellen's mother dies early, and her father is so consumed with family business that he asks Aunt Fortune Emerson to take over Ellen's life. Ellen, to her aunt's irritation, forms a firm friendship with the aunt's intended. Ellen's closest friend—the daughter of the local minister—is doomed to die soon and succeeds in doing just that. In the midst of life, tears flow. When Ellen and her friends are not crying, they are cooking. Warner's novel taught submission, the dangers of self-righteousness, and the virtues of a steadfast religion. Despite all the weeping, or maybe because of it, the book seemed to have been read by everyone of its time. E. Douglas Branch called it, "The greatest achievement of any of the lady novelists."[2]

Warner's popularity was exceeded only by Augusta Jane Evans Wilson for her *St. Elmo* (1867). Probably no other novel so literally touched the American landscape—thirteen towns were named, or renamed, St. Elmo, as were hotels, railroad coaches, steamboats, one kind of punch, and a brand of cigars. The popularity of Wilson's book may be gauged by a notice in a special edition of *St. Elmo* "limited to 100,000 copies." Only *Uncle Tom's Cabin* had greater sales, and Wilson was more than once called by her admirers the American Brontë.

Ridiculously melodramatic as the plot of *St. Elmo* is, it was so beloved that men and women publicly testified that their lives had been permanently changed for the better by reading it. The plot concerns an orphaned girl befriended by a wealthy woman whose dissolute son is immediately enamored of the young woman, is rejected by her, leaves home for several years, returns to plead for her love, is again rejected, and eventually becomes a minister to win the young woman's hand. They marry, another wicked man reformed by the power of a good woman.

If domestic novels took women by storm, dime novels performed almost the same miracle for men. They began when two brothers, Erastus and Irwin Beadle, republished Ann S. Stephens's *Malaeksa: The Indian Wife of the White Hunter* in June 1860. The story of a hunter and his Indian wife in the Revolutionary War days in upper New York state may be as melodramatic as any domestic novel, but its emphasis is more on thrills and chills than tears, and it apparently satisfied and intrigued male readers. Indeed, 65,000 copies of the 6- by 4-inch book of 128 pages sold in almost record time. The most popular of the early dime novels, also set in the Revolutionary period, appeared in October 1860. *Seth Jones: or, The Captives of the Frontier* sold 60,000 copies the first day; at least 500,000 copies were sold in the United States alone, and it was translated into ten languages.

For several years, dime novels cost ten cents, ran about 100 pages in a 7- by 5-inch format, and were aimed at adults. Some early genius of publishing discovered that many readers were boys who could hardly afford the dime cost. Thereafter, the novels dropped to a nickel, although the genre continued to be called the *dime novel*. The most popular dime novels were set in the West—the West of dime novels increasingly meant Colorado and points west—with wondrous he-men like Deadwood Dick and Diamond Dick. Dime novels developed other forms, such as mysteries and even early forms of science fiction, but none were so popular or so typical as the westerns.

Writers of dime novels never pretended to be writing great literature, but they did write satisfying thrills and chills for the masses. The books were filled with

These two half-dime novels illustrate the promised action, the purple prose, and the erudite vocabulary of their day.

stock characters. Early issues of the *Library Journal,* from 1876 onward for another thirty years, illustrate how many librarians hated dime novels for their immorality; but in truth dime novels were moral. The Beadles sincerely believed that their books should represent sound moral values, and what the librarians objected to in dime novels was nothing more than the unrealistic melodramatic plots and the stereotyped characters, more typical of the time than just the dime novel.

Bad Boy and Adventure Novels

Beginning with Thomas Bailey Aldrich's *The Story of a Bad Boy* in 1870, a new kind of literature developed around bad boys, imperfect but tough and realistic and anything but the good-little-boy figures in too many unrealistic books of the time. *The Story of a Bad Boy,* part-novel, part-autobiography, was an immediate success with readers and critics.

Mark Twain's *The Adventures of Tom Sawyer* (1876) and *Adventures of Huckleberry Finn* (1884) culminated and ended the genre. Aldrich and Twain told of real boys, sometimes moral or cruel or silly but always real. Other books once popular in the same strain, for example, George Wilbur Peck's *Peck's Bad Boy and His Pa* (1883), stressed silliness or prankishness to extremes.

A few adventure novels of the time deserve mention if for no other reason than that they remain readable even today. Noah Brooks's *The Boy Emigrants* (1876) is a romanticized but fascinating tale of boys traveling across the plains. Kirk Munroe is undeservedly ignored today, but his story of a young boy working in the mines, *Derrick Sterling* (1888), is great fun to read. John Bennett's *Master Skylark: A Story of Shakespeare's Time* (1898) is a witty, adventure-filled story, and John Meade Falkner's *Moonfleet* (1898) is almost as good a tale of piracy and derring-do as Robert Louis Stevenson's *Treasure Island* (1883).

Development of the American Public Library

The development of the public library was as rocky and slow as it was inevitable. In 1731, Benjamin Franklin suggested that members of the Junto, a middle-class social and literary club in Philadelphia, share their books with other members. That led to the founding of the Philadelphia Library Company, America's first subscription library. Other such libraries followed, most of them dedicated to moral purposes, as the constitution of the Salisbury, Connecticut, Social Library announced: "The promotion of Virtue, Education, and Learning, and . . . the discouragement of Vice and Immorality."[3]

In 1826, the governor of New York urged that school district libraries be established, in effect using school buildings for public libraries. Similar libraries were established in New England by the 1840s and in the Midwest shortly thereafter. Eventually, mayors and governors saw the wisdom of levying state taxes to support public libraries in their own buildings, not the schools, and by 1863, there were 1000 public libraries spread across the United States.

The first major report on the developing movement came in an 1876 document from the U.S. Bureau of Education. Part I, "Public Libraries in the United States of America, Their History, Condition, and Management," contained 1187 pages of reports and analyses on 3649 public libraries with holdings of 300 volumes or more.

That same year marks the beginning of the modern library movement. Melvil Dewey, then assistant librarian in the Amherst College Library, was largely responsible for the October 4, 1876, conference of librarians that formed the American Library Association the third day of the meeting. The first issue of the *American Library Journal* appeared the same year (it was to become the *Library Journal* the following year), the world's first professional journal for librarians. While there had been an abortive meeting in 1853, the 1876 meeting promised continuity the earlier meeting had lacked.[4]

In 1884, Columbia College furthered the public library movement by establishing the first school of Library Economy (later to be called Library Science) under Melvil Dewey's leadership. Excellent as these early public libraries were, they grew immeasurably under the impetus of Andrew Carnegie's philanthropy. A Scottish immigrant, Carnegie left millions of dollars for the creation of public libraries across the United States.

Fiction and Libraries

The growth of public libraries presented opportunities for pleasure and education of the masses, but arguments about the purposes of the public library arose almost as fast as the buildings. William Poole listed three common objections to the public library in the October 1876 *American Library Journal*: the normal dread of taxes; the more philosophical belief that government had no rights except to protect people and property—that is no right to tax anyone to build and stock a public library; and concern over the kinds of books libraries might buy and circulate.[5] In this last point, Poole touched on a controversy that raged for years, that is, whether a public library is established for scholars or the pleasure of the masses. Poole believed that a library existed for the entire community, or else there was no justification for a general tax. Poole's words did not quiet critics who argued that the library's sole *raison d'etre* was educational. Waving the banner of American purity in his hands, W. M. Stevenson maintained:

> If the public library is not first and foremost an educational institution, it has no right to exist. If it exists for mere pleasure, and for a low order of entertainment at that, it is simply a socialistic institution.[6]

Many librarians of the time agreed. Probably, a few agree even today.

The problem lay almost entirely with fiction. Indeed, the second session of the 1876 American Library Association meeting was devoted to "Novel Reading," mostly but not exclusively about young people's reading. A librarian announced that his rules permitted no fiction in his library. His factory-patrons might ask for novels, but he recommended other books and was able to keep patrons without supplying novels. To laughter, he said that he had never read novels so he "could not say what their effect really was."[7]

Teachers worried almost as much as librarians. A principal of a large endowed academy was approvingly quoted by a librarian for having said:

> The voracious devouring of fiction commonly indulged in by patrons of the public library, especially the young, is extremely pernicious and mentally unwholesome.[8]

That attitude persisted for years and is occasionally heard even today among teachers and librarians.

1900–1940: From the Safety of Romance to the Beginning of Realism

During the first forty years of the twentieth century, the western frontier disappeared, and the United States changed from an agrarian society to an urban one. World War I brought the certainty that it would end all wars. The labor movement grew along with Ford's production lines of cars, cars, cars. President Hoover came along, then the Wall Street crash of 1929 and the Great Depression. By 1938, three million young people from age 16 through 25 were out of school and unemployed, and a quarter of a million boys were on the road. Nazi Germany rose in Eastern Europe, and in the United States, Roosevelt introduced the "New Deal." When the end of the Depression seemed almost in sight, the New York World's Fair of 1939 became an optimistic metaphor for the coming of a newer, better, happier, and more secure life. But World War II lay just over the horizon, apparent to some, ignored by most.

Reading Interests Versus Reading Needs

In the high schools, which enrolled only a tiny fraction of eligible students in the United States, teachers faced pressure from colleges to prepare the young for advanced study, which influenced many adults to be more intent on telling young people what to read than in finding out what they wanted to read. Recreational reading seemed vaguely time-wasting, if not downright wicked. Young people nevertheless found and read books, mainly fiction, for recreation. Popular choices were series books from Stratemeyer's Literary Syndicate, including Tom Swift, Nancy Drew, the Hardy Boys, Baseball Joe, and Ruth Fielding. Non-Stratemeyer series books were also popular, as were individual books written specifically for young adults, along with some classics and best-sellers selected by the Book-of-the-Month Club when it began in 1926 and the Literary Guild when it began a year later.

Arguments over what students choose to read have raged for years, and the end is unlikely to come soon. In 1926, when Carleton Washburne and Mabel Vogel put together the lengthy *Winnetka Graded Book List,* they explained, "Books that were definitely trashy or unsuitable for children, even though widely read, have not been included in this list."[9] Apparently enough people were curious about the trashy or unsuitable to lead the authors to add two supplements.[10] *Elsie Dinsmore* was among the damned, and so were Edgar Rice Burroughs's *Tarzan of the Apes,* Eleanor Porter's *Pollyanna,* Zane Grey's westerns, books from the Ruth Fielding and Tom Swift series, Mark Twain's *Tom Sawyer Abroad,* and Arthur Conan Doyle's *The Hound of the Baskervilles. The Adventures of Sherlock Holmes,* however, was considered worthy of inclusion.

Representative of the other side of the argument is this statement by English professor William Lyon Phelps:

> I do not believe the majority of these very school teachers and other cultivated mature readers began in early youth by reading great books exclusively; I think they read *Jack Harkaway, an Old Sleuth,* and the works of Oliver Optic and Horatio Alger. From these enchanters they learned a thing of tremendous importance—the delight of reading. Once a taste for reading is formed, it can be improved. But it is improbable that boys and girls who have never cared to read a good story will later enjoy stories by good artists.[11]

Girls' Books and Boys' Books

Up to the mid–1930s, teachers and librarians frequently commented that girls' books were inferior to boys' books. Franklin T. Baker wrote that with the obvious exception of Alcott, girls' books of 1908 were "painfully weak" and lacking "invention, action, humor."[12] Two years later, Clara Whitehill Hunt agreed that many girls' books were empty, insipid, and mediocre.[13] In 1935, Julia Carter broke into a review of boys' nonfiction with what appeared to be an exasperated *obiter dictum:*

> Will someone please tell me why we expect the *boys* to know these things and still plan for the girls to be mid-Victorian, and consider them hoydens beyond reclaiming, when instead of shrieking and running like true daughters of Eve, they are interested in snakes and can light a fire with two matches?[14]

Such writers as Caroline Dale Snedeker, Cornelia Meigs, Jeanette Eaton, Mabel Robinson, and Elizabeth Forman Lewis responded to these kinds of criticism by writing enough good girls' books that in 1937 Alice M. Jordan wrote as if the difference in quality was a thing of the past:

> There was a time not long ago when the boys had the lion's share in the yearly production of books intended for young people. So writers were urged to give us more stories in which girls could see themselves in recognizable relationship to the world of their own time, forgetting perhaps that human nature does not change and the vital things are universal. Yet, nonetheless, the girls had a real cause to plead and right valiantly the writers have responded.[15]

Critics believed then, as they continued to insist for years, that girls would read boys' books, but boys would never read girls' books. At least part of the problem lay with stereotypes of boys' and girls' roles as expressed by two writers. Clara Vostrovsky, author of the first significant reading interest study, went back to ancient times for her stereotypes, suggesting that it was "probable" that the differences in reading interests between boys and girls lay "in the history of the race."[16] Psychologist G. Stanley Hall predicted reading interests of girls and boys on psychological differences:

> Boys love adventure, girls sentiment. . . . Girls love to read stories about girls which boys eschew, girls, however, caring much more to read about boys than boys to read about girls. Books dealing with domestic life and with young children in them, girls have almost entirely to themselves. Boys, on the other hand, excel in love of humor, rollicking fun, abandon, rough horse-play, and tales of wild escapades. Girls are less averse to reading what boys like than boys are to reading what girls like. A book popular with boys would attract some girls, while one read by most girls would repel a boy in the middle teens. The reading interests of high-school girls are far more humanistic, cultural and general, and that of boys is more practical, vocational, and even special.[17]

The simple truth, perhaps too obvious and discomforting to be palatable to some parents, English teachers, and librarians, was that boys' books were generally far superior to girls' books. That had nothing to do with the sexual or psychological nature of boys or girls but rather with the way authors treated their audience. Many authors insisted on making their girls good and domestic and dull (if a heroine were allowed some freedom to roam outside the house, she soon regretted it or grew up, whichever came first), perhaps because they thought parents and librarians wanted books that way. Boys were allowed outside the house not only to find work and responsibilities, of course, but also to find adventure and excitement in their books.

Changing English Classroom

By 1900, the library played a significant role in helping young adults find reading materials. Although many librarians reflected the traditional belief that classics should be the major reading of youth, other librarians helped young adults find a variety of materials they liked, not trash, but certainly popular books.

This would rarely have been true of English teachers, saddled as they were with responsibility for preparing young adults for college entrance examinations. At first, these examinations simply required some proof of writing proficiency, but in 1860 and 1870, Harvard began using Milton's *Comus* and Shakespeare's *Julius Caesar* as alternative books for the examination. Four years later, Harvard required a short composition based on a question about one of the following: Shakespeare's *The Tempest, Julius Caesar,* and *The Merchant of Venice,* Goldsmith's *The Vicar of Wakefield,* or Scott's *Ivanhoe* and *The Lay of the Last Minstrel.*

In 1894, the prestigious Committee of Ten on Secondary School Studies presented its report, and English became an accepted discipline in the schools, although not yet as respectable as Latin. Chaired by controversial Harvard president Charles W. Eliot, the committee was appointed by the National Education Association in July 1892 and met later that year to determine the nature, limits, and methods appropriate to many subject matters in secondary school. Samuel Thurber of the Boston Girls' High School was unable to promote his belief that a high school curriculum should consist almost entirely of elective courses, but as chairman of the English Conference, his report liberalized and dignified the study of English. Two important recommendations were that English be studied five hours a week for four years and that uniform college entrance examinations be established throughout the United States.

The result was the publication of book lists, mainly classics, as the basis of entrance examinations. Plays and books such as Shakespeare's *Twelfth Night* and *As You Like It,* Milton's Books I and II from *Paradise Lost,* Scott's *The Abbot* and *Marmion* or Irving's *Bracebridge Hall* virtually became the English curriculum as teachers, inevitably concerned with their students' entry into college, increasingly adapted the English curriculum to fit the list.

National Council of Teachers of English Begins

Out of the growing protest about college entrance examinations, a group of English teachers attending a national Education Association Table formed a Committee on College Entrance Requirements in English to assess the problem through a national survey of English teachers. The committee uncovered hostility to colleges presumptuous enough to try to control the secondary English curriculum through the guise of entrance examinations. John M. Coulter, a professor at the University of Chicago, tried to sound that alarm to college professors but without much success:

> The high school exists primarily for its own sake; and secondarily as a preparatory school for college. This means that when the high school interest and the college interest comes into conflict, the college interest must yield. It also means that the function of a preparatory school must be performed only in so far as it does not interfere with the more fundamental purpose of the high school itself.[18]

Some irate teachers recognized that the problem of college control would hardly be the last issue to face English teachers and formed the nucleus of the National Council of Teachers of English. The First Annual Meeting in Chicago on December 1 and 2, 1911, was largely devoted to resentment about actions of the National Conference on Uniform Entrance Requirements, particularly because that

In the decades before the 1929 stock market crash, American high schools developed in their present form. As with this public school in Prescott, Arizona, dedicated in 1910, many of them were the pride of their communities and lent credence to the idea that young people were a special group who needed to be protected from the harsh realities of ordinary life. (Photo courtesy of Arizona Historical Foundation, University Libraries, Arizona State University)

body had representatives from twelve colleges, two academies, and only two public high schools (principals, not English teachers). Wilbur W. Hatfield, then at Farragut High School in Chicago and soon to edit the *English Journal,* relayed instructions from the Illinois Association of Teachers of English that the new organization should compile a list of comparatively recent books suitable for home reading by students and that they should also recommend some books of the last ten years for study because the "present custom of using only old books in the classroom leaves the pupil with no acquaintance with the literature of the present day," from which students would choose their reading after graduation.[19]

James Fleming Hosic's 1917 report on the *Reorganization of English in Secondary Schools,* part of a larger report published under the aegis of the U.S. Bureau of Education, looked at books and teaching in ways that must have seemed muddle-headed or perverse to traditionalists. Looking at literature for the tenth, eleventh, and twelfth grades, Hosic chose works that pleased many, puzzled others, and alienated some. He explained that English teachers should lead students to read works in which they would, "find their own lives imaged in this larger life," and would gradually attain from the author's "clearer appreciation of human nature, a deeper and truer understanding. . . . It should be the aim of the English teacher to make [reading] an unfailing resource and joy in the lives of all."[20] Hosic's list included classics as well as modern works, such as Helen Hunt Jackson's *Ramona* and Owen Wister's *The Virginian* for the tenth grade, Rudyard Kipling's *The Light That Failed* and Mary Johnston's *To Have and To Hold* for the eleventh grade, and John Synge's *Riders to the Sea* and Margaret Deland's *The Awakening of Helena Richie* for the twelfth grade. Teachers terrified by the contemporary reality reflected in these books—and perhaps equally terrified by the possibility of throwing out age-old lesson plans and tests on classics—had little to fear. In many schools, nothing changed. *Silas Marner, Julius Caesar, Idylls of the King, A Tale of Two Cities,* and *Lady of the Lake* remained the most widely studied books. Most books were taught at interminable length in what was known as the "intensive" method with four to six weeks—sometimes even more—of detailed examination, while horrified or bored students vowed never to read anything once they escaped high school. A 1927 study by Nancy Coryell offered proof that the "intensive" method produced no better test results and considerably more apathy toward literature than the "extensive" method in which students read assigned works faster.[21] Again, however, in many schools nothing changed.

Fortunately, the work of two college professors influenced more English teachers. A 1936 study by Lou LaBrant on the value of free reading at the Ohio State University Laboratory School revealed that students with easy access to different kinds of books and some guidance read more, enjoyed what they read, and moved upward in literary sophistication and taste.[22] Earlier, University of Minnesota professor Dora V. Smith discovered that English teachers knew next to nothing about books written for adolescents. She began the long process of correcting that situation by establishing the first course in adolescent literature. She argued that it was unfair to both young people and their teachers "to send out from our colleges and universities men and women trained alone in Chaucer and Milton and Browning to compete with Zane Grey, Robert W. Chambers, and Ethel M. Dell."[23]

School Library

The development of the school library was almost as slow and convoluted as the development of the public library. In 1823, Brooklyn's Apprentice Library Association established a Youth Library where "Boys over twelve were allowed . . . as were girls whose access to the library were limited to one hour an afternoon, once a week." In 1853, Milwaukee School Commissioner Increase A. Lapham provided for a library open Saturday afternoons and recommended that schools spend $10 a year for books. Rules for the Milwaukee library were clear and more than a bit reminiscent of rules in some school and public libraries until the 1940s:

> (1) Only children over ten years old, their parents, teachers, and school commissioner could withdraw books; (2) books might be withdrawn between 2:00 P.M. and sunset on Saturdays and kept for one week; (3) withdrawals were limited to one book per person; and (4) fines were to be assessed for overdue or damaged books.[24]

Writers in the early years of the *Library Journal* encouraged the cultivation of friendly relations between "co-educators."[25] The National Education Association formed a Committee on Relations of Public Libraries to Public Schools, and its 1899 report announced that "The teachers of a town should know the public library, what it contains, and what use the pupils can make of it. The librarian must know the school, its work, its needs, and what he can do to meet them."[26]

A persistent question was whether schools should depend on the public library or establish their own libraries. In 1896, Melvil Dewey recommended to the National Education Association that it form a library department (as it had for other subject disciplines) because the library was as much a part of the educational system as the classroom.

The previous year, a branch of the Cleveland, Ohio, Public Library was established within Central High School, and in 1899, a branch of the Newark, New Jersey, Public Library was placed in a local high school. In 1900, Mary Kingston became the first library school graduate appointed to a high school library (Erasmus High School in Brooklyn). In 1912, Mary E. Hall, librarian at Girls' High School in Brooklyn, argued the need for many more professionally trained librarians in high school libraries:

(1) The aims and ideals of the new high school mean we must stop pretending that high school is entirely college preparatory. "It realizes that for the great majority of pupils it must be a preparation for life." (2) Modern methods of teaching demand that a textbook is not enough. "The efficient teacher today uses books, magazines, daily papers, pictures, and lantern slides to supplement the textbook." (3) Reading guidance is easier for the school librarian than the public librarian. "The school librarian has the teacher always close at hand and can know the problems of these teachers in their work with pupils."[27]

In 1916, C. C. Certain, as head of National Education Association committee, began standardizing high school libraries across the United States. He discovered conditions so mixed, from deplorable (mostly) to good (rarely) that his committee set to work to establish minimum essentials for high schools of various sizes. Two reports from the U.S. Office of Education indicate the growth of high school libraries. A 1923 report found only 947 school libraries with more than 3000 volumes, and these were mostly in the northeastern part of the United States. Six years later, the 1929 report found 1,982 school libraries with holdings of more than 3000 volumes, and the libraries were more equally spread over the country with New York having 211 such libraries and California having 191. The steady growth of high school libraries, however, slowed drastically during the Depression.

Edward Stratemeyer's Literary Syndicate

Whatever disagreements librarians and English teachers may have had about books suitable for young adults, they bonded together, although ineffectively, to oppose the books produced by Edward Stratemeyer and his numerous writers. Stratemeyer founded the most successful industry ever built around adolescent reading. In 1866, he took time off from working for his stepbrother and wrote on brown wrapping paper an 18,000-word serial, *Victor Horton's Idea,* and mailed it to a Philadelphia weekly boys' magazine. A check for $75 arrived shortly, and Stratemeyer's success story was under way. By 1893, Stratemeyer was editing *Good News,* Street and Smith's boys' weekly, building circulation to more than 200,000. This brought his name in front of the public, particularly young adults. Even more important, he came to know staff writers such as William T. Adams, Edward S. Ellis, and Horatio Alger, Jr. When Optic and Alger died leaving some uncompleted manuscripts, Stratemeyer was asked to finish the last three Optic novels, and he completed (or possibly wrote from scratch) at least eleven and perhaps as many as eighteen Alger novels.

His first hardback book published under his own name was *Richard Dare's Venture; or, Striking Out for Himself* (1894), first in a series he titled Bound to Succeed. By the close of 1897, Stratemeyer had six series and sixteen hardcover books in print. A major breakthrough came in 1898. After Stratemeyer sent a manuscript about two boys on a battleship to Lothrop and Shepard, one of the most successful publishers of young adult fiction, Admiral Dewey won his great victory in Manila Bay. A Lothrop editor asked Stratemeyer to place the boys at the scene of Dewey's victory. He rewrote and returned the book, and *Under Dewey at Manila; or, The War Fortunes of a Castaway* hit the streets in time to capitalize on all the publicity. Not one to miss an opportunity, Stratemeyer used the same characters in his next books, all published from 1898 to 1901 under the series title Old Glory. Using the same characters in contemporary battles in the Orient, Stratemeyer created another series called Soldiers of Fortune, published from 1900 through 1906.

By this time, Stratemeyer had turned to full-time writing and was being wooed by the major publishers, notably Grossett and Dunlap and Cupples and Leon. For a time he turned to stories of school life and sports, the Lakeport series (1904–1912), the Dave Porter series (1905–1919), and the most successful of his early series, the Rover Boys (30 books published between 1899 and 1926). These books were so popular that somewhere between 5 or 6 million copies were sold worldwide, including translations into German and Czechoslovakian.

Stratemeyer aspired to greater things, however. Between 1906 and 1910, he approached both his publishers, suggesting they reduce the price of his books to 50 cents. The publishers may have been shocked to find an author willing to sell his books for less money, but, as they soon realized, mass production of 50-centers increased their revenue and Stratemeyer's royalties almost geometrically. An even greater breakthrough came at roughly the same time, when he evolved the idea of his Literary Syndicate. Stratemeyer was aware that he could create plots and series faster than he could possibly write them. He advertised for writers who needed money and sent them sketches of settings and characters along with a chapter-by-chapter outline of the plot. Writers had a few weeks to fill in the outlines, and when the copy arrived, Stratemeyer tightened the prose and checked for discrepancies with earlier volumes of the series. Then the manuscript was off to the publisher and checks went out to the authors, from $50 to $100, depending on the writer and the importance of the series.

Attacks on Stratemeyer were soon in coming. Librarian Caroline M. Hewins criticized both Stratemeyer's book and the journals that praised his output:

> Stratemeyer is an author who misuses "would" and "should," has the phraseology of a country newspaper, as when he calls a supper "an elegant affair" and a girl "a fashionable miss," and follows Oliver Optic closely in his plots and conversations.[28]

Most librarians supported Hewins, but their attacks hardly affected Stratemeyer's sales. A far more stinging and effective attack came in 1913 from the Boy Scouts of America. Chief executive James E. West was disturbed by the deluge of inferior books and urged the organization's Library Commission to establish a carefully selected and recommended library to protect young men. Not long afterward, Chief Scout Librarian Franklin K. Mathiews urged Grosset and Dunlap to make better books available in 50-cent editions—to compete with Stratemeyer—and on

November 1, 1913, the first list appeared in a Boy Scout publication, "Safety First Week."

But that was not enough to satisfy Mathiews, who in 1914 wrote his most famous article under the sensational title "Blowing Out the Boy's Brains,"[29] a loud and vituperative attack, sometimes accurate but often unfair. Mathiews's attack was mildly successful for the moment, although how much harm it did to Stratemeyer's sales is open to question. Stratemeyer went on to sell more millions of books. When he died in 1930, his two daughters ran the syndicate, which still persists, presumably forever.

Series books were inevitably moral. Whatever parents, teachers, or librarians might have objected to about the unrealistic elements of the books or the poor literary quality, they would have agreed that the books were clearly on the side of good and right, if simplistically so. Series books—and many adult books as well—repeatedly underlined the same themes. Sports produced truly manly men. Foreigners were not to be trusted. School, education, and life should be taken seriously. The outdoor life was healthy, physically and psychologically. Good manners and courtesy were essential for moving ahead. Work in and of itself was a positive good and would advance one in life. Anyone could defeat adversity, any adversity, *if* that person had a good heart and soul. The good side (ours and God's) always won in war. Evil and good were clearly and easily distinguishable. And good always triumphed over evil (at least by the final chapter).

The Coming of the "Junior" or "Juvenile" Novel

Although for years countless books had been published and widely read by young adults, the term *junior* or *juvenile* was first applied to young adult literature during the early 1930s. Rose Wilder Lane's novel *Let the Hurricane Roar* had been marketed by Longmans, Green, and Company as an adult novel. A full-page blurb on the front cover of the February 11, 1933, *Publishers Weekly* bannered THE BOOK THAT MAKES YOU PROUD TO BE AN AMERICAN! and quoted an unnamed reader, presumably an adult, saying, "Honestly, it makes me ashamed of cussing about hard times and taxes." The tenor of the ad and ones to follow suggest an adult novel likely to be popular with young adults as well. It had been the same with the earlier serialization of the novel in the *Saturday Evening Post* and also with the many favorable reviews. Sometime later in 1933, Longmans, Green began to push the novel as the first of their series of "Junior Books," as they termed them.

That the company wanted to attract young adults to Lane's novel is not difficult to understand. Lane wrote of a threatening frontier world she had known in a compelling manner certain to win readers and admirers among young adults. *Let the Hurricane Roar* tells of newly married David and Molly and their life on the hard Dakota plains. David works as a railroad hand for a time, Molly waits for her baby to arrive, and both strive for independence and the security of owning their own fifty-acre homestead. When they realize that dream and the baby is born, all looks well, but David overextends his credit, grasshoppers destroy the wheat crop, and no nearby employment can be found. David heads east to find work and later breaks his leg, leaving Molly isolated on the Dakota plains for a winter. Neighbors flee the area, and Molly battles loneliness, blizzards, and wolves before David returns. In summary, *Let the Hurricane Roar* sounds melodramatic, but it is not. In a short, quiet, and loving work, Lane made readers care about two likable young adults living a tough life in a hostile environment. The book's popularity is attested to by its twenty-six printings between 1933 and 1958 and a recent television production and reissue in paperback under the title *Young Pioneers.*

The development of publishing house divisions to handle books lying in limbo between children's and adults' books grew after *Let the Hurricane Roar,* although authors of the time were sometimes unaware of the "junior" or "juvenile" branches as was John T. Tunis when he tried to market *Iron Duke* in 1934 and 1935. After sending the manuscript to Harcourt, Tunis was invited into the president's office. Mr. Harcourt clearly did not want to talk about the book but instead took the startled author directly to the head of the Juvenile Department. He explained that Harcourt wanted to publish the book as a juvenile, much to Tunis's bewilderment and dismay, since he had no idea what a "juvenile" book was. Thirty years later, he still had no respect for the term, which he called the "odious product of a merchandising age."[30]

Books That Young Adults Liked

Among the most popular books before World War I were those featuring a small child, usually a girl, who significantly changed people around her. At their best, they showed an intriguing youngster humanizing sterile or cold people. At their worst (and they often were), they featured a rapturously happy and miraculously even-dispositioned child who infected an entire household—perhaps a community—with her messianic drive to improve the world through cheer and gladness.

The type began promisingly with Kate Douglas Wiggin's *Rebecca of Sunnybrook Farm* (1904). Nothing Wiggin wrote surpassed *Rebecca,* which sold more than 1.25 million copies between 1904 and 1975. Living in a small town during the 1870s, the optimistic heroine is handed over to two maiden aunts while her parents cope with a large family. She is educated despite her imperfections, high spirits, and rebelliousness and at the close of the books seems cheerfully on her way upward to a better life.

Anne of Green Gables (1908) by Lucy Maud Montgomery was a worthy successor. As in Wiggin's book, Anne travels to an alien society. Here a childless couple who wants to adopt a boy gets Anne by mistake. Anne changes the couple for the better, but they also change her, and Anne's delightfully developed character goes far to remedy any defects in the book.

Wiggin and Montgomery generally managed to skim the sea of sentimentalism, that fatal syrupy deep beloved by bad writers. Occasionally, Rebecca and Anne waded out dangerously far, but their common sense, their impulsiveness, and their ability to laugh at themselves brought them back to shore. After them came the disaster: authors and character so enamored of humanity, so convinced that all people were redeemable and so stickily and uncomplainingly sweet and dear that they drowned in goodness, while many readers gagged. Eleanor Porter wrote the genre's magnum opus and destroyed it with *Pollyanna* (1913). *Pollyanna* is usually remembered as a children's book, but it began as a popular adult novel, eighth among bestsellers in 1913 and second in 1914.

Westerns provided a different type of popularity. The closing of the West heightened interest in an exciting, almost magical, era. A few writers, aiming specifically at young adults, knew the West so well that they became touchstones for authenticity in other writers. In *Pawnee Hero Stories and Folk Tales* (1898) and *By Cheyenne Campfires* (1926), George Bird Grinnell established an honest and generally unsentimentalized portrait of Native American life. Both he and Charles A. Eastman often appeared on reading interest studies as boys' favorites. Joseph Altsheler wrote more conventional adventure tales, including *The Last of the Chiefs* (1909) and *The Horsemen of the Plains* (1910). Far more sentimental but much more popular was Will James's *Smoky, The Cowhorse* (1926), originally published as an adult novel but soon read by thousands of young adults and twice filmed to appreciative audiences. The best-written and most sensitive western for young people was Laura Adams Armer's *Waterless Mountain* (1931). Unfortunately, enthusiastic librarians and teachers had little success in getting teenagers to read this slow-moving and mystical story about a young Navajo boy training to become a Medicine Priest.

The first great writer to focus on the West and its mystique of violence and danger mixed with open spaces and freedom was Owen Wister, whose *The Virginian: A Horseman of the Plains* (1902) provided a model of colloquial speech and romantic and melodramatic adventure for novelists to follow. The best of Zane Grey's books—certainly the most remembered and probably the epitome of the overly romanticized western—was *Riders of the Purple Sage* (1912), which was filled with such classic elements as the mysterious hero, the innocent heroine, evil villains, and the open land. Although Grey has been criticized by librarians and teachers—who seem in general to have read little or nothing of his work—anyone who wishes to know the western dream must read Grey.

With more young adults attending school and with the steadily rising popularity of sports—especially college football and professional baseball—more school-sports stories appeared. William Gilbert Patten, under the pen name of Burt L. Standish, was the first to introduce a regular, almost mythic, sports character recognized throughout America—Frank Merriwell. The Frank Merriwell books began as short stories later fashioned into hardback books. Three other writers who stand out for their realistic sports books include Owen Johnson with his *The Varmint* (1910), *The Tennessee Shad* (1911), and *Stover at Yale* (1911), which attacks snobbery, social clubs, fraternities, and anti-intellectualism. Ralph Henry Barbour wrote an incredible number of fine books, beginning with *The Half-Back* (1899). He invented the formula of a boy attending school and learning who and what he might become through sports. William Heyliger followed in a similar pattern with *Bartley: Freshman Pitcher* (1911) and his Lansing and St. Mary's series.

School stories for girls never had a similar number of readers, but a few deserve reading even today, including Laura Elizabeth Richard's *Peggy* (1899) and Marjorie Hill Allee's *Jane's Island* (1931) and *The Great Tradition* (1937). Best of them all is Mabel Louise Robinson's *Bright Island* (1937) about spunky Thankful Curtis who was raised on a small island off the coast of Maine and later attends school on the mainland.

1940–1966: From Certainty to Uncertainty

During the 1940s, the United States moved from the Depression into a wartime and then a postwar economy. World War II caused us to move from hatred of Communism to a temporary brotherhood, followed by Yalta, the Iron Curtain, blacklisting, and Senator McCarthy. We went from "Li'l Abner" to "Pogo" and from Bob Hope to Mort Sahl. Problems of the time included school integration, racial unrest, civil

Before World War II, books published for teenagers were clearly divided into "boys' books" and "girls' books," with the boys getting the more exciting stories. However, a surprising number of pre-1950s girls' books were designed to make girls think about careers.

rights, and riots in the streets. We were united about World War II, unsure about the Korean War, and divided about Vietnam. We went from violence to more violence and the assassinations of John Kennedy and Malcolm X. The 25 years between 1940 and 1965 revealed a country separated by gaps of all kinds: generational, racial, technological, cultural, and economic.

Educators were as divided as anyone else. Reading interest studies had become fixtures in educational journals, but there was little agreement about the results. In 1946, George W. Norvell wrote, "Our data shows clearly that much literary material being used in our schools is too mature, too subtle, too erudite to permit its enjoyment by the majority of secondary-school pupils." Norvell offered the advice that teachers should give priority to the reading interests of young adults in assigning materials that students would enjoy and in letting students select a portion of their own materials based on their individual interests. He thought that three-fourths of the selections currently in use were uninteresting, especially to boys, and that "to increase reading skill, promote the reading habit, and produce a generation of book-lovers, there is no factor so powerful as interest."[31]

Other researchers supported Norvell's contention that young adults' choices of voluntary reading rarely overlapped books widely respected by more traditional English teachers. In 1947, Marie Rankin surveyed eight public libraries in Illinois, Ohio, and New York and discovered that Helen Boylston's *Sue Barton, Student Nurse* was the most consistently popular book.[32] Twelve years later, Stephen Dunning surveyed fourteen school and public libraries and concluded that the ten most popular books were Maureen Daly's *Seventeenth Summer,* Henry Gregor Felsen's *Hot Rod,* Betty Cavanna's *Going On Sixteen,* Rosamund Du Jardin's *Double Date,* Walter Farley's *Black Stallion,* Sally Benson's *Junior Miss,* Mary Stolz's *The Sea Gulls Woke Me,* Rosamund Du Jardin's *Wait for Marcy,* James Summers's *Prom Trouble,* and John Tunis's *All American.*[33]

Near the height of the outpouring of published studies, Jacob W. Getzels assessed the value of reading interest surveys and found most of them wanting in "precision of *definition,* rigor of *theory,* and depth of *analysis.*"[34] He was, of course, right. Most reports were limited to a small sample from a few schools, and little was done except to ask students what they liked to read. The studies at least gave librarians and teachers insight into books young adults liked and brought hope that somewhere out there somebody was reading—a hope that for librarians and teachers needs constant rekindling.

In the mid-1950s, G. Robert Carlsen summarized the findings of published reading interest surveys as showing that young people select their reading first to reassure themselves about their normality and their status as human beings and then for role-playing:

> With the developing of their personality through adolescence, they come to a partially integrated picture of themselves as human beings. They want to test this picture of themselves in the many kinds of roles that it is possible for a human being to play and through testing to see what roles they may fit into and what roles are uncongenial.[35]

Carlsen's observations tied in with those of University of Chicago psychologist Robert J. Havighurst, who outlined the developmental tasks necessary for the healthy growth of individuals. (See Chapter 1, p. 33, for the tasks that Havighurst thought crucial to adolescence.)

An outgrowth of the tying together of reading interests and psychology was an interest in bibliotherapy. In 1929, Dr. G. O. Ireland coined the term while writing about the use of books as part of his treatment for psychiatric patients.[33] By the late 1930s and early 1940s, articles about bibliotherapy became almost commonplace in education journals, and by the 1950s, the idea of using books to help readers come to terms with their psychological problems was firmly entrenched. Philosophically, it was justified by Aristotle's *Poetics* and the theory of emotional release through catharsis, a theory with little support except for unverifiable personal testimonials.

One clear and easy application of bibliotherapy was the free reading program (sometimes too clear and too easy for the inept psychologist/English teacher who, finding a new book in which the protagonist had acne, sought the acne-ridden kid in class saying, "You must read this—it's about you"). Lou LaBrant, popularizer of free reading, sounded both a recommendation and a warning when she wrote:

> Certainly I can make a much wiser selection of offerings if I understand the potential reader. . . . [but] This does not mean, as some have interpreted, that a young reader will enjoy only literature which answers his questions, tells him what is to be done. It is true, however, that young and old tend to choose literature, whether they seek solutions or escape, which offers characters or situations with which they can find a degree of identification.[37]

Rise of Paperbacks

Young adult readers might assume paperbound books have always been with us. Despite the success of dime novels and libraries of paperbacks in the late 1800s, paperbacks as we know them entered the mass market in 1938 when Pocket Books offered Pearl Buck's *The Good Earth* as a sample volume in mail-order tests. In the spring of 1939, a staff artist created the first sketch of Gertrude the Kangaroo with a book in her paws and another in her pouch. It became Pocket Books' trademark. A few months later, the company issued ten titles in 10,000-copy editions, most of them remaining best-sellers for years. Avon began publishing in 1941; Penguin entered the U.S. market in 1942; and Bantam, New American Library, Ballantine, Dell, and Popular Library began publishing in 1943. By 1951, sales had reached 230 million paperbacks annually. Phenomenal as the growth was, paperbacks were slow to appear in schools despite an incredible number of titles on appropriate subjects. Librarians complained that paperbacks did not belong in libraries because they were difficult to catalog and easy to steal. School officials maintained that the covers were lurid and the contents little more than pornography. As late as 1969, a New York City high school junior explained, "I'd rather be caught with Lady Chatterley in hardcover than *Hot Rod* in paperback. Hard covers get you one detention, but paperbacks get you two or three."[38]

Regardless of "official" attitudes, by the mid-1960s paperbacks had become a part of young adults' lives. They are easily available, comfortably sized, and inexpensive. Fortunately, not all school personnel were resistant. The creation of Scholastic Book Clubs and widespread distribution of Reader's Choice Catalogs helped paperbacks get accepted in schools and libraries. Eventually, Bantam and Dell's Yearling books became the major suppliers of books written specifically for young adults.

Changes and Growth in Young Adult Literature

From 1941 to 1965, the quality of young adult literature rose steadily, if at times hesitatingly and uncertainly. Series books, so popular from 1900 to the 1940s, died out—except for Stratemeyer Syndicate stalwarts Nancy Drew, the Hardy Boys, and the new Tom Swift, Jr. series. They were killed by increasing reader sophistication combined with the wartime scarcity of paper. Many of the books that replaced the series celebrated those wonderful high school years by focusing on dating, parties, class rings, senior year, the popular crowd, and teen romances devoid of realities

GARY SOTO
On the Particulars of the World

I am new to children's writing and am only now getting to know some of the books in the field. What has struck me, now that I am reading YA novels, is that despite their other literary merits, the writing has so little that is obviously regional, obviously bent on nailing down a life that is wholly particular. Seldom are real rivers mentioned, or mountains, gangs, streets, cars; in short, the particulars of the world. Seldom do place names matter, names ringing of the familiar, such as Avocado Lake, Pinedale, Academy Cemetery, Francher's Creek, real names that might give rise to a reader's dreaming state of mind and curiosity for a faraway place. For the most part the novels I have been reading are homogenous and widespread in their feelings and cast of characters. They lack a sense of place. The stories could happen anywhere. And they often happen in a way that doesn't exclude anyone by race, thus, in a way, satisfying the book market, but also, in a way, dissatisfying any reader who knows what the real world is like. The characters are interchangeable, racially, that is.

I suppose because I was first trained as a poet and was told repeatedly to go to the particular—your block, your family, your friends, some dirt pile in the backyard—that I wrote about my hometown, Fresno, California. And then, more particularly, I looked to the southeast area of Fresno—the Roosevelt High area—the industrial area of south Fresno, where I grew up. My characters are Mexican-American, mostly playground kids, mostly the children of people whose parents work for Color Tile or a Safeway distribution center. I'm beginning to think that children's writing could learn to see regionality and particularity as underexplored territory. I'm beginning to think we don't have to satisfy everyone. We can remember the adult writers—Flannery O'Connor, Mark Twain, Sherwood Anderson, William Saroyan, Bernard Malamud—who had tenderness and longing toward place, even if that place scared the hell out of them when they were young.

Gary Soto's books include *Nickel and Dime*, University of New Mexico Press, 2000; *A Natural Man*, Chronicle, 1999; *Nerdlandia*, Putnam, 1999; and *Petty Crimes*, Harcourt Brace, 1998.

such as sex. The books often sounded alike and read alike, but they were unquestionably popular.

Plots were usually simple, with only one or two characters being developed, while others were stock figures or stereotypes. Books dealt almost exclusively with white, middle-class values and morality. The endings were almost uniformly happy and bright, and readers could be certain that neither their morality nor their intelligence would be challenged.

Taboos may never have been written down, but they were clear to readers and writers. Certain things were not to be mentioned—obscenity, profanity, suicide, sexuality, sensuality, homosexuality, protests against anything significant, social or racial injustice, or the ambivalent feelings of cruelty and compassion inherent in young adults and all people. Pregnancy, early marriage, drugs, smoking, alcohol, school dropouts, divorce, and alienation could be introduced only by implication and only as bad examples for thoughtful, decent young adults. Consequently, young adult books were often innocuous and pervaded by a saccharine didacticism.

Despite these unwritten rules, some writers transcended the taboos and limitations and made it possible for Stanley B. Kegler and Stephen Dunning to write in 1961, "Books of acceptable quality have largely replaced poorly written and mediocre books."[39] Among the authors bringing about this welcome change were four who appealed largely to girls (Florence Crannell Means, Maureen Daly, Mary Stolz, and James Summers) and four who appealed largely to boys (Paul Annixter, Henry Gregor Felsen, Jack Bennett, and John Tunis).

Means was unusual in developing minority protagonists. *Tangled Waters* (1936) about a Navajo girl on an Arizona reservation, *Shuttered Windows* (1938) about an African-American girl in Minneapolis who goes to live with her grandmother in South Carolina, and *The Moved Outers* (1945) about Japanese Americans forced into a relocation camp during World War II are rich portraits of young people with problems not easily solved.

During this period, Daly published only *Seventeenth Summer* (1942), which was incredibly popular and is still occasionally read, although by younger girls than its original audience. Daly was a college student when she wrote her story about shy and innocent Angie Morrow and her love for Jack Duluth during the summer between high school and college.

Stolz, the most prolific of the four, is still publishing. She writes magic, quiet, introspective books that appeal mostly to readers more curious about character than incident. Things happen in her books, but the focus is always on people—always lovingly developed. Her two best works are *Pray Love, Remember* (1945) and *A Love, or a Season* (1964). The former is a remarkable story of Dody Jenks, a popular and lovely and cold young woman who likes neither her family nor herself. The latter is a story of quiet and uneventful love suddenly turning torrid before either girl or boy is old enough to handle sex.

Summers's two best books are *Ring Around His Finger* (1957), a tale of young marriage told from the boy's point of view, and *The Limit of Love* (1959), a fine delineation of a sexual affair between two children. The girl begins to grow up, while the boy remains a boy dedicated to proving that the girl is ruining his life. Although both books were more about boys than girls, the readers were usually girls, curious about a boy's point of view. Critics worried about Summers's honesty, presumably fearing that young adult readers were too young to handle the emotional intricacies of sex.

Howard A. Sturzel, under the pen name of Paul Annixter, wrote widely but best known is *Swiftwater* (1950), a story mixing animals, ecology, symbolism, and some stereotyped characters into a rousing tale that remains a better than respectable book.

Felsen wrote run-of-the-mill prose, but not one of his fans cared because Felsen wrote about the joys and dangers of cars. *Hot Rod* (1950), *Street Rod* (1953), and *Crash Club* (1958) were widely read, often by boys who had never before read a book all the way through. Felsen was didactic, but his fans read for the material on cars and ignored his lessons. His best book was unquestionably *Two and the Town* (1952) about a young couple forced to marry. Tired as the book seems now, it was a groundbreaker widely opposed by teachers and librarians.

Bennett, a South African journalist, wrote several remarkable books for young boys, including *Jamie* (1963), *Mister Fisherman* (1965), and *The Hawk Alone* (1965), a brilliant book that never received its due. It is about an old white hunter who has hunted everything, done everything, and outlived his time.

Tunis, an amateur athlete and sports reporter, was the best of these writers. *Iron Duke* (1938), his first young adult novel, is about a high school runner who wants to enter the big time at Harvard. What that book promised, *All American* (1942) delivered in its attack on prejudice aimed at both Jews and African-Americans and the win-at-all-costs attitude. *Yea! Wildcats* (1944) eloquently mixes basketball with incipient totalitarianism in a small Indiana town. *Go, Team, Go!* (1954) is a fine story about the pressures brought to bear on high school coaches. Tunis preached too often, and sometimes the preaching was simply too much for readers to bear, but he knew sports and he cared deeply about boys and about games. At his best, he is still worth reading, and several of his books have recently been reissued.

Other Books Popular with Young Adults

While teachers in schools struggled to get kids to read Shakespeare, much as we still do today (see Film Box 2.1), the reading that young adults did on their own during these 25 years fell loosely into six areas: careers; sports and cars; adventure and suspense; love, romance, passion, and sex; society's problems; and personal problems and initiation.

Emma Bugbee, a reporter for the *New York Tribune,* began a deluge of career books with her *Peggy Covers the News* (1936). She wrote five Peggy Foster books that conveyed the ambivalent excitement and boredom of getting and writing the news. In presenting the picture of a young woman breaking into a male-dominated profession, the books served a purpose for their time. By far the most popular career books were about nursing, led by Helen Boylston's seven Sue Barton books followed by Helen Wells's 20 Cherry Ames books. Wells also wrote 13 books about flight stewardess Vicki Barr. Lucile Fargo's *Marion Martha* (1936) treated librarianship, and Christie Harris's *You Have to Draw the Line Somewhere* (1964) was about fashion designing.

Whatever freshness the vocational novel may once have had, by the late 1940s it was a formula and little more. Early in the book the insecure hero/heroine (more often the latter) suffers a mixture of major and minor setbacks but, undaunted, wins the final battle and a place in the profession. The novel passes rapidly and lightly over the job's daily grind, focusing instead on the high points, the excitement and events that make any job potentially, if rarely, dramatic.

We have already mentioned John Tunis and Henry Gregor Felsen in the sports and car category. Another notable is basketball writer John F. Carson with his *Floorburns* (1957), *The Coach Nobody Liked* (1960), and *Hotshot* (1961). C. H. Frick (pen name of Constance Frick Irwin) used clever plot twists to make her sports novels different. *Five Against the Odds* (1955) features a basketball player stricken with polio, and *The Comeback Guy* (1961) focuses on a too-popular, too-successful young man who gets his comeuppance and works his way back to self-respect through sports. Nonfiction was not yet as popular as it would become, but Jim Piersall's *Fear Strikes Out* (1955) and Roy Campanella's *It's Good to Be Alive* (1959) attracted young readers.

Until the late 1940s, interest in adventure or suspense was largely fulfilled by various kinds of war books, including vocational nonfiction such as Carl Mann's

FILM BOX 2.1

Shakespeare: Reverent Versions, Good Versions, Loving Versions, and Other Versions

Hamlet (1990, color, 120 min., PG; Director: Franco Zeffirelli; with Glenn Close, Alan Bates, Ian Holm, and Mel Gibson) A physical *Hamlet* with a weak Hamlet and a strong supporting cast, especially Holm as Polonius. The 1948 Laurence Olivier *Hamlet* (black and white, 153 min., Director: Olivier; with Jean Simmons, Olivier, and Eileen Herlie) is worth another look as an example of Freudian criticism. Also worth seeing is Kenneth Branaugh's 1996 version (color, 242 min., Director: Branaugh).

Henry V (1989, color, 137 min., NR; Director: Kenneth Branaugh; with Branaugh, Ian Holm, and Judi Dench) A fine Crispin speech and strong throughout, but Olivier's 1945 production also has many merits (color, 137 min., NR, Director: Olivier; with Robert Newton, Olivier, and Renee Asherson).

King Lear (1971, black and white, 137 min., PG; Director: Peter Brook; with Paul Scofield and Jack MacGowan) This is interesting to view alongside Akira Kurosawa's exceptional and bloody Japanese version, *Ran* (1985, color, 161 min., R; Director: Kurosawa).

Macbeth (1971, color, 140 min., R; Director: Roman Polanski; with Jon Finch and Francesca Annis) This dramatically effective film includes a bit of nudity. Look also at Orson Welles' version (1948, black and white, 89 min., NR; Director: Welles; with Jeanette Nolan). Again, the best of the *Macbeth* films is Akira Kurosawa's *Throne of Blood* (1957, black and white, 208 min., Director: Kurosawa). It's a Samurai *Macbeth*, but once you're over that, it's magnificent.

Othello (1942, black and white, 92 min., NR; Director: Orson Welles; with Michael MacLiammoir) A powerful *Othello*, but a recent version is also worth examining for a fine Othello and a brilliant Iago (1995, color, 166 min., NR; Director: Oliver Parker; with Laurence Fishburne and Kenneth Branaugh). And, as usual, Olivier's reading deserves a close look (1965, color, 166 min., NR; Director: Stuart Burge; with Olivier, Frank Finlay, and Maggie Smith).

Richard III (1955, color, 155 min., NR; Director: Laurence Olivier; with Olivier and Claire Bloom) is the standard, and Olivier is almost pure evil as Richard. Ian McKellen was better on the stage, but his filmed *Richard* works well (1995, color, 194 min., Director: Richard Loncraine). The best commentary about Richard is in *Looking for Richard,* (1996, color, 109 min., PG-13; Director: Al Pacino; with Pacino, Kevin Spacey, Alex Baldwin, and Winona Ryder). It's a documentary of Pacino's staging of *Richard* as Pacino discovers what the play is all about.

Romeo and Juliet (1968, color, 138 min., PG; Director: Franco Zeffirelli; with John McEnery, Michael York, Olivia Hussey, and Leonard Whiting) The young lovers are not particularly worth watching, but the supporting cast is.

Taming of the Shrew. (1967, color, 126 min., Director: Franco Zeffirelli; with Elizabeth Taylor, Richard Burton, and Michael Hordern) This is a badly underrated film, or maybe it's just a politically incorrect play. *10 Things I Hate about You* (1999, color, 97 min., PG-13; Director: Gil Junger), is a charming and effective retelling of the play.

Twelfth Night (1966, color, 134 min., PG; Director: Trevor Nunn; with Helena Bonham Carter, Ben Kingsley, and the magnificent Nigel Hawthorne)

Shakespeare in Love (1998, color, 122 min., R; Director; John Madden, with Gwyneth Paltrow, Joseph Fiennes, Geoffrey Rush, and Judi Dench) People ask about this most joyous recent film, "Is it true?" Who cares?

He's in the Signal Corps Now (1943) and vocational novels such as Elizabeth Lansing's *Nancy Naylor, Flight Nurse* (1944). More popular were true stories about battles and survivors, including Richard Tregaskis's *Guadalcanal Diary* (1943), Ernie Pyle's *Here Is Your War* (1943) and *Brave Men* (1944), Robert Trumbull's *The Raft* (1942), and Quentin Reynolds's *70,000 to One* (1946).

Perhaps as a reaction to the realities of war, the most popular series of books for both adults and young adults during the 1950s and 1960s centered about the fascinating James Bond, Agent 007. Ian Fleming caught the mood of the time with escapist excitement tinted with what appeared to be realities.

Also far removed from the grim realities of World War II were three historical novels that appealed to some young adults. Elizabeth Janet Gray's *Adam of the Road* (1942) revealed the color and music of the Middle Ages as young Adam Quartermain became a minstrel. Marchette Chute's *The Innocent Wayfaring* (1943) covers four days in June 1370 when Anne runs away from her convent school to join a band of strolling players, while in Chute's *The Wonderful Winter* (1954), young Sir Robert Wakefield, treated like a child at home, runs off to London to become an actor in Shakespeare's company.

Writers for young adults contributed several fine romances, including Margaret E. Bell's Alaskan story *Love Is Forever* (1954), Vivian Breck's superior study of young marriage in *Maggie* (1954), and Benedict and Nancy Freedman's *Mrs. Mike,* set in the northern Canadian wilderness. Elizabeth Goudge's *Green Dolphin Street* had everything working for it—a young handsome man in love with one of a pair of sisters. When he leaves and writes home his wishes, the wrong sister accepts. The true love, apparently overwhelmed by his unfaithfulness, becomes a nun. Passion, love, and adventure are all handled well by a first-rate writer. Kathleen Winsor was also one of a kind, although what one and what kind was widely debated. When her *Forever Amber* (1944) appeared, parents worried, censors paled, and young adults smiled as they ignored the fuss and read the book. Young people, especially in the last year or two of high school, have often been receptive to books about human dilemmas. Between 1940 and 1966, society changed rapidly and drastically with deeply disturbing consequences. There was a growing awareness that the democracy described in our Constitution was more preached than practiced. As the censorship applied to John Steinbeck's *The Grapes of Wrath* (1939) and *Of Mice and Men* (1937) lessened—although it never entirely disappeared—young readers read of the plight of migrant workers and learned that all was not well. Many were deeply disturbed by Alan Paton's stories of racial struggles in South Africa, *Cry the Beloved Country* (1948) and *Too Late the Phalarope* (1953). Still more were touched by the sentiment and passion of Harper Lee's *To Kill a Mockingbird* (1960) set in the American South.

Richard Wright and his books *Native Son* (1940) and *Black Boy* (1945) served as bitter prototypes for much African-American literature. The greatest African-American novel, and one of the greatest novels of any kind in the last fifty years, is Ralph Ellison's *Invisible Man* (1952). Existential in tone, *Invisible Man* is at different times bawdy (the incest scenes remind readers of Faulkner without being derivative), moving, and frightening, but always stunning and breathtaking.

Three African-American nonfiction writers are still read. Claude Brown painted a stark picture of African-American ghetto life in *Manchild in the Promised Land* (1965), whereas Malcolm X and Alex Haley, the latter better known for *Roots,* painted a no more attractive picture in *The Autobiography of Malcolm X* (1965). The most enduring work may prove to be Eldridge Cleaver's *Soul on Ice* (1968), an impassioned plea by an African-American man in prison who wrote to save himself.

Writings about African-Americans aimed at young adults were not long in coming. Lorenz Graham presented realistic African-American characters in *South Town* (1958), which today seems dated; *North Town* (1965); and *Whose Town?* (1969). Nat Hentoff's first novel for young adults, *Jazz Country* (1965), is a superb story of a white boy trying to break into the African-American world of jazz. It is an unusual topic, and perhaps neither African-Americans nor whites are comfortable with the themes or the characters, which is sad because Hentoff is a remarkable, compassionate, and honest writer. Nonfiction writing for young adults about African-Americans was mostly biographical. In the late 1940s and early 1950s, Shirley Graham wrote good biographies of Frederick Douglass, Benjamin Banneker, Phillis Wheatley, and Booker T. Washington. Elizabeth Yates won applause and the Newbery Award for *Amos Fortune, Free Man* (1950). Her account of a slave who gained freedom in 1801 and fought the rest of his life for freedom for other African-Americans has been attacked, however, by some groups as paternalistic, a word overused by African-American critics who assume that any white writer is inherently incapable of writing about African-Americans.

Intrigued and concerned as many young adults were about social issues and dilemmas, something far more immediate constantly pressed in on them—their own personal need to survive in an often unfriendly world. Anne Emery's books preached the status quo, especially acceptance of parental rules, but they also touched on personal concerns, with her best book being *Married on Wednesday* (1957). Mina Lewiton's *The Divided Heart* (1947) is an early study of the effects of divorce on a young woman, and Lewiton's *A Cup of Courage* (1948) is an honest and groundbreaking account of alcoholism and its destruction of a family. Later, Zoa Sherburne proved more enduring with her portrait of alcohol's effects in *Jennifer* (1959), although her best and most lasting book is *Too Bad About the Haines Girl* (1967), a superb novel about pregnancy, honest and straightforward without being preachy.

Something far more significant happened during this period, which was that the *bildungsroman,* a novel about the initiation, maturation, and education of a young adult, grew in appeal. Most bildungsroman were originally published for adults but soon read by young adults. Dan Wickenden's *Walk Like a Mortal* (1940) and Betty Smith's *A Tree Grows in Brooklyn* (1943) were among the first. None of these books won the young adult favor or the adult opposition as did J. D. Salinger's *The Catcher in the Rye* (1951). It is still the most widely censored book in American schools and still hated by people who assume that a disliked word (*that* word) corrupts an entire book. Holden Caulfield may indeed be vulgar and cynical and capable of seeing only the phonies around him, but he is also loyal and loving to those he sees as good or innocent. For many young adults, it is the most honest and human story they know about someone they recognize (even in themselves)—a young man caught between childhood and maturity and unsure which way to go. Whether *Catcher* is a masterpiece similar to James Joyce's *A Portrait of the Artist as a Young Man* depends on subjective judgment, but there is no question that Salinger's book captured—and continues to capture—the hearts and minds of countless young adults as no other book has.

Many teachers and librarians would have predicted just as long a life for John Knowles's *A Separate Peace* (1961) and William Golding's *Lord of the Flies* (1955), but fame and longevity are sometime things, and despite many articles in *English Journal* about the literary and pedagogical worth of both books, they seem to be in a state of decline.

Rise of Criticism of Young Adult Literature

Today we take criticism of young adult literature as discussed in Chapter Ten for granted, but it developed slowly. In the 1940s, journals provided little information on, and less criticism of, young adult literature except for book lists, book reviews, and occasional references in articles on reading interests or improving young people's literary taste. The comments that did appear were often more appreciative than critical, but given the times and the attitude of many teachers and librarians, appreciation or even recognition may have been more important than criticism.

In 1951, Dwight L. Burton wrote the first criticism of young adult novels, injecting judgments along with appreciation as he commented on works by Dan Wickenden, Maureen Daly, Paul Annixter, Betty Cavanna, and Madeleine L'Engle. Concluding his article, Burton identified the qualities of the good young adult novel and prophesied its potential and future:

> The good novel for the adolescent reader has attributes no different from any good novel. It must be technically masterful, and it must present a significant synthesis of human experience. Because of the nature of adolescence itself, the good novel for the adolescent should be full in true invention and imagination. It must free itself of Pollyannaism or the Tarkington–Henry Aldrich–Corliss Archer tradition and maintain a clear vision of the adolescent as a person of complexity, individuality, and dignity. The novel for the adolescent presents a ready field for the mature artist.[40]

In 1955, Richard S. Alm provided greater critical coverage of the young adult novel.[41] He agreed with critics that many writers presented a "sugar-puff story of what adolescents should do and should believe rather than what adolescents may or will do and believe." He cited specific authors and titles he found good and painted their strengths and weaknesses in clear strokes. He concluded by offering teachers some questions that might be useful in analyzing the merits of young adult novels.

A year later, Emma L. Patterson began her fine study of the origin of young adult novels showing that "The junior novel has become an established institution."[42] Her command of history, her knowledge of trends in young adult novels, her awareness of shortcomings and virtues of the novels, and her understanding of the place of young adult novels in schools and libraries made her article essential reading for librarians and teachers.

Despite the leadership of Burton, Alm, and Patterson, helpful criticism of young adult literature was slow in arriving, but biting criticism was soon forthcoming. Only a few months after Patterson's article, Frank G. Jennings's "Literature for Adolescents—Pap or Protein?"[43] appeared. The title was ambiguous, but if any reader had doubts about where Jennings stood, the doubt was removed with the first sentence: "The stuff of adolescent literature, for the most part, is mealy-mouthed, gutless, and pointless." The remainder of the article added little to that point, and although Jennings overstated his case, Burton, Alm, Patterson, and other sensible supporters would have agreed that much young adult literature, similar to much adult literature, was second-rate or worse. Jennings's article was not the first broadside attack, and it certainly would not be the last.[44]

Much of the literature written for young adults from 1940 through 1966 goes largely and legitimately ignored today. Some writers are still read, however, and more important than mere longevity is the effect that these authors had on books appearing after 1966. Readers before then could not have anticipated S. E. Hinton's *The Outsiders* or Paul Zindel's *The Pigman,* which were to appear in only a year or two, much less Isabelle Holland's *The Man Without a Face,* Norma Klein's *Mom, The Wolfman and Me,* Rosa Guy's *Ruby,* or Robert Cormier's *The Chocolate War.* These iconoclastic, taboo-breaking novels and others of today would not have been possible had it not been for earlier novels that broke ground and prepared readers, teachers, librarians, and parents for contemporary novels.

Notes

[1]Caroline Ticknor, *Hawthorne and His Publisher* (Houghton Mifflin, 1913), p. 141.

[2]E. Douglas Branch, *The Sentimental Years, 1836–1860* (Appleton, 1934), p. 131.

[3]Jesse H. Shera, *Foundations of the Public Library: The Origins of the Public Library Movement in New England, 1629–1885* (The University of Chicago Press, 1949), p. 238.

[4]A brief summary of the 1853 and 1876 library conventions can be found in Sister Gabriella Margeath, "Library Conventions of 1853, 1876, and 1877," *Journal of Library History* 8(April 1973):52–69.

[5]William F. Poole, "Some Popular Objections to Public Libraries," *American Library Journal* 1(October 1876):48–49.

[6]W. M. Stevenson, "Weeding Out Fiction in the Carnegie Free Library of Allegheny, Pa.," *Library Journal* 22(March 1897):135.

[7]"Novel Reading," *American Library Journal* 1(October 1876):98.

[8]"Monthly Reports from Public Librarians upon the Reading of Minors: A Suggestion," *Library Journal* 24(August 1899):479.

[9]Carleton Washburne and Mabel Vogel, *Winnetka Graded Book List* (American Library Association, 1926), p. 5.

[10]Carleton Washburne and Mabel Vogel, "Supplement to the Winnetka Graded Book List," *Elementary English Review* 4(February 1927):47–52; and 4(March 1927):66–73.

[11]William Lyon Phelps, "The Virtues of the Second-Rate," *English Journal* 16(January 1927):13–14.

[12]Franklin T. Baker, *A Bibliography of Children's Reading* (Teachers College, Columbia University, 1908), pp. 6–7.

[13]Clara Whitehill Hunt, "Good and Bad Taste in Girls' Reading," *Ladies Home Journal* 27(April 1910):52.

[14]Julia Carter, "Let's Talk About Boys and Books," *Wilson Bulletin for Librarians* 9(April 1935):418.

[15]Alice M. Jordan, "A Gallery of Girls," *Horn Book Magazine* 13(September 1937):276.

[16]Clara Vostrovsky, "A Study of Children's Reading Tastes," *Pedagogical Seminary* 6(December, 1899):535.

[17]G. Stanley Hall, "Children's Reading: As a Factor in Their Education," *Library Journal* 33(April 1908):124–125.

[18]J. M. Coulter, "What the University Expects of the Secondary School," *School Review* 17(February 1909):73.

[19]Wilbur W. Hatfield, "Modern Literature for High School Use," *English Journal* 1(January 1912):52.

[20]*Reorganization of English in Secondary Schools,* Department of the Interior, Bureau of Education, Bulletin 1917, No. 2. (Government Printing Office, 1917), p. 63.

[21]Nancy Gillmore Coryell, *An Evaluation of Extensive and Intensive Teaching of Literature: A Year's Experiment in the Eleventh Grade,* Teachers College, Columbia University, Contributions to Education, No. 275 (Teachers College, Columbia University, 1927).

[22]Lou LaBrant, *An Evaluation of the Free Reading Program in Grades Ten, Eleven, and Twelve for the Class of 1935.* The Ohio State University School, Contributions to Education No. 2 (Ohio State University, 1936). See also Lou LaBrant, "The Content of a Free Reading Program," *Educational Research Bulletin* 16(February 17, 1937):29–34.

[23]Dora V. Smith, "American Youth and English," *English Journal* 26(February 1937):111.

[24]Graham P. Hawks, "A Nineteenth-Century School Library: Early Years in Milwaukee,"*Journal of Library History* 12(Fall 1977):361.

[25]S. Swett Green, "Libraries and School," *Library Journal* 16(December 1891):22. Other representative articles concerned with the relationship include Mellen Chamberlain, "Public Libraries and Public School," *Library Journal* 5(November–December 1880):299–302; W. E. Foster, "The School and the Library: Their Mutual Relations," *Library Journal* 4(September–October 1879):319–341; and Mrs. J. H. Resor, "The Boy and the Book, or The Public Library a Necessity," *Public Libraries* 2(June 1897):282–285.

[26]"The Report of the Committee on Relations of Public Libraries to Public Schools," *NEA Journal of Proceedings and Addresses of the 38th Annual Meeting* (The University of Chicago, Press, 1899), p. 455.

[27]Mary E. Hall, "The Possibilities of the High School Library," *ALA Bulletin* 6(July 1912):261–63.

[28]Caroline M. Hewins, "Book Reviews, Book Lists, and Articles on Children's Reading: Are They of Practical Value to the Children's Librarians?" *Library Journal* 26(August 1901):58. Attacks on series books, especially Stratemeyer's books, persisted thereafter in library literature. Mary E. S. Root prepared a list of series books not to be circulated by public librarians, "Not to Be Circulated," *Wilson Bulletin for Librarians* 3(January 1929):446, including books by Alger, Finley, Castlemon, Ellis, Optic, and others, the others being heavily Stratemeyer. Two months later, Ernest F. Ayers responded, "Not to Be Circulated?" *Wilson Bulletin for Librarians* 3(March 1929):528–529, objecting to the cavalier treatment accorded old favorites and sarcastically adding, "Why worry about censorship so long as we have librarians?" Attacks continue today. Some librarians and English teachers to the contrary, the Syndicate clearly is winning, and students seem to be pleased.

[29]Franklin K. Mathiews, "Blowing Out the Boy's Brains," *Outlook* 108(November 18, 1914):653.

[30]John Tunis, "What Is a Juvenile Book?" *Horn Book Magazine* 44(June 1968):307.

[31]George W. Norvell, "Some Results of a Twelve-Year Study of Children's Reading Interests," *English Journal* 35(December 1946):532, 536.

[32]Marie Rankin, *Children's Interests in Library Books of Fiction,* Teachers College, Columbia University, Contributions to Education, No. 906 (Teachers College, Columbia University, 1947).

[33]Stephen Dunning, "The Most Popular Junior Novels," *Junior Libraries* 5(December 15, 1959):7–9.

[34]Jacob W. Getzels, "The Nature of Reading Interests: Psychological Aspects" in *Developing Permanent Interests in Reading,* ed. Helen M. Robinson, Supplementary Education Monographs, No. 84, December 1956 (University of Chicago Press, 1956), p. 5.

[35]G. Robert Carlsen, "Behind Reading Interests," *English Journal* 43(January 1954):7–10.

[36]G. O. Ireland, "Bibliotherapy: The Use of Books as a Form of Treatment in a Neuropsychiatric Hospital," *Library Journal* 54(December 1, 1929):972–974.

[37]Lou LaBrant, "Diversifying the Matter," *English Journal* 40(March 1951):135.

[38]S. Alan Cohen, "Paperbacks in the Classroom," *Journal of Reading* 12(January 1969):295.

[39]Stanley B. Kegler and Stephen Dunning, "Junior Book Roundup—Literature for the Adolescent, 1960," *English Journal* 50(May 1961):369.

[40]Dwight L. Burton, "The Novel for the Adolescent," *English Journal* 40(September 1951):363–369.

[41]Richard S. Alm, "The Glitter and the Gold," *English Journal* 44(September 1955):315.

[42]Emma L. Patterson, "The Junior Novels and How They Grew," *English Journal* 45(October 1956):381.

[43]*English Journal* 45(December 1956):226–231.

[44]See, for example, Alice Krahn, "Case Against the Junior Novel," *Top of the News* 17(May 1961):19–22; Esther Millett, "We Don't Even Call Those Books!" *Top of the News* 20(October 1963):45–47; and Harvey R. Granite, "The Uses and Abuses of Junior Literature," *Clearing House* 42 (February 1968): 337–340.

Titles Mentioned in the Text of Chapter Two

Alcott, Louisa May. *Behind a Mask: The Unknown Thrillers of Louisa May Alcott*, ed., Madeleine Stern. Morrow, 1975.

Alcott, Louisa May. *Little Women: Meg, Jo, Beth, and Amy. The Story of Their Lives. A Girl's Book.* 1868.

Alcott, Louisa May. *Little Women: Meg, Jo, Beth, and Amy. Part Second.* 1869.

Alcott, Louisa May. *A Long Fatal Love Chase*, ed., Kent Bicknell. Random House, 1995.

Alcott, Louisa May. *The Lost Stories of Louisa May Alcott*, eds., Madeleine Stern and Daniel Shealy. Citadel, 1993.

Alcott, Louisa May. *Plots and Counterplots: More Unknown Thrillers of Louisa May Alcott*, ed. Madeleine Stern. Morrow, 1976.

Aldrich, Thomas Bailey. *The Story of a Bad Boy.* 1870.

Alger, Horatio. *Ragged Dick: or Street Life in New York.* 1867.

Allee, Marjorie Hill. *The Great Tradition*. 1937.

Allee, Marjorie Hill. *Jane's Island*. 1931.

Altsheler, Joseph. *The Horsemen of the Plains*. 1910.

Altsheler, Joseph. *The Last of the Chiefs*. 1909.

Annixter, Paul (real name Howard A. Sturzel). *Swiftwater*. A. A. Wyn, 1950.

Appleton, Victor (Stratemeyer Syndicate pseudonym). Tom Swift series, 1910–1935.

Armer, Laura. *Waterless Mountain*, 1931.

Barbour, Ralph Henry. *The Crimson Sweater*. 1906.

Barbour, Ralph Henry. *The Half-Back*. 1899.

Bell, Margaret Elizabeth. *Love Is Forever*. Morrow, 1954.

Bennett, Jack. *The Hawk Alone*. Little, Brown, 1965.

Bennett, Jack. *Jamie*. Little, Brown, 1963.

Bennett, Jack. *Mister Fisherman*. Little, Brown, 1963.

Bennett, John. *Master Skylark: A Story of Shakespeare's Time*. 1897.

Benson, Sally. *Junior Miss*. Doubleday, 1947.

Boylston, Helen Dore. *Sue Barton, Student Nurse*. Little, Brown, 1936.

Breck, Vivian. *Maggie*. Doubleday, 1954.

Brooks, Noah. *The Boy Emigrants*. 1876.

Brown, Claude. *Manchild in the Promised Land*. Macmillan, 1965.

Buck, Pearl. *The Good Earth*. John Day, 1931.

Bugbee, Emma. *Peggy Covers the News*. Dodd, Mead, 1936.

Burroughs, Edgar Rice. *Tarzan of the Apes*. 1914.

Campanella, Roy. *It's Good to Be Alive*. Little, Brown, 1959.

Carson, John F. *The Coach Nobody Liked*. Farrar, Straus & Giroux, 1960.

Carson, John F. *Floorburns*. Farrar, Straus & Giroux, 1957.

Carson, John F. *Hotshot*. Farrar, Straus & Giroux, 1961.

Castlemon, Harry (real name, Charles Austin Fosdick). *Frank the Young Naturalist*. 1864.

Cavanna, Betty. *Going on Sixteen*. Ryerson, 1946.

Chute, Marchette. *The Innocent Wayfaring*. Scribner, 1943.

Chute, Marchette. *The Wonderful Winter*. Dutton, 1954.

Cleaver, Eldridge. *Soul on Ice*. McGraw-Hill, 1968.

Coolidge, Susan (real name, Sarah Chauncey Woolsey). *What Katy Did*. 1872.

Cormier, Robert. *The Chocolate War*. Pantheon, 1974.

Daly, Maureen. *Seventeenth Summer*. Dodd, Mead, 1942.

Deland, Margaret. *The Awakening of Helena Richie*. 1906.

Doyle, Arthur Conan. *The Adventures of Sherlock Holmes*. 1891.

Doyle, Arthur Conan. *The Hound of the Baskervilles*. 1902.

DuJardin, Rosamund. *Double Date*. Longman, 1953.

DuJardin, Rosamund. *Wait for Marcy*. Longman, 1950.

Ellison, Ralph. *Invisible Man*. Random House, 1952.

Emery, Anne. *Married on Wednesday*. Ryerson, 1957.

Falkner, John Meade. *Moonfleet*. 1898.

Fargo, Lucile Foster. *Marian Martha*. Dodd, Mead, 1936.

Farley, Walter. *Black Stallion*. Random House, 1944.

Felsen, Henry Gregor. *Crash Club*. Random House, 1958.

Felsen, Henry Gregor. *Hot Rod*. Dutton, 1950.

Felsen, Henry Gregor. *Street Rod*. Random House, 1953.

Felsen, Henry Gregor. *Two and the Town*. Scribner, 1952.

Finley, Martha (real name, Martha Farquharson). *Elsie Dinsmore*. 1867. The series ran from 1867–1905.

Freedman, Benedict and Nancy. *Mrs. Mike*. Coward, McCann, & Geoghegan, 1947.

Frick, Constance H. *The Comeback Guy*. Harcourt Brace Jovanovich, 1961.

Frick, Constance H. *Five Against the Odds*. Harcourt Brace Jovanovich, 1955.

Golding, William. *Lord of the Flies*. Coward, McCann, 1955.

Goudge, Elizabeth. *Green Dolphin Street*. Coward, McCann, 1944.

Graham, Lorenz. *North Town*. Crowell, 1965.

Graham, Lorenz. *South Town*. Follett, 1958.

Graham, Lorenz. *Whose Town?* Crowell, 1969.

Gray, Elizabeth. *Adam of the Road*. Viking, 1942.

Grey, Zane. *Riders of the Purple Sage*. 1912.

Grinnell, George Bird. *By Cheyenne Campfires*. 1926.

Grinnell, George Bird. *Pawnee Hero Stories and Folk Tales*. 1899.

Guy, Rosa. *Ruby*. Viking, 1976.

Haley, Alex. *Roots*. Doubleday, 1976.

Harris, Christie. *You Have to Draw the Line Somewhere*. Atheneum, 1964.

Hentoff, Nat. *Jazz Country*. HarperCollins, 1965.

Heyliger, William. *Bartley: Freshman Pitcher*. 1911.

Hinton, S. E. *The Outsiders*. Viking, 1967.

Holland, Isabelle. *The Man Without a Face*. Lippincott, 1972.

Jackson, Helen Hunt. *Ramona*. 1884.

James, Will. *Smoky, the Cowhorse*. 1926.

Johnson, Owen. *Stover at Yale*. 1911.

Johnson, Owen. *The Tennessee Shad*. 1911.

Johnson, Owen. *The Varmint*. 1910.

Johnston, Mary. *To Have and to Hold*. 1900.

Joyce, James. *Portrait of the Artist as a Young Man*. 1914.

Klein, Norma. *Mom, the Wolfman and Me*. Random House, 1973.

Knowles, John. *A Separate Peace*. Macmillan, 1960.

Lane, Rose Wilder. *Let the Hurricane Roar*. 1933.

Lane, Rose Wilder. *The Young Pioneers* (reissue of *Let the Hurricane Roar*). 1976.

Lansing, Elizabeth. *Nancy Naylor, Flight Nurse*. Crowell, 1944.

Lee, Harper. *To Kill a Mockingbird*. Lippincott, 1960.

Lewiton, Mina. *A Cup of Courage*. McKay, 1948.

Lewiton, Mina. *The Divided Heart*. McKay, 1947.

Malcolm X and Alex Haley. *The Autobiography of Malcolm X.* Grove, 1965.

Mann, Carl. *He's in the Signal Corps Now.* McBride, 1943.

Means, Florence Crannell. *The Moved-Outers.* Houghton Mifflin, 1945.

Means, Florence Crannell. *Shuttered Windows.* Houghton Mifflin, 1938.

Means, Florence Crannell. *Tangled Waters: A Navajo Story.* Houghton Mifflin, 1936.

Montgomery, Lucy Maud. *Anne of Green Gables.* 1908.

Munroe, Kirk. *Derrick Sterling.* 1888.

Optic, Oliver (real name, William Taylor Adams). *The Boat Club.* 1855.

Paton, Alan. *Cry, the Beloved Country.* Scribner, 1948.

Paton, Alan. *Too Late the Phalarope.* Scribner, 1953.

Peck, George Wilbur. *Peck's Bad Boy and His Pa.* 1883.

Piersall, James Anthony, and Albert Hirschberg. *Fear Strikes Out.* Little, Brown, 1955.

Porter, Eleanor. *Pollyanna.* 1913.

Pyle, Ernie. *Brave Men.* Holt, 1944.

Pyle, Ernie. *Here Is Your War.* Holt, 1943.

Reynolds, Quentin. *70,000 to One.* Random House, 1946.

Richards, Laura Elizabeth. *Peggy.* 1899.

Robinson, Mabel Louise. *Bright Island.* 1937.

Salinger, J. D. *The Catcher in the Rye.* Little, Brown, 1951.

Sherburne, Zoa. *Jennifer.* Morrow, 1959.

Sherburne, Zoa. *Too Bad about the Haines Girl.* Morrow, 1967.

Smith, Betty. *A Tree Grows in Brooklyn.* HarperCollins, 1943.

Standish, Burt L. (real name, William Gilbert Patten). Frank Merriwell series, 1901–1911.

Steinbeck, John. *The Grapes of Wrath.* Viking, 1939.

Steinbeck, John. *Of Mice and Men.* Viking, 1937.

Stevenson, Robert Louis. *Treasure Island.* 1883.

Stolz, Mary. *A Love, or a Season.* HarperCollins, 1953.

Stolz, Mary. *Pray Love, Remember.* HarperCollins, 1954.

Stolz, Mary. *The Seagulls Woke Me.* HarperCollins, 1951.

Stratemeyer, Edward. Dave Porter series. 1905–1919.

Stratemeyer, Edward. Lakeport series. 1904–1912.

Stratemeyer, Edward. Old Glory series. 1898–1901.

Stratemeyer, Edward. *Richard Dare's Venture; or, Striking Out for Himself.* 1894.

Stratemeyer, Edward. Rover Boys series. 1899–1926.

Stratemeyer, Edward. Soldiers of Fortune series, 1900–1906.

Stratemeyer, Edward. *Under Dewey at Manila; or, The War Fortunes of a Castaway.* 1898.

Stratemeyer, Edward. *Victor Horton's Idea.* 1886.

Summers, James. *The Limit of Love.* Ryerson, 1959.

Summers, James. *Prom Trouble.* Ryerson, 1954.

Summers, James. *Ring Around Her Finger.* Westminster, 1957.

Tregaskis, Richard. *Guadalcanal Diary.* Random House, 1943.

Trumbull, Robert. *The Raft.* Holt, 1942.

Tunis, John. *All-American.* Harcourt, 1938.

Tunis, John. *Go, Team, Go!* Morrow, 1954.

Tunis, John. *Iron Duke.* 1938.

Tunis, John. *Yea! Wildcats.* Harcourt, 1944.

Twain, Mark (real name, Samuel Clemens). *Adventures of Huckleberry Finn.* 1884.

Twain, Mark, *The Adventures of Tom Sawyer.* 1876.

Wetherell, Elizabeth (real name, Susan Warner). *The Wide, Wide World.* 1850.

Wickenden, Dan. *Walk Like a Mortal.* Morrow, 1940.

Wiggin, Kate Douglas. *Rebecca of Sunnybrook Farm.* 1904.

Wilson, Augusta Jane Evans. *St. Elmo.* 1867.

Winsor, Kathleen. *Forever Amber.* Macmillan, 1944.

Wister, Owen. *The Virginian: A Horseman of the Plains.* 1902.

Wright, Richard. *Black Boy.* HarperCollins, 1940.

Wright, Richard. *Native Son.* HarperCollins, 1940.

Yates, Elizabeth. *Amos Fortune, Free Man.* Aladdin, 1950.

Zindel, Paul. *The Pigman.* HarperCollins, 1968.

Information on the availability of paperback editions of these titles is available online from such book sellers as Barnes & Noble and Amazon.com, and through *Books in Print* compiled by R. R. Bowker Company and available either in person or online from major libraries.

YA Literature, Pop Culture, and the Mass Media

In the late 1980s and early 1990s, many of us who loved adolescent literature lamented a cutback by YA publishers who began focusing their attention on junior high and middle school readers because that's where the most students were. We assumed that once this big population bubble (the children of the baby boomers) was in high school, we would have another golden age of books written specifically for young adults. It has not been quite that simple.

Indeed, there was a population bubble whose members are now in high school or just beginning college. English teachers and librarians, however, weren't the only ones waiting for these young people, nor were they a generation to stand back and wait for us. Partly because of their sheer numbers and partly because of the eagerness of advertisers to attract this large body of potential lifelong customers, we are now in a youth-oriented (some would say "youth-dominated") era. Everywhere we look, we see evidence that today's young people—for better or for worse—have a sense of empowerment that previous generations did not feel. Many teenagers, along with many adults, look on the mass media as a modern-day equivalent of a fairy godmother—someone who occasionally grants instant fame, power, and riches, and who on a daily basis keeps us interested and entertained. See Focus Box 3.1, The Media as the Message in Fiction, for examples of how teenagers' lives are entwined with various aspects of modern media.

Time magazine covers provide an example of the increasing importance of the teen presence in the media. For example, in "the old days," the covers were a kind of *Who's Who* presenting world leaders and well-established politicians, performers, writers, producers, and winners of Nobel and Pulitzer Prizes. During the 1998–1999 school year, however, *Time* cover photos featured kid models for stories "The Latest on Ritalin," "Too Much Homework," "Growing Up Online," "How to Spot a Troubled Kid," and "Sports Crazed Kids." There were also cover stories relating the April, 1999 school shooting in Littleton, Colorado, to the March, 1998 one in Jonesboro, Arkansas, as well as a picture of 21-year-old Matthew Shepard, the gay college student killed in Laramie, Wyoming, in October of 1998. Celebrity

FOCUS BOX 3.1

The Media as the Message in Fiction

The Adventures of Blue Avenger by Norma Howe. Holt, 1999. Fifteen-year-old David Schumacher invents a cartoon alter ego, The Blue Avenger, to be "secret champion of the underdog, modest seeker of truth, fearless innovator of the unknown." When he turns 16, he decides to drop the *The* and become *Blue Avenger* himself. The results are both hilarious and tender.

The Great Interactive Dream Machine by Richard Peck. Dial, 1997. Peck uses his wit and humor to stimulate the imaginations of middle school and junior high computer users in this sequel to *Lost in Cyberspace* (Dial, 1995) starring computer geeks Josh and Aaron.

Hard Love by Ellen Wittlinger. Simon & Schuster, 1999. The setting for this unusual novel is the world of *zines* (desktop published magazines) as seen through the eyes of a high school junior who is grateful to find an outlet for his talent and interests. He meets a soul mate in Marisol, another zine writer, but there are too many complications for them to walk happily off into the sunset.

The Landry News by Andrew Clements, illustrated by Salvatore Murdocca. Simon & Schuster, 1999. Mr. Larson is a burned-out teacher, who is "inspired" to start a class-sponsored newspaper after one of his students writes an article for the town newspaper about his non-teaching. At last the fifth graders are excited by school and are developing real skills, but then the principal decides to use the newspaper as a way of firing Mr. Larson. Everyone learns something.

Making Up Megaboy by Virginia Walter, illustrated by Katrina Roeckelein. Dorling Kindersley Ink, 1998. The high-tech graphics, computerized photos, and varied type fonts seem especially fitting in this story of a 13-year-old boy who refuses to communicate except through the story he writes about Megaboy, a comic strip superhero he creates.

Monster by Walter Dean Myers, illustrated by Christopher Myers. HarperCollins, 1999. There are no pages of plain type in this story that a boy tells through a movie script he is writing about being charged as accessory to a crime. Scattered through the script are hand-printed pages from his journal, photos that resemble excerpted freeze frames, and tentative drawings of how he envisions the on-screen credits.

Toning the Sweep by Angela Johnson. Orchard, 1993. Emily's grandmother is terminally ill and is being taken away from the California desert home that she loves. In this three-generational story of African-American women, Emily uses a camcorder to make a record of the people and the places that are important to her grandmother and in the process learns a lot about herself.

Violet & Claire by Francesca Lia Block. HarperCollins, 1999. Violet dresses in "forever black" but dreams in technicolor, while Claire dresses and acts like a real-life Tinker Bell. As with Block's *Weetzie Bat*, the magic of movie making has seeped into Violet's soul and serves as a metaphor for this attractively designed 5-by-7-inch book.

---

portraits featured 23-year-old hip-hop singer Lauryn Hill; 26-year-old former White House intern Monica Lewinsky; 27-year-old Latin singer Ricky Martin, and in July the 20-somethings U.S. women's soccer team.

A dramatic illustration of the popular culture emphasis on youth occurred in mid-October of 1998 when the media carried stories about Riley Weston, a 32-year-old actress and writer, who had claimed to be a 19-year-old teenage genius. She wrote and guest starred in an episode of WB's teen drama *Felicity*. She had also signed a six-figure deal with Disney, but lost it when someone revealed to *Entertainment Tonight* that Weston was a better actress than anyone suspected. She had sliced thirteen years off her life without even having plastic surgery. When she was

The population surge in young adults has caused mainstream magazines to increase coverage of young people, so that for many teens it's a tossup as to whether they read standard adult magazines or magazines designed and marketed specifically to their age group.

interviewed by Mike Wallace on *60 Minutes* in February 1999, she defended her actions by saying that age should not matter. If her writing communicated to young people, then that should be what counted. Nevertheless as soon as her real age was revealed, her phone stopped ringing.

As part of the same *Sixty Minutes* program, Wallace also interviewed three veteran TV writers, apparently in their 50s or early 60s. All of them lamented what they viewed as Hollywood's mistaken emphasis on age. One had declared bankruptcy; another told how a 32-year-old producer had said "Well, if we do buy your idea would you have the energy to see it through to production?" while another confessed to leaving some of her most impressive jobs off her résumé. She said that when young producers see that someone was a writer for *M*A*S*H* or *All in the Family,* they view the person as a historical artifact.

Show business has so many teenage stars, especially in the field of music in which such teen pop stars as 17-year-old Britney Spears and the *Backstreet Boys* and *'N Sync* are known as "kiddie rappers", that in May 1999, there were plenty of performers to choose from when ABC aired a television special *21 Hottest Stars Under 21* sponsored by *Teen People.* The "do-it-ourselves" show business attitude is also seen in the publishing world in which teen and young adult authors are publishing their own books (see Focus Box 3.2, Teen Voices). Admittedly many of the teen authors have had considerable help from adults, but so have the teens in show business.

Teen authors are not a brand new phenomenon. Maureen Daly was in college when she wrote *Seventeenth Summer,* and S. E. Hinton was in high school when she wrote *The Outsiders,* but today young authors are publishing across different genres and with more vigor than in the past. The Internet is undoubtedly a factor in changing attitudes as well as the practicalities of publishing. When Charles Butz, a

FOCUS BOX 3.2

Teen Voices

After a Suicide: Young People Speak Up by Susan Kuklin. Putnam, 1994. Because most people feel awkward talking about suicide, Kuklin's interviews are all the more valuable and revealing. Other Kuklin interviews appear in *Irrepressible Spirit: Conversations with Human Rights Activists* (Philomel, 1996) and *Speaking Out: Teenagers Take on Race, Sex, and Identity* (Putnam, 1993).

Always Accept Me for Who I Am: Instructions from Teenagers on Raising the Perfect Parent by 147 Teens Who Know, compiled by J. S. Salt. Three Rivers Press/Random House, 1999. This 4-by-6-inch paperback resembles an autograph book with one or two kids' handwritten bits of advice on each page.

Conquering the Beast Within: How I Fought Depression and Won . . . And How You Can, Too by Cait Irwin. Random House, 1998. By the time the book was published, Irwin was a healthy 18-year-old attending college in Wisconsin. The text is handwritten and each page is decorated with Irwin's own drawings, befitting the side business she now has of designing murals.

Freedom's Children: Young Civil Rights Activists Tell Their Own Stories by Ellen Levine. Putnam, 1993. In straightforward but moving language, Levine presents thirty first-person accounts collected through interviewing adults who as children or teenagers in the South participated in the civil rights protests of the 1950s and 1960s.

Hearing Us Out: Voices from the Gay and Lesbian Community by Roger Sutton, photos by Lisa Ebright. Little, Brown, 1994. M.E. Kerr wrote the preface to this book which consists of interviews, many with young people. The photos add an air of authenticity and help readers identify with the heartfelt comments of those being interviewed.

The Heart Knows Something Different: Teenage Voices from the Foster Care System edited by Al Desetta, foreword by Jonathan Kozol. Youth Communication, Persea Books, 1996. The first-person accounts published here for a general adult audience were first published for other teenagers in *Foster Care Youth United*, a bimonthly magazine founded in 1993. New York City youth in foster care work on the magazine both with peers and adult editors. Some are volunteers and some are earning school credit.

No More Strangers Now: Young Voices from a New South Africa interviews by Tim McKee, photos by Anne Blackshaw. Dorling Kindersley Ink, 1998. A dozen teenagers from various backgrounds talk about their experiences living first under apartheid and now under the new system. They leave readers with respect for their pasts and hope for their futures.

Oh, Freedom!: Kids Talk about the Civil Rights Movement with the People Who Made It Happen by Casey King and Linda Barrett Osborne, illustrated by Joe Brooks, foreword by Rosa Parks. Knopf, 1997. Over two dozen young people conducted interviews with family members and other acquaintances who played roles in the Civil Rights movement.

Quiet Storm: Voices of Young Black Poets selected by Lydia Omolola Okutoro. Hyperion, 1999. Each of eight sections is introduced by a poem from an established poet such as Langston Hughes, Maya Angelou, Lucille Clifton, or Nikki Giovanni, followed by between five and eight "new" poems. An "About the Poets" afterword gives biographical information about the 41 young contributors, who were all under 20 when they wrote their poems.

The Shared Heart by Adam Mastoon. Morrow, 1997. **Two Teenagers in Twenty: Writings by Lesbian & Gay Youth** by Ann Heron. Alyson, 1994. These first person accounts lend immediacy to what young people feel and experience as they try to come to terms with their sexuality.

Voices from the Streets: Young Former Gang Members Tell Their Stories by Beth S. Atkin. Little, Brown, 1996. Journal entries, poems, casual observations, and interviews help readers understand why young people are attracted to the security of gangs.

What Are You? Voices of Mixed-Race Young People by Pearl Fuyo Gaskins. Holt, 1999. Helping Gaskins make her dream of writing this book come true are some eighty young writers who are identified by full or part names, ages, and racial mix. Hometowns and photographs are also included for many.

marketing manager at Electric Classifieds, Inc. in San Francisco, was talking to a reporter for a January 8, 1995, *New York Times* article, he compared the effects of the Internet to the effects of the printing press by saying that it takes "publishing out of the hands of the big corporations and places it into the hands of individuals, like what the printing press did in making literature available to the masses."

An example of young adult publishing power is the popular 1999 *Ophelia Speaks: Adolescent Girls Write about Their Search for Self.* It was put together by Sara Shandler, a college student, who when she was in high school read and disagreed with the basic premises in Mary Pipher's 1994 *Reviving Ophelia: Saving the Selves of Adolescent Girls* and so set out to present alternate viewpoints. She wrote 70,000 letters inviting young women to write their own stories. She put the book together from the 800 responses she received.

Perhaps today's young adults inherited their attitudes of empowerment from the 1960s flower children, who are their parents. In a 1995 article, "We Owe It All to the Hippies," published as part of a *Time* magazine Spring 1995, special issue "Welcome to Cyberspace," Stewart Brand, editor of the popular 1960s *Whole Earth Catalogue,* wrote that his generation perverted JFK's inaugural exhortation into "Ask not what your country can do for you. Do it yourself." He claimed that today's nonhierarchical and democratically run Internet is a result of the countercultural beliefs of computer hackers who wrested power from centralized mainframe computers under the control of IBM and gave it to millions of individuals with PCs.

> Our ethic of self-reliance came partly from science fiction. We all read Robert Heinlein's epic *Stranger in a Strange Land* as well as his libertarian screed-novel, *The Moon Is a Harsh Mistress.* Hippies and nerds alike reveled in Heinlein's contempt for centralized authority. To this day, computer scientists and technicians are almost universally science-fiction fans. Ever since the 1950s, for reasons that are unclear to me, science fiction has been almost universally libertarian in its outlook.

Today's young adults are the first generation who have grown up using computers and taking for granted what Brand calls the "democratic and nonhierarchical" structure of the Internet. While it will probably be decades before we will be able to assess the effects on literature of electronic communication tools, especially computers and the Internet, Eliza T. Dresang makes a start in her book *Radical Change: Books for Youth in a Digital Age.* She sets out four basic assumptions.

1. Children are capable and seeking connection.
2. The digital environment nurtures children's capabilities.
3. Handheld books offer digital-age connections.
4. Adults and youth are partners in the digital world.[1]

Following these assumptions, she proposes a framework for literary criticism revolving around what she thinks are the three biggest changes now occurring in books for children and teenagers.

- Changing forms and formats (See Focus Box 3.3, Fiction in New Formats, Focus Box 3.4, Picture Books for High Schoolers, and Focus Box 9.5, Stories in Verse on p. 299.)

FOCUS BOX 3.3

Fiction in New Formats

The Facts Speak for Themselves by Brock Cole. Front Street, 1997. Thirteen-year-old Linda has seen her mother's boyfriend shoot and kill a man with whom Linda has been sexually intimate. The book opens with Linda being questioned by the police. Rather than accepting the preliminary report written by a social worker, Linda writes her own account.

From the Notebooks of Melanin Sun by Jacqueline Woodson. Scholastic, 1995. The diary entries of 13-year-old Melanin Sun are identified by italics type in this story of an African-American boy coming to terms with the fact that his mother has a lesbian relationship with a white woman.

I Am the Cheese by Robert Cormier. Knopf, 1979. Cormier's book was a forerunner to today's experimental designs. Chapters alternate between Adam's drug-influenced memories and fantasies and the taped recordings of his sessions with Brint, who is either a psychiatrist or a government-sponsored interrogator.

Mind's Eye by Paul Fleischman. Holt, 1999. Readers get the feeling that they are hidden in a closet overhearing the conversations of three women in a nursing home. Sixteen-year-old Courtney was paralyzed in an accident while the other two are elderly. Surprisingly, it is the woman with Alzheimer's disease who helps Courtney the most. Other Fleischman books whose unusual formats make them good for out-loud reading or performing include his Civil War history *Bull Run* (HarperCollins, 1993) and his Newbery winning *Joyful Noise: Poems for Two Voices* (HarperCollins, 1988).

P.S. Longer Letter Later by Paula Danziger and Ann M. Martin. Scholastic, 1998. Two authors that most kids already know, (Martin for her *The Baby-Sitter's Club* series and Danziger for her *Amber Brown* books) join forces to write this lighthearted story through back-and-forth letters. There's lots of white space as they experiment with their names and with sending lists instead of letters and adding more and more P.S.'s. A sequel, *Snail Mail No More* followed in 2000, made up of e-mail messages.

The Perks of Being a Wallflower by Stephen Chbosky. MTV/Pocket Books, 1999. The setting is western Pennsylvania during the 1991–1992 school year when high school freshman Charlie has more to cope with than most kids meet in all four years. Charlie tells his story through long letters simply addressed to "Dear friend," which makes readers think of themselves as Charlie's friend.

Rats Saw God by Rob Thomas. Simon & Schuster, 1996. Steven Richard York, whose astronaut father named him after Richard Nixon, writes his story to make up for failing a semester of English. In it, he juxtaposes chapters about his senior year in California, where he has come to live with his mother and his sister, with chapters from his sophomore year in Houston where he lived with his father and went into a downward spiral after his girlfriend betrayed him.

3 NBs of Julian Drew by James M. Deem. Houghton Mifflin, 1994. A young boy so troubled that he writes in code, keeps his throughts in three notebooks, which in the course of his travels from Tempe, Arizona, to Wheeling, West Virginia, gradually get more readable.

- Changing perspectives (multiple points of entry to the information in a book)
- Changing boundaries (new ideas of what is appropriate and accessible to children)[2]

At much more mundane levels, any of us who are teaching literature classes undoubtedly feel the influence of the Internet on a daily basis. For example, teachers who have recently tried to teach students about the wonders of index cards and handwritten notes for writing research papers have undoubtedly felt challenged. Even getting students to go to a library isn't easy. In one of our short story classes, students

Books written by young people, or at least told through their voices, are becoming increasingly popular. See Focus Box 3.2 for examples.

sign up to introduce each of the authors. They used to bring in notes from books and photocopied pictures, but three or four years ago, a few students began getting their information electronically. This last semester every single student brought in computer-generated materials, and what made us realize that we had to change our teaching approach was the number of them who stood before the class and simply read—apparently for the first time—what they had printed out. They seemed to have the feeling that once they got a printout, their preparation was finished.

On a more positive note, however, a 1997 three-month-long survey conducted by an association of booksellers trying to measure the reading habits of middle-class Americans found that heavy computer users were also readers. The researchers contacted people through telephone interviews, over the Internet, and in person as they left bookstores. "The mean number of books purchased by individuals each year was twelve, but the people contacted over the Internet purchased three times as many." Chief editor Nora Rawlinson told a reporter for the *Fort Worth Star-Telegram* (June 15, 1997), "There's always been a concern that people who used computers a lot would read less, but now it's obvious they make up for computer time by eliminating some other leisure activity, maybe like watching less television."

We've been happily surprised at the Internet marketing techniques of such commercial booksellers as Amazon.com. They offer most books at a discount (which makes up for the shipping costs) and mail them to arrive at the customer's door within two or three days. They can discount their basic prices while offering a huge range of titles because their books are stored in warehouses, perhaps even a

FOCUS BOX 3.4

Picture Books for High Schoolers

From Slave Ship to Freedom Road by Julius Lester, paintings by Rod Brown. Dial, 1998. Brown's twenty-two paintings of American slaves work alongside Lester's carefully chosen words to communicate the hardships endured during the 250 years that slavery was an American business.

G Is for Googol: A Math Alphabet Book by David M. Schwartz, illustrated by Marissa Moss. Tricycle, 1998. This clever book goes from "A is for Abacus" to "Z is for Zillion." In between are "R is for Rhombicosidodecahedron" and "W is for When are we ever gonna use this stuff, anyway?"

Growing Up in Coal Country by Susan Campbell Bartoletti. Houghton Mifflin, 1997. Through a photo essay, Bartoletti lets readers understand the challenges and the hardships of the immigrant workers whose backs supported the coal mining industry of Pennsylvania.

Hiroshima No Pika by Toshi Maruki. Lothrop, Lee and Shepard, 1980. **Faithful Elephants** by Yukio Tsuchiya. Houghton Mifflin, 1988. These two stories look at World War II, including the dropping of the atomic bomb, from a Japanese perspective. American patriots have criticized both books for presenting children who are too young to understand complicated issues with only one side of the story. Because thinking and talking are needed, these are good books for reading aloud and discussing with older students.

The Inner City Mother Goose by Eve Merriam, illustrated by David Diaz. Simon & Schuster, 1996. New illustrations make this reissue of a 1962 controversial book more powerful. Merriam's parodies are shocking because of the contrast between the supposed innocence of nursery rhymes and the harsh realities of inner city life.

Maus I: My Father Bleeds History by Art Spiegelman. Pantheon, 1986. **Maus II; And Here My Troubles Began** by Art Spiegelman, Pantheon, 1991. When Spiegelman won the Pulitzer prize for using a comic book format to dramatize his father's Holocaust experience and the fallout on his own generation, he gave a tremendous boost to the development of the graphic novel.

The Octopus: Phantom of the Sea by Mary M. Cerullo, photos by Jeffrey L. Rotman. Cobblehill, 1997. Amazing underwater photographs along with Cerullo's writing help readers feel a kinship with these creatures who are as different from human beings as any alien created by the most inventive of movie directors.

Restless Spirit: The Life and Work of Dorothea Lange by Elizabeth Partridge. Viking, 1998. The author's father was a photographer and through him, Partridge was acquainted with Lange and the challenges she faced as a woman photographer in the 1930s and 1940s. More than sixty of Lange's photographs are included.

Rome Antics by David Macaulay. Houghton Mifflin, 1997. Macaulay puts his love of architectural drawing to work through using the viewpoint of a carrier pigeon flying over both ancient and modern Rome. Earlier Macaulay picture books appreciated by teenagers include his *Motel of the Mysteries* (1979), *Unbuilding* (1980), *The Way Things Work* (1988), and *Black and White* (1990), all Houghton Mifflin.

The Stinky Cheese Man and Other Fairly Stupid Tales by Jan Scieszka, illustrated by Lane Smith. Viking, 1992. Although issued as a children's book, readers of all ages enjoy these parodies of traditional tales. More interesting than the words is the visual layout and all the little running jokes that readers can trace.

Stephen Biesty's Incredible Body, written by Richard Platt, illustrated by Stephen Biesty. Dorling Kindersley Ink, 1998. Biesty's unique drawings trace two tiny explorers on their way through cutaways of the human body visiting the Hormone team, the Nerve team, the Blood team, and the Immune team. Other Biesty and Platt partnerships include *Stephen Biesty's Incredible Cross-Sections* (1992), *Man of War* (1993), *Castle* (1994), *Incredible Explosions* (1996), and *Incredible Everything* (1997), all Dorling Kindersley Ink.

Women in the Material World by Faith D'Aluisio and Peter Menzel, foreword by Naomi Wolf. Sierra Club, 1996. This collection of 375 full-color photographs grew out of the best-selling *Material World: A Global Family Portrait*. A team of women journalists travelled to twenty different countries to interview and photograph women in the various roles that they play.

As several critics have observed, kids in a digital age are more open to experiments in style and format and to books whose designs are influenced by the media that are included as subject matter in the plots. See Focus Boxes 3.1 and 3.3 for examples.

publisher's warehouse, rather than in high maintenance stores. The major advantage for customers is their sophisticated software that allows them to provide an abundance of information. For example, in July, 1999, someone hearing about Louis Sachar's *Holes,* could log onto Amazon.com and find seven pages of varied information attractively presented with lots of white space and different sizes and fonts of type. The first page included a photo of the cover, a discounted price, information about an audio cassette, a short list of other books that customers who bought *Holes* had purchased (these included Richard Peck's *A Long Way from Chicago: A Novel in Stories* and Anita Lobel's *No Pretty Pictures: A Child of War*), and news that the book was 65th in Amazon.com's current sales. At that time, 278 readers had submitted reviews. These reviewers gave *Holes* an average ranking of four and a half (out of five) stars. On the following pages were professional descriptions and reviews including an excerpt from Betsy Hearne's review printed in *The New York Times* and the complete review from *Horn Book.* Customers could click for further reviews. Customer comments began on page 4. Eight short paragraphs were printed (six from young readers and two from adults who were reading the book with youngsters). They were all dated within the previous week, and, again, viewers were invited to "Click here" if they wanted to read all 278 customer comments. A closing section told readers that customers who bought titles by Louis Sachar also bought titles by Barbara Park, J. K. Rowling, Bruce Coville, Jack Gantos, and Phyllis Reynolds Naylor. Readers were then given ten subject areas to click for similar books and were finally invited to click on one of the following:

- I have read this book, and I want to *review* it.
- *I am the Author,* and I want to comment on my book.
- *I am the Publisher,* and I want to comment on this book.

Such interactive communication is exactly what good teachers and librarians have been trying to promote for years. While not forgetting that the human touch is still needed, we can guide young readers to these kinds of resources.

Pokémon as Interactive Fiction

About ten years ago, we served on a best books committee that delayed publishing its list of recommended titles because we were waiting for those on the committee who were the most computer literate to provide examples of recommended interactive fiction. Finally we got a note saying they hadn't found anything wonderful "just yet," but "maybe, next year."

"Next year" never came, partly because we weren't sure what we were looking for. All we knew was that this new literature would be more sophisticated than the *Choose Your Own Adventure* books and it would have something to do with computers.

Ironically, when truly interactive literature finally arrived, we failed to recognize it. It snuck into the United States from Japan under the name of Pokémon or "pocket monsters." It is a sophisticated computer game developed from the imagination of a Japanese man who grew up in a rural area collecting and playing with such small creatures as beetles, snails, polliwogs, crickets, grasshoppers, butterflies, and frogs. It took him and fellow computer experts five years to program the game. When it arrived in the United States, it was preceded by television cartoons and comic books so that most of us dismissed it as entertainment for young children.

And then when Nintendo began selling Pokémon Gameboys for something like $80.00, along with $30.00 cartridges, trading cards, a related board game, T-shirts, caps, stuffed toys, and every other kind of paraphernalia anyone could dream up, we dismissed Pokémon again—this time because it was so commercialized.

However, the phenomenon has become almost impossible to ignore. While younger children are watching the cartoons and collecting the cards, young teens are the ones playing the game, which is a journey of adventure, caring, teaching, and learning. The good Pokémon player is not the one who vanquishes all foes or finishes first, but the one who explores, backtracks, learns, and enjoys the journey. The human characters in the cartoon and in the game include Ash Ketcham, a boy whose name fits into the slogan of "Gotta Catch 'em All!"; a girl named Misty, who is the Gym Leader of Cirulean City specializing in water Pokémon, a boy named Brock, who is the Gym leader of Pewter City specializing in rock Pokémon, and an older and wiser Dr. Oak and his son Gary. These people are all caregivers to their Pokémon, who could be any of 150 fascinating creatures living in Pokéballs and coming out at the bidding of their masters.

Gameboy players become caregivers of their own Pokémon (players can carry a maximum of six) as they journey forth on what is basically a romantic quest as outlined in Northrup Frye's *Anatomy of Criticism: Four Essays.*

The Romance involves the Journey, and the Journey involves the Hero, the Villain, the Quest, the Sage, the Prohibition, the Sacrifice, the Dragon, the

Treasure, and sometimes the rescue of the Maiden. The epiphany (mountain top, tower, island, lighthouse, ladder, staircase, Jack's beanstalk, Rapunzel's hair, Indian rope trick, etc.) connects Heaven and Earth.

On their idealized journeys in the Gameboys, players may meet and be challenged by such human characters as Ash, Misty, and Brock, who are aided by their own Pokémon. They might also be challenged by obstacles of nature so that they must get advice from characters they meet along the way or find technical help such as *flash,* which will enable them to escape from dark caves, or *cut,* which will help them get past bushes into restricted zones.

In the Northrop Frye sense of a romance, the good guys are Ash, Brock, and Misty while the bad guys are members of Team Rocket, who in the movie and the TV cartoons are appropriately named Jessie and James. The sage is Professor Oak and his Pokédex; the prohibition is "Don't be a bad Pokémon trainer"; the dragons are Giovanni and Persian; the sacrifice is a loss of Pokémon; while the treasure is the gaining of wisdom which is shown through learning techniques and acquiring tools and more numerous and more powerful Pokémon.

Game players have thousands of choices to make so that each story is truly unique. Players who want to look for water Pokémon head for Cirulean City, those who prefer such earthy Pokémon as Onyx, Zubat, and Golem head for a cave, while those who want to deal with ghosts and spirits head for Lavender City and its mausoleum-like tower and funereal music.

While each player creates a different story, all the stories fit into the genre of the picaresque novel as exemplified by Mark Twain's *Huckleberry Finn,* Charles Dickens's *The Pickwick Papers,* and Miguel Cervantes's *Don Quixote.* Stories about picaros are usually told in plain language about people without power, prestige, or authority, who embark on episodic journeys in which they are forced to live by their wits as they come in contact with people from other cultures and social classes.

The game is so complex that few adults have even the vaguest idea of how it is played. One of its great appeals to young people is that they get to be caregivers or beneficent dictators. Players have the responsibility of deciding whether to trade Pokémon, what skills or techniques their Pokémon should use, what kinds of further training and education their Pokémon should receive, and whether in a conflict they should run or stay and fight. If a Pokémon is injured, the caregiver must decide what antidotes, potions, and vitamins should be administered, and whether the Pokémon should be taken to a care center.

Clever language play helps readers and players remember the Pokémon characters. *Kangaskhan* carries a baby in a front pocket, *Tangela* is covered with tangled hair, and *Staryu* and *Starmie* are shaped like stars. As part of the game, most of the Pokémon evolve into more powerful or more complex creatures. For example *Koffing* evolves into *Weezing, Jigglypuff* into *Wigglytuff, Sandshrew* into *Sandslash,* *Magnemite* into *Magneton,* and *Venonat* into *Venomoth.* While other evolved sets do not use the same word parts, their meanings are related as when *Drowzee* evolves into *Hypno, Grimer* into *Muk, Growlith* into *Arcanine,* and *Caterpie* into *Metapod* and then into *Butterfree.*

Players also get lessons in symbolism. Green is used for plant-like creatures such as *Bulbasaur* and *Ivysaur;* blue for water creatures such as *Squirtle, Wartortle,* and *Blastoise;* brown for earth creatures such as *Geodude* and *Graveler;* and yellow and orange for fire creatures such as *Charmander* and *Charmeleon. Pikachu* is the little, yellow mouse-like creature who is everybody's favorite. Its name comes from the Japanese *pika* ("light") or *pika pika,* which some Japanese speakers say when they see a flashlight.

Popular media articles in the U.S. stress that Pokémon is most likely a passing fad of interest to children between 7 and 10 years of age. However, at the Pokémon "training fairs" that Nintendo sponsors in shopping malls, the serious players of the computer game as well as the board game are mostly young teenage boys. If they keep playing the game as they grow older, they will extend the interest level upwards so that the game may be for contemporary teenagers what Dungeons and Dragons was for young adults now in their 20s and 30s.

Even if the game itself dies from the over-marketing of related paraphernalia, there is little doubt that it has introduced a new kind of literature to millions of young people. And while it differs from what we as librarians and teachers consider "real" literature, serious players are nevertheless learning the literary and language skills that we have aspired to teach them. And most importantly, they are doing it with the kind of pleasure that will make them want to lose themselves in good books as well as in good games.

A Survey of Students' Relationships to Mass Media

We were so humble about writing this chapter on the interconnectedness of teenagers and books with magazines, newspapers, music, video games, movies, and television that, with the help of our graduate students who are teaching in public schools, in the early spring of 1999 we took an admittedly unscientific survey to get some idea of what young adults find appealing in the mass media. Our questionnaire was given to students in an inner city high school in Phoenix, Arizona, a suburban high school in Mesa, Arizona, a rural junior high school in Minnesota, and to some thirty randomly chosen teenagers from metropolitan Phoenix interviewed by students taking our adolescent literature class.

The biggest finding of the survey was that we are a deconstructed society. Just like adults, teenagers now have hundreds of magazines from which to choose, dozens of television channels, dozens of movies at theaters and hundreds or even thousands more available for borrowing at video rental shops. Because teenagers' tastes are as varied as adults' tastes, it is no wonder that teachers are frustrated when they try to find common references to illustrate literary points.

Another finding that supports what many others have observed is that a large portion of teenage entertainment circles around violence, especially with video games. Favorites of the 95 students who said they played video games were *Mario Kart, Goldeneye 007, Zelda, Final Fantasy, Mortal Combat,* and *Tomb Raiders.* According to our college students, these are all combat games of one kind or another. At the second tier of popularity were sports related games including NFL Blitz followed by Star Wars and World War II fighting games.

The most variety was shown when we asked respondents to name two or three favorite entertainment figures (musicians, actors, comedians, athletes). Of the 200 listed, those getting more than five votes include:

Basketball player Michael Jordan   11

Actress Drew Barrymore   9

Actress Katie Holmes	9
Actor Nicholas Cage	8
Comic actor Adam Sandler	8
Comedian/actor Robin Williams	8
Actor Ben Affleck	7
Actor Will Smith	7
Actor Ryan Phillippe	6
Actor Leonardo DiCaprio	5
Comedian Dana Carvey	5
Actor Harrison Ford	5
Baseball player Mark McGuire	5
Comic actor Jerry Seinfeld	5

When we asked about music, we found tastes equally diverse. Such categories as Disco, Techno, 80s music, New Age, Salsa, and Motown were listed by one student each. The most popular listings were:

Alternative	65
Rap	33
R & B	26
Hip Hop	25
Country	15
Rock	14
Oldies	13

Three people wrote down Classical, the same number as wrote down Christian Rock, Soft Rock, Dance, and Heavy Metal. In answer to our question about well-liked individuals, groups, or performances, students listed over 200 names, which, if nothing else, showed that they have good memories and when interested can remember such strange spellings as Aerosmith, DeeLite, Korn, Majic, Outkast, Phish, and Xcape. The names also showed that kids understand or at least make use of many of the poetic techniques that we keep trying to teach them in English classes; for example:

Alliteration: Bib Bib Bom Bom, Big Bad Voodoo Daddies

Allusion: Alice in Chains, Nirvana, War and Peace

Enigma: Nine Inch Nails, Notorious B.I.G., No Way Out, Nimrod

Incongruity: Bone, Thugs-n-Harmony, Grateful Dead, Led Zeppelin, Puff Daddy, Savage Garden, Third Eye Blind

Metaphor: Rage Against the Machine, Ride the Lightning

Repetition: Ozzy Ozbourne, Mighty Mighty Bosstones, Goo Goo Dolls, Never Say Never

Surprise: Smash Mouth, Weird Al Yankovich, Squirrel Nut Zippers

Wordplay: Everclear, Fugees, Hard Knocklife, Match Box, Maide Man, Metallica, 'N Sync, Tupac, U2

We were struck by the multicultural aspects of popular music. The interest shown in hip-hop, for example, supported news stories released when Lauryn Hill won the 1999 Grammy Award for Album of the Year with her "The Miseducation of Lauryn Hill." More than 81 million rap recordings were sold in 1998, an increase of 31 percent from 1997. For the first time hip-hop, or rap, outsold country music, and because white Americans purchase 71 percent of all records sold, it is obvious that many white kids are buying hip-hop music. In another example, when Latino singer Ricky Martin released his number 1-selling CD, "Livin' la Vida Loca," in May 1999, a crowd of 5,000 mainly young women described by music critic Christopher John Farley as "between the ages of *Dawson's Creek* and *Felicity* (with a few *Rugrats* and *Ally McBeals* mixed in)" gathered outside a Tower Records store in Manhattan all shouting, "Riiiiiickyyyyyyyyyyyyy!" in hopes of getting a glance of the new star. More surprising, however, was that in far away—both in miles and culture—Salt Lake City, Utah, Ricky Martin's CD also sold out within two hours. It is comforting to realize that kids can enjoy multicultural experiences without feeling the sense of duty that sometimes creeps into the multicultural lessons we plan for school classrooms.

The Ubiquitousness of Television

Television is so ubiquitous in today's homes, with even infants being offered their own Teletubbies program, that in August 1999, the American Academy of Pediatrics issued a statement identifying excessive television viewing as a public health issue.[3] Chief recommendations were that children less than 2 years old should not watch television, older children should not have television sets in their bedrooms, and when children come in for appointments and consultations pediatricians should have parents not only fill out a medical history but also a "media history," including questions about television, movies, video and computer games, music videos and the Internet as well as radio and books. Dr. Marjorie Hogan, the lead author of the report said that after taking into account all the research concerns about how viewing "can affect the mental, social and physical health of young people," the academy was laying out a plan and "trying to raise the bar a bit, as suggestions for optimal parenting." Although no reliable research has yet been done on how television viewing affects children younger than age 2, Dr. Hogan said the academy was basing its recommendations on their knowledge of what babies need for proper brain development. This includes close-up interaction with older people, and "the common-sense notion that, if they are watching television, babies are not getting those other essential stimuli."

In reference to older children, the report pointed to linkages between violence in movies and television and aggressive behavior as previously cited by studies from the American Medical Association, the American Psychological Association, the American Academy of Child and Adolescent Psychiatry, and the National Institute of Mental Health. "A bullet in the body is a physical health issue," said committee chair Dr. Miriam Baron. She went on to add that obesity is also a physical health issue and "Children who spend a lot of time in front of the TV set tend to gain weight."

In the previous edition of this textbook, we lamented the fact that teenagers were almost an ignored audience on television; a situation that is no longer true. During the 1997–1998 season, the industry sat up and took notice when the only network to gain viewers was Warner Brothers (WB), which increased its ratings by 19 percent. The other networks, except for CBS, which stayed basically the same, continued a downward trend. Although WB, which was created to guarantee an outlet for Warner Brothers productions, is still a relatively small network, it made its surprisingly big gains by going after the niche market of teenagers. At the turn of the century, WB has yet to make a profit but expects to be in the black at least by 2001. Investors' confidence is based on the belief that advertisers will give increasing support to the network because

1. Young people have a lot of money to spend.
2. They are easier to influence than are their elders.
3. They are forming buying patterns that will last a lifetime.

Jamie Kellner, WB founder, plans to stick to his goal of not seeking viewers over age 35; however, the network's ratings are also going up among 25-to-54-year-olds, which may say more about adult tastes than about the WB shows.

When we asked students to name two or three television shows they watch and like, 125 different shows were listed, most only a couple of times. Those listed more than ten times include:

Dawson's Creek	39
The Simpsons	37
Friends	36
Seventh Heaven	18
Buffy the Vampire Slayer	17
Ally McBeal	12
Seinfeld	10
Home Improvement	10

Of these popular shows, three (*Dawson's Creek, Seventh Heaven,* and *Buffy the Vampire Slayer*) are produced by WB. Writing in *Time* magazine under the title, "The Youth Brigade," James Collins said that "The key to the WB's success is this: babes, male and female. . . . the WB has the best-looking stars on TV. Is this business really so very complicated?"[4]

Dawson's Creek is about the life and loves of a group of young teens in the fictional seaside community of Capeside, Massachusetts. As of 1999, the show was WB's second highest rated show (coming in behind *Seventh Heaven,* an adult show) and was the top rated show among all teen shows. During the 1998–1999 season, an average of 5.4 million viewers tuned in every Wednesday. In the summer of 1999, a *Dawson's Creek* clothing line was announced so that in the fall teenagers could go back to school dressed like characters on the show. It was also announced that in its third season the characters would be allowed to move up to their junior year in high school (they had been spent two years as sophomores) so that more "mature" themes could be explored. The cast was being expanded to include more diversity, including a new high school principal advertised as "not your standard authoritarian."

Buffy the Vampire Slayer was the first WB show to gain widespread popularity. It had a head start with kids already interested in gothic literature (see Han Nolan's Author Box, p. 94). It was also one of the first to have its own Web site, which invites viewers to subscribe with

> For Buffy fans only! Explore the world of a Vampire Slayer from an insider's perspective by receiving news, photographs and personal messages from the stars — before anyone else. Join the Slayer's Circle today by submitting your e-mail address in the box below.

The gist of *Buffy the Vampire Slayer,* as described by *Arizona Republic* television critic Bill Goodykoontz (July 13, 1999) is that Buffy, played by Sara Michelle Gellar is a vampire slayer—"every generation has one." In keeping with the times, "she's an expert martial artist, a steely eyed protector of the world packaged in the body of a ditzy teenage girl." She is "supposed to be something of a romantic failure," which Goodykoontz finds hard to believe given her looks and her affinity to sexy tube tops. She lives with her single mom at the mouth of a canyon from which come all kinds of monsters, vampires, and creatures. Of course Buffy has a boyfriend and assorted other friends who help her, especially in the running battle she has against the evil mayor. While there's violence in the show, Goodykoontz describes "most, though not all" as the "cartoonish blood-free variety," where in the end good always wins out. The show's appeal comes from how well its writers "nail the loneliness, the awkwardness and the feeling of being different that just about everyone suffers on the way to a diploma." The show is also delightfully funny; for example, "As the mayor instructs a group of surly vampires in their gruesome maneuvers, he leaves them with a reminder, 'Boys, let's watch the swearing.'"

After the April 20, 1999 shootings at Columbine High School, part II of the season finale was postponed for nearly three months because the episode dealt with violence at Buffy's high school graduation. Goodykoontz praised the move, "but more for reasons of decorum than responsibility." He observed that after the Columbine shootings, "it's impossible to see this or any other show in the same light," but then added,

> Those intent on looking for the root of the nation's ills in such places as a fantasy show about high-schoolers killing 60-foot snakelike demons will find ammunition here (and anywhere else they look). But *Buffy's* great strength is its knowledge that the vast majority of violence in high schools is done to the teenage heart. If it takes an obvious metaphor to illustrate that, so be it. Think back to the first time you got dumped. If you didn't feel like a vampire on the wrong end of a wood stake, it wasn't really love.

Characters in the popular sitcoms from other networks, *Friends, Ally McBeal, Seinfeld,* and *Home Improvement,* are similar to those in adult books finding their way to popularity with teens. They feature characters older than teenagers but not so old as to be mired in family responsibilities and grim "adult" problems. While characters' lives are generally more exciting than real life, teenagers, just like many adults, are happy to engage in a willing suspension of disbelief and imagine themselves having similar friends with whom they carry on the same kinds of scintillating conversations.

HAN NOLAN
On "At Least She's Reading"

I made the decision before I even had children that I would allow them to read anything they wanted. This worked well with two of my children. They didn't always choose books I would have chosen for them but they selected books according to their own tastes and that was fine with me.

One child was different, however. When this child got into her teens she began to read vampire and horror books.

All right, I thought, they're not my taste but she's devouring these books. It's just good to see her reading. But she wasn't just reading; it went deeper than that. I noticed that she wanted to wear black all the time and she only wrote poetry about death. She had pulled her shades down in her bedroom and kept them down, and had started hanging out with the wrong crowd—all signals that I had an unhappy child on my hands. I knew that the books weren't the cause of her problems, but reading them did seem to make things worse. I'd go with her to the library and watch her pick out yet another adult vampire book and wonder what I should do. Finally, I told her what I felt, that the books seemed to be having a strong infuence on her, as were her new friends. I let her select the vampire book but I also helped her pick out another book that wasn't about vampires. Over the weeks and months that passed I worked hard on discovering where the darkness and fears were coming from, and I also worked on improving her reading selections. I'd go with her to the bookstore and help her select books just for her, books that supported her interests, just not her darker ones. As time passed, she stopped reading the vampire and horror books. More time passed and she pulled up the shades in her room and selected a new group of friends, and we were able to let her go back to making all her own choices again.

So, where do we draw the line? Where will you draw the line, and should you? I don't know if there is an easy answer. What a teen selects to read can often show the parent, librarian, or teacher, where her interests are, where her mind is, and when that teen might be hurting or in need of help.

I still believe in letting children and teens choose their own books, but I also believe it can be helpful for them to have some guidance in their reading selections when their own choices seem to be contributing to their problems rather than alleviating them. Imagine how a teen would feel if a teacher or librarian came up to her and said "I saw this book and thought of you. I knew you especially would like this." All teens want to feel special. Even if she doesn't care for the book, she's discovered someone cares about her. It couldn't hurt.

NOTE: This piece was written with the permission of Han Nolan's daughter, who is mentioned in the piece.

Han Nolan's books include *If I Should Die Before I Wake,* 1994; *Send Me Down a Miracle,* 1996; *Dancing on the Edge,* 1997; and *A Face in Every Window,* 1999, all from Harcourt Brace.

Animation

The high ranking of *The Simpsons* is especially impressive in that at the time of the survey the show was 10 years old and was still drawing in viewers. Various critics have tried to explain its success. In a *TV Guide* feature article identifying the twelve best episodes, critic David Owen wrote that *The Simpsons* is the only show his family watches "without simultaneously talking, reading or fighting. They don't want to miss anything."[5] Teachers taking our adolescent literature classes tell us that their students are ready for Edgar Allan Poe stories because they've already seen the parodies on *The Simpsons* Halloween specials.

The first animated cartoons were set to classical music and contained sophisticated allusions to world events and personalities or parodied famous literature. They were shown to adult audiences, first in burlesque halls and then in theaters. Even as late as 1960, *The Flintstones* premiered on prime-time television to an adult audience, but as technology improved and more cartoons were shown on television, the bright colors, the music, and the magical movements proved attractive to children as well as adults. When producers and product sponsors saw how much children liked cartoons, they dusted off old shorts and cranked up their production of new cartoons to be used as Saturday morning filler on television. One result was that people began to think of cartoons as being for children. On the negative side, this discouraged theater managers from going to the extra expense of showing cartoons before feature films; while on the positive side, it raised a generation of individuals with wide experience in viewing cartoons. These individuals are now playing leadership roles in producing such movies as *Toy Story* and *A Bug's Life,* along with animated films designed to appeal to adults such as the Biblical *Moses* released in 1998.

The success of *The Simpsons* on television has inspired other networks to create animated shows for prime time, several directly aimed at teenagers; for example, MTV's *Beavis and Butthead* and its spinoff *Daria,* along with Comedy Central's *South Park.* Other popular shows are Comedy Central's *Bob and Margaret* and *Dr. Katz* and Fox's *King of the Hill* and *The PJs.* Caryn James writing in *The New York Times* (June 22, 1998) gave as one reason for the trend, "With so little realism on the surface, animated characters can sneak up and irreverently hit plenty of nerves. The dunderheaded fathers of *The Simpsons* or *King of the Hill,* much less the boys of *South Park,* would never get on the air if they were breathing actors." Even though animated shows are relatively expensive to make, management does not have to arrange pay raises and weeks off for the stars, nor do they have to worry about child labor laws or the expense of having four airplanes fly overhead. And once a show is made, it can be broadcast over and over again.

Magazines

The 132 students who said they read magazines (31 said they did not) listed 107 different titles. Some were so specific that we were not surprised they were listed by only one respondent; for example, *Game Pro, Brio* (Christian), *Guitar Player, Handgunner, Paintball, Slam, Spin,* and *Word Up.* The big vote getters were:

Seventeen	47
YM (Young and Modern)	28

Teen	18
Sports Illustrated	14
Teen People	12
People	10
National Geographic	6
Cosmopolitan	5
Popular Science	5
Rolling Stone	5
Entertainment Weekly	4
Vogue	4

We were amused and surprised at how things have changed when we found the once proud *Mademoiselle* being listed as a favorite by the same number of students (1) who listed the *J. C. Penney Catalog.* We were also surprised to find only two students listing *MAD* magazine. Before we took the survey, we might have described *MAD* magazine as the quintessential magazine for teenagers, which indeed it used to be. As the co-editors Nick Meglin and John Ficarra philosophically explained in a *New York Times* article (June 30, 1997), however, the magazine is in some ways a victim of its own success. Across the board, today's humor is more in-your-face and coarse, and to stay on the edge *MAD* editors are pushing the boundaries still further so that some staff members no longer bring the magazine home to their kids. A majority of its 400,000 readers are adults who grew up with the magazine and have seen it evolve to keep up with their own cynical attitudes.

Also somewhat surprising were the five students who named *Cosmopolitan,* which is known as one of the most sexually frank of mass-marketed women's magazines. *Newsday* writer Paul D. Colford reported, however, that such other magazines as *Redbook, Glamour, Marie Clair,* and *New Woman* are following *Cosmopolitan's* lead in, "doing what certain men's publications have done effectively for a long time." They are, "increasing the amount of sexual information (and titillation), and luring buyers with suggestive cover lines" in hopes of boosting their single-copy sales.[6] Newsstand sales are more lucrative than subscription sales, but they have fallen 40 percent within the last decade. So as to remain acceptable in "home" environments, while at the same time being intriguing enough to garner attention at the newsstand, *Redbook,* for example, now prints two covers. The one being mailed into homes uses the word *love* on the cover, while the newstand copy uses the word *sex.* Magazines that do this also send their less daring covers to newsstands in particular areas of the country judged to be more conservative.

A Night Out at the Movies

When in 1984 we saw *The Breakfast Club,* we remember thinking, "This is YA lit!" The film was directed by John Hughes and starred Judd Nelson, Ally Sheedy, Emilio Estevez, Molly Ringwald, and Anthony Michael Hall as teenagers confined to early morning detention because of their various manifestations of teenage angst. Today, people in the movie business are looking back on *The Breakfast Club,* sort of like the way we in the book business look back on S. E. Hinton's *The Outsiders,* as the beginning of a movement (see Film Box 3.1).

FILM BOX 3.1

The World of Young Adults (see Appendix D)

American Graffiti (1973, color, 112 min., PG; Director: George Lucas; with Richard Dreyfuss, Ron Howard, and Cindy Williams) Young adults after a 1962 graduation learn something about what the real outside world is like.

The Breakfast Club (1985, color, 97 min., R; Director: John Hughes; with Molly Ringwald, and Ally Sheedy) Five young people confined to Saturday detention talk and rebel. Once regarded as a ground-breaker film, it's now hard to tell just what ground it broke.

Clueless (1995, color, 97 min., PG; Director: Amy Heckerling; with Alicia Silverstone and Stacey Dash) Jane Austen would probably be surprised to see this film based on her *Emma* set in 1990s Beverly Hills.

Election (1999, color, 104 min., R; Director: John Hughes; with Reese Witherspoon and Matthew Broderick) A student who has everything wants to be class president. A teacher tries to stop her. This is the best of the bunch, and a fine film by any standard.

October Sky (1999, color, 108 min., PG; Director: Joe Johnston; with Jake Gyllenhaal and Chris Cooper) A young boy in coal-mining, 1957 West Virginia wants more than a life in the mines.

Rushmore (1998, color, 93 min., R; Director: Wes Anderson; with Bill Murray and Jason Schwartzmann) A strange high school student so involved in activites he has no time for classes falls in love with a teacher.

Sixteen Candles (1984, color, 93 min., PG; Director: John Hughes; with Molly Ringwald and Paul Dooley) A 16-year-old endures a crush on a senior boy with thoughts of sex and other assorted embarrassments.

Slums of Beverly Hills (1998, color, 95 min., R; Director: Tamara Jenkins; with Natasha Lyonne and Alan Arkin) A father moves his motherless family to this or that place in Beverly Hills to allow them a good education.

Tex (1982, color, 103 min., PG; Director: Tim Hunter; with Matt Dillon and Meg Tilly) In S. E. Hinton's young adult novel, a motherless and, for all practical purposes, a fatherless boy is raised by his brother.

Twist and Shout (Danish, 1984, color, 99 min., R; Director: Billie August; with Lars Simonsen and Adam Tonsberg) Two friends grow up in the early days of the Beatles, one manipulated by his father, one to find love and sadness.

Reporter David Daley, writing in the *Hartford Courant*, quoted Courtney Love describing the film as "the defining moment of the 'alternative' generation." "Now," Daley says, "as the '80s teens who saw their high school angst reflected in Hughes' films start making movies of their own, his influence is unmistakable."[7] Jonathan Bernstein in his book *Pretty in Pink: The Golden Age of Teenage Movies* says that you can see Hughes' influence "in all the moments when they start to reveal their angst and the facades break down, and they start to blame their parents for their trauma and everything that's wrong now." Bernstein says that Hughes brought depth to what had been "a bubble gum genre." It was the first movie to take teen angst seriously and "opened the door for everything that's followed like *Dawson's Creek*." Kevin Williamson, the creator of *Dawson's Creek* and the screen writer of *I Know What You Did Last Summer* says that his goal is to be for the 90s what Hughes was for the 80s. In one of the *Dawson's Creek* shows, he paid tribute to *The Breakfast Club* by having the gang serve Saturday morning detention.

Teen stars Sara Michelle Gellar and Jennifer Love Hewitt have also acknowledged their admiration for the film. *The Breakfast Club* star Ally Sheedy said she first noticed how the influence of *The Breakfast Club* was spreading in the late 1980s when Winona Ryder starred in *Beetlejuice*. She sees it now in such movies as

Can't Hardly Wait, She's All That, Rushmore, and *Cruel Intentions*—all films that take high school insecurities, prom politics, graduation anxieties, and popularity seriously.

Fifteen years after the release of *The Breakfast Club,* director John Hughes is still thrilled at its success because when he first proposed it "the studio hated it. They walked out of the room furious. They said it wasn't funny, that it didn't have any story. They had no hope for it at all." But Hughes, who continued to think like a teenager throughout the 80s with the films *Sixteen Candles, Ferris Bueller's Day Off,* and *Pretty in Pink* always had confidence in the film. Besides, he knew enough about teen life to release the film in February. "When you're in high school," he explains, "there's nothing worse than the middle of February. Your winter jacket is dirty. There's not a holiday in sight. 'Wow, a movie that's just for me. I'm there!'" He credits the film's lasting to the fact that it deals with the kind of core high school feelings, like belonging and loneliness, that don't change.

On the survey we took, in reference to movies we asked students to "Name two or three movies that you have liked over the last few years." Respondents listed 194 different titles, with the most frequently cited being:

Titanic	32
Armageddon	26
Ever After	21
She's All That	20
Water Boy	13
Rush Hour	10
Braveheart	8
Can't Hardly Wait	8
Face Off	8
Independence Day	8
Patch Adams	8
Blade	7
Payback	7
The Truman Show	7
Happy Gilmore	6
Saving Private Ryan	6
Mulan	5
There's Something about Mary	5
What Dreams May Come	5

Movies made specifically for teens, including the horror films *I Know What You Did Last Summer, Scream,* and *Urban Legends,* along with *The Wedding Singer, Wild Things,* and *Star Wars* were mentioned by only four respondents each, while *The Rocky Horror Picture Show, The Faculty,* and *Friday the 13th* each received 3 votes. The survey was conducted before the spring and summer of 1999 when the teen films *American Pie, 10 Things I Hate About You, Never Been Kissed,* and *Cruel Intentions* were released.

Unscientific as our survey was, it is still probably safe to draw the following conclusions about movies:

- Teens are more attracted to movies made for general adult audiences than they are to those made specifically for teenagers, but this may be similar to the situation with general adult magazines, which are making efforts to attract young readers.
- The movies most popular with teens are filled with action and drama, and, yes, with violence as reflected in such films as *Armageddon, Ever After, Rush Hour, Braveheart,* and *Independence Day.*
- Many of the so-called "teen" movies are actually made and marketed to adults; in fact, they are rated "R," which, because of new legislation, means that teens under 18 should not be in the audience.

Some evidence indicates adults paid more attention than did teenagers to the screen version of Lois Duncan's *I Know What You Did Last Summer* (see her statement on p.100). Two months after the Columbine incident when screenwriters met in Hollywood at their annual three-day, Words into Pictures forum, Gary Dretzka wrote in *The Chicago Tribune* (June 20, 1999) that two of the seminars that attracted heavy media attention were entitled "Guns Don't Kill People . . . Writers Do" and "I Know What You Screamed Last Summer." The title of the second forum, which was identified as also being "the name of a slasher film parody currently in post-production" alludes not only to the film adapted from Duncan's book but also to Wes Craven's horror film *Scream,* which starred teen idol Drew Barrymore. Craven also produced *Scream 2* and *A Nightmare on Elm Street.* He is a former teacher, who explained that he was attracted to the horror genre in the early 1970s because "I got to express a lot of the cynicism, the irony, the passions that I felt about the war in Vietnam at that time, and authority figures in general . . . truth and lies in America." He thinks that "freedom to comment on the dark underbelly of the culture" is necessary to the health of a culture.

Rusty Cundieff, whose credits include *Tales from the Hood* and *Fear of a Black Hat,* tried to remember back and analyze the morbid curiosity that he felt as a youth:

> I never remember necessarily wanting to go out and think about what it would be like to stab somebody, but what I do remember is thinking, if I just had the power to do X to the bullies and kids who messed with me. . . . I would go to the library and get books about witchcraft to find a charm or incantation. But then, something happened that truly scared me and I went out and burned them in my grandmother's yard.

Here is a sampling of related comments:

> . . . because we have instant access to the news today, it seems as if, "Oh, my God, it's happening all over the place." In fact, I don't think it is. Everyone knows the name of those two kids in Littleton, but people don't know that millions of Armenians were killed by the Turks. I just don't believe we're living in a more violent time than we ever did.
>
> Brian Helgeland, screenwriter for *L. A. Confidential* and *Payback*

LOIS DUNCAN
On Sensationalized Violence

One of the most thrilling moments of my life occurred in 1997 when I learned that my young adult suspense novel *I Know What You Did Last Summer* was going to be a movie. Several of my other novels had been filmed for television, but this would be the first to be shown in a theater.

I was first in line at the box office, and settled into my seat with my box of popcorn, too excited to open it. The house lights dimmed, and onto the screen strode a fisherman who was not in my story. I thought I had walked into the wrong movie. But, no—within minutes I realized that those were, indeed, my teenage characters that the insane fisherman was chasing and decapitating with a boat hook.

I never did eat my popcorn.

I pride myself on being professional about the business side of my career. I understand that changes must be made when the written word is transferred to a visual medium. But the soul of a story should not be destroyed in the process. For a book that has been a mainstay in middle school literature classes for over 23 years, to be transformed into a slasher film without the knowledge and consent of the author, goes past what is acceptable.

I continued to watch in horror as a boy who was not in my book got shoved into a vat of boiling water, and my heroine opened the trunk of her car and found a body with crabs surging out of its mouth. Most of the action took place on a fishing boat (there was no boat in my story) where my heroine frantically tried to hide in an ice bin among the severed heads of her friends.

I Know What You did Last Summer was one of the books that earned me the Margaret A. Edwards Award for "a distinguished body of literature that provides young adults with a window through which to view the world." This is not the view of the world I intended to provide for them. As the mother of a murdered teenager, there is no way that I want to be part of desensitizing young people to violence and making blood a trigger for giggling and squealing.

Violence is a fact of life in today's society, and therefore it has its place in books and movies. I believe, however, that the people who create those books and films have a duty to treat the subject seriously and to show the terrible consequences, not only for the victim but for all those who loved the victim.

Today's e-mail brought a message from a 12-year-old who said "My mom and I were at the bookstore a couple days ago and I asked her to buy me your book. She told me no, because she thought it would be as bad as the movie."

I felt ashamed of a story I used to be proud of.

Lois Duncan's books include *Who Killed My Daughter?*, Delacorte, 1992; *Don't Look Behind You,* Dell, 1990; *The Third Eye,* Little, Brown, 1984; and *Killing Mr. Griffin,* Little, Brown, 1978.

When I first viewed my own movie with an audience, and they cheered when a man was shot, I was shocked because I had expected a completely different reaction. I had hoped for a stunned reaction—a realization that the character had just sealed her fate in a very powerful way. When the audience burst into applause, I was terrified to realize that I couldn't control how my work was received.

Callie Khouri, screenwriter for *Thelma & Louise*

It's unquestionable that there's a cause and effect between what goes up on the screen and behavior. I don't want to mess with the First Amendment, and, for that reason we have to look to ourselves and acknowledge what effect we have on the world. My core belief as a screenwriter is that cinema is the campfire around which young people gather in the global village and I think that when something goes on the screen, it takes on a greater importance.

William Mastrosimone, screenwriter for *The Burning Season* and *Extremeties*

In Japan, the movies, comic books and video games are even more violent and twisted than what we have here. The most popular comic book in Japan is called *Rapeman*. He has one particular bionic appendage and, in between crime fighting, he assaults women who are happy to have had a brief encounter with Rapeman. Meanwhile, they do not have the violence that we do here.

Steven De Souza, writer for the first two *Die Hard* movies

I believe that movies do have some kind of an impact, but, unlike so many of my friends in Congress, I don't know how much, I don't know where, and I don't know if there's a connecting link between seeing a movie and going out to buy a Tec-9 to blow someone's head off. None of the research—and God knows, I've read it until my eyes are blurry—has ever made that connecting link. But movies are powerful, so they must have some kind of impact.

Jack Valenti, President of the Motion Picture Association of America

From Comic Books to Graphic Novels

On our questionnaire, respondents were quick to point out that we forgot to ask about comic strips and comic books. We added the topic late, so we heard responses from only 27 students who said "yes," they read comic strips and 14 who said "no," they did not. Favorites listed by the 27 comic book readers included:

Garfield	13
Peanuts (Charlie Brown)	9
Calvin and Hobbes	4
Close to Home	4
Blondie	3
Baby Blues	3

Dilbert	3
Cathy	3

Eleven other strips were listed by one or two students. When the 100th anniversary of the comic strip was celebrated in 1995, statistics were released saying that in the United States, 86 million adults and 27 million kids are regular readers of comic strips in spite of the fact that their demise had been predicted over and over—first, when radio arrived, then when movies began to talk, then when television was developed, and now with the shrinking of newspaper space and the competition from the Internet.

In March 1996, when the International Museum of Cartoon Art opened in Boca Raton, some of the creators whose comic strips are featured were interviewed by the *Miami Herald* (March 3, 1996). Stan Lee, the creator of *Spider-Man,* observed, "There's virtually nobody who hasn't read a comic strip," while Jim Davis, creator of *Garfield,* said, "If you found a newspaper in an archaeological dig 100 years from now, I don't know if the headlines would tell us as much about what made us tick as the comics. They cut through the rhetoric, the jargon, and get right to the subject matter. . . . They're brutally honest." Jerry Robinson who drew *Batman* in its early years and created "The Joker" character, pointed to the role that comics have played in both American history and journalism. "They've permeated our culture—from Broadway plays and songs to TV and film. *Annie* and *Li'l Abner* on Broadway. Movies based on *Dick Tracy, Superman,* and *Batman.* They all started as comics." If it weren't for the comics, we wouldn't have animation as it is today.

When the Pathfinder landed on Mars in the summer of 1997, NASA scientists helped the 45 millions visitors to its Web sites relate to the event by naming specific rocks after the comic strip or cartoon characters Casper, Scooby-Doo, and Yogi. These comic names join other words from the comic strips that have been adapted into English: a *Dagwood* sandwich, a *Mickey Mouse* college course, a *Rube Goldberg* contraption, and most recently, a *Dilbert* situation.

One of our adolescent literature students, Daniel Salzman, was so concerned about our forgetting to include comic books in our first run of the questionnaire that, in spite of the fact that "back home" he had seven cardboard boxes of comics stored in his bedroom, he went out and purchased a new sampling and brought it to class. He divided his sampling into three categories. First were the innocent comic books, next were the adventure and hero tales, and third were adult or underground comics.

With Daniel's encouragement, we went for a Saturday afternoon visit to the largest comic book store in our area and found more teenage boys than we had ever seen in the young adult section of a library. We were surprised at how much the store resembled a library with its displays and shelves and shelves filled with comic books. They were arranged face out for browsing, but because most were wrapped in plastic, customers were forced to make their purchasing decisions solely on the basis of the covers, which may be why comic book covers are so crowded and sensationalized.

One section of the store was blocked off by an L-shaped string of large barrels, apparently acquired as surplus from heavy industry. Tables and chairs were set up for game playing of the Dungeons and Dragons type, snacking from vending ma-

Comic books can be divided into three basic types: the so-called innocent books such as the new Pokémon stories imported from Japan; the hero tales, which are the descendants of Superman; and horror and sex comics, which became popular with adults during World War II and are now produced by both underground and mainstream publishers.

chines, visiting with friends, or playing a small number of video games. The barrels, which were painted black with white tops, served as leaning posts and counter space and, most importantly, lent an aura of masculinity to the area which was filled with males ranging in age from about 12 to 25. In the half-hour we stayed, three fathers (no mothers) came in to shop with preteen sons. The only females were two young clerks identified by their T-shirts as employees.

It was easy to spot the three main types of comics that Daniel had described. "Innocent" comic books are the ones that began as newspaper comic strips in 1895 and gave the genre its name. Richard F. Outcault's 1895 *Hogan's Alley* (soon renamed *The Yellow Kid,* from which "yellow journalism" got its name) is generally considered to be the first comic strip, followed by Rudolph Dirk's *The Katzenjammer Kids,* Bud Fisher's *Mutt and Jeff,* George McManus's *Bringing up Father,* and George Herriman's *Krazy Kat.* "Innocent" comic strips have run the gamut from Chic Young's *Blondie* and Al Capp's *Li'l Abner,* to Walt Kelly's *Pogo* and Mort Walker's *Beetle Bailey,* and from Jeff MacNelly's *Shoe* and Jim Davis's *Garfield* to Berke Breathed's *Bloom County* and Bill Watterson's *Calvin and Hobbes.* Our student's current example of an innocent comic was a *Pokémon* book.

As long as comic strips appeared only in daily newspapers, they were limited to gags, but when in the 1930s comic books were created with original materials focusing on a single character, the door was opened to more complex characters and stories. The years between 1938 and 1945 are generally considered to be the golden age of comic books during which writers and artists developed the skills needed to communicate succinctly and precisely. The difficulties of the depression made readers long for escapist stories and romances with happy endings. Human interest comics such as Allen Saunders and Dale Connor's *Mary Worth,* Dahlia Messick's *Brenda Starr Reporter,* Stanley Drake's *The Heart of Juliet Jones,* and Nicholas Dallis's *Rex Morgan, M.D., Judge Parker,* and *Apartment 3-G* are considered the precursors to television's soap operas. In the 1950s, Chic Young's *Blondie* was the most popular comic strip in the world and is said to have been the model for television's family oriented sitcoms.

Fears of inner-city crime and the violence of World War II drew readers to crime and horror stories counterbalanced by adventure comics and patriotic stories such as Jack Kirby's *Captain America* and *Fighting American.* At U.S. Army Posts, ten times as many comic books were sold as the combined totals of such standard magazines as *Reader's Digest, Saturday Evening Post,* and *Life* magazine. Increased interest in technology, chemical warfare, and outer space helped to popularize science fiction comics and stories of such super heroes as *Superman, Batman, Captain Marvel,* and *Spider-Man.* It is these hero tales that, our student said, taught him to read and to recognize the literary archetypes and symbols that made him want to become an English major.

Steve Ditko's *Amazing Spider-Man* is interesting in relation to young adult literature because he was a teenager who got his magic powers when he was bitten by a radioactive spider. In spite of being a super human, he was plagued with mundane problems as shown in this line, "If this doesn't take the cake!! I can't go out in public as Spiderman until my mask is sewn up, and when it comes to sewing, I'm all thumbs!" Some critics think that the teenage Spider-Man was the forerunner of *Archie* comics, and to take it one step further, of romanticized adolescent literature.

The third type of comic books has such lurid and gruesome covers that it is hard to believe that today's models are less "offensive" than were the comic books of the early 1950s. The horror comics of the 1950s were so shocking that the U.S. Senate appointed a subcommittee headed by Estes Kefauver to Investigate Juvenile Delinquency as Encouraged by Comic Books. Even more alarming to the industry was that the British Parliament outlawed the importing of American comic books.

In 1954, to protect themselves from lawsuits and from outside censorship, America's comic book publishers formed an association and established the Comic Authority Code to monitor the editorial content and advertising allowed in comic books. An outgrowth of this action was the establishment of *Mad* as a magazine instead of a comic book so that it did not have to follow the guidelines. Another was the establishment of underground comics created and published by individuals or small companies who bypassed industry standards and mainline marketing. In such comics, many of which have worked their way back into general marketing, the topics of drugs, sex, violence, racism, elitism, blasphemy, risqué music, bodily functions, and crude language are made light of rather than preached against.

One of the defenses mounted for comic books during the 1950s controversy was that they taught children to read. The pictures and the balloons coming from characters' mouths help children comprehend higher level stories than what they can read in straight type. Also, the dialogues are printed in all capital letters, which are easier to see. Because of these helps to reading comprehension, many businesses and organizations produce comic books filled with persuasive or educational messages. Subjects range from maintenance instructions for new cars to the prevention of sexually transmitted diseases and messages against smoking, drinking, and drugs. For the last 40 years, an evangelical church group has produced a series of religious tracts, translated into forty-three languages, in the form of comic booklets about the size of baseball cards. Church members distribute them free by tucking them away at highway rest stops and leaving them in motels, on buses, at pay phones, and even in rental bowling shoes.

At the opposite end of the spectrum from these comic "booklets" are coffee table books in the form of beautifully printed, bound collections of comic strips. They usually have introductory and explanatory comments by the creators as in *The Calvin and Hobbes Tenth Anniversary Book* by Bill Watterson and *Bugs Bunny: Fifty Years and Only One Grey Hare* by Joe Adamson. These kinds of books are so far removed from the chap ("cheap") books, the dime novels, and the other pulp fiction that are the ancestors of today's comic books that few people call them comic books. Halfway between cheap giveaways and the coffee-table extravaganzas are the medium-sized collections that come in both hard and soft bindings as with Charles Schulz's various collections of *Peanuts* strips and Scott Adams's best-selling *The Dilbert Principle,* which was in part a collection of his comic strips.

The dubious heritage of comic books and the confusion over whether *comic* is describing content or format, has worked against the full-fledged acceptance of the relatively new genre of the *graphic novel.* In 1986 many people were shocked when Art Spiegelman won a Pulitzer Prize for *Maus: A Survivor's Tale,* in which he used a comic book format to retell his father's Holocaust memories through humanized mice. Spiegelman's success encouraged several mainstream publishers to take a new look at the genre and to publish other graphic novels; however, sales were disappointing so that the publication of graphic novels (also called serious comics) reverted to specialty publishers. Nevertheless, they are still being published and both *VOYA* and *School Library Journal* review them on a more-or-less regular basis. For example in the July 1999, issue of *School Library Journal,* Rich Taylor's *Batman in the Sixties* was described as "Campy and vibrant . . . A fascinating glimpse into the history of one of the most enduring characters in comic books."

Tom DeHaven, a professor at Virginia Commonwealth University, teaches a course in the graphic novel and in an article for the *New York Times Book Review* (May 31, 1998) wrote that he had a difficult job in cutting down the list to the dozen that he thought students would have time to read. The only one of those he settled on that we could find in our college library was Howard Cruse's *Stuck Rubber Baby.*

Graphic novels are a genre of which we will probably be seeing more because improved technologies make it easier for beginners to publish their own either electronically or through photocopying. For some students, turning standard pieces of literature into graphic novels is an excellent way for them to ponder and absorb the thoughts and the pictures in the minds of the original authors.

In a January 1997 *School Library Journal* cover story, "'Za'! Whoosh! Kerplow!' Build High-Quality Graphic Novel Collections with Impact," librarian Lora Bruggeman wrote about her experience in building a collection of 450 graphic novels (checked out by 4,400 individuals in one year) for the Downers Grove, Illinois, public library. From informal observations, she estimates that the collection gets the most use from male readers between ages 12 and 24 but with females becoming more interested. The Elfquest series from Warp Graphics, for example, is popular with both boys and girls, and as the collection gets better known, older readers are also checking out the books. Of the six major publishers of comic books, she recommends D.C. Comics (*Batman, Superman, Sandman, Watchmen,* and the Big Book series), Dark Horse Comics (*Star Wars, Predator, The Mask, The Alien* series, and *The Tale of One Bad Rat*) and Marvel Comics (*Spider-Man, X-Men, Incredible Hulk, Fantastic Four,* and *Star Trek*) as the ones publishing books appropriate for children and young adults. Other bits of advice include:

- Get acquainted with a manager of a local comic book store and deal through this person. He (it's unlikely to be a *she*) is able to offer comments on what's popular and has much better access than do standard library suppliers.
- You must get the books bound, but be sure your binder does not cover over the graphics or replace torn front pages with plain cardboard.
- It is best to shelve and display all graphic novels in the same area and to publicize the collection.
- Group the books according to how customers would look for them, which may sometimes be by series but other times by a particularly famous author.
- Use professional resources to help you choose; for example, Steven Weiner's *100 Graphic Novels for Public Libraries,* D. Aviva Rothschild's *Graphic Novels: A Bibliographic Guide to Book-Length Comics,* and Gale Research's yearbooks of *Contemporary Literary Criticism. School Library Journal, Publishers Weekly,* and *Booklist* occasionally carry reviews of graphic novels. Fuller sources for information are preview magazines put out by the publishers such as *Previews,* which carries titles from all publishers except for Marvel, which publishes its own *Marvel Vision.* Announcements of such annual prizes as the Eisners and the Harveys are also good sources.

Concluding Comments

The last question we asked students on the survey was "Do you see any connections between what you read and your other leisure time activities? If so, explain." Approximately 70 of the 161 students who filled out the survey responded affirmatively. Some drew connections to other entertainment as in "I read fantasy books with odd characters. I like TV shows with odd characters," "I read historical fiction and I like historical movies," "I read action-packed books and watch action-packed movies," and "I like to watch horror movies so I read horror books." Many more students drew connections to their own lives.

- Yes, I see a connection. I read *Guitar World*—I play guitar. I read *Rolling Stone*—I enjoy music.
- I read about the sports I like to play.
- I like to do things that I might see in books. Sometimes I can get ideas from the books.
- I like fantasy and good tragic, emotionally twisted stories; therefore, I dye my hair green and dress bizarre.

- I write stories, and to write stories you have to be articulate and have a large vocabulary. I've noticed people who read a lot have a large vocabulary and are articulate.
- I read Stephen King and like to write like him.
- I learn a lot from *Seventeen*'s advice on shopping, dating, and stuff.
- I like to work out and I like to debate, so I read *Men's Fitness* and controversial magazines.
- I like to model my life after the characters whom I admire.

As evidence in this chapter shows, both the literary world and the expectations of young readers have recently undergone significant changes. It would be a mistake, however, to view these changes as having happened overnight simply because of computers and the Internet. Instead, they are continuations of trends that have been developing over the twentieth century. Nevertheless, we prepared this chapter and made space for it early in this edition because the influence of the Internet has increased the speed with which these changes are occurring. Those of us who work professionally to encourage young people to read and to develop skills in literary appreciation need to think deeply about how these changes—across genres and across media—affect what we do. Listed below are some of the chief differences that we have observed in young people's literary experiences between the first edition of this text and the sixth.

- *Visuals are important.* In the mid-1980s we began noticing how many more full-color pictures were being put in informative books. Designers were making pages look like television screens with sidebars and cutlines providing the equivalent of "time out for commercials." In today's books, this trend has expanded so that even with fiction, young readers fan through a book and look disappointed if all they see are pages and pages of plain type. They expect photos, sketches, doodles, different fonts of type, lots of white space, and a variety of literary forms and techniques; for example, stories told through dialogue almost as in a play and through letters (or e-mail), journal entries, school assignments, interviews, notes, newsclippings, court transcriptions, psychologists' notes, or whatever else a creative author can think of putting between the covers of a book.
- *Readers are given choices.* One of the big publishing successes of the 1980s were the *Choose Your Own Adventure* books for preteens. At the end of a chapter, readers were given two choices of how the story might go. Depending on their preference, they were told which page to turn to and start reading. This trend of allowing reader choice has increased tremendously with materials being presented in shorter, more independent chunks, so that even with some novels, readers can decide the order of their reading, how much they read, and on which strand they focus. For example, the subtitle of Richard Peck's *A Long Way from Chicago* is *A Novel in Stories*. Paul Fleischman's *Whirligig* presents four basically separate accounts, while Virginia Euwer Wolff's *Bat 6* is 21 versions of the same story, each told by a different team member. With informative books, the trend is clearer. Many of them are written to resemble computer programs with hot keys, but instead of "click here for further information," the implied messages are "turn to . . .," "skim over," "follow the theme of your choice," or even "go to your computer and click on Web page. . . ."

- *Authors are encouraging multiple perspectives.* The "other" is being given increased space; history is being looked at from new viewpoints; and books are being written to let readers learn the background and the details that are left out of contemporary newscasts and out of most textbooks. Even poetry books are being arranged to show contrasting feelings from males and females, parents and children, and members of different ethnic groups.

- *Kids' own thinking and writing is given more respect.* Whether it's because we have a youth-oriented society with young people taking on more responsibility and power, because schools have changed their approaches to the teaching of writing, or because the easy availability of publishing on the Internet gives kids more confidence, we are seeing an increase in the numbers of young people whose ideas and thoughts are being published. This is especially true in collections of interviews, essays, and poems circling around topics of concern to teenagers.

- *Crossover books are commonplace.* Just as with television, which is viewed by all ages, more books are being published that can be appreciated by readers of different ages. The increasing importance of illustration makes this possible, along with nonlinear patterns of organization, which allow different readers to take away different concepts.

- *Young people's expectations for entertainment are high.* Because of the fast-moving excitement of video games and the quickness and drama of MTV Video and other television shows and movies, today's authors are pushed to compete in grabbing attention and keeping a story moving. They are also forced to compete with the sexuality and the violence of movies and popular music. In some ways, the freedom of expression in these kinds of popular media opens the door to more freedom in books, but in other ways, it encourages censorship. Parents and educators who feel they have no control over what their children can read on the Internet, view on cable television or at the local theater, or listen to on radio, feel that as a counterbalance they can at least exert control over what books their kids are offered at the local school.

- *The teen years are not a time for subtlety.* Young people looking for entertainment want real thrills and chills. If something is supposed to be funny, they want to laugh out loud; if it's supposed to be sexy they want to feel it, and if it's supposed to be informative they want the exact information they need in a format that is easy to navigate.

- *The literary canon is expanding.* All of the factors mentioned above contribute to an expansion of what is being offered to young people to read, view, and listen to. As with the question of censorship, however, the diversity of the offerings makes people feel out of control. This is why people keep asking for lists—the 100 best books, the 100 greatest films, the 20 books every high school student should read, etc. Every time such a list appears, however, it is immediately met with heavy criticism and counter suggestions simply because today's society is so diverse. Barring some science fiction–like dystopian future, gone are the days when we could recommend to a class of thirty students exactly what they should all read. Instead, we have to work with each student as an individual. We have to follow the advice and the modeling discussed by Han Nolan (see her statement on p. 94) and Robert Lipsyte (see his statement on p. 39). The wealth of literary material now available to virtually everyone makes our jobs harder rather than easier, but at least the situation is the mixed blessing covered in the cliché "When much is given, much is expected."

Notes

[1]Eliza T. Dresang, *Radical Change: Books for Youth in a Digital Age* (H. W. Wilson, 1999), p. xxiv

[2]Eliza T. Dresang, *Radical Change: Books for Youth in a Digital Age* (H. W. Wilson, 1999), p. 17.

[3]Lawrie Mifflin, "Pediatricians Urge Limiting TV Watching," *The New York Times* (August 4, 1999): A-1, A-11.

[4]James Collins, "The Youth Brigade," *Time* magazine (October 6, 1998):88–90.

[5]David Owen, "The Simpsons," *TV Guide* (January 3–9, 1998):cover story.

[6]Paul D. Colford, "In Women's Magazines, Everybody Seems to Be Doing It," *Newsday,* reprinted in *The Arizona Republic* (June 21, 1999):D–4.

[7]David Daley, "After 'Breakfast': Modern Teen Films Owe Debt to Groundbreaking 'Club,'" *Hartford Courant,* reprinted in *The Arizona Republic, The Rep* (April 1, 1999):22–23.

Titles Mentioned in the Text of Chapter Three

Adamson, Joe. *Bugs Bunny: Fifty Years and Only One Grey Hare.* Holt, 1990.

Bernstein, Jonathan. *Pretty in Pink: The Golden Age of Teenage Movies.* St. Martin's/Griffin, 1997.

Cruse, Howard. *Stuck Rubber Baby.* HarperPerennial, 1995.

Daly, Maureen. *Seventeenth Summer.* Dodd Mead, 1942.

Dresang, Eliza T. *Radical Change: Books for Youth in a Digital Age.* H. W. Wilson, 1999.

Duncan, Lois. *I Know What You Did Last Summer.* Little, Brown, 1973.

Frye, Northup. *Anatomy of Criticism: Four Essays.* Princeton University Press, 1957.

Heinlein, Robert. *Stranger in a Strange Land.* Putnam, 1961.

Heinlein, Robert. *The Moon Is a Harsh Mistress.* Putnam, 1966.

Hinton, S. E. *The Outsiders.* Viking, 1967.

Lobel, Anita. *No Pretty Pictures: A Child of War.* Greenwillow, 1998.

Peck, Richard. *A Long Way from Chicago: A Novel in Stories.* Dial, 1998.

Pipher, Mary. *Reviving Ophelia: Saving the Selves of Adolescent Girls.* Putnam, 1994.

Rothschild, D. Aviva. *Graphic Novels: A Bibliographic Guide to Book-Length Comics.* Libraries Unlimited, 1995.

Sachar, Louis. *Holes.* Farrar, Straus & Giroux, 1998.

Shandler, Sara, editor. *Ophelia Speaks: Adolescent Girls Write about Their Search for Self.* HarperPerennial, 1999.

Spiegelman, Art. *Maus I: A Survivor's Tale: My Father Bleeds History.* Pantheon, 1986.

Spiegelman, Art. *Maus II: A Survivor's Tale: And Here My Troubles Began.* Pantheon, 1991.

Watterson, Bill. *The Calvin and Hobbes Tenth Anniversary Book.* Andrews & McMeel, 1995.

Weiner, Steven. *100 Graphic Novels for Public Libraries.* Kitchen Sink Press, 1996.

Information on the availability of paperback editions of these titles is available online from such book sellers as Barnes & Noble and Amazon.com, and through *Books in Print* compiled by R. R. Bowker Company and available either in person or online from major libraries.

Modern Young Adult Reading

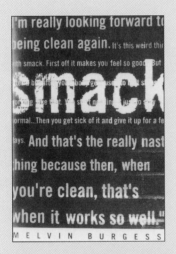

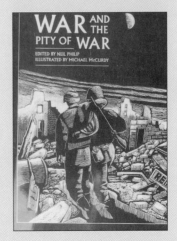

The New Realism
Of Life and Problems

With fantasy, folklore, humor, informative nonfiction, memoirs, poetry, and science fiction, age-level distinctions among readers are fairly fluid, but because stories about rites of passage from childhood to adulthood naturally have young people as their protagonists, in readers' minds they have become closely affiliated with young adults.

In standard literary criticism, such books are known as *bildungsroman*, or less commonly, *apprenticeship novels*, based on Goethe's 1795 *Wilhelm Meister's Apprenticeship*. Classic examples from British literature include Samuel Butler's 1903 *The Way of All Flesh*, James Joyce's 1914 *A Portrait of the Artist as a Young Man*, and Somerset Maugham's 1915 *Of Human Bondage*.

Contemporary books of this type published in the United States for a general adult audience but read and appreciated by sophisticated young adults include William Golding's *Lord of the Flies*, Harper Lee's *To Kill a Mockingbird*, Sylvia Plath's *The Bell Jar*, Chaim Potok's *The Chosen*, and, most famous of all, J. D. Salinger's *The Catcher in the Rye*.

In the late 1960s, societal, education, and business values had changed enough that publishers felt comfortable in encouraging writers to create serious coming-of-age stories to be read by teenagers themselves as they made that treacherous journey from childhood to adulthood. The books were wisely identified as *new realism* (as opposed to the romanticized stories that had been considered appropriate for children) or *problem novels* rather than as *bildungsroman*. Publishers were surprisingly successful in creating appealing formats and in marketing them to teen readers through libraries and schools.

In addition to their candor and the selection of subject matter, they differ from earlier books in four basic ways. The first difference lies in the choice of *characters*. These protagonists come mostly from lower-class families, which ties in with the second major difference, *setting*. Instead of living in idyllic, pleasant suburban homes, the characters in these books come from settings that are harsh, difficult places to live. To get the point across about the characters and where and how they live, authors used colloquial *language,* which is the third major difference. Authors began to write the way people really talked (e.g., in dialogue using profanity and ungrammatical constructions). That the general public allowed this change in language shows that people were drawing away from the idea that the main purpose of fictional books for young readers is to set an example of proper middle-class behavior.

The fourth difference also relates to this change in attitude, and that is the change in *mode.* As people began to think that the educational value of fiction is to provide readers with more vicarious experiences than would be either desirable or possible in real life, the mode of stories for young adults changed. It used to be that most of the books—at least most of the books approved of by parents and educators—were written in the comic and romantic modes. These were the books with upbeat, happy endings. As long as people believed that children would model their lives after what they read, of course they wanted young people to read happy stories because a happy life is what all of us want for our children.

 FOCUS BOX 4.1

Challenges—Physical and Emotional

All Together Now by Sue Ellen Bridgers. Knopf, 1979. When Casey Flanagan goes to spend the summer with her grandparents, she makes friends with 33-year-old Dwayne Pickens, who is retarded and thinks that Casey is a boy.

Am I Blue: Coming Out from the Silence edited by Marion Dane Bauer. HarperCollins, 1994. Several of the most popular writers for young adults have contributed stories to this well-received collection that centers on coming to terms with homosexuality.

Baby Be-Bop by Francesca Lia Block. Harper-Collins, 1995. Block uses her unusual style to explore homosexuality through telling the life story of Dirk McDonald, the gay young man who first appeared in *Weetzie Bat.*

Black Water by Rachel Anderson. Holt, 1995. One of the interesting details in this story of a nineteenth-century English boy with epilepsy is his meeting with Edward Lear, an epileptic who went to extraordinary lengths to keep his condition secret.

Blue Coyote by Liza Ketchum. Simon & Schuster, 1997. While Alex is searching for his lost friend, Tito, he learns some hidden truths about himself and begins to accept his homosexuality.

Don't Think Twice by Ruth Pennebaker. Holt, 1996. The setting is 1967 in a group home for pregnant teenagers. The story is told through the eyes of 17-year-old Anne Harper, but readers also get acquainted with some of the other residents.

Freak the Mighty by Rodman Philbrick. Scholastic, 1993. Kevin and Max are drawn together because they are both shunned by classmates, Max for being big and learning disabled and Kevin for being small and crippled. Their short but extraordinary friendship sticks in readers' minds.

Humming Whispers by Angela Johnson. Orchard, 1995. Having a sister who is schizophrenic is hard for a 14-year-old girl, but it is nothing compared to the fear she feels when she suspects that she may also be developing the condition.

Lena by Jacqueline Woodson. Delacorte, 1999. Lena is the poor white girl who leaves town because of her father's sexual abuse in Woodson's 1994 *I Never Meant to Tell You This* (Delacorte). Here she and her younger sister hitchhike from Ohio to Kentucky hoping to find a relative to take them in. That doesn't work, but they do find help in this honest look at what some children are called to endure.

The problem novel, however, is based on a different philosophy. The idea is that young people have a better chance to be happy if they have realistic expectations and if they know both the bad and the good about the society in which they live. This changed attitude opened the door to writers of irony and even tragedy for young people.

Irony differs from tragedy in that it may be less intense; similarly, instead of having heroic qualities, the protagonist is an ordinary person, much like the reader. Irony is a "tennis serve that you can't return." You can admire its perfection, its appropriateness, and even the inevitability of the outcome, but you just can't cope with it. There is a refreshing honesty in stories that show readers they are not the only ones who get served that kind of ball and that the human spirit, although totally devastated in this particular set, may rise again to play another match. Brock Cole's *The Facts Speak for Themselves,* Gary Soto's *Buried Onions,* Norma Fox Mazer's *When She Was Good,* Rob Thomas's *Rats Saw God,* Cynthia Rylant's *Missing May,* and Stephen Chbosky's *The Perks of Being a Wallflower* are books of this sort. (See Focus Box 4.1, Challenges—Physical and Emotional.)

Not the End of the World by Rebecca Stowe. Pantheon, 1992. Maggie's grandmother jovially explains to her tittering bridge friends that Maggie's crazy. All the way through, readers—along with Maggie—wonder about the truth of the "joke."

Petey by Ben Mikaelsen. Hyperion, 1998. Inspired by a real case, this is the heartbreaking story of a boy born in 1920 with cerebral palsy and mistakenly diagnosed as being mentally retarded.

Probably Still Nick Swansen by Virginia Euwer Wolff. Holt, 1988. Nick has "minimal brain damage" and at school is doomed to being in Room 19, home of the "droolers" and other misfits. Shana is on her way back to regular classes when she accepts Nick's invitation for a star-crossed date to the junior prom.

Speak by Laurie Halse. Farrar, Straus & Giroux, 1999, and **Boys Lie** by John Neufeld. Dorling Kindersley Ink, 1999. The protagonists in both books take steps to reclaim their reputations after having been taken advantage of by boys they dated.

Staying Fat for Sarah Byrnes by Chris Crutcher. Greenwillow, 1993. Eric and Sarah are drawn together because of their "terminal uglies." Eric is overweight, and Sarah is horribly scarred, both inside and outside, from burns inflicted on her when she was 3 years old.

When Zachary Beaver Came to Town by Kimberly Willis Holt. Holt, 1999. In this winner of the National Book Award, three boys, one the self-proclaimed fattest-boy-in-the-world, offer each other more than friendship in an original and touching story set in the small town of Antler, Texas.

Whistle Me Home by Barbara Wersba. Holt, 1997. Seventeen-year-old Noli views herself as pretty much of a loser until she finds a best friend in the sophisticated and handsome TJ. But then she has to come to terms with the fact that he is gay.

The Wild Kid by Harry Mazer. Simon & Schuster, 1998. This is an extraordinary story of adventure, survival, and most of all, friendship between "the wild kid" and Sammy who has Down's Syndrome.

Smack by Melvin Burgess. Holt, 1998. Readers share the years between ages 14 and 18 when Tar and Gemma's experimentation with drugs evolves into full-scale addiction to heroin. The story is told through ten different perspectives.

The Chocolate War as a Tragedy

Several of Robert Cormier's (see his statement below) books come close to being tragedies. In traditional literary criticism, tragedies have three distinct elements. First, there is a noble character who, no matter what happens, maintains the qualities that the society considers praiseworthy; second, there is an inevitable force that works against the character; and third, there is a struggle and an outcome. The reader of a tragedy is usually filled with pity and fear—pity for the hero and fear for oneself that the same thing might happen. The intensity of this involvement causes the reader to undergo an emotional release as the outcome of the story unfolds. This release, or catharsis, has the effect of draining away dangerous human emo-

ROBERT CORMIER
On Writing: A Mystery

Although I have been a writer most of my life, the act of writing still is mysterious to me.

One of the mysteries has to do with the way my novels *must* be written.

Let me explain it this way:

My favorite form of writing is using third person, present tense, with multiple viewpoints. *The Chocolate War* is an example of this approach. And so are *After the First Death*, *We All Fall Down*, and some others.

That approach allowed me to widen the scope of the story with a number of characters interacting with each other.

And yet I have written novels using a first-person narrator, sometimes in past tense, sometimes present tense.

I am not comfortable with the first-person telling of a story because it limits the action and forward progress to what that one character sees and knows. I feel hand-cuffed.

Yet, *I Am the Cheese*, *Fade*, and *Tenderness* employ a first-person telling, and I was satisfied with the outcome of those novels, or as satisfied as a writer can be, knowing that we all fall so far short of perfection.

Why did I use a first-person method for those particular stories?

That's where the mystery comes in.

I don't know why.

When I sat down, say, to write *I Am the Cheese*, Adam Farmer burst into life almost without my conscious effort. I remember writing several pages, the words flowing effortlessly when I suddenly realized that I was writing in the first person. I envisioned all the hazards that lay ahead: being confined to a limited viewpoint that would tie my hands in future scenes.

A further mystery:

The next chapter began with a question-and-answer format.

Hey, where did that come from?

And out of that Q&A exchange came a sudden shift to third-person, past-tense narration.

At that point, I stopped questioning the method and simply let the characters and events take over.

Well, not exactly take over.

I still had to direct them, had to follow the action that would flow from the inevitability of events, but I stopped worrying about the method of approaching and simply approached.

And that's what I mean by this mysterious thing called writing.

Writing is also a journey of constant discovery.

For instance, looking back I realized that in almost all my first-person novels, I departed from that method at some point and alternated with third-person chapters, most notably in *I Am the Cheese, Fade,* and *Tenderness.*

Here again, there's no real explanation.

My instincts told me that that was the right way to present those stories and I simply followed my instincts.

So probably it isn't so mysterious, after all.

Maybe it's just a matter of instinct—and luck.

Although I think it's more than that.

But I can't tell you what it is.

Robert Cormier's books include *Tenderness,* Delacorte, 1997; *Heroes,* Delacorte, 1998; and *The Chocolate War,* Pantheon, 1974.

tions and filling the reader with a sense of exaltation or amazed pride in what the human spirit is called on to undergo.

Robert Cormier's first YA book, *The Chocolate War,* remains our favorite example of a modern tragedy for young adults. It contains the kind of realism that many other books had been leading up to, and its message about conformity and human manipulation is all the more powerful because the young protagonist is so vulnerable. The religious symbolism serves as a contrasting backdrop to the terrible evil that pervades Trinity High School, where the protagonist is a freshman. The opening paragraph is the following simple line: "They murdered him." *Him* is 14-year-old Jerry Renault, who is being "tested" to see if he has enough guts to be on the football team.

The story begins and ends on the athletic field, where the shadows of the goal posts resemble a "network of crosses, empty crucifixes." On Jerry's third play at Trinity High, he is "hit simultaneously by three of them." He blinks himself back to consciousness and jumps to his feet:

. . . intact, bobbing like one of those toy novelties dangling from car windows, but erect.

"For Christ's sake," the coach bellowed, his voice juicy with contempt. A spurt of saliva hit Jerry's cheek.

Hey coach, you spit on me, Jerry protested. Stop the spitting, coach. What he said aloud was, "I'm all right, coach," because he was a coward about stuff like that, thinking one thing and saying another, planning one thing and doing another he had been Peter a thousand times and a thousand cocks had crowed in his lifetime.

Over the course of the book, Jerry gets the courage to think and do the same thing. He refuses to sell fifty boxes of chocolate that the corrupt teacher, Brother Leon, has assigned to each student. For the first ten days of the candy campaign, he simply follows the orders of the Vigils, a gang whose members, in the words of their head man, Archie Costello, "were the school." When the ten days are up, however, and the Vigils order Jerry to do a reversal and participate in the selling campaign, he dares to say, "No."

At first Jerry is a hero, but because this threatens the power of the Vigils, Archie uses his full potential in people management to turn the student body against Jerry. When all the chocolates except Jerry's are sold, Archie arranges a boxing match between Jerry and a bully who is trying to work his way into the Vigils. It is supposed to be set up "with rules. Fair and square," but what Archie really masterminds is a physical and psychological battering much worse than anything Jerry underwent at football practice.

The last chapter of the book could have begun with the same line as the first chapter—"They murdered him"—except that this time it would have been less of a metaphor. Although Jerry may recover physically from a fractured jaw and internal injuries, his spirit has been murdered. In the midst of the fight:

> A new sickness invaded Jerry, the sickness of knowing what he had become, another animal, another beast, another violent person in a violent world, inflicting damage, not disturbing the universe but damaging it. He had allowed Archie to do this to him.

After the fight, when the pain—"Jesus, the pain"—brings Jerry back to consciousness, the reader sees how changed he is because of what he tries to tell his friend Goober:

> They don't want you to do your thing, not unless it happens to be their thing, too. It's a laugh, Goober, a fake. Don't disturb the universe, Goober, no matter what the posters say.

In selecting *The Chocolate War* as a touchstone example, we asked ourselves several questions about the book. These same or similar questions could be asked when evaluating almost any problem novel (see Table 4.1). First, does the book make a distinctive contribution? Does it say something new, or does it convey something old in a new way? If so, is it something of value? Robert Cormier was praised by *The Kirkus Reviews* because with *The Chocolate War* he dared to "disturb the upbeat universe of juvenile books." He did not compromise by providing a falsely hopeful conclusion, nor did he sidestep the issue by leaving it open for readers to imagine their own happy ending. Until Cormier, most writers for young readers had chosen one of these two approaches. Yet Cormier was not being "difficult" just for the sake of being different. When he was questioned at a National Council of Teachers of English convention about his motives in writing such a pessimistic book for young readers, he answered that he had written three other novels and numerous short stories, all with upbeat endings, and that in *The Chocolate War* he was simply providing a balance. He then went on to say that today's young readers are a television generation. They have grown up thinking that every problem can be solved within a half-hour or an hour at the most, with time out for commercials. It

TABLE 4.1

SUGGESTIONS FOR EVALUATING THE PROBLEM NOVEL

A good problem novel usually has:	A poor problem novel may have:
A strong, interesting, and believable plot centering around a problem that a young person might really have.	A totally predictable plot with nothing new and interesting to entice the reader.
The power to transport the reader into another person's thoughts and feelings.	Characters who are cardboardlike exaggerations of people and are too good or too bad to be believed.
Rich characterization. The characters "come alive" as believable with a balance of good and negative qualities.	More characters than the reader can keep straight comfortably.
A setting that enhances the story and is described so that the reader can get the intended picture.	Many stereotypes.
A worthwhile theme. The reader is left with something to think about.	Lengthy chapters or descriptive paragraphs that add bulk but not substance to the book.
A smoothness of style that flows steadily and easily, carrying the reader along.	A preachy message. The author spells out the attitudes and conclusions with which he or she wants each reader to leave the book.
A universal appeal so that it speaks to more than a single group of readers.	Nothing that stays with the reader after the book has been put down.
A subtlety that stimulates the reader to think about the various aspects of the story.	A subject that is of interest only because it is topical or trendy.
A way of dealing with the problems so that the reader is left with insights into either society or individuals or both.	Inconsistent points of view. The author's sympathies change with no justification.
	Dialogue that sounds forced or inappropriate to the characters.
	"Facts" that do not jibe with those of the real world.
	Unlikely coincidences or changes in characters' personalities for the sake of the plot.
	Exaggerations that result in sensationalism.

is important for people to realize that all problems are not that easily solved. In real life, some problems may never be solved, and the solutions to others demand the utmost efforts of the most capable people in the world.

The plot of a book must be examined to see how closely it grows out of the characters' actions and attitudes. Is it an idea that could easily have been dropped into another setting or onto other characters? With Cormier's book, there wouldn't have been a story without the unique but believable personalities of both Jerry and Archie as well as of Brother Leon. The problem was not so bizarre or unusual that it overshadowed the characters, and the characters were not so unusual that readers could not identify with them or imagine themselves having to deal with people like them. It is because the characters at first appear to be such ordinary people that readers are drawn into the story. The theme is similar to that in Golding's *Lord of the Flies*, but because Golding's book is set on a deserted island in the midst of a war it could be dismissed as unrealistic. Cormier's book has an immediacy that is hard to deny. The problem is a real one that teenagers can identify with on the first or literal level, yet it has implications far beyond one beaten-up 14 year old and 20,000 boxes of leftover Mother's Day candy.

In looking at the setting, we might ask, is it just there or does it contribute something to the mood or the action or to revealing characterization? In *The Chocolate War,* the story would not have been nearly so chilling without the religious setting, which provided contrast. In some ways the evil in Archie is less hideous than that in Brother Leon, the corrupt teacher who enlists Archie's help in making his unauthorized investment pay off. The Brother hides behind his clerical collar and his role of teacher and assistant headmaster, while Archie only identifies himself as a nonbeliever in the so-called Christian ethic. When his stooge Obie asks him how he can do the things he does and still take Communion, he responds, "When you march down to the rail, you're receiving the Body, man. Me, I'm just chewing a wafer they buy by the pound in Worcester."

Another relevant question is the respect the author has for the intended audience. Cormier showed a great deal of respect for his readers: Nowhere did he write down to them. The proof of his respect is in some of the subtle symbolization that he worked into the story and the care with which he developed his style. For example, the irony of the whole situation is exemplified in the gang's name, the Vigils. He chose the name as a shortened form of *vigilante,* an accurate description of the way the gang worked. In response, however, to an interview question about whether or not the name was an ironic reference to vigil lights, the candles placed devotionally before a shrine or image, he agreed that the religious connotation, the image of the boys in the gang standing like vigil lights before Archie, who basked in the glow of their admiration, "was also very much a part of my choice."[1] Another example of Cormier's subtlety is the fact that Archie's name has such meanings as "principal or chief," as in *archvillain,* and "at the extreme, that is, someone or something most fully embodying the qualities of its kind," as in *archrival.*

A question that has to be asked somewhere in the evaluation process is how many people a particular book attracts as readers. *The Chocolate War* has gone through innumerable reprintings, so it's obviously being read, although many of those who read it are doing it as a class assignment either in a college young adult literature class or in a high school English class. It is ideal for class reading and discussion because there is more in the book than any one student sees at a first reading.

Post-Columbine Musings on the Value of Today's Problem Novels

When Robert Cormier was asked at a recent meeting of English teachers about the changing nature of school violence, he sadly admitted that he was as troubled as is everyone else. This was before the April 20, 1999, shooting at Columbine High School in Littleton, Colorado, in which teenagers Eric Harris and Dylan Klebold killed twelve of their classmates and a teacher and wounded several others before turning their guns on themselves. There had already been enough instances of teenagers using guns against each other that the audience was concerned. One participant mentioned that bringing guns into the picture changes the end results but not the beginnings of violence. For example, if Jerry had been shot instead of beaten up, he most likely would not have been there to share his disappointment with Goober; however, the way the alienation and the hostilities developed and escalated between Jerry and the Vigils would have been much the same.

Someone else pointed out that in relation to literature, the beginnings of the stories are the most interesting and are what we can work with. The simplest of video games can show people getting shot, but it takes great literature to help people understand the intensity of the emotions that might trigger such actions as well as to understand the emotional fallout on the victims' families and friends (see Focus Box 4.2, Explorations of Violence). Hoping to find quick and easy answers to the Columbine tragedy, people jumped on the fact that Harris and Klebold wore black overcoats, identified themselves as *Goths,* and communicated on the Internet with other aficionados of the dark side. After the first couple of days, however, cooler heads began pointing out that while struggles between good and evil abound in Gothic stories, they end with good overcoming evil, and there never was a vampire, a werewolf, or a human villain in a Gothic story who went to a school carrying rounds of ammunition and semiautomatic guns to shoot children.

 FOCUS BOX 4.2

Explorations of Violence

Breaking Rank by Kristen D. Randle. Morrow, 1999. A *School Library Journal* reviewer compared Randle's book to *The Outsiders* and to *West Side Story.* A girl steps outside of her suburban in-group, first to tutor a boy and then to be his girlfriend.

Buried Onions by Gary Soto. Harcourt Brace, 1997. When Eddie sits with the mortuary students at his community college in Fresno, California, he thinks they will get good jobs because people in his town are always dying.

The Buffalo Tree by Adam Rapp. Front Street, 1997. Rapp explores the violence in a juvenile detention center through the eyes of Sura, who is serving time for having stolen hood ornaments from cars.

Edge by Michael Cadnum. Puffin, 1999. The sell line on the book's cover is "Zach needs to see justice done." His father was shot during a robbery, and when the suspect goes free for lack of evidence Zach thinks it's up to him to settle the score.

Hate You by Graham McNamee. Delacorte, 1999. Alice is a songwriter but feels she can never sing her songs because her father once struck her in the throat, permanently damaging her vocal cords. Years later when she sees her father in a hospital dying from cancer, she starts on the road to emotional, if not physical, recovery.

Iceman by Chris Lynch. HarperCollins, 1994. Eric is a hockey player whose father lives out his aggressions through encouraging his son to play "tough." By the end of the book, Eric has grown enough to start sorting out just what this means.

Ironman by Chris Crutcher. Greenwillow, 1995. Bo Brewster is angry about being assigned to an anger-management class, but in this book which manages to be funny as well as powerful he makes progress. Other Crutcher books (*Running Loose, Stotan!,* and *The Crazy Horse Electric Game*) that explore sports related feelings are treated in Chapter Five.

Scorpions by Walter Dean Myers. Harper-Collins, 1988. Jamal's brother is in jail, and an old gang leader brings word to Jamal that he's to take over as leader of the Scorpions. He also brings Jamal a gun. Myers's *Monster* (Scholastic, 1999) is also about a sympathetic character caught, at least temporarily, in a web of violence.

Soulfire by Lorri Hewett. Dutton, 1996. Sixteen-year-old Todd Williams, an African-American living in Denver, shares his anguish over the gang-related death of his cousin, Tommy.

Tenderness: A Novel by Robert Cormier. Delacorte, 1997. In his inimitable style, Cormier makes murder all the more horrific because of a young serial killer's need for establishing intimacy and tenderness with the person he plans to kill.

Finger pointers then divided into two camps: those wanting to use the incident to campaign for stronger gun control and those wanting to blame the mass media for inuring kids to violence, and in the case of video games, for actually teaching kids how to use automatic weapons to kill the most people in the shortest amount of time. In between were people placing the blame on causes ranging from a weakened family life to the failure of parents to teach kids the difference between fantasy and reality, and from the lack of a network of support, evaluation, and treatment for troubled children to the ambivalence of teachers about getting involved when they observe students being cruel to other students.

In the late 1960s, when the problem novel was first developing as *the* genre in young adult literature, it played a relatively unique role in openly acknowledging that many young people lived lives far removed from the happy-go-lucky images shown in television commercials and sitcoms. The books on the Honor List from the 1960s and 1970s were new and interesting because they vividly demonstrated that young people worried about sex, drugs, money, peer pressure, and health problems. They also showed that not all teenagers had parents as kindly as Ward and June Cleaver, nor were all siblings as cute and competent as those portrayed on *The Brady Bunch.*

Such information does not come as news today, which means teenagers do not need to read young adult novels to learn they are not alone in having problems. The mass media does a thorough job of communicating that message. In fact, talk shows, soap operas, and even news programs and magazines make us privy to so many people's problems that we simply do not have the energy to empathize with all the sad stories we hear. We shrug our shoulders and turn off our tear ducts, which leaves us feeling alienated and dehumanized. Social observers have asked whether the tremendous public outpouring of sympathy at the deaths of such celebrities as England's Princess Diana and the United States's John F. Kennedy, Jr., might be evidence of a kind of emotional emptiness that people want desperately to fill?

Eric, the protagonist in Chris Lynch's *Iceman,* is a boy who feels this emptiness. Lynch communicated it by showing Eric at a funeral parlor where his older friend McLaughlin works. McLaughlin lets Eric peek, unseen, through a crack in the wood paneling. Eric watches three old friends come to say goodbye to a World War I comrade. As he watches, Eric suddenly understands why McLaughlin works there.

> Like a ghoul, he fed on it. Like a vampire sucking the life, the blood, he found that this was where to find it, the place where people *said* they were sad, they were hurt, said they didn't want to be alone. Where people let it rip and didn't give a damn who knew about it. I saw—and stole—more emotion raw and real in that room in twenty minutes than I'd gotten from my family in fourteen years.

Ameliorating the kind of emptiness that Eric felt is a role that well-written problem novels can fill in ways that fleeting glimpses of problems in the mass media cannot. Books have an advantage over the news media simply because of how much time is involved. For example, on television talk shows, suffering individuals are shuffled through their paces in less than an hour and then sent on their respective ways. In contrast, readers usually spend several hours with a book. Also, because few kids finish a book in a single sitting, they have time between readings to ponder the characters' problems and solutions.

From the production standpoint, authors of high-quality books spend several months or even years figuring out how best to communicate the crucial details that will help readers understand the heart of their story. They seek a balance between stories that are different enough to be interesting while common enough that readers can relate to them. In contrast, reporters and producers compete with each other to find something new and so look for stories further and further removed from people's ordinary experiences.

Certainly the shouting matches that make for high ratings on television talk shows do not serve as good models for the development of oral skills in problem solving. When a novel, however, is read by one or more students and discussed under the leadership of a knowledgeable adult (see Focus Box 10.4, Discussion Time on pp. 351), students can be led to think deeply about issues and problem solving. Solid discussions can counteract the tendency of people to make superficial decisions based on first impressions and emotions rather than through gathering and weighing solid information. One of the marks of emotional and intellectual maturity is understanding that there may be many viewpoints from which to judge the actions and beliefs of others. Another worthwhile lesson is recognizing the distance between knowing something is wrong and being able to do something about it.

Cynthia Voigt's *When She Hollers*—a title readers are to complete in their own minds with "make him pay"—does a superb job of illustrating how hard it is for Tish to confront the stepfather who has been abusing her. Even after she has sought out the help of an attorney and has a plan that gives her a chance, "Maybe even a

Even with grim stories of abuse, protagonists are shown to have the resilience to fight back.

pretty good chance," she turns down the offer of a ride home by telling the aptly named *Mr. Battle,* the attorney who is helping her,

> . . . that she wanted to walk so she'd have time to get ready, but she wasn't sure that was true. She thought maybe it was to give herself time to change her mind. She didn't have to tell Tonnie [her stepfather] about the paper, and the lawyer. She could get rid of the card in her pocket, with Mr. Battle's office phone number on it, and his home phone number. . . .
>
> Fear grew in her belly, like some speeded-up pregnancy, and shoved up against her heart and vibrated along her bones until she almost couldn't find the leg muscles to keep on walking, clump, clump, back to Tonnie's house.

But having come this far, Tish knows she cannot turn back, and when she gets to her own front door "bulging out with all the fury behind it," she rings the doorbell and then steps back so that she can confront Tonnie and say what she has to say outside in the open, rather than in Tonnie's house. She gets an image of how big the world is.

> . . . round like a picture in a book, with the Australians hanging off by their feet and smiling, and the Japanese sticking out of one side, smiling. She pictured how little a dot Tonnie's home made on that globe. Everything except for that tiny little dot *wasn't* his.

Wrapping her mind around this image and holding "it out in front of her, like a knife" gives her the courage to do what she has to do. This powerful story of a girl taking steps to save herself also illustrates another advantage that well-written problem novels have over superficial media treatments. Because most such treatments present a one-shot portrait, chosen to tug at the emotions of viewers or readers, they make a virtue of suffering and pain by portraying people as victims unable to move beyond their pain. In contrast, the best of the problem novels help young readers develop an internal locus of control through which they assume that their own actions and characteristics will shape their lives. They ask the question, "What am I going to do with my life?" while people with an external locus of control depend on luck, chance, or what others do. Their major life question is "What will happen to me?"

Although we all know adults who blame others for whatever happens to them and take little responsibility for making their own decisions, most of us would agree that we want to help young people feel responsible for their own lives. Books cannot substitute for real-life experiences, and one or two books, no matter how well written, are not enough to change a teenager's view of life. Skilled authors, however, can show what's going on in characters' minds, whereas cameras can show only what is externally visible. Authors of the problem novels have the space to develop various strands of their stories and to show characters making progress. This differs from television sitcoms as well as most series books, which preserve the status quo.

In the problem novels, young protagonists take steps toward maturity so that at the end of the book they are different in some significant way. For example, in the next-to-the-last chapter of Norma Fox Mazer's *When She Was Good,* Em is able to look back and remember the details of her sister's unexpected death, but in the final chapter, she is also able to find a happier memory. She remembers going with her mother to pick the elderberries that they brought home and put in a big pot for cooking. The book ends with these two sentences:

> She stirred cup after cup of sugar into the boiling pot of berries and scalded a dozen little jars and spread out the red rubber rings. When she was done, we had sweet jam for the rest of the year to spread on our toast each morning. And, oh, it was so good.

The memory of the "good" jam is a metaphor for the good thoughts that Em now manages to have. She can't change the past, but by being able to change the way she thinks about it, she is free to move forward with her life.

The point here is that in the most powerful stories, protagonists do not just wait for something to happen; they take responsibility. As one of our graduate students, Diana Kraus, wrote in her justification for wanting to teach Virginia Euwer Wolff's *Make Lemonade*:

> LaVaughn has a goal to go to college from which she never deviates. When her desperate friend asks for a loan (impossible to repay) of her college money, LaVaughn feels no ambivalence about saying, "No." She has enormous sympathy for her friend, she helps in every way she can, even side-stepping the truth to her mom, yet she does not jeopardize her own agenda. I think this is something many young adults, and especially girls, need to learn. It's okay, even good, to say "No," to put yourself first.

Hundreds of books present variations on this theme of taking responsibility for oneself. It is not hard to devise plots that include such incidents, but for authors to make them believable and bring enough life to the characters so that readers care is challenging.

What Are the Problems?

Good young adult authors treat candidly and with respect problems that belong specifically to young adults in today's world. Many of the problems that go along with modern adolescence did not exist in the nineteenth century, so, of course, they were not written about. At least in this one area, there is ample justification for books directed specifically to a youthful audience because there is a difference in the kinds of real-life problems that concern children, teenagers, and adults.

Family Relationships

A look at mythology, folklore, and classical and religious literature shows that the subject of family relationships is not what's new about the problem novel (see Film Box 4.1 Our Need for Family and Love and Focus Box 4.3, Parents and Kids for ex-

FILM BOX 4.1

Our Need for Family and Love (see Appendix D)

East of Eden (1955, color, 115 min., NR; Director: Ella Kazan; with James Dean, Raymond Massey, and Julie Harris) John Steinbeck's tale shows a terribly dysfunctional family.

Five Easy Pieces (1979, color, 98 min., R; Director: Bob Rafelson; with Jack Nicholson and Susan Anspach) A musical prodigy who now works on oil rigs comes home temporarily.

The Grapes of Wrath (1940, black and white, 129 min., NR; Director: John Ford; with Henry Fonda and Jane Darwell) In Steinbeck's best known novel, the Joad family leaves the dust of Oklahoma for the wonders of California.

The Great Santini (1980, color, 118 min., PG; Director: Lewis John Carlino; with Robert Duvall and Blythe Danner) A fighter pilot in peace-time 1962 has his only fight with his teenage son who is trying to become a man.

Hannah and Her Sisters (1986, color, 106 min., PG–13; Director: Woody Allen; with Allen, Mia Farrow, Michael Caine, and Diana Wiest) In one of Allen's greatest films, the family endures and delights despite adultery and drugs.

I Never Sang for My Father (1971, color, 93 min., PG; Director: Gilbert Cates; with Gene Hackman, Melvyn Douglas, and Dorothy Stickney) An old man near death and his son have never been able to talk of their love for each other.

My Left Foot (1989, color, 102 min., R; Director: Jim Sheridan; with Daniel Day-Lewis and Brenda Fricker) Writer and artist Christy Brown is born with cerebral palsy, but his life is often happy because his family loves him.

Tender Mercies (1983, color, 89 min., PG; Director: Bruce Beresford; with Robert Duvall and Tess Harper) A country singer on the way down finds hope and life with a widow and her son.

Tortilla Flat (1942, black and white, 105 min., NR; Director: Victor Fleming; with John Garfield and Frank Morgan) Perhaps this is minor Steinbeck, but it shows a loving view of the families of California fishermen and what's important in their lives.

Wild Strawberries (1957, black and white, 90 min., NR; Director: Ingmar Bergman) An elderly professor on his way to receive an award relives his life.

---

amples). Stories featuring inadequate or absent parents appeal to young readers because they provide opportunities for young people to assert their independence and prove that they can take care of themselves. Nevertheless, in real life, most kids want to be closer to their parents than they are (see Graham Salisbury's statement on p. 128). While many family stories are light enough to be placed in the next chapter under romances, Cynthia Voigt's Newbery Award–winning *Dicey's Song* is clearly heavy enough to be classified as a problem novel. It begins

> And They Lived Happily Ever After
> Not the Tillermans, Dicey thought. That wasn't the way things went for the Tillermans, ever. She wasn't about to let that get her down. She couldn't let it get her down that was what had happened to Momma.

Dicey's view that when parents are weak the children have to be that much stronger is a theme often illustrated through the way brothers and sisters pull together to close gaps in the family circle, as in Betsy Byars's *The Night Swimmers*, Vera and Bill Cleaver's *Where the Lilies Bloom* and *Trial Valley*, and S. E. Hinton's *Tex.* Jamaica Kincaid's *Annie John,* set on the Caribbean island of Antigua, is a

FOCUS BOX 4.3

Parents and Kids

Brad's Universe by Mary Woodbury. Orca, 1998. Astronomy is part of this book in which 14-year-old Brad looks for his place in the universe because it seems a lot more predictable and dependable than his family.

Broken Chords by Barbara Snow Gilbert. Front Street, 1998. Clara's mother conducts the local symphony and has spent her life preparing Clara for a career as a concert pianist, but at 17 Clara is no longer sure that's what she wants for herself.

Celine by Brock Cole. Farrar, Straus & Giroux, 1989. Celine, a 16-year-old artist, is left to make friends with her new, and almost embarrasingly young, stepmother when her father takes off on a European lecture tour.

A Day No Pigs Would Die by Robert Newton Peck. Knopf, 1973. The love that the boy Robert feels for his Pa is only one of the themes in this powerful story of a Vermont farm family from the 1920s.

Dear Nobody by Berlie Doherty. Orchard, 1992. Pregnant Helen writes longer and longer letters to the child she is carrying who over the course of the book becomes less and less of a nobody.

Dinky Hocker Shoots Smack by M. E. Kerr. HarperCollins, 1972. The first of M. E. Kerr's young adult books was inspired by her watching a do-gooder mother solving everyone's problems except those of her own daughter.

A Door Near Here by Heather Quarles. Delacorte, 1998. Four children try desperately to keep their family together when their divorced mother abandons herself to alcohol.

The Falcon by Jackie French Koller. Atheneum/Simon & Schuster, 1998. Troubled 17-year-old Luke feels like the falcon in a poem he wrote and published.

The Great Gilly Hopkins by Katherine Paterson. Crowell, 1979. Gilly manipulates her caregivers until she gets the wise and wonderful Trotter as a foster mother. But when Gilly's attempts to find her flower-child birth mother backfire, not even Trotter can help.

The Hanged Man by Francesca Lia Block. HarperCollins, 1994. Seventeen-year-old Laurel spins dangerously close to a breakdown as she tries purging herself of years of sexual abuse from her now deceased father.

Jack by A. M. Homes. Macmillan, 1989. Fifteen-year-old Jack is devastated when after his parents' divorce he learns that his father is gay. Shame and bewilderment are gradually replaced with respect and a realization that people's lives come with problems.

Missing Girls by Lois Metzger. Viking, 1999. Metzger sets her story in 1969 so that she can connect disagreements over Vietnam to the World War II experiences of Carrie's mother and grandmother.

The Moonlight Man by Paula Fox. Bradbury, 1986. In a memorable summer visit, Catherine ends up playing the role of the grown-up when she discovers that her father is a "falling-down-drunk."

Somewhere in the Darkness by Walter Dean Myers. Scholastic, 1992. Jimmy arrives home from school to find a tall, thin man waiting to introduce himself as the father who's been gone so long that Jimmy has to look at a photograph to verify the truth of what the man says.

Strays Like Us by Richard Peck. Dial, 1998. Their drug addicted mother is gone and their father is dying from AIDS, but because of Peck's talent as a writer readers feel hope for the kids in this sad story.

---

powerful exploration of a daughter's painful gaining of emotional independence from her mother.

In Paula Fox's *A Place Apart* and in Judy Blume's *Tiger Eyes,* the fathers of the families die unexpectedly (a heart attack and a shooting, respectively), and the mothers and daughters move to new locales, almost as if they are embarking on dual quests in search of a way to put their lives back together.

GRAHAM SALISBURY
On Fatherhood

As a boy I was all over the place, a shrimpy Tarzan in the jungles of Hawaii. It seemed like heaven.

Underneath it all, though, was a carefully constructed life, one that mercifully boarded up a few large holes. For the most part, I was far too free for my own good. I had no real father to define my limits or monitor my movements, and my kind and generous mother was too lost in her own emotional sorrows to spend her last ounce of hope on me.

So I roamed and wandered and explored.

As a writer, I still roam and wander and explore. Only now, some of it makes sense.

I remember one particular sizzling hot day in Kailua-Kona. The sky was cloudless, and the sea as soft and calm as a turquoise swimming pool. Every fishing boat in the harbor was out.

I was sitting on the concrete seawall that edged the bay, fishing with a bamboo pole and a barbless hook, catching luckless fish that I quickly tossed back. I was twelve years old and passing time. My stepfather had just moved us all to the Big Island from Honolulu and was still thinking about whether or not I had the brains and muscle to work as his deck hand on his new deep-sea charter fishing boat.

I should have been bored, sitting on the seawall wasting time like that. But I wasn't. The ocean was soothing to me. The lapping sound of waves, the perfect air. The whole *island* felt like that.

I noticed, down toward the pier, a man on the seawall walking my way, a small boy sitting on his shoulders. The man was dark—Hawaiian, Filipino, maybe even Samoan—and he wore only shorts. A white plastic sack hung from the fingers of his left hand. His right hand held the boy's knee, and the boy, who looked about three, was bouncing around as if on a horse, having a great time up there.

The man walked slowly, man-style, the way fishermen do, men of the islands like my stepfather, men born to ocean, boats, sand, and heat. He stopped a few yards away, his long black hair pulled into a knot behind his head. He was a big guy. A band of tattoos circled one of his biceps, and he looked like he might eat me if I made a wrong move.

He squatted down, and the boy slid off his shoulders. He came up to his father's knees, about. The two of them settled down and sat facing the sea with their feet dangling over the edge of the seawall.

The man noticed me watching them, and dipped his head, Howzit. I raised my hand half way, then quickly turned away.

After a few moments, I peeked back at them.

The man had opened the sack and was settling a plate lunch on his knees and handing another to the boy. Without speaking, the two of them sat eating with their fingers, each silently surveying the harbor.

The boy glanced over at me, and again I turned away.

When they'd finished their lunches, the man got up, and the boy, and they stuffed their Styrofoam plates into the plastic bag. The man took the boy's hand, and the two of them walked over to where I sat.

"Where's your fish bucket?" the man asked, his voice soft, friendly.

"Fish bucket?"

"To keep your fish in."

"Oh. These are just junk fish. I throw them back."

The man nodded and grinned. "I know what you mean," he said. He paused, as if thinking. Then said, "But I gotta tell you, boy, you may not like to eat this kind fish, and that's okay, but I gotta say, there's no such thing as a junk fish."

"Huh?"

He pointed his chin toward the water. "A fish is a work of art."

"What?"

He laughed at my confusion.

The boy looked over the edge into the water, pointing down at a handful of black crabs scurrying along the rocks below.

"A'ama," the man said. "Taste good. Eat 'um raw."

We all watched the crabs a moment, then the man winked at me and said, "Remember what I told you, boy. A work of art. Just like you."

He nodded.

Then they walked away.

Just as they were about to jump off the wall, the boy looked back at me. He waved, and I waved back. My hand was still in the air when I lost sight of him.

In that moment some feeling ran through me, some *thing* that, at twelve, I didn't begin to understand. But now I do. Emptiness. Because I'd just met the luckiest kid in the world.

Graham Salisbury's books include *Blue Skin of the Sea,* 1992; *Under the Blood-Red Sun,* 1994; *Shark Bait,* 1997; and *Jungle Dogs,* 1998, all from Delacorte.

Friends and Society

Peer groups become increasingly important to teenagers as they move beyond social and emotional dependence on their parents. By becoming part of a group, clique, or gang, teenagers take a step toward emotional independence. Even though they are not making truly independent decisions about such social conventions as clothing, language, and entertainment, their parents are no longer deciding on and enforcing their behavior. As part of a group, they try out various roles ranging from conformist to nonconformist, from follower to leader. These roles can be acted out by individuals within the group, or they can be acted out by the group as a whole, as, for example, when one gang challenges another gang. Group members in such a situation are caught up in a kind of emotional commitment that they would seldom feel as individuals.

All teenagers do not automatically find groups to belong to, and even if they do, they are still curious about other groups. This is where young adult literature comes in. It extends the peer group, giving teenagers a chance to participate vicariously in many more personal relationships than are possible for most youngsters in the relatively short time that they spend in high school. When they were children, making friends was a simple matter of playing with whomever happened to be nearby. Parents were responsible for locating in the "right" neighborhood near "good schools," so that children had no reason to give particular thought to differences in social and economic classes or ethnic backgrounds. Then quite suddenly their environments are expanded not only through larger, more diverse schools but also through jobs, extracurricular activities, public entertainment, shopping in malls, and church or community activities.

Tradition says that the United States is a democracy and that we do not have a caste system; anyone can grow up to be president. Real-life observations, however, do not support this, and that may be why books exploring differences in social classes are especially popular with young adults. Problems of group identification are a part of all of S. E. Hinton's books, especially *The Outsiders,* in which the *greasers* (i.e., the dirt heads) are in conflict with the *socs* (i.e., the society kids).

It is a mark of maturity in the field of young adult literature that no longer are just the big group distinctions being made. In *Tiger Eyes,* Judy Blume includes many subtle observations, which lead readers to see and judge inductively various status symbols in the high-tech, scientific community of Los Alamos (e.g., Bathtub Row, gun racks in pickup trucks, and tell-tale comments about Native Americans and Chicanos). It's also a mark of maturity that in *Remembering the Good Times,* Richard Peck's narrator has fun describing the various groups in his new school.

> There were suburbanites still maintaining their position and their Izod–and–L.L. Bean image . . . a few authentic Slos, the polyester people . . . punk . . . funk . . . New Wave . . . Spaces . . . people at the top of the line looked a lot like the Pine Hill Slos down at the bottom who'd been having to wear this type gear all along except with different labels.

In *The Friends,* Rosa Guy does a masterful job of leading her readers to see how Phyllisia is taught that she's too good for the neighborhood. Her family has immigrated to Harlem from the West Indies, and her overly strict, restaurant-owner father constantly instills in her a feeling of superiority. He is horrified when Phyllisia brings home poor "ragamuffin" Edith, with her worn coat, holey socks, turned-over shoes, and matted hair.

Living in a Multicultural World

Notice how often in these books about friendships, the stumbling blocks are related to ethnic or social class differences. This is an area of concern to young people because neighborhoods are no longer as segregated as they used to be and schools are bigger with students from many different groups attending. The demographic makeup of the United States is undergoing considerable change with both long-term and short-term effects; for example:

- Declining birth rates mean that the United States would have a net loss in population growth if it were not for rapidly increasing numbers of immigrants. In 1970, 4.7 percent of Americans were foreign born; in 1990, the figure was 8.6 percent; and in 2040, it is predicted to be 14.2 percent.[2]
- Today's immigrants are bringing in different family values, religion, and attitudes toward education. More than 80 percent of today's immigrants are His-

panic or Asian, as compared with "the old days," when most immigrants came from Europe.

- The United States is becoming one of the oldest populations in the world. By the year 2020, the fastest-growing segment of the population will be the very old—those over age 80.
- In 1990, 24 percent of all new births occurred outside of marriage, many to teenage mothers. Nineteen percent of new births were to women in the lowest income range.
- In 1990, 66 percent of women with children under age 18 were working outside the home.
- The population is being divided into extremes with the middle class shrinking and the numbers of those in "permanent" poverty and in "permanent" affluence growing. This is especially true for African-Americans with many being well-educated professionals whose lives are in sharp contrast with large numbers living under conditions as painful as anything known since the days of slavery.[3]

Although few people have these specific facts at hand, almost everyone realizes that changes are occurring, and to many people these changes are threatening. One of the results has been an increase in incidents of racism on high school and college campuses. While those are the incidents that grab public attention, there have also been many incidents showing the development of friendship and understanding across cultural and ethnic lines (see Focus Box 4.4, Relating Across Cultures). These are powerful books because the stories take place at the edges of groups where young people are brushing up against values and practices different from their own.

Among the most critically acclaimed books of the 1960s and early 1970s were Eldridge Cleaver's *Soul on Ice,* William H. Armstrong's *Sounder,* Maya Angelou's *I Know Why the Caged Bird Sings,* Sharon Bell Mathis's *A Teacup Full of Roses,* Alice Childress's *A Hero Ain't Nothin' But a Sandwich,* and Rosa Guy's *The Friends.* As powerful as these books were, they had a grimness and a sameness to them, and it's refreshing today to have them supplemented by books in which a variety of characters from different backgrounds face problems by working together.

We are not saying that reading one book or even a dozen books will change a skinhead into a loving individual or even into someone who would rather read a book than go cruising. We are saying, however, that for the majority of young readers, books can be a conversation starter and a way to focus needed attention on the matter of hostility related to racial, ethnic, and class differences.

In the fifth edition of this textbook, we provided Focus Boxes of books written about various ethnic groups. We pulled them together simply because we were so frequently asked to provide lists of books about members of minority groups, but for both philosophical and pedagogical reasons we feel uncomfortable in grouping books based on the race or ethnicity of the characters. We would rather focus on the experience that the characters are having, and we welcome the trend for "differentness" to include more than skin color. Hazel Rochman's professional book, *Against Borders: Promoting Books for a Multicultural World,* is a good illustration of diverse cultures coming together. Before she goes to the expected treatments of racial oppression and ethnic differences, she has chapters treating such themes as "The Perilous Journey," "The Hero and the Monster," "Lovers and Strangers," "Family Matters," and "Finding the Way Home."

The idea that authors can write only about their own ethnic group is being challenged by the many books now being written about interactions among people from different ethnic groups. See Focus Box 4.4 for examples.

We must realize as well that some authors prefer to focus on the similarities among all people rather than on differences between particular groups. For example, African-American author Lorenz Graham is quoted in Anne Commire's *Something About the Author* as saying

> My personal problem with publishers has been the difference between my image and theirs. Publishers have told me that my characters, African and Negro, are "too much like white people." And I say, "If you look closely you will see that people are people."[4]

Jamake Highwater expresses a counterbalancing view.

> In the process of trying to unify the world we must be exceedingly careful not to destroy the diversity of the many cultures of man that give human life meaning, focus, and vitality. . . . Today we are beginning to look into the ideas of groups outside the dominant culture, and we are finding different kinds of "truth" that make the world we live in far bigger than we ever dreamed it could be—for the greatest distance between people is not geographical space but culture.[5]

FOCUS BOX 4.4

Relating Across Cultures

Bat 6 by Virginia Euwer Wolff. Scholastic, 1998. World War II has been over for nearly four years, but pockets of prejudice are very much alive in the towns of Barlow and Bear Creek Ridge in rural Oregon. People choose not to notice until the prejudice erupts during the annual Bat 6 softball game.

The Brave by Robert Lipsyte. HarperCollins, 1991. Sonny Bear, an up-and-coming young boxer, leaves the Moscondaga reservation and ends up in Harlem where, fortunately, not all the people he meets are as devious as his self-appointed welcoming committee.

The Cay (Doubleday, 1969) and **Timothy of the Cay** (Harcourt, 1993) by Theodore Taylor. A 15-year-old white boy, Philip, and an elderly black man, Timothy, are the only survivors from a shipwreck. They are on an island, and Philip, who is blind, must overcome his aversion to blacks before he can accept Timothy's help.

Children of the River by Linda Crew. Delacorte, 1989. One of the first young adult novels to come to grips with the tremendous adjustments that today's refugees must make, Crew's story is about 17-year-old Sundara's life in Oregon after fleeing the Khmer Rouge in Cambodia.

The Circuit: Stories from the Life of a Migrant Child by Francisco Jiménez. University of New Mexico Press, 1997. Even though this collection of autobiographical stories was published by a university press, which means it didn't get the same kind of publicity and promotion as that provided by commercial presses, by 1999, it was already in its fifth printing.

Jubilee Journey by Carolyn Meyer. Harcourt Brace, 1997. Going on a family trip from Connecticut to a small town in Texas proves to be educational for 13-year-old Emily Rose Chartier who learns both about racism and her family.

Seedfolks by Paul Fleischman. HarperCollins, 1997. Fleischman traces the sprouting of the Gibb Street community garden in inner city Cleveland through the voices of thirteen young and old neighbors—Mexican, Haitian, Black, Vietnamese, Korean, British, Guatemalan, Rumanian, Indian, and Polish.

Sisters/Hermanas by Gary Paulsen. Harcourt Brace, 1993. Two girls, one an affluent American and one a Mexican girl trying to "make it" in a strange culture, cross paths and realize they have much in common.

Slave Day by Rob Thomas. Simon & Schuster, 1997. A Southern high school has "always" held a Slave Day auction to raise funds, but this year events and characters conspire to make the students, faculty, and townspeople rethink the whole activity.

Star of Luis by Marc Talbert. Clarion, 1999. When Luis's father joins the army at the beginning of World War II, Luis and his mother move to New Mexico to live with her father. By the time they return to Los Angeles, Luis has learned much about both himself and about various forms of prejudice.

The Starplace by Vicki Grove. Putnam, 1999. It is the beginning of the 1960s in Quiver, Oklahoma. Celeste Chisholm, the first black student at a previously all-white school, has a beautiful singing voice and becomes best friends with another singer. They both learn some things about prejudice.

When the Legends Die by Hal Borland. HarperCollins, 1963. In one of the first books about a young adult growing up in two cultures, Borland tells about a Ute boy raised by whites after the death of his parents. A 1972 movie starring Richard Widmark and Fredric Forrest was well received.

A White Romance by Virginia Hamilton. Philomel, 1987. Talley Barbour's life changes when she becomes best friends with a white girl and then is courted by a white boy who is into drugs and a whole different lifestyle. As the story progresses, Talley discovers some differences more important than skin color.

Zack by William Bell. Simon & Schuster, 1999. It is Zack's senior year in high school and his family (a black mother and a white father) move from the city of Toronto to a small town where, for the first time, Zack stands out because of his color.

By having characters from different groups involved in the same activities, authors can show a spectrum of actions and attitudes. Bruce Brooks's *The Moves Make the Man* is basically a quest story of accomplishment, and it almost does not matter that with the two best friends, one is African-American and the other is white. But when white Bix comes to dinner at African-American Jerome's house, big brother and future psychologist Maurice is disappointed that they are going to have a white guest because he had hoped for some "in-house observation." The rest of Jerome's family laughs at Maurice's disappointment and his pretentious pronouncement that, "Counseling across the color line is notoriously fruitless, due to preconditions of mistrust." But when Bix arrives, Jerome is surprised to see that his old friend has equally strange expectations. When he is introduced to younger brother Henri, Bix gives Henri an awkward high-five and says, "Dig it."

> Now, dig it is a very stupid thing to say when being introduced. Henri did not notice, but I did, and I thought it was queer. But when Maurice was there and I introduced him and he peered at Bix like to see if there was any chance of busting the color line with a little counseling anyway, and Bix grinned right into his stare and held out his hand and said, What be happening, Maurice my man?
>
> Maurice, who does not know jive talk from bird song, just looked confused and said Fine thank you and shook hands, but I was nearabout flipped. What be happening, Maurice my man? Where did Bix get this jive talking junk? It was ridiculous.

This light-hearted treatment of stereotypes is possible because today's young readers are more sophisticated about ethnic and racial differences. A generation ago, many white, middle-class readers had been so isolated from other racial groups that learning the generalities—what some would call the stereotypes—was a kind of progress. Today most teenagers are ready to go beyond those stereotypes.

This means that teachers, librarians, and reviewers should not present books and discuss them as if they represent *the* African-American point of view or *the* Asian-American point of view. Adults need to help young readers realize that people are individuals first and members of particular groups second. In John Patrick's play *The Teahouse of the August Moon,* one of the lines that gets a big laugh from the white, middle-class American audiences is about all Americans looking alike. The audience laughs because the tables are turned on an old joke, and a glimpse is provided of how ridiculous it is to think of any group of individuals as carbon copies of one another.

Perhaps for the sake of efficiency, history and social studies textbooks have to lump people together and talk about them according to the characteristics of the majority in the group, but good literature can counterbalance these generalizations and show individual perspectives. When students have read enough to go beyond the stereotypes of at least one group, they are more aware that the study of people as groups needs to be filled in with individual portrayals.

Something similar can be said about books set in other countries. Because of increased travel opportunities and the closer editorial and business relationships among the world's publishers, American companies are arranging to distribute more books originally published in other countries (see Focus Box 4.5, Teens in the World Around Us).

Because of an increase in travel and exchange programs, more young adults are coming to libraries and asking for both fiction and nonfiction from or about other countries. See Focus Box 4.5 for books set in other countries.

Body and Self

Books that treat problems related to accepting and effectively using one's physical body are treated in several sections of this text. When the physical problem is relatively minor, or is at least one that can be corrected, it might be treated as an accomplishment-romance, discussed in Chapter Five. Also, many nonfiction books as well as sports stories focus on the physical body, and in many realistic novels, physical problems serve as a concrete or visible symbol for mental growth, which is harder to show.

It is almost obligatory in realistic fiction for young protagonists to express dissatisfaction with their appearance. Part of this is because hardly anyone has a perfect body or has not envied others for their appearance or physical skill. A bigger part is that adolescent bodies are changing so fast that their owners have not yet had time to adjust. The reason they spend so much time looking in mirrors is to reassure themselves, "Yes, this is me!"

In 1970, Judy Blume surprised the world of juvenile fiction by writing a book that gave major attention to physical aspects of growing up. In *Are You There, God?*

Teens in the World Around Us

The Baboon King by Anton Quintana. Translated from Dutch by John Nieuwenhuizen. Walker, 1999. This grand adventure story takes place in East Africa with the hero being caught between two cultures. Ironically, it is a tribe of baboons who teach him about his own humanity.

Beyond the Mango Tree by Amy Bronwen Zemser. Greenwillow, 1998. Told by a 12-year-old, white American girl living in Liberia, this contemporary novel lets readers in on some of the not-so-positive aspects of living as a stranger in a culture, even if it is in a privileged position.

Close-Up by Szabinka Dudevszky, photos by Peter Kers, translated from Dutch by Wanda Boeke. Front Street, 1999. Fifteen teenagers all from the Netherlands talk about what it's like to live apart from their parents. Dudevszky got the idea of doing this book when in 1996 she conducted a series of interviews for an educational film and found that this topic aroused the most heartfelt statements.

Damned Strong Love: The True Story of Willi G. and Stephan K. by Lutz Van Dijk, translated from German by Elizabeth D. Crawford. Holt, 1995. Although this is a novel, it is based on an incident during World War II when two young men fell in love with each other. One was a Nazi soldier and the other a Polish actor.

The Eternal Spring of Mr. Ito by Sheila Garrigue. Simon & Schuster, 1994. Set in Canada during World War II, this is the story of the relationship between a Japanese-American gardener and an English girl sent to Canada for safekeeping.

Habibi by Naomi Shihab Nye. Simon & Schuster, 1997. Students accustomed to reading about immigrants coming to the United States might be intrigued by this story of a Palestinian American family moving from St. Louis to Jerusalem where 14-year-old Liyana gets acquainted with her father's family and learns about the tensions between Arabs and Israelis.

Haveli by Suzanne Fisher Staples. Knopf, 1993. In this sequel to the well-received *Shabanu: Daughter of the Wind* (Knopf, 1989), Staples continues the story of the strong-willed young woman who because of custom and family needs becomes the fourth wife of a powerful landowner in the Cholistan desert of Pakistan.

Letters from the Inside by John Marsden. Houghton Mifflin, 1994. Two Australian girls are penpals, each thinking that the other one has a wonderful life, but their letters gradually reveal that one is incarcerated and the other one is in her own kind of prison.

The Long Season of Rain by Helen Kim. Holt, 1996. The year is 1969 and the country is South Korea. When an orphaned boy is taken in by a family with several daughters the group dynamics are drastically changed.

No Turning Back: A Novel of South Africa by Beverley Naidoo. HarperCollins, 1997. Sipho is a 12-year-old black boy who lives on the streets in the suburbs of Johannesburg but eventually manages to find a home. Naidoo's earlier South African novels for preteens include *Journey to Jo'Burg: A South African Story* (Lippincott, 1986) and *Chain of Fire* (Lippincott, 1990).

One Bird by Kyoko Mori. Holt, 1995. A contemporary Japanese girl gradually learns to defy tradition and her father's demands as she welcomes and accepts her mother who had left the household because of her father's unfaithfulness. In Mori's earlier *Shizuko's Daughter* (Holt, 1993) a young woman comes to terms with her mother's suicide.

Peter by Kate Walker. Houghton, 1993. In this emotional story, a 15-year-old Australian boy tries to sort out the differences between the reality and the stereotypes of being gay.

Secret Letters from 0 to 10 by Susie Morgenstern, illustrated by Gill Rosner. Viking, 1998. Having won the French equivalent of our Newbery Award, Morgenstern's book is likely to appeal to preteens as it brings them into the sheltered life of a 10-year-old boy raised by his overly strict grandmother.

The Spring Tone by Kazumi Yumoto, translated from Japanese by Cathy Hirano. Farrar, Straus & Giroux, 1999. Tomomi, who is just entering junior high school, has a lot to cope with. Her grandmother has just died, she believes her father has deserted the family, her brother Tetsu is acting out, and she has nightmares about turning into a monster.

The Storyteller's Beads by Jane Kurtz. Harcourt/Gulliver, 1998. In this Ethiopian story set in the 1980s, Sahay and Rahel are part of a group making a dangerous trek to the Sudan in hopes of escaping the war and the famine in Ethiopia. When the men are turned back at the border, Sahay and Rahel go on even though Rahel is a blind Jewish girl and Sahay has been raised to hate and mistrust Jews.

Tonight by Sea by Frances Temple. Orchard, 1995. Paulie's uncle builds a boat planning for the family to escape by sea from the troubles of their Haitian community of Belle Fleuve. But before this comes about, Paulie is off on a journey of her own. Temple also wrote *Taste of Salt: A Story of Modern Haiti* (Orchard, 1992) and *Grab Hands and Run* (Orchard, 1993), which is about a family fleeing El Salvador.

It's Me, Margaret, Margaret Simon worries because her breasts are small and because she's afraid she will be the last one in her crowd to begin menstruating. A later Blume book, *Then Again, Maybe I Won't,* features Tony Miglione and his newly affluent family. He too worries about his developing body. In fact, he carries a jacket even on the warmest days so that he will have something to hide behind in case he has an erection. These books are read mostly by younger adolescents. But both junior and senior high students read Blume's *Deenie.* It is about a pretty teenager whose mother wants her to be a model, but then it's discovered that she has scoliosis and must wear an unsightly back brace. A minor point that goes unnoticed by some readers (but not by censors) is Deenie's worry that her back problems might be related to the fact that she masturbates. Because Blume ties physical development in with emotional and social development, her books are more fun to read (and more controversial) than are factual books about the development of the human body.

The problem novel does not stop with treating the more or less typical problems of growing up. Several of the books in Focus Box 4.1 treat mental and physical disabilities. Alden Carter's *Up Country* and Gary Paulsen's *Harris and Me* explore various aspects of parental alcoholism, while Robert Cormier's *We All Fall Down* explores teenage alcoholism.

Some of the most powerful problem novels are those that deal with death (see Focus Box 4.6, Dying Is Easy; Surviving Is Hard). In Gunnel Beckman's *Admission to the Feast,* 19-year-old Annika Hallin accidentally learns from a substitute doctor that she has leukemia. She flees by herself to her family's summer cottage, where she tries to sort out her reactions:

> I don't think I understood it until last night . . . that I, Annika, . . . will just be put away, wiped out, obliterated. . . . And here on earth everything will just go on. . . . I shall never have more than this little scrap of life.

Although Katherine Paterson's *Bridge to Terabithia* is considered a children's book because it's about two fifth-graders, we know several young adults who have read it and wept, as have many adults. Jean Ferris's *Invincible Summer* is a restrained

FOCUS BOX 4.6

Dying Is Easy; Surviving Is Hard

The Bell Jar by Sylvia Plath. HarperCollins, 1971. Mature teens are still fascinated by this story of a young woman who does more than flirt with suicide.

The Dark Light by Mette Newth, translated by Faith Ingwersen. Farrar, Straus & Giroux, 1998. Set in Norway more than a century ago, this is the intriguing story of 13-year-old Tora's heartbreaking attempts to figure out the meaning of life, God, happiness, and revenge as she lies dying of leprosy in a Bergen hospital.

The Eagle Kite by Paula Fox. Orchard, 1995. As a high school freshman, Liam learns that his father is dying of AIDS. His grief is complicated by anger as well as by the frustrations of change when his father moves out of the family apartment.

Homeless Bird by Gloria Whelan. Harper-Collins, 2000. Set in India, this is the story of a young bride who discovers that the money in her dowry was to be used for medical care for her 16-year-old groom who is dying of tuberculosis. In spite of the money, he dies and 13-year-old Koly is left a widow.

I Miss You, I Miss You by Peter Pohl and Kinna Gieth, translated from Swedish by Roger Greenwald. Farrar, Straus & Giroux, 1999. Having a sibling die is always traumatic, but it is worse for Tina because Cilla, killed by an automobile as she ran for the school bus just a few steps behind Tina, was her identical twin.

The Man Without a Face by Isabelle Holland. HarperCollins, 1972. The high-powered 1993 movie starring Mel Gibson gave a new burst of popularity to Holland's story of 14-year-old Charles who is left to adjust to the death of his friend and tutor.

My Brother Stealing Second by Jim Naughton. HarperCollins, 1989. While star athlete and favorite son Billy is drunk, he kills himself as well as a couple celebrating their wedding anniversary. His parents and brother, along with the daughter of the couple, suffer but survive.

Remembering Mog by Colby Rodowsky. Farrar, Straus & Giroux, 1996. It is Annie's high school graduation, but neither she nor her family can celebrate because the event is a grim reminder of her older sister's murder two years earlier.

Say Goodnight, Gracie by Julie Reece Deaver. HarperCollins, 1988. When Jimmy is killed by a drunk driver, Morgan realizes how much he meant to her, then and now.

Saying It Out Loud by Joan Abelove. Dorling Kindersley Ink, 1999. In this story from the 1960s, Mindy's mother has a brain tumor, which her father refuses to discuss. Two good friends help.

A Summer to Die by Lois Lowry. Houghton Mifflin, 1977. While her older sister is dying of leukemia, Meg finds comfort and solace in the help that comes from 70-year-old Will Banks, landlord, handyman, and photographer.

Tell Me Everything by Caroline Coman. Farrar, Straus & Giroux, 1993. Twelve-year-old Roz and her mother, Ellie, have an exceptionally close and spiritual relationship in their secluded mountain home. When Ellie is killed while trying to rescue a hiker, Roz must face her loss while also making a new life.

Someone Like You by Sarah Dessen. Viking, 1998. This is basically the story of Halley and Scarlett's friendship and how it is affected when one of them gets a boyfriend and gets pregnant and then that boyfriend dies.

but sad love story about two teenagers with leukemia. The boy, Rick, dies, but the book ends with readers and the girl, Robin, still uncertain about her prognosis and her future. Of course, she wants to live, but she consoles herself by thinking that if the treatments are unsuccessful, as Rick's were, if it were truly going to be "lights out, the end, eternal sleep, then what was there to worry about?" If she were going to be someplace, then Rick would be there too.

Sex-Related Problems

Among the books listed in Focus Box 4.1, Challenges—Physical and Emotional, are several relating to sex, but lest we leave the impression that we look at sex only as a problem, we hasten to add that discussions of the matter also appear in Chapter Five under "Love Romances" and in Chapter Nine under "Informational Books."

In trying to satisfy their curiosity, teenagers seek out and read the vivid descriptions of sexual activity in such books as Scott Spencer's *Endless Love* and William Hogan's *The Quartzsite Trip*, both published for adults but featuring young protagonists. Male and female readers have also been intrigued by Don Bredes's *Hard Feelings*, Terry Davis's *Vision Quest*, Jay Daly's *Walls*, and Aidan Chambers's *Breaktime*, all coming-of-age stories that focus on young men's sexual desires. Books intended primarily for young women are more likely to focus on romantic elements of a story, while only hinting at the characters' sexuality.

In the first edition of this textbook, we wrote that the three sexual issues treated in problem novels were rape, homosexuality, and premarital sex resulting in pregnancy. For the next two editions we added disease, incest, and child abuse, and for these last two editions we have added teenagers as parents. In the earlier books, pregnant girls had an abortion as in Paul Zindel's *My Darling, My Hamburger,* the baby died as in Ann Head's *Mr. and Mrs. Bo Jo Jones,* or the baby was given up for adoption as in Richard Peck's *Don't Look and It Won't Hurt.* In today's books the babies actually appear as in the highly acclaimed *Make Lemonade* by Virginia Euwer Wolff, *Gypsy Davey* by Chris Lynch, and *Like Sisters on the Home Front* by Rita Williams-Garcia.

While the physical aspects of sex-related problems are important parts of the stories, it's really the emotional aspects that interest most readers. A few years ago when Paul Zindel was speaking in Arizona, he commented on the fact that next to *The Pigman,* his most popular book was *My Darling, My Hamburger,* which is about pregnancy and abortion. Soon after the book was published in 1969, a Supreme Court decision made most abortions legal, and Zindel thought that would be the end of all sales because his book would seem terribly old-fashioned. It didn't turn out that way, however, because rather than settling the issue, the legalization of abortions increased interest in the moral and psychological aspects of the problem. Decision making was passed from the courts to every woman with an unwanted pregnancy. It is not only the woman herself who is involved, but also the father, the grandparents, and the friends.

Three landmark books opened the door to the treatment of homosexuality in books for young readers. They were John Donovan's *I'll Get There. It Better Be Worth the Trip* in 1969, Isabelle Holland's *The Man Without a Face,* and Lynn Hall's *Sticks and Stones,* both in 1972. The protagonists are male, and in all three books an important character dies. In none can a direct cause-and-effect relationship be charted between the death and the homosexual behavior, but possibilities for blame are there. Because the three books were all published within a relatively short period, critics were quick to object to the cumulative implications that homosexual behavior will be punished with some dreadful event. Despite this criticism, Sandra Scoppettone's *Trying Hard to Hear You,* published in 1974, was surprisingly similar, ending in an automobile accident that killed one of the teenage male lovers.

Books featuring female homosexuals were almost a decade behind the ones about males. In 1976, Rosa Guy published *Ruby,* which was a sequel to *The Friends.*

Ruby is Phyllisia's older sister, and in the book she has a lesbian relationship with a beautiful classmate. *Publishers Weekly* described the homosexuality in the book as "perhaps just a way-step toward maturity." This relaxed attitude toward female homosexuality was reflected in Deborah Hautzig's 1978 *Hey Dollface* and in Nancy Garden's 1982 *Annie on My Mind,* which was praised for its strong characterization and tender love story.

One of the strengths of M. E. Kerr's 1994 *Deliver Us from Evie* is that although it is an issues book intended to make readers give second thoughts to various aspects of lesbianism, it is not limited to the one issue. The narrator is Parr Burrman, who is almost 16 and tells the story in what one reviewer described as a voice "perfectly pitched between wit and melancholy."[6] It is the story of one year in the life of a Missouri farm family when they lose much of their farm to a flood and come close to losing Parr's sister, 18-year-old Evie, to community prejudices and family bad feelings. Kerr touches on the complications of friendships that cross socioeconomic and religious lines and, more importantly, on family dynamics when one player in a carefully structured pyramid pulls out.

In actuality, the big sex-related problems—rape, abuse, disease, homosexuality, and unwanted pregnancy—are experienced by relatively few teenagers, but nearly all young people wonder about the moral and social implications of experimenting with sexual activity, whether or not it leads to intercourse.

To get direct answers to their questions, young readers can turn to the informational books discussed in Chapter Nine. Because the questions they are most concerned with involve moral, emotional, and psychological issues, the fuller kinds of fictional treatments described here continue to be popular.

The Future of the Problem Novel From Realism to Postmodernism

We are willing to predict that authors will continue to write problem novels and young adults will continue to read them. As we demonstrated in Chapter Three, however, adolescent literature does not exist in a vacuum separate from the literature of the rest of the world. It is more than a coincidence that when the problem novel appeared in the late 1960s, great changes were taking place in American society and literature as a whole. The world was a new and scary place, with the imaginative fallout from the atomic bomb being a recognition that human extinction was quite possible.

In literature, belief in an ordered universe was gradually being replaced with theories about reader response and deconstructionism. The idea of deconstructionism is that what seems to be an event in a piece of literature is really a construct created through language. As a linguistic construct, it can also be undone or deconstructed through language. In a 1991 interview with CNN's Larry King, Norman Mailer illustrated the difference between how structuralists and deconstructionists might approach the same piece of literature. In structural terminology, a piece that is experientially true and is an author's honest attempt to depict people in ordinary situations without sentimentalizing or glossing over anything would probably be described as *realism*. In contrast, Mailer, representing the deconstructionist viewpoint, claims that as soon as a character—whether real or imagined—is written about, fiction results because the character now lives as imagined in people's minds rather than as a real person who can be talked to and touched. This is why in *Anatomy of Criticism,* Northrop Frye puts quotes around the term *realism* and why G. Robert Carlsen has written that

> If we evaluate literature by its realism alone, we should be forced to abandon most of the truly great literature of the world: certainly most of tragedy, much of comedy, and all of romance. We would be forced to discard the Greek plays, the great epics, Shakespeare, Molière. They succeed because they go beyond the externals of living and instead reach out and touch that imaginative life deep down inside where we live.[7]

As writers in the 1960s began searching for new ways to "touch that imaginative life," they experimented with postmodernism (a literary term invented as an almost joking corollary to the art term of *postimpressionism*) and with black humor, in which authors distorted their observations of people and events by exaggerating the negatives and minimizing the positives. Although bright and sophisticated teenagers were quick to appreciate some of these writings, including Ken Kesey's *One Flew Over the Cuckoo's Nest,* Kurt Vonnegut's *Slaughterhouse-Five,* and Joseph Heller's *Catch–22,* it is doubtful that authors for young people are ever going to be comfortable with the idea of writing about antiheroes suffering from alienation or with simply holding up life's absurdities.

Nevertheless, as authors of problem novels try not to repeat themselves and try to pluck psychic strings that remain untouched by superficial media stories, they are pulled in the same directions as writers for adults. Among the reasons that Kesey's, Vonnegut's, and Heller's writing is so appealing is that these authors juxtapose humor and pathos for the purpose of creating emotional tension or frustration. As Terry Heller has observed

> By repeatedly calling upon the reader to shift his interpretations of the incident, to laugh only to weep only to laugh only to weep again, [the author] suspends the reader between two poles.[8]

Another characteristic of black humorists is that they reject boundaries between realism and fantasy. Their writing exhibits what Bruce Friedman has described as "a nervousness, an upbeat tempo, a near hysteria or frenzy."[9] Some thirty years after Friedman observed this about the writing of such fellow authors as Thomas Pynchon, J. P. Donleavy, Vladimir Nabokov, Edward Albee, John Barth, Terry Southern, and James Purdy, it is almost a perfect description of Francesca Lia Block's books for young adults. While she focuses on the same kinds of problems as do other writers of YA problem novels, including loneliness, alienation, sexual problems, and love, she accepts wholeheartedly the deconstructionist idea of creating her own world and then working within it. Readers who are puzzled or troubled by her books are usually those accustomed to looking for a kind of "realism" that can be tested against their own observations or against statistics of probability.

Virginia Hamilton was one of the first writers to mix a fantasy element in a problem novel when in her 1982 *Sweet Whispers, Brother Rush* she had the ghost of

Teresa's uncle help the troubled 14-year-old understand her family's history and its relationship to her dearly beloved, retarded brother. In her 1990 *The Silver Kiss,* Annette Curtis Klause created a vampire ghost to help Zoë adjust to her mother's death, while Robert Cormier's 1988 *Fade* is about the struggles of young Paul Moreaux, who through his inherited ability to be invisible begins to understand the difference between good and evil. Lois Lowry's 1993 Newbery Award–winning *The Giver* is all the more interesting because it is set in a dystopian future society as is Peter Dickinson's 1989 *Eva.* Both of these books make use of a fading line between fantasy and reality as they pursue the major question faced by teenagers and treated in many problem novels: "Who am I?"

These various examples of imaginative stories are further discussed in later chapters. They are mentioned here to illustrate how physical and emotional problems are being treated in new ways. While we, along with many readers, continue to appreciate well-done problem novels of the kind that were considered an innovation in the late 1960s and the 1970s, we are at the same time pleased to realize that the field is not standing still. Many of today's writers are finding new ways to treat old problems.

Notes

[1] Alleen Pace Nilsen, "The Poetry of Naming in Young Adult Books," *ALAN Review* 7 (Spring 1980): 3–4, 31.

[2] "Immigrant Impact Grows on U.S. Population," *Wall Street Journal,* March 16, 1992.

[3] George Keller, Director of Strategic Planning for the University of Pennsylvania outlined these changes in a workshop at Arizona State University, February 14, 1992.

[4] Anne Commire, *Something about the Author,* Vol. 2 (Gale Research, 1971), pp. 122–23.

[5] Jamake Highwater, *Many Smokes, Many Moons* (Lippincott, 1978), pp. 13–14.

[6] Annotation of *Deliver Us from Evie,* "Editors' Choice '94", *Booklist* 91 (January 15, 1995): 859.

[7] G. Robert Carlsen, "Bait/Rebait: Literature Isn't Supposed to Be Realistic," *English Journal* 70 (January 1981): 8.

[8] Terry Heller, "Notes on Technique in Black Humor," *Thalia: Studies in Literary Humor* 2.3 (Winter 1979–80): 16.

[9] Bruce J. Freidman, ed. *Black Humor.* New York: Bantam, 1965.

Titles Mentioned in the Text of Chapter Four

Angelou, Maya. *I Know Why the Caged Bird Sings.* Random House, 1976.

Armstrong, William. *Sounder.* HarperCollins, 1969.

Beckman, Gunnel. *Admission to the Feast.* Holt, 1972.

Blume, Judy. *Are You There God? It's Me, Margaret.* Bradbury, 1970.

Blume, Judy. *Deenie.* Bradbury, 1973.

Blume, Judy. *Then Again, Maybe I Won't.* Bradbury, 1971.

Blume, Judy. *Tiger Eyes.* Bradbury, 1981.

Bredes, Don. *Hard Feelings.* Atheneum, 1977.

Brooks, Bruce. *The Moves Make the Man.* HarperCollins, 1986.

Butler, Samuel. *The Way of All Flesh.* Richards, 1903.

Byars, Betsy. *The Night Swimmers.* Delacorte, 1980.

Carter, Alden. *Up Country.* Putnam, 1989.

Chambers, Aidan. *Breaktime.* HarperCollins, 1979.

Chbosky, Stephen. *The Perks of Being a Wallflower.* MTV/Pocket Books, 1999.

Childress, Alice. *A Hero Ain't Nothin' But a Sandwich.* Coward, McCann, 1973.

Cleaver, Eldridge. *Soul on Ice.* McGraw-Hill, 1968.

Cleaver, Vera and Bill. *Trial Valley.* Lippincott, 1977.

Cleaver, Vera and Bill. *Where the Lilies Bloom.* HarperCollins, 1969.

Cole, Brock. *The Facts Speak for Themselves.* Front Street, 1997.

Commire, Anne. *Something About the Author,* Gale Research, 1971.

Cormier, Robert. *The Chocolate War.* Pantheon, 1974.

Cormier, Robert. *Fade*. Delacorte, 1988.

Cormier, Robert. *We All Fall Down*. Delacorte, 1991.

Daly, Jay. *Walls*. HarperCollins, 1980.

Davis, Terry. *Vision Quest*. Viking, 1979.

Dickinson, Peter. *Eva*. Delacorte, 1989.

Donovan, John. *I'll Get There. It Better Be Worth the Trip*. HarperCollins, 1969.

Ferris, Jean. *Invincible Summer*. Farrar, Straus & Giroux, 1987.

Fleischman, Paul. *Seedfolks*. HarperCollins, 1997.

Fox, Paula. *A Place Apart*. Farrar, Straus & Giroux, 1982.

Frye, Northrop. *Anatomy of Criticism*. Princeton University Press, 1957.

Garden, Nancy. *Annie on My Mind*. Farrar, Straus & Giroux, 1982.

Goethe, Johann Wolfgang von. *Wilhelm Meister's Apprenticeship*, 1795–96.

Golding, William. *Lord of the Flies*. Putnam, 1955.

Guy, Rosa. *The Friends*. Holt, 1973.

Guy, Rosa. *Ruby*. Viking, 1976.

Hall, Lynn. *Sticks and Stones*. Follett, 1972.

Hamilton, Virginia, *Sweet Whispers, Brother Rush*. Philomel, 1982.

Hautzig, Deborah. *Hey Dollface*. Morrow, 1978.

Head, Ann. *Mr. and Mrs. Bo Jo Jones*. Putnam, 1967.

Heller, Joseph. *Catch 22*, Simon & Schuster, 1961.

Hinton, S. E. *The Outsiders*. Viking, 1967.

Hinton, S. E. *Tex*. Delacorte, 1979.

Hogan, William. *The Quartzsite Trip*. Atheneum, 1980.

Holland, Isabelle. *The Man Without a Face*. Lippincott, 1972.

Joyce, James. *A Portrait of the Artist as a Young Man*. Huebisch, 1916.

Kerr, M. E. *Deliver Us from Evie*. HarperCollins, 1994.

Kesey, Ken. *One Flew Over the Cuckoo's Nest*. Viking, 1962.

Kincaid, Jamaica. *Annie John*. Farrar, Straus & Giroux, 1985.

Klause, Annette Curtis. *The Silver Kiss*. Delacorte, 1990.

Lee, Harper. *To Kill a Mockingbird*. Lippincott, 1960.

Lowry, Lois. *The Giver*. Houghton Mifflin, 1993.

Lynch, Chris. *Gypsy Davey*. HarperCollins, 1994.

Lynch, Chris. *Iceman*. HarperCollins, 1994.

Mathis, Sharon Bell. *Teacup Full of Roses*. Viking, 1975.

Maugham, Somerset. *Of Human Bondage,* Doran, 1915.

Mazer, Norma Fox. *When She Was Good*. Scholastic, 1997.

Paterson, Katherine. *Bridge to Terabithia*. Crowell, 1977.

Patrick, John. *The Teahouse of the August Moon*. Dramatists, 1953.

Paulsen, Gary. *Harris and Me*. Harcourt, 1993.

Peck, Richard. *Don't Look and It Won't Hurt*. Holt, 1972.

Peck, Richard. *Remembering the Good Times*. Delacorte, 1985.

Plath, Sylvia. *The Bell Jar*. HarperCollins, 1971.

Potok, Chaim. *The Chosen*. Simon & Schuster, 1967.

Rochman, Hazel. *Against Borders: Promoting Books for a Multicultural World*. American Library Association, 1993.

Rylant, Cynthia. *Missing May*. Orchard, 1992.

Salinger, J. D. *The Catcher in the Rye*. Little, Brown, 1951.

Scoppettone, Sandra. *Trying Hard to Hear You*. HarperCollins, 1974.

Soto, Gary. *Buried Onions*. Harcourt Brace, 1997.

Spencer, Scott. *Endless Love*. Knopf, 1979.

Thomas, Rob. *Rats Saw God*. Simon & Schuster, 1996.

Voigt, Cynthia. *Dicey's Song*. Atheneum, 1982.

Voigt, Cynthia. *When She Hollers*. Scholastic, 1994.

Vonnegut, Kurt, Jr. *Slaughterhouse-Five*. Delacorte, 1969.

Williams-Garcia, Rita. *Like Sisters on the Home Front*, Lodestar, 1995.

Wolff, Virginia Euwer. *Make Lemonade*. Holt, 1993.

Zindel, Paul. *My Darling, My Hamburger*. HarperCollins, 1969.

Zindel, Paul. *The Pigman*. HarperCollins, 1968.

Information on the availability of paperback editions of these titles is available online from such book sellers as Barnes & Noble and Amazon.com, and through *Books in Print* compiled by R. R. Bowker Company and available either in person or online from major libraries.

5

The Old Romanticism
Of Wishing and Winning

Romances serve as a counterbalance to the depressing realism of the problem novel. They have happy endings, and their tellers can exaggerate just enough to make the stories more interesting than real life. There is usually a quest of some sort in which the protagonist experiences doubts and undergoes severe trials, but he or she is successful in the end. This success is all the more appreciated because of the difficulties the protagonist has suffered. In bad moments, the extremes of suffering resemble a nightmare, but in good times the successes are like happy daydreams.

The word *romance* comes from the Latin adverb *romanice,* which means "in the Roman (i.e., the Latin) manner." It is with this meaning that Latin, Italian, Spanish, and French are described as romance languages. The literary meaning of *romance* grew out of its use by English speakers to refer to French dialects, which were much closer to Latin than was their own Germanic language of English. Later, it was used to refer to Old French and finally to anything written in French.

Many of the French stories read by English speakers were tales about knights who set out on bold adventures, slaying dragons, rescuing princesses from ogres, and defeating the wicked enemies of a righteous king. Love was often an element in these stories because the knight was striving to win the hand of a beloved maiden. Today, when a literary piece is referred to as a romance, it usually contains adventure or love or both.

The romance is appealing to teenagers because many romantic symbols relate to youthfulness and hope, and many of the protagonists even in traditional and classic tales are in their teens. They have reached the age at which they leave home or anticipate leaving to embark on a new way of life. This is more likely to be called "moving out" than "going on a romantic quest," but the results are much the same. Seeking and securing a "true love" usually but not always takes up a greater proportion of the time and energy of young adults than of middle-aged adults. The exaggeration that is part of the romantic mode is quite honestly felt by teenagers. Robert Cormier once said that he began writing about young protagonists when he observed that in one afternoon at the beach his own children could go through what to an adult would be a whole month of emotional experiences.

This range of emotions sometimes makes it difficult to decide whether a book is a realistic problem novel or a romance. Author Richard Peck has observed that teenage readers really want "romanticism masked as realism"—they want both the happy ending and the assurance that happy endings really do happen. This truism encourages authors of problem novels to incorporate at least some elements of romanticism in their problem novels, which makes for an overlap. Some of the "heavier" books talked about in this chapter and some of the "lighter" books talked about in Chapter Four might be one and the same.

Deciding whether to label a book a "problem novel" or a "romantic quest" could depend on which aspects of the book most strongly touched the reader's emotions. Because young people are characteristically viewed as optimists, a writer working with basically the same plot in a story to be published for a general adult audience might be inclined to present the adult story in an ironic mode but the young adult story in a romantic mode. For example, three popular quest stories about young protagonists that were published as somber adult novels are J. D. Salinger's *The Catcher in the Rye,* Hannah Green's *I Never Promised You a Rose Garden,* and Judith Guest's *Ordinary People.* In all three, worthy young heroes set out to find wisdom and understanding. They make physical sacrifices, including suicide

While the same problems may be treated in realistic problem novels and in romances, the approach will be different. For example, young people who have genuine worries about their changing bodies may be reassured by the lighthearted exaggeration in Rodman Philbrick's *Max the Mighty*.

attempts, and even though they receive help from wise and kindly psychiatrists (today's counterpart to the white witches, the wizards, and the helpful gods and goddesses of traditional romances), they must prove their worthiness through hard, painstaking work. This is what Deborah Blau's psychiatrist communicates in the phrase used for the book's title, *I Never Promised You a Rose Garden*. If Green's book had been a romance, there would have been no such reminder of life's difficulties. Readers could have imagined Deborah leaving the mental institution and living "happily ever after."

In contrast, *It Happened to Nancy* is a grim story that is nevertheless written in the romantic mode. It is advertised as a true story taken from the diary of an anonymous girl who "thought she'd found love but instead lost her life to AIDS." The editor is Beatrice Sparks, the same author who back in the late 1960s did *Go Ask Alice* (at the time identified as *anonymous*) about a young drug addict. Like Alice, Nancy dies at the end of the book, which is certainly a chilling touch of realism, but there are several other elements of the story that made Frances Bradburn ask questions similar to the ones that critics asked about *Go Ask Alice*: "Is this really a teen's diary, or is it Sparks's attempt to convey the reality of adolescent susceptibility to HIV/AIDS in a format that will impact [young adult] readers?"[1]

Among the romanticized elements that made Bradburn question the book's authenticity was the extreme vulnerability of 14-year-old Nancy, who, because she's asthmatic already, had a weakened immune system. Aside from the announcement on the cover of the book, there was little foreshadowing that Nancy's gentle and caring 18-year-old boyfriend would date rape her or that he would be a carrier of HIV. The rape, followed by the horror of the diagnosis of AIDS, truly fills the "nightmare" part of the definition of a romance, while the loving support she receives in her last months of life fills the "daydream" part of the definition. As Bradburn implied, young readers pick up the book because of the horror of the situation and they keep reading because of its poignancy.

Although no one wants to have Nancy's experience, the story is nevertheless wish-fulfilling in the way Nancy's friends, including a new boyfriend, stay close to her and lend support throughout her illness and in the way her divorced parents put aside their differences to care for her. People who work with such real-life tragedies say that neither of these situations is very likely. The strain of a gravely ill child is often the last straw in a fragile marriage relationship, and, as illustrated in Robin Brancato's *Winning* and Cynthia Voigt's *Izzy, Willy-Nilly*, old friends are likely to flee when they are made uncomfortable by a drastically changed situation.

The Adventure/Accomplishment Romance

The great satisfaction of the adventure or the accomplishment romance lies in its wish fulfillment, as when David slays Goliath, when Cinderella is united with the noble prince and given the fitting role of queen, and when Dorothy and Toto find their way back to Kansas. In every culture, there are legends, myths, and folk and fairy tales that follow the pattern of the adventure/accomplishment romance. In the Judeo-Christian culture, the biblical story of Joseph is a prime example. Early in life, Joseph was chosen and marked as a special person. When his brothers sold him as a slave to the Egyptian traders, he embarked on his quest for wisdom and knowledge. Just when all seemed lost, he received divine help being blessed with the ability to interpret dreams. This got him out of prison and into the Pharaoh's court. The climax of the story came years later, during the famine that brought his brothers to Egypt and the royal palace. Without recognizing Joseph, they begged for food. His forgiveness and his generosity were final proof of his worthiness.

A distinguishing feature of such romances is the happy ending, achieved only after the hero's worth is proved through a crisis or an ordeal. Usually as part of the ordeal the hero must make a sacrifice, be wounded, or leave some part of his or her body, even if it is only sweat or tears. The real loss is that of innocence, but it is usually symbolized by a physical loss, as in Norse mythology when Odin gave one of his eyes to pay for knowledge, or in J. R. R. Tolkien's *The Lord of the Rings* when Frodo, who has already suffered many wounds, found that he could not throw the ring back and so must let Gollum take his finger along with the ring. The suffering of the hero nearly always purchases some kind of wisdom, even though wisdom is not what the hero set out to find.

The adventure/accomplishment romance has elements applicable to the task of entering the adult world, which all young people anticipate. The story pattern includes the three stages of formal initiation as practiced in many cultures. First, the young and innocent person is separated both physically and spiritually from the nurturing love of most or all friends and family. This is one of the reasons that so many accomplishment stories include a trip (see Focus Box 5.1). Another reason for the trip (see Sharon Creech's statement on p. 149) is that the new environment provides new challenges and learning experiences. During the separation, the hero, who embodies noble qualities, undergoes a test of courage and stamina that may be mental, psychological, or physical. In the final stage, the young person is reunited with former friends and family in a new role of increased status.

Izzy, Willy-Nilly as an Adventure/Accomplishment Romance

Authors often dramatize mental accomplishments as physical ones because it is extremely hard to show something occurring inside someone's mind and heart. The physical challenge serves as a symbol for the mental or emotional one. The effect of this has been that adventure romances are more likely to feature males than females because males' lifestyles usually include more physically challenging activities (e.g., athletic competition, war, physical labor, and surviving on one's own). Today's authors, however, are consciously trying to write adventure/accomplishment stories about females.

Cynthia Voigt's *Izzy, Willy-Nilly* is a good illustration. Tenth-grader-cheer-leader-nice-girl Izzy has been in a serious automobile accident, and before she is really conscious, her leg is being amputated. Chapter Two is a flashback to before the accident. The author uses this chapter to set the background and to show readers that Izzy Lingard is a special person worthy of the challenge she will face. Izzy is the first of her group to be asked out by a senior, and she is strong enough not to succumb to the boy's teasing her because she has to ask her parents' permission before she accepts.

Because a romance is essentially the story of one person's achievement and development, everything else is a condensation. For the sake of efficiency, the personalities of the supporting characters are shown through symbols, metaphors, and significant details, all of which highlight the qualities that are important to the story. It

FOCUS BOX 5.1

Literal Journeys/Figurative Quests

Backwater by Joan Bauer. Putnam, 1999. Because Ivy Breedlove doesn't feel she fits in at a family reunion in the Adirondack Mountains, she sets out to learn about her Aunt Josephine with whom she is often compared.

Chasing Redbird by Sharon Creech. HarperCollins, 1997. Zinny does not travel far, only on an old Appalachian trail that she discovers and works to rebuild. Nevertheless, there's plenty to think about in this story of family relationships and young romance. Creech's *Bloomability* (HarperCollins, 1998) is also about a journey, but in it Dinnie is sent to a school in Switzerland where her uncle is headmaster.

Drive by Diana Wieler. Douglas & McIntyre/Publisher's Group West, 1998. Two brothers join up in this Canadian story—one as a musician and the other as his manager—travelling from one small town to the next looking for success and fame.

The Great Turkey Walk by Kathleen Karr. Farrar, Straus & Giroux, 1998. In this wish-fulfilling and lively quest story set in 1860, 15-year-old Simon Green goes in partners with his school teacher to buy 1,000 turkeys in Missouri, hoping to sell them to turkey-starved miners in Denver.

Out of Nowhere by Ouida Sebestyen. Orchard, 1994. When 13-year-old Harley is left at a desert campground by his mother and her boyfriend, he clings for comfort to an equally deserted pit bull. In a heartwarming story, he and the dog join three other "rejects" and make a new kind of family.

Rear-View Mirror by Paul Fleischman. HarperCollins, 1986. Seventeen-year-old Olivia Tate sets out on a commemorative bike trip in remembrance of the father she learned to love only a few months before his death. Fleischman's *Whirligig* (Holt, 1998) also shows how a journey provides time for reflection and growth.

Rules of the Road by Joan Bauer. Putnam, 1998. Sixteen-year-old Jenna Louise Boller is six-feet tall and feels ungainly and not particularly successful except in her after-school job at Gladstone's Shoes, but the story shifts gears when the company's elderly owner invites Jenna to be her driver for the summer.

---

is not really the villain whom the hero must ultimately defeat, but the villain stands in the way of the true accomplishment and gives the hero an enemy upon whom to focus. Without some scary, nightmarish, and usually life-threatening incident, the happy ending could not be appreciated.

The boy who asked Izzy for a date is the villain of the story. He is a "notorious flirt," who at the party gets so drunk that although he is not hurt when he plows his car into a tree, he does nothing to help Izzy. Then he lies to the police about Izzy doing the driving, and instead of apologizing for what happened, he manipulates Izzy's friend, hoping to influence what Izzy tells the police.

Izzy faces the physical loss of her leg and the challenge of learning to walk with a prosthesis, but the real challenge is the emotional one of acceptance. In the daytime, at least in front of other people, Izzy is cheerful. The first day that she dares to look down at the blanket covering her "leg-and-a-half" she begins her quest for emotional peace. Heroes in traditional romances often had visions or visits from divine beings. Izzie's "vision" comes through her mental image of a tiny little Izzy doll.

> My brain wasn't working. It was as if the little Izzy was running around and around in circles, some frantic wind-up Izzy, screeching No, no, no.

SHARON CREECH
On Journeys in Literature

Journeys have always been important to me. When I was young, my family took a car trip each summer, and the one we took when I was thirteen—from Ohio to Idaho, nearly 3,000 miles in the car—was particularly dramatic. What a vast and varied country! I wanted to memorize everything I saw and heard. That journey was later recreated in *Walk Two Moons,* and it was as exciting traveling with Salamanca Tree Hiddle across the States as it was taking that first trip so many years ago.

I love the way that each book—any book—is its own journey. You open the book, and off you go. You don't know who you're going to meet along the way, nor where you will go, and when you finish a book, you feel as if you've been on a journey. You are changed in some way — large or small — by having travelled with those characters, by having walked in their moccasins a while, by having seen what they've seen, heard what they've heard, felt what they've felt. These journeys echo all of our daily journeys: not knowing who we will meet today, tomorrow; who will affect our lives in small ways and profound ways; where we will go; what we will feel; what will happen to us?

This same journey motif extends to the writer's process, the creation process. When I begin writing a book, I have no idea who I will meet along the way, nor what they will see or hear or do. I usually have very little idea where we are all going together.

When students ask for advice or inspiration on writing, I often suggest that all they need to do is take someone on a journey. They don't have to know where they're going, and the journey can be as simple as walking from one block to the next. Just set off. Something will happen. The joy is in the journey—in the discovery of what will happen.

Sharon Creech's books include *Walk Two Moons,* 1994; *Bloomability,* 1998; *Absolutely Normal Chaos,* 1995; *Chasing Redbird,* 1997; and *Pleasing the Ghost,* 1996, all from HarperCollins.

But it was *Yes, yes, yes.*
And I knew it.
I knew it, but I couldn't believe it.

Izzy lays her head on the formica hospital table over her bed, and although she is not asleep, she has a nightmare.

I felt as if a huge long slide was slipping up past me, and I was going down it. I couldn't stop myself, and I didn't even want to. . . . Something heavy and wet and cold and gray was making me go down, pushing at the back of my bent neck and at my shoulders. At the bottom, wherever that was, something heavy and wet and cold and gray waited for me. It was softer than the ground when I hit it. I went flying off the end of the slide and fell into the gray. The gray reached up around me and closed itself over me and swallowed me up.

When a nurse comes in, Izzy wishes she would leave because Izzy is afraid she might cry, and, "We didn't cry, not the Lingards. We were brave and made jokes about things hurting. . . ." The nurse, a physical therapist, gives Izzy painful massages to toughen up her skin and muscles so she will be ready for the prosthesis. Izzy is hurt that the woman concentrates on her work and doesn't look at Izzy's face or talk with her. In her depressed mood, Izzy decides that it is because she is no longer a whole person. "I guessed if you'd finished working on the pizza dough, you wouldn't bend over and say goodbye to it. You don't talk to *things*. And that's what I was, a thing, a messed-up body."

The worst times for Izzy are at night, when she wakes up alone and cannot keep her "mind from going down that slide thinking of all the things that I managed not to think about during the days." She never knew until then, never even suspected, how it felt to be depressed.

I'd been miserable. I'd been blue. But depressed, no, I hadn't been that. I never knew how it felt to sigh out a breath so sad you could almost see tears in it. I never knew the way tears would ooze and ooze out of your eyes. I never knew the way something could hang like a gray cloud over all of your mind and you could never get away from it, never forget it.

Help comes to Izzy, not from her old friends, who are too involved in their own lives and too uncomfortable with her misfortune to stay long, but from the strange misfit Rosamunde—"not at all like Lisa and the rest"—who arrives to decorate Izzy's hospital room, and to play Yahtzee, and to bring fruit, good conversation, homemade turnovers, and piroshki.

When Izzy is released from the hospital, she does not go back to her old room on the second floor. Instead she is given her parents' bedroom on the first floor, and it's here in the middle of the night that Izzy, isolated from her family and in a strange and lonely place, undergoes the suffering that makes her eventual victory that much sweeter.

During a particularly bad time, Izzy sees the little doll in her head "standing there waving her detached leg at a crowd of people, like a safety monitor waving her stop sign." In contrast, the first day that someone at school forgets about Izzy's crutches, the little doll "gathered herself up and did an impossible back-flip, and then another and another." The book ends with Izzy seeing the little doll:

. . . standing alone, without crutches. . . . Her arms were spread out slightly. She looked like she was about to dance, but really her arms were out for balance. . . . The little Izzy balanced there briefly and then took a hesitant step forward—ready to fall, ready not to fall.

Other Symbols of Accomplishment

The motif of a worthy young hero embarking on a quest of wisdom appears in many more good books than those mentioned in this chapter because it fits well in biographies, adventure stories, historical fiction, fantasy, science fiction, and problem novels. Even when the quest is not the main part of a story, motifs that fit the quest romance are incorporated. For example, in traditional romances, the protagonist usually receives the vision or insight in a "high or isolated place like a mountain top, an island, or a tower."[2] In Virginia Hamilton's *M. C. Higgins, the Great,* the boy, M. C., comes to his realizations about his family and his role while he contemplates the surrounding countryside from a special bicycle seat affixed to the top of a tall steel pole standing in the yard of his mountain home. The pole is unique and intriguing, and M. C. earned it as a reward from his father for swimming across the Ohio River.

Robert Lipsyte's *The Contender* opens with Mr. Donatelli, the manager of a boxing gym, listening to the confident sound of young, African-American Alfred Brooks climbing the steps to his gym. Mr. Donatelli says he can tell who has what it takes to be a contender (readers are to interpret this as meaning a contender in life as well as in the boxing ring) by how they climb those stairs. A generation later, in another quest story, *The Brave,* this same Alfred Brooks helps Sonny Bear, a 17-year-old boxer from the Moscondaga Indian reservation, change the monster he feels inside himself into the dignified Hawk spirit of his people.

A railroad lantern named Spin Light that Jerome wins with his basketball skill is an intriguing symbol in Bruce Brooks's *The Moves Make the Man.* It enables him to go to a hidden, lonely court and play basketball after dark, but by the end of the book, readers share in Jerome's optimism that Spin Light will enable him to see more than his way around the basketball court.

In Chris Crutcher's *The Crazy Horse Electric Game,* pitching star Willie Weaver is seriously injured in a waterskiing accident. He runs away when it appears that on top of losing his athletic and speaking abilities, he is also losing his girlfriend. At first, he is concerned only with surviving, but then he gets involved with other people and attends an alternative school where, with help, he recovers many of his motor skills. He returns home strong enough to cope with all the changes that have occurred.

Some critics fear that when authors use such physical changes as Willie Weaver's almost miraculous recovery as a tangible or metaphorical way to communicate emotional or mental accomplishment, young readers interpret the physical achievement literally rather than figuratively. Teenagers are already overly concerned about their bodies and any defects they might have. Many physical challenges, including the common motif of obesity, cannot be totally overcome, so these critics prefer stories in which the protagonist comes to terms with the problem as does Izzy in *Izzy, Willy-Nilly* and the young Native-American boy in Anne Eliot Crompton's historical *The Sorcerer.* The boy is named Lefthand because he was injured by a bear and cannot hunt. In his tribe, this is a serious problem, because hunting is what the men do. There is no miraculous cure for his disability, but he gains both his own and his tribe's respect when he develops enough skill as an artist to draw the pictures of animals needed for the tribe's hunting rituals.

The acceptance of the compromised dream is an element of the romance pattern that is particularly meaningful to young adults. Many of them are just beginning to achieve some of their lifelong goals, and they are discovering the illusory nature of the end of the rainbow, which is a symbolic way of saying such things as, "When I graduate," "When we get married," "When I'm 18," or "When I have my own apartment." Like the characters in the romances, they are not sorry they have ventured, for they have indeed found something worthwhile, but it is seldom the pot of gold they had imagined.

Because the pattern of the romance has been outlined so clearly by critics, and because its popularity has passed the test of time with honors, it would seem to be an easy story to write. The plot has already been worked out. An author needs only to develop a likable protagonist, determine a quest, fill in the supporting roles with stock characters, and supply a few interesting details. It is far from being this simple, however. Sometimes, as in dance, the things that look the simplest are the hardest to execute. The plot must not be so obvious that the reader recognizes it as the same old thing. The good author develops a unique situation that on the surface appears to be simply a good story. Its appeal as a romantic quest should be at a deep, almost subconscious level, with readers experiencing a sense of *déjà vu*. It is as if their own life story is being told because the romantic quest is everyone's story.

Sports and the Game of Life

Notice how many of these symbols of accomplishment are related to athletics and physical prowess. This is because our society views sports as a metaphor for life; witness such clichés as *being a team player, quarterbacking a situation, having the inside track, making a close call,* and *setting the pace.* Players, and even fans, can experience virtually all the elements of a romantic quest in a single season or even in a single game. The best part is that with both books and films, this can happen without readers having to get blisters or sore muscles (see Film Box 5.1 and Focus Box 5.2).

Most sports books, whether fiction or nonfiction, include the training that is needed, the expected rewards, tangible or not, and the inevitable disappointments that make the rewards even sweeter. Early sports books in the 1890s and 1900s focused on the character-changing possibilities of sports along with an inning-by-inning or quarter-by-quarter account. The minute-by-minute account was almost never successful. But the excitement of sports—the euphoria that sometimes comes to players—and the potential character development has remained. Occasional nonfiction writers have focused almost exclusively on a player's character flaws, an iconoclastic approach that seems to have had its day.

The excitement of sports is what readers want just as winning is the only acceptable verdict for fans. Way back on June 5, 1974, the *Los Angeles Times* headlined the sports section, "There's Nothing Like the Euphoria of Accomplishment." *The New York Times* for August 11, 1974 headlined its sports section with an article (first published in *Dial* in 1919) "Baseball: A Boy's Game, A Pro Sport and a National Religion." And even further back to the May 17, 1913, *Outlook,* H. Addington Bruce in his article, "Baseball and the National Life," announced:

> Veritably baseball is something more than the great American game—it is an American institution having a significant place in the life of the people, and consequently worthy of close and careful analysis.

To deny or even to question the significant place of sports in many American lives is to misunderstand American life or values.

In the 1950s and early 1960s, such writers as H. D. Francis and John Carson wrote good novels filled with heroes reeking of sweat. Their heroes often examined the price of fame and the temptation to believe—always doomed—that fame would last. Writers as powerful as John Updike killed that dream much as F. Scott Fitzgerald had killed other dreams of society or business and glory and permanence. The

FILM BOX 5.1

Sports and Playing Around (see Appendix D)

Bang the Drum Slowly (1973, color, 97 min., NR; Director: John Hancock; with Michael Moriarty and Robert De Niro) Mark Harris's novel tells the story of a third-rate baseball catcher and the pitcher who loves him.

Body and Soul (1947, black and white, 104 min., NR; Director: Robert Rossen; with John Garfield, Lilli Palmer, and Canada Lee) A boxer works his way up to the championship any way he can.

Brian's Song (1970, color, 73 min., made for TV; Director: Buzz Kulik; with Billy Dee Williams and James Caan) Here's the real-life story of a deep friendship between black star running back Gayle Sayers and Southern white second-string Brian Piccolo.

Chariots of Fire (1981, color, 129 min., PG; Director: Hugh Hudson; with Ben Cross, Ian Holm, and Ian Charleson) Two men, one a Jew and one a Scottish missionary, have much to prove to themselves in the 1924 Olympics.

Hoop Dreams (1994, color, 169 min., PG–13; Director: Steve James) A documentary about two Chicago inner-city black kids who dream of playing basketball in college and in the pros.

A League of Their Own (1992, color, 124 min., PG; Director: Penny Marshall; with Geena Davis and Tom Hanks) During World War II, a women's baseball league was greatly admired.

The Loneliness of the Long Distance Runner (1962, British, black and white, 103 min., NR; Director: Tony Richardson; with Tom Courtenay and Michael Redgrave) At an English reform school, a young man is chosen to represent his school in a track meet.

Personal Best (1982, color, 124 min., R; Director: Robert Towne; with Mariel Hemingway and Patrice Donnelly) Two women competing for spots on the 1980 Olympic track team fall in and then out of love.

Raging Bull (1980, black and white/color, 128 min., R; Director: Martin Scorsese; with Robert DeNiro and Cathy Moriarty) The story of Jake La Motto and his determination to win in the ring.

The Set-Up (1949, black and white, 72 min., NR; Director: Robert Wise; with Robert Ryan and Audrey Totter) An over-the-hill fighter knows he can knock out his opponent; it's played in real time.

---

sentimental fiction of the 1950s and 1960s was never real, but it had a charm that we have lost, and with it some readers of more innocent sports books.

Baseball and basketball and football fans may dispute which sport is the most popular or has the most vociferous fans. But without question, baseball is the subject of the most books. Two books, Ron Smith's *The Sporting News Selects Baseball's Greatest Players* and Maury Allen's *Baseball's 100: A Personal Ranking of the Best Players in Baseball History*, try to do the impossible—rank the greatest players from the top down. Allen's top three are Willie Mays, Hank Aaron, and Babe Ruth, while Smith ranks the top three as Babe Ruth, Willie Mays, and Ty Cobb.

There's no shortage of biographies of outstanding baseball players. These are only a few of the best: Henry Aaron with Lonnie Wheeler's *I Had a Hammer: The Hank Aaron Story*; Joseph Durso's *DiMaggio: The Last American Knight*; Mark Ribowsky's *Don't Look Back: Satchel Paige in the Shadows of Baseball*; Rachel Robinson with Lee Daniels's *Jackie Robinson: An Intimate Portrait*; Michael Sokolove's *Hustle: The Myth, Life, and Lies of Pete Rose*; and Michael Seidel's *Ted Williams: A Baseball Life*. Fascinating as these books are to winter talk-show listeners, they all pale compared to Nicholas Dawidoff's *The Catcher Was a Spy: The Mysterious Life of Moe Berg*. Berg wasn't even a mediocre hitter, though he was a great catcher and an excellent handler of pitchers, but he was what none of the great baseball players were. He was an American spy in Japan before World War II and a spy in Europe. He

FOCUS BOX 5.2

An Armful of Great Books About Sports

The Curious Case of Sid Finch by George Plimpton. Macmillan, 1987. In this funny spoof of baseball and baseball fans, a pitcher throws 50 mph faster than anyone else. He's a Buddhist monk who learned to throw during his religious training in Tibet.

Friends Till the End by Todd Strasser. Delacorte, 1981. Soccer star and all-round good guy, David, agrees reluctantly to visit Howie, who is dying of leukemia. A powerful friendship develops.

In Lane Three, Alex Archer by Tessa Duder. Houghton Mifflin, 1987. In 1959, swimmer Alex (short for Alexandra) Archer is 15 and preparing for the 1960 Olympic Games in Rome.

The Natural by Bernard Malamud. Farrar, Straus, & Giroux, 1952. The mythical novel about Roy Hobbs and his famous bat is not Malamud at his best, but it is still powerful.

The Passing Game by Richard Blessing. Little, Brown, 1982. In one of the best YA novels ever, Craig Warren has potential greatness, but his playing is unsure.

Roughnecks by Thomas Cochran. Harcourt Brace, 1997. The Oil Camp High School Roughnecks prepare for the Louisiana AA State Football Championship against the Pineview High School Pelicans.

Safe at Second by Scott Johnson. Philomel, 1999. A great young pitcher has his choice of college scholarships or professional offers, then a line drive hits him in the face.

Shoeless Joe by W. P. Kinsella. Houghton Mifflin, 1982. A fan builds a ballpark for a legendary game with Shoeless Joe Jackson and other baseball immortals. See also *The Iowa Baseball Confederacy* (Houghton Mifflin, 1986) and *The Further Adventures of Slugger McBatt* (Houghton Mifflin, 1988).

Ultimate Sports: Short Stories by Outstanding Writers for Young Adults, edited by Don Gallo. Delacorte, 1995. Robert Lipsyte, Chris Crutcher, Norma Fox Mazer, Tessa Duder, and T. Ernesto Bethancourt are among the authors who contributed stories.

Zanballer by R. R. Knudson. Delacorte, 1972. Zan wants to play football rather than leading cheers, so she sets out to change the school. *Zanbanger* is the first of several less successful sequels.

---

graduated magna cum laude from Princeton with a major in modern languages, took a diploma from Columbia University Law School, and joined the Office of Strategic Services (OSS), the forerunner of today's Central Intelligence Agency (CIA). He was said to have known twenty-seven languages and to have joined his fellow baseball players at Princeton in yelling instructions to each other in Latin. He played for five big-league baseball clubs, with a lifetime batting average of .243, from 1923–1939. A fascinating and mysterious life.

The All-American Girls' Professional Baseball League founded during World War II because of the drafting of male athletes is the subject of Sue Macy's *A Whole New Ball Game*. Macy provides portraits of many players and their statistics and makes readers sorry that the league is dead. Barbara Gregorich in *Women at Play: The Story of Women in Baseball* points out that baseball has been played by women since Vassar College students formed two teams in 1866. In a 1931 exhibition game, a minor league pitcher named Jackie Mitchell struck out Babe Ruth in four pitches and Lou Gehrig in three, but the real news was that Mitchell was a woman. Russell Freedman's *Babe Didrikson Zaharias: The Making of a Champion* offers proof that women can be outstanding athletes, but Joan Ryan warns readers of the cost of athletic training and transitory fame in *Little Girls in Pretty Boxes: The Making and Breaking of Elite Gymnasts and Figure Skaters*.

See Focus Box 5.3 for other nonfiction books exploring relationships between heroic dreams and real life fulfillments.

Two particularly impressive books about baseball that are stories about love and friendship and fatherhood are Mark Harris's *Bang the Drum Slowly* and Donald Hall's *Fathers Playing Catch with Sons*. Harris's story of a second- or third-string catcher dying of leukemia is touching, just as it is also good baseball. Hall, a major poet, offers a warm and almost sentimental account of his love for sports, particularly baseball. The first two sentences of his introduction tie together the two worlds he loves and needs: writing and baseball.

> Half of my poet-friends think I am insane to waste my time writing about sports and to loiter in the company of professional athletes. The other half would murder to take my place.

Later, he distinguishes between baseball and football to the detriment of the latter.

> Baseball is fathers and sons. Football is brothers beating each other up in the backyard, violent and superficial.

Basketball is today's favorite spectator sport, so we should expect good basketball stories written for young adults. The story that James Bennett tells in *The Squared Circle* focuses on Sonny Youngblood, a high school star basketball player

FOCUS BOX 5.3

Sports Nonfiction—Real Life Dreams

Baseball: An Illustrated History by Geoffrey C. Ward and Ken Burns. Knopf, 1994. While this is attractive enough to be a coffee-table book, it is also informative enough to be a research tool.

Basketball: A History of Hoops by Mark Stewart. Watts, 1999. Part of a History of Sports series, this well-designed book is filled with intriguing details and information about how the game has been changed by becoming big business.

Men in Sports: Great Sport Stories of All Time, from the Greek Olympic Games to the American World Series by Brandt Aymar. Crown, 1994. Readers curious about virtually any sport from auto racing to billiards to cricket to polo to yacht racing and almost anything in between will find something of interest in Aymar's book.

Race Across Alaska: First Woman to Win the Iditarod Tells Her Story by Libby Riddles and Tim Jones. Stackpole Books, 1998. Students who read Gary Paulsen's Iditarod book

Woodsong (Bradbury, 1990) might enjoy this different perspective on the race.

The Story of Negro League Baseball by William Brashler. Ticknor & Fields, 1994. Brashler tells the stories that many of us don't know about such stars as Smokey Joe Williams, Bob Gibson, and Satchel Paige. Neil J. Sullivan does something similar in his book *The Minors: The Struggles and the Triumphs of Baseball's Poor Relations from 1876 to the Present* (St. Martin's Press, 1990).

Wait Till Next Year: A Memoir by Doris Kearns Goodwin. Simon & Schuster, 1997. In this lovely book, a historian remembers growing up in Rockville Centre, NY, and her passion for the Brooklyn Dodgers.

Winning Ways: A Photohistory of American Women in Sports by Sue Macy. Holt, 1996. In this book as in her *A Whole New Ball Game* (Holt, 1993), Macy presents wonderful photos and intriguing details to show that women have a sports heritage.

---

now entering Southern Illinois University as the hope of their athletic department. Whether Sonny even likes the sport is a question he avoids asking himself, mostly out of fear of the answer. His father long ago walked out, Sonny didn't like his high school coach, he is the only white player on the squad, he hates the fraternity he is ready to join, and if all that were not bad enough, a cousin who is an art professor wants Sonny to work out what he wants to do with his life. The ending is powerful and disturbing, but Sonny is on his way to somewhere.

John McFee's *A Sense of Where You Are: Bill Bradley at Princeton* is an admiring study of a Princeton all-American basketball player, a Rhodes Scholar at Oxford, a star player for the New York Knicks, a U.S. Senator, and later a presidential hopeful. Bradley's own book, *Value of the Game*, revisits his basketball life searching for values even though the game today has little in common with the game that Bradley played. David Halbertstam's biography of the greatest basketball player of all time, Michael Jordan, conveys a sense of Jordan's poetry and joy. *Playing for Keeps: Michael Jordan and the World He Made* should be a feast for any basketball fan.

Readers searching for a collection of short stories and poetry about basketball could hardly do better than Dennis Trudell's *Full Court*. The way coaches and institutions and fans use and then dump sports heroes is the concern of Darcy Frey, a magazine editor, in *The Last Shot*. Frey writes sympathetically, even lovingly, about three young black teens from New York's projects and one whose mother has escaped the projects. They are the stars of Abraham Lincoln High School's basketball program. College entrance exams threaten their futures. Frey is horrified, if not especially surprised, by the corruption in high school recruiting and by the uncaring college recruiting.

Sports books by young adult authors range from Jerry Spinelli's lighthearted look at wrestling in *There's a Girl in My Hammerlock* to such heavier and highly acclaimed wrestling stories as Rich Wallace's *Wrestling Sturbridge* and Terry Davis's *Vision Quest*. Will Weaver's three books, which have attracted positive attention from both readers and critics, are about baseball and far more. In *Striking Out*, Billy Baggs is a natural baseball player, but Billy's father, a farmer, needs Billy on the farm. The story is continued in *Farm Team* and *Hard Ball*.

Walter Dean Myers's *Hoops* and its sequel *The Outside Shot* show a young boy trying to escape his ghetto existence through basketball. Thomas J. Dygard has written some good football stories including *Quarterback Walk-On, Tournament Upstart*, and *Backfield Package*.

Chris Lynch uses ice hockey as the centering focus of his book *Iceman*, in which he explores the attitude among young American males that anger is "cool." Lynch's first book *Shadow Boxer* has some similarities as two brothers in an urban setting are constantly challenged on the street and are tempted to go into professional boxing even though their father died from injuries suffered in the ring. Lynch's most original book about athletes is *Slot Machine* in which a boy is sent to a special summer sports camp as a prelude to entering a private school. Elvin, the protagonist, is by turns cynical and amused, as he proves that he does not fit into any of the expected "slots."

Chris Crutcher is one of the most talented YA writers to combine sports and personal development stories. In *Running Loose,* Louie Banks wants to play football, but not the way his unethical coach wants it played. Crutcher's *Stotan!* is about swimming and how a team faces up to the serious illness of one of its members. In *The Crazy Horse Electric Game,* a star athlete suffers brain damage from a waterskiing accident. In *Ironman,* Bo Brewster, a bitter high school athlete forced to attend anger-management classes, writes letters to Larry King because he does not feel anyone else will listen. The short stories in *Athletic Shorts* feature some of the characters from Crutcher's novels.

Will Weaver (see his statement on p. 9) with his baseball stories is the newest author to add to the growing body of literature presenting sports-plus stories.

Animal and Nature Stories

Many children come to high school already familiar with the pattern of the accomplishment romance, which they met in such stories as Francis Hodgson Burnett's *The Secret Garden* and Kenneth Grahame's *The Wind in the Willows*. Animals play major roles in Allan Eckert's *Incident at Hawk's Hill,* Fred Gipson's *Old Yeller,* Sterling North's *Rascal,* Marjorie Rawlings's *The Yearling,* and Wilson Rawls's *Where the Red Fern Grows.* In many such stories, the animals are sacrificed as a symbol of the loss the young person undergoes in exchange for wisdom, but fortunately not all animals in such stories are sacrificed. Some of them live long, happy lives, providing companionship and even inspiration to the humans with whom they share the planet (see Focus Box 5.4, Accomplishment Romances Involving Animals and Michael Cadnum's statement). Readers who love animals probably also appreciate

 FOCUS BOX 5.4

Accomplishment Romances Involving Animals

Beardance by Will Hobbs. Atheneum/Simon & Schuster, 1993. Cloyd is a young Native American who risks his own life to guarantee the survival of the last grizzly bears found in the Rocky Mountains.

Bill by Chap Reaver. Delacorte, 1994. The only companion that Jess Gates, the motherless daughter of a moonshiner, has is her loyal dog Bill. When her father is sent to jail, Jess and Bill have to decide where to put their trust.

California Blue by David Klass. Scholastic, 1994. John discovers a new subspecies of butterfly in one of the old forests of California. He finds himself in conflict with his family and neighbors who work in the lumber business and do not want interference from environmentalists.

Call of the Wild by Jack London. Macmillan, 1903. This coming-of-age classic is set in the excitement of the Alaskan gold rush where both dogs and men were severely tested.

Every Living Thing by Cynthia Rylant. Bradbury, 1985. In these 12 short stories, people's lives are changed by their relationships with animals.

The First Horse I See by Sally M. Keehn. Philomel, 1999. There are no happily-ever-after guarantees in this book, but both humans and horses make progress when Willojean's grandfather lets her choose a horse.

Halsey's Pride by Lynn Hall. Atheneum/Simon & Schuster, 1990. Lynn Hall is a dog lover who wrote this story about a girl coming to live with her father and his prize-winning dog and learning to cope with her imperfections and life in general.

Mariposa Blues by Ron Koertge. Avon/Flare, 1993. Graham's dad is a horse trainer, but Graham decides to make his own decision about when a special horse is ready for competition.

Sniper by Theodore Taylor. Harcourt Brace Jovanovich, 1989. When Ben's parents go on a trip, they leave him in charge of their wild animal preserve, never dreaming of the challenges he will face.

A Solitary Blue by Cynthia Voigt. Atheneum, 1983. Jeff Greene, whose mother has left him and his father, feels as alone in the world as a beautiful blue heron that he observes in a Carolina marsh.

Taming the Star Runner by S. E. Hinton. Delacorte, 1988. Fifteen-year-old Travis moves from a detention center to his uncle's horse ranch, where everyone hopes he will be rehabilitated.

Under a Different Sky by Deborah Savage. Houghton Mifflin, 1997. Ben Stahler, who dreams of riding his horse in the Olympics, helps take care of horses belonging to the wealthy girls at a nearby boarding school. Other well-written animal stories by Savage include *To Race a Dream* (1994) and *A Rumour of Otters* (1986), both Houghton Mifflin.

MICHAEL CADNUM
On the Importance of Animals

The back door was open, afternoon sun all over the tangle of blackberry bushes and the clothes hanging on the line. My parrot Luke was perched on the back of a chair in the kitchen, keeping me company as I did the dishes. As though he had practiced it many times, Luke spread his wings and skimmed to the entrance of the back door. He took a few steps as I looked on, unable to speak, unable to make a move, afraid that I would startle my parrot into doing exactly what he was about to do.

Luke spread his wings, and did not fly so much as ascend, by an act of will, to the back porch rail. He hunched a little, cocking his eye upward at the sky, around at the autumn-bare backyard, everything bright with late sun. Another move, and my beautiful, yellow-crested green bird was on a wire fence overlooking the driveway. I was talking to him, calling his name, trying to keep the fear from my voice, holding out my hand. And just then a cat, one of those dry-grass colored tabbies from the neighborhood appeared through the geraniums.

This cat transformed from a friendly local tom to a hunter, closing in on my bright green Amazon parrot.

Luke was two years old, he had rarely been outdoors, and now he was singing that warbling, strangled cheer, his normal song when he was pleased. I was certain I would never hear this song again as he lofted upwards high over the neighboring house, into the birch tree up the street.

As my wife Sherina and I called to him, telephoned the fire department, did everything in our power, he winged away. Luke vanished from our lives.

When I am discovering the characters I write about, I often ask myself, what about the animals in their lives? Do they have a cat, or a dog? If they have an animal companion, what role does this animal play in the humor and affection of the family? When, in *Taking It,* Anna Charles lets a friend's family dog escape with her into Southern California, this tells us a great deal about Anna. She is lonely as well as reckless, and the dog offers a companionship that is both innocent and freely given—and which Anna cannot really appreciate.

In *Rundown,* my main character's interest in tropical birds is one of the things I like best about her. Myrna, the cat who has a litter of kittens in *Heat,* the battered wandering cat in *Zero at the Bone*—these animals, and the way my characters treat them—flavor the way I feel about the people in my books. I ask myself why Jennifer in *Rundown* doesn't take a greater interest in her new horse, and why Anna's father in *Taking It* has an aquarium filled with tropical fish. The way these individuals treat animals is a strong hint about the way they feel about life.

Someone found Luke, turned him in to the Animal Shelter. A week after he disappeared, Luke was back. He was sick, and dirty—but alive. Now after over twenty years of companionship, he still is full of surprises. He sings more loudly, more crazily—and more wonderfully—than ever. He often sits on my shoulder as I write.

Michael Cadnum's books include *Edge,* 1997; *Taking It,* 1995; and *Zero at the Bone,* 1996, all from Viking.

Elizabeth Hess's nonfiction *Lost and Found: Dogs, Cats, and Everyday Heroes at a Country Animal Shelter.* It's an account of the terrible things humans do to animals and the wonderful ways animals repay humans.

Jean George's *Julie of the Wolves* shows Julie separated from her Eskimo foster family when she runs away from the retarded Daniel, who plans to make her his wife in fact as well as name. She sets out with the vague, unrealistic goal of finding her pen pal in San Francisco. As she gains wisdom and confidence, she decides to live in the old ways. Amaroq, the great wolf, lends "miraculous" help to her struggle for survival on the Arctic tundra. The climax comes when Julie learns that her father still lives and that she has arrived at his village. When she learns that he has married a "gussack" and now pilots planes for hunters, the disillusioned Julie grieves for the wolves and the other hunted animals and vows to return and live on the tundra. The temperature falls far below zero and the "ice thundered and boomed, roaring like drumbeats across the Arctic." Despite all that Julie does to save him, Tornait, Julie's golden plover, who has been her faithful companion, dies from the cold. Tornait is the last symbol of Julie's innocence, and as she mourns his death, she comes to accept the fact that the lives of both the wolf and the Eskimo are changing, and she points her boots toward her father and the life he now leads.

Through her quest, Julie comes to understand that her life must change, but, unexpectedly, she also learns a great deal about her native land and the animals who live there. Readers are optimistic that Julie will not forget what she has experienced and that she will have some part in protecting the land and animals, although perhaps not to the degree that she desires.

Twenty years after *Julie of the Wolves* won the Newbery Award, Jean Craighead George wrote a sequel entitled *Julie*. Although it lacks the surprising originality of the earlier book, junior high readers are likely to enjoy reading more about Julie's continuing quest to save her wolves.

Of all the authors writing for young adults, Gary Paulsen is the one who most often uses nature as he explores the theme of a young person poised on the brink of a new stage of development or understanding. His books are further discussed in Chapter Six, but in relation to the genre of the accomplishment romance, he interestingly puts his characters at the right spot at the right time to receive inspiration and insight. In combination with the characters' own efforts, these insights bring them to a new level of maturity. One of our students, Laurie Platt, wrote her Honors College thesis on Paulsen's books and on what she called "catalysts for change," which she defined as the individuals, events, or settings that triggered emotional or intellectual growth.

With all three kinds of catalysts, nature plays a major part. In *The Monument*, when Rocky Turner follows and watches the artist who has been commissioned to create the Vietnam War memorial for the town of Bolton, Kansas, part of her learning comes from his desire to build a monument that would interrelate the natural aspects of the setting with the beliefs and emotions of the townspeople. The young narrator in *Harris and Me* takes on the task of initiating his city cousin into "the nature" of farm life. In *Dogsong,* the catalyst is the mystical, fortune-telling dreams that come to Russel "like heavy fog and steam rising from the ocean" as he journeys alone on a dogsled. In *Canyons,* Brennan Cole finds a skull and through a variety of dreams and voices understands that he needs to take the skull to its proper resting place, which turns out to be no easy task. When he finally gets there, Brennan stood:

And saw the world.

> That was the only way he could think of it—he saw the world. The desert lay below him. He stood on a flat almost-table of rock that jutted out, formed one side of the canyon, and below and away lay all the world he knew.

In this symbolically appropriate high place, Brennan feels a oneness with the Apache boy whose skull he is caring for and who a hundred years ago had stood at this same place and seen this same world.

In several of Paulsen's most popular books (e.g., *Hatchet, The Voyage of the Frog, The Island,* and *The Haymeadow*), he isolates his characters so that they are in fictional situations similar to the real-life one he wrote about in *Woodsong,* in which he and his dogs were totally dependent on each other during the two-and-a-half weeks it took to run the 1000-mile Iditarod dogsled race in Alaska. In *Tracker,* 13-year-old John Borne follows a doe for two days. He is so moved by the doe's tenacity that when he finally returns home, he explains to his worried grandparents, "A thing changed. A thing changed in hunting, in everything, and I walked after her but didn't shoot her." John's experience was the beginning of his understanding that,

> . . . his grandfather was going to die. He would die and there was nothing John could do about it—nothing touching the doe could do about it. Death would come.
>
> And the second thing was that death was a part of it all, a part of living. It was awful, a taking of life, but it happened to all things, as his grandfather said, would happen to John someday. Dying was just as much a part of Clay Borne [his grandfather] as living.

Westerns

The conquering of the American West is one of the great romantic quests of all time. As such, it caught the imagination of not only the United States but the entire world. Dime novelists of the 1870s and 1880s glorified the wildness and vitality of miners, cowboys, mountain men, soldiers, and outlaws. In 1902, Owen Wister's *The Virginian: A Horseman of the Plains* established the genre of the quiet and noble hero, the schoolmarm heroine, the hero's weak friend, and villains galore. Wister set up the archetypal showdown between good guys and bad guys. Jack Shaeffer's 1949 *Shane,* helped along by the Alan Ladd movie, added to the myth of the western loner-hero (see Film Box 5.2). All through the first third of the twentieth century, Zane Grey published his romanticized and highly popular westerns, a tradition carried on more recently by Louis L'Amour but with more skill and attention to historical detail.

Literally hundreds of writers have published westerns (stories set roughly between 1880 and 1895). Equally important in establishing the genre of the West have been movies and television. In 1990, Kevin Costner's *Dances with Wolves* surprised moviemakers and critics when it became the most successful film of the year. Expectations were that people had seen, heard, or read so many westerns that they would not come to see another one. Costner's story, however, had a new plot plus all the elements of the adventure/accomplishment romance, one of the oldest sto-

FILM BOX 5.2

Westerns: Cowboys and Horses and Gold—Maybe Even More (see Appendix D)

Bite the Bullet (1975, color, 131 min., PG; Director: Richard Brooks; with Gene Hackman and Candice Bergen) At the turn of the last century, cowboys set out on a 600-mile horse race.

Gunfight at the OK Corral (1957, color, 122 min., NR; Director: John Sturges; with Burt Lancaster and Kirk Douglas) Wyatt and Doc face the Clantons in this second best retelling—and that's high praise.

The Gunfighter (1950, black and white, 84 min., NR; Director: Henry King; with Gregory Peck and Millard Mitchell) An aging gunfighter tries to give up his life, but a young punk comes to town.

Little Big Man (1970, color, 139 min., NR; Director: Arthur Penn; with Dustin Hoffman, Faye Dunaway, and Richard Mulligan) Stories of the West long ago, told by 121-year-old Jack Crabb.

Lone Star (1996, color, 134 min., R; Director: John Sayles; with Chris Cooper and Kris Kristofferson) A small Texas border town uncovers a scandal about a former sheriff.

Lonely Are the Brave (1962, black and white, 107 min., NR; Director: David Miller; with Kirk Douglas and Walter Matthau) From Edward Abbey's novel, *The Brave Cowboy,* a cowboy who hates fences of any kind comes to town to help a friend break out of jail. When that doesn't work, the cowboy escapes into the hills.

My Darling Clementine (1946, black and white, 97 min., NR; Director: John Ford; with Henry Fonda and Victor Mature) This is the best of several retellings of the gunfight at the OK corral between the Earps and Holiday on one side and the Clantons on the other.

The Ox-Bow Incident (1943, black and white, 75 min., NR; Director: William A. Wellman; with Henry Fonda and Dana Andrews) An excellent movie is made from Walter Van Tilburg Clark's novel about a lynch mob and western justice.

The Searchers (1956, color, 155 min., NR; Director: John Ford; with John Wayne and Jeffrey Hunter) A young girl is taken by Commanches, and for years two men search for her.

The Seven Samurai (1954, Japanese, black and white, 141 min., NR; Director: Akira Kurosawa; with Toshiro Mifune and Takashi Shimura) In sixteenth-century Japan, villagers pay down-and-out samurai to protect them against bandits. Sound familiar? *The Magnificent Seven* (1960) is copied from it.

---

ries in the world. Its popularity shows that readers and viewers do not want a new story as much as they want a variation on a familiar theme.

In *Dances with Wolves,* a young soldier decides to volunteer for duty on the western frontier because he wants to see buffalos. He embarks on a more difficult task than anything he could have imagined. He arrives at the North Dakota post to find it abandoned, which results in the traditional period of isolation and contemplation necessary for the development of a hero. The fact that he works hard to salvage the abandoned post and do his duty as a completely unsupervised soldier shows viewers that he's a special person worthy of the friendships that develop, first with the wolf who plays with him and then with the Sioux Indians who are supposed to be his enemies.

By the time the other soldiers arrive and accuse the hero of treason because he has become friends with the Native Americans, viewers have no doubt who is the hero and who are the villains. They suffer with the hero when the villains shoot his wolf, and by the end they are clearly on his side when they see him riding off with the young woman whose life he has saved. It is appropriate that he looks different and that he is called by a new name because the ordeal he endured transformed him from a curious young soldier into a wise and caring man.

Of course, not all westerns follow the pattern of the romantic quest as closely as does *Dances with Wolves,* but most of them have some aspects of the adventure romance (e.g., the embarking on a literal journey that carries over into an intellectual and psychological journey, the exaggerated differences between the good guys and the bad guys, the taking of risks, the existence of life-threatening dangers, and the winning of someone's respect and/or love).

Most writers of westerns are aiming for a popular culture audience and, therefore, use a straightforward style that is easy to read. It is endemic to the genre that the heroes are involved in the same kinds of tasks as today's young adults—they are unencumbered individuals setting forth to find themselves a place to live, a way to earn their keep, and suitable companions. This means that teenagers can and do read many of the westerns written for a general adult audience (see Focus Box 5.5, Western Books Too Tough to Die). In fact, the first book officially published as a "junior novel" was a western. See the discussion in Chapter Two of Rose Wilder Lane's *Let the Hurricane Roar.*

 FOCUS BOX 5.5

Western Books Too Tough to Die

Borderlands by Peter Carter. Farrar, Straus & Giroux, 1990. Ben Curtis joins a cattle drive in 1871, meets an African-American man he learns to respect, and loses his brother in a gunfight.

The Brave Cowboy by Edward Abbey. Dodd Mead, 1956. A cowboy, an anachronism in our modern world, tries to help a friend break out of jail. Failing that, the cowboy flees, pursued by a lawman who won't give up.

Fire on the Mountain by Edward Abbey. Dial, 1962. When the government takes over his property to use as a missile range, an old rancher fights back.

The Last Picture Show by Larry McMurtry. Dial, 1966. The end of the West comes to dusty and drying-up Thalia, Texas, where even the movie theater shuts down.

Little Big Man by Thomas Berger. Dial, 1964. An old-timer tells of his life in the Old West, his capture by the Cheyennes, his work as a scout for General Custer, and other realities and myths. See also *The Return of Little Big Man* (Little, Brown, 1999).

The Man Who Killed the Deer by Frank Waters. Farrar, Straus & Giroux, 1942. A young Indian is caught between two cultures.

The Professor's House by Willa Cather. Knopf, 1925. A teacher, well known for his work on Spanish explorers in America, is lonely. The most intriguing section of the book is about Tom Outland and Mesa Verde National Park.

The Red Pony by John Steinbeck. Viking, 1938. One story, "The Leader of the People," tells what it was like to be westering way back then.

Roughing It by Mark Twain. American, 1872. Twain writes about the Nevada Silver find in the 1860s and his work at Virginia City's *Territorial Enterprise.*

Walking Up a Rainbow by Theodore Taylor. Harcourt Brace, 1994 (an earlier version was published by Delacorte in 1986). In the 1850s, 14-year-old Susan Darden Carlisle is left an orphan in Kanesville, Iowa. To save her family home, she sets out with the help of her elderly guardian and "the first American cowboy" to drive several thousand sheep from Iowa to California.

West of Everything: The Inner Life of Westerns by Jane Tompkins. Oxford University Press, 1992. Tompkins writes about western literature, western films, and everything between or around or near.

Although some of the westerns published specifically for young readers do not fit quite so clearly into the pattern of the romantic quest, most of them are easy reading filled with lots of action, and some provide readers with insights into lesser-known aspects of western history. For example, Kathryn Lasky's *The Bone Wars* is about teams of scientists competing for dinosaur fossils in the American West in the 1800s. Her powerful *Beyond the Divide,* told in journal form, is the story of Meribah Simon and her father, who in 1849 head west after Meribah's father is shunned for attending the funeral of a friend who had failed to observe Amish customs.

Young people growing up in single-parent or newly formed families may be interested in such books as Joan Lowry Nixon's *The Orphan Train Quartet,* which includes *A Family Apart, Caught in the Act, In the Face of Danger,* and *A Place to Belong.* The four stories are based on true accounts of homeless New York children sent to the frontier West for adoption. Isabelle Holland's *The Journey Home* is about two orphaned sisters, 12-year-old Maggie and 7-year-old Annie, who are taken to Kansas and adopted. Annie adjusts and likes the new life, but Maggie feels resentful partly because she's behind her classmates in school and she fears the farm animals. Patricia MacLachlan's *Sarah, Plain and Tall* is also about the forming of a new family. It's a children's story (a Newbery Award winner) of a mail-order bride who comes west to be the mother of Caleb and Anna. The 1991 television special starring Glenn Close was powerful enough to attract readers of all ages to the book.

Another appealing young adult western is Pam Conrad's *Prairie Songs,* about a young doctor and his beautiful wife who are welcomed as newcomers to a Nebraska prairie town. Their joy turns to sorrow, however, as the young wife slips into madness. Liza K. Murrow's *West Against the Wind* is set during gold rush times. Abigail Parker and her family set out for California, in search not for gold but for her missing father.

Gary Paulsen's first book for young adults was *Mr. Tucket,* published in 1969 and described in *Publishers Weekly* as a "real rock'em sock'em ripsnorter." Fourteen-year-old Francis Tucket is kidnapped by Pawnee Indians from an Oregon-bound wagon train. He escapes with help from a one-armed mountain man who over the course of a year teaches Francis how to live in the wilderness. In a 1995 sequel, *Call Me Francis Tucket,* the boy leaves his benefactor and sets off west to find his family. Of course, complications ensue.

Avi's *The Barn,* set in Oregon Territory during the 1850s, is a powerful yet simple story of three pioneer children and their dying father. The youngest child, Ben, is obsessed with the idea that they must build the barn that his now-paralyzed father has always wanted. The other children disagree, and in frustration Ben tries to enlist his father's support by asking him if he wants the barn built and then screaming, "If you mean *yes,* you *must* close your eyes!" The father closes his eyes, but it is never clear whether it was an accident or a purposeful communication. Nevertheless, the children begin work on an amazingly difficult task, all carefully detailed in the book. As they work, they prop their father in a wheelbarrow and bring him outside to watch, but in this sparse and moving story the higher the barn rises, the lower the father sinks.

Accomplishment Stories with Religious Themes

A different kind of accomplishment story is the one in which a young person is helped through a religious experience. In many ways, Cynthia Rylant's *A Fine White Dust* exemplifies this subgenre. The book's title comes from the chalklike dust that gets on Pete's fingers when he handles the "little bitty pieces of broken ceramic" that used to be a cross he had painted in Vacation Bible School—back before he got so old that it was not cool to go anymore. His best friend is a confirmed atheist, and he has "half-washed Christians for parents." Nevertheless, the summer that Preacher Man comes to town, "something religious" begins itching Pete, something that going to church could not cure.

Rylant's skill in developing Pete's character and revealing the depths of his emotions when he is saved and wooed and then betrayed by the Preacher Man won for her a well-deserved Newbery Honor Award. The twelve short chapters are almost an outline for a quest story beginning with "Dust" and a sense of ennui, moving through "The Joy," "The Wait," and "Hell," and ending with "The Light" and "Amen." In the end, Pete decides that, "The Preacher Man is behind me. But God is still right there, in front."

Books that unabashedly explore religious themes are relatively rare, partly because schools and libraries fear mixing church and state through spending tax dollars for religious books. Also, mainstream publishers fear cutting into potential sales by printing books with protagonists whose religious beliefs may offend some readers and make others uncomfortable. It has been easier for schools to include religious books with historical settings, such as Lloyd Douglas's *The Robe,* Scott O'Dell's *The Hawk That Dare Not Hunt by Day,* Elizabeth George Speare's *The Bronze Bow,* and Jessamyn West's *Friendly Persuasion.* Accepted also are books with contemporary settings that have proved themselves with adult readers, for example, Margaret Craven's *I Heard the Owl Call My Name,* Catherine Marshall's *A Man Called Peter,* and William Barrett's *Lilies of the Field.*

In lamenting the shortage of young adult books treating religious themes author Dean Hughes wrote

> We need to be careful that, in effect, we do not say to young people that they *should* be most concerned about pimples and clothes and dates and football games—or even sex. Part of being human is addressing oneself to questions about justice, creation, morality, and the existence of divinity.[3]

Patty Campbell made a similar point when she wrote that although nearly 60 percent of Americans attend some type of religious services, young adult fiction presents a world almost devoid of either personal or corporate religious practices. "Where," she asks, "are the church youth groups, the Hebrew or confirmation classes, the Bible study meetings that are so much a part of middle-class teenage American life? Where, too, is the mainstream liberal Protestant or Catholic practice and sensibility?" Practically the only religious characters developed in young adult books are villains who are "presented as despicable in direct proportion to the degree of their religious involvement."[4]

Examples of the "despicable" characters she was thinking about include the fanatical and unbending parents who make life miserable for their kids in Suzanne Newton's *I Will Call it Georgie's Blues,* Norma Howe's *God, The Universe, and Hot Fudge Sundaes,* and Kathryn Lasky's *Memoirs of a Bookbat.* In Stephanie Tolan's *A Good Courage,* Tie-Dye's hippie mother ends up in a religious commune that forces Tie-Dye to take control of his own future, whereas in M. E. Kerr's *Is That You, Miss Blue?* the hypocritical attitudes of the faculty members at a religious school inspire the students to come to the aid of a teacher who is fired because she "believes." In Bette Greene's *The Drowning of Stephan Jones,* homophobic ministers are at the heart of the evil treatment of two gay men, while in Lois Ruby's *Miriam's Well,* religious leaders do not let Miriam receive medical help. Jane Yolen and Bruce Coville's *Armageddon Summer* is not only about religion gone awry but also about love and survival. Marina and Jed are two teenagers caught up among the 144 "True Believers" chosen by Reverend Beelson to wait with him in an armed camp for the end of the world, predicted to occur on July 27, 2000.

In many ways, the negative portrayal of religion in books for teenagers is similar to the negative portrayal of parents and other authority figures. Such presentations serve as a foil to make the good qualities of the young protagonists shine all the brighter. Authors rely on the general assumption that religious people are good to provide contrast, as when the evil in Robert Cormier's *The Chocolate War* (see Chapter Four) is all the heavier because of the book's setting in a religious school.

Another reason that books for teenagers appear to have so many religious characters portrayed in a negative light is that the good characters go unnoticed. For example, in M. E. Kerr's *Little Little* one of Little Little's suitors is a dishonest evangelical preacher. When Kerr was criticized for this negative portrayal, she pointed out that Little Little's grandfather—the only person in the whole book who approached Little Little's dwarfism with common sense—was also a minister, but few readers noticed because he did his work in the manner expected from a competent clergyman in a mainstream church.

Although there are some good books focusing on broad religious themes and questions about whether there is a God and an afterlife (e.g., Aidan Chambers's *NIK: Now I Know,* Iris Rosofsky's *Miriam,* and Phyllis Reynolds Naylor's *A String of Chances*), what is more common is for an author to bring in religion as a small part of a bigger story. In Jim Naughton's *My Brother Stealing Second,* Bobby reminisces about his family's church experiences before his brother was killed, and in Sue Ellen Bridgers's *Permanent Connections,* Rob finds comfort by visiting a little country church. Katherine Paterson, who has attended theological school and served as a missionary in China, includes both implicit and explicit religious references in her books, most directly in *Jacob Have I Loved* and *Bridge to Terabithia.* Her 1999 *Preacher's Boy* is set in rural Vermont between May of 1899 and January of 1900. The excitement of a new century is part of the story, but rather than being worried about Y2K, Robbie Hewitt is worried about Darwin's theory of evolution and what is predicted to be the end of the world.

Madeleine L'Engle is devout, and along with some other writers of fantasy and science fiction, she includes religious overtones in her books; for example, the struggle between good and evil in *A Wrinkle in Time* and Vicky's hard-won acceptance of her grandfather's dying of leukemia in *A Ring of Endless Light.* Other books that include casual references to religious people and beliefs are Alice Childress's *Rainbow Jordan,* J. D. Salinger's *Franny & Zooey: Two Novellas,* Mary Stolz's *Land's End,* and Jill Paton-Walsh's *Unleaving.* Chaim Potok's *The Chosen, My Name Is Asher Lev,* and *In the Beginning* show what it is to come of age in a Hasidic Jewish community. Cynthia Voigt's *David and Jonathan* asks questions about religious and cultural differences; Marc Talbert's *A Sunburned Prayer* is about 11-year-old Eloy making a seventeen-mile pilgrimage on Good Friday to pray for his grandmother who is dying of cancer.

Of course, religious publishing houses provide books focusing on religious themes, but these are seldom useful in schools because they are aimed so directly at believers of a particular faith, and sometimes in their zeal to convert potential believers, the authors write polemics against other groups. Nevertheless, teachers and librarians are advised to visit local religious bookstores to see what is offered because some students may prefer to fill their independent reading assignments with books from these sources. Today's religious books range from biblical and western romances and adventures to self-help books and inspirational biographies. People who haven't taken a look at religious books over the past few years will probably be surprised at the slick covers and the upscale marketing techniques.

In relation to the accomplishment romance, an especially troublesome group consists of books in which a misguided life is set right by an end-of-the-book conversion. Teachers hesitate to discuss the credibility of such stories because they fear that in the process of building up literary sophistication, they may be tearing down religious faith. Nevertheless, teachers and librarians must seek out and support those authors and publishers who treat religious motifs with honesty as well as with respect for literary quality. They also must help parents and other critics realize that strong religious feelings, including doubts, are part of the maturation process and that reading about the doubts that others have or about imperfections in organized religion does not necessarily destroy one's own faith.

Kathleen Beck, a young adult librarian in Colorado, wrote an article for *VOYA* in which she recommended "Young Adult Fiction for Questioning Christians."[5] Her article was responding to the comment of one of the members of her ecumenical congregation who had observed about the teen members, "They don't know all the answers, but they sure know all the questions." Among the books she recommended that we have not already mentioned were Bruce Brooks's *Asylum for Nightface* in which a boy develops his own religious faith based on the orderliness of the world and in spite of his "self-indulgent, yuppy parents"; Cynthia Voigt's *Tree by Leaf* in which teenager Clothilde gets help in coming to terms with the wounds her father received fighting in World War I; Neal Shusterman's *What Daddy Did* in which a boy begins to understand the complexities of forgiveness when he goes to live with his grandparents after his father had killed his mother; and Gary Schmidt's *The Sin Eater* in which a boy is aided in understanding his father's suicide by the members of the Albion Grace Church of the Holy Open Bible, "whose theology is strict but who know the meaning of grace and compassion." In Han Nolan's *Send Me Down a Miracle*, M. E. Kerr's *What I Really Think of You*, and Gary Paulsen's *The Tent*, young people look questioningly at their parents' careers as evangelical preachers.

Among the more surprising books are those in which young people view themselves as religious figures. For example, in Michael Morpurgo's Honor List book *The War of Jenkins' Ear*, Christopher is an unusual student in an English boarding school who appears to be responsible for a healing, an escape from a vicious bull, and in holding down the violence between two warring groups of young people. When he confides that he is the reincarnation of Jesus, however, fellow students are flummoxed. Tres Seymour treats a similar reaction on the part of students in his *The Revelation of Saint Bruce*. High school senior Bruce Wells earns the name "Saint Bruce" because he refuses to go along with the crowd. Through Biblical allusions and references to mythology, the author gradually reveals Bruce's believable struggles as a modern day quest.

The Love Romance

The love romance is slightly different from the accomplishment romance or the adventure romance, but it shares many of their characteristics. Love stories are symbolically associated with youth and springtime. An ordeal or a problem must be overcome, which is followed by a happy ending. The "problem" is invariably the successful pairing of a likable young couple. An old definition of the love-romance pattern is, "Boy meets girl, boy loses girl, boy wins girl." This is a fairly accurate summary except that with teenage literature it is the other way around. Most of the romances are told from the girl's point of view. She is the one who meets, loses, and finally wins a boy.

The tone of the love romance is lighter than that of the adventure romance (see Focus Box 5.6). In a love story, the protagonist neither risks nor gains as much as in an adventure. Notwithstanding *Romeo and Juliet,* people seldom die, emotionally or physically, because of young love. For this reason, the love romance tends to be less serious in its message. Its power lies in its wish fulfillment. Women of all ages enjoy reading romances for the same reasons that people have always enjoyed either hearing or reading wish-fulfilling fantasies. The "open sesame" door to prosperity and the transformation of a cindermaid into a queen, a frog into a prince, and a

 FOCUS BOX 5.6

Love Stories with Something Extra

The Beetle and Me: A Love Story by Karen Romano Young. Greenwillow, 1999. Daisy Pandolfi wants to restore her father's abandoned 1957 Beetle; she also wants the new boy in town to get a crush on her. When her plans go awry, the story gets more interesting.

Cold Sassy Tree by Olive Ann Burns. Ticknor & Fields, 1984. Although this is the story of Will Tweedy growing up, it's also his grandfather's love story.

Forever by Judy Blume. Bradbury, 1975. Katherine and Michael become sexually involved, and although nobody gets punished, their love does not last forever.

"Hello," I Lied by M. E. Kerr. HarperCollins, 1997. Sixteen-year-old Lang expects to have a wonderful summer when his mother gets a job as cook for a legendary rock star in the East Hamptons. Lang is gay, but only his mother and his partner, Alex, know. He finds himself attracted to a French girl visiting for the summer and begins to question his wants and beliefs.

If Beale Street Could Talk by James Baldwin. Doubleday, 1974. In this mature story told in frank, black English, pregnant Tish loves Fonny, who has been jailed on a false charge.

If You Come Softly by Jacqueline Woodson.

Putnam, 1998. This story of love between a white girl and a black boy was chosen as one of the top ten books of 1998 by the Young Adult Library Services Association.

Love Among the Walnuts by Jean Ferris. Harcourt, 1998. If nothing else gives readers a clue that this is a melodramatic and romantic spoof, the names of the two protagonists should suffice: millionaire Horatio Alger Huntington Ackerman and aspiring actress Mousey Malone.

The Stone Fey by Robin McKinley, illustrated by John Clapp. Harcourt, 1998. A shepherdess, who is waiting for her fiancé to return, is entranced by a stone fey (or fairy), and is able to break his spell only through the help of her fiancé who comes to her in a dream. This fifty-two-page illustrated short story is a good introduction to the power of McKinley's writing in such books as *Beauty* (HarperCollins, 1978) and *A Knot in the Grain and Other Stories* (Greenwillow, 1994).

The Unlikely Romance of Kate Bjorkman by Louise Plummer. Delacorte Press, 1995. Kate Bjorkman is a high school senior who is six-feet tall and is much too smart and too funny to write a typical romance, but that's what makes this first-person story refreshing.

Scrooge into a kindly old man are all examples of the same satisfying theme that is the key to the appeal of love romances. In the teen romances, an ugly duckling girl is transformed by the love of a boy into a swan. In her new role as swan, she is not only popular and successful but also happy.

For the writer of a love story, probably no talent is more important than the ability to create believable characters. If readers do not feel that they know the boy and girl or the man and woman as individuals, they cannot identify with them and consequently will not care whether they make it or not. Another characteristic of the good love story is that it provides something beyond the simple pairing of two individuals. This something extra may be interesting historical facts, introduction to a social issue, glimpses into the complexity of human nature, or any of the understandings and concepts that might be found in quality books or movies. Stories come to life when an author is able to pick out and present the unexpected details that come from close observation.

Although most formula romances are aimed exclusively at a female audience, comparable to the way that most pornography is aimed at a male audience, some writers are trying to write romances that are also read by boys, even though they are not sports, adventure, or mystery stories. Hazel Rochman described such books as "domestic novels about boys in which heroes stay home and struggle with their feelings and their conscience rather than with tumultuous external events." Many such books are love stories, and as Rochman observed,

> The theme of so many girls' books finding that you love the boy next door after all has a new vitality from the male perspective, as in [Harry] Mazer's *I Love You, Stupid!* Sex is treated with honesty: in [Chris] Crutcher's *Running Loose,* after a long romantic buildup in which the couple drive and then ski to an isolated cabin for a weekend of lovemaking, the jock hero finds that he cannot perform. In [Richard] Peck's *Father Figure* and [Katie Letcher] Lyle's *Dark But Full of Diamonds,* the love for an older woman, in rivalry with the boy's own father, is movingly handled. . . . in *The Course of True Love Never Did Run Smooth,* [Marilyn] Singer's heroine finds strong and sexy a boy who is short, funny, and vulnerable.[6]

The most obvious difference between these boy-oriented romances and the larger body of love stories written from a girl's point of view is that their authors, who are mostly men, tend to put less emphasis on courtship and romance and more on sexuality. Rather than relying on discreet fade-outs, they allow their readers to know what happens, which sometimes means sexual intercourse. For the most part, the descriptions are neither pornographic nor lovingly romantic, but in such books as Chris Crutcher's *Running Loose,* Robert Lehrman's *Juggling,* Terry Davis's *Vision Quest,* and Aidan Chambers's *The Toll Bridge,* there is little doubt about the abundance of sexual feelings that the characters experience.

As an antidote to the lopsidedness of books that are either overly romantic or overly sexy, some adult critics suggest offering books in which boys and girls are as much friends as lovers. This is especially true in lighter books read by 11-, 12- and 13-year olds (see Focus Box 5.7). The romantic relationship is only part of a bigger story, and there is no indication of either partner exploiting or manipulating the other, as often happens in exaggerated romances or in pornographic or sex-oriented stories. As a ploy to attract male readers, because authors already feel con-

Love and Laughs for Junior High/Middle Schoolers

Bad, Badder, Baddest by Cynthia Voigt. Scholastic, 1998. In this sequel to *Bad Girls* (Scholastic, 1996), Gianette, a Creole orphan from New Orleans, has come to live with her grandmother and adds some spice to the Magalo and Mikey duo.

The Best School Year Ever by Barbara Robinson. HarperCollins, 1994. In this sequel to *The Best Christmas Pageant Ever* (HarperCollins, 1972) the Herdmans continue to make life interesting for their classmates.

Can of Worms by Kathy Mackel. Avon/Camelot, 1999. Mike Pillsbury has a reason for feeling that he doesn't fit in at his junior high; he's really an alien. Even he is surprised that when he finally gets a chance to go home, he doesn't want to leave.

The Cat Ate My Gymsuit by Paula Danziger. Delacorte, 1974. Danziger's first book combines humor with pathos in the everyday problems of overweight Marcy who hates to dress for P.E. Other funny Danziger books all from Delacorte include *The Pistachio Prescription* (1978), *Can You Sue Your Parents for Malpractice* (1979), *There's a Bat in Bunk Five* (1980), and *The Divorce Express* (1982).

Extreme Elvin by Chris Lynch. HarperCollins, 1999. It is the beginning of Elvin's freshman year at high school, and his friendships with Mikie and Frankie, as well as with his single mom, are going to be tested. Most of what happens will be more amusing to readers than to Elvin.

Flour Babies by Anne Fine. Little, Brown, 1992. When the boys in Room 8 are assigned to "experience parenthood" by taking care of a six-pound sack of flour for three weeks, Simon learns more than he thinks he will. This witty British author (see her statement on p. 28) also wrote *Alias Madame Doubtfire* (Little, Brown, 1988), the source of the popular movie starring Robin Williams, and *The Book of the Banshee* (Scholastic, 1994), another funny exploration of family relationships.

Green Thumb by Rob Thomas. Simon & Schuster, 1999. Witty and smart Grady Jacobs is a 13-year-old science fair winner and botanical genius. When he gets invited to participate in a rain forest experiment, he learns more than he bargained for.

I Love You, I Hate You, Get Lost: A Collection of Short Stories by Ellen Conford. Scholastic, 1994. Conford's witty writing and on-target dialogue make her a favorite for young readers. Among her other popular titles are *Dear Lovey Hart, I Am Desperate* (Little, Brown, 1975), *The Alfred G. Graebner Memorial High School Handbook of Rules and Regulations* (Little, Brown, 1976), *If This Is Love, I'll Take Spaghetti* (Four Winds, 1983), *The Things I Did for Love* (Bantam, 1987), and *Dear Mom, Get Me Out of Here!* (Little, Brown, 1992), which, in a change from Conford's other books, has a male protagonist.

Lockie Leonard, Scumbuster by Tim Winton. Simon & Schuster, 1999. This Australian sequel to *Lockie Leonard, Human Torpedo* (Little, Brown, 1992) proves that not all stories set in foreign countries are grim problem novels. Lockie is a 13-year-old surfer, his friend Geoff is into heavy metal music, and Lockie's true love (only temporarily) is an Elle McPherson look-alike surfer.

A Long Way from Chicago by Richard Peck. Dial, 1998. Between 1929 and 1935, Joey Dowdel and his sister Mary Alice spend a week each summer with their grandmother in downstate, rural Illinois. Although the humorous adventures recounted in this Newbery Honor Book are true-to-life, they bear similarities to Peck's delightful Blossom Culp ghost stories.

Sixth Grade Secrets by Louis Sachar. Scholastic, 1987. Laura Sibbie wavers between childhood with her smooth, long hair, and rebellion with her "Pig City" hat. Sachar plays with a similar theme in *The Boy Who Lost His Face* (Knopf, 1989).

Squashed by Joan Bauer. Delacorte, 1992. Ellie Morgan wants to lose 20 pounds for herself and gain 20 pounds for Max, the giant pumpkin she's growing for the Rock River Pumpkin Weigh-In. Other light-hearted Bauer books include *Thwonk* (Delacorte, 1995), starring photographer A. J. McCreary, and *Sticks* (Delacorte, 1996), starring pool player Mickey Vernon.

There's A Girl in My Hammerlock by Jerry Spinelli. Simon and Schuster, 1991. Even when Spinelli is treating serious themes, he zeroes in on the ironies and contradictions of adolescence as in *Space Station Seventh Grade* (Little, Brown, 1982), *Who Put That Hair in My Toothbrush?* (Little, Brown, 1984), and *The Library Card* (Scholastic, 1997).

fident that girls will read love stories, the narrator may be the boy, or there may be a mix with alternate chapters coming from the boy and the girl, as in Paul Zindel's *The Pigman* and in M. E. Kerr's *I'll Love You When You're More Like Me.*

The runaway popularity of formula love romances written especially for teenagers and published as original paperbacks was the big marketing surprise of the early 1980s. Formula romances most often feature girls 15, 16, or 17 years old with boyfriends who are slightly older. The target audience is supposedly girls between the ages of 12 and 16, although some 10 and 11 year olds are also finding them. The typical setting is a small town or suburb. There is no explicit sex or profanity. As one editor told us, "If there are problems, they have to be normal ones: no drugs, no sex, no alcohol, no bad parents, etc." This was not so true by the 1990s when the writers of formula romances began including strands of social criticism in their books, while the writers of "serious" fiction began looking for ways to lighten social issues.

Formula romances have many of the same qualities that publishers have developed for high-interest, low-vocabulary books. They are short books divided into short chapters. They have quick beginnings, more action than description, considerable use of dialogue, a straightforward point of view, and a reading level not much above fifth grade. Perhaps most important of all, the books are clearly labeled, so that readers know what they are getting. As shown by the popularity of movie sequels, television serials and reruns, and continuing columns in newspapers, although viewers and readers do not want to see or read precisely the same thing over and over again, they are comforted by knowing that a particular piece is going to be similar to something they have previously enjoyed.

Some adults worry that teenage readers take the books seriously, that they fail to recognize them as fantasy, and that they, therefore, model their behavior and attitudes—and, more important, their expectations—after those portrayed in the romances. A sampling of published quotations from critics illustrates a range of concern.

> . . . implicit in these hygienic stories are the old, damaging and limiting stereotypes from which we've struggled so hard to free ourselves and our children: that the real world is white and middle-class; that motherhood is women's only work; that a man is the ultimate prize and a woman is incomplete without one; and that in the battle for that prize, the weapons are good looks and charm, intelligence is a liability, and the enemy is the other woman.[7]

> There is an eternal paradox here. We read such romantic stories as an escape from reality and yet they form our ideals of what reality should be. Hence that frustration, that vague sense of failure and disappointment when a night out at the disco doesn't turn out the way it does in the magazines.[8]

In an attempt to appear wholesome enough to be mass marketed to girls in their early teens, many authors of formula romances encourage a kind of wish fulfillment that relates to the psychological ambivalence that young females feel about sexuality. On the one hand, girls want to be loved, not only because it is emotionally satisfying but also because dating and courtship are glamorous and exciting. On the other hand, many of them are not yet ready for a sexual relationship and would be happy to have the dating and the cuddling without the complications of sex. This makes authors gloss over the part that sex plays in male-female relationships. In many of the books, it is love at first sight, which must imply a physical attraction (i.e., a sexual attraction), yet the boys are portrayed as being almost platonically interested in the girl's thoughts and feelings rather than in her body. When Rainbow Jordan, the protagonist in Alice Childress's realistic book of the same name, learned that this was not the way it was in real life, she complained,

> True love is mostly featured in fairy tales. Sleepin' Beauty put off sex for a hundred years. When a prince finally did find her . . . he kiss her gently, then they gallop off on a pretty horse so they could enjoy the happy-ever-after. They never mentioned sex.

Defenders of formula romances most often focus on their popularity and the fact that they are recreational reading freely chosen by young girls who otherwise would most likely be watching TV. Teachers and librarians need to be especially careful in criticizing students' enjoyment of romances because young readers are as sensitive as anyone else to hints that they are gullible and lacking in taste and sophistication. So rather than making fun of love romances, one should approach them from a positive angle, offering readers a wide variety of books, including ones that treat boy-girl relationships not as the only thing of importance but as part of a bigger picture.

The various types of accomplishment and adventure stories, including love romances, are psychologically satisfying. More than any other genre, these stories match the particular stage of life that is young adulthood. Because of this match, and because the plots are straightforward and the reading levels are generally comfortable, the books discussed in this chapter are likely to remain among the most popular for young adult leisure time reading.

Notes

[1] Frances Bradburn, "Focus: Dear Diary," *Booklist* 90 (June 1 & 15, 1994): 1791.

[2] Glenna Davis Sloan, *The Child as Critic* (Teachers College Press, 1975), p. 33.

[3] Dean Hughes, "Bait/Rebait: Books with Religious Themes," *English Journal* 70 (December 1981): 14–17.

[4] Patty Campbell, "The Sand in the Oyster," *The Horn Book Magazine,* (September/October 1994): 619.

[5] Kathleen Beck, "I Believe It, I Doubt It: Young Adult Fiction for Questioning Christians," *VOYA* 21:2 (June 1998): 103–104.

[6] Hazel Rochman, "Bringing Boys' Books Home," *School Library Journal* 29 (August 1983): 26–27.

[7] Brett Harvey, "Wildfire: Tame but Deadly," *Interracial Books for Children Bulletin* 12 (1981).

[8] Mary Harron, "Oh Boy! My Guy," (London) *Times Educational Supplement* (July 1, 1983): 22.

Titles Mentioned in the Text of Chapter Five

Aaron, Henry and Lonnie Wheeler. *I Had a Hammer: The Hank Aaron Story*. HarperCollins, 1991.

Allen, Maury. *Baseball's 100: A Personal Ranking of the Best Players in Baseball History*. A & W, 1981.

Anonymous. *Go Ask Alice*. Prentice-Hall, 1969.

Avi. *The Barn*. Orchard, 1993.

Barrett, William. *Lilies of the Field*. Doubleday, 1962.

Bennett, James. *The Squared Circle*. Scholastic, 1995.

Bradley, Bill. *Values of the Game*. Artisan, 1998.

Brancato, Robin. *Winning*. Knopf, 1977.

Bridgers, Sue Ellen. *Permanent Connections.* Harper-Collins, 1987.

Brooks, Bruce. *Asylum for Nightface.* HarperCollins, 1996.

Brooks, Bruce. *The Moves Make the Man.* Harper-Collins, 1984.

Burnett, Francis Hodgson. *The Secret Garden.* 1911.

Chambers, Aiden. *NIK: Now I Know.* HarperCollins, 1988.

Chambers, Aiden. *The Toll Bridge.* HarperCollins, 1995.

Childress, Alice. *Rainbow Jordan.* Putnam, 1981.

Conrad, Pam. *Prairie Songs.* HarperCollins, 1985.

Cormier, Robert. *The Chocolate War.* Pantheon, 1974.

Craven, Margaret. *I Heard the Owl Call My Name.* Doubleday, 1973.

Crompton, Anne Eliot. *The Sorcerer.* Second Chance, 1982.

Crutcher, Chris. *The Crazy Horse Electric Game.* Greenwillow, 1987.

Crutcher, Chris. *Running Loose.* Greenwillow, 1983.

Davis, Terry. *Vision Quest.* Viking, 1979.

Dawidoff, Nicholas. *The Catcher Was a Spy: The Mysterious Life of Moe Berg.* Pantheon, 1994.

Douglas, Lloyd. *The Robe.* Houghton Mifflin, 1942.

Durso, Joseph. *DiMaggio: The Last American Knight.* Little, Brown, 1995.

Eckert, Allan W. *Incident at Hawk's Hill.* Little, Brown, 1971.

Freedman, Russell. *Babe Didrikson Zaharias: The Making of a Champion.* Clairon, 1999.

Frey, Darcy. *The Last Shot.* Houghton Mifflin, 1995.

George, Jean. *Julie.* HarperCollins, 1994.

George, Jean. *Julie of the Wolves.* HarperCollins, 1972.

Gipson, Fred. *Old Yeller.* HarperCollins, 1964.

Grahame, Kenneth. *Wind in the Willows.* 1908.

Green, Hannah. *I Never Promised You a Rose Garden.* Holt, 1964.

Greene, Bette. *The Drowning of Stephan Jones.* Bantam, 1991.

Gregorich, Barbara. *Women at Play: The Story of Women in Baseball.* Harcourt Brace, 1993.

Guest, Judith. *Ordinary People.* Viking, 1976.

Halbertstam, David. *Playing for Keeps: Michael Jordan and the World He Made.* Random House, 1999.

Hall, Donald. *Fathers Playing Catch with Sons.* North Point, 1985.

Hamilton, Virginia. *M. C. Higgins, the Great.* Macmillan, 1974.

Harris, Mark. *Bang the Drum Slowly.* Knopf, 1956.

Hess, Elizabeth. *Lost and Found: Dogs, Cats, and Everyday Heroes at a Country Animal Shelter.* Harcourt Brace, 1998.

Holland, Isabelle. *The Journey Home.* Scholastic, 1990.

Howe, Norma. *God, the Universe, and Hot Fudge Sundaes.* Houghton Mifflin, 1984.

Kerr, M. E. *I'll Love You When You're More Like Me.* HarperCollins, 1977.

Kerr, M. E. *Is That You, Miss Blue?* HarperCollins, 1975.

Kerr, M. E. *Little Little.* HarperCollins, 1981.

Kerr, M. E. *What I Really Think of You.* HarperCollins, 1982.

Klass, David. *Danger Zone.* Scholastic, 1996.

Lane, Rose Wilder. *Let the Hurricane Roar.* Longmans Green, 1933.

Lasky, Kathryn. *Beyond the Divide.* Macmillan, 1983.

Lasky, Kathryn. *The Bone Wars.* Morrow, 1988.

Lasky, Kathryn. *Memoirs of a Bookbat.* Harcourt, 1994.

Lehrman, Robert. *Juggling.* HarperCollins, 1982.

L'Engle, Madeleine. *A Ring of Endless Light.* Farrar, Straus & Giroux, 1980.

L'Engle, Madeleine. *A Wrinkle in Time.* Farrar, Straus & Giroux, 1962.

Lipsyte, Robert. *The Brave.* HarperCollins, 1991.

Lipsyte, Robert. *The Contender.* HarperCollins, 1967.

Lyle, Katie Letcher. *Dark But Full of Diamonds.* Putnam, 1981.

Lynch, Chris. *Iceman.* HarperCollins, 1994.

Lynch, Chris. *Shadow Boxer.* HarperCollins, 1993

Lynch, Chris. *Slot Machine.* HarperCollins, 1995.

MacLachlan, Patricia. *Sarah, Plain and Tall.* Harper-Collins, 1985.

Macy, Sue. *A Whole New Ball Game.* Holt, 1993.

Marshall, Catherine. *A Man Called Peter.* McGraw-Hill, 1951.

Mazer, Harry. *I Love You, Stupid!* HarperCollins, 1981.

McFee, John. *A Sense of Where You Are: Bill Bradley at Princeton.* Farrar, Straus & Giroux, 1999. (First published in 1965.)

Morpugo, Michael. *The War of Jenkins' Ear.* Philomel, 1995.

Murrow, Liza K. *West Against the Wind.* Holiday House, 1987.

Myers, Walter Dean. *Hoops.* Delacorte, 1981.

Myers, Walter Dean. *The Outside Shot.* Delacorte, 1984.

Naughton, Jim. *My Brother Stealing Second.* Harper-Collins, 1989.

Naylor, Phyllis R. *A String of Chances.* Atheneum, 1982.

Newton, Suzanne. *I Will Call It Georgie's Blues.* Viking, 1983.

Nixon, Joan Lowry. *The Orphan Train Quartet (A Family Apart, Caught in the Act, In the Face of Danger,* and *A Place to Belong).* Bantam, late 1980s.

Nolan, Han. *Send Me Down a Miracle.* Harcourt Brace, 1996.

North, Sterling. *Rascal: A Memoir of a Better Era.* E. P. Dutton, 1963.

O'Dell, Scott. *The Hawk That Dare Not Hunt by Day.* Houghton Mifflin, 1975.

Paterson, Katherine. *Jacob Have I Loved.* Crowell, 1980.

Paterson, Katherine. *Preacher's Boy.* Clarion, 1999.

Paulsen, Gary. *Call Me Francis Tucket.* Delacorte, 1995.

Paulsen, Gary. *Canyons.* Delacorte, 1990.

Paulsen, Gary. *Dogsong.* Bradbury, 1985.

Paulsen, Gary. *Harris and Me.* Harcourt Brace, 1993.

Paulsen, Gary. *Hatchet*. Bradbury, 1987.

Paulsen, Gary. *The Haymeadow*. Doubleday, 1992.

Paulsen, Gary. *The Island*. Orchard, 1988.

Paulsen, Gary. *The Monument*. Delacorte, 1991.

Paulsen, Gary. *Mr. Tucket*. Funk & Wagnalls, 1969.

Paulsen, Gary. *The Tent: A Parable in One Sitting*. Harcourt Brace, 1995.

Paulsen, Gary. *Tracker*. Bradbury, 1984.

Paulsen, Gary. *The Voyage of the Frog*. Orchard, 1989.

Paulsen, Gary. *Woodsong*. Bradbury, 1990.

Peck, Richard. *Father Figure*. Viking, 1978.

Potok, Chaim. *The Chosen*. Simon & Schuster, 1967.

Potok, Chaim. *In the Beginning*. Knopf, 1975.

Potok, Chaim. *My Name Is Asher Lev*. Knopf, 1972.

Rawlings, Marjorie Kinnan. *The Yearling*. Scribner's, 1938.

Rawls, Wilson. *Where the Red Fern Grows*. Doubleday, 1961.

Ribowsky, Mark. *Don't Look Back: Satchel Paige in the Shadows of Baseball*. Simon & Schuster, 1994.

Robinson, Rachel with Lee Daniels. *Jackie Robinson: An Intimate Portrait*. Harry Abrams, 1996.

Rosofsky, Iris. *Miriam*. HarperCollins, 1988.

Ruby, Lois. *Miriam's Well*. Scholastic, 1993.

Ryan, Joan. *Little Girls in Pretty Boxes: The Making and Breaking of Elite Gymnasts and Figure Skaters*. Doubleday, 1995.

Rylant, Cynthia. *A Fine White Dust*. Bradbury, 1986.

Salinger, J. D. *The Catcher in the Rye*. Little, Brown, 1951.

Salinger, J. D. *Franny & Zooey: Two Novellas*. Little, Brown, 1961.

Schmidt, Gary. *The Sin Eater*. Dutton, 1996.

Seidel, Michael. *Ted Williams: A Baseball Life*. Contemporary Books, 1991.

Seymour, Tres. *The Revelation of Saint Bruce*. Orchard, 1998.

Shaeffer, Jack. *Shane*. Houghton Mifflin, 1949.

Shusterman, Neal. *What Daddy Did*. Little, Brown, 1991.

Singer, Marilyn. *The Course of True Love Never Did Run Smooth*. HarperCollins, 1983.

Sokolove, Michael. *Hustle, The Myth, Life, and Lies of Pete Rose*. Simon & Schuster, 1990.

Smith, Ron. *The Sporting News Selects Baseball's Greatest Players*. Sporting News Publishing Co., 1998.

Sparks, Beatrice, editor. *It Happened to Nancy*. Avon/Flare, 1994.

Speare, Elizabeth George. *The Bronze Bow*. Houghton Mifflin, 1973.

Spinelli, Jerry. *There's a Girl in My Hammerlock*. Simon & Schuster, 1991.

Stolz, Mary. *Land's End*. HarperCollins, 1973.

Talbert, Marc. *A Sunburned Prayer*. Simon & Schuster, 1995.

Tolan, Stephanie. *A Good Courage*. Morrow, 1988.

Tolkien, J. R. R. *The Lord of the Rings*. Houghton Mifflin, 1974.

Trudell, Dennis, editor. *Full Court: A Literary Anthology of Basketball*. Breakaway, 1996.

Voigt, Cynthia. *David and Jonathan*. Scholastic, 1992.

Voigt, Cynthia. *Izzy, Willy-Nilly*. Atheneum, 1986.

Voigt, Cynthia. *Tree by Leaf*. Simon & Schuster, 1998.

Wallace, Rich. *Wrestling Sturbridge*. Knopf, 1996.

Walsh, Jill Paton. *Unleaving*. Farrar, Straus & Giroux, 1976.

West, Jessamyn. *Friendly Persuasion*. Harcourt Brace Jovanovich, 1956.

Wister, Owen. *The Virginian: A Horseman of the Plains*. Macmillan, 1902.

Yolen, Jane and Bruce Coville. *Armageddon Summer*. Harcourt, 1998.

Zindel, Paul. *The Pigman*. HarperCollins, 1968.

Information on the availability of paperback editions of these titles is available online from such book sellers as Barnes & Noble and Amazon.com, and through *Books in Print* compiled by R. R. Bowker Company and available either in person or online from major libraries.

Adventure, Mysteries, the Supernatural, and Humor
From Goose Bumps to Giggles

The genres discussed in this chapter are usually considered to provide pleasure rather than intellectual stimulation and growth. Remembering English teachers who pleaded with us to "read only the best—the classics," we feel vaguely worried if we are reading books simply to enjoy characters and their adventures. Somewhat defensively, we make claims that are hard to substantiate. For example, we claim that reading about adventures makes us more interesting people, mysteries are psychologically helpful to our inner–well-being, horror stories are a substitute for aggression, and having a sense of humor makes us healthy. These claims may have some truth, but they are hard to prove. We would be on safer ground if we simply accepted "Rosenberg's First Law of Reading: Never apologize for your reading tastes,"[1] and promoted the idea that reading for pleasure is a worthy activity and goal, in and of itself. If we, or our students, gain something more than pleasure, we should be grateful that serendipity is still at work in today's complex world.

The cover message on the September 6, 1999, *Time* magazine was "Why We Take Risks." The inside story was headlined "Life on the Edge" followed with the legend "Is everyday life too dull? Why else would Americans seek risk as never before?" After that came a litany of Americans at risk: skiing, mountain climbing, rock climbing, firefighting, race-car driving, even the most dangerous of them all, buying and trading options in futures on the Chicago Board of Trade.

Less than three weeks later Betsy Wade in "How Safe Are Thrill Rides?" in the Travel section of the September 26, 1999, *New York Times* worried about our propensity for thrills and chills. Her article was nominally about thrill rides in amusement parks and carnivals, but her comment seemed equally apropos of our apparent drive to test our mortality.

Proof that the adventurous spirit was not restricted to Americans, if proof was ever needed, came from the July 8, 1999, *New York Times* in an extended obituary of Thor Kappfjell, 32, who was certainly enamored of adventure. Kappfjell, a parachutist, died jumping off a 3,300-foot cliff in his native Norway, but his earlier exploits testified to his fearlessness. He had jumped from more than 200 mountains, towers, and buildings—including the Eiffel tower, the Empire State Building, and the World Trade Center.

Adventure books sell. A story in the May 31, 1999, *U.S. News and World Report* was entitled "Going to Extremes, Again. The Adventure-Book Craze Shows No Signs of Slowing." The author seemed to be a bit surprised and regretful that:

> First time authors with harrowing man-against-nature tales are now commanding six-figure advances, and obscure historians are hauling in contracts worth up to a million or more to retell legendary epics.

What shocking news—that the ancients loved and retold adventure stories of the gods and mortals like Hector and Achilles and Odysseus; that later writers told of the adventures of Don Quixote or Jonathan Wild or Tom Sawyer or Huck Finn or Sherlock Holmes; that popular writers of the nineteenth and twentieth centuries made their living by writing adventures—William Makepeace Thackeray, Charles Reade, Charles Dickens, Mark Twain, Rafael Sabatini, H. Rider Haggard, and many more—that people today often live such sedentary lives that they must seek adventure and temporarily leave their dull lives whenever they can.

Adventure Stories

"Once upon a time" is a magical phrase. In one way or another, it opens every adventure tale and suggests actions that precede and follow it with all the implied excitement that is inevitable. We may care about the people in these adventures, but we care equally—or more—about the actions to come. The greatest of these is implied violence, things we fear that will happen. The pace and tempo force the action to move faster and faster and to speed you into the tale.

The most commonly anthologized adventure story, almost devoid of characterization, is Richard Connell's "The Most Dangerous Game." This classic adventure short story reduces the cast to two people: the big game hunter Sanger Rainsford and the equally great big-game General Zaroff. The setting is simple, an apparently deserted island. Before being accidentally tossed ashore, Rainsford and a friend talked about the nature of hunting and debated whether a wild animal could feel fear or impending death. Rainsford had said, "Be a realist. The world is made up of two classes—the hunter and the huntee," but he regrets his glibness when he realizes that Zaroff is mad. Zaroff proposes that they play a hunting game. Rainsford will be given a head start, and Zaroff will track and attempt to bag him. Whoever wins, and it's clear Zaroff knows he will not lose, lays claim to Zaroff's castle and all he owns. Once Zaroff makes clear that the only animal he thinks is worth hunting is the only animal who *thinks,* few readers will be able to stop, and we're off into a frightening tale of danger.

Better adventure tales demand more than plot and a series of actions (see Table 6.1). Good writers provide believable characters, at least a likable and imperfect (and probably young) protagonist and a wily and dangerous antagonist (or villain), but because we are primarily interested in the action, we're likely to be irritated by long descriptive or meditative passages. Writers must reveal characterization through the plot—what could happen, what might happen, and how do all the incidents tie together.

TABLE 6.1

SUGGESTIONS FOR EVALUATING ADVENTURE STORIES

A good adventure story has most of the positive qualities generally associated with good fiction. In addition it usually has:	A poor adventure story may have the negative qualities generally associated with poor fiction. It is particularly prone to have:
A likable protagonist with whom young readers can identify	A protagonist who is too exaggerated or too stereotyped to be believable
An adventure that readers can imagine happening to themselves	Nothing really exciting about the adventure
Efficient characterization	Only stereotyped characters
An interesting setting that enhances the story without getting in the way of the plot	A long drawn-out conclusion after the climax has been reached
Action that draws readers into the plot within the first page or so of the story	

We want surprises and turns of the screw. Heroes become trapped and the only way to safety is through even greater jeopardy. Of the three basic conflicts, adventure tales usually focus on person against person, although person against nature and person against self may become important as the tale unfolds and the protagonist faces frustration and possible failure. Readers of adventure tales feel much the same way about taking a chance with adventure as did Susan Hiscock. For fifty years she and her husband sailed the globe, Hiscock never letting loose of her wanderlust. She was a fan of Arthur Ransome's books, and she and her husband painted a motto from Ransome over their cabin door: "Grab a chance and you won't be sorry for a might-have-been."[2] That's a great motto for reading or living.

The most important literary device found in adventure stories is verisimilitude. With so much emphasis on danger, writers must provide realistic details galore to assure us, despite some inner misgivings, that the tale is possible and believable. We must believe that whatever the hero's frustrations, the cliffhanging scenes are possible.

Robb White's *Deathwatch* epitomizes the elements of adventure novels—person versus person, person versus nature, person versus self, conflicts, tension, thrills, chills, and a hero frustrated at every turn by an inventive, devious, and cruel villain. The first paragraph forces us into the action and introduces the two actors:

> "There he is!" Madec whispered. "Keep still!" There had been a movement up on the ridge of the mountain. For a moment something had appeared between the two rock outcrops.
> "I didn't see any horns," Ben said.
> "Keep quiet!" Madec whispered fiercely.

We know from those few words that *Deathwatch* has something to do with hunting, although we have no reason yet to suspect that hunting will become an ominous metaphor. We recognize that the name *Madec* sounds harsh and seems vaguely related to the word *mad*, again without recognizing how prescient we are. Within the next few pages, we learn how carefully White has placed the clues before us. Ben crouches with his little .22 Hornet and watches Madec with his "beautifully made .385 Magnum Mauser action on a Winchester 70 stock with enough

power to knock down an elephant—or turn a sleeping Gila monster into a splatter"
and remembers that Madec had been willing to shoot anything that moved.

> Madec huddled over his gun. There was an intensity in his eyes far beyond
> that of just hunting a sheep. It was the look of murder.

And murder is present. Before long, Madec takes a shot at a bighorn sheep,
which turns out to be an old desert prospector—now quite dead—and he asks Ben
to quash the incident and forget it ever happened. Ben refuses, and the book is off
and running. So is Ben, running for his life, without gun, water, or food, amid hostile desert mountains and sand and a killing gun.

Madec personifies the maddened but crafty villain, able to read Ben's mind and
forestall his attempts to get clothes, weapons, or water. We are almost certain Ben
will win, but we wonder because Madec is an extraordinary opponent. We see Ben
change from a calm, rational young man to a frightened, desperate animal and then
into a cold, dangerous person who must think as Madec thinks to win out over the
villain. Madec begins with all the power on his side—guns, water, food, and wealth.
Given reality, we know that Madec must win, but given our sense of rightness and
justice, we believe that he cannot be allowed to win. Ben has little interest in right
or wrong after the first few pages. His interest is more elemental and believable—
simple survival until he can escape.

Adventure stories come in many forms and genres. Those who loved the film
Titanic may delight in Jennifer Carter and Joel Hirschhorn's *Titanic Adventure,* an
autobiography of a woman whose love of the sea and fascination with shipwrecks
ultimately led her to the Titanic. Don Lynch's *Titanic: An Illustrated History* is a
colorfully illustrated marvel by the historian of the Titanic Historical Society.

Two seafaring adventure writers for young adults are Iain Lawrence and Geraldine McCaughrean (see her statement on p. 241). In Lawrence's *The Wreckers,* a
young man who longs for the sea but is denied it by his businessman father, becomes involved in the dangerous business of looting wrecked ships. His adventures
continue in *The Smugglers.* McCaughrean's *The Pirate's Son,* packed with derring-
do, opens with the death of Nathan Gull's father and Nathan's being forced out of
his school because he has no money. Luckily for Nathan, Tamo White, son of a pirate, leaves school because he misses his homeland and takes Nathan with him.

Even if readers suffer from claustrophobia, some find satisfaction in vicariously spelunking. Michael Ray Taylor's *Cave Passages: Roaming the Underground
Wilderness* should assuage the latter need as Taylor takes readers into a number of
his adventures underground, from a Chinese burial cave to a sinkhole in Mexico.
Michael Coleman's *Weirdo's War* is the story of two boys who fall into an underground cavern and must work their way out.

Others prefer to enter the world of books about mountain climbing even if
they suffer from acrophobia. Arlene Blum's *Annapurna: A Woman's Place* tells of thirteen women climbers who tackle one of the world's great challenges. Two reached
the top, two died. Jim Wickwire's *Addicted to Danger* gives readers some sense of
what it means to battle mountains, against all odds doing what the human body
was never meant to endure. Julie Tullis's *Clouds from Both Sides* is the biography of
a woman who at 47 conquered K2 and died two days later. Tom Holzol and Audrey
Salkeld's *First on Everest: The Mystery of Mallory and Irvine* is about the two climbers
who in June 1924 were seen for the last time 800 feet from the summit of Everest.

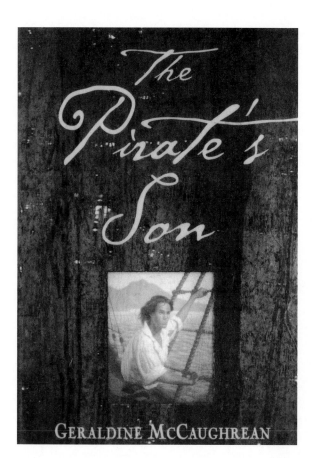

Travel, especially by ship, is a perfect setting for adventure.

Robert C. O'Brien's *Z for Zachariah* is a dystopian look at our future, but it is also a book of adventure. Julian F. Thompson's *The Grounding of Group Six* about some misfit teenagers whose parents have paid to have them killed is a mystery. Harry Mazer's *The Island Keeper* starts with a person-versus-self conflict when Cleo Murphy, fat and rich and lonely, decides on a whim to ditch plans for summer camp and spend the summer alone on Duck Island near her father's property. The elements conspire against her, and the story turns into a powerful tale of personal growth and survival.

William B. Karesh's *Appointment at the Ends of the World: Memoirs of a Wildlife Veterinarian* is an animal book, but it's also an adventure tale as Karesh hedgehops around the world to monitor wildlife populations. Other animal stories with goodly portions of adventure include Robert Westall's *Blitzcat* about World War II and a lost cat who finds his way into the homes and hearts of many people. A. M. Wilson's *Stray* is the tale of Pufftail, who has a few good times mixed with being mistreated by other cats or humans, while Chap Reaver's *Bill* is about a dog who protects a young girl from an alcoholic father and helps her search for buried treasure.

Patrick O'Brien's *The Hundred Days* is a page-turner of historical account of the Napoleonic wars and two men who appear in all of O'Brien's novels, Captain Jack Aubrey and a doctor and spy Stephen Maturin. It is also a wonderful adventure book. These books, and many more, have a common element, believable protagonists in danger, fighting their way out of danger and reminding us of the best in humanity and in ourselves.

Two writers who appeal to young adults because they write convincing adventures are Gary Paulsen and Will Hobbs. Paulsen may well be the most popular writer among young people today. His stories are widely admired by both young and adult readers. In *Hatchet,* 13-year-old Brian Robeson is the only passenger in a small plane when the pilot dies from a heart attack. The plane goes down far off course in the Canadian wilderness, and Brian must save himself from starvation and predators with only the help of his hatchet and his wits. In *Brian's Return,* he has found his way back to civilization, yet after two years he dreams of the quiet and happiness of the Northern woods compared to the miseries of the rat-race and the so-called civilization to which he has returned.

GARY PAULSEN
On Writing

If there were more space and time I would like to tell you how writing came to be for me, about the start of writing, of leaving all things secure—a job as an electronics engineer working in satellite tracking (part of what Tom Wolfe would call the right stuff but what was really the wrong stuff)—of throwing that life over, completely, to be a writer.

Madness.

A writer.

I would tell of the first tries, the first attempts to put words down and have them make sense, show a story, *be* a story and how dismal it was, how sad the first times. Feeble pawing, scratches at the door . . .

And the rejections.

If there were time and more time I would tell of all the rejections, every single one because every one became important, became the thing that kept me going more than anything. Dear author: you do not fit our format. Dear author, in the interests of brevity . . . Dear author, unfortunately at this time we are a bit overstocked on just about anything and everything you want to write about for the rest of your life and on and on . . . And then the pearls, the true saviors, the editors' letters. Dear Author, you show some promise. Dear Author, while we can't use this we would like to see other projects you may be working on . . .

And in the absence of acceptance the rejections, the rejection letters become the reason for writing; the knowledge that somebody out there is actually reading the work, evaluating it, judging it becomes important, must become important enough to take you through all the rough jobs, the dishwashing, the construction, the janitorial services, the grunt labor doing hot tar and gravel roofing in August in Denver, the truck driving, the replacing septic systems and demolitions work in the mountains. Writing through all of that, every night, studying and writing and the only pay a letter, a word.

An editorial comment. God, in the dark of failure, in the pit of it to get that, just that saving time spent by an editor who really read, who really understood, who really cared, who really wanted to help.

If there were time I would tell you of the editors, the ones who saved and the ones who hurt, the letters saved and read and reread, folded and refolded and finally taped to the wall so that when it was bad, when it was grinding down and bad and it didn't seem possible to sell work, to live as a writer, there would be the letter. Editorial comments. The only pay for long work, for life work.

If there were time and more time I would tell you of other writers. Every one, every single one I asked for help willingly gave it, helped with work, helped with salve for wounds, helped sometimes with small money and food and advice just as I try to help now and when you see that old cliché, see that bit of silliness that says writing is a lonely profession it is perhaps wise to remember the editors and other writers and wives and husbands and families and friends and publishers and sales people and book stores and libraries who all are part of it. Writing is a lonely profession as running the Iditarod is lonely—without the help of others, the support, the writer and dog runner cannot be alone.

And still more, if there were more time I would tell you of acceptance.

Acceptance.

What a small word to mean so much, no, to mean everything.

All of it comes down to that, to that one word:

Acceptance.

It finally becomes something that cannot be, cannot ever come; so many rejections, so many letters and comments and failures that it becomes a grail, something never achieved, something dreamed for, longed for, lusted for and never, never there and one day it comes.

The same kind of letter. So similar that at first it is thrown down as another rejection but a word catches, a different word jumps from the paper and there will never be another first like this one; not first love nor first hope nor first time never, no never one like this.

Dear author, we have decided to publish your book.

Can you *imagine?* Your life, your work, your hopes and thoughts and songs and breath—we have decided to publish your book. We have decided to publish *you*—God it thunders, burns into your mind, your soul.

I remember thinking that it didn't matter if I died right then. That nothing would be better, sweeter than that moment. Nothing. And nothing has been better.

If there were yet more time I would tell you of other moments and acceptances and failures that were not quite as big but close, close, and I would, finally, tell you stories . . .

Stories of love and death and cold and heat and ice and flame, stories sad and stories happy and stories of laughter and tears and places soft and hard, of dogs and the white-blink of arctic ice, stories of great men and beautiful women and souls and devils and gods, stories of lost dreams and found joys and aches and torture and great rolling hills and towering storms and things quick and hot and slow and dull, stories of graves and horses, pigs and kings, war and the times between wars, stories of childrens' cheeks and the soft hair at a woman's temple when it is moist, stories of rage and spirit and spit and blood and bodies on fences and hay so sweet you could eat the grass, oh God yes, stories of all things there are I would tell you, to make the hair go up on the back of the neck and stop the breath and bring life—stories that are everything, all of everything there is, these stories.

All these things I would try to do if there were only time.

But there is not. There is, sadly, only time to thank you for all you have done for me and to offer a hope that you will continue with me in this wonderful dance.

Thank you.

Gary Paulsen's books include *Hatchet,* Bradbury, 1987; *Woodsong,* Bradbury, 1990; *Harris and Me,* Harcourt Brace, 1993, *Nightjohn,* Delacorte, 1993; and *Soldier's Heart,* Delacorte, 1998.

Hobbs's interest in hiking, white-river rafting, archaeology, and natural history are reflected in his books. *Bearstone,* about a Native-American boy sent to live with an old rancher whose wife has died, combines adventure with a story of growth and friendship. His stories are more action-packed than Paulsen's and sometimes less introspective, though in *Downriver* the change that Jessie makes in her life is impressive. *River Thunder* is another of Jessie's rafting trips down the Colorado River, which gives the readers countless adventures and the characters plenty of room to mature. *The Maze* is about Rick Walker, a product of foster homes and neglect, who escapes into Canyonlands National Park in Utah and finds a man driven to restore condors into the wild.

Adventure stories are popular because boredom chafes at our souls and crowds out of our minds such practical concerns as safety and caution; however, the human body—at least our own—reminds us all too quickly of risk. This may be why we prefer our adventures to come through books or, even better, through movies (see Film Box 6.1) in which trick photography and special effects can make it easier for viewers to forget that losing is more common than winning.

Mysteries

Why are mysteries so enduringly popular? Basically, they are unrealistic and, as mystery writers cheerfully admit, usually have almost nothing to do with real-life detection by police or private agents. They demand that we suspend most of our disbelief, and the faithful gladly do so. Mysteries are mere games, but we love games. Some of us claim that we want to beat the detective to the murderer, but we rarely do, and when we do succeed, we feel cheated.

The popularity of mystery movies and the number of hotels, ships, and individuals who sponsor parties in which a mock murder takes place, with the partygoers playing detectives, shows the entertainment value of mayhem, murder, and suspense. Because of the high entertainment value of mysteries and their sometimes easy reading level, many mysteries published for a general audience find their way into the hands of young adults. For examples, see Focus Box 6.1, Popular Mystery Writers Accessible to Teens.

Daniel's detection of the guilty Elders in "The Story of Susanna" in the *Apocrypha* may be the world's first detective story. Critics generally agree, however, that the modern mystery begins with Edgar Allan Poe's "The Murders in the Rue Morgue," although "The Purloined Letter" is more satisfying today. Poe's detective, C. Auguste Dupin, is unquestionably the first criminal investigator.

Dime-novel imitations of Poe's Dupin soon appeared, notably Old Sleuth, Young Sleuth, Old King Brady, Cap Collier, and—best of them all—Nick Carter. What is usually said to be the first detective novel, published in 1868, is Wilkie Collins's *The Moonstone.* The world's greatest fictional detective appeared only a few years later when Sherlock Holmes (and his ever-faithful and often befuddled companion Dr. Watson) moved out of Arthur Conan Doyle's *A Study in Scarlet* and into the affections of thousands of readers.

Holmes was followed by other distinctive detectives—brilliant and cocky, like Jacques Futrelle's Professor S. F. X. Van Deusen, or brilliant and humble, like G. K. Chesterton's Father Brown. Others followed and won their fans—Agatha Christie's

FILM BOX 6.1

Adventure and Lots of Derring-Do (See Appendix D)

Breakheart Pass (1976, color, 95 min., PG; Director: Tom Gires; with Charles Bronson and Ben Johnson) Troops on a train carrying supplies to an Army post high in the Rockies suffer a diptheria epidemic. Almost none of the motley group on board are what they seem to be. All that snow makes it a great movie to see in a hot summer.

Flight of the Phoenix (1965, color, 147 min., NR; Director: Robert Aldrich; with James Stewart, Hardy Kruger, and Ian Bannen) Survivors work to put a plane back in order after it goes down in the Sahara.

The Great Train Robbery (1979, color, 111 min., PG; Director: Michael Pressman; with Sean Connery, Lesley-Anne Down, and Donald Sutherland) Three people set out to rob the gold on a moving train.

Gunga Din (1939, black and white, 117 min., NR; Director: George Stevens; with Cary Grant, Douglas Fairbanks, Jr., and Victor McLaglen) Kipling's book is nominally the inspiration for the film, but the tale of three Engish soldiers in nineteenth-century India and how they save the day for the queen still works its magic.

In the Line of Fire (1993, color, 123 min., R; Director: Wolfgang Petersen; with Clint Eastwood, and John Malkovich) An assassin plays mind games with a secret service agent protecting the president.

The Man Who Would Be King (1975, color, 129 min., PG; Director: John Huston; with Sean Connery and Michael Caine) Two British soldiers find a place where civilization has not arrived and the people will buy their tale of being gods. Taken from a Kipling short story.

Raiders of the Lost Ark (1981, color, 115 min., PG; Director: Stephen Spielberg; with Harrison Ford and Karen Allen) Indiana Jones, archeologist and adventurer, is in search of the Biblical ark. He's noble and his enemies are evil. Adventures galore, one right after another.

Runaway Train (1985, color, 111 min., R; Director: Andrei Konchalovsky; with Jon Voight and Eric Roberts) Two convicts escaping from an Alaskan prison highjack a train. Another wonderful one to see on a hot summer afternoon.

The 39 Steps (1935, black and white, 81 min., NR; Director: Alfred Hitchcock; with Robert Donat and Madeleine Carroll) From John Buchan's spy novel in which an innocent businessman is dragged into international espionage.

Where Eagles Dare (1969, color, 155 min., PG; Director: Brian G. Hutton; with Richard Burton and Clint Eastwood) A small band of soldiers sent into World War II Germany to rescue an officer learn there's a spy in their midst. Thrills, spills, and chills.

Miss Marple and Hercule Poirot, Erle Stanley Gardner's Perry Mason, Dashiell Hammett's Sam Spade, and Raymond Chandler's Philip Marlowe. Where they left off, contemporary writers and detectives have picked up.

Writer and critic Hillary Waugh has said that the skeletons on which mysteries hang are "nothing more nor less than a series of ironclad rules." The rules are essential to present the puzzle properly and to ensure fair play. He lists them as follows:

Rule One: All clues discovered by the detective must be made available to the reader.

Rule Two: The murderer must be introduced early.

Rule Three: The crime must be significant.

Rule Four: There must be detection.

FOCUS BOX 6.1

Popular Mystery Writers Accessible to Teens

Nevada Barr is a National Park Service Ranger and so is her fictional Anna Pigeon whose detective work takes her to Georgia's Cumberland Island in *Endangered Species* (Putnam, 1997), to Carlsbad Caverns National Park in *Blind Descent* (1998), and to the Statue of Liberty and Ellis Island in *Liberty Falling* (1999), all from Putnam.

Stephanie Barron has caught many of the nuances of Jane Austen's work in *Jane and the Genius of the Place* (1999), *Jane and the Wandering Eye* (1998), and *Jane and the Man of the Cloth* (1997), all from Bantam.

Rita Mae Brown lists her cat Sneaky Pie Brown as both coauthor and codetective in her *Murder She Meowed* (1996) and *Cat on the Scent* (1999), both from Bantam.

Sue Grafton is the creator of Kinsey Millhone, a private investigator working her way through the alphabet in such books as *"A" is for Alibi* (Holt, 1982) and *"O" is for Outlaw* (Holt, 1999).

Peter J. Heck uses Mark Twain to unravel mysteries. He did an especially good job catching Twain's voice in *A Connecticut Yankee in Criminal Court* (Berkley, 1996).

Sue Henry writes about Alaskan State Trooper Alex Jensen who in *Murder on the Iditarod Trail* (Little, Brown, 1991) investigates a series of killings. *Death Takes Passage* (Avon, 1997) recreates the 1897 sea voyage that brought miners to the gold rush.

Laurie R. King writes about Sherlock Holmes, married and settled down to a life of bliss and detection. The series is a bit uneven, but *The Moor* (St. Martin's, 1998) is atmospheric and brooding and elegant.

Ed McBain (Evan Hunter) writes police procedurals about the officers in the 87th Precinct in Isola (presumably New York City). Detective Steve Carella is the star in such books as *Romance* (Warner, 1995), *Nocturne* (Warner, 1997), and *The Big Bad City* (Simon & Schuster, 1999).

Sharyn McCrumb takes her titles from the folk ballads of Southern Appalachia where she has set such stories as *The Ballad of Frankie Silver* (Dutton, 1998), *She Walks These Hills* (Scribner, 1994), and *If Ever I Return, Pretty Peggy-O* (Scribner, 1990).

Peter Robinson's *In a Dry Season* (Twilight, 1999) is a police procedural set in Northern England when a drought causes a drop in the water level of a lake and a body is discovered.

Troy Soos sets his stories in the baseball world of the early twentieth century with Mickey Rawlings, utility infielder for the Red Sox in *Murder at Fenway Park* (Kensington, 1994), the Detroit Tigers in *Hunting a Detroit Tiger* (Kensington, 1997), and the Cincinnati Reds in *The Cincinnati Red Stalkings* (Kensington, 1998).

Dana Stabenow's mysteries take place in Alaska and feature Native-American investigator Kate Shugak, who in *A Cold-Blooded Business* (Berkley, 1994) deals with corrupt politicians and businessmen wanting to rape Alaska's mineral deposits, while she deals with an equally big game hunter in *Hunter's Moon* (Putnam, 1999).

Rule Five: The number of suspects must be known, and the murderer must be among them.

Rule Six: The reader, as part of the game of fair play, has the right to expect that nothing will be included in the book that does not relate to or in some way bear on the puzzle.[3]

Types of Mysteries

The characteristics of the traditional murder mystery are well known and relatively fixed, although devotees are always interested in variations on the theme of murder.

A mystery short story may settle for theft, but a novel, of course, demands murder. Accompanying crimes such as blackmail or embezzlement may add to the delights of murder, but they never replace murder. The ultimate crime normally takes place a few chapters into the book, after readers have been introduced to major and minor characters, including the victim and those who might long for his death. The detective appears, clues are scattered, the investigation proceeds, the detective solves the case, the guilty are punished, the innocent are restored to their rightful place, and the world becomes right again.

Shannon Ocork classifies mysteries into these six types.

1. *The amateur detective:* At least in the older stories, the amateur detective was male (e.g., C. August Dupin or Sherlock Holmes and later Rex Stout's Nero Wolfe). These detectives are altruistic and usually optimistic. They are bright and see what others do not. Sometimes called traditional, golden-age, or classic mysteries, these flourished from the 1920s through the 1940s.

2. *The cozy mystery:* These stories are close to the amateur detective stories. They are usually set in a small English village, although New England is increasingly popular. Agatha Christie, who began writing in the 1920s, is the most obvious writer of cozies. She scattered her best books throughout her life. Her 1939 *And Then There Were None* is her best book without a detective. Others include her 1950 *A Murder Is Announced,* a Miss Marple book, and her 1968 *By the Pricking of My Thumbs,* in which the usually tiresome Tommy and Tuppence Beresford stumble into a believable mystery.

3. *The puzzle:* These stories are exercises in ingenuity as we are led into an intricate murder, with the detective daring us to figure out the end of the story. Ellery Queen's early mysteries had a "Challenge to the Reader" about three or four chapters from the end, when the writer announced that we had all the clues Queen had and should be able to solve the mystery. Luckily, we rarely succeeded.

4. *The private detective:* These hard-boiled mysteries differ from other mysteries in significant ways. Private detectives lack altruistic motives. They enter cases for pay rather than for love of the chase or intellectual fondness for the puzzle. Working out of a cheerless office and around even less cheerful people, they are tired and cynical about the courts, the police, class distinctions, and life in general. Many are former police officers who left the force under a cloud. They have seen too much of the seamy world to feel hope for anything or anyone, and they know that detective work is hard and mostly routine and dull. With patience, any bright person could do what they do. Not only does violence come with the territory, it is the territory. Moreover, we are surprised, even disappointed, if the violence is not there.

5. *The police procedural:* Police procedurals are often the most believable mysteries because the central characters are officers doing their mundane jobs and tracking down murderers with scientific methods and machines available only to the police. The books of Ed McBain are probably the most popular police procedurals today.

6. *The thriller:* These are usually spy thrillers. They may have bits of mystery tucked into them, but as in Ian Fleming's James Bond series, the mystery involves not so much who did it as how our hero can escape his latest impossible situation with even more than his usual derring-do.[4]

Tony Hillerman's Books

In the February 1992 *English Journal*, the editors published responses to the question, "Who is your favorite writer of detective fiction?" Tony Hillerman won by a margin of ten to one. One of the reasons for Hillerman's popularity is that he does such a good job of establishing atmosphere. He does what the fine mystery writer P. D. James has argued that all writers must do—give a sense of place. For example, Hillerman begins *The Listening Woman* by letting us see, hear, and feel the world of the Indian reservation.

> The southwest wind picked up turbulence around the San Francisco Peak, howled across the emptiness of the Moenkopi plateau, and made a thousand strange sounds in windows of the old Hopi villages at Shongopovi and Second Mesa. Two hundred vacant miles to the north and east, it sand-blasted the stone sculptures of Monument Valley Navajo Tribal park and whistled eastward across the maze of canyons on the Utah-Arizona border. Over the arid immensity of the Nokaito Bench it filled the blank blue sky with a rushing sound. At the hogan of Hosteen Tso, at 3:17 p.m., it gusted and eddied, and formed a dust devil, which crossed the wagon track and raced with a swirling roar across Margaret Cigaret's old Dodge pickup truck and past the Tso brush arbor.

Hillerman's place may not be our place, or a place we know, but it is a place we can recognize, and it is a place we will soon know. Hillerman has come close to breaking the boundary of mystery writers and being accepted as a fine novelist without regard to a specific genre. His Navajo police novels began appearing in 1970 with *The Blessing Way,* in which we meet officer Joe Leaphorn's talent at detection as well as the villain who uses Navajo religion to protect himself. The Indian lore and the religious aspects of the book are accurate, just as they are in later Hillerman novels, including *The Dance Hall of the Dead, The Listening Woman, The Ghostway, The Skinwalkers, Coyote Waits,* and *Sacred Clowns.* Joe Leaphorn and Jim Chee, Hillerman's detectives, have the best of two worlds, the Anglo and the Native American. Although they are often confused about who and what they are, they always find that ultimately they are Native American. If *The Fallen Man* is a bit less suspenseful than earlier books, Hillerman's *The First Eagle* is a marvelous adventure as Joe Leaphorn, now retired and a private detective, is on his first case searching for a biologist who is tracking infectious diseases.

Mysteries Written for Young Adults

Mysteries written specifically for teenagers are usually shorter than books described in the previous section. Protagonists are unlikely to be professional detectives and far more likely to be bright and energetic young people, not yet cynical about the world. Violence is more likely to be underplayed, possibly at the edge of the story. The victim is often connected to the protagonist—a family member, a friend, an admired adult, a boyfriend or girlfriend—and the protagonist is virtually forced to enter the game and examine the puzzle.

Two young adult mystery writers stand out: Patricia Windsor, and Joan Lowery Nixon. Windsor's *The Christmas Killer* is set in a Connecticut town terrrorized by a killer. Rose Potter has a series of dreams in which a murdered girl appears and hints at where her body can be found. The police question whether Rose is believable, or even sane, wonder if she is involved in the murder, and finally realize that Rose is in danger. Sections dealing with Rose alternate with the ramblings of the deranged killer about his need for blood. At one point he says,

> Killing is not a bad thing. Death is easeful, death is kind. I am friends with death. It cools the boiling blood. Blood is as red as a Christmas ribbon. Blood ties a body like a Christmas package. Blood is the color of Christmas berries, baubles, all things of joy. Why shouldn't I find joy in blood?

He finds joy in all things red, and in the last two paragraphs of the book, imprisoned though he is, readers learn that the story may have yet another chapter.

> Let a little time pass. I will send her a letter, tied up in my own blood and sealing wax. She will know me from my work. And she will think of me again.
> And, before long, I will escape this place, and I will be seeing her again.

Here's a fine story, not long on mystery but full of suspense and wonders and fears. It's an eerie and scary book, just right for the night when a reader is home alone with the fierce wind and the blowing shutters and the creaking house.

Joan Lowery Nixon's thrillers are even more popular with young people. *Whispers from the Dead* is about a near-death drowning and a spirit who seems to shadow the protagonist thereafter. *The Dark and Deadly Pool* concerns a young girl who discovers a body floating in a pool, a typical ploy for Nixon, who is eager to grab her readers' attention. Cody Garnett's friend in *Spirit Seeker* is accused of murder, and Cody sets out to find the truth. In *Who Are You?*, a file is kept on high school art student Kristi Evans. When the person keeping the file is shot, Kristi is drawn into a world of art and forgery.

A few other writers deserve our attention and readership from young adults. M. E. Kerr's books about John Fell are mysterious and fun to read. Walter Dean Myers's *The Mouse Rap* is one of those rare mysteries, lighthearted and happy, yet telling a mystery that is unusually entertaining. Avi's *Wolf Rider* may not be Avi at his best, but the eerie phone calls Andy Zadinski gets would be a real worry to any of us. Chap Reaver's *Mote* is a fast-moving and increasingly intriguing book about Mote, the protagonist's friend accused of murder. *The Man in the Woods* by Rosemary Wells is an atmospheric thriller about a young girl who is in danger because she knows more than she should about a murder. *The Ghost in the Tokaido Inn* by Dorothy Hoobler and Thomas Hoobler features 14-year-old Seikei, who is the son of a tea merchant but proves to have the qualities of a samurai in this Sherlock Holmes kind of mystery set in eighteenth-century Japan.

Stories of the Supernatural

The aim of every writer is to grab the reader's attention immediately and to hold it. Robbie Branscum's first two paragraphs in *Me and Jim Luke,* a book nearly thirty years old, is a model of how to get the reader involved.

> I knew the hand was dead the minute it touched my naked shoulder next to my overall strap. I couldn't have moved if my life had depended on it, and I

reckoned it did. I sort of froze, and at the same time I felt like messing all over myself. I tried to holler, but no matter how wide I got my mouth open no sound came out. I could see the light of the lantern Jim Luke carried get further and further away, and finally it was plumb out of sight. The moon was plenty bright enough to see by, but Lord I didn't want to see the thing that had hold of me. I knew if I did, I would die for sure.

Once I heard Grandpa and Grandma talking, and they said that when a body passed on, their lives passed before their eyes. It didn't seem fair in my case because the good Lord hadn't given me much time to pass before me. But, again in my case, I'd rather think about what little living I had done than the dying I was going to do shortly, from stark raving fear.

What a marvelous beginning: the fear of death mixed with the reality of somebody else's death, the inability to move but the need to move for obvious bodily needs, the darkness that surrounds him as Jim Luke moves steadily away, and the brightness of the moon, which might be a comfort, but not tonight, when he does not want to see the dead body with its slowly swinging arm.

Fears of death, the unknown, and the supernatural probably go back to prehistoric times, when shadows in a cave and light and dark mystified and frightened humans. We have demanded answers to the unknown but have rarely found them, and so we have settled on myths and legends about superior and unseen beings. Such explanations are satisfying because when we are fighting the inexplicable, they make winning more pleasing and losing more acceptable.

Amidst all our modern knowledge and sophistication, we hold onto our fascination with the unknowable. We delight in chambers of horrors, tunnels of terror, and haunted houses. We claim to be rational beings, yet we read astrology charts. We mock the superstitions of others yet hold as pets one or two of our own, joking all the time while we toss salt over our shoulder, avoid walking under ladders, and knock on wood. We follow customs without wondering why they came about. Black is assumed to be the appropriate dress for funerals because it is dark and gloomy and demonstrates solemnity. We may not know that black was worn at a time lost in history because spirits, sometimes malignant or perhaps indignant, were thought to linger near a corpse for a year. Wearing black made it more difficult for these evil spirits to see the living. As long as spirits were around, danger lurked; hence, long mourning periods in black dress.

Greek and Roman literature abounds with supernatural elements, but so does Elizabethan literature. Whether Shakespeare believed in ghosts or witches is anyone's guess. Certainly, his audiences often did, and they apparently delighted in or were frightened by incidents in plays such as *Macbeth, Hamlet,* and *The Tempest.*

The Gothic novel of unexplained terror and horror began with Horace Walpole's *The Castle of Otranto* in 1764. Success bred imitators, and Clara Reeves's *The Old English Baron* appeared in 1780; William Beckford's *Vathek* was published in 1786. The two greatest of the gothics appeared in the 1790s: Ann Radcliffe's *The Mysteries of Udolpho* and Matthew Gregory Lewis's *The Monk.* Although Jane Austen did much to demolish the fad with *Northanger Abbey* in 1818, that posthumously published novel did not prevent Mary Shelley's 1818 *Frankenstein, or the Modern Prometheus,* the apotheosis of the genre, from winning admirers. The Romantic poets and prose writers continued to be half in love with the dark and the unknown, as much of Coleridge and Keats and the novels of the Brontë sisters illustrate.

Some radio shows capitalized on our fears, as anyone old enough to have enjoyed radio shows "Inner Sanctum" or "The Whistler" will testify. The supernatural never worked as well on television, perhaps because it is too literal a medium. Horror movies, however, have almost always been popular with the masses, and they have sometimes produced masterpieces of our internal struggles against evil or the unknown; for example, *The Mummy* (1932), *The Bride of Frankenstein* (1935), *Village of the Damned* (1960), *The Innocents* (1961), *Rosemary's Baby* (1968), *The Abominable Dr. Phibes* (1971), and *The Haunting* (1963 and 1999).

Supernatural novels have well-established ground rules. Settings are usually in an eerie or haunted house or in a place where a mysterious event occurred years ago. Some thrillers occur in more mundane places, perhaps a brownstone in New York City or a hotel shut down for the season, but readers know the mundane remains calm only for a short time before frightening events begin and strange people come out to play. Darkness is usually essential, but not always physical darkness. The protagonist is oblivious to evil for a time but ultimately recognizes the pervasive power of the darkness of the soul. Sometimes the wife or husband sells out to evil and entices the spouse to join in a black mass. Rituals or ceremonies are essential. Family curses or pacts with the Devil have become commonplaces of the genre.

Alfred Hitchcock, that master of suspense, reminds us over and over that the most terrifying things can happen in the most commonplace settings. On a lovely day in the middle of a South Dakota cornfield in *North by Northwest*, Cary Grant is suddenly attacked by a crop-dusting airplane. In *The Birds*, a placid setting alongside the ocean suddenly turns to terror when sweet little birds begin to tear into human flesh.

In the 1989 edition of this textbook, Robert Westall observed that supernatural books break quite naturally into horror stories and ghost stories. The horror stories make the point that "the human organism is a frail thing of flesh subject to an infinity of abuse, and that it is painful and undignified for the human spirit to have to dwell in it." Such a depressing fact may be well worth saying but not over and over again. Even the books by such ingenious and powerful writers as Poe and Lovecraft are not something you would want to read if you were "on the way to build the Taj Mahal, or paint the Sistine Chapel ceiling, or even have a happy love affair."

> On the other hand, the ghost story is about the undying spirit, not the dying flesh. . . . [Ghosts] add an exciting fifth dimension to the often-boring four dimensions of real life. They make it possible for us to escape into the land of the impossible where, delightfully, anything can happen. They are also a comfort; a reassurance of our own immortality. I would adore to spend my first few years of death as a ghost, drifting round the world painlessly in the company of other friendly ghosts, seeing all the things I never got round to seeing in life because there were other boring earthbound things to be done.

He went on to explain that we need ghost stories:

> In terms of love and the passing of time, we are all haunted houses, full of rooms we have shut off because of loss, or fear, or regret. To spend all our time wandering through such rooms would lead to madness. But to wander sometimes can be agonizingly sweet and rich. And never to dare to wander through them can make life a dusty boring hell.[5]

Annette Curtis Klause's *The Silver Kiss* is a good illustration of the genre. Nearly every night Zoë comes home to a dark and empty house. Her mother is in the hospital dying of cancer, and as early as page 2 readers get clues about supernatural elements. Zoë is almost as thin as her mother, "a sympathy death perhaps, she wondered half seriously. . . . Wouldn't it be ironic if she died, too, fading out suddenly when her look-alike went?" On page 3, Zoë remembers happier times with her mother, but even here there's a shadow: "You're a dark one," her mother said sometimes with amused wonder. "You're a mystery."

Zoë likes to walk in the neighborhood park and sit in front of the old-fashioned gazebo, where one night "a shadow crept inside, independent of natural shades." Then she saw his face.

> He was young, more boy than man, slight and pale, made elfin by the moon. He noticed her and froze like a deer before the gun. They were trapped in each other's gaze. His eyes were dark, full of wilderness and stars. But his face was ashen. Almost as pale as his silver hair.

In her first meeting with Simon, a 200-year-old vampire from Bristol, England, Zoë recognizes how beautiful he is, he flees, and she cries. The story within a story, in which Simon explains how he became a vampire, is brilliant in its own right, but then so is the book's ending when Zoë and Simon must part.

Klause's *Blood and Chocolate* has proved popular among young people and reviewers. A clan of werewolves, existing since time began, have lost their leader in a fire. They now intend to live in Virginia, led by Vivian, daughter of the late head of the clan. Going to school, she meets a boy who attracts her. She is sure she knows and can trust him, so Vivian shows him who and what she is, and he is frightened and repelled.

Therein lies the dilemma. Can we accept someone disturbingly different though we mostly admire and trust the person? Are we willing to go below the surface in judging people? That is the essence of much supernatural literature, from *Frankenstein* to that of Anne Rice and Stephen King.

Rice is one of the most popular writers of vampire literature, widely read by adults and young adults alike. *Memnoch the Devil,* fifth in her "Vampire Chronicles," tells of Satan (Memnoch) and his war with God, in which the vampire Lestat is wooed by the Devil and taken on a trip to heaven and hell. The sixth in the series, *The Vampire Armand,* is a finer book chronicling the history of Armand as he develops after being kidnapped and then reborn as a vampire.

Leading all the writers in the field is Stephen King, a former high school English teacher who frequently includes likable young people among his characters. The fact that he writes about them without condescension is not lost on the audience. "The Langoliers" (from *Four Past Midnight*) is the story of a late-night flight from Los Angeles to Boston. The plane goes through a time rip, and the only passengers who survive are the ten who happened to be sleeping. Fortunately, one of them is a pilot; otherwise there wouldn't have been much of a story to tell. There is also the blind Dinah, a young girl on her way to Boston for an operation on her eyes. She has such a superdeveloped sense of hearing that she is mistaken by the mad Craig Toomy, the ultimate yuppie gone awry, as the chief Langolier. The character most closely filling the role of a young adult hero on a romantic quest is Albert Kaussner, a gifted violinist on his way to enroll in a Boston music conservatory. In his own mind, he's not Albert or Al, but Ace Kaussner, "The Arizona Jew" and "The Fastest Hebrew West of the Mississippi." The journey turns out to be much more difficult than anything faced by Ace's mythical heroes of the Old West, and it even requires him to sacrifice his beloved violin. At the end of the trip, he is rewarded with his first love and the feeling of growth and confidence that comes with having passed a difficult test.

Stephen King's first book, *Carrie*, appeared in 1974 and sold well for a then unknown writer. From that point on, King maintained his place as *the* writer of the genre. Carrie is a young outsider, the daughter of religious fanatics, and the brunt of cruel jokes. She possesses the power of telekinesis, and she uses it to destroy the school, the students, and the town in a fit of justified rage. *Salem's Lot*, although better characterized, is something of a letdown after *Carrie*, as are *The Stand* and *The Shining*, which is possibly better known through its film version than as a novel. *Firestarter* is far better, with its portrait of an 8-year-old girl with the power to start fires merely by looking at an object. A government agency, "The Shop," learns about the child and launches a search for her. King effectively indicts this bureaucracy become evil. *Firestarter* may not be King's best book, but it is his most penetrating study of character and the United States. King's later books include *Different Seasons*, a collection of four novelettes; *Cujo*, a messy and disappointingly obvious horror tale of the lovable St. Bernard dog gone mad; and *Christine*, the story of a 1958 Plymouth Fury gone equally mad. *Pet Sematary* is an acknowledged variation of W. W. Jacobs's 1904 "The Monkey's Paw," which has a power that cannot be ignored, although it remains something of a prolonged ghastly joke. *The Tommyknockers* and *It* added a chill or two to King's repertoire, but little more.

Three recent books by King make clear his creativity and power. *Desperation* is set in an old Nevada mining town where a mad lawman is as played out as are the mines. He runs over a few townspeople and almost anyone foolish enough to take Route 50. *Bag of Bones* is in part a commentary on the horrors and misfortunes of being a writer, in part the story of a writer who finds ghosts when he goes to a favorite vacation retreat. *The Girl Who Loved Tom Gordon* is the story of a 9-year-old girl lost in the woods and haunted by something stalking her.

Among young adult writers specializing in supernatural themes, Lois Duncan (see her statement on p. 100) has been consistently popular. In *Summer of Fear*, Rachel Bryant's family is notified that relatives have died in a car crash, leaving 17-year-old Julia, behind. The girl, who looks surprisingly mature, arrives and changes the lives of everyone around her. Trickle, the family dog, suspects something is wrong, but Trickle does not live too long, and neither does anyone else who gets in Julia's way. Duncan's *Stranger with My Face* and *The Third Eye* were enjoyable but lacked the power of *Summer of Fear*. See Focus Box 6.2 for other examples of supernatural stories written for teens.

More support for allowing young adults to read supernatural books comes from Jeanine Basinger, chair of film studies at Wesleyan University. While her words were aimed at horror films, they apply equally well to books:

It never really goes away, this appetite for horror films. The millennium is approaching. We have all of these tragedies on our minds. In modern life it's just one damn thing after another, and we seek to explain it to one another. And if

 **FOCUS BOX 6.2**

The Supernatural in YA Books

Back of Beyond: Stories of the Supernatural by Sarah Ellis. Simon & Schuster/McElderry, 1997. In each story, ordinary young people are going about their everyday lives and then they realize that somehow things are not so ordinary anymore.

The Dark Angel by Meredith Ann Pierce. Little, Brown, 1982. A servant girl tries to save her vampire master from his evil deeds.

Fade by Robert Cormier. Delacorte, 1988. Paul Moreaux, a young French Canadian, discovers that he has inherited a family gift/curse that comes to only one person in each generation: the ability to be invisible.

In Camera and Other Stories by Robert West-all. Scholastic, 1992. Westfall fans who enjoy these supernatural stories will also want to read his *The Haunting of Chas. McGill and Other Stories* (Greenwillow, 1993), and *Rachel and the Angel and Other Stories* (Scholastic, 1988).

Last Vampire series by Christopher Pike. Pocket Books, 1994 on. Sita is a 5,000-year-old vampire who is coping with a modern world but whose history is given in flashbacks. As with vampire stories for adults, sex and violence play a role.

The Lion Tamer's Daughter: And Other Stories by Peter Dickinson. Delacorte, 1997. In the title story, Keith is drawn into the dark side of a circus when he meets a duplicate of his long-time friend. In each of the other stories, teenagers are equally surprised when events and characters from another world become involved with their world.

Midnight Magic by Avi. Scholastic, 1999. It's the year before Columbus set sail and 12-year-old Fabrizio is working as a servant to Mangus the Magician in the Kingdom of Pergamontio. Little does he know that he will soon be confronting a ghost. Avi's *Devil's Race* (Lippincott, 1984) is also recommended.

Never Trust a Dead Man by Vivian Vande Velde. Harcourt, 1999. In his medieval village, life is going well for 17-year-old Selwyn until he is imprisoned in a burial cave and visited by Witch Elswyth, who magically unleashes a host of complications, both funny and scary.

Nightmare Hour by R. L. Stine. Harper-Collins/Parachute, 1999. Just in time for Halloween, Stine came out with a hardback collection of ten original stories designed to attract teenreaders who are likely to remember his name from their childhood reading.

Short Circuits: Thirteen Shocking Stories by Outstanding Writers for Young Adults edited by Donald R. Gallo. Dell, 1992. Several of these suspenseful and ghostly stories are recommended for humorous read-alouds.

Skellig by David Almond. Delacorte, 1999. When Michael sets out to explore the new property his family just bought, he looks in an old shed and discovers Skellig, who at first appears to be an ailing man but as the story progresses is revealed to be something more. Also recommended is Almond's *Kit's Wilderness* (Delacorte, 2000).

Thwonk by Joan Bauer. Delacorte, 1995. If cupids with the power to shoot love arrows count as supernatural beings, then this is both a funny and a supernatural romance starring a high school photographer and the boy of whom she secretly takes pictures.

The Tricksters by Margaret Mahy. McElderry, 1987. Mahy's strength is in creating believable characters even though their situations are less than believable. Earlier recommended books include *The Changeover* (Atheneum, 1984) and *The Haunting* (Atheneum, 1982).

Vampires edited by Jane Yolen. HarperCollins, 1991. After reading this collection of original short stories, readers will be tempted to take a second look at their acquaintances. Yolen teamed up with illustrator David Wilgus in the 1990s to do a series of *Here There Be Dragons, . . . Unicorns, . . . Angels, . . . Witches,* and *. . . Ghosts* for Harcourt Brace.

there's some experience that gives closure to it, gives an explanation or at least gives us reassurance that we're not the only ones having the scaries, it reassures us.[6]

From Chills to Giggles

Something in the human mind encourages crossovers between fear and amusement as shown by how often people who have suffered a fright burst out laughing as soon as the danger is over. Humor about death can be traced back at least as far as the early Greeks. English speakers refer to this blend of humor and horror as *Gothic* because we trace it back to the Gothic cathedrals, where grotesque gargoyles and other frightening figures in tapestries, paintings, sculptures, and stained glass windows were created to represent the devil and to frighten people into "proper" beliefs and behavior. Instead, people coped with their fears by turning such icons into objects of amusement.

Gothic humor isn't nearly so scary when it comes with a smile. Shown here at the International Society for Humor Studies conference in Ithaca, New York, is Joan Bauer looking askance at the prop that Paul Zindel was using for his speech about the contrasting elements that make dark humor fascinating.

People still do this at Halloween with spider webs, skeletons, black cats, bats, rats, ghosts, coffins, tombstones, monsters, and haunted houses. Halloween developed out of the sacred or "hallowed" evening preceding All Saints Day, which falls on November 1. The holiday is now second only to Christmas in the amount of money expended for costumes, parties, and candy to be given to trick-or-treaters.

The world has had great fun with Mary Shelley's 1818 story of *Frankenstein, or the Modern Prometheus,* but when it was written many people viewed it as a cautionary tale against medical experimentation. As Paul Zindel pointed out in the last edition of this textbook, Shelley's story followed close on the heels of the development of autopsies and of dissection for purposes of medical study. Such practices made people nervous and fearful. One way of calming such fears was by laughing at them. While Shelley's story was itself rich in Gothic details with a complex plot and fully developed characters, hundreds of parodies and imitations are comic in nature.

Gothic novels underwent a similar kind of transformation from scary to funny when the same year that Shelley published *Frankenstein* (1818), Jane Austen published *Northanger Abbey* as a gleeful parody of the earlier novels. Later Gothic stories in the mid and late 1800s included some darkly humorous moments caused by visits from the dead, for example, Edgar Allan Poe's *The Fall of the House of Usher,* Emily Brontë's *Wuthering Heights,* and Charles Dickens's *A Christmas Carol* with its Ghosts of Christmas Past, Christmas Present, and Christmas Future. In *Bleak House,* Dickens creates a character who spontaneously combusts; in *Little Dorrit* the prison resembles a haunted castle, and in *Great Expectations* Pip meets the criminal in a graveyard and has a hallucinatory vision of Miss Havisham's hanged body "with but one shoe to the feet."

Bram Stoker's 1897 *Dracula* is not the first story about a vampire, but it is the one that established such western traditions as vampires' need for periodically sucking blood, the requirement of a prolonged relationship before a human can be turned into a vampire, vampires sleeping in coffins during the day and arising for action only after dark, the impossibility of killing vampires with ordinary human weapons, and the use of such conventional techniques for repelling vampires as garlic, a silver crucifix, and a wooden stake through the heart.

Stoker based his story on a fifteenth-century legend about Prince Vlad Tepes, the tyrannical ruler of Transylvania and Walachis, now Romania. During the twenty-four-year reign of dictator Nicolae Ceausescu, who in 1989 was executed for crimes against the people (including an alleged 60,000 deaths), Bram Stoker's story was censored throughout Romania, as were some twenty American films. This was because Westerners were comparing Ceausescu to Dracula, and he understandably did not want to further the image. After the revolution, however, popular singers and cartoonists revived the story, and a cartoon on the subject was first-place winner in an International Black Humor Festival "Humorror," held in Bucharest in 1997, the centennial year of the publication of Stoker's book.

Mark Twain made great fun of bad poetry about death. In his *Adventures of Huckleberry Finn,* he may have been thinking of Julia Moore, known as "The Sweet Singer of Michigan," who never lost an opportunity to write about the dead, particularly the recent dead. Granted that she wrote in dead earnest, her poetry now can be read only as amusing or odd. One of her major works concerned a little girl named Libbie:

> One morning in April, a short time ago,
> Libbie was alive and gay:

Her savior called her, she had to go,
Ere the close of that pleasant day.

While eating dinner, this dear little child
Was choked on a piece of beef.
Doctors came, tried their skill awhile,
But none could give relief.

A contemporary of Julia Moore, Howard Heber Clark, who tilled the same poetic field, may have helped to kill obituary verse with this tribute to little Willie.

Willie had a purple monkey climbing on a yellow stick,
And when he sucked the paint all off it made him deathly sick.
And in his latest hours he clasped that monkey in his hand,
And bade good-bye to earth and went into a better land.

Oh! no more he'll shoot his sister with his little wooden gun;
And no more he'll twist the pussy's tail and make her yowl, for fun.
The pussy's tail now stands out straight; the gun is laid aside;
The monkey doesn't jump around since little Willie died.

Although Clark's little Willie was presumably not meant to be funny, a series of poems about another little Willie (sometimes called little Billy) were meant to make us laugh. Harry Graham, an English soldier in the Coldstream Guard who wrote under the pen name Co. D. Streamer, produced enduring and widely quoted masterpieces in 1902 with his *Ruthless Rhymes for Heartless Homes* with poems like this one:

Billy, in one of his nice, new sashes,
Fell in the fire and was burned to ashes.
Now, although the room grows chilly,
I haven't the heart to poke poor Billy.

So popular were his sadistic verses that papers printed new catastrophes by many imitators, most of them about Little Willie and his latest nastiness or disaster so the form became known as "Little Willie Poems." Here are two of the imitators:

Dr. Jones fell in the well,
And died without a moan.
He should have tended to the sick
And left the well alone

Little Willie, mean as hell,
Drowned his sister in the well.
Mother said, while drawing water,
"Gee, it's hard to raise a daughter."

Bud Abbott and Lou Costello were among the earliest film comedians to take advantage of the possibilities of film for stretching viewers' emotions between the frightening and the ridiculous. Their 1948 *Abbott and Costello Meet Frankenstein* still appears on all-time best comedy lists, with such other comedies as *Abbott and*

Costello Meet the Killer, Boris Karloff (1948), *Abbott and Costello Meet Dr. Jekyll and Mr. Hyde* (1953), and *Abbott and Costello Meet the Mummy* (1955).

In the mid 1960s, *The Munsters* was a popular television show. Also, Charles Addams's ghoulish cartoons, which had been published in *The New Yorker,* were adapted into the pseudoscary *The Addams Family.* A generation later, children who had enjoyed watching these television shows took their own children to theaters to see the feature films *The Addams Family* (1991) and *Addams Family Values* (1993) starring Anjelica Huston, Raul Julia, and Christopher Lloyd. Laughs come mostly from the surprise of seeing ordinary family life conducted in a spooky old mansion by scary looking individuals with such names as Uncle Fester, Morticia, Gomez, Wednesday, and Pugsley.

Other Gothic movies that made people both shiver and laugh include the 1975 *Rocky Horror Picture Show,* a spoof of a Gothic novel, which originally failed at the box office, but soon developed a cult following; the 1984 *Ghostbusters* starring Bill Murray and Dan Aykroyd; the 1986 *Little Shop of Horrors* starring Steve Martin, Rick Moranis, and a plant that eats people; and also in 1986, *The Witches of Eastwick* based on John Updike's novel and starring Jack Nicholson, Cher, Susan Sarandon, Michelle Pfeiffer, and Veronica Cartwright.

In 1975, Richard Peck published his first Blossom Culp book *The Ghost Belonged to Me,* a delightfully funny book about a boy who finds a charming, although somewhat outspoken young woman from the past century, living in the family barn. Sequels include *Ghosts I Have Been, The Dreadful Future of Blossom Culp,* and *Blossom Culp and the Sleep of Death.*

Folklore collector Alvin Schwartz was happily surprised when his 1981 *Scary Stories to Tell in the Dark* and its sequels *More Scary Stories to Tell in the Dark* and *Scary Stories 3: More Tales to Chill Your Bones* began winning state contests where children voted on their favorite books. The stories he collected were kids' versions of some of the scary urban legends published in such adult books as Jan Harold Brunvand's *The Vanishing Hitchhiker: American Urban Legends and Their Meanings* and Paul Dickson and Joseph C. Goulden's *There Are Alligators in Our Sewers and Other American Credos.* A similar but newer book that includes such stories as "The Stolen Kidney," "The Scuba Diver in the Forest Fire," and "Aliens in Roswell, New Mexico," is Thomas Craughwell's *Alligators in the Sewer: And 222 Other Urban Legends.*

The *Alligators in the Sewer* allusion relates to our primitive fears of monsters coming out of caves and underground passages. According to the urban legend, during the 1960s hippies all over the country were flushing marijuana down toilets to keep from being arrested. By now this well-fertilized marijuana has flourished and spread throughout the sewer systems of the world providing food for baby alligators, turtles, and other animals small enough to slip into sewer systems. These turtles are the same ones that by the 1980s had developed into the popular fantasy figures, the Teenage Mutant Ninja Turtles.

In the mid 1980s, writer Robert Lawrence Stine, who had written joke books for Scholastic as well as a *How To Be Funny* manual under the pen name of Jovial Bob Stine, created the *Goosebumps* series for 8-, 9-, and 10-year-olds and the *Fear Street* series for young teens using the pen name of R. L. Stine. Although by now interest has somewhat peaked, Stine's books became a publishing phenomenon. As of 1996, the books and related merchandise (T-shirts, CD-ROMS, TV shows, videos, and games) had grossed $450 million, and Stine became known as the "best-selling children's author in history."

Stine's *Fear Street* series was similar to the 1984 movie *A Nightmare on Elm Street* and its four sequels in that the neighborhood plays as important a role as do any of the characters. The advantage of centering a story on a street is that the story can continue even after specific characters have disappeared through foul play or other mysterious circumstances. Stine's Fear Street was named after a mansion built by the Fear family in the 1800s. Behind the mansion is Fear Cemetery, Fear Woods, and Fear Lake.

While some parents were grateful that their children were reading, others objected to both the *Goosebumps* and the *Fear Street* books, as well as to scary books by Christopher Pike and many lesser imitators. While some thought such books were a waste of time, others worried that they might influence children to believe in ghosts, voodoo, and other bugaboos. One horrified mother said after looking at a title in Stine's *Goosebumps* series:

> After reading the back cover of one of the books, I had a horrible nightmare and I was screaming for someone to come and save me.

She added that the books put "fear in the hearts and minds of children," so much so that her 3-year-old nephew refused to sleep in his Goosebumps sleeping bag.[7] Librarian Patrick Jones entered the debate with a 1999 book *What's So Scary About R. L. Stine,* in which he argues that horror books are more helpful than harmful.

In the 1990s, it was hard for Americans not to be aware of Gothic humor because of Warner Brothers' several *Batman* films. The comic book characters of Batman and Robin were originally created almost as a parody or a reversal on the all-American image of Superman. By the time the movies were made, however, Batman and his apprentice, Robin, were folk heroes in their own right. To stress the Gothic connection, New York City was renamed Gotham City and its underground tunnels and sewer systems were made to serve as modern substitutes for the secret passageways, hidden entries, and basement crypts of the castles and mansions in Gothic novels. The maidens in distress who proved themselves to be every bit as resourceful as those in Gothic novels were played by Kim Basinger, Michelle Pfeiffer, and Nicole Kidman. Michael Keaton, Val Kilmer, and George Clooney played Batman, with the creepy but funny bad guys being played by Jim Carrey, Jack Nicholson, and Danny DeVito.

Even the U.S. Postal System joined the Gothic humor fad by releasing stamps and assorted paraphenalia in honor of Boris Karloff playing Frankenstein and Bela Lugosi playing Dracula in the 1931 movies.

Other Humor

Rafael Sabatini began his first novel, *Scaramouche,* with a one-sentence characterization of his hero: "He was born with a gift of laughter and a sense that the world was mad." The ability to laugh at ourselves and the madness of the world is nature's gift to a perpetually beleaguered humanity. The need seems even more desperate today, although probably every previous generation could have made the same claim, so we laugh at almost everything and anything. At a time when taxes, death, and sex are serious matters indeed, they are also the staples of humor. We are pleased when we find something, anything, to laugh at. See Joan Bauer's statement on

In 1997, even the United States Post Office joined in the Gothic humor fad by creating stamps in honor of Boris Karloff playing Frankenstein and the Mummy, Lon Chaney, Sr., playing the Phantom of the Opera, and Lon Chaney, Jr., playing the Wolf Man. In addition to the stamps, the marketing campaign included T-shirts, computer mousepads, and stationery items.

p. 199. We are even more pleased when we discover someone who consistently makes us laugh. As Steve Allen reminds us:

> Without laughter, life on our planet would be intolerable. So important is laughter to us that humanity highly rewards members of one of the most unusual professions on earth, those who make a living by inducing laughter in others. This is very strange if you stop to think of it; that otherwise sane and responsible citizens should devote their professional energies to causing others to make sharp, explosive barking-like exhalations.[8]

Given their enforced world of school and an ever-demanding society, young people need laughter every bit as much as adults, maybe even more so. What do young people find funny? Lance M. Gentile and Merna M. McMillen's article, "Humor and the Reading Program," offers a starting point. Their stages of children's and young adult's interest in humor, somewhat supplemented, are as follows:

- *Ages 10–11.* Literal humor, slapstick (e.g., The Three Stooges) laughing at accidents (banana-peel humor) and misbehavior, sometimes mildly lewd jokes (usually called "dirty jokes"), and grossness.
- *Ages 12–13.* Practical jokes, teasing, goofs, sarcasm, more lewd jokes, joke-riddles, sick jokes, elephant jokes, grape jokes, tongue twisters, knock-knock jokes, moron jokes, TV blooper shows, and grossness piled on grossness.

JOAN BAUER
On Hooking Students with Humor

I like the word *hook*. It floods my mind with images. Captain Hook reaching to snatch a lost boy. My teenage daughter's wall covered in hooks of various sizes upon which she hangs mysterious treasures. I think of boxing where a short *hook* is delivered with a circular motion, the hook check in ice hockey which knocks the puck away from an opponent, the hook-up of our technological age that connects different parts to one another forming a system, or, as Webster's calls it, "a state of cooperation or alliance often between antagonistic elements." Depending on the day, this last definition can well describe a young adult classroom.

Using humor as a hook with students incorporates all of these approaches. Humor reaches out and grabs us; it is a tool upon which to hang other things; it can define character, develop plot, be quick, sharp, and deliver its message with lightning clarity; it can change the very nature of a classroom because laughter builds bridges between people. It can connect different people, seemingly unconnectable, to universal truths.

Humor teaches us about ourselves in non-threatening ways. Take obsession—a subject, sadly, in which I excel. I am passionately obsessive about my work—writing fuels me and it never, ever stays just in my office. It oozes out everywhere and touches all that I do. Depending on the occasion, this can either be wonderfully charming or bleakly inappropriate. When it is the latter, being able to laugh at myself very often saves the day.

Humor, I've come to believe, can be taught. I'm not advocating stand-up comedy classes in the library, but we would do well to heed the words of William Zinsser: "What I want to do is to make people laugh so that they'll see things clearly." When Woody Allen quips that his mother's two passions are God and carpeting, we understand instantly. We know people like that; perhaps we're like that. His statement rings so clearly that it is forever etched in our minds—like a remarkable photograph that captures an image or feeling. Every writer, every humorist, strives to find those defining words that say it all. I believe pointing out those words to students and discussing the layers of what they mean beneath the surface laugh will teach profound lessons and hook students up to a lifetime appreciation of the power of laughter.

Mark Twain said the secret ingredient in humor isn't joy, but pain. Humor often squeezes laughter from painful experiences. Does that mean we're laughing at the pain? Not at all. It means we've snatched hope from the midst of difficulty. And hope is humor's most sacred gift.

Joan Bauer's books include *Welcome Stairways,* 2000; *Backwater,* Putnam, 1999; *Rules of the Road,* Putnam, 1998; *Thwonk,* Delacorte, 1995; and *Squashed,* Delacorte, 1992.

- *Ages 14–15.* More and more lewd jokes (some approaching a mature recognition of the humor inherent in sex); humor aimed at schools, parents, and adults in authority, *Married with Children* and their ilk; and grossness piled on even greater grossness. Young adults may still prefer their own humor to their parents' humor, but they are increasingy catching on to adult humor and may prefer it to their own.
- *Ages 16 and up.* More subtle humor, satire and parody now acceptable and maybe even preferable, witticisms (rather than last year's half-witticisms, which they now detest in their younger brothers and sisters). Adult humor is increasingly part of their repertoire, partly because they are anxious to appear sophisticated, partly because they *are* growing up.[9]

Despite what must seem obvious truth to good teachers and librarians—that a sense of humor is essential for survival of educators and students—some deadly serious people wonder if this (or any other time, presumably) is the time for levity. The answer is, of course, yes—this is the time (and so is any other time). Many young people may be surprised to find that they laugh at the same things their parents laugh at in the movies (see Film Box 6.2).

Our job at school is not just to repeat the same kinds of humor that students get on the Comedy Channel or through lists of jokes on the Internet but to help students mature in their taste and appreciation. We need to educate students to catch onto a multitude of allusions and to have the patience required for reading and appreciating subtle kinds of humor. See Focus Box 6.3, Adult Humorists Accessible to Kids.

At one of the International Society for Humor Studies meetings, Jacque Hughes, who teaches at Central Oklahoma University in Edmond, presented an example of how drawing relationships between raucous humor and more subtle humor can help students move to new levels of appreciation. She was having a hard time getting her 18-year-old freshmen to understand the dark humor in Flannery O'Connor's "A Good Man Is Hard to Find." Then she happened to see *National Lampoon's Vacation* starring Chevy Chase. It was wonderfully funny, and because most of her students had seen the movie, class members were able to compare the personalities and the incidents. When they realized that the similarities were too extensive—and too funny—to be coincidental, they gained a new appreciation for O'Connor's skill to do only with words what cost the movie producers millions of dollars to do with words and film.

It takes skill and practice, along with a broad, cultural background of knowledge, to understand a full range of humor. In the *New York Magazine* (July 17, 1995), readers sent in some thoughtful letters as a follow-up to an article on today's depressing state of stand-up comedy. One writer answered his own question of "Why were the Bennys, the Aces, the Allens (Steve and Fred, both), Berles, Benchleys, Parkers, Woollcotts intuitively brilliant and where are their kind now?" with the observation that these earlier comedians "were the products of a literate society, widely read or with extensive cultural experience, which gave them backgrounds upon which to draw. . . . They knew how to think and were well edited, either by erudite editors or by perceptive audiences." Another reader wrote that the place to look for delightful wit today is not in the comedy clubs but "in written form, in comic novels and essays." Most of our students aren't going to find this kind of humor unless we help prepare them.

FILM BOX 6.2

Spoofs and Parodies and Some Silly, Some Clever Stuff (See Appendix D)

Airplane (1980, color, 88 min., PG; Director: David and Jerry Zucker and Jim Abrahams; with Julie Hagerty, Robert Hays, and Leslie Nielsen) In this put-down of disaster movies, there are so many jokes—both visual and linguistic—that if you don't like one, you'll like the next one or the next dozen or so.

Dick (1999, color, 90 min., PG-13; Director: Andrew Fleming; with Kirsten Durst, Michelle Williams, and Dan Hedaya) Two giggly 15-year-old girls accidentally penetrate the secrets of Watergate and using Deep Throat as their name, tell reporters what they've found.

Dr. Strangelove: Or How I Learned to Stop Worrying and Love the Bomb (1964, black and white, 93 min., PG; Director: Stanley Kubrick; with Peter Sellers, George C. Scott, and Sterling Hayden) How a mad general, with the help of inept generals, can end our world.

The Naked Gun (1988, color, 85 min., PG-13; Director: David Zucker; with Leslie Nielsen and Priscilla Presley) Related to the hallowed files of the TV series *Police Squad,* this is almost as funny as the TV show with the adventures of Lt. Frank Drebin.

Roxanne (1987, color, 107 min., PG; Director: Fred Schepisi; with Steve Martin, Daryl Hannah, and Shelley Duvall) An updating of *Cyrano de Bergerac.*

Sleeper (1973, color, 88 min., PG; Director: Woody Allen; with Allen and Diane Keaton) A man frozen in 1973 wakes 200 years later.

Support Your Local Sheriff (1969, color, 93 min., G; Director: Burt Kennedy; with James Garner, Joan Hackett, and Walter Brennan) A stranger rides into a western town and saves it from bad people. Almost every western film cliché gets its comeuppance.

Wag the Dog (1997, color, 97 min., R; Director: Barry Levinson; with Robert de Niro, Dustin Hoffman, and Anne Heche) When the President makes another sexual goof, his aides hire PR people and a Hollywood producer to focus all of us on other news. Art sometimes becomes reality.

Waiting for Guffman (1997, color, 84 min., R; Director: Christopher Guest; with Eugene Levy and Guest) A pseudodocumentary of producing a musical to celebrate Blaine, Missouri's 150th anniversary.

Young Frankenstein (1974, black and white, 105 min., PG; Director: Mel Brooks; with Gene Wilder, Marty Feldman, and Peter Boyle) Brooks's affectionate salute to the original Frankenstein movies.

While few people appreciate having jokes explained to them, analyzing humor can be a good way to entice students into other kinds of literary analysis. Humor is an obvious emotion, and students are genuinely interested in figuring out what causes them to smile or laugh. While philosophers, psychologists, linguists, anthropologists, writers, actors, and comedians have all tried to figure out why people laugh, no one has come up with a proven system. All the reviewers we know, however, have come to agreement that Louis Sachar's *Holes* is a very funny book. It won both the Newbery Award and the National Book Award and was listed on practically every "Best Book" list created for 1998. *Holes* consists of two stories. One is set in the present featuring young Stanley Yelnats, while the other one is set in the past and is about Stanley's ancestors. When the contemporary story would get too grim, Sachar would slip in a chapter from the past.

As explained very early in *Holes,* Stanley and his family seem to have more than their share of bad luck "all because of his no-good-dirty-rotten-pig-stealing-great-great-grandfather!" The very next line says that Stanley smiled when he

FOCUS BOX 6.3

Humorous YA Fiction (See also Focus Box 5.7 Love and Laughs for Junior High/Middle Schoolers, pp. 170)

Are You There God? It's Me, Margaret by Judy Blume. Bradbury, 1970. Blume's greatest strength as a writer is that she balances her serious themes with humor whether in this early book she wrote for young teens or whether in her later books for older readers including *Forever* (1975), *Starring Sally J. Freedman as Herself* (1977), and *Tiger Eyes* (1981), all from Bradbury.

The Arizona Kid by Ron Koertge. Little, Brown, 1988. In a *School Library Journal* article, Roger Sutton praised Koertge for being able to treat the subject of homosexuality with humor and respect for both the characters and the reader. Other Koertge books that combine humor and seriousness are *Tiger, Tiger, Burning Bright* (Orchard, 1994) and *Confess-O-Rama* (Orchard/Kroupa, 1996).

Alex Icicle: A Romance in Ten Torrid Chapters by Robert Kaplow. Houghton Mifflin, 1984. It would be hard not to smile after reading Kaplow's overly dramatic opening lines: "I am a sick man. I am a diseased man. I am not even a man, merely a boy. *And yet I love her.*"

Harris and Me: A Summer Remembered by Gary Paulsen. Harcourt Brace, 1993. When the son of an alcoholic couple is dumped off on a farm with some odd relatives, his cousin Harris greets him with a warm, "We heard your folks was puke drunks, is that right?"

If I Love You, Am I Trapped Forever? by M. E. Kerr. HarperCollins, 1973. Alan Bennett, the narrator, describes himself as "The most popular boy at Cayuta High. Very handsome. Very cool. Dynamite," but then Duncan Stein comes to town and Alan's life and world begin to

crumble. Among Kerr's other humorous books, all from HarperCollins, are *Dinky Hocker Shoots Smack* (1972), *Little Little* (1981), *Him She Loves?* (1984), and *I'll Love You When You're More Like Me* (1977).

The Pushcart War by Jean Merrill. W. R. Scott, 1964. This gentle and most effective satire of human cupidity is told as straight, factual history of "the war" which began when a truck driver crushes a pushcart and propels its owner into a pickle barrel.

The Secret Diary of Adrian Mole, Aged 13 3/4 and **The Growing Pains of Adrian Mole** by Sue Townsend. Grove Press, 1986, first published in England in 1982. These very funny books are taken from Adrian's diaries as he recounts his life struggles, in which no one (especially the BBC) fully appreciates the value of his sensitive writings, in which the beloved Pandora does not long for Adrian's caresses as much as Adrian longs to caress Pandora.

The Snarkout Boys and the Avocado of Death by Daniel Pinkwater. Lothrop, 1982. Pinkwater writes about nonconformists who do things with vigor. His quirky sense of humor is revealed through surprising allusions and frenetic energy. His *Young Adult Novel* (Crowell, 1982) is about the Wild Dada Ducks, five boys determined to upset the routine at Himmler High School.

Weetzie Bat by Francesca Lia Block. HarperCollins, 1989. Weetzie Bat, Dirk, and Slinkster Dog have their sad moments, but overall they are three of the hippest and funniest characters in all of YA literature.

thought of this because "It was a family joke," but as shown in Louis Sachar's statement some readers are just like Stanley and his family in forgetting that this is a joke.

Stanley is mistakenly accused of theft, found guilty, and sentenced to Camp Green Lake Juvenile Correction Facility, where every day each of the boys must dig a five-foot by five-foot hole supposedly to strengthen their character. Actually the warden is forcing the boys to help her (yes, the warden is a woman) look for buried treasure. Stanley figures he'll lose weight or die digging, but his friend and fellow

criminal Zero tries another way: he runs off. Stanley sets out after Zero, knowing little about the environment and forgetting to fill up his canteen. Stanley and Zero save themselves, partly through their own devices and partly through a series of coincidences that even Sachar realizes is a bit much. However, he lets readers in on the joke by entitling his denouement "Filling in the Holes."

LOUIS SACHAR
On the Moral of the Story?

After winning the Newbery Medal for *Holes,* I found myself giving interviews to newspapers, magazines, and TV reporters all over the country. One question I kept being asked was what did I want kids to learn from the book. What was my message? What morals was I hoping to teach children?

I seemed to give a particularly good answer when I spoke to the *Houston Chronicle.* The reporter wrote that I said, "The best moral kids get from any book is just the capacity to empathize with other people, to care about the characters and their feelings. So you don't have to write a preachy book to do that. You just make it a fun book with characters they care about, and they will become better people as a result." I always have a difficult time answering interviewers' questions — especially on TV where I'm given thirty seconds to tell about a two-hundred-and-fifty-page book that took a year and half to write — but I also have trouble with newspapers as well. So I was proud that I was able to come up with a good answer to that question, and, in fact, I even believe it's true.

But that certainly was not on my mind when I was writing *Holes.* I was just struggling to put all the elements of the story together: plot, character development, theme, etc.

It's hard to imagine anyone asking an author of an adult novel, what morals or lessons he or she was trying to teach the reader. But there is a perception that if you write for young people, then the book should be a lesson of some sort, a learning experience, a step toward something else.

It's not just reporters who feel this way. Some teachers and possibly even the students themselves believe this. Some fan letters read like class assignments. I received one recently which said something like, "Your book taught me that the acts of your great-great-grandfather can affect your life." Here, it seemed, the teacher required the students to write a letter to an author and say what lessons they learned from the book.

I didn't write the book for the purpose of teaching kids that something their great-great-grandparents did long ago might have cursed them and their descendants for all eternity. I included the curse only because I think most adolescents can identify with the feeling that their lives must be cursed.

The book was written for the sake of the book, and nothing beyond. It was meant to be enjoyed. If there's any lesson at all, it is that reading is fun.

(Continued)

> When I finish reading a book I love, I feel somehow enriched by it. My favorite books have become a part of me. That's so much more significant than anything as mundane as a moral or a lesson.
>
> I'm thinking about this now in this moment of reflection. It's not something that concerns me while I'm writing a book. When I type the words on my computer, it's hard for me to even imagine that real people will actually read them someday.
>
> Mostly when I write, I'm just trying to please one reader, myself. I try to write a story I like. And knowing myself as I do, I would not presume to try to teach myself a lesson. Although I often do surprise myself.
>
> Louis Sachar's books include *Holes,* Farrar, Straus & Giroux, 1987; *There's a Boy in the Girls' Bathroom,* Knopf, 1987; *Sideways Stories from Wayside School,* Morrow, 1978; *Dogs Don't Tell Jokes,* Knopf, 1991; and the Marvin Redpost series, 1990s, Random House.

To illustrate the complexity and the interrelatedness of narrative humor, in Table 6.2 we list several of the features that humor scholars identify as being what people find funny. We illustrate them with examples from Sachar's *Holes.* The chart will, of course, be more meaningful to those who have read the book, so if nothing else, we hope it will encourage you to do just that.

Evidence of the power of Sachar's humor is the difficulty we had in pulling out succinct examples of humor because a well-developed book (see Focus Box 6.4) differs from stand-up comedy in being more than a series of one-liners. For example, Sachar carried some of his jokes throughout the entire book as when Stanley first gets to camp and the guard tells him, "You're not in the Girl Scouts anymore." The guard regularly repeats this idea sometimes by just reminding the boys they aren't Girl Scouts, while at other times he asks, "You Girl Scouts having a good time?" Near the end of the book, when Stanley's lawyer and the Attorney General drive into the camp and the Warden wonders if it's "them," the guard tells her, "It ain't Girl Scouts selling cookies." This all leads up to the ironic denouement when readers are told that the camp is "bought by a national organization dedicated to the well-being of young girls. In a few years, Camp Green Lake will become a Girl Scout camp."

Another difficulty in making the chart was matching specific examples with the designated features because many of Sachar's jokes serve several purposes. At the same time Sachar is surprising readers or making them feel superior to a particular character, he is puzzling them with incongruous details, which he later resolves, thereby bringing more smiles. For example, on first seeing this description of the animals who share the amenities of Camp Green Lake Detention Center, readers probably do not realize they are being let in on a crucial plot element. Instead they just sit back and enjoy a standard three-part joke in which a comedian sets up a pattern and then surprises listeners by breaking the pattern.

> Here's a good rule to remember about rattlesnakes and scorpions: If you don't bother them, they won't bother you.
>
> Usually.
>
> Being bitten by a scorpion or even a rattlesnake is not the worst thing that can happen to you. You won't die.

FOCUS BOX 6.4

Adult Humor Accessible to Teens

Anguished English by Richard Lederer. Wyrick, 1987, Dell, 1989. Read this book in short chunks to get the fullest pleasure from the truly funny errors that Lederer gleaned from unpublished writings.

archy and mehitabel by Don Marquis. Doubleday, 1927. The poems in this classic are printed without capitals because they are composed on an old typewriter by archy, a giant cockroach who positions himself on the frame of the typewriter and dives off head first to hit the keys.

The Best of Bombeck: At Wit's End, Just Wait Until You Have Children of Your Own, I Lost Everything in the Post-Natal Depression by Erma Bombeck. Budget Book Service, 1994. Three of Bombeck's most popular books are reprinted in this collection. When Bombeck died of kidney failure in 1996, she had twelve books in print, mostly adapted from her popular newspaper columns.

Fables for Our Time by James Thurber. Harper & Brothers, 1940. Thurber's fables are the most accessible of his writings, but students can also be led to such stories as "The Night the Bed Fell," "University Days," "The Catbird Seat," and "The Secret Life of Walter Mitty." *The Thurber Carnival,* originally printed in 1945, had its thirtieth printing in 1998.

The Hitchhiker's Guide to the Galaxy by Douglas Adams. Ballantine, 1980. Arthur Dent and Ford Prefect are on a perilous and very funny journey through the galaxy. The stories were originally produced in England as radio shows and so work well as read-alouds or on tape.

Poetry for Cats: The Definitive Anthology of Distinguished Feline Verse by Henry Beard. Villard, 1994. Beard founded *The National Lampoon* and then resigned to write his own very funny books including several sports "daffynitions" done with Roy McKie.

Politically Correct Bedtime Stories: Modern Tales for Our Life & Times by James F. Garner. Macmillan, 1994. Clever teenagers will learn something about political correctness from these spoofs of stories they all know.

Russell Baker's Book of American Humor, edited by Russell Baker. Norton, 1993. This well-rounded collection would be a good resource to have in a classroom for students—and teachers—who need a break from routine and hard work.

Side Effects by Woody Allen. Random House, 1989. Some critics think that Allen's compilations of stories and essays are wittier and have better one-liners than do his films. Sophisticated students can also enjoy *Getting Even* (Random House, 1971) and *Without Feathers* (Random House, 1975).

Lake Wobegon Days by Garrison Keillor. Viking Penguin, 1985. Keillor came up with the idea for his well-known *Prairie Home Companion* radio show about Lake Wobegon and its residents, while listening to the Grand Ol' Opry in Nashville and imagining what a Minnesota gospel show would be like. Books related to the show include *Happy to Be Here: Even More Stories and Comic Pieces* (1983), and *Leaving Home: A Collection of Lake Wobegon Stories* (1987), both Viking Penguin.

The World According to Dave Barry by Dave Barry. Random House, 1994. In 1998, newspaper columnist Dave Barry won the Pulitzer Prize for commentary the same year that he published *Dave Barry's Greatest Hits* (Columbine/Fawcett). Other titles are *Dave Barry Slept Here: A Sort of History of the United States* (Random House, 1988) and *Dave Barry's Complete Guide to Guys: A Fairly Short Book* (Fawcett, 1996).

Usually. . . .

But you don't want to be bitten by a yellow-spotted lizard. That's the worst thing that can happen to you. You will die a slow and painful death.

Always.

TABLE 6.2

SOME FEATURES OF NARRATIVE HUMOR AS ILLUSTRATED BY INCIDENTS IN LOUIS SACHAR'S *HOLES*

Ambiguity

Stanley Yelnats is the name of either Stanley, his father, or his grandfather?

The whole story would have collapsed if *Zero*'s name hadn't been a shortened form of *Zeroni* instead of a reference to the contents of his brain.

When Stanley finds the gold cap with *K.B.* on it, he thinks it might be the cap to the pen of a famous writer, but readers figure out that the *K.B.* stands for both *Kate Barlow* and the *Kissing Bandit*.

Upon seeing the name *Mary Lou* on the back of the sunken boat, Stanley and Zero imagine a boy rowing across the lake with a beautiful girlfriend; readers know that *Mary Lou* was a 50-year-old donkey who lived on onions.

Exaggeration

The digging of five-foot-by-five-foot holes every day by every boy was surely an exaggeration.

The characters are eccentrics, especially those bigger-than-life ones from the 1890s including the Kissing Bandit, Kate Barlow, who "died laughing," the mean sheriff, the too-good-to-be-true "onion man," and the too-bad-to-be-true townspeople including Trout Walker and Linda.

Equally exaggerated is Stanley's great grandfather who carried his wealth in his suitcase and after losing it to Kate Barlow spent three weeks wandering in the desert. He was saved by the "Thumb of God," and married the nurse who took care of him at the hospital because he thought she was an angel—literally.

Hostility

There is enough hostility to go all around. When Stanley first gets to camp, the guard asks him if he's thirsty and when Stanley gratefully says, "Yes, thanks," the guard tells him to get used to it because "You're going to be thirsty for the next 18 months."

Stanley fantasizes about his new "friends" coming to his old school and intimidating his nemesis.

The warden puts rattlesnake venom in her nail polish so when she slaps Mr. Sir and scratches his face, he writhes in pain and his face is swollen for days.

Incongruity

There could hardly be a more incongruous set of characters ranging from Clyde "Sweet Feet" Livingston to Warden Walker and from Madame Zeroni to poor love-sick Elya Yelnats.

Stanley had thought about becoming an F.B.I. agent, but he realizes the group meeting with Mr. Pendanski is not "the appropriate place to mention that."

Readers laugh right along with the other boys when Stanley innocently responds to Mr. Pendanski's lecture about there being only one person responsible for Stanley's predicament: "My no-good-dirty-rotten-pig-stealing-great-great-grandfather."

Incongruity Resolution

The whole story revolves around Sachar resolving such incongruities as the boys being covered with the dreaded lizards but not being bitten, why the warden made the boys dig so many holes, why Zero never learned to read, how Zero and Stanley were tied together by "fate," how Stanley's great grandfather was saved on the desert, and why the curse is now lifted.

Irony

Not only is there no lake at Camp Green Lake, there is no greenery except in the two trees whose shade is owned by the warden.

The townspeople of Green Lake said that God would punish Kate Barlow for kissing a black man, but instead God punishes the town so that no rain falls and the Lake dries up so that not only its shape but also its surface is like a frying pan.

In his search for Zero, when Stanley comes up on the old, wrecked boat, he realizes that someone probably drowned in the very spot where he might die of thirst.

Superiority

Throughout the story kids feel superior to the adults, and well they might, judging by the Warden, Mr. Sir, and Mr. Pendanski.

The whole adult society is made to look ridiculous so that readers agree with Stanley's "Well, duh!" when he reads the sign at the entrance to the camp declaring it "a violation of the Texas Penal Code to bring guns, explosives, weapons, drugs, or alcohol onto the premises."

Readers cheer when Zero and Stanley, who are the lowest on the totem pole of the camp, are the ones who get out and become something less—"but not a lot less"—than millionaires.

Everyone feels superior to the pot-headed Myra who does not have sense enough to choose to marry Stanley's great-great-grandfather.

Surprise or Shock

Readers are as surprised as is Stanley at the sneakers falling from the sky and hitting him on the head.

When Zero tells Stanley that he knows he didn't steal Clyde Livingston's sneakers, Stanley shakes his head because when he tells the truth nobody believes him, and now when he lies, he still isn't believed.

Stanley and Zero's adventure is one surprise after another starting with Stanley finding Zero and Zero finding the "Sploosh" and ending with their finding the trunk with Stanley Yelnats's name on it.

A Trick or a Twist

An intriguing new setting is provided for the old trick of convincing someone that by lifting a calf every day, his strength will increase at the same rate that the animal gains weight.

Word Play

The recreation hall is named the *W-R-E-C-K* room.

The boys all have descriptive names: *Zigzag, Magnet, Squid, Armpit, Caveman, Barf Bag,* and *Xray.*

The macho guard is named *Mr. Sir* (he's doubly a man), while the boys call *Mr. Pendanski* ("pen-dance-key") *Mom.*

Sachar constantly plays with the word *holes* as when Stanley finds the lipstick tube initialed with *K.B.* and "digs that hole into his memory," and Sachar entitles the denouement, "Filling in the Holes."

In conclusion, this chapter has been about literature that is sometimes treated as "nonessential" mostly because it tugs at emotional more than intellectual parts of our brains. In today's high tech world, however, it may be that this is the very kind of reading that serves to remind us of our humanity and our need to reach out and understand the emotions of others.

Notes

[1]Betty Rosenberg, *Genreflecting: A Guide to the Reading Interests in Genre Fiction.* (Libraries Unlimited, 1982), in place of a dedication page.

[2]London *Independent,* June 30, 1995, p. 18.

[3]Hillary Waugh, "What Is a Mystery?" *The Basics of Writing and Selling Mysteries and Suspense: A Writer's Guide* 10 (1991): 6–8.

[4]Shannon Ocork, "What Type of Mystery Are You Writing?" *The Basics of Writing and Selling Mysteries and Suspense: A Writer's Digest Guide* 10 (1991): 10–12.

[5]Robert Westall, "On Nightmares for Money," *Literature for Today's Young Adults* (Scott, Foresman, 1989), pp. 166–167.

[6]Rick Lyman, "The Chills! The Thrills! The Profits!" *New York Times.* August 31, 1999, p. B1.

[7]Mary Ann Grossman, "Now *These* Books Will Give You Goosebumps," Saint Paul (MN) *Pioneer Express,* January 15, 1997, p. 6A.

[8]Steve Allen, *Funny People* (Stein & Day, 1981) p. 1.

[9]Lance M. Gentile and Merna M. McMillan, "Humor and the Reading Program," *Journal of Reading* 21 (January 1978): 343–350.

Titles Mentioned in the Text of Chapter Six

Avi. *Wolf Rider.* Macmillan, 1986.

Blum, Arlene. *Annapurna: A Woman's Place.* Sierra Club Books, 1980.

Branscum, Robbie. *Me and Jim Luke.* Doubleday, 1971.

Brunvand, Jan Harold. *The Vanishing Hitchhiker: American Urban Legends and Their Meanings.* Norton, 1984.

Carter, Jennifer and Joel Hirschhorn. *Titanic Adventure.* New Horizon, 1999.

Christie, Agatha. *And Then There Were None.* Dodd, Mead, 1939.

Christie, Agatha. *By the Pricking of My Thumbs.* Dodd, Mead, 1968.

Christie, Agatha. *A Murder Is Announced.* Dodd, Mead, 1950.

Coleman, Michael. *Weirdo's War.* Orchard, 1998.

Craughwell, Thomas J. *Alligators in the Sewer: And 222 Other Urban Legends.* Black Dog & Leventhal,1999.

Dickson, Paul and Joseph C. Goulden. *There Are Alligators in Our Sewers and Other American Credos.* Delacorte, 1983.

Duncan, Lois. *Summer of Fear.* Little, Brown, 1976.

Duncan, Lois. *The Third Eye.* Little, Brown, 1984.

Duncan, Lois. *Stranger with My Face.* Little, Brown, 1981.

Hillerman, Tony. *The Blessing Way.* HarperCollins, 1970.

Hillerman, Tony. *Coyote Waits.* HarperCollins, 1990.

Hillerman, Tony. *The Dance Hall of the Dead.* HarperCollins, 1973.

Hillerman, Tony. *The Fallen Man.* HarperCollins, 1996.

Hillerman, Tony. *The First Eagle.* HarperCollins, 1998.

Hillerman, Tony. *The Ghostway.* HarperCollins, 1985.

Hillerman, Tony. *The Listening Woman.* HarperCollins, 1978.

Hillerman, Tony. *Sacred Clowns.* HarperCollins, 1993.

Hillerman, Tony. *The Skinwalkers.* HarperCollins, 1987.

Hobbs, Will. *Bearstone.* Atheneum, 1989.

Hobbs, Will. *Downriver.* Atheneum, 1991.

Hobbs, Will. *River Thunder.* Bantam, 1997.

Hobbs, Will. *The Maze.* Morrow, 1998.

Holzol, Tom and Audrey Salkeld. *First on Everest: The Mystery of Mallory and Irvine.* Henry Holt, 1986.

Hoobler, Dorothy and Thomas Hoobler. *The Ghost in the Tokaido Inn,* Philomel, 1999.

Jones, Patrick. *What's So Scary About R. L. Stine?* Scarecrow, 1998.

Karesh, William B. *Appointment at the Ends of the World: Memoirs of a Wildlife Veterinarian.* Warner, 1999.

King, Laurie R. *The Moore.* St. Martin's, 1998.

King, Stephen. *Bag of Bones.* Scribner, 1998.

King, Stephen. *Carrie.* Doubleday, 1974.

King, Stephen. *Christine.* Viking, 1983.

King, Stephen. *Cujo.* Viking, 1981.

King, Stephen. *Desperation.* Viking, 1996.

King, Stephen. *Different Seasons.* Viking, 1982.

King, Stephen. *Firestarter.* Viking, 1980.

King, Stephen. *Four Past Midnight.* Viking, 1990.

King, Stephen. *The Girl Who Loved Tom Gordon.* Scribner, 1999.

King, Stephen. *It.* Viking, 1986.

King, Stephen. *Pet Sematary.* Doubleday, 1983.

King, Stephen. *Salem's Lot.* Doubleday, 1975.

King, Stephen. *The Shining.* Doubleday, 1977.

King, Stephen. *The Stand.* Doubleday, 1978.

King, Stephen. *The Tommyknockers.* Putnam, 1987.

Klause, Annette Curtis. *Blood and Chocolate.* Delacorte, 1997.

Klause, Annette Curtis. *The Silver Kiss.* Delacorte, 1990.

Lawrence, Iain. *The Smugglers.* Delacorte, 1999.

Lawrence, Iain. *The Wreckers.* Delacorte, 1998.

Lewis, Matthew Gregory. *The Monk.* Grove Weidenfeld, 1952 (originally published in 1797).

Lynch, Don and Robert D. Ballard. *Titanic: An Illustrated History*. Hyperion, 1997.

Mazer, Harry. *The Island Keeper*. Delacourte, 1981.

McCaughrean, Geraldine. *The Pirates Son*. Scholastic, 1998.

Myers, Walter Dean. *The Mouse Rap*. Harper & Row, 1990.

Nixon, Joan Lowery. *The Dark and Deadly Pool*. Delacorte, 1987.

Nixon, Joan Lowery. *The Haunting*. Delacorte, 1998.

Nixon, Joan Lowery. *Spirit Seeker*. Delacorte, 1995.

Nixon, Joan Lowery. *Whispers from the Dead*. Delacorte, 1989.

Nixon, Joan Lowery. *Who Are You?* Delacorte, 1998.

O'Brian, Patrick. *The Hundred Days*. Norton, 1999.

O'Brien, Robert C. *Z for Zachariah*. Atheneum, 1975.

Paulsen, Gary. *Brian's Return*. Delacorte, 1999.

Paulsen, Gary. *Hatchet*. Bradbury, 1987.

Peck, Richard. *Blossom Culp and the Sleep of Death*. Delacorte, 1986.

Peck, Richard. *The Dreadful Future of Blossom Culp*. Delacorte, 1983.

Peck, Richard. *The Ghost Belonged to Me*. Viking, 1975.

Peck, Richard. *Ghosts I Have Been*. Viking, 1977.

Reaver, Chap. *A Little Bit Dead*. Delacorte, 1994.

Reaver, Chap. *Mote*. Delacorte, 1990.

Rice, Anne. *Memnoch, the Devil*. Knopf, 1995.

Rice, Anne. *The Vampire Armand*. Knopf, 1998.

Sachar, Louis. *Holes*. Farrar, Straus & Giroux, 1998.

Schwartz, Alvin, collector. *More Scary Stories to Tell in the Dark*. Lippincott, 1984

Schwartz, Alvin, collector. *Scary Stories to Tell in the Dark*. Lippincott, 1981.

Schwartz, Alvin, collector. *Scary Stories 3: More Tales to Chill Your Bones*. HarperCollins, 1991.

Taylor, Michael Ray. *Cave Passages: Roaming the Underground Wilderness*. Scribner, 1996.

Thompson, Julian F. *The Grounding of Group Six*. Avon, 1983.

Tullis, Julie. *Clouds from Both Sides*. Sierra Club Books, 1987.

Wells, Rosemary. *The Man in the Woods*. Dutton, 1984.

Westall, Robert. *Blitzcat*. Scholastic, 1989.

White, Rob, *Deathwatch*. Doubleday, 1972.

Wickwire, Jim. *Addicted to Danger*. Pocketbooks, 1998.

Windsor, Patricia. *The Christmas Killer*. Scholastic, 1991.

Information on the availability of paperback editions of these titles is available online from such book sellers as Barnes & Noble and Amazon.com, and through *Books in Print* compiled by R. R. Bowker Company and available either in person or online from major libraries.

CHAPTER

7

Fantasy, Science Fiction, Utopias, and Dystopias

Fantasy and science fiction are related to each other and to humankind's deepest desires, but it is not always easy to draw a clear-cut line between the two. Ursula LeGuin offered this distinction:

> The basic concept of fantasy, of course, is this; you get to make up the rules, but then you've got to follow them. Science fiction refines the canon: you get to make up the rules, but within limits. A science-fiction story must not flout the evidence of science, must not, as Chip Delaney puts it, deny what is known to be known.[1]

Or, as Walter Wangerin, Jr., said in a lecture to a college audience:
"Fantasy deals with the 'immeasurable' while science fiction deals with the "measurable."[2]

No matter what the definitions or distinctions, the boundaries between science fiction and fantasy are fuzzy, so that more often than not the two genres are treated together (witness two important journals about these areas—*Science Fiction Chronicle: The Monthly Science Fiction and Fantasy Newsmagazine* and *The Magazine of Fantasy and Science Fiction*). Advertisements for the Science Fiction Book Club often mix choices of science fiction and fantasy with horror, the supernatural, mythology, folklore, and some selections that seem impossible to pigeonhole. Anyone who teaches or is around young people knows that in this area books cross genre lines and age lines. Young adults read what adults read, and books that may have been published for young readers (e.g., Robin McKinley's *Beauty* or Lloyd Alexander's *Prydain* series) are now also read by adults.[3]

What Is Fantasy?

Fantasy comes from a Greek word meaning "a making visible." Perhaps more than any other form of literature, fantasy refuses to accept the world as it is, so readers can see what could have been (and still might be), rather than merely what was or must be.

The appeal of fantasy may be, simply, that it is so elemental. Some see its most comparable form of communication in music, which may be why so many composers have been influenced by it. Fantasy sings of our need for heroes, for the good, and for success in our eternal fight against evil. Composers of works as dissimilar as Stravinsky's *Firebird* and Mahler's *Song of the Earth* and Strauss's *Thus Sprach Zarathustra* have sung that song. Writers sing similar songs when they tell stories of great heroes, usually of humble means and beginnings, seeking truth, finding ambiguities, and subduing evil, at least temporarily. On its lighter side, musicians sing of beauty and love and dreams and dreamers, as in Mozart's *The Magic Flute* or Ravel's *Daphnis and Chloë* and Tchaikovsky's *Swan Lake*. Writers sing their lighter tales through stories about Beauty and the Beast, the happier and younger life of Arthur, and many of the old folktales and legends that are childhood favorites.

Ray Bradbury agrees that fantasy is elemental and essential.

> The ability to "fantasize" is the ability to survive. It's wonderful to speak about this subject because there have been so many wrong-headed people dealing with it. We're going through a terrible period of art, in literature and living, in psychiatry and psychology. The so-called realists are trying to drive us insane, and I refuse to be driven insane. . . . We survive by fantasizing. Take that away from us and the whole damned human race goes down the drain.[4]

Fantasy allows us—or even forces us—to become greater than we are, greater than we could hope to be. It confronts us with the major ambiguities and dualities of life—good and evil, light and dark, innocence and guilt, reality and appearance, heroism and cowardice, hard work and indolence, determination and vacillation, and order and anarchy. Fantasy presents all these, and it provides the means through which readers can consider both the polarities and the many shadings in between.

Conventions of Fantasy

Jo-Ann Goodwin's comment about the nature of fantasy is worth repeating for its accuracy and succinctness.

> Classic fantasy is centered around quests. The quest may have any number of different motives—spiritual, political, sexual, material—but its presence in the text is essential. The quest expresses the desire to accomplish a thing fraught with difficulty and danger, and seemingly doomed to failure. It also enables fantasy writers to deal with rites of passage; the central figure grows in stature as the quest evolves. Typically, the journey will be full of magical, symbolic and allegorical happenings which allow the hero to externalize his or her internal struggles: thus Odysseus must pass through Charybdis and Scylla and the Knight of Temperance must extricate himself from Acracia and the Bower of Bliss.
>
> Fantasy also deals with flux. The central characters operate in a world turned upside down, amid great wars and events of a cataclysmic nature. The possible outcomes are open and endlessly variable; the responsibility carried

by the hero is enormous. In fantasy, the imagined world is always a global village. No action can take place in isolation. Every decision taken by the hero affects someone else, and sometimes the fate of nations. It is a deeply social genre.[5]

Heroes must prove worthy of their quest, although early in the story they may be fumbling or unsure about both themselves and their quests.

The quest may be ordained, required, or, occasionally, self-determined. The hero may briefly confuse good and evil, but the protagonist ultimately recognizes the distinction. When the obligatory battle comes between the powers of good and evil, the struggle may be prolonged and the outcome in doubt. But eventually good prevails, although the victory is always transitory.

John Rowe Townsend, both a fine writer of young adult novels and one of the most perceptive and honored critics of the field, maintained that the quest motif is a powerful analogy of life's pattern:

> Life is a long journey, in the course of which one will assuredly have one's adventures, one's sorrows and joys, one's setbacks and triumphs, and perhaps, with luck and effort, the fulfillment of some major purpose.[6]

We all begin our quest, that long journey, seeking the good and being tempted by the evil that we know we must ultimately fight. We face obstacles and barriers throughout, hoping that we will find satisfaction and meaning during and after the quest. Our quests may not be as earthshaking as those of fantasy heroes, but our emotional and intellectual wrestling can shake our own personal worlds. In the December 1971 *Horn Book Magazine,* Lloyd Alexander wrote about this kind of comparison.

> The fantasy hero is not only a doer of deeds, but he also operates within a framework of morality. His compassion is as great as his courage—greater, in fact. We might consider that his humane qualities, more than any other, are really what the hero is all about. I wonder if this reminds us of the best parts of ourselves?[7]

Tamora Pierce notes an important element of the appeal of fantasy to young people.

> Fantasy, more than any other genre, is a literature of empowerment. In the real world, kids have little say. This is a given; it is the nature of childhood. In fantasy, however short, fat, unbeautiful, weak, dreamy, or unlearned individuals may be, they find a realm in which those things are negated by strength. The catch—there is *always* a catch—is that empowerment brings trials. Good novels in this genre never revolve around heroes who, once they receive the "Spatula of Power," call the rains to fill dry wells, end all war, and clear up all acne. Heroes and heroines contend as much with their granted wishes as readers do in normal life.[8]

Fears of Fantasy

Attacks on fantasy are common and predictable. Fantasy is said to be childishly simple reading. It is true there are simple fantasies, but anyone who has read Walter Wangerin, Jr.'s, *The Book of the Dun Cow* or Evangeline Walton's Mabinogion series knows that fantasy need not be childish or simple. Fantasies are often difficult and demand close reading, filled as they are with strange beings and even stranger lands with mystical and moral overtones and ambiguities.

Fantasy has also been labeled escapist literature, and, of course, it is in several ways. Fantasy allows readers to escape the mundane and to revel in glorious adventures. For some readers (perhaps for all readers at certain times), escape is all that's demanded. For other readers, venturing on those seemingly endless quests, encountering all those incredible obstacles, and facing all those apparently tireless antagonists to defend the good and defeat the evil lead to more than mere reading to pass time. The escape from reality sends those readers back to their own limited and literal worlds to face many of the same problems they found in fantasy. See Film Box 7.1 and Focus Box 7.1 for illustrations. (See also Focus Box 2.1 p. 47 Old Stories in New Dress.)

In the most illogical objection (and more common than we could have predicted only a few years ago), fantasy has been attacked for being unreal, untrue, and imaginative (the term *imaginative* seems to have replaced *secular humanism* as one of today's leading bogeymen). To critics who believe that using imagination leads to unwillingness to face reality, fantasy doubtless seems dangerous. But fantasy is about reality, as Ursula K. LeGuin explained nearly twenty years ago:

> For fantasy is true, of course. It isn't factual, but it is true. Children know that. Adults know it too, and that is precisely why many of them are afraid of fantasy. They know that its truth challenges, even threatens, all that is false, phony, unnecessary, and trivial in the life they have let themselves be forced into living. They are afraid of dragons because they are afraid of freedom.
>
> So I believe we should trust our children. Normal children do not confuse reality with fantasy—they confuse them much less often than we adults do (as a certain great fantasist pointed out in a story called "The Emperor's New Clothes"). Children know perfectly well that unicorns aren't real, but they also know that books about unicorns, if they are good books, are true books.[9]

Seven Significant Writers of Fantasy

While several contemporary authors have produced fantasies that have been critically acclaimed, seven fantasy writers lead all the rest. For many enthusiasts, J. R. R. Tolkien is the writer against whom all other writers in the field are measured. *The Hobbit, or There and Back Again* began in 1933 as a series of stories that Tolkien told his children at night about a strange being, Bilbo, the Hobbit. His three-part *The Lord of the Rings* is even better known, revealing his love of adventure and his fascination with language.

Alan Garner is one of the most widely respected writers in the genre and that largely for one book. *The Owl Service* (1968) appeared in the early days of modern adolescent literature in the United States and created something of a sensation

FILM BOX 7.1

What Is Fantasy and What Is Real? (see Appendix D)

Birdy (1984, color, 120 min., R; Director: Alan Parker; with Matthew Modine and Nicholas Cage) From William Wharton's novel, this is the story of a young man who spends his entire life wanting to escape reality and become a bird.

The Ghost and Mrs. Muir (1947, black and white, 104 min., NR; Director: Joseph L. Mankiewicz; with Gene Tierney and Rex Harrison) A young widow slowly falls in love with the ghost of a sea captain.

King of Hearts (British, 1966, color, 102 min., NR; Director: Phillipe De Broca; with Alan Bates and Genevieve Bujod) A British soldier enters a French town in World War II and discovers that the only people there are inmates of the local asylum.

Ladyhawke (1985, color, 124 min., PG–13; Director: Richard Donner; with Michelle Pfeiffer, Rutger Hauer, and Matthew Broderick) In this underrated film, a shape-spell is cast on lovers never allowing them to see each other.

Lost Horizon (1937, black and white, 132 min., NR; Director: Frank Capra; with Ronald Colman, Jane Wyatt, and Sam Jaffe) James Hilton's best-selling novel is translated into a film about the human wish to leave our troubled world and find the perfect society.

The Purple Rose of Cairo (1985, black and white/color, 82 min., PG; Director: Woody Allen; with Mia Farrow and Jeff Daniels). A depression-era waitress spends her time going to movies to escape her drab life. Then a movie character leaves the screen and temporarily enters her life.

The Secret of Roan Inish (1995, color, 103 min., PG; Director: John Sayles; with Jeni Courtney and Richard Sheridan) Old legends are retold in this atmospheric film about the island of Roan Inish (Island of the Seals).

The Seventh Seal (Swedish, 1957, black and white, 96 min., NR; Director: Ingmar Bergman; with Max Von Sydow and Gunnar Björnstrand) A cynical knight on his way home from the Crusades plays chess with Death.

The Thief of Bagdad (British, 1940, color, 106 min., NR; Director: Ludwig Berger; with Sabu and Conrad Veldt) These Arabian nights adventures are complete with flying carpets and more. The silent version filmed in 1924 is equally good and fun to compare.

The Wizard of Oz (1939, black and white/color, 101 min., NR; Director: Victor Fleming; with Judy Garland, Bert Lahr, and Ray Bolger) L. Frank Baum's childhood classic becomes one of the greatest American films with its good and bad witches, flying monkeys, and the yellow brick road.

among the few teachers and librarians who read it. Based on the Mabinogion, a collection of Welsh legends and myths, the three young characters in the story find a set of dishes. As the three get to know each other better, they also find that the pattern reflects a story of love and jealousy and hatred, one of the Mabinogion's tales of a triangular love that ends disastrously. *Red Shift*, Garner's later work, is rewarding for students who can stay with it, but it is a tough go.

Best known for her Earthsea books, Ursula LeGuin has maintained her popularity with young and adult readers. *A Wizard of Earthsea*, set in a land of vast oceans and multitudinous islands, focuses on a young boy who senses he is capable of becoming a wizard. He is named Ged, and while he generally comports himself satisfactorily, he once showed off his magic and raised an evil spirit who followed him thereafter. Ged appears in *The Tombs of Atuan*, but the chief character is Tenar, dedicated from his youth to the Powers of the Earth. In *The Farthest Shore*, Ged, now an Archmage and the most powerful of wizards, accompanies a young man on a mission to seek out evil.

FOCUS BOX 7.1

Reality May Not be Fantasy, but Fantasy Is Reality

The Camelot Chronicles edited by Mike Ashley. Carroll and Graf, 1992. Ashley presents retellings of Arthurian legends and stories.

Circle of Magic: Daja's Book by Tamora Pierce. Scholastic, 1998. In Pierce's third Circle book, Daja is now an outcast from her people.

Dark Shade by Jane Louise Curry. McElderry, 1998. Time travel back to 1758 reveals some surprising ways in which the past affects the present.

Fortress in the Eye of Time by C. J. Cherryh. Prism, 1995. Two men—one a human and one a Shapling—are forced to work together to save the land.

A Glory of Unicorns edited by Bruce Coville. Scholastic, 1998. Coville, who has written books for preteens about unicorns, collected these twelve stories about his favorite creatures and their interactions with people.

In the Rift by Marion Zimmer Bradley and Holly Lisle. Baen, 1998. Kate must save not only our own world but also the parallel world of Glenraven.

Of Two Minds by Carol Matas and Perry Nodelman. Simon & Schuster, 1995. Two young people live in a world ruled by a dictator who controls the population.

The One-Armed Queen by Jane Yolen. TOR, 1998. A one-armed young woman learns who and what she is in a world of intrigue.

A Wizard's Dozen edited by Michael Stearns. Harcourt Brace, 1993. Magic and mystery are woven throughout Stearns's collection of short stories.

Xone of Contention by Piers Anthony. TOR, 1999. To stave off a divorce, a couple visits the planet of Xanith where magic exists.

Readers had long assumed that the Earthsea series was complete, but more than twenty years after the first book, *Tehanu: The Last Book of Earthsea* appeared. Tenar and Ged reappear, but the principal character is a much-abused child, Therru, who is to become the greatest of all opponents of evil. *Tehanu* is a far darker book than the other three and is different in another way as well. While the other three books were told from the perspective of the powerful Ged and Tenar, this is told from the perspective of the—apparently—powerless.

Rewriting fairy tales is nothing new, but Robin McKinley's *Beauty: A Retelling of the Story of Beauty and the Beast* and the recent *Rose Daughter* are so amusing and so spirited that in this one narrow niche of fantasy she leads all the rest. McKinley's Beauty is strong and unafraid and loving. When her father steals a rose from the Beast's garden and forfeits his life, Beauty is eager to save her father. She says,

> "He cannot be so bad if he loves roses."
> "But he is a beast," said her father helplessly.
> I saw that he was weakening, and wishing only to comfort him, I said, "Cannot a Beast be Tamed."

The answer to that question, in both *Beauty* and *Rose Daughter* is yes, with time and kindness and love.

Anne McCaffrey's series of novels about Pern, once a colony of Earth, is required reading for anyone into fantasy. Every 200 years Pern is threatened by shimmering spores, organisms that devour all organic matter. Dragons destroy the threads as they fall. The name Pern comes from *Parallel Earth Resources Negligible*. Beginning with *Dragonflight* in 1968, followed by *Dragonsong, Dragonsinger,* and

Dragondrums, McCaffrey set an exceptionally high standard for other writers of fantasy.

Many of her books have considerable science fiction mixed with the fantasy, not unusual for writers working either genre. McCaffrey has long maintained that she writes science fiction, not fantasy, and in an interview in 1999, McCaffrey was asked again in which genre she wrote. She answered,

> We keep having to settle that question. *I write science* fiction. It may seem fantasy because I use dragons, but mine were biogenetically engineered; ergo, the story is science fiction.[10]

She may protest and she has a point, but most readers are likely to continue to think of her as a writer of fantasy. So it goes.

After writing several successful books of mystery and adventure set in Victorian England, Philip Pullman (see his statement) turned even more successfully to fantasy in the first two of his projected three-volume series under the general title "Dark Materials." *The Golden Compass* introduces readers to Lyra Belacqua and her demon (an animal companion that reflects both its owner's personality and that of its own personality) and her education at Oxford. *The Subtle Knife,* the second book, introduces readers to Will Parry whose father has been lost in the Arctic. Will sets out to find his father and in the journey slides into another universe and meets Lyra.

Both books are filled with adventures and a constant stream of wonders. Both introduce magic. In the first book, readers learn about the golden compass, which can foretell the future. In the second, the subtle knife, called Aesahaettr, is entrusted to Will. It can cut through anything, real or magical. The significance of the knife and the seriousness of Pullman's book is revealed when a witch remarks that the name of the knife "sounds as if it meant 'god-destroyer.' "

Clockwork—or All Wound Up, Pullman's most recent fantasy, is a brief but powerful tale of an apprentice clockworker who has failed to create a figure to add to the town clock. As he bewails what he has not done, a friend tells a story of the mad sorcerer, Dr. Kalmenius, and soon the doctor appears before the clockworker and the story begins. It's a tale of love and evil and failure and peace.

The most recent addition to the list of significant writers of fantasy is new to the field and to the publishing world, but she may yet surpass all the rest, in sales if nothing else. J. K. Rowling's first three volumes about Harry Potter in a projected ten-volume series have surprised almost everyone in publishing. By October 1999, the three books had sold almost two-million copies in Great Britain and more than five-million copies in the United States. The books have been translated into twenty-eight languages. Even more surprising, the last of the published three, *Harry Potter and the Prisoner of Azkaban,* received a full, four-column review in the *New York Times Book Review.* The series generally has led the best-selling charts for fiction for several weeks. Perhaps even surpassing that, *Time* magazine gave six pages to the Harry phenomenon in the September 20, 1999, issue. All in all, amazing for a work aimed at children and maybe adolescents. In truth, however, adults are just as taken by the series as any other group.

Why is Harry so popular? Even a cursory reading of the series would suggest some answers. Harry is a remarkable character. He is almost impossible to dislike; he's an incredibly apt student of magic at the Hogwarts School of Witchcraft and Wizardry; he's athletic in the game played by wizards, Quidditch (played in midair

PHILIP PULLMAN
On "Where do you get your pictures from?"

"Where do you get your ideas from?" is without any doubt the number one question people ask writers.

I'm always stuck for an answer to that, because I don't think of my books as being made of ideas in the first place. They're made of pictures (even when they only look like words). *The Golden Compass,* for instance, began with a picture in my mind, a picture of a girl hiding in a wardrobe and overhearing something she shouldn't have. I wrote the story to find out what that was, and what happened next. I didn't think of it as an *idea;* it was a picture.

Maybe that's what people mean by the question, though. Maybe they mean, "Where do you get your pictures from?"

And again, I'm stuck, because I have pictures in my head all the time. Doesn't everyone? Most people probably call them daydreams. They come out of books, as well, and items I see on the TV or read about in the newspaper; they come from all over the place. But then, these pictures come to everyone else at the same time as coming to me; so again, where's the difference?

I can only suppose that when you've been writing stories and novels for a long time you get in the habit of looking at the pictures (or ideas, or whatever you want to call them) and seeing whether you can twist them into a more interesting shape. Of playing *What if . . . ?* of thinking "Hey, that's just like *Cinderella,* except that . . ."

In other words, taking them on a bit further. Playing with them. Because the really interesting questions aren't, "Where do they come from?" but "Why did you do *this* with that idea?" and "How did you develop that story once you had the first picture?" and "What's a good way of making a story take an unexpected direction?"

Questions like that, technical ones, are actually the most interesting ones for me. I could talk about them for a long time, and I'm always interested to hear or read what other writers have said about them.

And if you want to write a book, stop worrying about where your ideas are going to come from, and start playing with pictures instead.

Of course, you still have to sit down and *write* the damn thing . . .

But that's another story.

Philip Pullman's books include *The Golden Compass,* 1996; *The Subtle Knife,* 1998, and *The Ruby in the Smoke,* 1987, all from Knopf.

by boys on broomsticks); he's clearly a fighter; and he has friends that are attractive to readers.

His parents were murdered by the evil Voldemort, and there are enough reminders of Luke Skywalker and Darth Vader and other aspects of *Star Wars* to fascinate readers for years. In a *School Library Journal* interview, Rowling was asked what young readers are most curious about. She answered, "They were very keen to

When *Harry Potter and the Sorcerer's Stone* was brought to the United States by Scholastic, in 1998, it went immediately to number 1 on the *New York Times* bestseller list. The same thing happened with *Harry Potter and the Chamber of Secrets*, so Scholastic moved up by several months the 1999 publication of the third book *Harry Potter and the Prisoner of Azkaban* because they were losing sales to anxious readers who were ordering the British version through Amazon.com.

know whom I'm going to kill." And shortly a related question was posed. "The first two Harry Potter books are very lighthearted. Will the series remain that way?" Rowling answered,

> The books are getting darker, and that's inevitable. If you are writing about Good and Evil, there comes a point where you have to get serious. This is something I really have had to think about.[11]

Other Kinds of Fantasy

Animal Fantasies

Animal stories aimed at instructing humans are as old as Aesop and as recent as yesterday's book review. Many students come to high school having already enjoyed books such as E. B. White's *Charlotte's Web,* Jane Langton's *The Fledgling,* Robert C. O'Brien's *Mrs. Frisby and the Rats of NIMH,* Kenneth Grahame's *The Wind in the Willows,* and Richard Adams's *Watership Down.*

They may be ready to read Walter Wangerin, Jr.'s, *The Book of the Dun Cow,* a delightfully funny theological thriller retelling the story of Chauncticleer the Rooster. Supposedly the leader for good against evil (the half-snake, half-cock—

Cockatrice—and the black serpent—Wyrm), Chaunticleer is beset by doubts. He is aided by the humble dog, Mondo Cani, some hilariously pouting turkeys, and assorted other barnyard animals. Although this may sound cute, it is not, and the battle scenes are among the bloodiest, ugliest, and most realistic that readers are likely to find in fantasy. *The Book of Sorrows* was a disappointing sequel.

Readers who do not know fantasy may associate the genre with high seriousness, but readers of the genre know how funny some fantasy writers can be. Peter Beagle's fantasies stand out for their quiet wit, even in treating a serious theme. The title of *A Fine and Private Place* comes from Andrew Marvell's "To His Coy Mistress":

> The Grave's a fine and private place,
> But none, I think, do there embrace.

The grave is a lively and often funny place in Beagle's novel with a living human talking to a delightfully tough old raven. In *The Last Unicorn,* a lonely unicorn seeks the company of others of its kind, helped by the magician Schmendrick, who is incapable of telling any story without wild elaboration. Stopping at a town early in the quest, Schmendrick tells of his adventures.

> During the meal Schmendrick told stories of his life as an errant enchanter, filling it with kings and dragons and noble ladies. He was not lying, merely organizing events more sensibly.

Fantasy and the Mabinogion

The *Mabinogion* is a collection of medieval Welsh tales, first published in English in 1838 to 1849 by Lady Charlotte Guest. The eleven stories fall into three parts: The four branches of the Mabinogi (tales to instruct young bards) deal with Celtic legends and myths of Pywll, prince of Dived; Branwen, daughter of Llyr; Manawyddan, son of Llyr; and Math, son of Mathonwy. There are also four independent tales and four Arthurian romances. Several writers have used the Mabinogi myths and legends as a basis for their books.

Lloyd Alexander's Prydain Chronicles consists of five volumes about Taran, the young Assistant Pig-Keeper. The opening book of this rich fantasy, *The Book of Three,* introduces the main characters, especially Taran, and sends him on his quest to save his land, Prydain, from evil. He seeks his own identity as well, for none know his heritage. Taran's early impatience is understandable but vexing to his master, Dalben, who counsels patience "for the time being."

> "For the time being," Taran burst out. "I think it will always be for the time being, and it will be vegetables and horseshoes all my life."
> "Tut," said Dalben, "there are worse things. Do you set yourself to be a glorious hero? Do you believe it is all flashing swords and galloping about on horses? As for being glorious. . . ."
> "What of Prince Gwydion?" cried Taran. "Yes, I wish I might be like him."
> "I fear," Dalben said, "that is entirely out of the question."
> "But why?" Taran sprang to his feet. "I know if I had the chance. . . ."
> "Why?" Dalben interrupted. "In some cases," he said, "we learn more by looking for the answer to a question and not finding it than we do from learning the answer itself."

Taran, youthful impetuousness and righteous indignation aglow, is bored by Dalben's thoughts and wants action, and that he finds soon enough in the books that follow: *The Black Cauldron, The Castle of Llyr, Taran Wanderer,* and *The High King.*

Evangeline Walton (real name, Evangeline Walton Ensely) stands out among writers who have used the *Mabinogion* as a basis for fantasy. Her four-part series, *The Prince of Annwn: The First Branch of the Mabinogion, The Children of Llyr: The Second Branch of the Mabinogion, The Song of Rhiannon: The Third Branch of the Mabinogion,* and *The Virgin and the Swine: The Fourth Branch of the Mabinogion* (the last volume was reprinted in 1970 as *The Island of the Mighty: The Fourth Branch of the Mabinogion*), is among the best of retellings of the old Welsh legends. Walton's quartet is both mythology and ecology, for the author makes the earth a divinity that must not be despoiled by humanity. In an afterword to the first book, Walton writes,

> When we were superstitious enough to hold the earth sacred and worship her, we did nothing to endanger our future upon her, as we do now.

King Arthur and Other Myths in Fantasy

Arthurian legends have long been staples of fantasy. T. H. White's *The Once and Future King* (a source, for which it can hardly be blamed, for that dismal musical, *Camelot*) is basic to any reading of fantasy. In four parts, *The Sword in the Stone, The Witch in the Wood, The Ill-Made Knight,* and *The Candle in the Wind,* White retells the story of Arthur—his boyhood, his prolonged education at the hands of Merlin, his seduction by Queen Morgause, his love for Guinivere and her affair with Lancelot, and Mordred's revenge and Arthur's fall. A later work, *The Book of Merlyn: The Unpublished Conclusion* to *The Once and Future King,* should, like most work left unpublished at an author's death, have been allowed to remain unpublished and largely unknown.

Among the shorter retellings of the legends, no one has surpassed the series by Rosemary Sutcliff. *The Sword and the Circle: King Arthur and the Knights of the Round Table, The Light Beyond the Forest: The Quest for the Holy Grail,* and *The Road to Camlann: The Death of King Arthur* are masterfully written by a writer who loves the legends and has a firm grasp on the materials and the meanings.

Marion Zimmer Bradley's *The Mists of Avalon* focuses on the conflict between the old religion, the Celtic, represented by Morgan Le Fay (here called Morgaine) and the new religion of Christianity, represented by Guinivere (here called Gwenhyfar).

Young readers curious about the Arthurian world have a choice of several good books. Leading the list, as usual, is Katherine Paterson whose *Parzival: The Quest of the Grail Knight* complements our knowledge of Arthur's knights and Wagner's *Parsifal.* Nancy Springer's *I Am Mordred* related the sad, even accursed life of Arthur's bastard son. Pamela Service's two books combining fantasy and science fiction begin 500 years after a nuclear weapon destroyed the Earth. *Winter of Magic's Return* has two survivors rescuing yet another person, in this case Merlin who has been enchanted for 2,000 years. The trio set off to find Arthur. In the sequel, *Tomorrow's Magic,* Arthur takes over England.

Fantasy on Other Worlds: Here There Be Dragons

Several other writers have written marvelous tales of dragons and fantastic worlds. Jane Yolen's *Dragon's Blood, Heart's Blood,* and *A Sending of Dragons* comprise a series with two extraordinarily likeable young people fighting for their lives and for their dragons. Patricia C. Wrede's *Dealing with Dragons, Searching for Dragons, Calling on Dragons,* and *Talking to Dragons* are funny adventure stories. Her best work can be found in *Book of Enchantments.*

Diana Wynne Jones always tells a good story, often peopled with dragons and such. In *Dark Lord of Derkholm,* a world is controlled by dictatorial Mr. Chesney. When Derk, a stumblebum of a wizard, is selected to play a part in an adventure, Chesney's world begins to collapse. Patricia McKillip's *The Forgotten Beasts of Eld* is a remarkable story about the rational and the emotional sides of humanity followed by three others in the series.

Marion Zimmer Bradley's Darkover books are among the most popular of books set in another world. Colonists from Earth come to the planet Darkover with its one sun and four multicolored moons, but over 2000 years they lose touch with their home planet and evolve new cultures and new myths. *Darkover Landfall* serves as a good introduction, although almost any book in the series will serve equally well. *The Best of Marion Zimmer Bradley's Fantasy Magazine,* a collection of her short fiction along with brief prefaces, serves to remind readers how powerfully Bradley can write.

What Is Science Fiction?

In 1953, Robert A. Heinlein, asked the question: "But what, under rational definition, is *science fiction?*" He went on to answer the question by defining the genre as speculative fiction based on the real world, with all its "established facts and natural laws." Although the result can be extremely fantastic in content, "it is not fantasy: it is legitimate—and often very tightly reasoned—speculation about the possibilities of the real world."[12] (See Focus Box 7.2 on p. 226.)

There are other conventions, although none are as important as Heinlein's. Characters voyage into space and face all sorts of dangers. (Science fiction is, after all, more adventure than philosophy, although the latter is often present.) Other planets have intelligent or frightening life forms, although they may differ drastically from Earth's humans. Contemporary problems are projected hundreds or thousands of years into the future, and those new views of overpopulation, pollution, religious bickering, political machinations, and sexual disharmony often give readers a quite different perspective of our world and our problems today.

Prophecies are not required in science fiction; nevertheless, some of the richest books of Isaac Asimov and Arthur C. Clarke have been prophetic. (Ray Bradbury, conversely, has said, "I don't try to predict the future—I try to prevent it.")

Occasionally a scientifically untenable premise may be used. On the August 15, 1983, "Nightcap" talk show on Arts Cable Television, Isaac Asimov said, "The best kind of sci-fi involves science." Then he agreed that, "Time travel is theoretically impossible, but I wouldn't want to give it up as a plot gimmick." Essentially, he was agreeing with Heinlein but adding that plot and excitement counted even more. The internal consistency and plausibility of a postulated imaginary society creates its own reality.

Ray Bradbury argues that the appeal of science fiction is understandable because science fiction is important literature, not merely popular stuff. Opening his essay on "Science Fiction: Why Bother?" he compares himself to a fourth-rate George Bernard Shaw who makes an outrageous statement and then tries to prove it. Bradbury says, "Science fiction is the most important fiction being written today." He adds that it is not "part of the Main Stream. It *is* the Main Stream."[13]

Carl Sagan, the late Cornell University astronomer/author, added his testimony, writing that it was science fiction that brought him to science. Kurt Vonnegut, Jr., also applauded science fiction through character Eliot Rosewater in *God Bless You, Mr. Rosewater, or Pearls Before Swine.* Stumbling into a conversation of science fiction writers, Rosewater drunkenly tells them that he loves them because they are the only ones who:

> . . . know that life is a space voyage, and not a short one either, but one that'll last billions of years. You're the only ones with guts enough to really care about the future, who really notice what machines do to us, what wars do to us, what cities do to us, what big, simple ideas do to us, what tremendous misunderstanding, mistakes, accidents and catastrophes do to us.

He goes on to praise them for being "zany enough to agonize over time and distances without limit, over mysteries that will never die, over the fact that we are right now determining whether the space voyage for the next billion years or so is going to be Heaven or Hell."

Science fiction writer and scientist Arthur C. Clarke agrees with Rosewater on the admittedly limited but still impressive power of science fiction to scan the future. In his introduction to *Profiles of the Future,* Clarke writes:

> A critical—the adjective is important—reading of science-fiction is essential training for anyone wishing to look more than ten years ahead. The facts of the future can hardly be imagined *ab initio* by those who are unfamiliar with the fantasies of the past.
>
> This claim may produce indignation, especially among those second-rate scientists who sometimes make fun of science-fiction (I have never known a first-rate one to do so—and I know several who write it). But the simple fact is that anyone with sufficient imagination to assess the future realistically would inevitably be attracted to this form of literature. I do not for a moment suggest that more than one percent of science-fiction readers would be reliable prophets; but I do suggest that almost a hundred percent of reliable prophets will be science-fiction readers—or writers.[14]

Why does science fiction appeal to young adults and to adults? First and probably most important, it is exciting. Science fiction may have begun with the "rah-rah-we're-off-to-Venus-with-Buck-Rogers" sensational fiction, and although it has gone far beyond that, the thrill of adventure is still there. Science fiction writers do not write down to their audience, and this is recognized and admired. Science fiction allows anyone to read imaginative fiction without feeling the material is kid stuff. Science fiction presents real heroes to readers who find their own world often devoid of anyone worth admiring, of heroes doing something brave, going to the ultimate frontiers, even pushing these frontiers further back, all important at a time when many young people wonder if any new frontiers exist.

Science fiction has a heritage of fine writers and important books. Some critics maintain that the genre began with Mary Wollstonecraft Shelley's *Frankenstein, or The Modern Prometheus* in 1818. Others argue for Swift's *Gulliver's Travels* in 1726 or the much earlier Lucian's *The True History* in the second century A.D. No matter, for nearly everyone agrees that the first major and widely read writer was Jules Verne, whose *Journey to the Center of the Earth* in 1864 and *Twenty Thousand Leagues Under the Sea* in 1870 pleased readers on several continents. The first American science fiction came with Edgar Allan Poe's short story, "The Unparalleled Adventures of One Hans Pfaall," which appeared in the June 1835 issue of *Southern Literary Messenger* and was included in *Tales of the Grotesque and Arabesque* in 1840. Hans Pfaall's balloon trip to the moon in a nineteen-day voyage may be a hoax, but the early trappings of science fiction are there. Dime novels occasionally used science fiction, particularly in the "Frank Reade" series, as did some books from the Stratemeyer Literary Syndicate, particularly in the Tom Swift and Great Marvel series.

These books were readable and fun, and they were read over and over by many people who had no idea how good most of the stories were. Most critics, however, were snobs about science fiction. Some fans didn't consider the genre respectable, but the fact that science fiction, or whatever it was called in the early days, was not part of mainstream writing may have made it more attractive to readers who were not seeking literary respectability so much as they were looking for books that were entertaining.

Many boys like science fiction because it provides an opportunity to read romances without feeling the stigma attached to "girls' love stories."

For better or worse, academic respectability came to science fiction in December 1959, when the prestigious and often stuffy Modern Language Association began its science fiction journal, *Extrapolation*. Two other journals, *Foundation* (in England) and *Science-Fiction Studies* (in Canada), began publishing in the early 1970s. Colleges and secondary schools offered courses in the genre, and major publishers and significant magazines recognized and published science fiction.

Four writers are usually regarded as being *the* fathers of science fiction—Isaac Asimov, Arthur C. Clarke, Robert Heinlein, and Ray Bradbury. One writer is often hailed as the writer most likely to become a science fiction master, Orson Scott Card.

The prolific Asimov—more than 500 books—wrote so much on so many fields that he comes the closest to begin a truly renaissance figure, but whatever his contributions to the study of the Bible or Shakespeare, no one could question his contributions to science fiction. His multivolume "Foundation" series established a basis for a multidimensional society that an incredible number of readers have temporarily inhabited and accepted.

Arthur C. Clarke may be less widely read than Asimov, but few could argue that *Childhood's End* is one of the classics in the field. *2001: A Space Odyssey,* the basis of the movie (Film Box 7.2) and developed from one of Clarke's short stories, may in book and film form be the most widely cited of any work in science fiction.

After several young adult books, Robert A. Heinlein moved on to adult material and never looked back. Books for the young such as *Farmer in the Sky* and *Pokayne of Mars* may be largely forgotten, but for many young people, these books provided a vision of the future new to them. Later books, particularly *The Moon Is a Harsh Mistress* and *Stranger in a Strange Land,* are both better written and far more powerful visions of a deeply troubled universe. Heinlein may have been unable to picture a believable, strong woman, as critics often claim, but he wrote exceptionally fine science fiction.

Ray Bradbury may be less interested in the mechanics of science fiction than any other major writer, but he may have been the most sensitive of them all about humanity's ability to befoul Earth and the rest of the universe. He seemed to have almost no interest in how his characters moved from Earth to Mars, but *The Martian Chronicles* is a marvelous set of semirelated short stories about the problems of being human in a universe that does not treasure our humanity.

Almost anything by Orson Scott Card is magical, but one novel is usually cited as his best novel thus far—with other great ones to come. *Ender's Game* came out of Card's reading of Asimov's first three "Foundation" books and is set in a somewhat vague future time when humans fear another attack from the insectoid Buggers. Seventy years earlier, a military genius in Earth's army saved the world, and the military are now looking for one more military genius who can save Earth again. Peter and Valentine Wiggin have the military genius but the wrong temperament to be the proper choice, but Andrew Wiggin (who wants to be called Ender) has both the temperament and the genius, and he becomes the tactician who can understand and, therefore, defeat the enemy.

Ender's Game is a complex book, as are its sequels, *Speaker for the Dead* and *Xenocide*. *Ender's Shadow* is not another sequel, no matter what the title, because it retells the story of *Ender's Game* with another main character, this time Ender's assistant, Bean. Unquestionably, Card has written the most significant science fiction in the last twenty years. If there are limits to his ability, readers have not found them.

FILM BOX 7.2

Science Fiction, or What's Out There (see Appendix D)

Aliens (1986, color, 135 min., R; Director: James Cameron; with Sigourney Weaver) This sequel to the 1979 **Alien** occurs 57 years after the earlier flight. Another expedition is sent to a planet run by aliens to learn what happened to the human colony.

Blade Runner (1982, color, 118 min., R; Director: Ridley Scott; with Harrison Ford and Rutger Hauer) Taken from Philip K. Dick's *Do Androids Dream of Electric Sheep?*, this twenty-first century movie is about an ex-policeman hired to find androids who have escaped to Los Angeles.

Close Encounters of the Third Kind (1977, color, 135 min., PG; Director: Steven Spielberg; with Richard Dreyfuss) Spielberg's movie is remembered as our first encounter with aliens.

E.T.: The Extra-Terrestrial (1982, color, 115 min., PG; Director: Steven Spielberg; with Dee Wallace and Drew Barrymore) A loveable alien is accidentally stranded on our planet and needs help getting home.

Invasion of the Body Snatchers (1956, black and white, 80 min., NR; Director: Don Siegel; with Kevin McCarthy and Dana Wynter) In this movie that is better than the 1978 remake, the pods are here, but no one takes them seriously.

Starship Troopers (1998, color, 129 min., R; Director: Paul Verhoeven; with Caspar Van Dien and Jake Busey) In this adaptation from Robert A. Heinlein's novel, viewers can join the troopers and kill all the giant insects coming our way.

Star Trek: The Voyage Home (1986, color, 119 min., PG; Director: Leonard Nimoy; with William Shatner and Nimoy) Finding humpback whales helps the Enterprise save Earth.

Star Wars (1977, color, 121 min., PG; Director: George Lucas; with Harrison Ford and Carrie Fisher) Modern space adventure begins here complete with comedy provided by robots R2D2 (named after Reel 2, Dialogue 2) and C3PO.

2001: A Space Odyssey (1968, color, 139 min., G; Director: Stanley Kramer; with Keir Dullea and Gary Lockwood) Kramer's movie was ahead of its time in exploring what happens when your computer no longer obeys you.

Westworld (1973, color, 88 min., PG; Director: Michael Crichton; with Richard Benjamin and Yul Brynner) A futuristic, western theme park promises love and adventure but delivers mayhem when a cowboy robot goes beserk.

Types of Science Fiction

The most obvious type, and probably the first to be read by many later fans of science fiction, is the simple-minded but effective story of wild adventure, usually with a touch of sociological or environmental concern. Isaac Asimov's "Lucky Starr" series, written under the Paul French pseudonym, begins with *David Starr: Space Ranger* and a story of an overly populated Earth in need of food. It's a poor book, but it's better adventure than most because Asimov simply could not tell a dull story. Robert Heinlein's early juvenile books suffer from the same fate, particularly the episodic but often thrilling *The Rolling Stones*.

H. G. Wells's *The War of the Worlds* spawned many imitations as we read about this group of aliens invading Earth and that group of aliens attacking another threatened outpost of civilization. The visits of the aliens, however, continue to appeal to us, partly because they combine the best of two worlds—science fiction and horror. William Sleator's *Interstellar Pig* may sound like an odd or funny book, but it is not. Sixteen-year-old Barney is intrigued to discover that three different neighbors moved next door. Soon, Barney and the three are playing a board game called

FOCUS BOX 7.2

Science Fiction Tells Us of Our Future So We Can Know the Present

The Alien Years by Robert Silverberg. Prism, 1998. Aliens landing on the Earth and controlling it may spell the end of humanity.

Blue Mars by Kim Stanley Robinson. Bantam, 1996. An antiaging drug being used on Mars begins to lose its effect.

Dune by Frank Herbert. Chilton, 1965. Herbert's story about political machinations, battles, and power struggles on the planet Arrakis ranks as a sci-fi classic.

Forever Peace by Joe Haldeman. Ace Books, 1997. A soldier, able to manipulate a robot, has an attack of conscience.

The Man Who Fell to Earth by Walter Tevis. Del Rey, 1963. An alien comes to Earth hoping to save his own people with major help from earthlings, but his ship crashes in the backwoods, leaving him momentarily helpless.

Phoenix Cafe by Gwyneth Jones. TOR, 1998. Earth is almost destroyed in the twenty-fourth century, 300 years after an alien invasion.

Seize the Night by Dean Koontz. Bantam, 1998. To stop a mad scientist, a man must rescue four kidnapped children.

Tomorrowland edited by Michael Cart. Scholastic, 1999. Cart collects ten stories about the future from prominent YA authors.

2041 edited by Jane Yolen. Delacorte, 1991. Twelve short stories of our future world.

Virtual World by Chris Westwood. Viking, 1998. A new virtual reality game makes players into gods.

Interstellar Pig, and Barney learns fast enough that he stands between the neighbors and the destruction of Earth. John Wyndham's (pseudonym of John Beynon Harris) *The Midwich Cuckoo* is set in an apparently tranquil small town in England. Suddenly and briefly, the town stops dead, and nine months later a number of children with strange eyes and even stranger attitudes are born.

Time travel has been a theme in science fiction since H. G. Wells's *The Time Machine*. Jack Finney's *Time and Again* and its sequel *From Time to Time* begin with Simon Morley charged with taking part in a government secret mission. He is transported back to New York City of the 1880s along with a sketch book and a camera and a clear mind for taking detailed notes. He meets the usual corrupt officials, but he also meets Julia and he falls in love, and that makes up for what he does not like. He returns to the present only to learn that the government wants him to continue his work and to change history, or as it puts it, "to correct mistakes of the past which have already affected the present for us."

From Time to Time is, in the minds of some reviewers, one of those rarities, a sequel better than the original.

The wonder and danger of space travel is an obvious theme in much science fiction. In Larry Niven and Jerry Pourelle's *The Mote in God's Eye,* humans have colonized the galaxy. An alien society sends emissaries to work with the humans and the aliens accidentally die. The humans must send representatives dashing through space to ward off disaster and war. Ben Bova's *Mars* reminds us of the excitement of watching mortals first going into space.

Science frightens most of us some time or other, and the mad scientist or the threat of science gone sour or insane is another theme that runs through science fiction. In a note in Bantam's 1954 revision of Ray Bradbury's *The Martian Chronicles,* Clifton Fadiman describes Bradbury as "a moralist who has caught hold of a simple, obvious but overwhelmingly important moral idea—that we are in the grip of a psychosis, a technology-mania, the final consequences of which can only be universal murder and quite conceivably the destruction of our planet."

William Sleator's *House of Stairs* illustrates how mad psychologists can become to prove a point. Five young people are brought to an experimental house made up almost entirely of stairs madly going everywhere, and the young people learn how cruel scientists can be in attempting to find something adults think is important. Isaac Asimov's *The Ugly Little Boy* is the most touching use of this theme that we know. Scientists have trapped a young Neanderthal boy and have brought him back to our time, all in the name of science. A nurse is hired to take care of him until he is sent back to his own time. The boy is a terrified mess, and the nurse is horrified by him, but her native compassion and his normal need for a friend bring the two together.

The holocaust of a nuclear explosion is a constant fear for all humanity, just as it is for science fiction writers. Robert O'Brien's *Z for Zachariah* begins after the blast. Ann Burden believes that she is the sole survivor because the valley she lives in is protected from fallout. Then she discovers another survivor, and she learns that she is in danger. The book ends somewhat enigmatically with Ann looking for yet more survivors and the hope that decency and compassion survive somewhere out there. Louise Lawrence also writes about the final explosion, and *Andra, Children of the Dust,* and *Moonwind* are powerful stories about survivors. Vonda N. McIntyre's finest novel, *Dreamsnake,* is a mystical story of a world recovering from nuclear war and a young woman who becomes a healer.

Perhaps the gloomiest view of the future is in Philip K. Dick's *Do Androids Dream of Electric Sheep?* (reissued as *Blade Runner* in 1982 when the film adaptation came out). A cop/bounty hunter searches for human-created androids who have escaped from another planet to come back to a horribly drizzling and bleak Earth.

Jane Donawerth made some excellent points in her significant and helpful article in the March 1990 *English Journal;* she noted that between 1818 when Mary Wollstonecraft Shelley published *Frankenstein, or the Modern Prometheus* and the 1930s, women were among the most important writers dealing with technological utopias and similar topics that foreshadowed science fiction:

> But the times when such visions were welcomed did not last; at least in *Amazing Stories* and in *Wonder Stories,* the women virtually disappeared by the mid–1930s. I think that editorial policy, or simply civic pressure on the women, kept their stories from earning money that could go, instead, to a man supporting a family during the Depression.[15]

By the time women returned to science fiction in the 1940s, they used masculine-sounding pen names, for example, Andre Norton and Leigh Brackett. Today, however, science fiction readers have a number of women writers to turn to, notably Ursula K. LeGuin with *The Left Hand of Darkness* and *Dispossessed: An Ambiguous Utopia,* both studies in gender restrictions. Joanna Russ mines much the same field in her books.

Harry Turtledove's *Worldwar: In the Balance* is another type of science fiction in which the author changes history, a type of "what if" book. In *Worldwar,* the first of four projected volumes, the time is 1942, the Allies are at war with the Axis powers, and an alien force of lizardlike things invades Earth with a technology that far surpasses human knowledge. Turtledove continues his fascination with alternative histories in his and Richard Dreyfuss's *The Two Georges,* with an America in which the Revolutionary War was not fought. In *The Great War: Walk in Hell,* Turtledove announces a new historical lineup of players, the South, which won the Civil War, is now allied with France and England and at war with the thirty-four United States, and, in turn, the United States is now allied with Prussia. Philip K. Dick's *The Man in the High Castle* postulates that Germany and Japan have won World War II, and the Nazis have taken over most of the United States. Robert Harris's *Fatherland* is set in the 1960s, Germany has supposedly won World War II, and the Holocaust has not yet been uncovered.

Cyberpunk is one of the wildest, rampaging kinds of science fiction today. Gene LaFaille defines cyberpunk as

> A subgenre of science fiction that incorporates our concern about the future impact of advanced technologies, especially cybernetics, bionics, genetic engineering, and the designer drug culture, upon the individual, who is competing with the increasing power and control of the multinational corporations that are extending their stranglehold on the world's supply of information.[16]

Cyberpunk is about technology and the power of communication, particularly power used to manipulate people. Bruce Sterling's *Mirrorshades: The Cyberpunk Anthology* is 15 years old, but it still has enough variety to give readers opportunity to see what cyberpunk is and what its ramifications can be. William Gibson's *Neuromancer* was the novel that brought cyberpunk to readers' attention. The antihero of *Neuromancer* gives way to far more likable characters in *Virtual Light.* Neal Stephenson's *Snow Crash* is about a strange computer virus that does all kinds of weird and horrible things to computer hackers. David Brin's *Earth* describes the powerful implications of information technology on society at large.

Science fiction was never as popular on radio as it deserved to be, though "Dimension-X" and "X Minus One" had many fans, but science fiction was popular on television. From Rod Serling's "The Twilight Zone" on through the ever-new casts of "Star Trek," viewers seemed to find TV science fiction irresistible. A recent entry in the field, "The X-Files," seems to have been different enough that it has found an audience. N. E. Genge's *The Unofficial X-Files Companion* is a record of the plots and characters along with the serial killers, cults, werewolfs, robots, and other strangenesses that have roamed through "X-Files" episodes.

Humor is not often the strongest feature of science fiction, but Douglas Adams's *The Hitchhiker's Guide to the Galaxy* is rich in humor, a genuinely funny spoof of the genre. The books that follow in the series are not nearly as happily done, but Adams's first book began as a BBC radio script, progressed to a television script, and ultimately became a novel. When Arthur Dent's house is due for demolition to make way for a highway, he finds Ford Prefect, a strange friend, anxiously seeking a drink at a nearby pub. Ford seems totally indifferent to Arthur's plight because, as he explains, the world will soon be destroyed to make way for a new galactic freeway. Soon the pair are safe aboard a Vogon Construction Fleet Battleship, and that is the most easily explained of the many improbabilities that follow. Any reader desperate to know the meaning of life can find a simple answer in this book.

Two other recent books should amuse science fiction fans and possibly others. Christopher Buckley's *Little Green Men* tells of the leader of Majestic Twelve (MJ–12), a group formed to convince cold-war Russia that the United States had UFO technology. Now MJ–12 proposed that because the original purpose for the organization was moot, a new purpose should be found, in this case convincing the American public that an alien invasion was likely, thus assuring that Congress would vote for increased military spending.

Eric Idle, one of Monty Python's Flying Circus, satirizes science fiction and all sorts of people in *The Road to Mars: A Post-Modern Novel*. Set in the twenty-fifth century, it relates the work of Professor William Reynolds and an android who writes a dissertation on what makes people laugh.

Keeping Up-to-Date on Science Fiction

The *Voice of Youth Advocates* yearly reviews many books in "Best Science Fiction, Fantasy & Horror." It is a most helpful guide. Don D'Ammassa's yearly brief listing, "The Best Science Fiction, Fantasy, and Horror Novels," in *Science Fiction Chronicle* is less helpful than his analysis of the year's authors, books, and trends appearing immediately before his lists.

Utopias and Dystopias

Utopias and dystopias are neither science fiction nor fantasy, but they share characteristics with both. Readers must suspend disbelief and buy into the author's vision, at least for the duration of the story. As with science fiction, utopian and dystopian books are usually set in the future, with technology having played a role in establishing the conditions out of which the story grows. Unlike science fiction and more like fantasy, however, once the situation is established, authors focus less on technology and more on sociological and psychological or emotional aspects of the story. A utopia is a place of happiness and prosperity; a dystopia is the opposite.

Three interesting young adult books are dystopias. One is Bruce Brooks's *No Kidding*, which tells a serious story of a boy realizing that he cannot, and in fact doesn't want to, make all the decisions for his alcoholic mother and his strange little brother. The story is set in a Washington, D. C., of the future, where 69 percent of the population is alcoholic and children are a treasured commodity because so many people have been made sterile by sitting in front of cathode ray tubes. The story is about two young brothers, Sam and Ollie. Sam is rehabilitating his mother at the same time he attempts to direct and control the foster parents who want to adopt the younger Ollie. Sam is shocked when he finds out that even with all his help Ollie feels a need for something he doesn't have and regularly sneaks out at night to meet with a cultlike religious group.

Despite the grim plot, *No Kidding* is filled with some wonderful kidding about schools, social workers, educational jargon, and the wishful thinking that any problem can be corrected if only we can give it a name and obtain federal funding. Sam goes to an AO (Alcoholic Offspring) school, where, in a tough moment, the counselor confesses to the school nurse that she has not been trained as a generalist counselor, only as an AO specialist:

I have *no* certification outside AO programs. My thesis was on the doctrinal interface between quantified behavior-analysis patterns and AOCLEP. Quantified! I am trained to deal with kids who are tested every week for theoretical knowledge of specific AO doctrine *and* behavioral adjustment in AO alignments. At my previous school a kid would come in and say "I aggressed on the math teacher's car in a third-level postdenial anger/pity syndrome, and I broke the windshield." I would say, "What's your denial factor?" and he would say "Eight," and I would say "Index of control achievement?" and he would say "Six," and I would know *exactly* what to do with him. . . . Now, what am I supposed to do with a kid who knows nothing except that he threw a rock at a car?

Peter Dickinson's *Eva* is a fascinating story about the daughter of a famous scientist devoting his life to working with chimpanzees. In this futuristic world, chimpanzees are relatively important because all the big animals have vanished. The scientist, his wife, his 13-year-old daughter Eva, and a chimpanzee named Kelly are driving home from an outing when they get in a horrible wreck. Eva remembers nothing but slowly wakes to a controlled environment. Over several weeks she discovers that her mind has been planted in Kelly's body.

The rest of the book is about the next thirty years of Eva's life. The technology is intriguing to read about, but it's the psychological and the social aspects that leave readers pondering ideas about ecology, parent-child and male-female relationships, mass media advertising, medical ethics, and young adult suicide.

Of the three young adult books, Lois Lowry's *The Giver* is the most powerful and disturbing. Jonas lives in an apparently perfect society. At the Ceremony of 12 when the elders assign each young person his career, Jonas is selected to be "our next receiver of memory." Jonas discovers that this job requires him to learn everything that the society has forgotten, in effect things such as color or music or anything else his people have given up for the common good. *The Giver* is brief but gripping, and any reader will be caught up in the story of people who have willingly given up their freedom and their imagination for the supposed "good of the people."

Utopias and dystopias are never likely to be popular with the masses because they usually lack excitement and fast-moving plots. Writers of adventure or fantasy or science fiction begin with a story (the more thrilling the better) and later, if ever, add a message. Writers of utopias and dystopias think first of the message and then devise a story to carry the weight of the message.

The books are usually about dissatisfaction with contemporary society. Many people have no drive to think seriously about societal issues—or to think at all. Readers who do not share the anger or irritation of utopian writers easily miss the allusions needed to follow the story or find the message. For these reasons, utopian literature is likely to appeal only to more thoughtful and intellectual readers. Although these young adults may not share the anger of the writer, given their idealism, they probably share the writer's concerns about society and humanity.

The centuries-old fascination with utopias is suggested by the Greek origin of the word, which includes two meanings, "no place" and "good place." Most of us, in idle moments, dream of a perfect land, a perfect society, a place that would solve all our personal problems and, if we are altruistic enough, all the world's problems as well. In our nightmares, we also dream of the opposite, the dystopias, which are diseased or bad lands. But few of us do more than dream, which may explain why some people are so intrigued with authors who transfer their dreams to the printed page.

In his *Republic* in the fifth century B.C., Plato presented his vision of the ideal world, offering suggestions for educating the ruling class. With wise philosopher-kings, or so Plato maintains, the people would prosper, intellectual joys would flourish (along with censorship, for Plato would ban poets and dramatists from his perfect society), and the land would be permanently safe.

Later utopias were geared less to a ruling class and more to a society that would preserve its peace and create harmony and happiness for the people. Sir Thomas More's *Utopia* (1516) argued for mental equality of the sexes, simple laws understandable to all, and common ownership of everything. Whether More intended his book as a practical solution to society's problems is doubtful, but he probably did mean it as a criticism of contemporary English life. Utopias, after all, are personal and reflect an author's enthusiasm for (or abhorrence of) certain ideas. That was clearly true of two early utopias, Francis Bacon's *The New Atlantis* (1627) and Tommaso Campanella's *City in the Sun* (1623).

During the late 1800s, the popularity of such utopias as Samuel Butler's *Erewhon* (1872) and *Erewhon Revisited* (1901), William Dean Howell's *A Traveler from Altruia* (1894), and Edward Bellamy's *Looking Backward* (1888) paralleled the popularity of people's real-life attempts to seek better lives through various utopian schemes. In the United States, utopian communities at places such as Harmony, Pennsylvania; New Harmony, Indiana; Brook Farm, Massachusetts; Fruitlands, Massachusetts; Oneida, New York; Nauvoo, Illinois; and Corning, Iowa, were rarely more than temporarily satisfactory.

Utopian communities have been the setting for several novels. Elizabeth Howard's *Out of Step with the Dancers* shows a celibate Shaker community in 1853 through the eyes of Damaris as she accompanies her converted father to a strange new life. Religious pacifism in the face of the Civil War is the subject of Janet Hickman's *Zoar Blue,* about the German separatist community of Zoar, Ohio. Lynn Hall's excellent *Too Near the Sun* focuses on 16-year-old Armel Dupree and his Icarian community near Corning, Iowa. To the shame of his family, Armel's older brother has sought life in the outside world. Armel now wonders if he should follow his brother as he views the ideal community composed of less than ideal people.

Yearning for the simpler life, in which we dream of being part of something greater than ourselves, is natural. For some young people, however, the search has led to religious groups less like communes and more like cults. Robert Coover explored the power and madness of a cult in *The Origin of the Brunists.* In that novel, a mining explosion kills ninety-seven people, but one survivor believes that God has saved him to proclaim the approaching end of the world. Two sound nonfiction works give insights about cults and why and how they are often so successful in attracting the most sincere young adults—Willa Appel's *Cults in America: Programmed for Paradise* and David G. Bromley and Anson D. Shupe, Jr.'s, *Strange Gods: The Great American Cult Scare.* The frightening consequences of the assault on the Branch Davidian compound in Waco, Texas, in early 1993 is the subject of Dick J. Reavis's *The Ashes of Waco: An Investigation,* not the last of the cult problems but a particularly troubling one because of the death of many children.

Dystopias are more dramatic and exaggerated than their counterparts and for that reason are more successful in attracting young adults. Dystopias warn us of society's drift toward a particularly horrifying or sick world lying just over the horizon. They are sometimes misinterpreted as prophecies alone, but books such as Aldous Huxley's *Brave New World* and George Orwell's *Nineteen Eighty-Four* and

Animal Farm are part prophecy, part warning. Readers who get to know and care about the Savage and Winston Smith are never again able to regard a discussion of individual freedom in an abstract way.

A theme that we'll certainly see more of is that of disasters caused by ecological carelessness. Thomas Baird's *Smart Rats* is a disturbing exploration of this theme. Everything is rationed, including children (one per family); the government is all-powerful except when it comes to solving problems; contaminated areas are said to be harmless, and areas that the government does not want entered are said to be infested with killer rats, from which the book gets its title. Inspired by all the terrible things that are happening both inside and outside his family, 17-year-old Laddie Grayson connives his way into a forbidden area of the library and reads about the effects of various chemicals. In this truly depressing book, Laddie keeps his theories to himself about an insecticide that his pregnant mother encountered, but he realizes what he must do. He also enrolls in a special school to become part of the "system." The question for readers is whether Laddie can remain inside the system without becoming corrupt.

To attract young adult readers, dystopian books have to have something extra because, with a few exceptions, young adults are optimistic and imaginative. Adults might read dystopian books on the premise that misery loves company, but teenagers have not lived long enough to lose their natural curiosity, and they have not been weighed down with adult problems such as failing health, heavy family responsibilities, expenses surpassing income, and dreams gone bankrupt. So even when teenagers read dystopian books, they probably wear rose-colored glasses, feeling grateful for the world as it usually is.

David Macaulay's *Motel of the Mysteries* is a wonderful spoof of scientific arrogance unmasked as a wild guessing game. The book begins with the ominous description of the burial of the North American continent under tons of third-class and fourth-class mail (caused by an accidental reduction in postal rates). Since the year 3850, scholars have wondered about the lost civilization, but it is left to 42-year-old Howard Carson to stumble and fall into a secret chamber. There he discovers a "gleaming secret seal" (DO NOT DISTURB) and a "plant that would not die." He enters the chamber and finds a body atop a "ceremonial platform" near a statue of the "deity WATT" and a container, "ICE," designed to "preserve, at least symbolically, the major internal organs of the deceased for eternity." Later, he enters the inner chamber and there finds another body "in a highly polished white sarcophagus" behind translucent curtains. Near this body is a "sacred urn" and a "sacred parchment" holder and the "sacred collar" with a headband beating a ceremonial chant, "Sanitized for Your Protection." The drawing of Howard Carson playing savant and the many artifacts recovered from the motel bedroom and bathroom add to the fun. Museum goers will particularly enjoy the concluding section of the book devoted to "Souvenirs and Quality Reproductions" from the Carson excavations now for sale.

The books we've talked about in this chapter start with life as we know it and attempt to stretch readers' imaginations. All of us need to dream, not to waste our lives but to enrich them. To dream is to recognize humanity's possibilities. In a world hardly characterized by undue optimism, the genres treated here offer us challenges and hope, not the sappy sentimentalism of "everything always works out for the best" (for it often does not) but realistic hope based on our noblest dreams of surviving. If we go down, we do it knowing that we have cared and dreamed and found something for which we are willing to struggle.

Notes

[1] Ursula LeGuin, "On Teaching Science Fiction," in Jack Williamson, ed., *Teaching Science Fiction: Education for Tomorrow* (Oswick Press, 1980), p. 22.

[2] Walter Wangerin, Jr., in a lecture, "By Faith, Fantasy," quoted in John H. Timmerman's *Other Worlds: The Fantasy Genre* (Bowling Green University Popular Press, 1983), p. 21.

[3] This point, with many more examples, is made repeatedly by Leslie E. Owen in "Children's Science Fiction and Fantasy Grow Up," *Publishers Weekly* 232 (October 30, 1987): 32–37.

[4] Mary Harrington Hall, "A Conversation with Ray Bradbury and Chuck Jones," *Psychology Today* 1 (April 1969): 28–29.

[5] Jo-Anne Goodwin, "In Defence of Fantasy," *Independent Magazine,* London, July 25, 1993, p. 32.

[6] John Rowe Townsend, "Heights of Fantasy," in Gerard J. Senick, ed., *Children's Review,* vol. 5. (Gale Research, 1983), p. 7.

[7] Lloyd Alexander, "High Fantasy and Heroic Romance," *Horn Book Magazine* 47 (December 1971): 483.

[8] Tamora Pierce, "Fantasy: Why Kids Read It, Why Kids Need It," *School Library Journal* 39 (October 1993): 51.

[9] Ursula LeGuin, "Why Are Americans So Afraid of Dragons?" *PNLA* (Pacific Northwest Library Association) *Quarterly* 38 (Winter 1974): 18.

[10] Michael Cart, "Miss M," *School Library Journal* 45 (June 1999): 25.

[11] Roxanne Feldman, "The Truth about Harry," *School Library Journal* 45 (September 1999): 139.

[12] Robert Heinlein, "Ray Guns and Rocket Ships," *Library Journal* 78 (July 1953): 1188.

[13] Ray Bradbury, "Science Fiction: Why Bother?" *Teacher's Guide: Science Fiction* (Bantam, n.d.), p. 1.

[14] Arthur Clarke, *Profiles of the Future* (Holt, 1984), p. 9.

[15] Jane Donawerth, "Teaching Science Fiction by Women," *English Journal* 79 (March 1990): 39–30.

[16] Gene LaFaille, "Science Fiction: Top Guns of the 1980s," *Wilson Library Bulletin* 65 (December 1990). 34.

Titles Mentioned in the Text of Chapter Seven

Adams, Douglas. *The Hitchhiker's Guide to the Galaxy.* Harmony, 1979.

Adams, Richard. *Watership Down.* Macmillan, 1974.

Alexander, Lloyd. *The Black Cauldron.* Holt, 1965.

Alexander, Lloyd. *The Book of Three.* Holt, 1964.

Alexander, Lloyd. *The Castle of Llyr.* Holt, 1966.

Alexander, Lloyd. *The High King.* Holt, 1968.

Alexander, Lloyd. *Taran Wanderer.* Holt, 1967.

Appel, Willa. *Cults in America: Programmed for Paradise.* Holt, 1983.

Asimov, Isaac. *The Ugly Little Boy.* TOR, 1958.

Bacon, Francis. *The New Atlantis.* 1627.

Baird, Thomas. *Smart Rats.* HarperCollins, 1990.

Beagle, Peter. *A Fine and Private Place.* Viking, 1960.

Beagle, Peter. *The Last Unicorn.* Viking, 1968.

Bellamy, Edward. *Looking Backward.* 1888.

Bova, Ben. *Mars.* Bantam, 1992.

Bradbury, Ray. *The Martian Chronicles.* Doubleday, 1950.

Bradley, Marion Zimmer. *The Best of Marion Zimmer Bradley's Fantasy Magazine.* Warner, 1994.

Bradley, Marion Zimmer. *Darkover Landfall.* DAW books, 1972.

Bradley, Marion Zimmer. *The Mists of Avalon.* Knopf, 1983.

Bradshaw, Gillian. *Hawk of May.* Simon & Schuster, 1982.

Bradshaw, Gillian. *Kingdom of Summer.* Simon & Schuster, 1982.

Brin, David. *Earth.* Bantam, 1990.

Bromley, David G., and Anson D. Shupe, Jr. *Strange Gods: The Great American Cult Scare.* Beacon Press, 1982.

Brooks, Bruce. *No Kidding.* HarperCollins, 1989.

Buckley, Christopher. *Little Green Men.* Random House, 1999.

Butler, Samuel. *Erewhon.* 1872.

Butler, Samuel. *Erewhon Revisited.* 1901.

Campanella, Tommaso. *City in the Sun.* 1623.

Card, Orson Scott. *Ender's Game.* TOR, 1985.

Card, Orson Scott. *Ender's Shadow.* TOR, 1999.

Card, Orson Scott. *Speaker for the Dead.* TOR, 1986.

Card, Orson Scott. *Xenocide.* TOR, 1991.

Clarke, Arthur C. *Childhood's End.* Houghton Mifflin, 1953.

Coover, Robert. *The Origin of the Brunists.* Viking, 1977.

Dick, Phillip K. *Do Androids Dream of Electric Sheep.* Doubleday, 1968.

Dick, Phillip K. *The Man in the High Castle.* Putnam, 1962.

Dickinson, Peter. *Eva.* Delacorte, 1989.

Finney, Jack. *From Time to Time.* Simon & Schuster, 1995.

Finney, Jack. *Time and Again.* Simon & Schuster, 1970.

French, Paul. *David Starrs Space Ranger.* Doubleday, 1952.

Garner, Alan. *The Owl Service.* Walck, 1967.

Garner, Alan. *Red Shift*. Macmillan, 1973.

Genge, N. E. *The Unofficial X-Files Companion*. Crown, 1995.

Gibson, William. *Neuromancer*. Ace, 1984.

Gibson, William. *Virtual Light*. Bantam, 1993.

Grahame, Kenneth. *The Wind in the Willows* (originally published in 1908).

Hall, Lynn. *To Near the Sun*. Follett, 1970.

Harris, Robert. *Fatherland*. Random House, 1992

Heinlein, Robert A. *Farmer in the Sky*. Scribner, 1950.

Heinlein, Robert A. *The Moon Is a Harsh Mistress*. Putnam, 1966.

Heinlein, Robert A. *Podkayne of Mars*. Putnam, 1963.

Heinlein, Robert A. *The Rolling Stones*. Scribner, 1952.

Heinlein, Robert A. *Stranger in a Strange Land*. Putnam, 1961.

Hickman, Janet. *Zoar Blue*. Macmillan, 1978.

Howard, Elizabeth. *Out of Step with the Dancers*. Morrow, 1978.

Howell, William Dean. *A Traveler From Altruia*. 1894.

Huxley, Aldous. *Brave New World*. HarperCollins, 1932.

Idle, Eric. *The Road to Mars: A Post-Modern Novel*. Pantheon, 1999.

Jones, Diana Wynne. *Dark Lord of Derkholm*. Greenwillows, 1998.

Langton, Jane. *The Fledgling*. HarperCollins, 1980.

Lawrence, Louise. *Andra*. Harper & Row, 1971. First American Edition. 1991.

Lawrence, Louise. *Children of the Dust*. HarperCollins, 1980.

Lawrence, Louise. *Moonwind*. HarperCollins, 1986.

LeGuin, Ursula K. *Dispossessed: An Ambiguous Utopia*. Harper, 1974.

LeGuin, Ursula K. *The Farthest Shore*. Atheneum, 1972.

LeGuin, Ursula K. *The Left Hand of Darkness*. Ace, 1969.

LeGuin, Ursula K. *Tehanu: The Last Book of Earthsea*. Macmillan, 1990.

LeGuin, Ursula K. *The Tombs of Atuan*. Atheneum, 1972.

LeGuin, Ursula K. *A Wizard of Earthsea*. Parnassus, 1968.

Lowry, Lois. *The Giver*. Houghton Mifflin, 1993.

Lucian. *The True History*. 2nd Century A.D.

Macaulay, David. *Motel of the Mysteries*. Houghton Mifflin, 1979.

McCaffrey, Anne. *Dragondrums*. Atheneum, 1979.

McCaffrey, Anne. *Dragonflight*. Ballantyne, 1968.

McCaffrey, Anne. *Dragonsinger*. Atheneum, 1977.

McCaffrey, Anne. *Dragonsong*. Atheneum, 1976.

McIntyre, Vonda N. *Dreamsnake*. Houghton Mifflin, 1978.

McKillip, Patricia. *The Forgotten Beasts of Eld*. Atheneum, 1974.

McKinley, Robin. *Beauty: A Retelling of the Story of Beauty and the Beast*. HarperCollins, 1978.

McKinley, Robin. *Rose Daughter*. Greenwillow, 1997.

More, Thomas. *Utopia*. 1516.

Niven, Larry and Jerry Pournell. *The Mote in God's Eye*. Simon & Schuster, 1974.

O'Brien, Robert C. *Mrs. Frisby and the Rats of Nimh*. Atheneum, 1971.

O'Brien, Robert C. *Z for Zachariah*. Atheneum, 1975.

Orwell, George. *Animal Farm*. Harcourt Brace Jovanovich, 1954.

Orwell, George. *Nineteen Eighty-Four*. Harcourt Brace Jovanovich, 1948.

Paterson, Katherine. *Perzival: The Guest of the Grail Knight*. Lodestar, 1998.

Plato. *The Republic*. 5th Century B.C.

Pullman, Philip. *Clockwork—or All Wound Up*. Scholastic, 1998.

Pullman, Philip. *The Golden Compass*. Knopf, 1996.

Pullman, Philip. *The Subtle Knife*. Knopf, 1997.

Reavis, Dick J. *The Ashes of Waco: An Investigation*. Simon & Schuster, 1995.

Rowling, J. K. *Harry Potter and the Chamber of Secrets*. Scholastic, 1997.

Rowling, J. K. *Harry Potter and the Prisoner of Azkaban*. Scholastic, 1999.

Rowling, J. K. *Harry Potter and the Sorcerer's Stone*. Scholastic, 1998.

Service, Pamela. *Tomorrow's Magic*. Atheneum, 1987.

Service, Pamela. *Winter of Magic's Return*. Atheneum, 1985.

Shelly, Mary Wollstonecraft. *Frankenstein, or the Modern Prometheus*. 1818.

Sleator, William. *House of Stairs*. Dutton, 1974.

Sleator, William. *Interstellar Pig*. Dutton, 1984.

Springer, Nancy. *I Am Mordred*. Philomel, 1998.

Stephenson, Neal. *Snow Crash*. Bantam, 1992.

Sterling, Bruce, editor. *Mirrowshades: The Cyberpunk Anthology*. Morrow, 1986.

Stewart, Mary. *The Crystal Cave*. Morrow, 1970.

Stewart, Mary. *The Hollow Hills*. Morrow, 1973.

Sutcliff, Rosemary. *The Light Beyond the Forest: The Quest for the Holy Grail*. Dutton, 1979.

Sutcliff, Rosemary. *The Road to Camlann: The Death of King Arthur*. Dutton, 1982.

Sutcliff, Rosemary. *The Sword and the Circle: King Arthur and the Knights of the Round Table*. Dutton, 1981.

Swift, Jonathan. *Gulliver's Travels*. 1726.

Tolkien, J. R. R. *The Hobbit or There and Back Again*. Houghton Mifflin, 1938, rev. ed. 1951.

Tolkien, J. R. R. *The Lord of the Rings*. Houghton Mifflin. Composed of three parts: *The Fellowship of the Rings*, 1954, rev. ed. 1967; *The Two Towers*, 1955, rev. ed. 1967; and *The Return of the King*, 1956, rev. ed. 1967.

Turtledove, Harry. *The Great War: Walk in Hell*. Del Rey/Ballantine, 1999.

Turtledove, Harry. *Worldwar: In the Balance*. Ballantine, 1994.

Turtledove, Harry and Richard Dreyfuss. *The Two Georges*. TOR, 1996.

Verne, Jules. *Journey to the Center of the Earth*. 1864.

Verne, Jules. *Twenty Thousand Leagues Under the Sea*. 1870.

Vonnegut, Kurt, Jr. *God Bless You, Mr. Rosewater, or Pearls Before Swine*. Holt, 1965.

Walton, Evangeline. *The Children of Llyr: The Second Branch of the Mabinogion*. Ballantine, 1971.

Walton, Evangeline. *The Island of the Mighty: The Fourth Branch of the Mabinogion*. 1973, (first printed as *The Virgin and the Swine: The Fourth Branch of the Mabinogion*).

Walton, Evangeline. *The Prince of Annwn: The First Branch of the Mabinogion*. Ballantine, 1974.

Walton, Evangeline. *The Song of Rhiannon: The Third Branch of the Mabinogion*. Ballantine, 1972.

Wangerin, Walter, Jr. *The Book of the Dun Cow*, HarperCollins, 1978.

Wangerin, Walter, Jr. *The Book of Sorrows*. Harper-Collins, 1985.

Wells, H. G. *The Time Machine*. 1895.

Wells, H. G. *The War of the Worlds*. 1898.

White, E. B. *Charlotte's Web*. HarperCollins, 1952.

White, T. H. *The Once and Future King*. Putnam's 1958.

Wrede, Patricia C. *Book of Enchantments*. Jane Yolen Books, 1996.

Wrede, Patricia C. *Calling on Dragons*. Harcourt Brace, 1993.

Wrede, Patricia C. *Dealing with Dragons*. Harcourt Brace, 1990.

Wrede, Patricia C. *Searching to Dragons*. Harcourt Brace, 1991.

Wrede, Patricia C. *Talking to Dragons*. Harcourt Brace, 1993.

Wyndham, John. *The Midwich Cuckoos*. M. Joseph, 1957.

Yolen, Jane. *Dragon's Blood*. Delacorte, 1982.

Yolen, Jane. *Heart's Blood*. Delacorte, 1984.

Yolen, Jane. *A Sending of Dragons*. Delacorte, 1987.

Information on the availability of paperback editions of these titles is available online from such book sellers as Barnes & Noble and Amazon.com, and through *Books in Print* compiled by R. R. Bowker Company and available either in person or online from major libraries.

CHAPTER

8

History and History Makers
Of People and Places

The United States has always viewed history in its own way. More than a century ago, Ralph Waldo Emerson described the great American tradition as "trampling on tradition," and Abraham Lincoln said that Americans had a "perfect rage for the new." By the beginning of the twentieth century, however, Americans were feeling more confident and were ready to look back. American history became a standard part of the school curriculum, thousands of towns erected statues of Abraham Lincoln and Ulysses S. Grant, and historical pageants flourished, including in the South, where Confederates began to look back with pride on their role in the Civil War.

As interested as we may be in history, we are always more concerned about the present, and we find ourselves imposing present-day values on the past. In 1927, Henry Seidel Canby wrote, "Historical fiction, like history, is more likely to register an exact truth about the writer's present than the exact truth of the past."[1] Historian Michael Kammen developed a similar point in *Mystic Chords of Memory. Time* magazine reviewer Richard Stengel praised Kammen for showing how "Throughout American history, facts have been transformed into myths and myths transformed into beliefs." Immigrants came to the United States to escape the past, but once they were settled here they contributed to a "kind of ethnic American syllogism: the first generation zealously preserves; the second generation zealously forgets; the third generation zealously rediscovers." Kammen wrote that after World War II, Americans were tied together by a sense of patriotism, but in the 1960s this was replaced by a decade of questioning. In the 1970s, it turned to nostalgia (i.e., "history without guilt"), which continued in the 1980s with a "selective memory and a soothing amnesia." History became a growth industry, and under President Reagan "public history was privatized, so that it was Coca Cola, not the U.S. government, that brought you the centennial of the Statue of Liberty."[2]

Despite the flaws that Kammen points out, the history "growth industry" has generally been positive for the education of young people.

Trade Books for History Study

Kammen's book focuses on people's predilection for comfortable myths (i.e., nostalgia), as opposed to factual history, but what he says is more true of popular entertainment than of history-related trade books. Moreover, it is not as true of trade books as it is of textbooks. Textbook writers often rely on comfortable myths because to be adopted in a school district the books must go through so many committees and stages of approval that by the time they get to classrooms they are likely to be extremely bland. If a point of view is expressed, it is likely to be in support of the status quo. For example, a 1983 state of Texas mandate on textbook selection reads, "Positive aspects of the USA's history must be stressed in world history texts used in public schools." In commenting on this mandate, Betty Carter and Richard Abrahamson observed that "Those negatives—the sorry mistakes that have dotted our past and may well affect our future—are either left out, glossed over, or presented in a favorable light." For example, a history book prepared under this philosophy might present the Spanish-American War as "little more than a dramatic charge up San Juan Hill" and America's ignoring of Hitler's rise to power and his evil intentions as a "failure to communicate with Eastern Europe." Carter and Abrahamson warn that such distortions "turn the drama of history into a whitewash."[3]

Fortunately the writers of history-related trade books are freer to pursue particular points of view because their books are purchased individually or by libraries, which endorse, at least on paper, having a great variety of opinions and points of view. With trade books, writers also have frequent chances to incorporate new attitudes and new findings (see Focus Box 8.1) because individuals and libraries provide a steady market. Reviewers and other evaluators stand guard, so that over the last several years increasing emphasis has been given to the importance of authenticity and the use of primary sources. Nonfiction writer Brent Ashabranner, for example, has said that one of the things he's learned from reviewers is how seriously they feel about documentation. After his first few books were criticized, he has been much more careful with his bibliographies and has taken special pains to let readers know where he received his information. He thinks extensive footnotes interrupt the flow of reading, so he tries to put the information "into the text in a way that doesn't interfere with the prose but assures the reader that I didn't just make things up."[4]

Books created from letters and diaries reassure readers that they are reading authentic history, and relying on primary sources goes a long way toward keeping authors and subsequently their readers from wallowing in nostalgia. The standard practice in history books now is for the author to include a foreword or afterword discussing the methods of research and giving suggestions for further reading.

We need to help students develop skills to interpret the clues that authors give to distinguish between what is known and what is only believed but is really unproved or unprovable. A good book to start with, because of its format, is Dorothy and Thomas Hoobler's *The Fact or Fiction Files: Lost Civilizations*. On one side of the pages are the facts as they are known about such mysteries as Stonehenge and the carved heads on Easter Island. On the other side, the authors present hypotheses and conjectures. Another good book to illustrate these differences is William Loren Katz's *Breaking the Chains: African-American Slave Resistance*. Katz spends a good deal of time discussing and refuting some of the myths and historical misrep-

Nonfiction: History from New Angles

The Ancient City: Life in Classical Athens & Rome by Peter Connolly and Hazel Dodge. Oxford University Press, 1998. Peter Connolly did the grand illustrations and cut-away drawings to show how life was lived in these ancient and glorious capitals.

Black Legacy: A History of New York's African Americans by William Loren Katz. Simon & Schuster/Atheneum, 1997. Katz begins his book in 1609 when the first Africans came to New York (many as free individuals rather than as slaves) and ends with David Dinkins's election as mayor in 1989.

Bound for America: The Forced Migration of Africans to the New World by James Haskins and Kathleen Benson, illustrated by Floyd Cooper. Lothrop, 1999. A timeline, careful use of primary source material, exceptional wash-and-oil paintings, and clear writing make this forty-eight-page continuation of *African Beginnings* (Lothrop, 1998) an effective introduction to a sad part of American history.

Forbidden Love: The Secret History of Mixed-Race America by Gary B. Nash. Holt/Edge, 1999. Nash includes vignettes about the successful lives of mixed-race Americans, while also showing that " . . . there is more genetic variation within any grouping we call 'race' than between any two such groups."

Growing Up in Coal Country by Susan Campbell Bartoletti. Houghton Mifflin, 1996. In this well-researched and well-illustrated account of northeastern Pennsylvania, readers learn why child labor laws and safety regulations were needed for the mining industry.

Navajo Code Talkers: Native American Heroes by Catherine Jones. Tudor, 1998. In World War II, the Navajo Code Talkers of the U.S. Marine Corps worked with their Dineh (Navajo) language, which had never been written down and had to be adapted to modern warfare. It was the only code never broken.

The Salem Witch Trials by Lori Lee Wilson. Lerner, 1997. Differences between Western and non-Western perceptions of witches and a discussion of Arthur Miller's play *The Crucible* with parallels to the McCarthy era are some of the unique aspects of this well-done history, which could be read alongside Kathryn Lasky's *Beyond the Burning Time* (MacMillan, 1983) and Ann Rinaldi's *A Break with Charity* (Harcourt, 1992).

The Way Things Never Were: The Truth about the "Good Old Days" by Norman H. Finkelstein. Simon & Schuster/Atheneum, 1999. Readers will be grateful for today's lifestyles after reading about unsafe automobiles, unhealthy diets, and doctors who made housecalls but had very little of real use in their black bags.

resentations about slavery that have allowed people to believe that most slaves were satisfied with their lot.

Another good way to show young readers that there are different opinions and different ways of looking at history is to encourage the use of several books on the same subject. When a topic is to be studied, instead of assigning all students to read the same book, bring in individual copies of various books, so that students can choose. Encourage them to trade with one another, to skim, and to read excerpts. Then after they have immersed themselves in their topic, they can make some kind of presentation to the class or work together on a culminating activity that illustrates the different viewpoints.

By making connections, students can understand not only the *who, what,* and *when* of things but also the *why.* For example, Malcolm C. MacPherson's *Time Bomb: Fermi, Heisenberg, and the Race for the Atomic Bomb* is a good companion book to Carl B. Feldbaum and Ronald J. Bee's *Looking the Tiger in the Eye: Confronting the Nuclear Threat.*

One of the most useful activities is for teachers and librarians to pull together groups of related books. For example, students can better appreciate Walter Dean Myers's *Malcolm X: By Any Means Necessary* if they also have access to other books about the history of African-Americans. See Chapter Eleven on thematic units for further discussion of this point.

Historical Fact and Fiction

Most of us read historical novels because we are curious about other times, places, and peoples; we also read them because, most important, we want adventure, suspense, and mystery. Movies as old as *Gone with the Wind* (1939) and *The Scarlet Pimpernel* (1935) and as new as *Elizabeth* (1998), *Braveheart* (1995), and *Rob Roy* (1995) pique our interest, however ignorant we may be of the times and places described. Historical adventures remain readable much longer than contemporary, realistic stories (e.g., Sir Walter Scott's *Ivanhoe* [1819], Alexandre Dumas's *The Count of Monte Cristo* [1844], Mary Johnston's *To Have and to Hold* [1900], Rafael Sabatini's *Scaramouche* [1921], Helen Waddell's *Peter Abelard* [1933], Elizabeth Goudge's *Green Dolphin Street* [1944], and Margaret Walker's *Jubilee* [1966]).

As with any literary form, there are standards for judging historical novels. (See Table 8.1). They should be historically accurate and steeped in the sense of time and place. We should recognize totems and taboos, food, clothing, vocations, leisure activities, customs, smells, religions, literature, and all that goes into making

TABLE 8.1

SUGGESTIONS FOR EVALUATING HISTORICAL FICTION

A good historical novel usually has	A poor historical novel may have
A setting that is integral to the story	A story that could have happened any time or any place. The historical setting is for visual appeal and to compensate for a weak story
An authetic rendition of the time, place, and people being featured	
An author who is so thoroughly steeped in the history of the period that he or she can be comfortably creative without making mistakes	Anachronisms in which the author illogically mixes up people, events, speaking styles, social values, or technological developments from different time periods
Believable characters with whom young readers can identify	Awkward narrations and exposition as the author tries to teach history through characters' conversations
Evidence that even across great time spans people share similar emotions	
References to well-known events or people or other clues through which the reader can place the happenings in their correct historic framework	Oversimplification of the historical issues and a stereotyping of the "bad" and the "good" guys
Readers who come away with the feeling that they know a time or place better. It is as if they have lived in it for at least a few hours	Characters who fail to come alive as individuals having something in common with the readers. They are just stereotyped representatives of a particular period

one time and one place unique from another. Enthusiasts forgive no anachronism, no matter how slight (see Geraldine McCaughrean's statement on Getting the Facts Right in Fiction). Historical novels should give a sense of history's continuity, a feeling of the flow of history from one time into another, which is, for good reason, different from the period before. As writers allow us to feel that flow of history, however, they should particularize their portraits of one time and one place. Historical novels should tell a lively story with a sense of impending danger, mystery, suspense, or romance.

Historical novels allow us—at their best they force us—to make connections and to realize that despair is as old and as new as hope, that loyalty and treachery, love and hatred, compassion and cruelty were and are inherent in humanity, whether it be in ancient Greece, Elizabethan England, or post-World War I Germany. As with most writers, historical novelists may want to teach particular lessons. Christopher Collier, for example, makes no pretense about why he and his brother write about the American Revolution in their fine historical novels:

> . . . [T]he books I write with my brother are written with a didactic purpose to teach about ideals and values that have been important in shaping the course of American history. This is in no way intended to denigrate the importance of the dramatic and literary elements of historical novels. Nothing will be taught, and certainly nothing learned, if no one reads the books.[5]

Collier later added that "there is no better way to teach history than to embrace potential readers and fling them into a living past."[6] Sheila A. Egoff clearly felt happy about the historical novel when she wrote, "For most adults over fifty years of age, childhood reading is almost synonymous with historical romance."[7] Patty Campbell in 1980, however, questioned whether young adults read historical novels today.

> This reviewer has long been convinced that young adults lack a sense of history to a significant degree. They will accept a good YA novel with a historical setting if the other elements of the story are appealing enough to overcome that drawback, but, in general, so-called historical fiction is sudden death on the YA shelf.[8]

In our adolescent literature classes, we have students read something like thirty books in a semester spread across various genres. Historical fiction is often one of the last blanks to get filled in, but when students come to us complaining that they can not find a good piece of historical fiction to read, we ask them which books they've read, and invariably they tell us about two or three that we consider to be historical fiction, but that they have put in some other category. They act almost surprised to learn that they have already enjoyed something "historical."

One reason for their surprise is their stereotyped view that historical fiction must be grand and imposing, like a movie spectacle starring Charlton Heston, or

GERALDINE MCCAUGHREAN
On Getting the Facts Right in Fiction

I remember, as a child, dimly resenting historical novels laden with improving historical facts—as if a story were the sugar needed to get down unpalatable medicine. Long, badly integrated, easy-to-skip digressions featured perpendicular architecture or details of the 17th-century lace trade. "Hello," I used to think, "someone is trying to educate me here." (Books like that still happen.)

So when I came to write my first novel (*A Little Lower than the Angels*), I did no historical research whatsoever. What I did not know about, I wrote my way round. Apart from avoiding dire anachronisms, I did not feel any other "duty" toward facts. I was writing fiction, after all.

Later on, I was approached to write a big, adult, historical novel. To my great unease, I realized there was no way I was going to get by without doing extensive research, and I did. That was when I discovered an entirely new way of writing fiction—one born out of all the fascinating facts and extraordinary details I could squirrel together into a card-index file. The things I read gave me ideas for incidents, characters, and whole new plot-lines. And such bizarre, incredible things have happened in real life that there was no shortage of material.

When I based a children's novel on a newspaper cutting about a worked-out gold mining town (*Gold Dust*), I again found that I had to do research on South American gold-mining, flora, fauna, language, local beliefs. . . . Once again, the research part wrote the story.

But gradually, I began to feel my feet clogging with a great weight of facts, slowing me down, demanding to be included. The weight of research finally broke the novel's back, and I had to set it aside for several months before coming back to it, with fiction and fiction alone in mind.

I have never been able fully to recover the unalloyed joy I felt while writing my first, unresearched books. Somehow I keep making the same mistake—burdening myself with facts and background information in the effort to "get things right."

When I go into schools, the first thing I do is contradict that well-worn advice of teachers, "Write about what you know about." I never took it to heart as a child, and I can't see any merit in it, as far as recreational writing is concerned. Any act of imagination should take children as far as they want—to places they may never go (especially that most exotic of all locations: the Past), with people they may never meet, embarking on adventures that will never befall them in real life; fulfilling their wildest dreams.

I doubt if I shall ever dare to write another novel without a card-index file on one hand and a pile of reference books on the other. But I am quite sure I would do better if I followed my own advice and got back to "making it up as I go along."

Geraldine McCaughrean's books include *The Pirate's Son,* Scholastic, 1998; *A Little Lower Than the Angels,* Oxford University Press, 1987; *Gold Dust,* Oxford University Press, 1993; and *The Golden Hoard/Silver Treasure/Bronze Cauldron* and *Crystal Pool Myths and Legends of the World* published in England by Orion Children's Books.

exaggerated like a "bodice ripper" romance. Actually, historical fiction includes mysteries, comedies, adventures, realistic problem stories, and whatever other genres can be listed (see Focus Box 8.2). The only thing they have in common is that they are set in the past.

 FOCUS BOX 8.2

Historical Fiction

The All-True Travels and Adventures of Lidie Newton by Jane Smiley. Knopf, 1998. Lidie marries an abolitionist and moves with him to the Kansas Territory where a war rages between Southern and Northern sympathizers.

Black Horse for the King by Anne McCaffrey. Harcourt, 1996. McCaffrey's first historical novel is set in fifth-century Roman Britain. Young Galwyn finds a way to advance in life and war.

The Burning Road by Ann Benson. Delacorte, 1999. A neurologist seeking a cure for a modern epidemic reads the journal of a late fourteenth century doctor.

Fragments of the Ark by Louise Meriwether. Pocket Books, 1994. Told from an African-American viewpoint and set in 1861, this is the story of South Carolina slave Peter Mango, a trained navigator who turns his gunboat over to the Northern side.

Frontier Wolf by Rosemary Sutcliff. Dutton, 1980. A young Roman commander of a unit of frontier scouts in northern England must begin a retreat from the forces of native tribes.

Frozen Summer by Mary Jane Auch. Holt, 1998. In western New York the year of 1816 is known as "the year without a summer," because the weather was so cold crops could not grow. Remembrance, called "Mem," tries to hold her family together in this sequel to the carefully researched *Journey to Nowhere* (Holt, 1997).

Gib Rides Home by Zilpha Keatley Snyder. Delacorte, 1998. Snyder's best storytelling efforts went into this story based on the life of her father, who in the early 1900s grew up in an orphanage.

A Murder for Her Majesty by Beth Hilgartner. Houghton Mifflin, 1986. When her father is killed and rumor hath it that Queen Elizabeth I wants him dead, Alicia takes refuge as a boy singer in the York Cathedral.

Quest for a Maid by Frances Mary Hendry. Farrar, Straus & Giroux, 1990. Despite witches and storms, Meg manages to bring a young girl who is the heir to the throne from Norway to Scotland.

The Raging Quiet by Sherryl Jordan. Simon & Schuster, 1999. The cast of characters in this love story from the Middle Ages includes a 16-year-old girl, her drunken and soon-to-be deceased older husband, a young boy who is deaf, and a village full of superstitious people eager to cast aspersions and place blame.

The Sheriff of Nottingham by Richard Kluger. Viking, 1992. Robin Hood is only a minor character in this revisionist tale of a fine man serving a rotten king.

The Squire, His Knight, and His Lady by Gerald Morris. Houghton Mifflin, 1999. Along with *The Squire's Tale* (Houghton Mifflin, 1998), this lively and humorous book is a crossover between fantasy and historical fiction.

Stealing Freedom by Elisa Carbone. Knopf, 1998. Slave Ann Maria Weems was born in the 1840s on the plantation of a kind master and his not-so-kind wife. Her story documents many of the complications brought by changes preceding the Civil War.

Susannah by Janet Hickman. Greenwillow, 1998. Susannah is 13 when her mother dies and her father decides to join a Shaker community on the Ohio frontier.

Tales from the Homeplace: Adventures of a Texas Farm Girl by Harriet Burandt and Shelley Dale. Holt, 1997. Twelve-year-old Irene is the character at the center of these episodic stories from the 1930s based on the author's own family histories.

We used to define historical fiction as any story that happened before or during World War II, but as we have grown older and readers of YA fiction seem to have grown younger, we find ourselves using the Vietnam era as the dividing line between "historical" and "contemporary."

Outstanding Writers of Historical Fiction

For years, British critics have acclaimed Rosemary Sutcliff as the finest writer of British historical fiction for young people. From her finest early novel in 1954, *The Eagle of the Ninth,* through her 1990 *The Shining Company,* she clearly had no peer in writing about early Britain. We must find a way for librarians and teachers to get her books to the right young readers, those who care about history and a rattling good story and who are not put off by a period of time they know little about. *The Shining Company* may be harder to sell than Sutcliff's earlier books about the Normans and the Saxons (e.g., *The Shield Ring* and *Dawn Wind*) because it is set in a more obscure time, seventh-century Britain. Sutcliff knew about the cries of men and the screams of stricken horses and the smell of blood and filth, and she cared about people who make history, whether knaves or villains or, in this case, naive men who trusted their king and themselves beyond common sense.

Leon Garfield's world is the eighteenth century, with an occasional detour into early nineteenth-century England. Beginning with *Jack Holborn* in 1965 and continuing with his more recent books, including *The Empty Sleeve,* Garfield set a standard for historical writing that few can match. Garfield's eighteenth century is the world of Fielding and Smollett, lusty, squalid, ugly, bustling, and swollen, full of life and adventure and the certainty that being born an orphan may lead you ultimately to fame and fortune. Garfield does not fear conventions, but his stories also play with reality versus illusion, daylight versus dreams, flesh versus fantasy. His ability to sketch out minor characters in a line or two and make them come alive is impressive. Of a man in *The Sound of Coaches,* he wrote, "He was one of those gentlemen who affect great gallantry to all the fair sex except their wives." Of the protagonist we are told, "although jealousy was ordinarily foreign to Sam's nature, they did, on occasion, talk the same language." Garfield's epigrams are equally effective, for example, "Many a man is made good by being thought so."

Wit, humor, and liveliness permeate Garfield's books. Perhaps the funniest are *The Strange Affair of Adelaide Harris* and its sequel, *The Night of the Comet.* In *Adelaide,* Bostock and Harris, two nasty pupils in Dr. Bunnion's Academy, become so entranced with stories of Spartan babies abandoned on mountaintops, there to be suckled by wolves, that they borrow Harris's baby sister to determine for themselves the truth of the old tales. Therein begins a wild comedy of errors and an even wilder series of coincidences and near duels and wild threats that hardly lets up until the last lines.

Scott O'Dell's death ended a career of excellent historical novels. *The King's Fifth* is probably his most convincing work, with its picture of sixteenth-century Spaniards and the moral strains put on anyone involved in the search for gold and fame. It is convincing, often disturbing, and, like most of O'Dell's historical novels, generally worth pursuing. Students coming to high school with a good reading background probably already know O'Dell from his *Island of the Blue Dolphins* and *Sing Down the Moon,* both of which present original and positive portrayals of young Native American women suffering at the hands of white settlers in the middle to late 1800s.

O'Dell was a pioneer in featuring strong young women in these two books, but within the last couple of decades several good writers have followed his lead, so that good historical books about women and minorities are much easier to find. The rollicking sea adventure, *The True Confessions of Charlotte Doyle*, by Avi is a brilliant example even if it has to be read with a willing suspension of disbelief.

In *The Birchbark House*, Louise Erdrich writes about Omakayas, a young Ojibwa girl living in the mid-1800s on an island in Lake Superior. Cynthia DeFelice specializes in stories about preteens. In *Nowhere to Call Home*, her heroine is 12-year-old Frances (Frankie), who in 1930 is awakened by the sound of a gunshot. Her once-wealthy father, now bankrupt, has committed suicide. Frankie is left a penniless orphan, and there begins her adventure of dressing as a boy and riding the rails along with thousands of other young adventurers during the Depression. Irene Hunt's *No Promises in the Wind* is a brilliant picture of the Depression and the hopelessness of two small boys during the time.

Ann Rinaldi has written a number of excellent historical novels using real historical figures and teaching readers about a time and a place. Five of her books are particularly fine—*Wolf by the Ears; A Break With Charity: A Story About the Salem Witch Trials; The Fifth of March: A Story of the Boston Massacre; Finishing Becca: A Story About Peggy Shippen and Benedict Arnold;* and *Cast Two Shadows*, a Civil War story.

Rinaldi tackled a particularly ambitious subject in *Wolf by the Ears*, a fictional story of Sally Hemmings's family. Sally was a mulatto slave in Thomas Jefferson's household, and some historians believe that Jefferson fathered several of her children. Rinaldi's book implies that this is true, but the question is never clearly answered, even though the protagonist, supposedly Jefferson's daughter, asks it often enough. The book's title comes from Jefferson's statement about slavery: "as it is, we have the wolf by the ears, and we can neither hold him, nor safely let him go. Justice is in one scale, and self-preservation the other."

Carolyn Meyer began her writing career doing nonfiction, but then began coming up against blank walls where she could find no more information. Because she wanted the stories to continue, she began asking, "What if?" and so began her career as a writer of fiction. Her most highly acclaimed historical fiction is probably *White Lilacs*, while others include *Where the Heart Still Beats: The Story of Cynthia Ann Parker* and *Mary, Bloody Mary*, about the youth of the woman who became one of England's most unpopular rulers.

Historical novels come in all times and all places. Readers interested in prehistoric times would enjoy Joan Wolf's *The Reindeer Hunters* and Peter Dickinson's *A Bone from a Dry Sea*. Even more excitement waits in medieval Europe. Karen Cushman has two brilliant works that ought to appeal to slightly younger students—*Catherine, Called Birdy* and *The Midwife's Apprentice*. The best of the bunch is Frances Temple's *The Ramsay Scallop*. Temple describes the apprehension that 13-year-old Eleanor of Ramsey feels as she awaits marriage to 22-year-old Lord Thomas of Thornham. Thomas is no happier about his upcoming marriage because he has become cynical about life and religion after fighting in the Crusades. Father Gregory sets them off on a pilgrimage to the cathedral in Santiago, Spain, and asks that they remain chaste during the trip. Temple's portraits of the people and the time and the friendships they form and the deceit and pain they meet are brilliant.

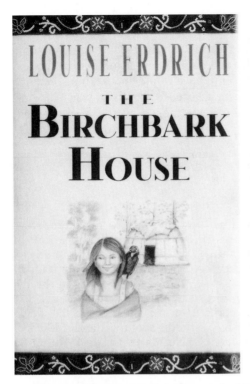

With historical fiction, today's authors are looking for less obvious stories and are making an effort to include girls as protagonists.

If readers want to travel to the Orient, they can do so in Malcolm Bosse's *The Examination* with its picture of two quite different brothers in sixteenth-century China and Erik Christian Haugaard's novels about the life of the Samurai. *The Samurai's Tale* is about a captured boy who becomes the first servant of a Lord in feudal sixteenth-century Japan. More recently, Haugaard's *The Revenge of the Forty-Seven Samurai* is a tale of honor and revenge in Japan two centuries later.

Phillip Pullman's novels about Victorian England have appealed to many readers. *The Ruby in the Smoke* is about Sally Lockhart and a missing ruby and a deep, dark mystery. Two other books complete the series—*Shadow in the North* and *The Tiger in the Well.*

The United States has been the subject of a number of historical novels. Kathryn Lasky's *Beyond the Burning Time* is a fine novel focusing on the terrors of the Salem witch trials, and *Beyond the Divide* is a novel of the western movement. James Lincoln Collier and Christopher Collier's *My Brother Sam Is Dead* is only one of many excellent Collier books. Howard Fast's *April Morning* is more than 30 years old, but it is still worth reading by anybody who cares about young people and their place in the Revolutionary War. Katherine Paterson's *Lyddie* presents the manufacturing world of the 1840s and Lyddie's place therein.

Another book written from the perspective of a young person is *The Perilous Journey of the Donner Party* by Marian Calabro. Calabro tells her meticulously researched story of a group of unfortunate western settlers stranded in an early California snowstorm. Her heroine is 12-year-old Virginia Reed, the young survivor who throughout the months of the ordeal hid her rag doll inside her clothes.

Books About War

It is increasingly difficult to distinguish between fiction and nonfiction, and that is especially true in memoirs and reminiscences and fiction about war. Struggling to survive in war is not an adventure we would choose, but so many people have been forced into horrible circumstances that books about war—histories, diaries, letters, interviews, fiction—are among the most powerful books young people can read

 FOCUS BOX 8.3

War's Effect on Young People

Ain't Gonna Study War No More by Milton Meltzer. Harper and Row, 1985. Meltzer traces pacifism in the United States starting with the Quakers who refused to fight Indians and moving on to the mid-1980s.

America Storms the Beaches: 1944 by John Devaney. Walker, 1993. Devaney uses books, articles, and interviews to make clear how significant the war was between September and December 1944.

Darkness Be My Friend by John Marsden. Houghton Mifflin, 1999. This is fourth in a series of books about a war not too far in the future. See also the earlier books—*Tomorrow, When the War Began* (1995), *The Dead of Night* (1997), and *A Killing Frost* (1998), all from Houghton Mifflin.

The Dreams of Maihe Mehan by Jennifer Armstrong. Knopf, 1996. An Irish immigrant tries to keep her brother from fighting in the Civil War.

Fallen Angels by Walter Dean Myers. Scholastic, 1988. Richie Oerry would do anything to get out of Harlem. He joins the Army, and then comes Vietnam.

Hiroshima: A Novella by Laurence Yep. Scholastic, 1995. Although the story is centered around Hiroshima residents, 12-year-old Sachi and her sister Riko, Yep also tells the story of the dropping of the atomic bomb from other perspectives, including from the crew of the Enola Gay bomber.

Johnny Got His Gun by Dalton Trumbo. Lippincott, 1939. Filled with patriotic fervor, Joe enlists, but after battle he has no arms or legs, and he is blind, deaf, and mute.

Linger by M. E. Kerr. HarperCollins, 1993. When Private Robert Peel is sent to the Persian Gulf War, the restaurant where he worked becomes a center for patriotism. Then Peel and friends are hit with friendly fire.

Live from the Battlefield: From Vietnam to Baghdad, 35 Years in the World's War Zones by Peter Arnett. Simon & Schuster, 1994. One of the most respected news correspondents talks about war and soldiers and politics.

No Man's Land: A Young Soldier's Story by Susan Campbell Bartoletti. Blue Sky, 1999. A 14-year-old boy joins the Confederate army, in part to spite his father.

Sergeant Dickinson by Jerome Gold. Soho, 1999. The Vietnamese surround the company of narrator Ray Dickinson, a radioman in Vietnam, and an assault is coming soon.

A Short Wait Between Trains: An Anthology of War Stories by American Writers edited by Robert Benard. Dell, 1991. The writers of these short stories include Ralph Ellison, Ambrose Bierce, and Eudora Welty.

Voices from Vietnam by Barry Denenberg. Scholastic, 1995. These anecdotes and horror stories all come from the Vietnam War, the longest War in American history.

War and the Pity of War edited by Neil Philip. Clarion, 1998. Philip starts his poetry collection with ancient Greece and moves forward to today.

With Every Drop of Blood: A Novel of the Civil War by James Lincoln Collier and Christopher Collier. Delacorte, 1994. Fourteen-year-old Johnny joins a wagon train to bring food to the Southern forces. He's captured by a black soldier about his age, and with that begins his education into reality.

(see Focus Box 8.3). War is one of the topics treated in the movies, starting with D. W. Griffith's 1915 *The Birth of a Nation* and continuing on to Steven Spielberg's 1998 *Saving Private Ryan* (see Film Box 8.1). Newspaper and magazines banner headlines of this or that war and TV assaults us with horrible scenes of carnage and tearful scenes of survivors.

We are preoccupied with war, perhaps because it is so inherently terrifying and evil and, in the minds of many of us, inevitable. The Bible is full of battles, but so is the *Iliad*. War serves as background for an endless succession of wars—Sophocles's *Antigone,* Stephen Crane's *The Red Badge of Courage* (Civil War), William March's *Company K* (World War I), James Jones's *The Thin Red Line* (World War II), and Jerome Gold's *Sergeant Dickinson* (Vietnam).

Young adults are conscious of the nearness of war though they likely know little of the realities of war and even less about the details of past wars. Reading literature about war, fiction or not, acquaints young people with the ambiguous nature

 FILM BOX 8.1

War Is Dangerous to Our Health (See Appendix D)

Apocalypse Now (1979, color, 150 min., R; Director: Francis Ford Coppola; with Marlon Brando, Martin Sheen, and Robert Duvall) Joseph Conrad's *The Heart of Darkness* is played out in Vietnam with an agent sent into the backwaters to kill an officer.

The Deer Hunter (1978, color, 183 min., R; Director: Michael Cimino; with Robert De Niro, Meryl Streep, and Christopher Walken) This three-hour movie shows the before and after in the lives of three steelworkers who leave Pennsylvania to fight in Vietnam.

The Execution of Private Slovik (1974, color, 120 min., made for TV; Director: Lamont Johnson; with Martin Sheen, and Ned Beatty) Private Slovik is the only American soldier since the Civil War to be executed by a firing squad for desertion.

Glory (1989, color, 122 min., R; Director: Edward Zwick; with Matthew Broderick and Denzel Washington) The 54th Regiment of the Massachusetts Voluntary Infantry, an all-black company, goes into battle during the Civil War.

Grand Illusion (1937, black and white, 117 min., NR; Director: Jean Renoir; with Jean Gabin, Erich von Stoheim, and Pierre Fresnay) French prisoners of war in a German World War I prison camp illustrate truths about war and social class.

Midnight Clear (1992, color, 107 min., R; Director: Keith Gordon; with Ethan Hawke and Gary Sinese) From William Wharton's novel, a young troop of American soldiers in World War II face equally young German soldiers, and both sides agree, temporarily, to hold a truce.

Paths of Glory (1957, black and white, 86 min., NR; Director: Stanley Kubrik; with Kirk Douglas and Adolphe Menjou) When a French general in World War I finds that his men failed to take a goal, he picks three at random to die for the company's cowardice.

Platoon (1986, color, 120 min., R; Director: Oliver Stone; with Willem Dafoe and Tom Berenger) Life during the Vietnam War is horrifying, frustrating, and harrowing.

Regret to Inform (1999, color, 72 min., NR; Director: Barbara Sonneborn) In 1968 Sonneborn's husband was reported dead in Vietnam. In 1992, she went to Vietnam to document what other war widows—American and Vietnamese—have suffered.

Saving Private Ryan (1998, color, 170 min., R; Director: Steven Spielberg; with Tom Hanks, Edward Burns, and Matt Damon) This story of landing at Omaha Beach and fighting inward in France has undeniable power, even though it was a bit overrated when it came out and by now is a bit underrated.

of war, on one hand illustrating humanity's evil and horror, on the other hand revealing humanity's decency and heroism.

Civil War literature, once pretty well summarized by Crane's *The Red Badge of Courage,* has several books worth young people's time. Three of the best are Milton Meltzer's *Voices from the Civil War: A Documentary History of the Great American Conflict,* Annette Tapert's *The Brothers' War: Civil War Letters to Their Loved Ones from the Blue and the Gray,* and Gary Paulsen's *Soldier's Heart: Being the Story of the Enlistment and Due Service of the Boy Charley Goddard in the First Minnesota Volunteers.*

Meltzer's book combines his own voice with voices of those alive during the war—in journals, public records, ballads, and letters. It brilliantly covers virtually everything about the war, for example, slavery, politics, songs, battles, death, and civilians. Tapert's collection of letters is even more personal and touching. David Ash served with the 37th Illinois Volunteer Infantry. On March 11, 1862, three days after the Union victory at the Battle of Pea Ridge in Arkansas, Ash wrote about the aftermath of the battle.

> It is the hardest sight a person could behold to see the dead lying round after they bring them in. They lay them in a pile until they get time to bury them. There was twenty-one killed out of one regiment and one hundred and nineteen wounded. Albert Hilliard was laying alongside of me when he was shot, says he, "Oh, Dave, I am shot." It was the hardest thing I have done to call the roll the first time after the battle, so many of our boys killed or wounded.

Paulsen's work is an almost understated account of 15-year-old Charley who enlists and is acclaimed by women and young boys for his bravery and rides in trains and wonders if he will ever get into battle. At his first battle at Manassas he learns what carnage can be with bullets whispering of death and a cannon ball neatly removing the head of a soldier next to him. Charley lived through the war, but he came out physically and mentally wounded and died in his mid-twenties.

G. Clifton Wisler's *Mr. Lincoln's Drummer* may be less dramatic, but the story of Willie Johnston, the youngest person to receive the Congressional medal of Honor, who was at age 11 a drummer with the Third Vermont Regiment, is impressive. Joyce Hansen's *Between Two Fires: Black Soldiers in the Civil War* is a brief account of the more than 180,000 black troops who made up 11 percent of the Union forces.

World War I produced some honest and realistic novels. Rudolph Frank's *No Hero for the Kaiser* was so powerful that Hitler banned it in Nazi Germany in the 1930s. Fourteen-year-old Jan and his dog are the only survivors when German troops take his Russian village. The troops befriend him and save him from being sent to a prison camp. He helps them, and they talk of the Kaiser making him a German citizen. At a great ceremony, the soldiers learn what he thinks of war, and they are deeply troubled.

The most frequently cited book about World War I is again told from the German point of view. Erich Maria Remarque's *All Quiet on the Western Front* is a bitter account of a young German student Paul and his friends and fellow students who are persuaded to join the army by their teacher Kantorek, who fills them with nationalistic propaganda and patriotic fervor. They march off, find what war is really like, and die, one by one.

Pat Barker's award-winning British trilogy, *Regeneration, The Eye in the Door,* and *The Ghost Road* convey the spirit of the times that led men to enlist for King and country and the inevitable horror and insanity that followed. Lt. Billy Prior is the center of the books, a bright young man from the wrong side of the railroad tracks, a man ordinarily unlikely to be allowed to move up in society. The books are about both the war and the apparently eternal social order before the war and the changing society after it.

During World War II, Ernie Pyle was the American soldier's favorite war correspondent, partly because he preferred talking to soldiers in the ranks rather than to officers, and partly because he reported honestly what he saw, not what was good for the morale of soldiers or civilians. For example, in *Ernie's War: The Best of Ernie Pyle's World War II Dispatches* (edited by David Nichols) he writes about the death of Captain Henry T. Waskow, one of the most "beloved" men Pyle found in the war. He told of Waskow's men coming in, gently, to see and honor the body. Pyle ended his account this way.

> Then a soldier came and stood beside the officer, and bent over, and he spoke to the dead captain, not in a whisper but awfully tenderly, and he said: "I sure am sorry, sir." Then the first man squatted down, and he reached down and took the dead hand, and he sat there for a full five minutes, holding the dead hand in his own and looking intently into the dead face, and he never uttered a sound all the time he sat there.
>
> And finally he put the hand down, and then reached up and gently straightened the points of the captain's shirt collar, and then he sort of re-arranged the tattered edges of his uniform around the wound. And then he got up and walked away down the road in the moonlight, all alone.
>
> After that the rest of us went back into the cowshed, leaving the five dead men lying in a line, end to end, in the shadow of the low stone wall. We lay down on the straw in the cowshed, and pretty soon we were all asleep.

Jack Stenbuck's *Typewriter Batallion,* with its seventy-three dispatches from World War II, conveys much of the horror that we get from Ernie Pyle's material. Annette Tapert's *Lines of Battle: Letters from American Servicemen, 1941–1945* makes the horror even more personal.

Few books about World War II, or any other war, succeed so well in creating a revulsion to the blood and messiness as does Farley Mowat's *And No Birds Sang.* After Mowat's company encountered and killed six truckloads of German soldiers, Mowat said,

> It was not the dead that distressed me most—it was the German wounded. There were a great many of these, and most seemed to have been hard hit.
>
> One ghastly vignette from that shambles haunts me still: the driver of a truck hanging over his steering wheel and hiccuping great gouts of cherry-pink foam through a smashed windscreen, to the accompaniment of a sound like a slush pump sucking air as his perforated lungs labored to expel his own heart's blood . . . in which he was slowly drowning.

Mowat's book is hardly the only honest account, but it reeks of death and lost dreams, and anyone wanting to know what war is like should not miss it.

Six novels about World War II are worth reading. William Wharton's *A Midnight Clear* is about six high-I.Q. American soldiers in an intelligence and reconnaissance platoon sent to determine whether there are German troops near a French chateau. The six play bridge and chess and word games and begin to believe they have nothing to do with the war. Then the Germans show up, and instead of warfare, everyone engages in a snowball fight. They sing Christmas carols and set up a Christmas tree and wonderful peace reigns. Then war starts again and the killing resumes, and what had been warm is now bloody.

English novelist Robert Westall writes about young people who refuse to stay outside the war in *The Machine Gunners* and the sequel, *Fathom Five*. The first novel begins in an English coastal town during 1940 and 1941. Rumors of a German invasion are rife, and Chas McGill wants to help win the war. Chas and his friends locate a downed German plane, find the machine gun in working order, and hide it. When a school is hit by a German plane somewhat later, Chas steals sandbags to create a fortress, a safe place to display the machine gun. The rear gunner of the downed plane stumbles into their fortress and becomes the boys' prisoner. All this childish innocence dies when adults discover the fortress, the German is shot, and the young people are rounded up by their parents. *Fathom Five* is a rousing spy story set later in the war and the story of Chas's lost love and lost innocence. Westall had an amazing ability to portray the ambivalence of young people, and the alienation they feel mixed with love and duty.

Peter Carter's *The Hunted* is set in 1943 France when Italian troops are heading home after the Italian surrender to the Allies. Corporal Vito Salvani is fleeing when he finds a young Jewish boy, Judah, and takes the boy with him. A fanatic collaborator with the Nazis, Palet, believes the boy has jewels on him, and he sets out after the Italian and the boy, an example of evil hunting down good. *The Hunted* is a big book, but it stays with the reader long after it's been finished.

Harry Mazer's *The Last Mission* is set near the end of World War II. Jack Raab uses his older brother's identification to lie his way into the Air Force to destroy Hitler and to save democracy, all by himself; that dream lasts only a short time before Jack learns that the Air Force involves more training and boredom than fighting. When Jack does go to war, his first twenty-four bombing raids go well, but on the last mission, his plane is hit, all his buddies die, and he is captured. When he returns home, the principal at his old high school asks him to talk.

"I'm glad we won," he said. "We couldn't let Hitler keep going. We had to stop him. But most of all, I'm glad it's over." Had he said enough? There was a silence . . . a waiting silence. There was something more he had to say.

> "I don't like war. I thought I'd like it before. But war is stupid. War is one stupid thing after another. I saw my best friend killed. His name was Chuckie O'Brien. My whole crew was killed." Now he was talking, it was coming out, all the things he'd thought about for so long. "A lot of people were killed. Millions of people. Ordinary people. Not only by Hitler. Not only on our side. War isn't like the movies. It's not fun and songs. It's not about heroes. It's about awful, sad things, like my friend Chuckie that I'm never going to see again." His voice faltered.
>
> "I hope war never happens again," he said after a moment. "That's all I've got to say."

> He sat down. He hardly heard the applause. The floor of the radio room was still slippery with Chuckie's blood . . . Dave was still fumbling with his chute . . . the plane was still falling through the sky.

James Forman's finest work, too little known, is *Ceremony of Innocence.* Hans and Sophie Scholl, brother and sister in Nazi Germany, print and distribute literature attacking Hitler. Arrested by the Gestapo, they are urged by friends to escape. A lawyer, who Hans suspects is a Nazi, encourages them to plead insanity. They refuse, endure the mock trial, are found guilty, and are taken away to be executed. Hans is the last to die by the guillotine.

> Hans heard the sound of rollers, and at last there burst from his throat a cry, uttered in a great voice, a voice that combined anger, reproof, and an overwhelming conviction for which he was willing to die.
> "Long live freedom!"
> Then the greased blade fell. His teeth met through his tongue, and it was over.

Readers curious about the White Rose, a German movement to end the war, can find information in Richard Hanser's *A Noble Treason: The Revolt of the Munich Students Against Hitler;* Hermann Vinke's *The Short Life of Sophie Scholl;* Annette E. Dumbach and Jud Newborn's *Shattering the German Night: The Story of the White Rose;* and Inge Jens's *At the Heart of the White Rose: Letters and Diaries of Hans and Sophie Scholl.*

A few good books about life in Germany during World War II are Bernt Engelmann's *In Hitler's Germany: Daily Life in the Third Reich* and Wendelgard von Staden's *Darkness Over the Valley.* Barbara Gehrts's *Don't Say a Word* shows life in a Berlin suburb through the eyes of a daughter of an officer in the Luftwaffe. T. Degens's *The Visit* begins after the end of the war when young Kate Hofmann reads her aunt's diary to find out exactly how she died. Kate learns that her aunt had been a member of the Hitler Youth, and worse discoveries follow that.

Vietnam was the most unpopular war in American history, and for some time few novels or books about it were published. Now they abound in great numbers. Nonfiction such as Elizabeth Becker's *America's Vietnam War: A Narrative History* may help young readers unravel the strangeness that was Vietnam. What it was like to be in Vietnam from the point of view of the run-of-the-mill American soldier can be learned through Mark Baker's *Nam: The Vietnam War in the Words of the Men and Women Who Fought There;* Al Santoli's *Everything We Had: An Oral History of the Vietnam War by Thirty-Three American Soldiers Who Fought It;* and Kathryn Marshall's *In the Combat Zone: An Oral History of American Women in Vietnam.*[9]

When teacher Bill McCloud tried to decide what to tell his junior high students about Vietnam, he wrote to people involved in the war to get their advice. The result is his book *What Should We Tell Our Children About Vietnam?* Responses came from more than 100 people as different as Garry Trudeau, Jimmy Carter, Pete Seeger, Kurt Vonnegut, Alexander Haig, Henry Kissinger, and Barry Goldwater. Another unusual book on Vietnam is Laura Palmer's *Shrapnel in the Heart: Letters and Remembrances from the Vietnam Veterans Memorial.* All items left at the Vietnam

Memorial are saved by the U.S. Park Service, and from these letters, notes, and personal memorabilia Palmer chose deeply moving examples.

Unhappily, war does not stop with Vietnam. The incredible mess that has killed hundreds of thousands of people, many of them children and innocent civilians, in Serbia, Bosnia, and Croatia goes on, apparently without end. Zlata Filipovic's *Zlata's Diary: A Child's Life in Sarajevo* is precisely what the title says, a diary of the horrors and the friendship and the love and the blood that a fifth-grade girl in Sarajevo sees and feels every day. Ji Li Jiang's *Red Scarf Girl: A Memoir of the Cultural Revolution* is also just what the title says in telling about a time when a young Chinese girl was asked to betray her family.

Of all the many books on war, none has a more horrible indictment of the absurdity and cruelty of war than Roger Rosenblatt's *Children of War.* Rosenblatt circled the globe seeking out children in Belfast, Israel, Cambodia, Hong Kong, and Lebanon whom he asked about themselves and what war had done to them. A 9-year-old girl in Cambodia had made a drawing, and after a year of help by an American psychologist, she was able to explain how the instrument in the drawing worked. Rosenblatt writes:

> The children harvesting rice include Peov. She is the largest of the three. Whenever a child refused to work, he was punished with the circular device. The soldiers would place it over the child's head. Three people would hold it

Stories about war are especially touching when told through the eyes of young people. See Focus Box 8.3 for examples.

steady by means of ropes. . . . A fourth would grab hold of the ring at the end of the other rope. . . . When the rope with the ring was pulled . . . the child would be decapitated. A portable guillotine.

But it wasn't the soldiers who worked the device. It was the children.

Literature of the Holocaust

Only a few years back, anyone wishing to read about the Holocaust would read Anne Frank's *The Diary of a Young Girl*. Advanced students might find a few other sources, mostly historical, and the most mature students might view Alain Resnais's powerful short film "Night and Fog." Today an outpouring of films and books about the Holocaust means that no one can pretend not to know about the happenings and the evils that went with it.

 FILM BOX 8.2

The Holocaust (See Appendix D)

Anne Frank Remembered (1995, black and white/color, 123 min., PG; Director: Jon Blair) Kenneth Branaugh narrates and Glen Close reads excerpts from the diary and from interviews with people who knew Anne.

Au Revoir les Enfants (1988, color, 103 min., PG; Director: Louis Malle) Two boys become friends in 1944 Nazi-occupied France. One is a Catholic, the other a Jew hiding his identity by going to a Catholic boarding school where Nazis come looking for Jews.

The Diary of Anne Frank (1959, black and white, 156 min., NR; Director: George Stevens; with Millie Perkins and Shelley Winters) The movie is based on the diary and the Broadway play. The 1980 TV version is equally good.

Escape from Sobibor (1987, color, 150 min., made for TV; Director: Jack Gold; with Alan Arkin and Rutger Hauer) This television film is about the largest concentration camp breakout during World War II.

Life Is Beautiful (1998, Italian, color, 122 min., PG–13; Director: Roberto Benigni; with Benigni and Nicoletta Braschi) A Jew and his son are sent to a Nazi concentration camp. The father convinces his son that everything in the camp is a game and there is nothing to worry about.

Night and Fog (1975, French, black and white/color, 31 min., NR; Director: Alain Resnais) A voice-over shows us color photography of concentration camps as they are in 1975 and then in black and white as they were when human beings were slaughtered by the millions. This great short film may be the most intense view of the Holocaust we can stand to watch.

Playing for Time (1989, color, 150 min., made for TV; Director: David Mann; with Jane Alexander and Vanessa Redgrave) While other Auschwitz prisoners marched to their deaths, an orchestra made up of prisoners played on. Arthur Miller wrote the deeply moving script.

Schindler's List (1993, black and white/color, 195 min., R; Director: Steven Spielberg; with Liam Neeson, Ben Kingsley, and Ralph Fiennes) A war profiteer under the Nazis saves 1000 Jews he hires to work in his crockery plant.

Shoah (1986, black and white, 563 min. [5 video cassettes], NR; Director: Claude Lanzmann) Holocaust survivors tell their stories.

Sophie's Choice (1982, color 157 min., R; Director: Alan J. Pakula; with Meryl Streep and Kevin Kline) A Polish-Catholic woman was in a German concentration camp for two years and lost her two children. Now, in America, she needs to justify her existence.

Experiencing the Holocaust So It Won't Happen Again

The Beautiful Days of My Youth: My Six Months in Auschwitz and Plaszow by Ana Novac, translated from the French by George L. Newman. Holt, 1997. As Nazis kill and cremate concentration camp victims, Novac keeps a diary of the horrors.

Dancing on the Bridge of Avignon by Ida Vox. Houghton Mifflin, 1995. In Nazi-occupied Holland, Rosa de Jong finds solace in playing her beloved violin while being Jewish becomes more and more dangerous. See also *Anna Is Still Here* (Houghton Mifflin, 1993) and *Hide and Seek* (Houghton Mifflin, 1991).

Good Night, Maman by Norma Fox Mazer. Harcourt Brace, 1999. Karin Levi and her older brother flee Paris when the Nazis come. They are caught and sent to the only refugee camp on American soil at Fort Ontario in Oswego, New York.

Hiding to Survive: Stories of Jewish Children Rescued from the Holocaust by Maxine B. Rosenberg. Clarion, 1994. With dignity and restraint, fourteen Americans now in their 50s and 60s tell what they remember about being hidden. Pathos is added by then-and-now photos.

In Kindling Flame: The Story of Hannah Senesh, 1921–1944 by Linda Atkinson. Lothrop, Lee and Shepard, 1985. Senesh, a Hungarian Jew, was a resistance fighter. See also *Hannah Senesh: Her Life and Diary* (Schocken, 1972).

I Was There by Hans Peter Richter. Holt, 1972. The Third Reich destroys a Jewish family.

One, by One, by One: Facing the Holocaust by Judith Miller. Simon & Schuster, 1990. A journalist examines how West Germany, Austria, France, the Netherlands, Russia, and the United States each handled its responsibility for the Holocaust.

Return to Auschwitz by Kitty Hart. Atheneum, 1982. More than thirty years after surviving Auschwitz, Hart returns to the camp to help make an English documentary.

Reunion by Fred Uhlman. Farrar, Straus & Giroux, 1977. Two close friends, one the son of a Jewish doctor, one the son of an aristocrat, know the Nazi regime is soon to come.

Stella by Peter Wyden. Simon & Schuster, 1992. A Jewish boy denied an education, attends a Jewish school in Berlin. He falls in love with Stella and finds out much later that she was one of the Nazi's chief informants against German Jews.

Stories in Water by Donna Jo Napoli. Dutton, 1997. Roberto lives in Vienna during World War II and sneaks into a theater to see an American Western. German soldiers arrive, round up all the young males, including Roberto and his Jewish friend Samuele, and send them on a train to a labor camp.

Walk the Dark Streets by Edith Baer. Farrar, Straus & Giroux, 1998. After the Germans enter her city, Jews know they must flee.

Witnesses to War: Eight True-Life Stories of Nazi Persecution by Michael Leapman. Viking, 1998. Leapman, a British journalist who directed a film for the BBC, became intrigued with what happened after the war to the thousands of children of all races who were stolen from their parents and given to German families to raise.

One book of that outpouring is the 1995 definitive edition of Anne Frank's *Diary*, in which Anne becomes far more human and far less saintly. A number of passages touch on Anne's interest in sex and love, and Anne's entry for March 24, 1944, is sexual and analytical. The definitive edition should please readers who want to read about a human being with all her faults. It should almost equally please censors, who will have new reasons to find fault with a nearly perfect book. Miep Gies's *Anne Frank Remembered*, the autobiography of the woman who helped hide the Frank family, adds more detail and should be read alongside Anne's *Diary*.

Most young adults seek out books about young people caught in the Holocaust because they are better able to identify with people their own age or slightly older.

A book that is similar to Anne Frank's *Diary* is Etty Hillesum's *An Interrupted Life: The Diaries of Etty Hillesum, 1941–1943*. Being 27 years old, Hillesum probably knew precisely what her fate was to be. Her diary begins, "Here goes, then," and she writes of her love affairs, her graduate study at the University of Amsterdam, and her friends and ideas. She seems to have had little interest in politics until Jews were required to wear the yellow star. That jolted her, but she never sought to escape. In her last days, she volunteered to go with a group of condemned Jews to Westerbork Camp. She must have known that Westerbork was the usual first step to Auschwitz. Her journal complements Anne's *Diary*; Etty's irony and sophistication neatly counterpoint Anne's simplicity and innocence. *An Interrupted Life* is completed in *Letters from Westerbork*.

Students continue to read and love Johanna Reiss's *The Upstairs Room* and its sequel *The Journey Back*. The first book is a true story of the author and her sister, two young Jewish girls in Holland, kept safely in hiding by a gentile family for over two years during the Nazi occupation. The girls detest having to stay inside all the time, but when they learn from an underground newspaper what is happening to Jews across Europe, they realize how precarious is their life. The second book is about their trip back to their hiding place after the war. Karen Ray's *To Cross a Line* is about Egon Katz, a 17-year-old Jewish baker's apprentice who was certain that if he followed all the rules, he'd be safe. Then the Gestapo shows up with a warrant for him. Kati David's *A Child's War: World War II Through the Eyes of Children* is an account of World War II through the eyes of 15 children, 8 girls and 7 boys. Those eyes tell stories of fear and death and every horror that war brings about.

Thomas Keneally's *Schindler's List* should be read alongside any work about the Holocaust. But then so should the accounts of inmates of the concentration camps in Sylvia Rothchild's *Voices from the Holocaust*. Hazel Rochman and Darlene Z. McCampbell's *Bearing Witness: Stories of the Holocaust* is a marvelous collection of material that will shock readers just as other selections will give them pictures of real heroes. Hanna Volavkova's *I Never Saw Another Butterfly: Children's Drawings and Poems from Terezin Concentration Camp, 1941–1944* and Chana Byers Abells's *The Children We Remember* are unquestionably the most painful reading because they detail the massacre of the innocent.

Milton Meltzer does his usual fine job of collection and reporting in *Never to Forget: The Jews of the Holocaust*. Ten years later, he wrote a book about a much smaller number of people, *Rescue: The Story of How Gentiles Saved Jews in the Holocaust*. As he explained in the introduction:

> Now I have come to realize the great importance of recording not just the evidence of evil, but also the evidence of human nobility. Love, not hatred, is what the world needs. Rescue, not destruction. The stories in the book offer reason to hope. And hope is what we need, the way plants need sunlight.

Two other books deserve to be read alongside Meltzer—Eva Fogelman's *Conscience and Courage: Rescuers of Jews During the Holocaust*, and Maxine B. Rosenberg's *Hiding to Survive: Stories of Jewish Children Rescued from the Holocaust*. Ina R. Friedman's *The Other Victims: First Person Stories of Non-Jews Persecuted by the Nazis* is a worthy addition to Holocaust literature.

Ruth Minsky Sender's three volumes on her life from 1939 Poland to today show the horrors of the time. *The Cage* has 16-year-old Riva and her brothers taken by the Nazis to a concentration camp. It's a painful book, but it's also a brave book. *To Life* deals with post-World War II and Riva searching for her family. *The Holocaust Lady* is about Riva, now Ruth, who marries and comes to the United States and starts a family and decides that she must remember the past so that others will never relive it.

Some recent books have focused on the obvious fact that bigotry endures. In Lois Ruby's *Skin Deep,* Dan comes from a fatherless home. When multiethnic quotas keep him off the swimming team and from getting a job at the University of Colorado, he turns to the local skinheads for support, adopting their dress code but never quite accepting their racism. Han Nolan's *If I Should Die Before I Wake* portrays a young girl, a neo-Nazi initiate, who is in a coma from a motorcycle accident. In her dreams in the hospital, she becomes a young Jewish girl whose family lives in a ghetto and then Auschwitz. *The Wave* by Morton Rhue (pen name of Todd Strasser) has proved incredibly popular with many young people. In a high school history class, students wonder why the non-Nazi Germans let the Holocaust happen. The teacher responds by introducing students to a new movement, The Wave, which captures the imaginations and the hearts of students apparently longing for indoctrination and belief in certainties.

The best of all these books is Fran Arrick's *Chernowitz!* Bob Cherno, 15, looked back on his fights with Emmett Sundback, a bigot who ridiculed Bob's Jewishness. When Bob's school shows a film about the concentration camps, some students who have ridiculed Bob leave in tears because they understand the horrors of the Nazis' treatment of Jews and other minorities. To Arrick's credit, Sundback does not change and remains the horrible creep that he was.

Japanese Internment Camps in World War II

The most shameful American action during World War II began in February 1942, when President Roosevelt ordered the forced evacuation of anyone of Japanese ancestry on the West Coast into detention camps scattered in desolate places inland. More than 120,000 people were deported for the remainder of the war. Jeanne Wakatsuki Houston and James D. Houston's *Farewell to Manzanar* describes the first author's life in a camp ringed by barbed wire and guard towers and with open latrines. That three-year ordeal destroyed the family's unity and left them with a burdening sense of personal inadequacy that took years to remove.

John Armor and Peter Wright discovered many photographs that Ansel Adams took for his ironically titled 1944 book, *Born Free and Equal,* and Armor and Wright wrote a text to go with Adams's pictures and titled the book *Manzanar.* With a commentary by John Hersey, *Manzanar* is largely a record of a people who had a right to be bitter but were instead making conditions at the camp work for them.

In February 1983, a Congressional committee concluded its deliberations and agreed that internment of Japanese-American citizens was a "grave injustice." The commission said that the relocation was motivated by "racial prejudices, war hysteria, and failure of political leadership," not by any military considerations.[10] Five years later, the House passed and sent on to President Reagan legislation giving apologies and $20,000 tax-free payments to Japanese-American survivors of World War II internment camps. Typical of bureaucratic bumbling, it was 1990 before the first checks were sent out. American justice may be slow—in this case 45 years—but it often may arrive.

Personal Experiences

Death is an eternal mystery, as anyone who has read *Hamlet,* Dickinson's poetry, or Edgar Lee Masters's *Spoon River Anthology* knows full well. Young adults sometimes complain about the "morbid" or "sick" literature adults foist on them: *Macbeth,* Romantic poetry, "Thanatopsis," *Death of a Salesman, Oedipus Rex,* and "A Rose for Emily." In reality, both adults and young adults may be preoccupied with death, but they prefer to choose their own literature. Surely it could be argued that reading such literature helps young adults develop an appreciation of their own lives as well as a code of values to hold dear in the dread times to come.

Books about young people dying have been popular for years, including Doris Lund's *Eric,* about her son's losing battle with leukemia; John Gunther's *Death Be Not Proud,* about his son's slow death from a brain tumor; and three different versions of the story of Chicago Bears running back Brian Piccolo and his struggle with cancer. The favorite of this last group is usually William Blinn's *Brian's Song,* created from the television movie, which is still shown in reruns. The movie plot came originally from a chapter in Gale Sayers's *I Am Third.* Jeanne Morris wrote the most complete version of the story in *Brian Piccolo: A Short Season.* She and Piccolo worked together on the manuscript during his hospitalization.

Because readers identify with the young protagonists, it's particularly satisfying when they win their struggle against an illness or a disability. Two books by young cancer patients are wise and funny by turns. Although they bring tears to their readers, that is clearly not their purpose. Matthew Lancaster's *Hang Toughf* is a solid little classic in which a 10-year-old author gives sound advice to other kids who have cancer. As he says, it's not fair, "but it happened, and you and I have to accept it." And if your hair falls out, then "if your friends laugh at you, they're not very good friends." Eight-year-old Jason Gaes hated other books about kids with cancer because they always died, and he had cancer and he hadn't died, so he wrote *My Book for Kids with Cansur,* almost as good as (and sometimes funnier than) *Hang Toughf.* Erma Bombeck tuned into the same theme with the help of young cancer patients for her book *I Want to Grow Hair, I Want to Grow Up, I Want to Go to Boise: Children Surviving Cancer.*

Edie Clark's *The Place He Made* and Edith Kunhardt Davis's *I'll Love You Forever, Anyway* are two warm and wonderful books about two people who learn to survive the death of someone they deeply love. *Paula* by Isabel Allende comes from an important political person who found something far more troubling than her political battles—the slow death of her 27-year-old daughter, Paula.

More Upbeat Personal Experiences

Most personal experience stories are not about death and illness but instead about adventures, successes, and experiences the writers feel so strongly that they wish to share them with readers. Some are career stories, for example, former surgeon-general C. Everett Koop's *Koop: The Memoirs of America's Family Doctor.* Janet Buell in *Ancient Horsemen of Siberia* spells out the complications, both technological and social, of excavating the burial site of a Pazyryk woman and her horses and other possessions from a frozen tomb in southern Siberia. She also shows how archeologists use such information to make educated guesses about ancient peoples. A companion volume is *Greenland Mummies* about the discovery of 500-year-old mummified corpses on a Greenland fjord.

Partly because of their fondness for animals, many readers appreciate Jane Goodall's *My Life with the Chimpanzees.* Animal lovers might also like Anne E. Neimark's *Wild Heart: The Story of Joy Adamson.* This 110-page biography, with an album of 34 photos, will lead some students to read Adamson's own books. Other animal-related books include Diane Ackerman's *The Moon by Whale Light: And Other Adventures Among Bats, Penguins, Crocodilians, and Whales,* and Candace Savage's *Wolves.*

Although Farley Mowat's books are not as upbeat, they make fascinating reading. In *A Whale for the Killing,* he thought he had found the perfect place to live until he discovered his neighbors were savages who took pleasure in killing a trapped whale. His angry prose also typifies *Never Cry Wolf* and *Sea of Slaughter.* He's less angry in his earlier *The Dog Who Wouldn't Be* and *Owls in the Family. Born Naked* is Mowat's childhood memories of 1920s and 1930s Canada. Given Mowat's irritation with people in most of his books, *Born Naked* is a relatively quiet and gentle book.

Some authors tell their own quite ordinary stories of growing up in ways that make young readers feel privileged to get acquainted with a new friend. Annie Dillard's *An American Childhood* tells about growing up in the 1950s and 1960s. Tobias Wolff's *This Boy's Life* is set at about the same time, in Seattle, where he grew up longing to be a "boy of dignity."

Sometimes memories are incredibly funny to readers, although just how amusing the events were to the writer early in his life is open to question. The first paragraph in Mark Salzman's *Lost in Place: Growing Up Absurd in Suburbia* is witty and certainly likely to grab the attention of most readers:

> When I was thirteen years old I saw my first kung fu movie, and before it ended I decided that the life of a wandering Zen monk was the life for me. I announced my willingness to leave East Ridge Junior High School immediately and give up all material things, but my parents did not share my enthusiasm. They made it clear that I was not to become a wandering Zen monk until I had finished high school. In the meantime I could practice kung fu and meditate down in the basement. So I immersed myself in the study of Chinese boxing and philosophy with the kind of dedication that is possible only when you don't yet have to make a living, when you are too young to drive and when you don't have a girlfriend.

The success of personal experience books, as well as autobiographies, depends largely on the quality of the writing because there isn't a plot for readers to get excited about, and honest accounts lack the kinds of literary exaggeration that make for intriguing villains and heroes. One aspect of personal experience books that makes them attractive to young readers is that they are by people looking back on experiences they had when they were young. For example, Robin Graham, author of *Dove,* (see Focus Box 8.5 for other personal experience stories on our Honor List) was only 16 when he set sail on his own boat to go around the world. Steven Callahan, author of *Adrift: Seventy-Six Days Lost at Sea,* was 29 when he set sail. Bruce Feiler in *Under the Big Top* is an adult, but he remembers back to his childhood when he learned to juggle with a handful of oranges and when he first developed his love affair with the circus.

In the personal experience books about adult protagonists that teenagers enjoy, the adults are likely to be unencumbered by family responsibilities. For example,

FOCUS BOX 8.5

Honor List: Biographies and Personal Experiences (See also the Personal Memoirs by Honor List Authors on p. 8.)

Abigail Adams: Witness to a Revolution by Natalie S. Bober. Simon & Schuster/Atheneum, 1995. Some 2,000 letters written by Abigail Adams (wife of one U.S. president and mother of another) were saved by grateful recipients. These letters were a major source of information for Bober, who warned, "We must not look at the eighteenth century through a lens ground in the 1990s."

Columbus and the World Around Him by Milton Meltzer. Franklin Watts, 1990. Meltzer brought his usual careful research and writing to this biography, which helps readers understand the controversy over the 500th anniversary of Columbus's arrival in the Americas.

Dove by Robin L. Graham. HarperCollins, 1972. Young readers like this true story of a 16-year-old doing something that most kids can only dream about. He set off in his own boat and sailed around the world.

Eleanor Roosevelt: A Life of Discovery by Russell Freedman. Clarion, 1993. More than 120 photos, along with intriguing details and insights, make this large-format biography especially appealing.

The Life and Death of Crazy Horse by Russell Freedman. Holiday, 1996. As white people flocked to the West, the Oglala Sioux leader, Crazy Horse, recognized that a fight to the death was likely. He was foreseeing the Battle of the Little Big Horn.

The Long Road to Gettysburg by Jim Murphy. Clarion, 1992. Murphy used the personal journals of John Dooley, an 18-year-old Southern lieutenant, and Thomas Galway, a 17-year-old Union corporal, as the centerpiece of his retelling of the story of the Battle of Gettysburg.

Unconditional Surrender: U. S. Grant and the Civil War by Albert Marrin. Atheneum, 1994. Marrin nicely balances this story of a man whose life alternated between peaks of success and depths of failure.

---

mature young readers enjoy such travel books as Peter Matthiessen's *African Silences,* Charles Kuralt's *A Life on the Road,* and Bruce Chatwin's *What Am I Doing Here?*

Whether to consider a book a personal experience or an autobiography is often up to the reader. For example, Maya Angelou's *I Know Why the Caged Bird Sings* and its three sequels are usually considered to be autobiographies because they move chronologically through Angelou's life, but it might be argued that they are personal experience stories because each book is about only a part of her life. There is also a crossover between personal experience accounts and the new journalism discussed in Chapter Nine.

Biographies

The Greeks enjoyed stories about the gods of Mount Olympus and hero tales about the moral descendants of the gods. Hero tales, however, had an added feature that helped listeners identify with the protagonists. Unlike the gods, who live forever, heroes had one human parent, which meant that they were mortal. The most that the gods could risk in any undertaking was their pride, but heroes could lose their lives.

When we're reading modern fiction, we know that the author can always bring the protagonist out alive; however, in true hero tales—biographies—protagonists risk their lives, just as readers would in the same situation. This adds credibility and intensity because the reader thinks, "If this happened to someone else, then it might happen to me."

John Dryden introduced the word *biography* to English readers in his 1683 edition of Plutarch's *Parallel Lives*. While the term may have been new, the form was well known to readers who had long read the lives of famous generals and politicians and religious leaders. People today remain fascinated by biographies. Where else can we see the uniqueness and authenticity of one person's life and, at the same time, emotions and problems that all human beings face.

Some of the best biographers for young people also write other kinds of informative books, so they are featured in Chapter Nine. To learn about the kinds of biographies they write, check the information on Russell Freedman, James Cross Giblin, James Haskins, Albert Marrin, Milton Meltzer, and Fredrick L. and Patricia McKissack in the next chapter.

Traditionally, biographies—especially those for young readers, for example, Parson Weems's biography of George Washington—were about heroic figures whose lives were models for mere mortals to emulate. Today's biographies for young adults are likely to be written more objectively, providing a balance of both strengths and weaknesses. They demonstrate how the subject and the reader share similar emotions. Both have fears and insecurities, and both succumb to temptations and vanities. After reading a good biography, the reader feels a kinship with the subject, not so much in spite of as because of the character's human frailties.

To say that a biography is written "objectively" does not mean that it is written without feeling. For biographies to ring true, the author must become immersed in the subject's life so that he or she can write with passion and commitment. This implies a point of view, not one imposed by an author who set out to prove a preconceived idea but a unifying force that guided the person's life and was discovered by the author through his or her research.

Few of us admit to selecting the biographies we are going to purchase and promote on the basis of how we feel about the subject, but that's like one of those old clichés, such as "Never judge a book by its cover," that is honored more in word than in deed. Someone could write a Ph.D. dissertation on how American values have changed over the last thirty years as reflected by whose biographies were put on the shelves of libraries.

In the early 1960s, readers at almost any library would find a predominance of biographies about white men who were inventors, statesmen, soldiers, and business leaders. During the 1970s, the imbalance became so obvious, particularly in school libraries, that educators and publishers took steps to correct the situation by preparing biographies about previously unsung heroes, including members of minority groups, women, handicapped individuals, and people whose contributions were not in military, political, or business spheres. Of course, there is still room for good books presenting new information on both traditional and nontraditional heroes (see Focus Box 8.6); for example, Rhoda Blumberg's *What's the Deal?: Jefferson, Napoleon, and the Louisiana Purchase* gives new insights into two historical giants. She makes the story of the greatest "deal" in American history read like a suspense novel. Steven H. Jaffe, in his *Who Were the Founding Fathers? Two Hundred Years of Reinventing American History,* presents alternate stories about George Washington,

More Excellent Biographies (See also Focus Box 5.3 Sports Nonfiction, p. 156)

Alexander Graham Bell: Making Connections by Naomi Pasachoff. Oxford University Press, 1996. The focus of this biography is on Bell's work as an educator, particularly with the deaf. An insert illustrates the interconnectedness of sound, speech, and hearing, and how Bell's inventions aided the process.

An American Hero: The True Story of Charles A. Lindbergh by Barry Denenberg. Scholastic, 1996. This is the sixth well-written and attractively designed book that Denenberg has written for young readers. He is especially good at presenting various sides to controversies as he did in his *Voices from Vietnam.*(Scholastic, 1997).

Behind the Mask: The Life of Queen Elizabeth I by Jane Resh Thomas. Clarion, 1998. Thomas's highly acclaimed biography needs to be in every high school library not only for background reading when studying British literature but also to entice students into looking at women in history.

Clara Schumann: Piano Virtuoso by Susanna Reich. Clarion, 1999. Photos, advertisements, programs, letters, and diary entries add interest to this story of the remarkably talented young woman who married composer Robert Schumann when he was one of her father's students. Readers learn not only about the musical world of the 1800s but also about the complications of raising a large family and battling the mental illness that struck Robert Schumann.

The Ingenious Mr. Peale: Painter, Patriot, and Man of Science by Janet Wilson. Simon & Schuster/Atheneum, 1996. A lively biography of a lively individual, Wilson's book shows an early American managing to balance three distinctively different careers.

Leonardo da Vinci for Kids: His Life and Ideas by Janis Herbert. Chicago Review, 1998. Herbert writes not just about Leonardo's art but about his interests in science and technology as shown through his designs for diving suits and hang gliders. Web sites are listed for further information.

Mother Jones: Fierce Fighter for Workers' Rights by Judith Pinkerton Josephson. Lerner, 1997. People who have heard of Mother Jones only as the name of a periodical will appreciate this account of one of America's first and most effective labor organizers and reformers.

Samuel Adams: The Father of American Independence by Dennis Brindell Fradin. Clarion, 1998. Decades before other Americans saw the necessity for breaking with England, Samuel Adams was convinced it had to be done and set out to convince other powerful colonists to help including his cousin John Adams and his friends John Hancock and Paul Revere.

Shadow Catcher: The Life and Work of Edward S. Curtis by Laurie Lawlor. Walker, 1994. Curtis spent thirty years taking pictures of Native Americans. Lawlor continues Curtis's work by documenting and bringing to people's attention the plight of Native Americans in the early 1900s.

Thomas Jefferson, and Benjamin Franklin. The stories teach a powerful lesson about political spin as well as history in general.

One of the best new biographies is Norman H. Finkelstein's *With Heroic Truth: The Life of Edward R. Murrow.* Readers will come away not only with a new appreciation of an individual but also with insights into twentieth century American history and into the establishment of current practices and standards in broadcast media.

Young adults interested in dance will appreciate Frances Mason's *I Remember Balanchine: Recollections of the Ballet Master by Those Who Knew Him* and Agnes de Mille's *Martha: The Life and Work of Martha Graham.* Russell Freedman's *Martha Gra-*

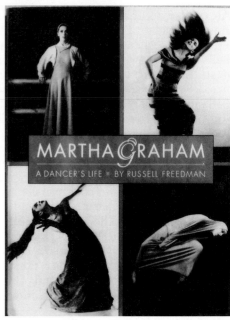

Well-done biographies have the advantage of teaching about both individuals and the times in which they lived and influenced those around them.

ham: A Dancer's Life is beautifully laid out and illustrated. Ellen Levine's *Anna Pavlova: Genius of the Dance* (see Levine's statement on p. 263) is another excellent book.

Young readers who have particular favorite authors should enjoy biographies about those favorites. Many teens remember Roald Dahl's *Charlie and the Chocolate Factory* with fondness, but whether they will enjoy Jeremy Treglown's *Roald Dahl: A Biography,* learning that he was not a nice person, may be questionable. Almost certainly, fans of Dr. Seuss will love Judith Morgan and Neil Morgan's *Dr. Seuss and Mr. Geisel: A Biography.* Fans of *The Little Prince,* and they are legion, who read Stacy Schiff's *Saint-Exupery: A Biography* will get a picture of a man of action, a lover of flying, and a man who wrote some exceptional books. With Daniel Dyer's *Jack London: A Biography,* there's bound to be a circular effect with its readers searching out London's fiction and readers of his fiction getting extra pleasure from the biography. Whether Jay Parini's *John Steinbeck: A Biography* convinces readers that Steinbeck is a major writer is unclear, but young adults who love *Of Mice and Men* and *The Grapes of Wrath* will surely enjoy Parini's book. Catherine Reef has also written a biography, *John Steinbeck,* which is a large-size book with plenty of photos and brief excerpts from Steinbeck's writing. Sharon O'Brien's *Willa Cather,* published in part of Chelsea House's Lives of Notable Gay Men and Lesbians series, is a solid study of Cather's life and work, not just her sex life.

Stephanie Cowell's *Nicholas Cooke* tells Shakespeare's story through this fictional friend who is an actor, a doctor, a soldier, and a priest as well as a friend of Kit

ELLEN LEVINE
On a Grand Adventure

I write to engage my reader. In nonfiction the challenge is particularly great because many young people equate nonfiction with encyclopedias, which to them means cell-aching boredom. For me, however, nonfiction is a grand adventure. How, for example, do people solve daily living problems that result from the total destruction of their world, as in the great San Francisco earthquake of 1906. Well, some strapped roller skates to the feet of bathtubs in order to push their belongings to safety. This is not boring. How do veterinarians crack the mystery of a diagnosis when their patients can't speak? Or, why should anyone today care about Anna Pavlova, born in 1881, who once said, "I am haunted by the need to dance"?

For me, there can also be another concern, and that's to try to contribute to the development of an ethical being (my reader), one capable of taking moral positions even if it means standing alone against the crush of some popular belief. Such a person, adult or child, is a true hero, and each one of us has the potential to be heroic.

Young people equate the civil rights movement, to take an example, with Martin Luther King and other famous adults. And so it is important for them to know that "ordinary" folks like their parents and kids like themselves were essential to the success of the movement. They should know that before Rosa Parks, a teenager, a real person named Claudette Colvin in Montgomery, Alabama, refused to give up her bus seat when ordered by the driver. They should also know that the Supreme Court case holding that bus segregation was unconstitutional has Colvin's not Parks's name on it.

Once, before speaking to students in a Michigan school, I chatted with four fourth-grade boys, all African-American. Among other subjects, I have written about the underground railroad and the civil rights movement of the 1950s and '60s. One of the boys asked me, "Why do you write so much stuff on black people?" A good question that I tried to answer. Some might dismiss this in today's parlance as "politically correct." Nonsense. It's about right and wrong. That's not to say there aren't complexities and subtleties in any story. But there aren't "two sides" in the moral sense to every issue. The fact that you may tell the story of white southern slave owners without caricature, doesn't for a moment take away from the evil of slavery.

How do young people learn morality? How do they choose heroes? There are bullies in the schoolyard as well as in the political arena, and it takes courage to defy them whatever the context. How do we teach that courage to act with compassion toward another?

One young white girl, after reading my book on the underground railroad, somewhat wistfully asked her parents, "Don't we have any black ancestors?" She was hungry to be part of that ethical as well as physical adventure. And how gloriously color-blind. One can only hope adulthood doesn't corrupt the grandness of her wish.

Ellen Levine's books include *Darkness over Denmark: The Danish Resistance and the Rescue of the Jews,* Holiday House, 1999; *A Fence Away from Freedom: Japanese Americans and World War II,* Putnam, 1995; *Anna Pavlova: Genius of the Dance,* Scholastic, 1995; and *Freedom's Children: Young Civil Rights Activists Tell Their Own Stories,* Putnam, 1993.

Morley. Dominic Shellard's *William Shakespeare* is a good introduction to Elizabethan England and the history of the theater. It also does a good job of demonstrating the difference between what is actually known about the period and why other "facts" are still disputed.

There is always a place for biographies about women and men who have changed the world. Patricia C. McKissack and Fredrick McKissack's *Sojourner Truth: Ain't I a Woman?* is a compelling life of a woman who began as a slave and ultimately emerged as a powerful African-American voice in the United States. Ellen Chesler's *Woman of Valor: Margaret Sanger and the Birth Control Movement in America* is the life of a nurse who became a militant socialist and ultimately saved many other women's lives. Carolyn G. Heilbrun's *The Education of a Woman: The Life of Gloria Steinem* portrays the woman who may have had more power in the women's movement than any other.

Collective Biographies

Collective biographies (i.e., one book presenting the stories of several individuals) have become increasingly popular because authors can write about individuals whose lives may not have been chronicled fully enough to provide information for an entire book. Collective biographies are also an efficient way to get information about previously ignored individuals into a library. Authors usually bring together the stories of people who have something in common. This development of a unifying theme may be the best way to show trends and connections among various subjects. For example, Russell Freedman's *Indian Chiefs,* the biographies of six western Indian chiefs during the 1800s, is a stronger condemnation of Anglo treatment of Native Americans than it would have been had he told only one of the stories. In a similar way readers get a broader picture than if they were reading about only one first lady when they read *The Smithsonian Book of the First Ladies: Their Lives, Times, and Issues,* edited by Edith P. Mayo with a foreword by Hillary Rodham Clinton. Mayo is curator of the Division of Political History in the American part of the Smithsonian Institution, so she had all of her experience plus the resources of the Smithsonian to use for this beautifully designed and illustrated history of forty-three remarkable women.

William Drake's *The First Wave: Women Poets in America, 1915–1945* shows that many women are interested in literary endeavors through presenting accounts of twenty-seven highly acclaimed poets, including Marianne Moore, Edna St. Vincent Millay, and Amy Lowell. Jim Haskins's *One More River to Cross: The Stories of Twelve Black Americans* counters the stereotype that African-Americans have succeeded only as entertainers and athletes by presenting the stories of businesswoman C. J. Walker, explorer Matthew Henson, diplomat Ralph Bunche, congresswoman Shirley Chisolm, and astronaut Ronald McNair. Peter Irons's *The Courage of Their Convictions: Sixteen Americans Who Fought Their Way to the Supreme Court* shows the variety of problems the justices are asked to solve.

Ruth Ashby and Deborah Gore Ohrn's *Herstory: Women Who Changed the World* is a marvelous collection of brief comments (1–3 pages) about women from Queen Hatshepsut in the fifteenth century B.C. to Rigoberta Menchú of contemporary Guatemala. In between those women are brief comments about Jane Austen, Charlotte Perkins Gilman, Beatrix Potter, Mary Leakey, Barbara Jordan, and many others, 120 in all. Two collective biographies of writers by Rebecca Carroll should attract young people. *I Know What the Red Clay Looks Like: The Voice and Vision of Black Women Writers* has excerpts from fifteen black authors, including Rita Dove, Gloria Naylor, Lorene Cary, and Nikki Giovanni. *Swing Low: Black Men Writing* has works by sixteen authors, including Henry Louis Gates, Jr., Ishmael Reed, and August Wilson.

Gold Rush Women by Claire Rudolf Murphy and Jane G. Haigh takes a look at the women who flocked to Alaska in the 1890s, when gold was discovered. One-tenth of the adventurers looking for riches were women. The authors give short biographies of twenty-three women including two native women who helped discover the gold and then taught survival skills to newcomers, two sisters who opened a bank, an African-American woman who gave birth on the trail, and a woman who panned gold by lantern light and became one of the first millionaires. Ina Chang's *A Separate Battle: Women and the Civil War* looks beyond Scarlett O'Hara to show what real women did during the Civil War.

In *The Greatest Generation,* newscaster Tom Brokaw tells the stories of some fifty Americans who came of age during the depression and World War II. Their stories are grouped into such categories as Ordinary People, Women in Uniform and Out, Heroes, Shame, and Love, Marriage and Commitment. While the book was printed for an adult audience, it is accessible to older teens who might be interested in learning about their grandparents' generation. Studs Terkel's *Coming of Age: The Story of Our Century by Those Who've Lived It* includes the voices of more than seventy people, the youngest of whom is 70 and the oldest 99. The cast ranges from well-known people such as dancer Katherine Dunham and actress Uto Hagen to scholar John Kenneth Galbraith to the unknowns of the world. Similar to all of Terkel's collective biographies, this one ranges from charming chitchat to resounding ideas. A more specific group is looked at in *Hell Fighters: African American Soldiers in World War I* by Michael L. Cooper. In 1916, when the Fifteenth New York Voluntary Infantry of the National Guard went to serve in France, it was segregated from other soldiers, deprived of basic uniforms and equipment, and controlled by white officers. General John J. Pershing intervened on their behalf, and in May of 1918, they were renamed the 369th Regiment and, because of their bravery in combat, came home to a hero's welcome in Harlem.

We rarely think about young people changing the course of the world, but Ellen Levine's *Freedom's Children: Young Civil Rights Activists Tell Their Own Stories* should make young people proud of other young people. Joseph Berger's *The Young Scientists: America's Future and the Winning of the Westinghouse* tells of Berger's study of the winners of the annual national Westinghouse Science Talent Search. Berger notes one of the major problems with " . . . most science classes. Students learn scientific concepts and facts that they feed back on tests. They do not learn methods of research, and they do not perform any research." Berger becomes excited, and so will readers, as he learns how dedicated these young scientists are and how they have developed their own research.

Debunking versus Fawning Biographies

We need to keep our wits about us as we read biographies because the authors may have agendas not immediately clear to readers. They may want subtly to poison the reader or to vent their spleens about any number of things, from the subject of the biography to an institution or anything at all.

Controversy erupted in September of 1999, when bits of *Dutch: A Memoir of Ronald Reagan* were released ahead of the September 30th publication date. Pulitzer Prize–winning author Edmund Morris assumed the "dread title of authorized biographer" for President Reagan in 1985. He had been working on the book for fourteen years, and in the process bemoaned his fate and confessed to fellow historians attending at least one scholarly conference that he was suffering from writer's block and just could not make the story come alive. He finally got off square one by reinventing his own life and making himself a character in the story coming in and out of Reagan's life ever since he glimpsed the future president on a Dixon High School football field.

Critics were quick to offer opinions. Some defended the use of such a dramatic device because today's biographers have to compete with every celebrity whose life is being laid out for public consumption. Others were appalled that what they had anticipated for so long as the "definitive" biography of Reagan, was coming out as a mixture of fact and fiction. Charles Krauthammer, writing in *Time,* listed several recent biographies (all with political impact) in which great chunks have been proved false, but the books are still assigned to college students and respected and defended as "postmodern" or as people "personalizing" their groups' stories. Books that are in fact banal and formulaic, Krauthammer wrote, are "harder to dismiss" when they are presented as truth. He concluded:

> At least Morris is not out to deceive. His invention . . . is just a device, open and bold. Yet that very openness tells us how far we've come in bending the notion of historical truth. Morris' Morris could not have happened 10 or 20 years ago. He stands on the shoulders of giants: the brazen confabulators who make up their histories and the slavish academics who justify them.[11]

In the debunking biography, a popular hero or an institution or anything treasured by many people is taken down from a pedestal. Although such books are certainly "antihero," they differ from true examples of the literary meaning of the term in that the subject of a debunking biography is not written about with sympathy. Among the most famous are Kitty Kelley's *Nancy Reagan: The Unauthorized Biography* and Christina Crawford's *Mommie Dearest,* which debunked actress Joan Crawford for the way she played her real-life role of mother. Jim Bouton's *Ball Four: My Life and Hard Times Throwing the Knuckleball in the Big Leagues* was a debunking of professional baseball, and Samuel Wilson Fussell's *Muscle: Confessions of an Unlikely Body Builder* debunked weightlifting. Books such as these serve as antidotes for gullibility and excessive hero worship. Not to read debunking books is to miss one facet of humanity, but to read only debunking books is to produce only debunkers, and that we already have in sufficient number.

Fawning biographies are just as extreme as are the vicious ones. Michiko Kakutani commenting on contemporary biographies wrote:

> It's not surprising that a society obsessed with the Bobbitts, the Menendez brothers, Amy Fisher, and Tonya Harding should spawn a growing number of gossipy, speculative and just plain tasteless biographies. Indeed, this development is indicative, in many respects, of broader currents in our society at large, for biography writing has served, throughout its history, as a kind of mirror of the cultural Zeitgeist.

Borrowing a phrase from Freud, Joyce Carol Oates has called this disturbing new subgenre "pathography." Kakutani says that the motifs are "dysfunction and disaster, illnesses and pratfalls, failed marriages and failed careers, alcoholism and breakdowns and outrageous conduct." She went on to describe how sensationalized some of these books are "wallowing in squalor and foolishness," playing with the "shrill theme" of "failed promise," if not outright "tragedy."[12]

Autobiographies

Autobiographies have an immediate and obvious appeal to readers. "Who," we ask ourselves, "would know more about this person than the person? Who could better tell us this person's story?" The truth may be that almost any other good writer could have been more honest and could have written a better story. Even a tiny bit of thought might suggest to us that most people are poor witnesses of their lives. Most of us want to look good to others. Most of us might even leave out a significant piece of our lives that still embarrasses us or humiliates us or leaves us feeling unsure of ourselves and our motives. Most of us know friends who are incapable of telling us precisely, much less accurately, what happened at certain turns in their lives.

This is not to say that autobiographies are automatically untrustworthy, only that they may not tell the whole story or that certain parts may be left out, possibly for good reason, possibly not. Writers of autobiographies are not necessarily out to con us, but they may be. Worse yet, they may even con themselves. In today's media-oriented world, autobiographies may simply be business ventures designed to promote a celebrity's fame. In the introduction to comedian Tim Allen's *Don't Stand Too Close to a Naked Man* he jokingly explained that he was practically forced to write his book because:

> Hyperion [his publisher] is owned by Disney, which also owns my television show. Disney owns Disneyland and Disney World. Disney also owns Euro-Disney, Tokyo-Disney, and a Disney store in every city, town, and hamlet in the world. *They also have my cat.*

He ended his introductory chapter with, "And if all goes well and you buy lots and lots of copies, maybe Disney will give me back my cat."

Throughout the 1990s comedians were among the most popular celebrity authors. For three years in a row, the nonfiction division of Bantam books made its highest profits on comedians' books: Jerry Seinfeld's *Signlanguage* in 1993, Paul Reiser's *Couplehood* in 1994, and Ellen DeGeneres's *My Point . . . And I Do Have One* in 1995.

Jim Koncz, one of our doctoral students, studied ten of these autobiographies written by comedians who were starring in their own shows. Brett Butler, the star of *Grace Under Fire,* wrote *Knee Deep in Paradise,* which Koncz found to be the best written and to provide the most genuine information and insights into Butler's life; however, it was one of the least popular. The most popular, such as *Signlanguage,* which was on the *New York Times* best-seller list for thirty-three weeks, were extensions of the shows and the personalities demonstrated in performances. Koncz's conclusion was that most buyers did not care as much about the real person as about the comedy character.

It's probably a good idea for adults to discuss with kids the whole concept of celebrity biographies and autobiographies and the role of ghost writers or "book doctors." An article in the *New York Times Book Review* (January 5, 1997) mentioned that Charles Barkley and O. J. Simpson, both "claimed to have been misquoted in their ghostwritten autobiographies—thus inviting jeers, catcalls and obloquy." John Callahan, the disabled cartoonist who shocks the sensibilities of the politically correct, was more than candid in acknowledging the help he received on his *Don't Worry, He Won't Get Far on Foot.* In his thank-you's, he wrote,

> Finally, David Kelly, working from hundreds of hours of my tapes, drafted each chapter and then rewrote it again and again and again and *again* until no trace of his own voice remained. "We're not going to have one of those goddam *as-told-to* books," he would snarl. And we don't.

While celebrity autobiographies and biographies are the ones that get in the news and are likely to be requested from libraries, some of them present problems for educators. One such problem comes from Andy Warhol's statement that each of us will have "15 minutes of fame." The problem is that it takes more than fifteen minutes for a book to be written, published, and purchased, so schools and libraries are usually a step behind. By the time a biography or autobiography of some new celebrity has gone through a rigorous selection procedure, the subject may no longer be of interest.

Many of the books also present questionable or outright immoral concepts. For example, Wilt Chamberlain's *A View from Above* has a chapter, "On Sex and Love: What Rules the World," which makes clear that he believes he is lucky because he has had sexual relations with nearly 20,000 women. That may impress Chamberlain, but it is likely to bother most adults. Adults have also been bothered by the popularity of Vincent Bugliosi's *Helter Skelter: The True Story of the Manson Murders,* which is still read by young people as Charles Manson periodically pops up in the news.

With questionable books, it's usually better that teenagers have a chance to read the whole book rather than just get the smatterings of sexual or violent titillation that appear in the media. One thing we can feel confident in suggesting is that when it comes to selecting books about which you are unsure, check out your initial reaction with others. Talk to colleagues, parents, and students. Perhaps it's the last group that is most important to include in discussions about book selection because unless someone starts young people along such a line of thinking, they may never understand that reading about someone's life does not necessarily mean emulating everything about that person. As librarian Mary Mueller observed:

> Our past and present are full of personages who lived outside traditional rules. They often used poor judgment or acted in a less-than-exemplary fashion. . . . How can we expect our students to really see the personality of Harry Truman without letting them see the tenacity, salty language, and temper that so characterized him?[13]

Connections Between History and Biography

We borrowed the title for this chapter from an "Up for Discussion" piece, which Mueller wrote for *School Library Journal* entitled "History and History Makers: Give YAs the Whole Picture."[14] Mueller, a librarian at Rolla Junior High School in Missouri, was recommending biographies and histories as mutually complementary because individuals are shaped by the times and circumstances of their lives, which they, in turn, influence and shape for themselves as well as for those around them and those who will follow. In making a plea for librarians to be assertive in recommending biographies alongside history books, she pointed out how few books about the 1960s, the civil rights movement, and the Vietnam War include information about the "rich, complex character of Lyndon Johnson, a man who greatly influenced all three and who is extremely important to any understanding of these happenings and the era in which they occurred." She also argued for updating the 900s sections in our libraries, noting that in times of shrinking budgets we hesitate to weed out historical books and feel more justified in spending money for a new computer book than for a biography of someone who lived 200 years ago.

We'll end this chapter with the same plea that Mueller made; there are so many changes in attitudes and outlooks, "to say nothing of revisionists' theories," that history and biography sections need just as much loving care and attention—including weeding, replacing, and promoting—as do any other sections of a library.

Notes

[1]Henry Seidel Canby, "What Is Truth?" *Saturday Review of Literature* 4 (December 31, 1927): 481.

[2]Richard Stengel, "Books: American Myth 101," *Time,* December 23, 1991, p. 78.

[3]Betty Carter and Richard F. Abrahamson, *From Delight to Wisdom: Nonfiction for Young Adults* (Oryx Press, 1990), p. 180.

[4]Betty Carter and Richard F. Abrahamson, "A Conversation with Brent Ashabranner," in *From Delight to Wisdom: Nonfiction for Young Adults* (Oryx Press, 1990), p. 101.

[5]Christopher Collier, "Criteria for Historical Novels," *School Library Journal* 29 (August 1982): 32.

[6]Christopher Collier, "Fact, Fiction, and History: The Role of the Historian, Writer, Teacher, and Reader," *ALAN Review* 14 (Winter 1987): 5.

[7]Sheila A. Egoff, *Thursday's Child: Trends and Patterns in Contemporary Children's Fiction* (American Library Association, 1981), p. 159.

[8]Patty Campbell, "The Young Adult Perplex," *Wilson Library Bulletin* 55 (November 1980): 214.

[9]Larry R. Johannessen's *Illumination Rounds: Teaching the Literature of the Vietnam War* (NCTE, 1992) is an uncommonly helpful source of information on teaching or using material in secondary schools. So are Johannessen's article, "Young-Adult Literature and the Vietnam War," *English Journal* 82 (September 1993): 43–49; and articles by Perry Oldham, "Some Further Thoughts on Teaching Vietnam Literature," *English Journal* 82 (December 1993): 65–67; Christie N. Bradley, "Teaching Our Longest War: Constructive Lessons from Vietnam," *English Journal* 78 (April 1989): 35–38; and Fred A. Wilcox, "Pedagogical Implications of Teaching Literature of the Vietnam War," *Social Education* 52 (January 1988): 39–40.

[10]Judith Miller, "Wartime Internment of Japanese Was 'Grave Injustice,' Panel Says." *New York Times,* February 25, 1983, p.1.

[11]Charles Krauthammer, "The Case of the Suspect Bios." *Time,* October 4, 1999, p. 122.

[12]Michiko Kakutani, "Biography as a Blood Sport." *New York Times,* May 20, 1994, pp. B1, B6.

[13]Mary E. Mueller, "Up for Discussion: History and History Makers: Give YAs the Whole Picture." *School Library Journal* 37 (November 1991): 55–56.

[14]Mary E. Mueller, "Up for Discussion: History and History Makers: Give YAs the Whole Picture." *School Library Journal* 37 (November 1991): 55–56.

Titles Mentioned in the Text of Chapter Eight

Abells, Chana Byers. *The Children We Remember,* Greenwillow, 1986.

Ackerman, Diane. *The Moon by Whale Light: And Other Adventures Among Bats, Penguins, Crocodilians, and Whales.* Random House, 1991.

Allen, Tim. *Don't Stand Too Close to a Naked Man.* Hyperion, 1994.

Allende, Isabel. *Paula.* HarperCollins, 1995.

Angelou, Maya. *I Know Why the Caged Bird Sings.* Random House, 1970.

Armor, John and Peter Wright. *Manzanar.* Times Books, 1989.

Arrick, Fran. *Chernowitz!* Bradbury, 1981.

Ashby, Ruth and Deborah Gore Ohrn, eds. *Herstory: Women Who Changed the World.* Viking, 1995.

Avi. *The True Confessions of Charlotte Doyle.* Orchard, 1990.

Baker, Mark. *Nam: The Vietnam War in the Words of the Men and Women Who Fought There.* Morrow, 1981.

Barker, Pat. *The Eye in the Door.* Dutton, 1993.

Barker, Pat. *The Ghost Road.* Dutton, 1995.

Barker, Pat. *Regeneration.* Dutton, 1991.

Becker, Elizabeth. *America's Vietnam War: A Narrative History.* Clarion, 1992.

Berger, Joseph. *The Young Scientists: America's Future and the Winning of the Westinghouse.* Addison-Wesley, 1994.

Blinn, William. *Brian's Song.* Bantam, 1972.

Blumberg, Rhoda. *What's the Deal?: Jefferson, Napoleon, and the Louisiana Purchase.* National Geographic, 1998.

Bombeck, Erma. *I Want to Grow Hair, I Want to Grow Up, I Want to Go to Boise: Children Surviving Cancer.* HarperCollins, 1989.

Bosse, Malcolm. *The Examination.* Farrar, Straus & Giroux, 1994.

Bouton, Jim, edited by Leonard Shecter. *Ball Four: My Life and Hard Times Throwing the Knuckleball in the Big Leagues.* World, 1970.

Brodie, Fawn M. *Thomas Jefferson: An Intimate History.* Norton, 1974.

Brokaw, Tom. *The Greatest Generation.* Random House, 1998.

Buel, Janet. *Ancient Horsemen of Siberia.* 21st Century, 1998.

Buell, Janet. *Greenland Mummies.* 21st Century, 1998.

Bugliosi, Vincent, and Curt Gentry. *Helter Skelter: The True Story of the Manson Murders.* Norton, 1974.

Butler, Brent. *Knee Deep in Paradise.* Hyperion, 1996.

Calabro, Marian. *The Perilous Journey of the Donner Party.* Clarion, 1999.

Callahan, John. *Don't Worry, He Won't Get Far on Foot.* Random House, 1989.

Callahan, Stephen. *Adrift: Seventy-six Days Lost at Sea.* Thorndike, 1986.

Carroll, Rebecca. *I Know What the Red Clay Looks Like: The Voice and Vision of Black Women Writers.* Crown, 1994.

Carroll, Rebecca. *Swing Low: Black Men Writing.* Crown, 1994.

Carter, Peter. *The Hunted.* Farrar, Straus & Giroux, 1994.

Chamberlain, Wilt. *A View from Above.* Villard, 1991.

Chang, Ina. *A Separate Battle: Women and the Civil War.* Lodestar, 1991.

Chatwin, Bruce. *What Am I Doing Here?* Viking, 1989.

Chesler, Ellen. *Woman of Valor: Margaret Sanger and the Birth Control Movement in America.* Simon & Schuster, 1992.

Clark, Edie. *The Place He Made.* Villard, 1995.

Collier, James Lincoln and Christopher Collier. *My Brother Sam Is Dead.* Scholastic, 1991.

Cooper, Michael L. *Hell Fighters: African American Soldiers in World War I.* Dutton, 1997.

Cowell, Stephanie. *Nicholas Cooke.* Norton, 1993.

Crawford, Christina. *Mommie Dearest.* Morrow, 1978.

Cushman, Karen. *The Midwife's Apprentice.* Clarion, 1995.

Cushman, Karen. *Catherine, Called Birdy.* Clarion, 1994.

David, Kati. *A Child's War: World War II Through the Eyes of Children.* Four Walls Eight Windows, 1990.

Davis, Edith Kunhardt. *I'll Love You Forever, Anyway.* Fine, 1995.

DeFelice, Cynthia. *Nowhere to Call Home.* Farrar, Straus & Giroux, 1999.

DeGeneres, Ellen. *My Point . . . And I Do Have One.* Bantam, 1995.

Degens, T. *The Visit.* Viking, 1982.

deMille, Agnes. *Martha: The Life and Work of Martha Graham.* Random House, 1991.

Dickinson, Peter. *A Bone from a Dry Sea.* Delacorte, 1992.

Dillard, Annie. *An American Childhood.* HarperCollins, 1987.

Drake, William. *The First Wave: Women Poets in America, 1915–1945.* Macmillan, 1987.

Dumbach, Annette E. and Jud Newborn. *Shattering the German Night: The Story of the White Rose,* Little, Brown, 1986.

Dyer, Daniel. *Jack Landon: A Biography.* Scholastic, 1998.

Engelmann, Bernt. *In Hitler's German: Life in the Third Reich.* Pantheon, 1987.

Erdrich, Louise. *The Birchbark House.* Hyperion, 1999.

Fast, Howard. *April Morning.* Crown, 1961.

Feiler, Bruce. *Under the Big Top.* Scribner, 1995.

Feldbaum, Carl B. and Ronald J. Bee. *Looking the Tiger in the Eye: Confronting the Nuclear Threat.* HarperCollins, 1988.

Filipovic, Zlata. *Zlata's Diary: A Child's Life in Sarajevo.* Penguin, 1994.

Finkelstein, Norman H. *With Heroic Truth: The Life of Edward R. Murrow.* Clarion, 1997.

Fogelman, Eva. *Conscience and Courage: Rescuers of Jews During the Holocaust.* Anchor, 1994.

Forman, James. *Ceremony of Innocence.* Hawthorne, 1970.

Frank, Anne. *Diary of a Young Girl: The Definitive Edition.* Doubleday, 1995.

Frank, Rudolph. *No Hero for the Kaiser.* Lothrop, Lee & Shepard, 1986. First published 1931.

Freedman, Russell. *Indian Chiefs.* Holiday, 1986.

Freedman, Russell. *Franklin Delano Roosevelt.* Clarion, 1990.

Freedman, Russell. *Martha Graham: A Dancer's Life.* Clarion, 1998.

Friedman, Ina R. *The Other Victims: First Person Stories of Non-Jews Persecuted by the Nazis.* Houghton Mifflin, 1990.

Fussell, Samuel Wilson. *Muscle: Confessions of an Unlikely Body Builder.* Poseidon, 1991.

Gaes, Jason. *My Book for Kids with Cansur.* Melius & Peterson, 1987.

Garfield, Leon. *The Empty Sleeve.* Delacorte, 1988.

Garfield, Leon. *Jack Holborn.* Pantheon, 1965.

Garfield, Leon. *The Night of the Comet.* Delacorte, 1979.

Garfield, Leon. *The Sound of Coaches.* Viking, 1974.

Garfield, Leon. *The Strange Affair of Adelaide Harris.* Pantheon, 1971.

Gerhts, Barbara, *Don't Say a Word.* McElderry, 1986.

Gies, Miep. *Anne Frank Remembered.* Simon & Schuster, 1987.

Goodall, Jane. *My Life with the Chimpanzees.* Pocket Books, 1988.

Graham, Robin. *Dove.* HarperCollins, 1972.

Gunther, John. *Death Be Not Proud.* HarperCollins, 1949.

Hansen, Joyce. *Between Two Fires: Black Soldiers in the Civil War.* Watts, 1993.

Hanser, Richard. *A Noble Treason: The Revolt of the Munich Students Against Hitler.* Putnam, 1979.

Haskins, Jim. *One More River to Cross: The Stories of Twelve Black Americans.* Scholastic, 1992.

Haugaard, Erik Christian. *The Revenge of the Forty-Seven Samurai.* Houghton Mifflin, 1955.

Haugaard, Erik Christian. *The Samurai's Tale.* Houghton Mifflin, 1984.

Heilbrun, Carolyn G. *The Education of a Woman: The Life of Gloria Steinem.* Dial, 1995.

Hillesum, Etty. *An Interrupted Life: The Diaries of Etty Hillesum; 1941–1943.* Pantheon, 1984.

Hillesum, Etty. *Letters from Westerbork.* Pantheon, 1986.

Hoobler, Dorothy and Thomas Hoobler. *The Fact or Fiction Files: Lost Civilizations.* Walker, 1992.

Houston, Jeanne Wakatsuki and James D. Houston. *Farewell to Manzanar.* Houghton Mifflin, 1973.

Hunt, Irene. *No Promises in the Wind.* Follett, 1979.

Irons, Peter. *The Courage of Their Convictions: Sixteen Americans Who Fought Their Way to the Supreme Court.* Free Press, 1988.

Jaffe, Steven H. *Who Were the Founding Fathers? Two Hundred Years of Reinventing American History.* Holt, 1996.

Jens, Inge. *At the Heart of the White Rose: Letters and Diaries of Hans and Sophie Scholl.* Harper & Row, 1987.

Jiang, Ji Li. *Red Scarf Girl: A Memoir of the Cultural Revolution.* HarperCollins, 1997.

Johannessen, Larry R. *Illumination Rounds: Teaching the Literature of the Vietnam War.* National Council of Teachers of English, 1992.

Kammen, Michael. *Mystic Chords of Memory.* Knopf, 1991.

Katz, William Loren. *Breaking the Chains: African-American Slave Resistance.* Atheneum, 1990.

Kelly, Kitty. *Nancy Reagan: The Unauthorized Biography.* Simon & Schuster, 1991.

Keneally, Thomas. *Schindler's List.* Simon & Schuster, 1982.

Koop, C. Everett. *Koop: The Memoirs of America's Family Doctor.* Random House, 1991.

Kuralt, Charles. *A Life on the Road.* Putnam, 1985.

Lancaster, Matthew. *Hang Tough!.* Paulist, 1985.

Lasky, Kathryn. *Beyond the Divide.* Macmillan, 1983.

Lasky, Kathryn. *Beyond the Burning Time.* Scholastic, 1994.

Lawrence, R. D. *In Praise of Wolves.* Holt, 1986.

Levine, Ellen. *Anna Pavlova: Genius of the Dance.* Scholastic, 1995.

Levine, Ellen. *Freedom's Children: Young Civil Rights Activists Tell Their Own Stories.* Putnam, 1993.

Lund, Doris. *Eric.* Lippincott, 1974.

MacPherson, Malcolm C. *Time Bomb: Fermi, Heisenberg and the Race for the Atomic Bomb.* Dutton, 1986.

March, William. *Company K.* Smith and Haas, 1933.

Marshall, Kathryn. *In the Combat Zone: An Oral History of American Women in Vietnam.* Little, Brown, 1987.

Mason, Frances. *I Remember Balanchine: Recollection of the Ballet Master by Those Who Knew Him.* Doubleday, 1991.

Masters, Edgar Lee. *Spoon River Anthology.* Macmillan, 1962.

Matthiessen, Peter. *African Silences.* Random House, 1991.

Mazer, Harry. *The Last Mission.* Delacorte, 1979.

Mayo, Edith P., ed. *The Smithsonian Book of the First Ladies: Their Lives, Times and Issues.* Holt, 1996.

McCloud, Bill. *What Should We Tell Our Children About Vietnam?* University of Oklahoma Press, 1989.

McKissack, Patricia C. and Frederick McKissack. *Sojourner Truth: Ain't I a Woman?* Scholastic, 1992.

Meltzer, Milton. *Never to Forget: The Jews of the Holocaust.* HarperCollins, 1976.

Meltzer, Milton. *Rescue: The Story of How Gentiles Saved Jews in the Holocaust.* HarperCollins, 1988.

Meltzer, Milton. *Voices from the Civil War: A Documentary History of the Great American Conflict.* Crowell, 1989.

Meyer, Carolyn. *Mary, Bloody Mary.* Harcourt, 1999.

Meyer, Carolyn. *Where the Heart Still Beats: The Story of Cynthia Ann Parker.* Harcourt, 1993.

Meyer, Carolyn. *White Lilacs.* Harcourt, 1993.

Morgan, Judith and Neil Morgan. *Dr. Seuss and Mr. Giesel: A Biography.* Random House, 1995.

Morris, Edmund. *Dutch: A Memoir of Ronald Reagan.* Random House, 1999.

Morris, Jeanne. *Brian Piccolo: A Short Season.* Rand McNally, 1971.

Mowat, Farley. *Born Naked.* Houghton Mifflin, 1994.

Mowat, Farley. *The Dog Who Wouldn't Be.* Little, Brown, 1957.

Mowat, Farley. *Never Cry Wolf.* Little, Brown, 1963.

Mowat, Farley. *And No Birds Sang.* Little, Brown, 1980.

Mowat, Farley. *Owls in the Family.* Little, Brown, 1961.

Mowat, Farley. *Sea of Slaughter.* Atlantic, 1985.

Mowat, Farley. *A Whale for the Killing.* Little, Brown, 1972.

Murphy, Claire Rudolf and Jane G. Haigh. *Gold Rush Women.* Alaska Northwest, 1997.

Myers, Walter Dean. *Malcolm X: By Any Means Necessary.* Scholastic, 1993.

Neimark, Anne E. *Wild Heart: The Story of Joy Adamson.* Harcourt, 1999.

Nolan, Han. *If I Should Die Before I Wake.* Harcourt Brace, 1994.

O'Brien, Sharon. *Willa Cather.* Chelsea House, 1995.

O'Dell, Scott. *Island of the Blue Dolphins.* Houghton Mifflin, 1960.

O'Dell, Scott. *The King's Fifth.* Houghton Mifflin, 1966.

O'Dell, Scott. *Sing Down the Moon.* Houghton Mifflin, 1970.

Palmer, Laura. *Shrapnel in the Heart: Letters and Remembrances from the Vietnam Veterans Memorial.* Random House, 1987.

Parini, Jay. *John Steinbeck: A Biography.* Holt, 1995.

Paterson, Katherine. *Lyddie.* Dutton, 1991.

Paulsen, Gary. *Soldier's Heart: Being the Story of the Enlistment and Due Service of the Boy Charley Goddard in the First Minnesota Volunteers.* Delacorte, 1988.

Pullman, Phillip. *The Ruby in the Smoke.* Knopf, 1987.

Pullman, Phillip. *Shadow in the North.* Knopf, 1988.

Pullman, Philip. *The Tiger in the Well.* Knopf, 1990.

Pyle, Ernie. *Ernie's War: The Best of Ernie Pyle's World War II Dispatches.* David Nichols, ed., Random House, 1986.

Ray, Karen. *To Cross a Line.* Orchard, 1994.

Reef, Catherine. *John Steinbeck.* Clarion, 1996.

Reiser, Paul, *Couplehood.* Bantam, 1994.

Reiss, Johanna. *The Journey Back.* Crowell, 1976.

Reiss, Johanna. *The Upstairs Room.* Harper & Row, 1972.

Remarque, Erich Maria. *All Quiet on the Western Front.* Putnam, 1929.

Rhue, Morton (Todd Strasser). *The Wave.* Dell, 1981.

Richter, Elizabeth. *Losing Someone You Love: When a Brother or Sister Dies.* Putnam, 1986.

Rinaldi, Ann. *A Break with Charity: A Story about the Salem Witch Trials.* Harcourt Brace Jovanovich, 1992.

Rinaldi, Ann. *Cast Two Shadows.* Harcourt, 1998.

Rinaldi, Ann. *The Fifth of March: A Story of the Boston Massacre.* Harcourt Brace Jovanovich, 1993.

Rinaldi, Ann. *Finishing Becca: A Story about Peggy Shippen and Benedict Arnold.* Harcourt Brace Jovanovich, 1994.

Rinaldi, Ann. *Wolf by the Ears.* Scholastic, 1991.

Rochman, Hazel and Darlene Z. McCampbell, eds. *Bearing Witness: Stories of the Holocaust.* Orchard, 1995.

Rosenberg, Maxine B. *Hiding to Survive: Stories of Jewish Children Rescued from the Holocaust.* Orchard, 1995.

Rosenblatt, Roger. *Children of War.* Doubleday, 1983.

Rothchild, Sylvia, ed. *Voices from the Holocaust.* New American Library, 1981.

Ruby, Lois. *Skin Deep.* Scholastic, 1994.

Salzman, Mark. *Lost in Place: Growing Up Absurd in Suburbia.* Random House, 1995.

Santoli, Al. *Everything We Had: An Oral History of the Vietnam War by Thirty-Three American Soldiers Who Fought it.* Random House, 1981.

Sayers, Gayle. *I Am Third.* Viking, 1970.

Schiff, Stacy. *Saint-Exupery: A Biography.* Knopf, 1994.

Seinfeld, Jerry. *Signlanguage.* Bantam, 1993.

Sender, Ruth Minsky. *The Cage.* Macmillan, 1986.

Sender, Ruth Minsky. *The Holocaust Lady.* Macmillan, 1992.

Sender, Ruth Minsky. *To Life.* Macmillan, 1988.

Sexton, Linda Gray. *Searching for Mercy Street: My Journey Back to My Mother, Ann Sexton.* Little, Brown, 1994.

Shellard, Dominic. *William Shakespeare.* Oxford, 1999.

Stenbuck, Jack. *Typewriter Battalion.* Morrow, 1995.

Sutcliff, Rosemary. *Dawn Wind.* Walck, 1961.

Sutcliff, Rosemary. *The Eagle of the Ninth.* Walck, 1954.

Sutcliff, Rosemary. *The Shield Ring.* Oxford University Press, 1957.

Sutcliff, Rosemary. *The Shining Company.* Farrar, Straus & Giroux, 1990.

Tapert, Annette, ed. *The Brothers' War: Civil War Letters to Their Loved Ones from the Blue and the Gray.* Times Books, 1988.

Tapert, Annette, ed. *Lines of Battle: Letters from American Servicemen, 1941–1945.* Times Books, 1987.

Temple, Frances. *The Ramsay Scallop.* Orchard, 1994.

Terkel, Studs. *Coming of Age: The Story of Our Century by Those Who've Lived it.* New Press, 1995.

Treglown, Jeremy. *Roald Dahl: A Biography.* Farrar, Straus & Giroux, 1994.

Vinke, Hermann. *The Short Life of Sophie Scholl.* Harper & Row, 1980.

Volavkova, Hanna, ed. *I Never Saw Another Butterfly: Children's Drawings and Poems from Terezín Concentration Camp, 1941–1944.* Schocken, 1978.

von Staden, Wendelgard. *Darkness over the Valley.* Tickner and Fields, 1981.

Westall, Robert. *Fathom Five.* Greenwillow, 1979.

Westall, Robert. *The Machine Gunners.* Greenwillow, 1976.

Wharton, William. *A Midnight Clear.* Knopf, 1982.

Wisler, G. Clifton. *Mr. Lincoln's Drummer.* Dutton, 1994.

Wolf, Joan. *The Reindeer Hunters.* Penguin/Dutton, 1995.

Wolff, Tobias. *This Boy's Life.* Atlantic Monthly Press, 1989.

Information on the availability of paperback editions of these titles is available online from such book sellers as Barnes & Noble and Amazon.com, and through *Books in Print* compiled by R. R. Bowker Company and available either in person or online from major libraries.

CHAPTER

9

Nonfiction
Information, Poetry, and Drama

Fiction usually gets the lion's share of attention when it comes to reviewing and recommending books for teenagers; however, we should pay more attention to nonfiction because it gets the lion's share of the budget when it comes to school and library purchases. Many teenagers, as well as many adults, go for years without reading a novel or even a short story, but virtually everyone reads nonfiction whether in newspapers, in magazines, on the Internet, or on a cereal box. In this chapter, we look at three quite different kinds of nonfiction: information books, poetry, and drama. What they have in common is that readers come to them seeking something. What they seek may be just general information or answers to specific questions, but just as often, readers of nonfiction are seeking pleasure and a refreshing change of pace.

Information Books

When the American Library Association made history by awarding its coveted 1988 Newbery Medal to Russell Freedman's *Lincoln: A Photobiography*, Milton Meltzer, who has long championed the cause of nonfiction, applauded by saying,

> It was a terrific thing to do, but it took fifty years to do it. The few books they gave prizes to before, that were called nonfiction, really were not. Instead, they were books written in the outmoded vein of biography that was highly fictionalized, had invented dialogue, and sometimes concocted scenes. That's all changed today, but it took a long time.[1]

In their 1990 *Nonfiction for Young Adults: From Delight to Wisdom*, Betty Carter and Richard F. Abrahamson cited 22 research studies. Among the reported findings:

- An interest in reading nonfiction emerges at about the fourth grade and grows during adolescence.

- Interest in reading nonfiction crosses ability levels; one study showed that nonfiction made up 34 percent of the leisure reading of academically able teenagers and 54 percent of the control group's leisure reading.
- Nonfiction makes up a much larger proportion of boys' reading than of girls' reading.
- One study categorized the seven most popular types of nonfiction as cartoon and comic books, weird but true stories, rock stars, ghosts, magic, stories about famous people, and explorations of the unknown.
- Remedial readers prefer informative nonfiction and read "primarily to learn new things."
- Students choose nonfiction for a variety of reasons often unrelated to school curricular matters, as shown by the fact that computer-related books are popular in schools with no computers and books on the Ku Klux Klan are frequently checked out in junior highs in which recent American history is not studied.
- When students gave reasons for reading particular books, it became clear that the purpose of the reading is guided more by the student than by the type of book. One boy read books on subjects he already knew about because it made him feel smart; others preferred how-to books so that they could interact with the author while learning to draw, care for a pet, program a computer, make a paper airplane, and so on; and still others preferred *The Guinness Book of World Records*. Even here purposes differed. Some read the book to discover amazing facts, but others read it to imagine themselves undergoing strange experiences.

Narrative or Storytelling in Nonfiction

When Thomas Keneally's 1982 *Schindler's List* won a Pulitzer Prize in fiction, there was considerable controversy over whether the book was eligible because it was supposedly a journalistic account of a true event. E. L. Doctorow spoke to the same issue when he said in his acceptance speech for the National Book Critics Circle Award for *Ragtime*, "There is no more fiction or nonfiction only narrative."

Three hundred English teachers who responded to a survey asking for ten adolescent novels and ten adult novels worthy of recommendation to teenagers gave further evidence that in people's minds, fiction and nonfiction are blending together. Among twenty nonfiction titles recommended as novels were Piers Paul Read's *Alive*, James Herriot's *All Creatures Great and Small*, Robin Graham's *Dove*, Peter Maas's *Serpico*, Doris Lund's *Eric*, Alvin Toffler's *Future Shock*, Maya Angelou's *I Know Why the Caged Bird Sings*, Dee Brown's *Bury My Heart at Wounded Knee*, Claude Brown's *Manchild in the Promised Land*, Eldridge Cleaver's *Soul on Ice*, and John H. Griffin's *Black Like Me*.

The blending of fiction and nonfiction has occurred from both directions. On one side are the nonfiction writers who use the techniques of fiction, including suspense, careful plotting and characterization, and literary devices, such as symbolism and metaphor. On the other side are the novelists who collect data as an investigative reporter would. In *Midnight Hour Encores*, Bruce Brooks acknowledged thirty-two individuals for talking to him "about music in relentless detail," and at the beginning of *Izzy, Willy-Nilly*, Cynthia Voigt acknowledged help from medical personnel who taught her about physical and mental aspects of amputation. Readers are so accustomed to finding "real" places and events in novels that following the popular success of Robert J. Waller's *The Bridges of Madison County, National Geographic Magazine* had a hard time convincing readers that they could not buy or even look at a historical feature on Iowa bridges because Waller's story was purely fictional.

Brooks's, Voigt's, and Waller's books are fiction in the sense that fictional names are used and they combine bits and pieces of many individual stories. Nevertheless, in another sense, these stories are more real and actually present a more honest portrayal than some pieces labeled nonfiction that are true accounts of bizarre or strange happenings.

Literature—fiction and nonfiction—is more than a simple recounting or replaying of the life that surrounds the writer. It is a distillation and a crystallization. Only when an author skillfully chooses descriptive details and develops believable dialogue does an account of an actual event become real to the reader. Certainly Alex Haley's *Roots* became real to millions of television viewers as well as to millions of readers, yet the book contains many fictional elements in both subject matter and presentation. Part of Haley's success comes from his ability to select powerful incidents and details. Good writers of nonfiction do not simply record everything they know or can uncover. With Haley's book, readers' imaginations were captured by the fact that on September 29, 1967, he "stood on the dock in Annapolis where his great-great-great-great-great-grandfather was taken ashore on September 29, 1767," and sold as a slave to a Virginia plantation owner. From this point, Haley set out to trace backward the six generations that connected him to a 16-year-old "prince" newly arrived from Africa. What the public might not stop to consider as they read about this dramatic incident is that it is setting the stage for only a small portion of Haley's "roots." In the generation in which Haley started his story with the young couple, Omoro and Binta Kinte, and the birth of their first son, Kunta, there were 256 parents giving birth to 128 children, each one of whom is also a great-great-great-great-great-grandfather or grandmother to Alex Haley. The point is that even though Haley was writing nonfiction, he had an almost unlimited range of possibilities from which to choose, and he made his choices with the instinct of a storyteller rather than a clerk, who might have put together a more complete but less interesting family history.

New Journalism

Roots is part of the genre sometimes labelled *new journalism*. Truman Capote called it the "most avant-garde form of writing existent today" and coined the term *nonfiction novel* for *In Cold Blood,* an account of an especially brutal murder and the subsequent trial. Other terms that are used include *creative nonfiction, literary journalism, journalistic fiction,* and *advocacy journalism.* Although its roots were growing right along with journalism in general, it did not begin to flower until the 1950s and 1960s. Part of the reason for its development is the increased educational level of the American public. Newspaper readers and television viewers, including young adults, are not satisfied with simplistic explanations. They want enough background information that they can feel confident in coming to their own conclusions.

Affluence, combined with modern technology, helps make the new journalism possible. Compare similar incidents that happened 126 years apart. In 1846, a group of travelers who came to be known as the Donner party were trapped in the high Sierras by an early snow. They had to stay there all winter without food except for the flesh of their dead companions. After they were rescued, word of their ordeal gradually trickled back east, so that for years afterward sensationalized accounts were made up by writers who had no chance to come to the scene or interview the survivors.

In 1972, a planeload of Uruguayan travelers crashed in the Andes mountains. As in the Donner party, some people knew each other before the trip, but others were strangers. During the terrible weeks of waiting to be rescued, they all got to know each other and to develop intense relationships revolving around leadership roles and roles of rebellion or giving up. They endured unspeakable hardships. Many died; those who lived did so because they ate the flesh of those who died. In this situation, however, the people were rescued by helicopters after two of the men made their way out of the mountains. Word of their 2 1/2–month ordeal was flashed around the world, and by the time the sixteen survivors, mostly members of a rugby team, had been flown back to Uruguay, reporters from many nations were there. A press conference was held, and the journalists were told about the cannibalism.

This was the second surprise in the story. The first had been their survival. The drama of the situation naturally fired imaginations all around the world. Lippincott suggested to author Piers Paul Read that this was the kind of story that would make a good book. He went to Uruguay, where he stayed for several months interviewing survivors, rescuers, family, and friends of both the deceased and the survivors, and the government officials who had been in charge of the search. More than a year later, Lippincott published *Alive: The Story of the Andes Survivors,* which was on the *New York Times* best-seller list for seven months, was made into a movie, and will probably continue to be read by young adults for the next several years, both in and out of school.

The fact that the survivors were in their early twenties undoubtedly helps teenagers to identify with the story, but so do the literary techniques that Read used. He focused on certain individuals, presenting miniature character sketches of some and fully developed portraits of others. The setting was crucial to the story, and he described it vividly. He was also careful to write so that the natural suspense of the situation came through. His tone was consistent throughout the book. He admired the survivors but did not shy away from showing the negative aspects of human nature when it is sorely tried. In a foreword he said that the only liberty he allowed himself was the creation of dialogue between the characters, although, whenever possible, he relied on diaries and remembered comments and quarrels as well as his acquaintance with the speaking styles of the survivors.

"New journalism" combines factual information with emotional appeal. Such books might be classified as biography, history, drama, essay, or personal experience, but regardless of classification, they serve as a bridge between childhood and adult reading because of the straightforward, noncondescending style that is characteristic of good journalism.

Nonfiction best-sellers often outsell fiction best-sellers, and television producers know they can add millions of viewers if they advertise a program as "a documentary" rather than "a drama." Popular movies are done in "nonfiction" style, whereas on television more viewers watch "live" than fictionalized police shows.

Even the success of the tabloids depends on their nonfiction format. The majority of readers do not really believe all those stories about Elvis Presley still being alive or about women giving birth to aliens or apricot pits curing cancer; yet, for the

FILM BOX 9.1

The Power of the Media, The Power of Language (see Appendix D)

All the President's Men (1976, color, 128 min., PG; Director: Alan J. Pakula; with Robert Redford, Dustin Hoffman, and Jason Robards) The Watergate cover-up is brought to light through the work of two *Washington Post* reporters.

Being There (1979, color, 130 min., PG; Director: Hal Asby; with Peter Sellers and Melvyn Douglas) A simple-minded gardener becomes a guru for national politicians.

Broadcast News (1987, color, 131 min., R; Director: James L. Brooks; with William Hurt, Holly Hunter, and Albert Brooks) A TV news director falls for a pretty-face anchor whose journalistic values are dubious.

A Face in the Crowd (1957, black and white, 125 min., NR; Director: Elia Kazan; with Andy Griffith and Patricia Neal) In this badly underrated film, a homespun bum becomes a national idol with his songs and stories.

The Front (1976, color, 94 min., PG; Director: Martin Ritt; with Woody Allen and Zero Mostel) During the Hollywood-Ten blacklist of scriptwriters, a friend agrees to submit scripts under his name.

The Lost Honor of Katharina Blum (1975, German, color, 106 min., R; Director: Volker Schlondorff; with Margaretha von Trotta and Angela Winkler) In Heinrich Boll's novel, a woman sleeps one night with a terrorist and is accused by the mass media of being his accomplice.

Network (1976, color, 121 min., R; Director: Sidney Lumet; Peter Finch, Faye Dunaway, William Holden, and Robert Duvall) An over-the-hill newscaster threatens to kill himself, and network ratings go up.

Quiz Show (1994, color, 133 min., PG-13; Director: Robert Redford; with John Turturro, Rob Morrow, and Ralph Fiennes) A professor and member of a famous American literary family cheats on a game show.

The Stunt Man (1980, color, 129 min., R; Director: Richard Rush; with Peter O'Toole, Steven Railsback, and Barbara Hershey) A man fleeing police kills a movie stunt man. The film's director promises to protect the fugitive if he will become the stunt man.

Three Days of the Condor (1975, color, 117 min., R; Director: Sydney Pollack; with Robert Redford, Cliff Robertson, and Max von Sydow) A reader for an American intelligence unit stumbles onto something politically dangerous, and only he is left when the unit is wiped out.

fun of it they are willing to give themselves over to a momentary suspension of disbelief, something we used to talk about mainly in relation to fantasy and science fiction. These kinds of changes are in and of themselves interesting to both teenagers and young adults. See Film Box 9.1 The Power of the Media, The Power of Language.

Evaluation of Nonfiction

Evaluating nonfiction for young readers is more complicated than evaluating fiction because

1. People select informational books primarily on the basis of the subject matter, and because there is such a variety in subjects, people's choices vary tremendously, resulting in a lack of consensus on what is "the best."

2. Informative books on such topics as computers and car repair become dated more quickly than fiction books. Students preparing to take the SAT tests, wanting advice on handling money, or planning for a career need the most recent information. The constant turnover of informative books leaves us with few touchstone examples.

3. The transitory nature of informative nonfiction books discourages teachers and critics from giving them serious consideration as instructional materials. Although well-written personal experience narratives have longer life spans, people who have made up their minds that they are not interested in nonfiction find it easy to ignore all nonfiction.

4. Reviewers and prize givers may not feel competent to judge the technical or other specialized information presented in many informative books. Also, many reviewers, especially those working with educational journals, come from an English-teaching tradition, and they tend to focus on books that would be used in conjunction with literature rather than biology, home economics, social studies, industrial arts, history, or business classes.

5. In evaluating nonfiction, there is no generally agreed-upon theory of criticism or criteria for judgment.

We suggest that the evaluation situation can be improved by readers looking at fiction and nonfiction in similar ways. Replace looking at plot and characterization with looking at the intended audience and the content of the book. (What is it about? What information does it present?) Then look at the appropriateness and success with which each of the following is established. Examining a nonfiction book carefully enough to be able to describe the setting or scope and the theme, tone, and style will give you insights into how well it is written and packaged. Also, for information books, look at the more specific suggestions in Table 9.1.

Setting/Scope Informative books may be historical, restricted to regional interests, or have a limited scope. In evaluating these, one needs to ask whether the author set realistic goals, considering the reading level of the intended audience and the amount of space and back-up graphics available.

Theme Informational books also have themes or purposes that are closely tied to the author's point of view. Authors may write in hopes of persuading someone to a particular belief or to inspire thoughtfulness, respect, or even curiosity. Some authors shout out their themes; others are more subtle. You need to consider consistency as you evaluate the theme. Did the author build on a consistent theme throughout the book?

Tone The manner in which an author achieves a desired goal—whether it is to persuade, inform, inspire, or amuse—sets the tone of a book. Is it hard-sell, strident, one-sided, humorous, loving, sympathetic, adulatory, scholarly, pedantic, energetic, or leisurely? Authors of informative books for children used to take a leisurely approach as they tried to entice children into becoming interested in their subject. Today's young readers, however, are just as busy as their parents and most likely go to informative books for quick information rather than leisure time entertainment. A boy or girl who wants to repair a bicycle does not want to read the history of the Wright brothers and their bicycle shop before getting to the part on slipped gears.

TABLE 9.1

SUGGESTIONS FOR EVALUATING INFORMATIVE NONFICTION

A good piece of informative writing usually has:	A poor piece of informative writing may have:
A subject of interest to young readers, written about with zest. Information that is up-to-date and accurate.	Obsolete or inaccurate information or illustrations. Even one such occurrence causes the reader to lose faith in the rest of the book.
New information or information organized in such a way as to present a different point of view than in previously available books.	Evidence of cutting-and-pasting in which the author merely reorganized previously prepared material without developing anything new in content or viewpoint.
A reading level, vocabulary, and tone of writing that are at a constant level appropriate to the intended audience.	Inconsistencies in style or content, for example, college-level vocabulary but a childish or cute style of writing.
An organization in which basic information is presented first so that chapters and sections build on each other.	An awkward mix of fiction and nonfiction techniques through which the author unsuccessfully tries to slip information in as an unnoticed part of the story.
An index and other aids to help readers look up facts if they want to return to the book for specific information or to glean ideas and facts without reading the entire book.	A reflection of out-of-date or socially unfair attitudes, for example, a history book that presents only the history of white upper-class men with a title and introduction that give the impression that it is a comprehensive history of the time period being covered.
Adequate documentation of the sources of information, including some original sources.	A biased presentation in which only one side of a controversial issue is presented with little or no acknowledgment that many people hold different viewpoints.
Information to help interested students locate further readings on the subject.	In how-to books, frustrating directions that oversimplify or set up unrealistic expectations so that the reader is disappointed in the result.
In how-to-books, clear and accurate directions including complete lists of the equipment and supplies needed in a project.	
Illustrations that add interest as well as clarity to the text.	
A competent author with expertise in the subject matter.	

Style The best informative books also have style. As author Jane Langton said when she was asked to serve as a judge, the good books "exude some kind of passion or love or caring . . . and they have the potential for leaving a mark on the readers, changing them in some way."[2] George A. Woods, former children's editor of the *New York Times Book Review,* said that he selected the informational books to be featured in his review mostly on his own "gut-level" reactions to what was "new or far better than what we have had before." He looked for a majesty of language and uniqueness and for books that would add to children's understanding by making them eyewitnesses to history.[3] A problem in examining an author's style is that each book must be judged according to the purpose the author had in mind. From book to book, purposes are so different that it is like the old problem of comparing apples and oranges. Some books are successful simply because they are different—more like a mango than an apple or an orange. Their value is that they are providing something not previously available as with Dee Parmer Woodtor's *Finding a Place Called Home: A Guide to African-American Genealogy and Historical Identity.* Had it been available when Walter Dean Myers (see his statement on Finding One's Identity) was a

WALTER DEAN MYERS
On Finding One's Identity

My earliest conscious identity was as my mother's darling boy. The memory of this period of warmth and intimacy with the woman who first gave me the gift of reading still brings me pleasure. My introduction to school changed my self-concept in important ways. I discovered that most of my classmates could not read, which surprised me. The first idea of being "bright" entered my thoughts. But I also became aware, painfully so, that the other children and my first-grade teacher had difficulty understanding me. I began speech therapy and began to layer my identity with that disability as well. Seeing my frustration in reading before a class, a teacher suggested that I write something to read instead of reading from a book. I began to write poems, which were praised by the teacher.

School, on the whole, was a joyous experience on the elementary level. I identified with the heroes we were given: George Washington, Thomas Jefferson, the wise Benjamin Franklin, and the brave Patrick Henry. We did plays in which we were colonists at Thanksgiving or threw tea into Boston Harbor. Unconscious of differences between myself and my white classmates, I was identifying as an American. But then one day I turned the page in our history books and encountered the concept of race. There was a picture of a small group of Africans, their heads down, marching from a boat. They were identified not as Africans, of course, but as "slaves."

From that day on, the identity of race—it was Negro in those days—dominated my identity. When we read *Huck Finn* I struggled against being Nigger Jim. I wanted to be the brave, adventuresome Huck. Unconsciously, I began to accept the values, or rather the lack of values, assigned to people of my race.

I began to reject the devalued race. If Negroes were physical, liked finger-popping music, and were never serious, then I would be intellectual, study classical music, and always be serious. In retrospect, I was simply looking for those human values that the school ascribed to white Americans but neglected to give to black Americans.

The logical extension of my identity as an intellectual was the continuation of my education on the college level. The revelation that my parents would not be able to send me to college was devastating. It seemed perfectly logical for me to drop out of high school.

A gang and then the army gave me acceptable macho identities over the next few years, acceptable because I did not see alternatives. It certainly doesn't take much imagination for me to understand the lure of today's gangs.

(Continued)

After the army and a series of menial jobs, I started writing again. I wrote about things I knew—Harlem, basketball, gangs, the army. The values that I did not find in books as a child I was now putting into the books.

A few years ago I began writing a history book. In the book I wanted to talk about the Africans—Africans, not slaves—who had helped to create the United States. The book was a result of all of the experiences of my life, of my turning to books, of my racial conflicts, of my need to bring value to who I am. I knew that my own family had been held on a plantation in what is now West Virginia. I delayed going to the plantation until the book was nearly finished, and I approached it with trepidation. But I did not feel the pain that I expected and soon realized that in the years of writing, I had re-created a surety of identity that could not be threatened, not even by the shadow of enslavement.

This is what I want to do with my writing, to bring value to the young people who read my books, to allow them to discover their own identities without harmful value prejudices. In so doing, I feel more value in my own existence. It's a good feeling.

Walter Dean Myers's books include *Monster,* HarperCollins, 1998; *At Her Majesty's Request,* Scholastic, 1998; *Now Is Your Time,* HarperCollins, 1991; *Somewhere in the Darkness,* Scholastic, 1992; and *Fallen Angels,* Scholastic, 1988.

teenager, it probably would have meant a lot to him with its attractive layout, its photos, and its straight-forward and accessible writing style.

Contemporary Influences on the Publishing of Informational Books

Before the 1950s, what was published for young readers was in the main fiction (novels or short stories), poetry, or textbook material to be used in school. Few publishers thought that young readers would be interested in factual books unless they were forced to study them as part of their schoolwork. Then the Russians launched Sputnik, and Americans were sincerely frightened that Russia was scientifically and technologically ahead. In 1961, Congress passed the National Defense Education Act, which gave millions of dollars to school libraries for the purchase of science and math books (later expanded to include all books). Publishers competed to create informative books that would qualify for purchase under the Act and would attract young readers.

The rise in the popularity of nonfiction has paralleled the information explosion and the rise in the power and influence of the mass media. Today there is simply more information to be shared between reader and writer. Television, radio, movies, newspapers, magazines, and now the Internet all communicate the same kinds of information as do books, but people expect more from books because the other media are limited in the amount of space and time that they can devote to information on any one topic. Moreover, whatever is produced by the mass media must be of interest to a *mass* audience, whereas individual readers select books. Of course, publishers want masses of individual readers to select their books. Nevertheless, there is more room for experimentation and the development of minority viewpoints in books than in the kinds of media that are supported by advertisers and that, therefore, must aim to attract the largest possible audience.

Many writers take the same subjects that are treated on television and write about them in more detail or from unexpected viewpoints. They try to answer the questions that cursory news reports do not have time or space to probe (see Focus Box 9.1, Going Beyond the Headlines). Readers also have more faith in books than in news stories that are necessarily put together overnight or in Internet stories for which it is often impossible to check the sources.

Need for Scientific Literacy

At a meeting of the Conference on College Composition and Communication in St. Louis, science writer Jon Franklin spoke on a panel entitled "Nonfiction: The Genre of a Technological Age." Formerly a science writer for the *Evening Sun* in Baltimore and now a teacher of journalism at the University of Maryland in College Park, Franklin's topic was "Literary Structure: A Growing Force in Science Journalism." He pointed out how in the past decade, more than half the winners of the Pulitzer Prize in nonfiction had been science books, and how the increasingly important role of scientific writing in newspapers and magazines is changing basic concepts of journalism. The upside-down pyramid, in which the key points are stated first with the details being filled in later so an editor can cut the story whenever the available space is filled, does not work for science writing because it results in oversimplification. Science stories have to be written inductively, building from the small to the large points because most scientific developments and concepts are too complex for readers to understand unless they get the supporting details first.

Franklin worries about the development of a new kind of elitism based on scientific literacy. He says that if people feel uncomfortable with scientific writing, they are likely to resent and reject scientific concepts. He gives as an example the censorship battles that have developed over beliefs in creationism versus evolution. He proposes a two-pronged approach to keep the gap from widening between the scientifically literate and those who reject all science. On the one hand, science writers have to work harder to find organizational patterns and literary techniques that make their material understandable and interesting. On the other hand, schools must bring the reading of technological and scientific information into the curriculum with the goal of preparing students to balance their lifetime reading. See Focus Box 9.2 for recommended titles.

Books to Support and Extend the School Curriculum

Informational books purchased by school libraries are usually referred to as "books to support the curriculum," but a more accurate description would probably be "books to extend the curriculum." These books seldom help students who are doing poorly in class. Instead, they provide challenges for successful students to go further than their classmates. They also serve as models for research, and they go beyond the obvious facts to present information that is too complicated, too detailed, too obscure, or too controversial to be included in textbooks. A legitimate complaint often voiced about history books is that they focus on war and violence

FOCUS BOX 9.1

Going Beyond the Headlines

The Adventures of Sojourner: The Mission to Mars that Thrilled the World by Susi Trautmann Wunsch. Mikaya, 1998. The Sojourner rover is the hero in this sixty-page book, which explains why scientists worked to launch the Mars Pathfinder. Stunning photographs accompany details about the December 1996 launch and the landing on July 4, 1997. Timelines, charts, and information about relevant Web sites are also given.

The Bone Detectives: How Forensic Anthropologists Solve Crimes and Uncover Mysteries of the Dead by Donna M. Jackson, photos by Charlie Fellenbaum. Little, Brown, 1996. All the facts that are too creepy to be published in the newspapers are included in this book about how the dead can provide clues for clever detectives.

Braving the Frozen Frontier: Women Working in Antarctica by Rebecca L. Johnson. Lerner Discovery Series, 1997. This was a wonderfully appropriate behind-the-scenes book for the 1999 news story about the challenges of dropping medical equipment for a woman doctor in Antarctica who was diagnosed with breast cancer. But even without such a news event, this is an illuminating book about a place where relatively few humans will ever live.

Breaking Ground, Breaking Silence: The Story of New York's African Burial Ground by Joyce Hansen and Gary McGowan. Holt, 1998. Discovery in New York of an African burial ground from the 1700s has allowed archaeologists to learn much about a people who left very little about themselves in writing.

Fire in Their Eyes: Wildfires and the People Who Fight Them by Karen Magnuson Beil. Harcourt, 1999. An abundance of full-color photographs in this sixty-four-page book make it a good choice for either skimming or reading for solid information. It ends with a useful glossary of terms.

Gladiator by Richard Watkins. Houghton Mifflin, 1997. Watkins illustrates his eighty-page history of the seven centuries of the Roman games with charcoal and pencil drawings that are both dramatic and realistic. The statistical and political information about these public celebrations of death lend a different perspective to the question of modern violence.

Gone A-Whaling: The Lure of the Sea and the Hunt for the Great Whales by Jim Murphy. Clarion, 1998. The controversy over contemporary whaling can be better understood against this well-researched and well-presented background. Murphy focuses on the role of teenage boys and includes a chapter showing that African-Americans and women sometimes participated because they had more freedom on ship than on land.

How TV Changed America's Mind by Edward Wakin. Lothrop, 1996. Arranged by decades from the 1950s to the 1990s, this accessible history includes photos of key events and a generous bibliography also arranged by decades.

My Life in Tap by Savion Glover and Bruce Weber. Morrow, 2000. The author is the young dancer who has added hip-hop and rap to revitalize the art of tap dancing.

Once a Wolf: How Wildlife Biologists Fought to Bring Back the Gray Wolf by Sy Montgomery, photos by Jim Brandenburg. Houghton Mifflin, 1999. Part of the Scientists in the Field series, this fascinating book with its full-color photos documents the demise of wolves from the lower forty-eight states and the efforts of biologists to reintroduce them into Yellowstone National Park and other areas.

Restless Earth: Disasters of Nature, National Geographic Society, 1997. The full-color photos in this glossy, oversized book are almost better than watching television because readers can hold them still for concentrated study. The extensive write-ups also provide more details than can usually fit into a news story.

Nonfiction—History, Science, and Technology

Bodies from the Bog by James M. Deem. Houghton Mifflin, 1998. As peat bogs have been cut for fuel on the plains of northern Europe, several well-preserved corpses have been found. Deem provides information about the bogs and about the amazing forensic methods being used to eke out information from a time long past and little known. Full-color photos, as well as historical ones, add interest.

Close Encounters: Exploring the Universe with the Hubble Space Telescope by Elaine Scott. Hyperion, 1998. *Close Encounters* is a follow-up to Scott's *Adventure in Space: The Flight to Fix the Hubble* (Hyperion, 1995) and is equally detailed and well illustrated as she explains the purpose of the various instruments on the Hubble and includes full-color photos as well as artists' renditions.

Discovering the Inca Ice Maiden: My Adventures on Ampato by Johan Reinhard. National Geographic, 1998. Reinhard is the anthropologist who in 1995 found the frozen mummy of a girl from the Inca Empire who was about 14 years old when she died from a skull fracture. The full-color photos are fascinating as is his account of the excitement and the meaning of the find as well as the steps necessary to protect it.

Invisible Enemies: Stories of Infectious Disease by Jeanette Farrell. Farrar, Straus & Giroux, 1998. Farrell makes fighting against such diseases as smallpox, leprosy, tuberculosis, and AIDS as exciting as either real-life or fictional battles against enemies that can be seen and heard.

Just What the Doctor Ordered: The History of American Medicine by Brandon Marie Miller. Lerner People's History Series, 1997. This eighty-eight-page book starts with American Indian ceremonies and remedies and goes on through the part that illness and disease played in the Revolutionary and Civil Wars, turn-of-the-century dental care, Lydia E. Pinkham's Vegetable Tonic for Female Problems, and on into today's laser surgery.

Shoes: Their History in Words and Pictures by Charlotte and David Yue. Houghton Mifflin, 1997. The only really new shoe design of the last century is the sneaker, but that doesn't keep readers from being fascinated by the wealth of shoes in this fascinating history.

Tracking Dinosaurs in the Gobi by Margery Facklam. 21st Century Books, 1997. In the 1920s, Roy Chapman Andrews led the first American expedition to the Gobi desert in search of fossils. They made such amazing discoveries that Andrews became the model for the fictional character of Indiana Jones. Facklam tells not only his story but more recent ones as well.

and leave out life as it was lived by most people. Another complaint is that they leave out the experiences of women and minorities. Well-written and well-illustrated trade books serve as a counterbalance to these omissions.

Teenagers are especially interested in books that present the extremes of life's experiences, which is why various editions and adaptations of *The Guinness Book of World Records* remain popular. Whatever is the biggest, the best, or the most unusual is of interest, which partly explains the popularity of Penny Colman's *Corpses, Coffins, and Crypts: A History of Burial*; Frederick Drimmer's *Incredible People: Five Stories of Extraordinary Lives*; and Rosemary Guiley's *The Encyclopedia of Ghosts and Spirits*, which a *School Library Journal* reviewer described as "a miracle—a reference book that's also a terrific read" in maintaining the "enticing lure of the supernatural" while presenting both beliefs and skepticism.

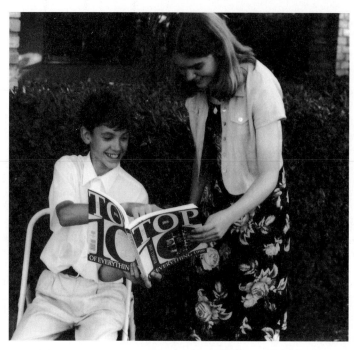

One of the reasons for the popularity of trivia books, as with Dorling Kindersley's *Top 10 of Everything,* is that the items are short and intriguing enough that kids can share them with each other.

Books presenting bits and pieces of miscellaneous information provide instant entertainment and intriguing facts that readers can share with others. Good examples are Russell Ash's *Factastic Book of 1001 Lists* and *Junior Chronicle of the 20th Century.* In 336 oversized pages, each including several full-color photographs, the editors give the major events of each year. They were clever in finding at least one youth-oriented photo for each double-page spread.

Succinctness and easy accessibility are also selling points when encouraging teenagers to dip into collections of essays as opposed to books that need to be read in their entirety. Students who have enjoyed Robert Cormier's fiction might look on his *I Have Words to Spend: Reflections of a Small-Town Editor* as a chance to share thoughts with the kind of uncle or grandfather they wish they had been lucky enough to have. Teenagers can also enjoy Russell Baker's, Erma Bombeck's, and Andy Rooney's collections of newspaper columns.

Space in this text allows us to present only a sample of the many books available as companion reading, or even replacement reading, for typical textbooks (see Focus Boxes 9.2 and 9.3 for some suggestions). When selecting such books, librarians and teachers should remember that teenagers most often pick them up to find specific information. Because young readers lack the kind of background knowledge that most adults have, it is especially important that informative books be well organized and indexed in such a way that readers can look up facts without reading the whole book. Unclear references or confusing directions are especially troublesome in how-to books, which range from books as practical and personal as Ron Volpe's *The Lady Mechanic's Total Car Care for the Clueless* and Deborah Heiligman's

FOCUS BOX 9.3

Nonfiction—Humanities and the Arts

Art Attack: A Short Cultural History of the Avant-Garde by Marc Aronson. Clarion, 1998. Many adults will be grateful for this clear and interesting history of modern art. Aronson provides information to help readers turn his book into a multisensory experience by suggesting music to listen to while reading and telling where on the Internet readers can find more information and full-color reproductions of some of the art pieces about which he writes and presents in black and white.

Chuck Close, Up Close by Jan Greenberg and Sandra Jordan. Dorling Kindersley Ink, 1998. Chuck Close became famous in the late 1960s and has continued to paint huge portraits in an abstract and unique style that reminds viewers of computer art or some other mechanical process. As usual with Dorling Kindersley Ink, the reproductions are beautifully done. A section on "What Is a Portrait?" goes beyond the work of Chuck Close to include portraits done in different styles by other artists.

Circus: An Album by Linda Granfield. Dorling Kindersley Ink, 1998. We considered putting this in the Focus Box on Picture Books because each of the large, double-spread pages has several pictures (photos, drawings, posters, boxed sidebars, tickets, and programs), but if readers just look at the pictures they will miss out on some fascinating information both about the history and the future of circuses.

In Search of the Spirit: The Living National Treasures of Japan by Sheila Hamanaka and Ayano Ohmi. Morrow, 1999. Hoping to keep traditional arts alive, the post-war Japanese government established a program to honor and support elderly artists and to encourage them to pass on their skills. Approximately 100 men and women have received the honor of being a Living National Treasure. Six of them are pictured and their crafts explained in this beautifully designed book.

Keeping Secrets: The Girlhood Diaries of Seven Women Writers by Mary E. Lyons. Holt, 1995. These excerpts from the diaries of nineteenth-century girls who grew up to become well-known writers may encourage aspiring writers to keep their own journals.

Lives of the Musicians: Good Times, Bad Times (and What the Neighbors Thought) by Kathleen Krull. Harcourt Brace Jovanovich, 1993. Although the publishers recommend "ages 8–12," we've found that teenagers and adults—including nonmusical ones—are intrigued by the brief stories of twenty musical geniuses and the clever illustrations by Kathryn Hewitt. Companion volumes (all Harcourt Brace Jovanovich) include *Lives of the Artists: Masterpieces, Messes (and What the Neighbors Thought)*; and *Lives of the Writers: Comedies, Tragedies (and What the Neighbors Thought)*; and *Lives of the Athletes: Thrills, Spills (and What the Neighbors Thought)*. In 1999, Krull also published *They Saw the Future: Oracles, Psychics, Scientists, Great Thinkers, and Pretty Good Guessers* with Simon & Schuster/Atheneum.

The Paper's Papers: A Reporter's Journey through the Archives of the New York Times by Richard Shepard. Times Books, 1996. This general adult book has lots to say to teens who aspire to careers in journalism. Shepard worked for the *New York Times* between 1946 and 1991 and used his long experience and access to the paper's files to write this lively history of a great newspaper.

Quotations for Kids, edited and compiled by J. A. Senn, illustrated by Steve Pica. Millbrook, 1999. Humorous full-color cartoons add interest to the over 2,000 quotations in this 256-page book. They are arranged alphabetically by subjects likely to appeal to young people. Sources are clearly identified, including the name of the character who spoke the line if it comes from fiction.

Talking with Tebe: Clementine Hunter, Memory Artist by Mary E. Lyons. Houghton Mifflin, 1998. Clementine Hunter, known as Tebe, died in 1987 at the age of 101. She was an African-American primitive artist who lived in Louisiana and worked as a manual laborer. Even though she never learned to read or write, she was nationally known and respected, and her art pieces are displayed in many museums. Lyons gathered quotes from Tebe that were published in newspaper and magazine articles or preserved in taped interviews.

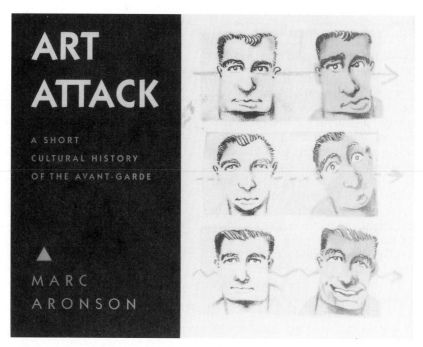

See Focus Box 9.3 for new nonfiction relating to humanities and the arts.

The New York Public Library Kid's Guide to Research to such ambitious social action books as Arlene Hirschfelder's *Kick Butts! A Kid's Action Guide to a Tobacco-Free America* and Catherine Paladino's *One Good Apple: Growing Our Food for the Sake of the Earth*.

How-to books are seldom best-sellers, simply because they are so specialized that they appeal to fairly limited audiences. The challenge for the teacher or librarian is to let students know about their availability. Once students find their way into the library to check out a book that helps them accomplish a particular goal, they are likely to return for other books. If they are disappointed by ambiguous or hard-to-understand directions or come-on statements that make projects look easier than they are, they may lose interest in both the project and the library.

With sports books, obviously the first thing a reader looks for is the particular sport; consequently, authors choose titles that practically shout to potential readers. The sports books that stand out from the crowd usually have a believable and likable personality behind them (see Focus Box 5.3, p. 156 Sports Nonfiction—Real-Life Dreams). Many such books are inspirational as much as instructive, but one thing to watch for in a how-to sports book is whether costs are mentioned. It is almost cruel for an author to write a glowing account of a child star in tennis, gymnastics, skating, swimming, or dancing and leave young readers with the impression that all it takes is hard work. Those readers whose parents do not have time or money for transportation, lessons, entry fees, equipment, and clothes should be let in on the secret that there's more to how you play the game than meets the eye. A similar warning needs to be given about books telling kids how to establish their own businesses or how to get into show business. Such wish-fulfilling books about unusual successes are likely to set the stage for disappointment among the thousands of more typical kids who find themselves working in fast-food restaurants or as grocery store courtesy clerks for minimum wages. There's a need for more books about these less glamorous jobs as well as for the kind of commonsense guidance found in Neale S. Godfrey's *Godfrey's Ultimate Kid's Money Book.*

For academically inclined high school students, it is important to bring books about college to their attention early on because the actual application process takes eighteen months, and its success or failure may depend on what classes a student took as a freshman. High school libraries should have recent editions of such books as *The Fiske Guide to Colleges* and the Princeton Review's guide to *Visiting College Campuses* as well as various practice books designed to help students do well on admissions examinations.

Books helping students plan their future careers are equally important. As with sports-related books, the ones that are the most fun to read are biographical or personal experience accounts (see Chapter Eight) such as those written by James Herriot on his veterinary practice or by Farley Mowat on being a naturalist. For more complete information on a wider range of jobs, see the *Careers without College* series from Peterson's Guides, the *Career Horizons* books from VGM, and the *Careers and Opportunities* series from Rosen.

Nonfiction to Help Teenagers Learn Who They Are and Where They Fit

When young adult specialist Patty Campbell spoke at an American Library Association annual meeting, she pointed out that teenagers are so wrapped up in what the psychologists have labeled the "adolescent identity crisis" that they have neither the time for nor the interest in sitting down and reading about the world in general. What they are looking for are books that help them decide on who they are and where they fit into the scheme of things. Informative books they judge to be helpful include sex education books, some physical and mental health books, selected how-to books, and biographies or true accounts of experiences teenagers can imagine themselves or their acquaintances having. Nearly all the other information books published for teenagers are read under duress—only because teachers assign reports and research papers.

Teenagers especially appreciate books that give advice on managing one's life and being successful right now. Marie Hardenbrook, librarian at McClintock High School in Tempe, Arizona, says that over the last few years her "Inspirational" display and booklist has been consistently popular. She includes such sports-related books as Richard E. Peck's *Something for Joey*, William Blinn's *Brian's Song*, Steve Cameron's *Brett Favre: Huck Finn Grows Up*, and Shannon Miller's *Winning Every Day: Gold Medal Advice for a Happy, Healthy Life.* The runaway best-loaners, however, are Jack Canfield's books including two volumes of *Chicken Soup for the Teenage Soul: 101 Stories of Life, Love, and Learning; Chicken Soup for the Pet Lover's Soul: Stories about Pets as Teachers, Healers, Heroes, and Friends;* and *Chicken Soup for the Woman's Soul: 101 Stories to Open the Hearts and Rekindle the Spirits of Women.* Other books that kids appreciate from her display and booklist are Adeline Yen Mah's *Falling Leaves: The True Story of an Unloved Chinese Daughter,* James McBride's *The Color of Water: A Black Man's Tribute to His White Mother,* and Brad Steiger's *Animal Miracles: Inspirational and Heroic True Stories.*

See Focus Box 9.4, Information About Bodies and Minds for books that answer the more specific kinds of questions that kids ask about both themselves and each other; for example,

Information about Bodies and Minds

Adolescence: The Survival Guide for Parents and Teenagers by Elizabeth Fenwick and Dr. Tony Smith. Dorling Kindersley Ink, 1996. Main sections include "The Milestones of Adolescence," "Learning to Live Together," "The Adolescent and the Outside World," and "The Adolescent in Trouble." Full-paged photos and boxed inserts add variety to this nearly 300-page book.

Anorexia and Bulimia by Paul R. Robbins. Enslow, 1998. Part of the Diseases and People Series, this book is informative and up to date providing similar information to that in Nancy J. Kolodny's *When Food's a Foe* (Little, Brown, 1992) or Michael Maloney and Rachel Kranz's *Straight Talk about Eating Disorders* (Facts On File, 1991).

The Body Project: An Intimate History of American Girls by Joan Jacobs Brumberg. Random House, 1997. As one reviewer said, Brumberg shows how a body born just 12 years ago, can have a 100-year history. Brumberg explores the social and emotional costs that have come to young women in the twentieth century as a result of consumerism, the mass media, and changing social attitudes.

Changing Bodies, Changing Lives: Expanded Third Edition by Ruth Bell and the other coauthors of *Our Bodies, Ourselves* and *Ourselves and Our Children,* together with members of the Teen Book Project. Times Books, 1998. Comments from teenagers, along with photos and drawings, are scattered throughout this large, 410-page book, which was created under the philosophy that the more young people know about themselves and their bodies, the better able they will be to manage their lives. Besides the chapters on sex education, there are chapters on "Emotional Health Care," "Eating Disorders," "Substance Abuse," and "Living with Violence."

Drinking: A Risky Business by Laurence Pringle. Morrow, 1997. Besides presenting the personal aspects of drinking, Pringle includes a chapter on the history of the U.S. temperance movement and the economics of the alcohol industry. The personal health message is comparable to what he did in *Smoking* (Morrow, 1996).

Girls Speak Out: Finding Your True Self by Andrea Johnston, introduction by Gloria Steinem. Scholastic, 1997. This guide to self-esteem tries to provide for individual readers the kind of conversation and talk that takes place in the "Girls Speak Out" weekend programs affiliated with the YWCA. A chapter near the end provides "Who I Am" statements from thirty participants.

How Sex Works by Elizabeth Fenwick and Richard Walker. Dorling Kindersley Ink, 1994. The description on the cover of "A clear, comprehensive guide for teenagers to emotional, physical, and sexual maturity," explains the goal of this ninety-six-page book. The photos are appealing, but some readers have sensed a mismatch between the young looking models on the cover and the explicitness of the information.

Intimate Universe: The Human Body by Anthony Smith. Random House, 1998. Published to accompany the eight-part televised series *Intimate Universe* broadcast by TLC (The Learning Channel) and the BBC (British Broadcasting Channel), this oversized book with its dramatic photos, including many microscopic views, traces the body from conception through death.

It's Perfectly Normal: A Book about Changing Bodies, Growing Up, Sex, and Sexual Health by Robie H. Harris, illustrated by Michael Emberley. Candlewick, 1994. A light-hearted approach is communicated through a bird and a bee arguing their way through the pages of what is actually a serious discussion prepared for readers in middle school or junior high.

The Right Moves: A Girl's Guide to Getting Fit and Feeling Good by Tina Schwager and Michele Schuerger, illustrated by Mike Gordon and Marieka Heinlen. Free Spirit, 1998. Humorous line drawings lend a light touch to this book with its focus on developing a positive self-image, choosing nutritious foods, and exercising regularly.

Straight Talk About Teenage Pregnancy by Paula Edelson. Facts on File, 1998. If readers wait until they are pregnant to get this book, they won't get their money's worth because a good portion of it focuses on how to avoid pregnancy. However, there's still plenty of "straight talk" about parenting, adoption, and abortion. Resources are described including Web sites that are pro-choice and pro-life.

Outspoken: Role Models from the Lesbian and Gay Community by Michael Thomas Ford. Morrow, 1998. Through interviews, Ford tells the stories of six men and women who after the turmoil they felt as teenagers have come to accept their sexual identity.

Can I get AIDS from French kissing?

Do I have diabetes?

Why do I feel like crying all the time?

How serious is herpes?

What's the difference between just trying a drug and becoming addicted?

If I'm pregnant, what are my options?

What's an STD?

Is being fat really unhealthy?

What causes pimples?

What happens if someone has Hodgkin's disease?

My mother has breast cancer. Is she going to die?

Is anorexia nervosa just in a person's head?

Why does my grandfather say such strange things? Will I be like that when I'm old?

What will happen if I have venereal disease and don't go to the doctor?

The best books offering answers to such questions have good indexing, clear writing, suggestions for further reading, and, where appropriate, information about Web pages, telephone numbers, and support groups.

The exploration of sexual matters in books for young readers is an especially sensitive area for the following reasons:

1. Young adults are physically mature, but they probably have had little intellectual and emotional preparation for making sex-related decisions.
2. Parents are anxious to protect their children from making sex-related decisions that might prove harmful.
3. Old restraints and patterns of behavior and attitudes are being questioned, so that there is no clear-cut model to follow.
4. Sex is such an important part of American culture and the mass media that young people are forced to think about and take stands on such controversial issues as homosexuality, premarital sex, violence in relation to sex, and the role of sex in love and family relationships.
5. Talking about sexual attitudes and beliefs with their teenage children may make parents uncomfortable, especially if the father and the mother have different views. This means that many young people must get their information outside of the home.

While some books focus specifically on a problem such as AIDS or pregnancy, it is more common for books to cover emotional as well as physical aspects of sexual activity. No single book can satisfy all readers, and this is true of those dealing with sex education. An entire collection must be evaluated and books provided for a wide range of interests, attitudes, beliefs, and lifestyles. Those who criticize libraries for including books that present teenage sexual activity as the norm have a justified complaint if the library does not also have sex education books that present, or even promote, abstinence as a normal route for young people.

Materials dealing with sex are judged quite differently from those on less controversial topics. For example, in most subject areas, books are given plus marks if they succeed in getting the reader emotionally involved, but with books about sex, some adults feel that it is better for young readers to be presented with straightforward, "plumbing manuals"—the less emotional involvement the better. Other adults argue that it is the emotional part that young people need to learn. Coming to agreement is not at all easy because adults have such varying attitudes and experiences as shown by M. E. Kerr's statement below.

Well-planned and well-written books can present information about different viewpoints, and teachers and librarians are performing a worthwhile service if they bring such books to the attention of young people. As we mentioned in Chapter Three, a new trend in women's magazines is to use sex-related articles as a selling

M. E. KERR
On Gay Books

When I attended an Episcopalian boarding school in Virginia, in the forties, I wrote an essay about a "Negro lady." My teacher wrote in the margin, "Negro women are never referred to as ladies. Only white women."

My brother, at the time, was in a military school in Florida. When I went there with my family to visit him, we passed several large hotels with a sign at the entrance: RESTRICTED. My father explained to me that no Jews were allowed there.

He always pointed out how wrong prejudice was. He would say, "Imagine the world had never known a Marian Anderson, an Einstein, a George Washington Carver, or a Jonas Salk."

He was a vigorous defender of all peoples except when it came to homosexuals. All he would say in our behalf was that it was wrong to look down on anybody, "including them."

Today it is hard for me imagine that time when prejudice flourished. But my father's tolerant, dismissive attitude regarding homosexuality, is one I often encounter when I am asked to give presentations in schools. Now that publishers are labeling YA literature "10 up," or "Junior High up," I more and more find myself speaking to fifth and sixth graders, as well as older kids. Some teachers make it clear ahead of time that "this isn't an audience for your gay novels," and some teachers simply don't order them. A principal once met me in the parking lot and said, "We like your books a lot, Ms. Kerr, but these children are too young for *Night Kites*, *Deliver Us from Evie*, or *Hello, I Lied*." (They were sixth, seventh, and eighth graders.)

I understand that most often neither the teachers nor the principals are responsible for this blackout—nor are most parents—it is usually only a few parents, more likely just one who, experience has proven, is bound to cause big trouble around this issue.

Of course kids know about gays; any kid who watches TV does. There are gay characters in sitcoms now, on soaps, on talk shows and featured in movies and made for TV dramas. Gay performers are on MTV, and there are gay rock stars, singers, and composers.

The failure to mention us to children, and to discuss books about us, puts us in a special category. Kids know we're there, but they sense that somehow we're reprehensible. Educators are not protecting the child with this blackout, they are protecting the prejudice.

Hate mongers can feel safe calling out "Fag!" and "Dyke!" and the joke about the male who lisps is okay to tell. Take that attitude to its limit and you have 21-year-old Matthew Sheppard kidnapped, robbed, tied to a fence, beaten in the head with a .357 Magnum, tortured with cigarettes, and left to die in freezing temperatures. His murderers claimed he made a pass at one of them.

The *Wall Street Journal* recently published some of the findings of the 1997 Massachusetts Youth Risk Behavior Survey stating that lesbian, gay, bisexual and transgendered children are more than four times as likely as their heterosexual counterparts to be threatened with a weapon at school. They are more than five times as likely to skip school because of feeling unsafe en route to or at school. They are more than four times as likely to be in a fight resulting in medical treatment. And as a result of this abuse, they are more than five times as likely to attempt suicide.

What is the fault of telling 10-, 11-, and 12-year-olds-and-up that no one knows for sure why some people realize a love with someone of the same sex, but it is a fact of life?

Why can't we ask them to imagine a world which had never known W. H. Auden, Phillip Johnson, Leonardo da Vinci, Walt Whitman, Bernice Abbott, Willa Cather, Mary Renault, and Rosa Bonheur?

M. E. Kerr's books, all from HarperCollins, include *Blood on the Forehead*, 1998; *Deliver Us from Evie*, 1994; and *"Hello", I Lied*, 1997.

point. In magazines for young women, many of the articles are written as though their purpose is sex education, when in fact they border on what *Playboy* editors once described as "pious pornography." Women who have inhibitions or feel guilty about sex can think and talk about sexuality as long as they are doing it to learn something, especially if they are made to feel that they are being unselfish in learning to "please their man." Ironically, the easy availability of such magazines, as well as all the sexually oriented material available on the Internet, probably cuts down on the number of young people going to a library in search of sex education materials. This is too bad because there is little or no control over what gets on the Internet, and magazine articles designed to entice buyers may be more wish-fulfilling than accurate in providing the kinds of well-rounded information that young people need.

When helping young adults make reading decisions in this area, we need to consider the reader's purpose. If the reader wants basic information, nonfiction is far superior because it can present a wider range of information in a clear, unambiguous way. But if the reader desires to understand the emotional and physical aspects of a particular relationship, an honest piece of fiction usually does a better job.

The important thing for adults to remember is that they should provide both kinds of material in conjunction with a listening ear and a willingness to discuss questions. Schools and libraries need to seek community help in exchanging ideas and developing policies. Family values must be respected, but honest, accurate information must also be available for those who seek it. Charting a course along this delicate line is more than any one individual should be expected to do, which is why people need to communicate with each other. Professionals working with books are also obligated to find and study the latest, most authentic information and to bring that information to those who are helping to shape policies and practices. The general public may get away with objecting to or endorsing ideas and books that they have never explored or read. Not so for the professional charged with leading a group to consensus or compromise. The more you know about the materials, and the more you understand about individual and group differences, the better able you are to participate in book selection, discussion, and, sometimes, defense.

Authors of Nonfiction for Young Adults

Some nonfiction authors are so productive that it makes one wonder if they have something like the Stratemeyer Syndicate helping them write their books. What's more likely is that they approach the task like journalists doing research for newspaper features. They write on current topics and bring together other people's research, making it accessible to teenagers.

Not all educators appreciate the kind of journalistic work that goes into these authors' books because they think it would be better training for students to go directly to the magazine and journal articles that the authors go to for their information. The argument is similar to the one that college teachers of freshman composition have over whether it is best to use a source book when students do research papers or to have students go only to primary sources. There's something to be said for both sides. Teachers and librarians, however, should at least be aware of the issue and should help students go beyond relying on any one book when they are researching controversial issues.

As the role of nonfiction has become increasingly recognized in the young adult market, a group of significant authors has emerged. Brent Ashabranner, Janet Bode, Howard and Margery Facklam, Kathlyn Gay, Margaret O. Hyde, William Loren Katz, Michael Kronenwetter, Susan Kuklin, Patricia Lauber, Frederick L. McKissack, Patricia C. McKissack, and Jim Murphy are writers whose names frequently appear on lists of recommended nonfiction. The McKissacks's *Rebels Against Slavery: American Slave Revolts* was a 1997 Coretta Scott King Award Honor Book, while their *Let My People Go: Bible Stories Told by a Freeman of Color* was praised for combining African-American history and Bible literature. *Booklist* editors praised their *Young, Black, and Determined: A Biography of Lorraine Hansberry* for the way it allowed readers to "drink in the whole civil rights history" of America in the middle of the twentieth century. Patricia Lauber has long been an acclaimed science writer for children, but publishers are now labeling some of her beautifully illustrated books as "gr. 4–up" or "gr. 5–up." Among her books that we have seen teenagers relate to are *Painters of the Caves, Volcano: The Eruption and Healing of Mt. St. Helens, Summer of Fire: Yellowstone, 1988,* and *Seeing Earth from Space.*

In addition to these authors, the ones described next can usually be trusted to provide the something extra that comes when a writer is truly involved in the subject and puts heart and soul into a book. We are not claiming that the following authors, introduced in alphabetical order, are the only ones about whom this could be said, but we are willing to say that they are among a growing body of nonfiction writers who prepare their books with the same kind of care and feeling that goes into the best fiction writing.

Russell Freedman

Nearly thirty years elapsed between the time that Russell Freedman wrote his first book *Teenagers Who Made History* in 1961 and when he won the Newbery Award in 1988 for *Lincoln: A Photobiography.* Since then he has been honored with the Laura Ingalls Wilder Award given every five years to honor a lifetime contribution. Among his most recent books are *Martha Graham: A Dancer's Life* and *Babe Didrikson Zaharias: The Making of a Champion.* These have between 175 and 200 pages and as such are longer than his earlier books. Freedman began his career by focusing mostly on books about animals for primary and middle grade readers. A turning point came when he attended an exhibition of historical photographs and found himself "communicating" with the young faces that stared out at him from the old photos. He searched out these and other pictures for a book *Immigrant Kids.* Since then he has made a specialty out of finding evocative photographs to use not as decoration but as an integral part of his books. His timing was perfect for communicating with a generation of young readers who had grown up watching television. He won the Orbis Pictus Award and the Boston Globe/Honor Book award for his 1990 *Franklin Delano Roosevelt.* His 1991 *The Wright Brothers* was a Newbery Honor Book and so was his 1993 *Eleanor Roosevelt: A Life of Discovery.* In his 1994 *Kids at Work: Lewis Hine and the Crusade Against Child Labor,* he wrote directly about the power of photography by telling the story of an early photographer who took it upon himself to document the conditions under which U.S. children labored.

James Cross Giblin

Giblin's background as an editor of children's books stands him in good stead when he writes informational books. He chooses unlikely topics and then does enough research and careful planning and writing so that his readers find new and interesting information. His *The Riddle of the Rosetta Stone: Key to Ancient Egypt* is a fascinating detective story about how a large stone slab covered with writing in three different languages enabled linguists to decipher one of the world's first writing systems. Giblin's *The Truth About Unicorns* serves as an excellent model for research as it traces the history of beliefs, superstitions, stories, and art about this mythical creature. His *Charles A. Lindbergh, A Human Hero* was chosen for several best-book lists based on Giblin's meticulous research and the skillful way that he balanced information about "an all-too-human-hero."

James (Jim) Haskins

As with many other authors of nonfiction, James Haskins writes both for children and for young adults. He's been a stockbroker, a high school teacher in New York, and a faculty member at several colleges, including Staten Island Community College, Manhattanville College, Indiana University, and Purdue. In 1979, he published an adult book, *Diary of a Harlem Schoolteacher*. For young adults, his main contribution has been to recognize the need for biographies and other books about minorities. In contrast to so many of us who bemoan the lack of a particular kind of book, Haskins set out to put his pencil (more likely his word processor) where his mouth is. Since the mid-1970s, he has consistently prepared books on African-American heroes and African-American history as well as on such topics as rights for people with disabilities, the American labor movement, and women leaders in other countries (e.g., Corazon Aquino and Indira Gandhi). Among his most recent books are *Spike Lee: By Any Means Necessary*; *Bound for America: The Forced Migration of Africans to the New World* illustrated by Floyd Cooper; *African American Entrepreneurs*; *Power to the People: The Rise and Fall of the Black Panther Party*; *Get on Board: The Story of the Underground Railroad*; *I Have a Dream: The Life and Words of Martin Luther King, Jr.*; *Thurgood Marshall: A Life for Justice*; *I Am Somebody! A Biography of Jesse Jackson*; and *Freedom Rides: Journey for Justice*.

Albert Marrin

Albert Marrin earned a Ph.D. in history from Columbia University in 1968 and shortly thereafter began publishing history-related books. We first took notice of his books in 1985 when his *1812: The War Nobody Won* was chosen as a *Boston Globe—Horn Book* Honor Book for Nonfiction. Since then, his books including *Virginia's General: Robert E. Lee and the Civil War* and *Unconditional Surrender: U.S. Grant and the Civil War* have consistently appeared on best-book lists and received starred reviews. *School Library Journal* praised his *The Spanish-American War* for delineating "how American jingoists, expansionists, 'big navy' advocates, yellow journalists, and filibusterers maneuvered the nation into taking part in what politicians called 'A splendid little war!'" Other highly recommended history books include *Empires Lost and Won: The Spanish Heritage in the Southwest*; *Struggle for a Continent: The French and Indian Wars*; *America and Vietnam: The Elephant and the Tiger*; *Cowboys, Indians, and Gunfighters: The Story of the Cattle Kingdom*; and *The War for Independence*. His biographies include *Hitler*; *Stalin: Russia's Man of Steel*; *The Sea King: Sir Francis Drake and His Times*; *Commander in Chief Abraham Lincoln and the Civil War*; and *Terror of the Spanish Main: Sir Henry Morgan and His Buccaneers*.

Milton Meltzer

Of all the nonfiction writers for young adults, Milton Meltzer is the one most consistently recognized as a spokesperson and champion of the genre. He focuses on social issues and for the third edition of this textbook wrote that except for inventing facts, he used almost all the same techniques as do writers of fiction. Literary devices help him draw readers into the situation and the story that he is telling and they help to enrich and deepen readers' feelings for people whose lives may be far different. He believes that it is not so much a question of fiction vs. fact, but of truth vs. falseness. His conclusion was that both fiction and nonfiction can lie about reality; but they can also tell the truth.

Meltzer investigates whatever topics he finds interesting with one area of research triggering questions about another so that he has moved from poverty to crime to terrorism and on to racism, slavery, war, and politics. His 1998 *Food: How We Hunt and Gather It, How We Grow and Eat It, How We Buy and Sell It, How We Preserve and Waste It, and How Some Have Too Much and Others Have Too Little of It* grabbed attention for the length of its title as well as for its subject matter. Meltzer pioneered an in-their-own-words technique using historical journals, diaries, letters, and news accounts to bring out the personalities of his subjects and to illustrate how their lives have been shaped by their situations. Examples include *Lincoln in His Own Words* and *Frederick Douglass: In His Own Words*, both illustrated by Stephen Alcorn. Among his most acclaimed titles are *The Many Lives of Andrew Carnegie; The Bill of Rights: How We Got It and What It Means; Columbus and the World Around Him; Voices from the Civil War; Never to Forget: The Jews of the Holocaust*; and *Rescue: The Story of How Gentiles Saved Jews in the Holocaust.*

Laurence Pringle

Laurence Pringle is a respected and prolific writer of science-related books for young readers. For an earlier edition of this text, he discussed the challenge of being "fair" when writing about decision making that involves both social and scientific knowledge and attitudes. Because idealistic young readers may be especially vulnerable to one-sided arguments, he says that writers have a responsibility to present all sides of an issue and to show the gray as well as the black and white. He quickly adds, however, that being fair is not the same as being objective, "anyone who is well informed on an issue is not neutral," but that does not mean that he or she can not work "to help kids understand the issues so they can make their own decisions." Among Pringle's recent well-received books are *Drinking, A Risky Business* and *Jackal Woman: Exploring the World of Jackals*, in which he introduces middle school readers to the life of a behavioral ecologist, Patricia Moehlman. She was trained by Jane Goodall and is doing for jackals what Goodall did for chimpanzees. Other titles include *Chemical and Biological Warfare: The Cruelest Weapons; Oil Spills: Damage, Recovery and Prevention; Living Treasure: Saving Earth's Threatened Biodiversity; Global Warming*; and *Rain of Trouble: The Science and Politics of Acid Rain.*

Poetry

Marc Aronson is a senior editor at Henry Holt where he works with the Edge imprint. In a speech he presented about the development of American adolescent literature at a 1997 conference in Rome, he told how poetry books have been a surprising success in young adult literature. One of Holt's best sellers in 1994 was Lori

M. Carlson's *Cool Salsa: Bilingual Poems on Growing Up Latino in the United States.*
He gave part of the credit to the fact that Carlson had found hip poems in three languages: English, Spanish, and Spanglish. He then explained:

> Poetry has been out of favor in America for a good long time. It was seen as either incredibly boring, or impossibly difficult to understand. Neither made it a good match for teenagers. But that has changed. The popularity of rap music has made adolescents very conscious of the power of words, rhythm, and rhyme. The revival of the Beat poets as emblems of rebellion, sexuality, and coolness has encouraged teenagers to drink espresso, grow beards, read Kerouac, and recite their own poetry.[4]

Poetry was the focus topic of the April 1999 issue of *VOYA*. Besides a listing of some thirty-five recommended poetry anthologies, there were articles about monthly teen poetry events at the public library in Ft. Lauderdale, Florida; Poetry Slams (teens reading their own poems, short stories, or other writing) at the Central Rappahannock Regional Library in Fredericksburg, Maryland; a coffeehouse setting for poetry readings at the public library in East Brunswick, New Jersey; and poetry readings by English as a second language (ESL) students at the Berkeley, California Public Library.

Perhaps the most surprising news story about teenage poetry readings was the one that appeared in *Time* magazine (Sept. 13, 1999) under the title "Who Are the New Beat Poets? Hint: They're Blue." The story was about a "Take 5" program put on by the Chicago police department, which has been sponsoring poetry readings in local station houses in hopes of establishing better relations with teenagers. While teenagers as well as professional poets have been participating, the biggest surprise has been police officers themselves stepping forward to share their thoughts. *Time* quoted Officer Linda Griffith:

> He allows me to walk the danger,
> He lets me extend help to a stranger,
> My flesh crawls and I miss him when he's not under my wing.
> I don't let people see or touch him, it's a private thing.
> So you should be grateful and understand what I've done.
> If and when I let you touch the butt of my gun.

Readers' appreciation for poetry develops in much the same way as their appreciation for prose. They begin with an unconscious delight in sounds—the repetition and rhythm of nursery rhymes, songs, and television commercials. Then they go on to the fun of riddles, puns, playground chants, and autograph rhymes. Soon they get involved in such simple plots as those found in limericks and the humorous verses of Jack Prelutsky and Shel Silverstein. By the time children are in the middle grades, their favorite poems are those that tell stories, for example, Robert Browning's "The Pied Piper of Hamelin," Henry Wadsworth Longfellow's "Hiawatha's Childhood" and "The Midnight Ride of Paul Revere," Robert Service's "The Cremation of Sam McGee," James Whitcomb Riley's "The Gobble-Uns'll Get You if You Don't Watch Out," and Edgar Allan Poe's "The Raven."

Books that are helpful in introducing students to performance with something less daunting than a whole play include *The Actor's Book of Contemporary Stage Monologues* edited by Nina Shengold, *100 Monologues: An Audition Sourcebook for New Dramatists* edited by Laura Harrington, *Scenes and Monologues from the New American Theatre* edited by Frank Pike and Thomas G. Dunn, and *Sometimes I Wake Up in the Middle of the Night,* monologues written by students of the Walden Theatre Conservatory. Don Gallo's *Center Stage: One-Act Plays for Teenage Readers and Actors* works well in classrooms.

Notes

[1]"A Conversation with Milton Meltzer," in *Nonfiction for Young Adults: From Delight to Wisdom* by Betty Carter and Richard F. Abrahamson (Oryx Press, 1990), pp. 53–54.

[2]Milton Meltzer, "Where Do All the Prizes Go? The Case for Nonfiction," *Horn Book Magazine* 52 (February 1975): 23.

[3]George A. Woods, personal correspondence to Alleen Pace Nilsen, Summer 1978.

[4]Marc Aronson, "When Coming of Age Meets the Age That's Coming: One Editor's View of How Young Adult Publishing Developed in America," *VOYA* 21:5 (December, 1998): 340–342.

[5]Richard W. Beach and James D. Marshall, *Teaching Literature in the Secondary School.* Harcourt Brace Jovanovich, 1991, p. 384.

[6]Paul Janeczko, "On Collecting Poems," *Literature for Today's Young Adults* by Kenneth L. Donelson and Alleen Pace Nilsen (Longman, 1997), p. 345.

[7]Luella B. Cook, "Reading for Experience," *English Journal* 25 (April 1936): 280.

[8]Rick E. Amidon, "Toward a Young Adult Drama," *English Journal* 76 (September 1987): 59.

[9]Lowell Swortzell, "Broadway Bound? Or Beyond?" *English Journal* 76 (September 1987): 52.

Titles Mentioned in the Text of Chapter Nine

Angelou, Maya. *I Know Why the Caged Bird Sings.* Random House, 1970.

Ash, Russell. *Factastic Book of 1001 Lists.* Dorling Kindersley Ink, 1999.

Baldwin, Neil. *To All Gentleness, William Carlos Williams: The Doctor Poet.* Atheneum, 1984.

Blinn, William. *Brian's Song.* Bantam, 1976.

Bradbury, Ray. *When Elephants Last in the Dooryard Bloomed.* Knopf, 1973.

Brooks, Bruce. *Midnight Hour Encores.* HarperCollins, 1986.

Brown, Claude. *Manchild in the Promised Land.* Macmillan, 1965.

Brown, Dee. *Bury My Heart at Wounded Knee: An Indian History of the American West.* Holt, 1971.

Cameron, Steve. *Brett Favre: Huck Finn Grows Up.* Masters, 1997.

Canfield, Jack. *Chicken Soup for the Pet Lover's Soul: Stories about Pets as Teachers, Healers, Heroes, and Friends.* Health Communications, 1998.

Canfield, Jack. *Chicken Soup for the Teenage Soul: 101 Stories of Life, Love, and Learning, I and II.* Health Communications, 1997, 1998.

Canfield, Jack. *Chicken Soup for the Woman's Soul: 101 Stories to Open the Hearts and Rekindle the Spirits of Women.* Health Communications, 1996.

Capote, Truman. *In Cold Blood.* Random House, 1966.

Carlson, Lori. *Cool Salsa: Bilingual Poems on Growing Up Latino in the United States.* Holt, 1994.

Carter, Betty and Richard F. Abrahamson. *Nonfiction for Young Adults: From Delight to Wisdom.* Oryx Press, 1990.

Cleaver, Eldridge. *Soul on Ice.* McGraw-Hill, 1968.

Colman, Penny. *Corpses, Coffins, and Crypts: A History of Burial.* Holt, 1997.

Cormier, Robert. *I Have Words to Spend: Reflections of a Small-Town Editor,* edited by Constance Senay Cormier. Delacorte, 1991.

Dias, Patrick and Michael Hayhoe. *Developing Response to Poetry.* Open University Press, 1988.

Doctorow, E. L. *Ragtime.* Random House, 1975.

Drimmer, Frederick. *Incredible People: Five Stories of Extraordinary Lives.* Atheneum, 1997.

Dunning, Stephen. *Teaching Literature to Adolescents: Poetry.* Scott, Foresman, 1966.

Fiske, Edward B. *The Fiske Guide to Colleges.* Random House, yearly.

Freedman, Russell. *Babe Didrikson Zaharias: The Making of a Champion.* Clarion, 1999.

Freedman, Russell. *Eleanor Roosevelt: A Life of Discovery.* Clarion, 1993.

Freedman, Russell. *Franklin Delano Roosevelt.* Clarion, 1990.

Freedman, Russell. *Immigrant Kids.* Dutton, 1980.

Freedman, Russell. *Kids at Work: Lewis Hine and the Crusade Against Child Labor.* Clarion, 1994.

Freedman, Russell. *Lincoln: A Photobiography.* Clarion, 1987.

Freedman, Russell. *Martha Graham: A Dancer's Life.* Clarion, 1998.

Freedman, Russell. *Teenagers Who Made History.* Holiday House, 1961.

Freedman, Russell. *The Wright Brothers.* Holiday House, 1991.

Gallo, Donald, R., ed. *Center Stage: One-Act Plays for Teenage Readers and Actors.* HarperCollins, 1990.

Giblin, James Cross. *Charles A. Lindbergh, A Human Hero.* Clarion, 1997.

Giblin, James Cross. *The Riddle of the Rosetta Stone: Key to Ancient Egypt.* Crowell, 1990.

Giblin, James Cross. *The Truth About Unicorns.* HarperCollins, 1991.

Glenn, Mel. *Class Dismissed! High School Poems.* Clarion, 1982.

Godfrey, Neale S. *Godfrey's Ultimate Kid's Money Book.* Simon & Schuster, 1998.

Gould, Jean. *American Women Poets: Pioneers of Modern Poetry.* Dodd Mead, 1980.

Graham, Robin. *Dove.* HarperCollins, 1972.

Griffin, John Howard. *Black Like Me.* Houghton Mifflin, 1977.

Guiley, Rosemary Ellen. *The Encyclopedia of Ghosts and Spirits.* Facts on File, 1992.

Haley, Alex. *Roots.* Doubleday, 1976.

Harrington, Laura. *100 Monologues: An Audition Sourcebook for New Dramatists.* Mentor, 1989.

Haskins, James. *African American Entrepreneurs.* Wiley, 1998.

Haskins, James. *Bound for America: The Forced Migration of Africans to the New World.* Lothrop, 1999.

Haskins, James. *Diary of a Harlem Schoolteacher.* Grove Press, 1979.

Haskins, James. *Freedom Rides: Journey for Justice.* Hyperion, 1995.

Haskins, James. *Get on Board: The Story of the Underground Railroad.* Scholastic, 1993.

Haskins, James. *I Am Somebody! A Biography of Jesse Jackson.* Enslow, 1992.

Haskins, James. *I Have a Dream: The Life and Words of Martin Luther King, Jr.* Millbrook, 1993.

Haskins, James. *Power to the People: The Rise and Fall of the Black Panther Party.* Simon & Schuster, 1997.

Haskins, James. *Spike Lee: By Any Means Necessary.* Walker, 1997.

Haskins, James. *Thurgood Marshall: A Life for Justice.* Holt, 1992.

Heiligman, Deborah. *The New York Public Library Kid's Guide to Research.* Scholastic, 1998.

Herriot, James. *All Creatures Great and Small.* St. Martin's, 1972.

Hirschfelder, Arlene. *Kick Butts! A Kid's Action Guide to a Tobacco-Free America.* Simon & Schuster/Messner, 1998.

Jacobus, Lee A., ed. *The Bedford Introduction to Drama,* 3rd ed. Bedford, 1997.

Janecsko, Paul. *Poetspeak: In Their Work, About Their Work.* Bradbury, 1983.

Junior Chronicle of the 20th Century. Dorling Kindersley Ink, 1997.

Keneally, Thomas. *Schindler's List.* Simon & Schuster, 1982.

Lauber, Patricia. *Painters of the Caves.* National Geographic, 1998.

Lauber, Patricia. *Seeing Earth from Space.* Orchard/Watts, 1990.

Lauber, Patricia. *Summer of Fire: Yellowstone, 1988.* Orchard/Watts, 1991.

Lauber, Patricia. *Volcano: The Eruption and Healing of Mt. St. Helens.* Bradbury, 1986.

Lund, Doris. *Eric.* HarperCollins, 1974.

Maas, Peter. *Serpico,* Viking, 1973.

Mah, Adeline Yen. *Falling Leaves: The True Story of an Unloved Chinese Daughter.* Broadway Books, 1998.

Marrin, Albert. *America and Vietnam: The Elephant and the Tiger.* Viking, 1992.

Marrin, Albert. *Commander in Chief Abraham Lincoln and the Civil War.* Dutton, 1997.

Marrin, Albert. *Cowboys, Indians, and Gunfighters: The Story of the Cattle Kingdom.* Atheneum, 1993.

Marrin, Albert. *1812: The War Nobody Won.* Atheneum, 1985.

Marrin, Albert. *Empires Lost and Won: The Spanish Heritage in the Southwest.* Simon & Schuster/Atheneum, 1997.

Marrin, Albert. *Hitler.* Viking, 1987.

Marrin, Albert. *The Sea King: Sir Francis Drake and His Times.* Atheneum, 1995.

Marrin, Albert. *The Spanish-American War.* Atheneum, 1991.

Marrin, Albert. *Stalin: Russia's Man of Steel.* Viking, 1988.

Marrin, Albert. *Struggle for a Continent: The French and Indian Wars.* Atheneum, 1987.

Marrin, Albert. *Terror of the Spanish Main: Sir Henry Morgan and His Buccaneers.* Dutton, 1998.

Marrin, Albert. *Unconditional Surrender: U.S. Grant and the Civil War.* Macmillan, 1994.

Marrin, Albert. *Virginia's General: Robert E. Lee and the Civil War.* Atheneum, 1994.

Marrin, Albert. *The War for Independence: The Story of the American Revolution.* Atheneum, 1988.

McBride, James. *The Color of Water: A Black Man's Tribute to His White Mother.* Riverhead, 1996.

McKissack, Fredrick L. and Patricia C. McKissack. *Young, Black, and Determined: A Biography of Lorraine Hansberry*. Holiday, 1998.

McKissack, Patricia C. and Fredrick L. McKissack, illustrated by James E. Ransome. *Let My People Go: Bible Stories Told by a Freeman of Color*. Simon & Schuster/Atheneum, 1998

McKissack, Patricia C. and Fredrick L. McKissack. *Rebels Against Slavery: American Slave Revolts*. Scholastic, 1996.

Meltzer, Milton. *The Bill of Rights: How We Got It and What It Means*. Crowell, 1990.

Meltzer, Milton. *Columbus and the World Around Him*. Watts, 1990.

Meltzer, Milton. *Food: How We Hunt and Gather It, How We Grow and Eat It, How We Buy and Sell It, How We Preserve and Waste It, and How Some Have Too Much and Others Have Too Little of It*. Millbrook, 1998.

Meltzer, Milton. *Frederick Douglass: In His Own Words*. Harcourt, 1995.

Meltzer, Milton. *Lincoln in His Own Words*. Harcourt, 1993.

Meltzer, Milton. *The Many Lives of Andrew Carnegie*. Watts, 1997.

Meltzer, Milton. *Never to Forget: The Jews of the Holocaust*. HarperCollins, 1976.

Meltzer, Milton. *Rescue: The Story of How Gentiles Saved Jews in the Holocaust*. HarperCollins, 1988.

Meltzer, Milton. *Voices from the Civil War*. Crowell, 1989.

National Council of Teachers of English and Bowker (Joseph Mersand, Committee Chair). *Guide to Play Selection*, 1975.

Paladino, Catherine. *One Good Apple: Growing Our Food for the Sake of the Earth*. Houghton Mifflin, 1999.

Peck, Richard E. *Something for Joey*. Bantam, 1978.

Pike, Frank and Thomas G. Dunn, ed. *Scenes and Monologues from the New American Theatre*. Mentor, 1980.

Pringle, Laurence. *Chemical and Biological Warfare: The Cruelest Weapons*. Enslow, 1993.

Pringle, Laurence. *Drinking, A Risky Business*. Morrow, 1997.

Pringle, Laurence. *Global Warming*. Arcade, 1990.

Pringle, Laurence. *Jackal Woman: Exploring the World of Jackals*. Scribner's, 1993.

Pringle, Laurence. *Living Treasure: Saving Earth's Threatened Biodiversity*. Morrow, 1991.

Pringle, Laurence. *Oil Spills: Damage, Recovery and Prevention*. Morrow, 1993.

Pringle, Laurence. *Rain of Trouble: The Science and Politics of Acid Rain*. Macmillan, 1988.

Read, Piers Paul. *Alive: The Story of the Andes Survivors*. Lippincott, 1974.

Rosenblatt, Louise. *The Reader, the Text, the Poem: The Transactional Theory of the Literary Work*. Southern Illinois University Press, 1978.

Shank, Theodore J. *A Digest of 500 Plays: Plot Outlines and Production Notes*. Crowell-Collier, 1963.

Shengold, Nina, ed. *The Actor's Book of Contemporary Stage Monologues*. Penguin, 1987.

Steiger, Brad. *Animal Miracles: Inspirational and Heroic True Stories*. Adams Media Corp, 1999.

Toffler, Alvin. *Future Shock*. Random House, 1970.

Voigt, Cynthia. *Izzy, Willy-Nilly*. Macmillan, 1986.

Volpe, Ron. *The Lady Mechanic's Total Car Care for the Clueless*. Griffin, 1998.

Walker, Alice. *The Color Purple*. Harcourt Brace Jovanovich, 1982.

Walker, Alice. *Good Night, Willie Lee. I'll See You in the Morning*. Dial, 1979.

Waller, Robert J. *The Bridges of Madison County*. Warner, 1992.

Woodtor, Dee Parmer. *Finding a Place Called Home: A Guide to African-American Genealogy and Historical Identity*. Random House, 1999.

Information on the availability of paperback editions of these titles is available online from such book sellers as Barnes & Noble and Amazon.com, and through *Books in Print* compiled by R. R. Bowker Company and available either in person or online from major libraries.

PART Three

Adults and the Literature of Young Adults

Evaluating, Promoting, and Using Young Adult Books

Chances are that you are studying adolescent literature because you expect to work, or are already working, in a situation that calls for you to bring young adults in touch with books. This chapter begins with a section on evaluation, including the evaluation of literature for and about minorities, followed by discussions centered around common professional roles for adults who work with books and young readers: librarians, reading teachers, social studies teachers, parents, and counselors or youth workers. (See Chapter Eleven for specific information for English teachers.) These areas were chosen to give focus and organization to the information, but there is considerable overlap.

Everyone working with young readers and books needs to be skilled in suggesting the right book for the right student or at least pointing someone in the right direction. When two people are talking about a book they both enjoyed, there is no way to divide the conversation into such discrete categories as literary analysis, personal feelings, sociological implications, and evaluation of potential popularity. Librarians find themselves discussing books as if they were classroom teachers. Teachers can adopt some of the promotional techniques that librarians use, and librarians can use some book discussion tactics that teachers use. In short, the organization of this chapter may make it appear that librarians work with young readers and books quite differently from teachers or counselors. In reality, nearly all adults who work with young readers and books have much the same goals and share many of the same approaches.

All of us meet wide-ranging differences in abilities and personalities, which implies great differences in interests. Those interests demand an alert and prepared adult who is aware of them, who can uncover them, and who is familiar with an enormous number of titles to meet them. To an inexperienced person, the information about books that a librarian or teacher can call forth seems magical, but developing that repertoire takes time, patience, and hard work. Reading many young adult books comes with the territory for the professional, but so does reading professional books, magazines of all sorts, several newspapers, adult books, and much,

much more. The professional likes to read (or would not be working with books), so that makes the job easier and more fun, but the professional reads beyond the areas that are personally enjoyable. For example, whether a professional likes science fiction or not, he or she must know titles of new science fiction. When young adults ask a teacher or librarian for another book like *The Martian Chronicles* (or the *Redwall* books or *The Hitchhiker's Guide to the Galaxy* or *The Perks of Being a Wallflower* or *The Color Purple*), they pay that person a sublime compliment. Woe unto the teacher or librarian who says, "I'm sorry, but I don't know anything about science fiction," or "Why don't you broaden your reading background just a bit?" Such a response kills interest and will probably turn kids away from reading.

In any given group, a teacher or librarian might find students like the following (and gradations in-between): Rachel reads nothing at all (she did once, but now that she has become a woman she has put away childish things); Brenda reads nothing because her reading skills are so poor she is virtually illiterate; Candy read a book once, her first book all the way through, and she hated it; Del reads magazines and an occasional sports biography if he's in an intellectual mood; Emily reads Sweet Valley High romances; José reads all kinds of books as long as they're science fiction; George reads a few books but always classics ("He's going to college," his mother says proudly); Howie reads only religious books and has already warned the teacher about the Satanic powers in *Lord of the Flies*; Imogene reads anything that is popular—Danielle Steele, Anne Rice, best-sellers, and novelizations of movies and television specials; Jon reads classics, football stories, mysteries, and everything else and refuses to be pigeonholed; and Lynn reads all the time, perhaps too much (she's bright but socially immature). Serving the needs of such a diverse group is far from easy, but when the job is well done, it's a valuable contribution.

Evaluating Young Adult Literature

The role of the evaluator of books for young adults is more important than ever because more books are being published and publishers are opting for shorter life spans for all books. With so many ephemeral books around, there's a greater need for knowledgeable people to find and promote the excellent ones. It is ironic that when there are more books to choose from, most schools and libraries have less money to spend. Also, book prices have increased more than budgets, so that if a purchasing mistake is made, especially with a series or a set of books, a proportionately larger bite is taken out of school, library, and personal budgets.

Writing About Books

If you devote your professional life to working with young people and books, chances are that at some level you will be involved in evaluating books and helping to decide which ones will receive prizes and get starred reviews and which ones should be ignored or receive "Not Recommended" labels. Teachers and librarians working with books for young people have more opportunity to be among the decision makers than do those working with books for adults because fewer than two dozen people in the United States are full-time reviewers of juvenile books. The bulk of the reviewing is done by teachers and librarians who evaluate books both as part of their assigned workloads and as a professionally related hobby. Whether or not you wish to be one of these reviewers, you need to know what is involved, so that you will understand how the work of these people can help you in selecting the books that are best for your purposes. The sheer number of books published each year makes it necessary that book lovers share the reading responsibilities and pool their information through written evaluations.

Evaluation underlies nearly all writing about books. Even when someone is simply making notes to serve as a reminder of the contents of a book, that person is making an evaluation and concluding that the book is worth remembering. Three concerns run throughout the evaluation of young adult literature:

1. What different types of writing meet specific needs, and how can they do it best?
2. Should reviews of young adult books be less promotional and more critical?
3. Is the writing and scholarship in the field aimed too much at the uses of literature rather than at the analysis of the literature itself?

Keeping a Record of Your Reading

The type of writing most often done by teachers and librarians is the making of note cards or, in this day of word processors, typing paragraph-length descriptions filed according to whatever organization is most helpful to the writer. This might be alphabetical or by subject matter, age level, or genre. The advantage to the computerized annotations is that they can be pulled out and reorganized for many different purposes, including booktalking, creating a display, or making a bibliography tailored to a teacher's request for books on the Holocaust, for example, or books about Native Americans. Regularly going over your write-ups jogs your memory about the books you have read and can personally recommend, and when a title or author slips your mind, you can probably find what you need by doing word searches through your write-ups.

Comments vary according to the needs of the writer but should include at least the following:

Author's name and complete book title.

Publisher (both hardback and paperback) with original publication date.

A short summary of the story, including the characters' names and other details that make this book different.

A brief evaluation and any ideas about how you might make special use of the book.

Librarians sometimes write their descriptions in the form of a booktalk identifying a page they could read aloud, while reading teachers note the level of reading

Shipwreck at the Bottom of the World: The Extraordinary True Story of Shackleton and the Endurance by Jennifer Armstrong. Crown, 1998. 134 pp. 40 B&W photos. Ages 12—up.

From August 1914 until August 1916, British explorer Sir Ernest Shackleton and his crew of 27 men, which included two doctors, several scientists, and one stowaway, made an incredible journey. They planned to be the first men to cross Antarctica, the most hostile place on earth. Instead, their ship was caught in ice when they were still 100 miles from land. Pressure from the ice gradually crushed the ship and during the next 19 months they set new records for human endurance and bravery as they worked to save themselves. Not one man died. The amazingly clear photographs and diary entries are available because from the beginning the plan was to document the trip for the patrons who financed it. On the night they had to leave the camp they had made by the frozen-in ship, Shackleton set an example for his men by dumping onto the snow the gold coins from his pockets as well as the inscribed Bible which the Queen had given him. He kept only a page from the Book of Job about the hoary frost of Heaven.   **Bottom of p. 51—52 is good for reading aloud.**

difficulty, and English teachers may mention how the book might illustrate a particular literary principle. A youth worker might make a note about the potential of the book as a catalyst to get kids talking along certain lines, whereas a teacher who anticipates that the book could be controversial is wise to note positive reviews and honors.

Even if you prepare your notes on a computer, teachers and librarians tell us it is also a good idea to do a printout on card stock. Of course it makes sense to have a hard copy backup to your computer files, but more important is the fact that a box of cards on your desk is a constant reminder. It is also more accessible and easier to use on the spur of the moment. The sample card above is for a beautifully designed book that grabs readers' attention for either leisure-time reading or for filling assignments related to history and biographies or even photography and journalism.

Writing Annotations

Annotations are similar to note cards, but they are usually written for someone else to see rather than for the writer's own use. Because they are usually part of an annotated bibliography or list in which space is at a premium, as in the Focus Boxes throughout this text, writers must make efficient use of every word. Communicating the plot and tone of a book as well as a recommendation in only one or two interesting sentences is challenging, but no one wants to read lists of characters and plot summaries all starting with "This book . . ." That annotations can be intriguing as well as communicative is shown by the following two samples for Virginia Hamilton's *Sweet Whispers, Brother Rush*. To save space, the bibliographical information given on the lists is not reprinted here.

See Appendix B for magazines and journals devoted to the evaluation and promotion of literature for young readers.

Poetic, many-layered novel of 14-year-old Teresa's devotion to her retarded and doomed brother Dab. A strong story of hope and the power of love.
School Library Journal, December, 1982

Fourteen-year-old Tree learns a lot about her family and the interconnections between their past and present tragedies from Brother Rush, her uncle's ghost.
Booklist, March 15, 1983

Notice how both writers communicated the age of the protagonist, the fact that it was a family story, and, through the use of *doomed* and *tragedies,* that it was a fairly serious book. The writers also hinted at mystery and intrigue, the first one through "Poetic, many-layered . . . hope and the power of love" and the second one through the reference to "Brother Rush, her uncle's ghost."

How much you put in an annotation depends on its purpose. If you are recommending titles on a book mark, space is so limited that you will probably want to use just descriptive phrases and key words rather than whole sentences, and for that purpose the most important part might be the library's call number. Several of the journals shown in the photograph on p. 317 print cumulative booklists showing the best books of a particular year or in a particular genre. A key sentence is excerpted or adapted from the original review, and the date of the review is given for those who want to go back and get a fuller picture.

Writing Reviews

A problem in reviewing juvenile books is that more books are published than can be reviewed in the media. (See Appendix B for major reviewing sources for young adult books.) In addition to these, dozens of national publications carry occasional review articles, and many library systems sponsor reviewing groups whose work is published either locally or through such nationally distributed publications as *Book Waves*, from the Bay Area (northern California) Young Adult Librarians, and *Books for the Teen Age*, from the Young Adult Services Office of the New York Public Library. Also, some teachers of children's and young adult literature work with their students to write regular review columns for local newspapers.

The field of juvenile reviewing is sometimes criticized for being too laudatory because the reviews are written by book lovers who are anxious to "sell" literature. One reason is that it's the publishers of well-established authors who can afford to send out review copies. Also, those editors who have room for only a limited number of reviews devote their space to the books they think are the best, so of course the reviews are usually positive.

The fact that juvenile books are reviewed mostly by librarians and teachers working on a part-time basis slows down the reviewing process, especially if they take time to incorporate the opinions of young readers. With adult books, reviews often come out before or simultaneously with the publication of the book, but with juvenile titles it is not uncommon to see reviews appearing a full year or more after the book was released. Once young adult books are launched, however, they are likely to stay afloat much longer than adult bestsellers because teachers work them into classroom units, librarians promote them, and paperback book clubs keep selling them for years. Children continue to grow older and to advance in their reading skill and taste, so that every year a whole new set of students is ready to read *A Separate Peace, The Catcher in the Rye,* and *The Outsiders.* As a result, reviews, articles, and papers continue to cover particular titles years after their original publication dates.

People generally evaluate books based on literary quality, reader interest, potential popularity, or what the book is teaching (i.e., its social and political philosophy). Evaluators should make clear their primary emphasis lest readers misunderstand them. For example, a critic may review a book positively because of its literary quality, but a reader will interpret the positive review as a prediction of popularity. The book is purchased and put on the shelf, where it is ignored by teenagers. Consequently the purchaser feels cheated and loses confidence in the reviewing source.

In an attempt to resolve that kind of conflict, when Mary K. Chelton and Dorothy M. Broderick founded *VOYA (Voice of Youth Advocates),* they devised the

TABLE 10.1

VOYA EVALUATION CODE

Quality	Popularity
5Q: Hard to imagine it being better written	5P: Every young adult was dying to read it yesterday
4Q: Better than most, marred only by occasional lapses	4P: Broad general young adult interest
3Q: Readable without serious defects	3P: Will appeal without pushing
2Q: A little better editing or work by the author would have made it 3Q	2P: For the young adult reader with a special interest in the subject
1Q: Hard to understand how it got published	1P: No young adult will read unless forced to for assignments

evaluation code shown in Table 10.1. Each review is preceded by a *Q* number, indicating *quality,* and a *P* number, indicating *popularity.* They suggest that a fringe benefit to using such a clearly outlined code is that it helps librarians analyze their buying patterns. Those who lean heavily toward either quality or popularity see their biases and are able to strike a more appropriate balance.

A quite different set of criteria from either popularity or literary quality is that of social or political values. Most reviewers—whether or not they realize it—are influenced by their personal feelings toward how a book treats social issues. For example, Sue Ellen Bridgers's *Notes for Another Life* was highly recommended and praised in *Horn Book Magazine,* the *New York Times Book Review,* and the *Bulletin of the Center for Children's Books,* but when Janet French reviewed the book for *School Library Journal* she wrote:

> The blurb suggests that this is "a family chronicle for all ages." It would have been more accurate to describe it as a propaganda vehicle for female domesticity. Good women subordinate their talents and yearnings to the home and their children; all other paths lead to havoc. For a riveting story of four deserted children, lead readers instead to Cynthia Voigt's marvelous upbeat *Homecoming.*[1]

This review was written in such a way that readers can easily recognize that the reviewer's opinion was shaped by her disagreement with the plot. For a reviewer to use this as the basis for a negative recommendation is perfectly justifiable *if* the situation is made clear. The problem comes when reviewers reject books based on such social issues but don't admit to themselves, much less to their readers, that their feelings have been influenced by whether a story sharpens or dulls whatever personal ax they happen to be grinding.

There are as many reviewing styles as there are journals and individual reviewers. Nearly all reviews contain complete bibliographical information, including number of pages and prices, perhaps a cataloguing number, the intended age level, a summary statement of the contents, and some hint of the quality of the book as evaluated by the reviewer. A few years ago, an issue of *Top of the News* (the ALA publication now called *Journal of Youth Services in Libraries)* had as its feature topic

"Reviews, Reviewing, and the Review Media." Editor Audrey Eaglen solicited answers to the question, "What makes a good review?"[2] Here are excerpts from some of the responses:

> An intelligent review . . . is never obsequious, if it is favorable. It is never flip, if it is unfavorable. It never quotes from the front flap.
>
> Rosemary Wells, author

> Are there any clever devices or intriguing aspects of the book which could be used to pique the interest of a group and "sell" the book? Also I need to be alerted to potentially controversial issues, be it strong language, explicit sex, violence, or whatever, not so I can avoid buying the book, but so I can plan and prepare and thereby deal with a conflict should it arise.
>
> Katherine Haylman, school librarian

> How attractive is the cover? While we might feel that no one should judge a book by its cover, the truth is that everyone does.
>
> Dorothy Broderick, editor and educator

> I want a clear-cut commitment as to recommendation or nonrecommendation. I don't have the time to read every book published, and I'm hoping that some literate person will help me decide where to invest my reading hours.
>
> Walter Dean Myers, author

> Does the book have magic for YA's? Are there format faults, for example, does the size and shape make it look like a baby book? Is the word *children* used anywhere on the dust jacket? And if there is going to be a film or television tie-in, who are the stars and when will it be released?
>
> Patty Campbell, author and critic

Writing reviews is a skill that improves with practice and effort. A good way to begin developing this skill is to study several reviews of the same book as they appear in different publications. Note the essentials that seem to be the same in each review and then compare the information that is different. See if you can explain the differences in light of the source's reading audience.

For the person reading reviews, one of the biggest problems is that they all run together and begin to sound the same. To keep this from happening, reviewers need to approach their task with the same creative spirit with which authors write books. They need to think of new ways of putting across the point that a book is highly recommended or that it has some unique quality that readers should watch for, as in these two excerpts of reviews that were written by authors reviewing books written by other authors. Granted, authors probably have had more practice in working with words, and therefore their skill is greater than that of most reviewers, but they probably also try harder because they know how important it is to do something to make a review stand out, to give the reader something by which to remember the book.

The first excerpt is taken from a review of Alice Childress's *Rainbow Jordan*, written by Anne Tyler for the *New York Times Book Review*:

Rainbow is so appealing that she could carry this book on her own, but she doesn't have to. There's Miss Josie, who gives us her clearer view to balance what Rainbow tells us. . . . And there's the mother herself—short-tempered, inconsistent, sometimes physically abusive, not much of a mother at all, really. Seen through Rainbow's adoring eyes, she's at least someone we can understand ("Life is complicated," Rainbow says, "I love her even now while I'm putting her down."). In fact, Rainbow's story moves us not because of her random beatings or financial hardships, but because Rainbow needs her mother so desperately that she will endlessly rationalize, condone, overlook, forgive. She is a heartbreakingly sturdy character, and *Rainbow Jordan* is a beautiful book.[3]

Katherine Paterson made these comments about Virginia Hamilton's *Sweet Whispers, Brother Rush* as part of an article she wrote for the *New York Times Book Review:*

There are those who say that Virginia Hamilton is a great writer but that her books are hard to get into. This one is not. It fairly reaches off the first page to grab you, and once it's got you, it sets you spinning deeper into its story. Needless to say, this is not a conventional ghost story. In fact, the function of the ghost in this book is to provide 14-year-old Tree Pratt with a place from which to view her world. . . . In this book everyone we meet, including the ghost, is wonderfully human. . . . The language too is of Miss Hamilton's own special kind, which uses the speech forms of the young to enhance rather than restrict the music of the book.[4]

Writing Scholarly and Pedagogical Articles

A fourth kind of writing about young adult books is made up of articles or papers that go into more depth than is possible in reviews. Because most reviewers of juvenile books have little hope of coming out with a "scoop" or of being the first one to pass judgment on a new book, they focus on deeper treatments or on tying several books together. Dorothy Mathews analyzed the writing about adolescent literature that appeared in professional journals over a five-year period.[5] She categorized the writing into three types. First were those articles that focus on the subjective responses of readers to particular books, such as reader surveys, lists of popular titles, and reviews written from the point of view of how the book is likely to affect young readers. Articles of this kind are primarily descriptive.

The second type was also descriptive and consisted of pedagogical articles giving teachers lists of books that fit together for teaching units; ideas for book promotion; and techniques for teaching reading, social studies, or English. They may include brief comments on the literary qualities of the novels, but, again, the writer's primary intention is to be informative.

The third kind of writing was that restricted to the books themselves. It is in this group that Matthews thinks hope lies for developing a body of lasting scholarly knowledge that will be taken seriously by the academic community. These papers include discussions of adolescent literature as a genre, historical background of the field, relationships between authors and their work, patterns that appear in young adult novels, and themes and underlying issues. More of this kind of literary analysis is being done as authors write books serious enough to support it. Examples of some of these articles are included in Appendix C, "Some Outstanding Books and Articles About Young Adult Literature."

Twayne Publishers paved the way for some serious extended criticism of young adult literature when they inaugurated a Young Adult Authors subset in their United States Authors series. More than a dozen books have been completed under such titles as *Presenting Judy Blume, Presenting Sue Ellen Bridgers, Presenting Robert Cormier,* and so on. Rosa Guy, S. E. Hinton, M. E. Kerr, Norma Klein, Kathryn Lasky, Norma Fox Mazer, Walter Dean Myers, Zibby Oneal, Richard Peck, William Sleator, Mildred Taylor, Barbara Wersba, and Paul Zindel are among the authors featured so far. The same company has also done books on specific genres; for example, *Presenting Young Adult Science Fiction* by Suzanne Reid, *Presenting Young Adult Fantasy Fiction* by Cathi Dunn MacRae, and *Presenting Young Adult Horror Fiction* by Cosette Kies.

Also, a look into a recent edition of *Dissertation Abstracts International* shows an increasing number of dissertations being written on young adult literature. The majority of topics, however, deal more with social or pedagogical issues than with literary ones.

To summarize, writing about young adult books falls into four categories: descriptions for personal use, annotations, reviews, and scholarly or pedagogical writing. Most of you will be involved in the first kind, that is, making note cards for your own use. But some of you will also be making annotations, writing reviews, and doing scholarly or pedagogical analyses. This latter kind of writing and critiquing can be especially intriguing because significant changes have occurred within recent years and relatively few scholars have worked with young adult literature. This means there is ample opportunity for original research and observation, whether from the viewpoint of a literary scholar, a teacher, a librarian, or a counselor or youth worker. The field as a whole will grow strong as a result of serious and competent criticism and analysis.

Deciding on the Literary Canon

Educators are finding themselves in the midst of a lively debate over what books should be taught in U.S. classrooms. An oversimplification of the issue is to say that on one side are those who believe in acculturation or assimilation. They think that if we all read approximately the same books, we will come away with similar values and attitudes and, hence, be a more united society. On the other side are those who believe in diversity and want individuals and groups to find their own values, attitudes, and ways of life reflected in the literature they read. This latter group views the traditional literary canon as racist and sexist, with its promotion in schools serving to keep minorities and women "in their place."

Katha Pollitt, contributing editor of *The Nation,* made some interesting observations when she wrote that, "In a country of real readers a debate like the current one over the canon would not be taking place." She described an imaginary country where children grow up watching their parents read and going with them to well-supported public libraries where they all borrow books and read and read and read. At the heart of every school is an attractive and well-used library, and in classrooms children have lively discussions about books they have read together, but they also read lots of books on their own, so that years later they don't remember whether "they read *Jane Eyre* at home and Judy Blume in class, or the other way around."

Pollitt wrote that in her imaginary country of "real readers—voluntary, active, self-determined readers," a discussion of which books should be studied in school would be nothing more than a parlor game. It might even add to the aura of writers not to be included on school-assigned reading lists because this would mean that their books were "in one way or another too heady, too daring, too exciting to be ground up into institutional fodder for teenagers." The alternative would be millions of readers freely choosing millions of books, each book becoming just a tiny part of a lifetime of reading. Pollitt concluded her piece with the sad statement that at the root of the current debate over the canon is the assumption that the only books that will be read are those that are assigned in school: "Becoming a textbook is a book's only chance: all sides take that for granted." She wonders why those educated scholars and critics who are currently debating this issue and must be readers themselves have conspired to keep secret two facts that they surely must know:

> . . . if you read only twenty-five, or fifty, or a hundred books, you can't understand them, however well chosen they are. And . . . if you don't have an independent reading life—and very few students do—you won't *like* reading the books on the list and will forget them the minute you finish them.[6]

Pollitt's argument puts even more of a burden on those of us who have as our professional responsibility the development of lifelong readers. We are the ones who should be raising our voices to explain the limitations of expecting children to read just what is assigned in class. We are also the ones with the responsibility of helping students develop into the kinds of committed and enthusiastic readers that Pollitt described in her imaginary country.

In the meantime, we also have an obligation to become knowledgeable about the issues that underlie the current debate over the literary canon and to assist schools and libraries in making informed choices with the resources they have. We, as authors of this textbook, have already committed ourselves to the idea of an expanded canon. Some of the harshest critics of adolescent literature are those in favor of promoting only the traditional canon; others tolerate adolescent literature only because they view it as a means to the desired end of leading students to appreciate "real" literature.

At the 1991 National Council of Teachers of English convention in Seattle, Washington, Rudolfo Anaya, author of *Bless Me, Ultima* and a professor of creative writing at the University of New Mexico, predicted that the biggest literary change that will occur in the 1990s will be the incorporation of minority literature into the mainstream. He did not mean just the inclusion on booklists of the names of authors who are members of minority groups but also the incorporation of new styles and ideas into the writing of nonminority authors.

One of the ways that Anaya's prediction is coming true is through the incorporation into mainstream literature of the kinds of magical realism that for a long time has been common in Hispanic literature. Another way is through the desegregation of characters. See Focus Box 4.4, Relating Across Cultures, on p. 133 for examples.

Anaya went on to explain that Mexican-Americans have a different world view. When he was in college, he loved literature and read the standard literary canon with enthusiasm and respect, but when he went to write his own stories he couldn't use Hemingway or Milton as models. He could create plots like theirs, but then he was at a standstill because nowhere in the literary canon did he find people like the ones he knew. His Spanish-speaking family has lived in eastern New Mexico for more than 100 years. The harsh but strangely beautiful landscape and the spirit of the Pecos River had permeated his life, as had stories of *La Grande,* the wise old woman who had safely pulled him from his mother's body even though the umbilical cord was wrapped around his neck. There were also stories of *La Llorona,* a woman who had gone insane and murdered her children and whose tortured cries traveled on the wind around the corners of his childhood home. All his life, such dramatic dreams and stories were woven in and out of reality, but nowhere in the literature that he studied in school did he find such stories.

Anaya worked on *Bless Me, Ultima* for seven years, during which he felt he was "writing in a vacuum. I had no Chicano models to read and follow, no fellow writers to turn to for help. Even Faulkner, with his penchant for the fantastic world of the South, could not help me in Mexican/Indian New Mexico. I would have to build from what I knew best." He went on to explain:

> I began to discover that the lyric talent I possessed, as the poet I once aspired to be, could be used in writing fiction. The oral tradition which so enriched my imagination as a child could lend its rhythm to my narrative. Plot techniques learned in Saturday afternoon movies and comic books could help as much as the grand design of the classics I had read. Everything was valuable, nothing was lost.[7]

Anaya's observations about not having models to follow and being forced to create a new narrative style to tell a story coming from his own experience relates to the frustration that teachers and librarians often express when they go to look for young adult novels about minority characters. They look for the same kinds of coming-of-age stories that are typical in mainstream young adult literature except they want the characters to have brown skin and "different" names. The absence of such books, especially such books written by Native American authors, is in itself part of the cultural difference. We've noticed that the more closely a book with a Native American protagonist resembles what we described in Chapter One as a typical young adult book, the greater the chance that the author is not a Native American and that the protagonist is of mixed parentage or is living apart from the native culture.

Young adult books containing mystical elements tied in with Native American themes are another example of how Anaya's prediction that ethnic writing will become incorporated into the mainstream is coming true. Not everyone, however, is pleased to see this kind of incorporation because they view the books as contaminated or impure. The authors have used old legends and beliefs for their own purposes, interweaving them with contemporary situations and ideas. Also, several of the authors are not Native Americans.

Being in the blood line of a particular group, however, does not guarantee acceptance by the group. For example, most high school teachers think they are contributing to an awareness of cultural diversity and the enlargement of the literary canon by leading students to read Maxine Hong Kingston's *Woman Warrior.* But noted Chinese writer Frank Chin criticizes Kingston, along with Amy Tan for *The Joy Luck Club* and David Henry Hwang for his plays, *F. O. B.* and *M. Butterfly.* He accuses these writers of "boldly faking" Chinese fairy tales and childhood literature. Then he goes on to ask and answer the question of why the most popular "Chinese" works in the United States are consistent with each other but inconsistent with Chinese culture and beliefs:

> That's easy: (1) all the authors are Christian, (2) the only form of literature written by Chinese Americans that major publishers will publish (other than the cookbook) is autobiography, an exclusively Christian form [based on confession]; and (3) they all write to the specifications of the Christian stereotype of Asia being as opposite morally from the West as it is geographically.[8]

Chin's comments are in an essay, "Come All Ye Asian American Writers," that is used as an introduction to an anthology entitled *The Big Aiieeeee!,* apparently put together for use in college classes. The 619-page book is too intimidating for most high school students, but they could appreciate many of the individual stories, poems, and essays. The book's title comes from the sound in movies, television, radio, and comic books assigned to "the yellow man" who "when wounded, sad, or angry, or swearing, or wondering" either "whined, shouted, or screamed, 'Aiieeeee!'"

Chin's introductory essay illustrates the complexities involved in the whole matter of ethnic differences. As Chin goes on to state his case, he brings in religion

See Focus Box 10.1 for books to help people feel knowledgeable and comfortable when working with materials portraying various ethnic and social groups.

FOCUS BOX 10.1

Books to Help Adults with Multicultural Materials

Against Borders: Promoting Books for a Multicultural World by Hazel Rochman. American Library Association, 1993. A highly respected critic and anthologist writes about her own experience as an immigrant to the United States from South Africa and then presents her philosophy about going beyond political correctness. She uses a thematic approach in part one "Journeys Across Cultures," while in part two she presents resources focusing on specific events and ethnic groups.

Authorizing Readers: Resistance and Respect in the Teaching of Literature by Peter J. Rabinowitz and Michael W. Smith. National Council of Teachers of English and Teachers College Columbia University, 1998. This thoughtful book probes what goes on in the minds of both authors and readers as they meet unconventional ideas.

Multicultural Voices in Contemporary Literature, updated and revised by Frances Ann Day. Heinemann, 1999. Reviews, activities, biographical profiles, and a resource list are given for over 120 books.

No Small World: Visions and Revisions of World Literature, edited by Michael Thomas Carroll. National Council of Teachers of English, 1996. Fifteen scholars contributed essays offering new perspectives on the literary canon, problems with translation and the compiling of anthologies, and how to introduce unfamiliar traditions to readers.

Peace in the Streets: Breaking the Cycle of Gang Violence by Arturo Hernandez. Child Welfare League of America, 1998. Hernandez goes a step beyond working with materials and talks about working with kids. He presents an eight-step blueprint for adults to follow in creating a network to shepherd at-risk youth.

Reading Across Cultures: Teaching Literature in a Diverse Society, edited by Theresa Rogers and Anna O. Soter, foreword by Rudine Sims Bishop. Teachers College Columbia University and National Council of Teachers of English, 1997. Fifteen educators contributed chapters with such titles as "Negotiating the Meaning of Difference: Talking Back to Multicultural Literature," "No Imagined Peaceful Place: A Story of Community, Texts, and Cultural Conversations in One Urban High School English Classroom," "Out of the Closet and onto the Bookshelves: Images of Gays and Lesbians in Young Adult Literature," and "Reader Response Theory and the Politics of Multicultural Literature."

Teaching and Using Multicultural Literature in Grades 9–12: Moving Beyond the Canon, edited by Arlette Willis. Christopher-Gordan, 1998. Ten contributors in addition to the editor have written chapters on literature from such specific groups as African-Americans, Puerto Ricans, Asian- and Pacific-Americans, Native Americans, Mexican-Americans, and Caribbean-Americans. Introductory and concluding chapters discuss both philosophy and methods.

Teaching the Short Story: A Guide to Using Stories from Around the World, edited by Bonnie H. Neumann and Helen M. McDonnell. National Council of Teachers of English, 1996. A page or more is devoted to each of 175 stories by outstanding writers from dozens of different countries. Information about the author is followed by a summary of the story and then observations about possible comparisons. While the underlying premise of the book is that people should know about other cultures, the message is taught inductively rather than through overt preaching.

and gender differences as well as differences caused by race, history, social class, and politics. In answer to the kind of criticism he offers, Kingston has explained:

> Sinologists have criticized me for not knowing myths and for distorting them; pirates [those who illegally translate her books for publication in Taiwan and China] correct my myths, revising them to make them conform to some traditional Chinese version. They don't understand that myths have to change, be

useful or be forgotten. Like the people who carry them across oceans, the myths become American. The myths I write are new, American. That's why they often appear as cartoons and Kung Fu movies. I take the power I need from whatever myth. Thus Fa Mu Lan has the words cut into her back; in traditional story, it is the man, Ngak Fei the Patriot, whose parents cut vows on his back. I mean to take his power for women.[9]

Knowledge of these opposing viewpoints should not frighten teachers back into the comforts of the established canon; instead, it should help teachers prepare for meeting the challenges involved in going beyond the "tried and true."

Teaching Ethnic Literature

Most educators feel a duty to bring ethnic-based literature to young people in hopes of increasing general understanding. Besides that lofty goal, here are some additional reasons for making special efforts to bring ethnic books to young people:

- Young readers can identify with characters who straddle two worlds because they have similar experiences in going between the worlds of adulthood and childhood.
- Motifs that commonly appear in ethnic-based stories—including loneliness, fear of rejection, generational differences, and troubles in fitting into the larger society—are meaningful to teenagers.
- Nearly all teenagers feel that their families are somehow different, and so they can identify with the theme of family "differentness" that often finds its way into stories about immigrant families.
- Living in harmony with nature is a common theme, especially in Native American literature, and this theme appeals to today's ecology-minded youth.
- As movies, television programs, mass media books, and magazines inundate teens with stories and photos of people who are "all alike," readers find it refreshing to read about people who have their own individuality.
- Myths and legends that are often brought into ethnic-based literature satisfy some deep-down psychological and aesthetic needs that are not met with contemporary realism or with the romanticism masked as realism that currently makes up the main body of fiction provided for young adults.

One of the most important concepts that needs to be taught is that there are large differences among people typically identified as a group. When Europeans first came to the American continent, there were more than thirty distinct nations speaking perhaps 1000 different languages. During the past 500 years, these people have had such common experiences as losing their lands, being forced to move to reservations, and having to adapt their beliefs and lifestyles to a technological society. These experiences may have affected their attitudes in similar ways, but still it is a gross overgeneralization to write about Native Americans as if they were one people holding the same religious and cultural views. Although in a single class it would be impossible to study dozens of different Native American tribes, a compromise solution might be to study the history and folklore of those tribes who lived, or are living, in the same geographical area as the students. With this approach, it is important for students to realize that they are looking at only one small part of a bigger group, and that if they studied a different group they would learn equally interesting but different facts.

Similar points could be made about the thoughtlessness of talking about Africa as if it were one country and as if one set of folktales could represent a continent that contains nearly 12 million square miles and over 40 independent countries.

Asian Americans also resent being lumped together. The Chinese and Japanese, the two groups who have been in the United States the longest, come from countries with a long history of hostility toward each other. A refugee from Vietnam or Cambodia has very little in common with someone whose ancestors came to California in the 1850s. Likewise, Puerto Ricans in New York have quite a different background from southwestern Mexican-Americans. Even in the Southwest, people whose families have lived there from the days before Anglo settlers arrived resent being grouped with people who just came over the border from Mexico.

We need to teach about the histories of groups whose literature is being read to help readers understand the bitterness that finds its way into some ethnic literature. Readers who get impatient with Hispanic authors for including words and phrases in Spanish will probably be a little more tolerant if they realize that today's generation of Mexican-American authors went to school in the days before bilingual education. In their childhoods, many of them heard nothing but Spanish and were amazed to arrive at English-speaking schools where they would be punished for speaking the only language they had ever known.

While Rudolfo Anaya broke new literary ground with his *Bless Me, Ultima,* many other minority writers are breaking new ground by changing the format of stories and translating them from an oral tradition into a written form. Before printing presses, typewriters, word processors, movies, radio, and television, people had more of an incentive to remember and tell the stories that communicated the traditions and values of a society. Even today, oral traditions play an important role, as seen on television talk shows as well as with kids telling stories at slumber parties and summer camp and workers and travelers whiling away long, boring hours. Many minority writers are experimenting in translating oral stories into written and printed formats, which means that some of the first publications to come from particular groups are more likely to be poetry and short stories than novels.

There are many beautifully designed collections (see Focus Box 10.2, Anthologies of Multicultural Materials) presenting art, poetry, photographs, essays, observations, interviews, and short stories. Besides the obvious advantage that anthologies present a variety of pieces short enough for classroom and library use, the differences in the statements demonstrate that members of groups are first and foremost individuals. They have their own thoughts, feelings, and values, just as do the members of one's own family, one's own church, and one's own neighborhood.

This is probably a lesson that works better through demonstration than through lecturing. Jim Burke in *The English Teacher's Companion* gives two examples of ways that teachers might introduce Sandra Cisneros's *The House on Mango Street.*

Scenario One

"Okay guys, today we're going to be getting a new book called *The House on Mango Street* by a Latina author. I thought it was really important that we read an author from a different culture since so many students here are Latino."

FOCUS BOX 10.2

Anthologies of Multicultural Materials

American Dragons: Twenty-five Asian American Voices, edited by Laurence Yep. Harper-Collins 1993. The metaphor in the title relates to the old belief that dragons appear in many guises and are always adaptable. These stories proving the adaptability of Asian Americans are grouped under *Identity, In the Shadow of Giants, The Wise Child, World War Two, Love, and Guides.*

American Eyes: New Asian-American Short Stories for Young Adults, edited by Lori M. Carlson. Holt, 1994. These well-written stories about immigrants from Japan, China, Vietnam, Korea, and the Philippines are an antidote to readers thinking of all Asians as the same.

American Indian Trickster Tales, selected and edited by Richard Erdoes and Alfonso Ortiz. Viking Penguin, 1998. In Native American folklore, Trickster stories take center stage. In this rich collection, two highly respected scholars have collected dozens of stories clearly documented and identified as to their sources. A useful appendix describes the fifty-four groups from which the stories come.

The Big Aiiieeeee! An Anthology of Chinese American and Japanese American Literature, edited by Jeffery Paul Chan, Frank Chin, Lawson Fusao Inada, and Shawn Wong. Meridian, 1991. The editors are on a campaign to get more of what they view as "authentic" Asian literature before the American public.

The Girl Who Dreamed Only Geese: And Other Tales of the Far North, retold by Howard Norman, illustrated by Leo and Diane Dillon. Harcourt/Gulliver, 1997. These lively tales from the Arctic will bring smiles while also letting readers or listeners learn about Inuit cultures and beliefs.

Her Stories: African American Folktales, Fairy Tales, and True Tales by Virginia Hamilton, illustrated by Leo and Diane Dillon. Scholastic, 1995. Hamilton carefully documents these stories collected from African-American women. Hamilton's other well-done anthologies illustrated by the Dillons include *Many Thousand Gone: African Americans from Slavery to Freedom* (Knopf, 1993) and *The People Could Fly* (Knopf, 1985).

Las Christmas: Favorite Latino Authors Share Their Holiday Memories, edited by Esmeralda Santiago and Joie Davidow. Random House, 1998. The twenty-five contributions are organized under "Stories," "Poems and Songs," and "Menu." Jose Ortega did the illustrations, which are nicely placed to provide white space and variety.

Latino Voices, edited by Frances R. Arparicio. Millbrook Press, 1994. The poetry and the short stories, along with excerpts from fiction and biographies, do a good job of illustrating the variety that exists among and within the groups that make up America's fastest growing minority.

Navajo: Visions and Voices across the Mesa by Shonto Begay. Scholastic, 1995. Begay is an artist living on the Navajo reservation in Arizona. While his paintings are the core of the book, he includes chants, poems, stories, and first-person observations to help readers understand a unique community.

The Space Between Our Footsteps: Poems and Paintings from the Middle East, selected by Naomi Shihab Nye. Simon & Schuster, 1998. Nearly forty paintings are spaced throughout this attractive 144-page book of poems celebrating the Middle East by showing deep feelings for such universal topics as school, childhood, love, fear, and family.

Talking Leaves: Contemporary Native American Short Stories, edited by Craig Lesley. Laurel, 1991. Short stories from thirty-five authors are arranged alphabetically. While some are too complex for most high school students, several are short enough for reading out loud.

Where Angels Glide at Dawn: Stories from Latin America, edited by Lori M. Carlson and Cynthia L. Ventura. HarperCollins, 1990. These ten stories do a good job of reflecting the pride that individuals feel about their home countries including Argentina, Chile, El Salvador, Mexico, Panama, Peru, and Puerto Rico. Several include strands of magical realism.

Scenario Two

(after reading a brief section from Cisneros's book) "So, we've been talking about this whole idea of growing up, about creating an identity for oneself, what it means, how and when it happens. *Huck Finn* allowed us to talk about some important aspects of that whole experience. And Nathan McCall's book told us what it was like for him to grow up as a young black man in the sixties. I thought it would be interesting to see what this other book has to say about the experience since unlike Huck she didn't take off but stayed on Mango Street. I love this book a lot. It took her five years to write this 120-page book. It's like a poem almost, the language and images are so intense.[10]

As Burke explains, the second scenario is clearly better in that the teacher grabbed students' interest by reading an excerpt and then linked the book to what the class had been doing. By emphasizing the book's literary quality, she helped students see why they were reading the book. The teacher in the first scenario left students with the idea that they were reading *The House on Mango Street* to be politically correct.

We'll conclude this section with a plea for all those working with books and young adults to continue seeking out and promoting the use of minority literature. Educators have shied away from working with minority literature because:

- They didn't study it when they were in school and so they feel less prepared than when teaching mainstream literature.
- They fear censorship both because of prejudice against minorities and because of the fact that some minority writers use language considered inappropriate for schoolbooks.
- Minority literature is harder to find, especially minority literature that has been given a "seal of approval" by the education establishment (i.e., positive reviews and suggestions for teaching).
- Ethnic identification is such a sensitive topic that teachers fear that when they are discussing a piece of literature either they or their students may say something that will offend some students or hurt their feelings.

Being a professional means that you do not shy away from responsibilities just because they are challenging. Instead, you prepare, so that you can be successful— at least most of the time—in the work you have chosen for your career.

Using Young Adult Literature in the Library

When discussing public libraries, we used to assume that every library has a young adult librarian and a special section serving teenagers. Although this may be the ideal arrangement, there are certainly many libraries where this has never been the practice and many others where shrinking budgets are making young adult librarians an endangered species. A fairly common approach is for libraries to enlarge their children's sections to "Youth Sections" serving readers up to age 15 or 16 while sending everyone else to the adult division. Some of the problems with such an arrangement, cited in a *Voice of Youth Advocates* article ("Whose Job Is It Anyway?"[11]), are the following:

- Teenagers enter a children's section reluctantly, and their size, voices, and active natures intimidate the children who are there.
- The purpose of young adult services is to provide a transition from the children's collection to the resources of the total library, and when a librarian accompanies a teenager looking for something into the larger adult collection there's no one left to serve the children.
- It is difficult for the same person who runs programs for preschoolers, prepares story hours for older children, and reviews hundreds of children's books to switch gears to the fads and multiple interests of teenagers.
- Young adult librarians deal not only with "safe" young adult books, but also with adult materials of interest to young adults. These are often controversial and are likely to prove more problematic to a children's librarian whose training has engendered different perceptions and attitudes.
- Without "sponsorship" by knowledgeable young adult librarians, there may not be enough circulation for serious, high-quality books, which results in a greater reliance on popular taste (e.g., formula romances and series books).

Certainly these worries are valid, and we all need to do what we can to persuade decision makers that young adult librarians serve an important role. If the choice is between having a library open only four days a week and having separate librarians for children and teenagers, however, most library boards vote to keep the library open. This dictates more flexibility and more challenge for the librarian who serves both age groups. Parents who have both teenagers and young children vouch for the differences between the two, yet they manage somehow. Many librarians have to do the same. We hope this textbook helps.

Matching Books with Readers

Most people working with books and young readers have come to accept the idea that there is no such thing as one sacred list of books that every student should read. The best that can be hoped for are agreeable matches between particular books and particular students. To bring such matches about, adults need to be acquainted with a wide range of books and with individual students. A commonly used technique in getting to know students is to ask them what books they have previously enjoyed and then to suggest something similar or something by the same author. An alternative is to ask young readers to describe the book they would most like if an author were going to write just for them and then to suggest three or four books that contain elements they have mentioned.

Other people use written forms or reader interest surveys in which students write down their hobbies, the kinds of classes they are taking, what they want to do for a career, what books they have read, and the kinds of stories they most enjoy. The problem with such forms is that they are usually filled out and then stored in a drawer. No one has time to interpret them. One of our students who is a junior high librarian, however, designed a reader interest survey for her students. She added their reading test scores and programmed her library computer with 100 of the best books she had read. All her students received individual computer printouts suggesting six books that they would probably like and that would be within their reading level.

Similar commercial programs are becoming available, but what made this program successful was that the librarian had read and personally reacted to each book that she listed in the program. The individualized printouts served as conversation starters from which one-to-one relationships developed. Although she worked hard to initiate the project, she considered it worth the effort because once the machinery was set in order, it could be done for hundreds of students almost as easily as for thirty, and she could continue to update it with the new books she was reading.

Commercial programs and CD-ROMS allow students to search for books using key words. Many YA authors have their own Web sites, and clever booksellers (see Chapter 3, p. 86 about Amazon.com) do on an international level the same kind of promotional work that teachers and librarians have for years been doing locally.

Many teachers encourage students to write letters directly to authors, which is all well and good, but before you do this read what author Robin McKinley has to say.

ROBIN MCKINLEY
On The School Assignment Letter

I love—how could I not?—getting letters from people who have so much enjoyed or been moved by my books that they go to the trouble of writing me a letter about it. I like knowing my books are read, and I am interested in knowing *how* they are read; and while the great majority of the mail I receive is positive, the only dispraise I ignore is the sort based on the reader's annoyance that I've written some other book than the one he or she wanted. I have learned useful things about what I've gotten both right and wrong by letter-writers who tell me about the books I did write. With the exception of the very, very rare crazy or abusive letter, I answer all this book mail.

I also personally answer about 80 percent of the school assignment letters I receive. I answer them for the kids' sake. I'm sure I guess wrong sometimes about students' motives and understanding. I can't tell which letter-writers already have a pretty clear idea about the ramifications of the hierarchies they live in, with grown-ups at the top and young people at the bottom; I can't always see when a complimentary letter is insincere, composed because that's what goes down with adults. But my judgment is a bit clouded by the fact that letters which begin with any of the variations on "I am writing to you for a school assignment" instantly make my blood pressure rise; and the ones that end with "I get extra credit if you answer this" send me into orbit.

The School Assignment Letter dilemma is on my mind more than usual because of a recent round of correspondence with a librarian who took exception to the standard letter I send to the other 20 percent of school-assignment-letter-writers, which ends, having begun by saying that I like hearing from readers who have enjoyed my books, "I object to being made into a school assignment. . . . My *books* are what I'm offering to my audience, not my *self*. I'm not a homework project. I Am A HUMAN BEING. I have my own life, and more demands on my time than I can meet successfully *before* this week's book mail arrives." She wrote back that I "didn't care about anyone else's feelings," that she would never purchase another of my books for any of the libraries under her supervision ("even if you win the Newbery again"), and that she was planning on burning the ones already on her shelves. I answered that letter, too, making the same points I hope I am making in this essay, and sent copies to administrators at the school the students had written from. No one replied.

I am at a loss to understand how authors have been so dehumanized in so many teachers' and librarians' minds that blind school assignment letters to an author can appear to be a good idea. Every popular or award-winning children's book writer I've ever spoken to gets school-assignment letters. Some authors mind less than I do. Some mind more. My "I am not a homework project" letter—although it has evolved over the years—has gone out hundreds of times, and the aforementioned is the first response to it I've ever received—and it certainly wasn't to thank me for successfully communicating my point of view.

It is not only the involuntariness of my involvement in these school assignments that is so inexplicable. How can a teacher declare that a student will receive extra credit if the author responds? The author is not under the teacher's authority. If this is not moral blackmail, what is it? Nor are circumstances under the teacher's control. What if the student wrote the most charming, perceptive letter anyone has ever written and the author has an earache and is too wretched to answer any letters? What if the letter is eaten by the Great Postal Dragon, and the author never sees it? Nor is the cost to the recipient of school-assignment letters limited to the spiritual. Perhaps ten percent of the students who write include return postage; my yearly expenditure on stamps for book mail comes to a splashy weekend holiday for my husband and me that we don't get—or, perhaps more to the point, about one-quarter of the new furnace and fittings our elderly, cold house urgently needs. Surely the myth that writers are all wealthy is not still current? Those of us who earn enough of a living to give up our day jobs are in the minority; school budgets for enrichment programs are not leaner than most writers' royalty checks. And the energy I use to answer letters is the same creative energy that I need to write my books: coherent sentence production is coherent sentence production, and I've only got a few good hours of it a day, and after that I'm an excellent washer of dishes and walker of dogs. Let me stress that the *voluntary* book mail I receive—and this includes the letters that say "I was thinking about writing to you and my teacher/librarian/parent/older-person-with-authority encouraged me"—is worth it. Absolutely. I don't in the least begrudge the price of the personal enrichment program of acknowledging the letters from readers who *want* to write to me. I am a storyteller, and the *teller* only functions if she has an audience.

What is most discouraging about the book-burning librarian's letter is that she insists on missing the crux of what both my letters to her school district were trying to convey, about the ordinary humanity of authors, and the parameters of their profession. You don't expect your car mechanic to fix your bicycle, gratis, in his spare time. Lucky you if he (or she) is willing to, but you are unlikely to boycott his gas station and write him hate mail if he isn't. And I bet at the very least you ask first and say thank-you afterward. For the several thousand school-assignment letters I have answered in the last fifteen-plus years, I can remember once that I was asked in advance and twice that I was later thanked for having responded.

Robin McKinley's books include *The Hero and the Crown*, Greenwillow, 1985; *Deerskin*, Putnam, 1993; *Rose Daughter*, Greenwillow, 1997; and *Spindle's End*, Putnam, 2000. Her web site address is http://www.sff.net/people/robin-mckinley/.

Perhaps reading an author's Web page could be as effective, or for a special occasion, a teacher might arrange through a publisher to have an on-line or e-mail conversation with an author.

Another way that librarians and teachers use their computers to find suggestions for books or other resources is to communicate with colleagues through Internet or commercial e-mail accounts. The following list of such sources, prepared by Chris Crowe, Professor of English at Brigham Young University, was up-to-date in January of 2000, but some may have dropped off and others may have been added. If you manage to get on one such list, you will probably see references to other active lists. Most of the listservs provide interactive dialogue with others who have interest or expertise in the field, while the Web sites are static "bulletin boards" that contain a variety of information. The basic description is followed by the e-mail message you should send (leave the "Subject" space blank) if you wish to join the group.

DISCUSSION LISTSERVS
CHILD_LIT

Children's Literature: Criticism and Theory. An unmoderated discussion group for scholars, teachers, authors, and anyone else interested in books for children and young adults. Subscription message:

To: listserv@email.rutgers.edu

Subject: (leave this blank)

Message: SUBscribe child_lit (your name)

KIDLIT-L

An international forum for teachers, librarians, authors, and students interested in the study and teaching of literature for children and young adults. Subscription message:

To: listserv@bingvmb.cc.binghamton.edu

Subject: (leave this blank)

Message: SUBSCRIBE KIDLIT-L (type in your own name)

PUBYAC

The discussion forum for Children and Young Adult Services in Public Libraries. Subscription message:

To: majordomo@nysernet.org

Subject: (leave this blank)

Message: subscribe PUBYAC

YALSA-L

Young Adults Library Services Association of the American Library Association. A listserv for young adult librarians. Subscription message:

To: listproc@ala.org

Subject: (leave this blank)

Message: subscribe YALSA-bk (type in your own name)

WORLD WIDE WEB SITES

The ALAN Homepage

Offers information about the NCTE's Assembly on Literature for Adolescents (ALAN), its activities, and links to related YA literature Web sites, including *The ALAN Review*.

http://english.byu.edu/alan/

Betty Carter's "Young Adult Literature on the World Wide Web"

Betty Carter's article in the Winter 1996 issue of *The ALAN Review* suggests many Web sites of interest to readers and to YA literature specialists.

http://scholar.lib.vt.edu/ejournals/ALAN/winter96/libCONN.html

Booktalks—Quick and Simple

A guide to nearly 700 booktalks for middle and high school students indexed by author, subject, title, and interest. This impressive site also offers additional information about selected YA authors and books.

http://rms.concord.k12.nh.us/booktalks/

The Bulletin of the Center for Children's Books Homepage

Contains information on children's and YA books, including book reviews and lists of award-winning books.

http://edfu.lis.uiuc.edu/puboff/bccb/

Carol Hurst's Children's Literature Web Site

Information on children's and YA literature: book reviews, author bios, teaching materials, suggestions for using literature across the curriculum, and more.

http://www.carolhurst.com/

Child_Lit & The Classroom

A web page developed from the Child_Lit listserv. It offers suggestions on using on-line material in classes, sample assignments, and an archive of discussions from the listserv.

http://www.gen.umn.edu/faculty_staff/stan/childlit/

The Children's Book Council

Classroom ideas, previews of new books, discussions about current issues and trends, links to authors' Web sites, bibliographies, and news about the publishing business.

http://www.cbcbooks.org/

Children's Book Publishers

Nearly all publishers have homepages that feature their books and their authors. This Web site has links to more than twenty-five publishers of books for children and young adults.

http://www.scils.rutgers.edu/special/kay/publish.html

Children's Literature Authors and Illustrators

Provides access to more than fifty links to biographical home pages from Cormier to Stine, Alcott to Zolotow.

http://www.ucet.ufl.edu/~jbrown/chauth.html

The Children's Literature Web Guide

Provides access to children's/YA literature announcements and award lists, lists of recommended books, topical bibliographies, lesson plans, information about authors, and much more. This is one of the most comprehensive Web sites on YA and children's literature anywhere.

http://www.ucalgary.ca/~dkbrown/index.html

Electronic Resources for Youth Service

Provides lists of award-winning books, book reviews, on-line literature, author and publisher links, listservs, news groups, associations, and resources for teachers and librarians interested in young adult literature.

http://www.chebucto.ns.ca/Education/ERYS/

Fairrosa Cyber Library

Contains a reference section, author information, articles, book lists, links to other sites, and more.

http://dalton.org/libraries/fairrosa

The Internet Public Library Youth Division Homepage

Includes a range of resources for YA students, YA author interviews, author biographies, and links to authors' homepages.

http://www.ipl.org/youth/

Kay E. Vandergrift's Special Interest Homepage

Information for teachers and students interested in children's and YA literature. It includes sample syllabi, information on censorship, and a wide range of topics related to YA literature.

http://www.scils.rutgers.edu/special/kay/

MIRAGe Readers' Advisory Links

A truly impressive Web site filled with links to sites of nearly all genres and reading interests, including sites about YA literature and sites for young adults.

http://www.prairienet.org/mirage/ra.html#General

New Mexico State University Library Gopher

Contains recent information about teaching materials, resources, syllabi, and other information pertaining to children's and YA literature.

gopher://lib.nmsu.edu/11/.subjects/Education/.childlit

Notes from the Windowsill

An independent, electronic journal of reviews of books for children and young adults. It also offers themed annotated lists of books and indexes to back issues.

http://www.armory.com/~web/notes.html

The Young Adult Library Services Association (YALSA) Home Page

Features a variety of information, including news, award winning books, sites for young adults, information for librarians, booklists, and links to related sites.

http://ala8.ala.org/yalsa/

Young Adult Literature: Middle & Secondary English—Language Arts

Offers information and links to a broad range of literature for young adults, including African-American history and literature, authors' homepages, feminism/women, Southern literature, sports, and much more.

http://falcon.jmu.edu/~ramseyil/yalit.htm

Electronic aids are wonderful, but nothing can substitute for a large and varied reading background and the ability to draw relationships between what students tell or ask and what the librarian remembers about particular books. Experience sharpens this skill, and those librarians who make a consistent effort to read a few new books every month rapidly increase their repertoire of books.

Booktalks

With all their other responsibilities, few librarians have as much opportunity as they would like to guide individual reading on a one-to-one basis. The next best thing is to give presentations or booktalks to groups. A booktalk is a short introduction to a book, which usually includes one or two paragraphs read from the book. Booktalks are comparable to movie previews or teasers in presenting the characters and a hint of the plot, but they never reveal the ending. Joni Bodart has described booktalking as a kind of storytelling that resembles an unfinished murder mystery in being "enticing. It is a come-on. It is entertaining. And it is fun, for both the listener and the booktalker."[12]

The simplest kind of booktalk may last only sixty seconds. In giving it, the booktalker must let listeners know what to expect. For example, it would be unfair to present only the funniest moments in a serious book—a reader might check it out expecting a comedy. If a book is a love story, some clue should be given, but care needs to be taken because emotional scenes read out loud and out of context can sound silly. The cover of a book often reveals its tone, which is one of the reasons for holding up a book while it is being discussed or for showing slides or color overheads if a presentation is being given to a large audience.

Booktalks need to be carefully prepared ahead of time. It takes both concentration and skill to select the "heart" of a story. People who try to ad-lib have the advantage of sounding spontaneous, but they also run the risk of using up all their time telling about one or two books or of getting bogged down in telling the whole story, which would defeat the purpose. Most young readers do not want to hear a 10- or 15-minute talk on one book, unless it is dramatic and used as a change of pace along with several shorter booktalks. Even with short booktalks, people's minds begin to wander after they've listened for 10 or 15 minutes. The ideal approach is for the teacher or librarian to give booktalks frequently but in short chunks.

This may not be practical, however, if the person giving the booktalk is a visitor (e.g., a public librarian coming to a school to encourage students to sign up for library cards and begin to use the public library). In situations such as this, the librarian can arrive in class with a cart full of books ready to be checked out. A half-hour or so can be devoted to the booktalks, with the rest of the time saved for questions and answers, browsing, sign-up, and check-out. In cases like this, it's good to have a printed bibliography or bookmark to leave with students for later use in the library.

This kind of group presentation has the advantage of introducing students to the librarian, which is especially important for helping students feel at ease in public libraries. Students who already feel acquainted are more likely to initiate a one-to-one relationship, a valuable part of reading guidance. Group presentations also give students more freedom in choosing books that appeal to them. When a student asks a librarian to recommend a good book, the librarian has time to tell the student about only two or three titles, and the student probably feels obligated to take one of these books whether or not it sounds appealing. But when the librarian presents 10 to 15 different titles, students can choose from a much larger offering. This also enables students to learn about and to select books that might cause them embarrassment if they were recommended on a personal basis. For example, if a girl is suspected of having lesbian leanings, it may not help the situation for the librarian to hand her Nancy Garden's *Annie on My Mind*. But if this were included among several books introduced to the class and the student chose it herself, it might fill a real need. The fact that the librarian talks about it, showing that she has read it, opens the door for the girl to initiate a conversation if she so desires.

Another advantage to group presentations is that they are efficient. If a social studies class is beginning a unit on World War II in which everyone in the class is required to read a novel having something to do with the war and also write a small research paper, it makes sense for the librarian to give the basic information in one group presentation. Being efficient in the beginning enables the librarian to spend

TABLE 10.2

DO'S AND DON'TS FOR BOOKTALKING

Do	Don't
1. Prepare well. Either memorize your talks or practice them so much that you can easily maintain eye contact.	1. Don't introduce books that you haven't read or books that you wouldn't personally recommend to a good friend as interesting.
2. Organize your books so that you can show them as you talk. To keep from getting confused, you might clip a note card with your talk on it to the back of each book.	2. Don't "gush" over a book. If it's a good book and you have done an adequate job of selecting what to tell, it will sell itself.
3. When presenting excerpts, make sure they are representative of the tone and style of the book.	3. Don't tell the whole story. When listeners beg for the ending, hand them the book. Your purpose is to get them to read.
4. Even though you might sometimes like to focus on one or two themes, be sure, over the months you meet with any group, that you present a wide variety of books. Include informative books that young readers would probably like to know about but might be too embarrassed to ask for.	4. Don't categorize books as to who should read them, for example, "This is a book you girls will like"; or show by the books you have brought to a particular school that you expect only Asian-Americans to read about Asian-Americans and only Native Americans to read about Native Americans, and so forth.
5. Experiment with different formats, for example, a short movie, some poetry, or one longer presentation along with your regular booktalks.	5. Don't give literary criticisms. You have already evaluated the books for your own purposes, and if you do not think they are good, do not present them.
6. Keep a record of which books you have introduced to which groups. This can be part of your evaluation when you compare before and after circulation figures on the titles you have talked about. Also, good record keeping helps you not repeat yourself with a group.	
7. Be assertive in letting teachers know what you will and will not do. Perhaps distribute a printed policy statement explaining such things as how much lead time you need, the fact that the teacher is to remain with the group, and how willing you are to make the necessary preparation to do booktalks on requested themes or topics.	

time with individual students who have specific questions rather than making an almost identical presentation to thirty individuals. Table 10.2 gives some suggestions taken from an article by Mary K. Chelton, "Booktalking: You Can Do It" (*School Library Journal,* April, 1976). Other sources of information include an American Library Association book and videotape featuring Hazel Rochman and entitled "Tales of Love and Terror: Booktalking the Classics, Old and New," and Joni Richard Bodart's *Booktalk! Booktalking and School Visiting for Young Adult Audiences.*

Displays

Making displays is another effective way to promote books. Most young adults have some common needs, although they might not admit them or even be aware of them. The sensitive adult who knows books can quietly alert students to titles and authors that might prove worthwhile. It can be done simply; indeed, the simpler and less obvious, the better—perhaps nothing more than a sign that says "Like to watch Oprah Winfrey?—You'll Love These" (personal experiences and social issues books, although not identified in just that way), or "Did You Cry Over *Gone with the Wind?*" (books about love problems and divorce). None of these simple gimmicks involves much work, but what's more important is that they do their job without the librarian seeming pushy or nosy. No book report is required and no one will know whether John checks out Howard Fast's *April Morning* because his father recently died or because he likes American history.

When it comes to promoting books, librarians should not be ashamed to borrow ideas from the world of commerce. After all, we are competing directly for students' time and interest and indirectly for a share of the library budget and the taxpayers' dollars. Attractive, professional-looking displays and bulletin boards give evidence that things are happening in the library (or the classroom), and they help patrons develop positive attitudes toward books and reading. Even if there is no artwork connected with a display, it can encourage reading simply by showing the front covers of books.

Preparing displays can bring the same kind of personal satisfaction that comes from creatively decorating a room or painting a picture. People who have negative feelings about making displays have probably had experiences in which the results did not adequately compensate for the amount of time and effort expended. One way to correct this imbalance is to follow some general principles that help to increase the returns on a display while cutting down on the work.

1. Go window shopping in the best stores—the ones that appeal to the young adults that you are wooing—and when you see a display that you like, adapt its features to your own purposes.
2. Promote more than one book and have multiple copies available. Enthusiasm wanes if people have to put their names on a list and wait. Use color photocopies of the book jackets, so that as the books are checked out, your display won't look skimpy.
3. Tie the displays into current happenings. Connect them with popular movies, the school play, a neighborhood controversy, or various anniversary celebrations.
4. Use displays to get people into the library. Offer free bibliographies and announce their availability through local media.
5. Put your displays in high-traffic areas where everyone, not just those who already use the young adult collection, will see them.
6. Use interchangeable parts, so that it isn't necessary to start from scratch each time. To get variety and height into a display, use wood-stained fruit baskets and crates, leaning boards with screwed-in hooks for holding books, or cardboard boxes covered with drapes. To focus attention on the books, plain backgrounds are better than figured ones.
7. Take advantage of modern technology. Buy stick-on letters and use your computer and your desk-top publishing skills to prepare attractive bibliographies and signs.

The changing location of portable displays is in itself an attention getter. A portable display can be as small as a foot-square board set in the middle of a table or as large as a camper's tent set up in the middle of a room and surrounded by books about camping, hiking, backpacking, ecology, and nature foods. If space is a problem, small bulletin boards can be hung from the ceiling or stood against pillars or walls. They can do double duty (e.g., dividing the children's section from the young adult section or separating a reading corner with its casual furniture from the desks and tables set aside for study). Give students a sense of ownership over the displays by involving them as much as possible. Art teachers are usually happy to work with librarians to have a place where student work can be attractively displayed alongside such art-related books as Louise Plummer's *My Name is Sus5an Smith. The 5 Is Silent;* Gary Paulsen's *The Monument;* Brock Cole's *Celine;* and Zibby Oneal's *In Summer Light.* When you do a display of books about animals, include snapshots of students under the headings of "The Comforts and Delights of Owning a Dog," or "The Comforts and Delights of Being Owned by a Cat."

Occasionally, students working as library interns or helpers enjoy the challenge of doing displays all by themselves. Whatever is interesting and different is the key to tying books in with real life. An ordinary object—a kitchen sink, a pan full of dirty dishes, or a torn and dirty football jersey—is out of the ordinary when it appears as part of a display. Also, don't overlook the possibility of putting up posters such as those offered by the American Library Association or tying commercial posters in with books. Remember the part that the poster message, "Don't disturb the universe," played in Cormier's *The Chocolate War.*

Programs

Stores have special sales and events to get people into the marketplace, where they will be tempted to buy something. In the same way, ambitious librarians put on young adult programs to do something special for those who regularly use the library and, at the same time, to bring nonusers into the library. Advice from people whose libraries have been especially active in arranging programs includes

1. Take a survey, or better, talk with your teenage clientele to see what their interests and desires are.
2. Avoid duplicating the kinds of activities that students do in school and in conjunction with other community agencies.
3. Include young adults in planning and putting on programs so that the library can be a showcase for young adult talent.
4. Work with existing youth service agencies to cosponsor events, or plan them in conjunction with school programs so as to have the beginning of an audience and the nucleus of a support group.
5. Do a good job of publicizing the event. The publicity may influence people unable to come so they will feel more inclined to visit the library at some other time.
6. Have a casual setting planned for a relatively small group, with extra chairs available in case more people come than you expect. Bustling around at the last minute to set up extra chairs gives an aura of success that is more desirable than having row on row of empty chairs.

Program possibilities include outdoor music concerts featuring local teenage bands, teenage poetry readings in a coffeehouse setting, chess tournaments, and

To make quick and easy library displays, incorporate whatever you happen to have that is new and interesting as with this "jackalope" to bring attention to folklore and this souvenir teapot to set off fantasy books.

showings of original movies or videos. Workshops are held in computer programming, photography, creative writing, bicycle repair, and crafts. Guest speakers are often invited to discuss subjects that schools tend to shy away from, such as self-defense and rape prevention, drug and birth control information, and introductions to various hotlines and other agencies that help young adults.

Large-scale workshops are sometimes held in libraries to which various schools bring their students. For example, in a town with three high schools, one big day on choosing careers may be planned at the community library. Guest speakers who could not give up three days of their time may be willing to make a single appearance, and special exhibits and displays can be set up once rather than three times.

Regardless of the topic or format of a program, librarians should view programs as opportunities to encourage library visitors to become regular book users. The following practices help:

Regardless of why kids come to a public library, use their presence as an opportunity for making them feel at home by routing traffic past displays and the young adult area and by distributing bookmarks or other information about YA books and activities.

1. Hold the program so that it is in or near the young adult book section. If this is impractical, try routing traffic past the young adult area or past displays of young adult books.
2. Pass out miniature bibliographies, perhaps printed on a bookmark or in some other easy-to-carry format.
3. Schedule the program to end at least a half-hour before the library closes, so that participants can browse and sign up for library cards.
4. Place paperback book racks where they are as tempting as the displays that grocery and discount stores crowd into checkout areas.
5. For ten minutes at the start of the program, while waiting for latecomers to straggle in, do a welcome and warm-up by giving a few booktalks related to the subject of the evening.

Some libraries have had success with book discussion groups in which teenagers serve as readers and critics. These usually work best if their evaluations can be shared, for example, on a bulletin board, in a teen opinion magazine, through a display of recommended books, in a monthly column in a local newspaper, through the periodic printing and distribution of annotated lists of favorites, or on a library Web site.

When an author is invited to speak, the host librarian needs to begin publicity several weeks in advance to be sure that people are reading the author's books. English and reading teachers should be notified so that they can devote some class time to the author's work. A panel of students who especially enjoyed the author's work might be set up to interact with the author at the end of the formal presentation. Another way to involve students, and perhaps teachers, would be to invite three or four to have lunch or dinner with the guest author. (Check this out first because some speakers prefer to be left alone to gather their thoughts before making a presentation.) If you are setting up an author's visit, it is usually best that you first write the publisher of the author's most recent book. State how much money, if any, you have available. Sometimes publishers pay for an author's transportation, but you will usually need to pay at least for food and housing and, if possible, to offer an honorarium. If you have no money, say so immediately, and then be patient, flexible, and grateful for whomever you get. An author might be scheduled to speak in or near your area and might then come to you as an extra. Also, it is highly possible that there are young adult authors living in your own state. The Children's Book Council (568 Broadway, Suite 404, New York, NY 10012) has a brochure *Inviting Children's Book Authors and Illustrators to Your Community*, which can be requested for a fee of $2.00 plus stamps totalling 78 cents.

Magazines

As discussed in Chapter Three, magazines and their place in the reading habits of Americans have changed considerably. There are now magazines for every taste and interest—even a few that please teachers. The vast number from which to choose makes librarians' jobs harder rather than easier. See Focus Box 10.3 for recommendations of magazines published directly for teens. It was prepared in the fall of 1999 by Diane Tuccillo, youth services librarian for the Mesa, Arizona, Public Library.

Educators must realize that many students who won't pick up books are eager to read the latest magazines in their areas of interest. With many of the teen magazines, poor readers can feel their first success with the printed word because much of the information is communicated through easy-to-read layouts and photographs. Also, the material, which is presented in short, digestible chunks, is of prime interest to teens. Some of the magazines are read by both boys and girls, but because of the abundance of advertising money for cosmetics and fashions, many magazines are purposely designed to appeal only to girls. Others are financed by advertisements for products usually purchased by boys.

There's no limit to the challenges that good students can find in magazines. A much higher percentage of adult Americans read magazines rather than books, and yet in school we give people little help in introducing them to magazines or in picking out the ones they will get the most from. It is almost as if kids find magazines despite teachers, not because of them. We would do well to change our attitudes and look on magazines as taking up where books leave off in presenting up-to-date information on a wide variety of topics chosen to be especially interesting to young adults. We need to make special efforts to teach the skills necessary to do research in all kinds of modern periodicals. As pointed out in Chapter Nine, many contemporary writers of informative books for teenagers get most of their information from magazines and journals. If teenagers can learn to get such information themselves, then they won't be limited to reading only about those topics and viewpoints chosen by someone else as "appropriate" for teens.

FOCUS BOX 10.3

Selected Magazines Popular with Young Adults

Prepared by Diane Tuccillo, Senior Librarian/ YA Coordinator, Mesa (Arizona) Public Library.

Campus Life. A nonpreachy, upbeat, frank, and relevant magazine for Christian youth containing articles, advice columns, and reviews. ISSN 0008–2538. $19.95 per year. Order from Christianity Today, Inc., P.O. Box 37060, Boone, IA 50037–0060. wwwcampuslife.net

Cicada. A literary magazine just for teens featuring stories, poetry, opinions, and artwork. ISSN 1097–4008. $35.97 for six issues. Order from Cicada, Box 7705, Red Oak, IA 50591–0705. www.cicadamag.com

Electronic Gaming Monthly. Contains news, reviews, previews, and more on a myriad of computerized games. ISSN 1058–918X. $24.97 per year. Order from ZD Inc., P.O. Box 3338, Oak Brook, IL 60522–3338. www.videogames.com/misc/mags/egm.html

Jump. Like *Teen*, *Seventeen*, and *YM*, this magazine contains articles and features for contemporary teen girls. ISSN 1092–6984. $15.90 for eight issues. Order from Weider Publications, Inc., 21100 Erwin Street, Woodland Hills, CA 91367. www.jumponline.com

MAD. This is the classic magazine of wacky, offbeat humor that teens love. ISSN 0024–9319. $24.00 per year. Order from Mad Magazine, P.O. Box 52345, Boulder, CO 80322–2345. www.madmag.com

Right On! A zine that gives a high-interest look at today's popular black entertainment personalities. ISSN 0048–8305. $29.95 per year. Order from Sterling/Macfadden Partnership, 233 Park Avenue South, New York, NY 10003. www.rightonmag.com

Scholastic Choices. News and pertinent articles on contemporary issues of concern to teens as well as tips for self-improvement are found in this informative YA magazine. ISSN 0883–475X. $10.75 for eight issues for students; $21.75 for a teacher's edition; quantity discounts available. Order from Scholastic, Inc., 2931 E. McCarty Street, P.O. Box 3710, Jefferson City, MO 65102–3710. www.choicesmag@scholastic.com

Starlog. Articles, reviews, and lots of full-color photos give this zine high appeal to fans of science fiction films and other SF media. ISSN 01910–4626. Order from Starlog Group Inc., 475 Park Avenue South, New York, NY 10016. E-mail only at communications@starloggroup.com

Teen People. Biographies of all kinds of stars plus fashion trends for both guys and girls are featured in this hip, article-packed teen zine. ISSN 1096–2832. $14.77 for ten issues. Order from Teen People, P.O. Box 61680, Tampa, FL 33661. E-mail only at letters@teenpeople.com or call 1-800-284-0200.

Warp. THE cool magazine for guys into "skate, snow, style and sound." ISSN 1083–3579. $11.95 for six issues. Order from Subscription Department, Warp, P.O. Box 469014, Escondido, CA 92046.

Using Young Adult Books in the Reading Classroom

Now that many teachers, schools, and school districts have adopted a whole-language approach to teaching reading, writing, and speaking skills to children, the role of trade books as opposed to textbooks and exercise sheets has become much more acceptable in teaching reading. Under the best circumstances, students come to high school having read many books and being eager to read many more. Under the worst circumstances (i.e., when students arrive in high school unable to read or not wanting to read), the idea of teaching them with genuine literature instead of with workbooks and exercises is at least familiar.

Including a section on reading in this text is in some sense superfluous because this whole book is devoted to teaching and promoting reading, but the interests and responsibilities of teachers of reading differ in some ways from those of English teachers or of librarians. One difference is that except for remedial programs, teaching reading as an academic discipline in the high schools is a fairly recent development. The assumption used to be that normal students had received enough formal instruction in reading by the time they completed elementary school. They were then turned over to English teachers who taught mostly literature, grammar, and composition. Certainly English teachers worked with reading skills, but they were not the primary focus. Today more and more states are passing laws setting minimal reading standards for high school graduation, and this has meant that reading has become almost a regular part of the high school curriculum. In some schools, all ninth-graders now take a reading class; in other schools, such a class is reserved for those who test one or two years below grade level. Depending on how long it takes them to pass the test, students may take basic reading classes for several semesters.

In the teaching profession, the reluctant reader is nearly always stereotyped as a boy from the wrong side of town, someone S. E. Hinton would describe as an outsider, a greaser. Actually, reluctant readers come in both male and female varieties and from all social and I.Q. levels. Many of them have fairly good reading skills; they simply don't like to read. Others are poor readers partly because they get so little practice. What these students have in common is that they have been disappointed in their past reading. The rewards of reading—what they received either emotionally or intellectually—have not come up to their expectations, which were based on how hard they worked to read the material. They have therefore come away feeling cheated. The reading profession has recognized this problem and has attempted to solve it by lowering the price the student has to pay (i.e., by devising reading materials that demand less effort from the student). These are the controlled vocabulary books commonly known as "high-low books," meaning high interest, low vocabulary. They are only moderately successful because the authors are rarely creative artists; they are educators who have many priorities that come before telling a good story. An alternative approach is making the rewards greater rather than reducing the effort. This is where the best adolescent literature comes into the picture. It has a good chance of succeeding with reluctant readers for the following reasons:

1. It is written specifically to be interesting to teenagers. It is geared to their age level and their interests.
2. It is usually shorter and more simply written than adult material, yet it has no stigma attached to it. It isn't written down to anyone, nor does it look like a reading textbook.
3. There is so much of it (almost 800 new books published every year) that individual readers have a good chance of finding books that appeal to them.
4. As would be expected, because the best young adult books are the creations of some good contemporary authors, the stories are more dramatic, better written, and easier to get involved in than the controlled vocabulary books.
5. The language used in good adolescent literature is more like the language that students are accustomed to hearing. In this day of mass media communication, a student who does not read widely may still have a fairly high degree of

literary and language sophistication gained from watching television and movies.

Taking all this into account, some types of adolescent literature will still be enjoyed more than others by reluctant readers. In general, reluctant readers want the same things from the books they read that the rest of us want, but they want them faster and in less space. If it's information they are looking for, they want it to be right there. If they are reading a book for thrills and chills, they want it to be really scary. If they're reading for humor, they want it to be really funny. And if they're not sure about committing themselves for a large chunk of time, they want books in which they can get a feeling of accomplishment from reading short sections, paragraphs, or even sentences, as with various kinds of trivia books.

The Young Adult Library Services Association (YALSA) puts together an annual list, "Quick Picks for Reluctant Young Adult Readers." Selection criteria for the "Quick Picks" list includes short sentences, short paragraphs, simplicity of plot, uncomplicated dialogue, a sense of timeliness, maturity of format, and appeal of content. Fiction must include "believability of character and plot as well as realistic dialogue." This list, along with another YALSA list, "Popular Paperbacks for Young Adults," can prove helpful for reading teachers. The lists are available on the American Library Association's (ALA) Web site, www.ala.org/yalsa. The ALA also publishes a yearly book *ALA's Guide to Great Reading,* which includes all of their "Best Book" lists ready for photocopying.

Guided Reading Classes

The push for higher reading scores has opened the high school curriculum to reading classes for all students, not just those with low reading scores. Most high schools offer study skills courses in which skimming, speed reading, and selecting main ideas are taught. Some high schools also offer classes in what used to be called "free reading," but with the back-to-the-basics swing that occurred in the 1980s today are called *individualized* or *guided reading.* Rather than being a semester-long course, such programs are more likely to be incorporated into a six-week unit or a twice-a-week program as part of regular English or reading classes.

One of the chief reasons for providing kids time to read in class is to prevent the drop-off in reading that usually occurs when students begin high school and their social and work schedules leave little time for reading. A classroom library is provided containing multiple copies of popular young adult and adult titles from which students make their own selections. It is wise for teachers to send a note of explanation to parents that includes the statement that the choice of books is up to the student and his or her parents. It helps at the beginning for either the teacher or the librarian to give booktalks; once the class is started, students can recommend "good books" to each other.

When students finish a book, they hold a conference with the teacher, who preferably has also read the book. The purpose is not to test the student as much as it is to encourage thinking about the book and the author's intentions and to give teachers an opportunity to suggest other books that will help the student progress. Teachers need to show that they respect the reading of popular young adult books by being familiar with many of them and by being genuinely interested in what students have to say about them. The class is doomed to failure if teachers view it as a kind of focused study hall in which their job is to do little more than keep control and keep kids reading. It's also doomed to failure if students view it as a "cake" class, and for this reason successful teachers are fairly stringent as they devise various systems for giving credit. Students keep records of the number of books (or number of pages) read, they assist the teacher in judging the difficulty of the material, they mark their improvement over the semester (perhaps shown by a test score or by the number of pages the student reads in a class period), and they receive grades on their preparation for the individual conferences.

Various studies summarized by Dick Abrahamson and Eleanor Tyson in "What Every English Teacher Should Know About Free Reading"[13] have shown:

- Free reading is enjoyed by both students and teachers.
- Over a semester, students pick a variety of books, ranging from easy to difficult and from recent to classic.
- Reading skills improve, with some of this improvement undoubtedly related to attitude change.
- Students taught through free-reading are more likely to read as adults and to foster reading activities with their children.
- Individual conferences help literature come alive for students.
- The conferences also help to break down barriers between students and teachers.
- Good teachers employ the concept of reading ladders (e.g., helping a girl move from a Sweet Dreams romance to a Norma Fox Mazer or an M. E. Kerr book and on to *Gone with the Wind* and *Jane Eyre*).

With so many benefits, why isn't the course taught more often? Part of the reason is an image problem. *Free reading* smacks of "free love" and the permissiveness of the 1970s. Although the connotations of such a course title might attract students, these same connotations fly in the face of those who believe "You get what you pay for." Besides, the course is already suspect because of its avowal of quantity over quality; i.e., "reading by the pound," and its emphasis on pleasure for students. More people than we care to think about are sure that if students are having a good time they can't also be learning.

Another problem is that the teacher's role is practically invisible. Being able to listen to students while working ever so subtly to suggest books that will raise levels of reading and improve skills without discouraging young readers takes a knowledge of hundreds of books plus tact and considerable talent in communication. Yet this teaching occurs in private sessions between two people. One of our favorite graduate students is a high school reading teacher who teaches an individualized reading class along with some of the more traditional remedial reading classes. She laughs in frustration about her principal's visits to her individualized reading class. After popping his head into her room on several different occasions and seeing the kids reading and her talking with a student at her desk, he sent her a note requesting that she let him know "when you are going to be teaching," so that he could come and observe.

She's still trying to educate him about the type of class she's teaching. It is not for the dysfunctional or disabled reader. It is for the average, or above-average, student who simply needs a chance to read and discuss books. In effect, it is one last try on the part of the school to instill in young people the habit of reading for pleasure (see Ann Martin's statement on p. 349 on the Joy of Reading). Some people

ANN MARTIN
On The Joy of Reading

Recently I was having dinner with friends, and their two-year-old asked me for another piece of the ice-cream cake that was sitting just out of her reach. I cut off a very thin slice, since Rachel had already eaten two much larger ones, and slid it onto her plate. Rachel stared at the skimpy piece and pronounced in a wounded tone, "This is terrible."

That's exactly how I used to feel as a child when I read a book that didn't deliver whatever I thought had been promised; for instance, when I read a mystery and the hauntings in the big old mansion turned out not to be hauntings but the results of explainable, everyday phenomena. The flickering lights? Why, they weren't supernatural flickering lights at all, just a burglar roaming the house with a flashlight. Cheat! I would think. I wanted a real mystery, with ghosts and unresolved conflicts from the past. I was far more willing to suspend disbelief for the joys of a good mystery than I was to settle for lackluster, if logical explanations. The latter, quite simply, was not fun.

This is why when someone (usually an adult) now asks me what I hope kids will "get" from my books, I respond, "Pleasure." I can't imagine that a child who has just spent hours in school, then hours more at soccer practice, followed by homework at the computer and maybe a piano lesson, would want to sit down and read a story with a thinly disguised lesson about why it is better to give than to receive, or why stealing is wrong.

Of course, I would like for children to believe these things. I believe these things. And I have strong feelings about many, many other things. It's impossible not to let these feelings infuse what I write. But when I begin working on a book, *Leo the Magnificat*, for instance, I think about what the readers believe the story is going to deliver and that is the story I try to write. I hope that first and foremost, *Leo* is an enjoyable story about a church cat. I hope that kids will have fun reading it and will come away satisfied that the story delivered what was promised. If they also come away with some new thoughts on death, on compassion, on homeless people and animals—fantastic.

I can think of few pleasures greater than the pleasure of reading, and of turning others on to that pleasure, which is why I almost never think about what children will "get" from my books, apart from the great joy of reading.

Ann Martin's books include the Babysitters series from Scholastic, *Ten Kids, No Pets*, Holiday House, 1988; *Leo the Magnificat*, Scholastic, 1996; and with Paula Danziger *P.S. Longer Letter Later*, Scholastic, 1998.

still find such a concept an anathema, while others think it just comes naturally and, therefore, does not need to be "taught."

While we're not sure it can be taught, we want to at least give kids a chance to "absorb" it. Those who lack the skills for this kind of self-selected and self-paced reading need expert help from a professional reading teacher. Preparing teachers for such a challenging role is beyond the scope of this book.

Using Young Adult Books in the Social Studies Class

Turning facts into believable stories that touch readers' emotions is the biggest contribution of fiction to the social studies class. It is important for readers to realize, however, that many different books need to be read because each book presents a limited perspective. Stereotypes exist in people's minds for two reasons. One is that the same attitudes are repeated over and over, so that they become a predominant image. Another is that an individual may have had only one exposure to a particular race, group, or country. For example, readers of Chaim Potok's *The Chosen* don't learn everything about Hasidic Jews, but they know a lot more than they did before they read the book, and their interest may have been piqued, so that they will continue to watch for information and to read other books.

Nearly everyone agrees that by reading widely and sharing their findings, social studies class members can lead each other to go beyond stereotypes. For this to happen on more than an ad hoc or serendipitous basis, however, the teacher needs to identify clear-cut goals and then seek help from professional sources and other teachers and librarians in drawing up a selective list of books to be offered to students.

Social studies teachers have always recognized the importance of biographies and of the kind of historical books featured in Chapter Eight, but they may not be as aware of the many books, both fiction and nonfiction, that are available to help them teach students about contemporary social issues. See Chapter Nine for nonfiction books treating topics of interest to teenagers, such as ecology; the sex-related issues of pornography, rape, abuse, abortion, and prostitution; and medicine and health care, including questions about transplants, surrogate parenting, euthanasia, animal rights, and experiments on humans. Books on government ask questions about individual rights as opposed to the welfare of the group. Such questions range from whether the state has a right to require motorcycle helmets and seat belts to whether it should legislate drugs and sexual preference.

Social studies teachers also miss a powerful resource if they fail to bring the kind of fiction discussed in Chapter Four and in Focus Box 10.4 into their classes when they talk about current social problems. When they are talking about other countries, they need to remember that one of the great values and pleasures of literature is that it frees us to travel vicariously to other times and places. Movies, television, and photographs allow people to see other places, but literature has the added dimension of allowing the reader to share the thoughts of another person. One never feels like a stranger in a country whose literature one has read, and as today's jet age shrinks the distances between countries and cultures, it is more important than ever that people realize that members of the human race, regardless of where or how they live, have more similarities than differences.

Parents and Young Adult Literature

"Tell me a story."
"Read just one more!"
"Can we go to the library today?"
Such requests are among the pleasant memories that parents have of their young children. These memories become even more cherished when parents look

FOCUS BOX 10.4

Discussion Time

Heroes by Robert Cormier. Delacorte, 1998. Two young men return from World War II to their hometowns. Readers gradually learn that both are horribly damaged, but the damage shows more on Francis Joseph Cassavant than it does on Larry LaSalle. Other Cormier books that force hard thinking and discussion are *The Bumblebee Flies Anyway* (Pantheon, 1974), *I Am the Cheese* (Pantheon, 1977), *After the First Death* (Pantheon, 1979) and *We All Fall Down* (Delacorte, 1991).

Babylon Boyz by Jess Mowry. Simon & Schuster, 1997. The title refers to the sin-filled neighborhood in Oakland, California, where 14-year-old Dante and his basically homeless friends find a suitcase filled with cocaine and must decide what to do with it.

Blackwater by Eve Bunting. HarperCollins, 1999. A 13-year-old boy who is being hailed as a hero for trying to save his drowning friends suffers from guilt because he knows that if it had not been for his horseplay, they would not have been in danger.

Dirty Laundry: Stories About Family Secrets, edited by Lisa Rowe Fraustino. Viking, 1998. Among the eleven YA writers who have contributed stories to this collection are Bruce Coville, Chris Crutcher, Richard Peck, Rita Williams-Garcia, and M. E. Kerr. Just as in readers' own families, there are both light-hearted and serious secrets that inspire comparisons and pondering over why particular things are kept secret.

Keeping Christina by Sue Ellen Bridgers. HarperCollins, 1993. In an unusual book for young adults, Bridgers tells a story showing that being a friend to someone cannot always solve that person's problems and in fact may cause problems for the one doing the befriending.

Scorpions by Walter Dean Myers. HarperCollins, 1988. Jamal's brother is in jail, and an old gang leader brings word to Jamal that he's to take over as leader of the Scorpions. He also brings Jamal a gun.

Skin Deep by Lois Ruby. Scholastic, 1994. As a *Booklist* reviewer observed, this complex novel is more than "skin deep." Ruby tells the story of Dan and Laurel and what happens to their relationship when Dan joins a neo-Nazi skinhead group.

Stone Cold by Peter Hautman. Simon & Schuster, 1998. At 16, Doyle is a surprisingly good poker player. He leaves school and after a few rough starts actually ends up on the winning side. The question readers will wonder and argue about is whether he made the right decision, not just for now but forever.

The Tulip Touch by Anne Fine. Little, Brown, 1997. As Natalie looks back on the intense relationship she shared over the years with a classmate named Tulip, she gains important insights about friendship, accountability, and manipulation. The book is so powerful that readers will probably want to share their reactions with others.

---

at these same children, now teenagers rushing off to part-time jobs or after-school sports or spending so much time with friends that they no longer seem to have time to do required school assignments, much less read a book. When parents ask us what they can do to encourage their teenage children to read, we find it easier to tell them what *not* to do because we've observed at least three clear-cut roads to failure.

1. Don't nag. There's simply no way to force young adults to read, much less to enjoy it.
2. If you choose to read the books your teenagers are reading, don't do it as a censor or with the intent of checking up on your child or your child's school.

3. Don't suggest books to your teenager with the only purpose being to teach moral lessons.

Lest we appear unduly pessimistic, we hasten to add that we have also seen some genuinely rewarding reading partnerships between teenagers and their parents. These successful partnerships have resembled the kind of reading-based friendships that adults have with each other. Mutual respect is involved, and the partners take turns making suggestions of what will be good to read. Conversations about characters, plots, authors, and subject matter come up naturally, with no one asking teacher-type questions and no one feeling pressured to talk about what he or she has just read.

Teenagers enjoy being in a helping role (i.e., being experts whose opinions are valued). Some of the best partnerships we've seen have been between our students whose teenage children have volunteered to read and share their opinions on the books they've seen their mothers reading (sorry we can't remember any fathers in this role, although we have known fathers who do read and serve as examples). A key to enticing young people to read is simply to have lots of books and magazines available. But they need to be available for genuine browsing and reading by everyone in the family, not purchased and planted in a manner that will appear phoney to the teenager. A teenager who has never seen his or her parents read for pleasure will surely be suspicious when parents suddenly become avid readers on the day after parent-teacher conferences.

Perhaps a more important benefit than modeling behavior is that when parents read some of the best new books (the Honor List is a good starting place), they gain an understanding of what is involved in being a teenager today. Parents who have read some of the realistic problem novels have things to discuss with their children whether or not the children have read the books. Even when children are not interested in heart-to-heart discussions, parents are more understanding if they've read about the kinds of turmoil that teenagers face in struggling to become emotionally independent. In our own classes, and we understand the same is true for others teaching young adult literature, we are getting an increasing number of adult students who are there simply because they enjoy reading and talking about the young adult fiction that was not being written when they were teenagers. Those who are parents of teenagers consider it serendipitous if their teenagers also get interested and begin reading the same books.

A more structured approach is for parents to work with youth groups and church groups or to volunteer as a friend of either the public library or the school library. These kinds of activities provide parents with extra opportunities to involve young people in sharing reading experiences. In such situations, it is often a benefit to have other young people involved and for parents to trade off, so that they aren't always the leader for the particular group in which their child is a member.

Clarifying Human Relations and Values

Workers with church and civic youth groups, teachers of classes in human relations, and professional counselors working with young adults have all found that reading and discussing the kinds of books listed in Focus Box 10.4 can be useful.

When we talk about using books to help students understand their own and other people's feelings and behavior, we sometimes use the term *bibliotherapy*. It is a word that goes in and out of fashion, at least in reference to the informal kind of work that most teachers and librarians do with young adults. Its technical meaning is the use of books by professionally trained psychologists and psychiatrists in working with people who are mentally ill. Because of this association with illness, many "book" people reject the term. They reason that if a young adult is mentally ill and in need of some kind of therapy, the therapy should come from someone trained in that field rather than from someone trained in the book business or in teaching and guiding normal and healthy young adults.

Most people agree, however, that normal and healthy young adults can benefit psychologically from reading and talking about the problems of fictional characters. All teenagers have problems of one type or another, and simply finding out that other people have them too provides some comfort. We are reassured to know that our fears and doubts have been experienced by others. David A. Williams, a communications professor at the University of Arizona, said in a newspaper interview that he would die happy if he could "prove that a positive correlation exists between the rise in anxiety in the country and the decline of pleasure reading." Research done during the 1950s and 1960s showed that anxiety is directly related to a poor concept of oneself. "It seems to me," he said, "that the human being's major concern in life is to determine what it means to be a human being." The paradox is that before people can see themselves, they have to get outside of themselves and look at the whole spectrum of human experience to see where they fit in. "When we are feeling anxious it is usually because we have a narrow perspective which sees only what it wants to see." Someone who is anxiety-ridden, paranoiac, or resentful selects experiences from life to validate those feelings. For people like this, reading can put things back into perspective. "When we read about others who have suffered similar anxieties, we don't feel so cut off and, although the world doesn't change, we change the way we look at it."[14]

As books put things back into perspective, they open up avenues of communication that successful discussion leaders tap into. It is important, however, for adults to be careful in guiding students to read and talk about personal problems. No one should be forced to participate in such a discussion, and a special effort should not be made to relate stories to the exact problem that a group member is having. In fact, it would probably be best to avoid matching up particular problems with particular students. When someone is in the midst of a crisis, chances are that he or she does not want to read and talk about someone else in a similar predicament. As a general rule, one would probably get the most from such a discussion before or after—rather than during—a time of actual crisis.

Such discussions are usually held in clubs, church groups, classes on preparation for marriage and human relations, and counseling and support group meetings at crisis centers and various institutions to which young people are sent. Because membership in these groups changes from meeting to meeting and there are no pressures for participants to do outside reading as "homework," a leader will probably be disappointed or frustrated if the discussion is planned around the expectation that everyone will have read the book. A more realistic plan is for the leader to give a summary of the book and a 10- to 20-minute prepared reading of the part that best delineates the problem or the topic for discussion. Using fairly well-known books, including ones that have been made into movies, increases the chances of participation. Using popular books also makes it easier for students whose appetites have been whetted to find the book and read it on their own.

In an adult group of professionals, the same purpose would be accomplished by reading a case study that would then be discussed. But case studies are written for trained adults who know how to fill in the missing details and how to interpret the symptoms. Teenagers are not psychologists, and they are not social workers or philosophers. Literature may be as close as they will ever come to discussing the kinds of problems dealt with in these fields. What follows the oral presentation can be extremely varied, depending on the nature of the group, the leader's personality, and what the purpose or the goal of the discussion is. The literature provides the group—both teenagers and adults—with a common experience that can serve as the focus for discussion. Pressures and tensions are relieved because everyone is talking in the third person about the characters in the book, although in reality many of the comments will be about first-person problems.

In 1999, Greenwood Press launched a series of professional books edited by Joan F. Kaywell under the heading, "Using Literature to Help Troubled Teenagers." Published titles include one on family issues edited by Kaywell, one on identity issues edited by Jeffrey S. Kaplan, one on societal issues edited by Pamela S. Carroll, and one on health issues edited by Cynthia Ann Bowman. Forthcoming titles will include one on abuse also edited by Kaywell, and one on end-of-life issues edited by Janet Allen. Chapters, which focus on the characters in specific YA books, are co-authored by specialists in young adult literature and mental health workers whose practices include teenagers.

Reading and discussing books can in no way cure mental illness, but reading widely about all kinds of problems and all kinds of solutions helps keep young people involved in thinking about moral issues. As shown in Table 10.3, about what

TABLE 10.3

THE POWERS AND LIMITATIONS OF YOUNG ADULT LITERATURE

What literature can do:	What literature cannot do:
1. It can provide a common experience or a way in which a teenager and an adult can focus their attention on the same subject.	1. It cannot cure someone's emotional illness.
2. It can serve as a discussion topic and a way to relieve embarrassment by enabling people to talk in the third person about problems with which they are concerned.	2. It cannot guarantee that readers will behave in socially approved ways.
3. It can give young readers confidence that, should they meet particular problems, they will be able to solve them.	3. It cannot directly solve readers' problems.
4. It can increase a young person's understanding of the world and the many ways that individuals find their places in it.	
5. It can comfort and reassure young adult readers by showing them that they are not the only ones who have fears and doubts.	
6. It can give adults as well as teenagers insights into adolescent psychology and values.	

young adult literature can and cannot do when it is used as a tool to teach about human relations and values, the positives outweigh the negatives.

This chapter has shown that using and promoting books with young readers is a shared opportunity and responsibility. It belongs not only to librarians and English and reading teachers but also to everyone who works closely with young people and wants to understand them better. It can serve as a medium through which to open communication with young adults about their concerns.

Notes

[1]Janet French, "Review of *Homecoming*," *School Library Journal* 28 (September 1981): 133.

[2]Audrey Eaglen, "What Makes a Good Review," *Top of the News* 35 (Winter 1979): 146–152.

[3]Anne Tyler, "Looking for Mom," *New York Times Book Review,* April 26, 1981, p. 52.

[4]Katherine Paterson, "Family Visions," *New York Times Book Review,* November 14, 1982, p. 41.

[5]Dorothy Mathews, "Writing about Adolescent Literature: Current Approaches and Future Directions," *Arizona English Bulletin* 18 (April 1976): 216–19.

[6]Katha Pollitt, "Why We Read: Canon to the Right of Me . . .," *The Nation,* September 23, 1991, reprinted in *The Chronicle of Higher Education,* October 23, 1991.

[7]*Rudolfo Anaya Autobiography as Written in 1985.* Copyright 1991 Rudolfo Anaya (TQS Publications; P.O. Box 9275; Berkeley, CA 94709), pp. 16–17.

[8]*The Big Aiiieeeee!: An Anthology of Chinese American and Japanese American Literature,* edited by Jeffery Paul Chan, Frank Chin, Lawson Fusao Inada, and Shawn Wong (New American Library, 1991), p. 8.

[9]Maxine Hong Kingston, "Personal Statement," in *Approaches to Teaching Kingston's THE WOMAN WARRIOR,* edited by Shirley Geok-lin Lim (Modern Language Association, 1991), p. 24.

[10]Jim Burke, *The English Teacher's Companion: A Complete Guide to Classroom, Curriculum and the Profession* (Boynton Cook, 1999), p. 252.

[11]Dorothy M. Broderick, "Whose Job Is It Anyway?" *VOYA* 6 (February 1984): 320–26.

[12]Joni Bodart, *Booktalk! Booktalking and School Visiting for Young Adult Audiences* (H. W. Wilson, 1980), p. 2–3.

[13]Dick Abrahamson and Eleanor Tyson, "What Every English Teacher Should Know About Free Reading," *The ALAN Review* 14 (Fall 1986): 54–58, 69.

[14]"Feeling Uptight, Anxious? Try Reading, UA Prof Says," *Tempe Daily News,* December 15, 1977.

Titles Mentioned in the Text of Chapter Ten

ALA's Guide to Great Reading. American Library Association, yearly.

Adams, Douglas. *The Hitchhiker's Guide to the Galaxy.* Crown, 1980.

Allen, Janet, ed. *Using Literature to Help Troubled Teenagers Cope with End-of-Life Issues.* Greenwood, forthcoming.

Anaya, Rudolfo. *Bless Me, Ultima.* TQS Publications, 1972.

Blume, Judy. *Forever.* Bradbury, 1975.

Bodart, Joni Richard. *Booktalk! Booktalking and School Visiting for Young Adult Audiences.* H. W. Wilson, 1980.

Bowman, Cynthia Ann, ed. *Using Literature to Help Teenagers Cope with Health Issues.* Greenwood, 1999.

Bradbury, Ray. *The Martian Chronicles.* Doubleday, 1958.

Bridgers, Sue Ellen. *Notes for Another Life.* Knopf, 1981.

Brönte, Charlotte. *Jane Eyre,* 1847.

Burke, Jim. *The English Teacher's Companion: A Complete Guide to Classroom, Curriculum, and the Profession.* Boynton Cook, 1999.

Campbell, Patricia J. *Presenting Robert Cormier, Updated Edition.* G. K. Hall/Twayne, 1989.

Carroll, Pamela S., ed. *Using Literature to Help Troubled Teenagers Cope with Societal Issues.* Greenwood, 1999.

Chan, Jeffery Paul, Frank Chin, Lawson Fusao Inada, and Shawn Wong, eds. *The Big Aiiieeeee! An Anthology of Chinese American and Japanese American Literature.* Meridian, 1991.

Chbosky, Stephen. *The Perks of Being a Wallflower.* MTV/Pocket Books, 1999.

Childress, Alice. *Rainbow Jordan.* Putnam, 1981.

Cisneros, Sandra. *The House on Mango Street.* Random House, 1984.

Cole, Brock. *Celine*. Farrar, Straus & Giroux, 1989.

Cormier, Robert. *The Chocolate War*. Pantheon, 1974.

Fast, Howard. *April Morning*. Crown, 1961.

Garden, Nancy. *Annie on My Mind*. Farrar, Straus & Giroux, 1981.

Golding, William. *Lord of the Flies*. Putnam, 1955.

Hamilton, Virginia. *Sweet Whispers, Brother Rush*. Putnam, 1982.

Hinton, S. E. *The Outsiders*. Viking, 1967.

Hipple, Theodore. *Presenting Sue Ellen Bridgers*. G. K. Hall/Twayne, 1990.

Kaplan, Jeffrey S., ed. *Using Literature to Help Troubled Teenagers Cope with Identity Issues*. Greenwood, 1999.

Kaywell, Joan F., ed. *Using Literature to Help Troubled Teenagers Cope with Family Issues*. Greenwood, 1999.

Kies, Cosette. *Presenting Young Adult Horror Fiction*. Twayne, 1991.

Kingston, Maxine Hong. *The Woman Warrior: Memoirs of a Girlhood Among Ghosts*. Knopf, 1976.

Knowles, John. *A Separate Peace*. Macmillan, 1960.

MacRae, Cathi Dunn. *Presenting Young Adult Fantasy Fiction*. G. K. Hall/Twayne, 1998.

Mitchell, Margaret. *Gone with the Wind*. Macmillan, 1936.

Oneal, Zibby. *In Summer Light*. Viking, 1985.

Paulsen, Gary. *The Monument*. Delacorte, 1991.

Potok, Chaim. *The Chosen*. Simon & Schuster, 1967.

Plummer, Louise. *My Name Is Sus5an Smith. The 5 Is Silent*. Delacorte, 1991.

Reid, Suzanne. *Presenting Young Adult Science Fiction*. G. K. Hall/Twayne, 1998.

Salinger, J. D. *The Catcher in the Rye*. Little, Brown, 1951.

Tan, Amy. *The Joy Luck Club*. Putnam, 1989.

Twain, Mark (real name Samuel Clemens). *Adventures of Huckleberry Finn*. 1884.

Voigt, Cynthia. *Homecoming*. Atheneum, 1981.

Walker, Alice. *The Color Purple*. Harcourt Brace Jovanovich, 1982.

Weidt, Maryann N. *Presenting Judy Blume*. G. K. Hall/Twayne, 1989.

Zindel, Paul. *The Pigman*. HarperCollins, 1968.

Information on the availability of paperback editions of these titles is available online from such book sellers as Barnes & Noble and Amazon.com, and through *Books in Print* compiled by R. R. Bowker Company and available either in person or online from major libraries.

CHAPTER

11

Literature in the English Class
Short Stories, Novels, Creative Writing, Film, and Thematic Units

In response to requests from previous users of this textbook, we devote this chapter to a discussion of standard approaches to the teaching of literature in high school. Although we recognize that there is no single best way to teach and that schools, classes, students, and goals vary from school to school, from teacher to teacher, and from parent to parent, the methods of teaching literature to young people discussed here have proved their worth for large numbers of teachers and their students.

Principles of Teaching English

We believe in five principles about English teachers and the teaching of literature. We have developed these principles from our own experiences and from the writings and thoughts of many others in both books and journals. See Appendix C for a listing.

1. *English teachers must never forget that literature should be both entertaining and challenging.* Teachers must alert students to literature that the students will find challenging and satisfying through talking about individual works in many genres, perhaps in a genre unit, a thematic unit, or free reading. Is this easy to do? No, not always, but it might convince a few students that teachers care about reading and kids. If the literature does not provide entertainment and challenge, English teachers have failed.

2. *English teachers must know a wide range of literature.* Teachers should know classics of English and American literature, of course; they should also know American popular literature and young adult literature and something about Asian and European literature (e.g., Asian folktales, Norwegian drama, French short stories, or Russian novels). They should know women writers and ethnic writers, especially, but not exclusively from the United States, and what they

do not know about literature, they should learn. That demands that English teachers read all sorts of literature—the great, the new, the popular, the demanding, and the puzzling. Why do they read? Because they are readers themselves and because they are always looking for books that might work with students. One of life's joys for English teachers, and maybe its greatest annoyance, is that they view every poem, every film, every newspaper article, every football game, every everything for its potential use in class.

3. *English teachers ought to know enough about dramatic techniques and oral interpretation to be comfortable reading aloud to students.* We need teachers eager and able to read material to students that just might interest, intrigue, amuse, or excite them, material that might make young people aware of new or old books or writers or techniques or ideas. Outside of speech or drama, no classes require so much oral performance from teachers as English classes. Poetry must be read aloud. So must drama. Reading fiction aloud is half the fun of teaching short stories. If students are to learn how to read poetry or drama, it will come from English teachers comfortable with their own oral reading. One added benefit is that common devices in literature, such as metaphor or irony or ambiguity, are often more apparent when heard rather than read. Obviously, the availability of poetry or fiction on tapes or CDs means other voices can be heard, but that does not mean the teacher's voice should be silent. Granted, Ian McKellen's reading of Shakespeare exceeds the grasp of us mortals, but McKellen is not there to explain why he read a passage from *Richard III* or *Macbeth* or *Othello* as he did. English teachers are there to explain why they chose to read a particular passage and why they read it as they did.

4. *English teachers must remember the distance in education and sophistication between them and their students.* No matter what the rapport between them, it is almost equally easy for teachers to overestimate as to underestimate their students, although experienced teachers would surely prefer the first error to the second. Choosing material for an entire class is never easy and often seems impossible. Some materials—say a *New Yorker* short story or a T. S. Eliot poem or a Harold Pinter play—assume a sophistication that high school students often do not have, although sometimes their glibness in class temporarily fools a neophyte. On some occasions, a class is ready for the Pinter, but while waiting for that class, it's tempting for teachers to choose material that challenges no one and that no one greatly enjoys. Selecting literature for 15, 35, or 45 students is almost inevitably an exercise in frustration and failure. That comes with the territory, but it is no excuse for not trying to meet all students' needs with that one fabulous, never-to-be-forgotten classroom novel, poem, short story, or play. Experienced English teachers know this, but most parents and other citizens do not. Teachers should try to let others in on the secret.

5. *Finally, English teachers should teach and use only literature they enjoy.* Teachers should not be expected to fake enthusiasm or interest. If a teacher doesn't like Robert Frost's poetry or Stephen Crane's *The Red Badge of Courage,* the teacher has no business using Frost or Crane. It is permissible for both teachers and young people not to like a work or an author, assuming, of course, the teacher has read and responsibly considered the author or work in question (we can be a bit more charitable toward students on this point). If teachers do not like highly regarded modern works such as Raymond Carver's short stories or Athol Fugard's *"Master Harold" . . . and the Boys* or Sharon Olds's poetry, they

shouldn't teach them. There are too many stories, plays, and poems out there about which teachers are presumably enthusiastic. (Obviously, this point follows our second point, that teachers are incurable, wide readers.)

None of this implies that teachers cannot change their minds about literature or writers, just as teachers know that occasionally it is great fun and profitable to work with literature about which they feel ambivalent. Nor does this imply that students should be discouraged from reading and talking about works for which the teacher has no great enthusiasm.

Our five principles for teaching literature extend to works in the curriculum guide as well as the literary canon of great books. We are not being unduly critical of the manner in which many literature curriculum guides are developed by noting that they are created by human beings with certain strengths and weaknesses, and they are fallible. As long as they are taken as guides, teachers may be helped, particularly beginning teachers, but when curriculum guides are taken as biblical edicts, absurdity reigns, and any value disappears.

Assuming teachers have a wide knowledge of literature, they can find a variety of works of equal quality to teach. What is gained from a bored teacher presenting Poe's poetry to an equally bored class? It is much better to assume that in the four years of high school these students will have one English teacher who likes Poe. And if it doesn't happen? There are worse disasters. What if no teacher wants to teach Shakespeare? We cannot imagine an English department so devoid of taste or ability, but if one exists, it is surely preferable that students leave school ignorant of Shakespeare than that they be bored by him.

Forcing teachers to teach something they do not like encourages classroom dishonesty. Teachers spout trite and obvious interpretations of literature taken from the teacher's guide, and students regurgitate on tests what they neither care about nor understand. Such dishonesty inevitably breeds boredom with literature and contempt for learning.

Literature that a teacher thinks worth teaching, however defined, ought to encourage honest teaching and honest responses from kids. As Louise Rosenblatt has pointed out again and again:

> No one else can read a literary work for us. The benefits of literature can emerge only from creative activity on the part of the reader himself. He responds to the little black marks on the page, or to the sounds of the words in his ear, and he "makes something of them." The verbal symbols enable him to draw on his past experiences with what the words point to in life and literature.[1]

Allowing young people to respond to literature slows down the teacher and the lesson because thinking takes time and brainpower. Time is required to build trust, especially for students accustomed to memorizing and spitting back whatever the teacher has said. Some students simply do not believe that a teacher wants their opinions, sometimes for good reason. Students have to be convinced that responding honestly to literature is worth the trouble and hard work. An invitation to what appears to be an intellectual coup d'état does not come easily from a teacher, and the acceptance does not come easily from students.

Using Young Adult Literature in English Classes

One of the reasons we endorse young adult literature for English classes is that students can believe a teacher who asks for their honest response to a book that features a contemporary young person facing a problem that students are more likely to face than their teacher. Young adult literature is often recommended as a bridge to appreciating literary techniques, but its role in developing the trust needed for a response-centered approach to literature may be even more important.

Teachers who believe in the value of young adult literature for either of these purposes sometimes forget that many English teachers still make fun of young adult books. To us, the criticisms often seem irrational and defensive, almost as if the books threaten teachers and their worlds. Nevertheless, young adult converts must be aware of the following protestations. We could not resist offering some counterarguments, even though we realize we're preaching to the choir.

1. *No one around here knows anything about it. If it was really worth knowing, we'd have heard about it.* It's been around quite a long time now, and since the publication of books by S. E. Hinton, Paul Zindel, Robert Lipsyte, Norma Fox Mazer, Harry Mazer, Robert Cormier, Rosa Guy, Gary Paulsen, and many more, lots of people have heard about it. In any case, the statement is a rationalization for learning nothing new. Ignorance is not an impressive justification for anything.

2. *Adolescent literature has no heritage and no respectability.* It has a heritage going back more than 130 years. Some people respect it, but few respect something they have not read.

3. *We teach only the greatest of literature, and that automatically eliminates adolescent literature from our consideration. Why should we demean ourselves or our students—and their parents—by stooping to something inferior?* We wonder how the greatest of literature was chosen for this curriculum. Were these great books chosen from a list supplied by a college teacher or by some independent body? How great are they for high school students? How long has it been since the teacher read any adolescent books? Some students—and not just the slowest—get little pleasure from reading. We believe it is the English teacher's responsibility to help students find pleasure in reading. We wonder if only the greatest will do that.

4. *We can't afford thirty or forty copies of something we don't know. That's why we don't use adolescent books.* Maybe you ought to read some of the books. That may tell you whether you'd want to use a class set, and it might suggest that individual titles are better than a set of anything.

5. *Kids have to grow up and take themselves and their work seriously. I do. We expect them to. That takes care of adolescent literature as far as my school is concerned.* We take our work and our kids seriously, too. We'd also like them to enjoy some of their reading. Bruce Brooks's and Sue Ellen Bridgers's books contain plenty of serious stuff, but they also provide the joy of discovering similarities between readers and characters.

6. *Adolescent literature has no permanence. Something is popular today, and something else is popular tomorrow. Great literature is timeless and unchanging. How can we be expected to keep track of ephemera?* What a wonderful justification for reading nothing new. Yes, new books come out all the time. Some new books have a chance to escape the dustheap. Some don't. Most adolescent books don't

last, but Alcott's *Little Women* and Twain's *Huckleberry Finn* have been around a long time. Also, consider that S. E. Hinton's *The Outsiders,* Robert Lipsyte's *The Contender*, and Paul Zindel's *The Pigman* are over 30 years old. Will they last? That's anyone's guess. We would put money on a bet that some of Robert Cormier's and Katherine Paterson's books will last. For that matter, we can think of a dozen other young adult writers who seem likely to last.

7. *Why have kids spend time in class reading something they can easily read on their own? Shouldn't class time be spent on books that are challenging, books that kids won't find on their own, books that will make kids stretch intellectually?* Some of those kids may not find those books as challenging as Cormier's *After the First Death* or Alan Garner's *The Owl Service* or Alice Childress's *A Hero Ain't Nothin' But a Sandwich,* and these three titles, among many more, are challenging emotionally and intellectually. Besides, what is there about *The Pearl* or *Silas Marner* or *The Old Man and the Sea* that makes their difficulties worth stretching for? The painful truth is that many young people do not find reading enjoyable, and even though they may not find *Silas Marner* on their own, they also won't find Lowry's *The Giver* or Voigt's *Homecoming*, which might come closer to reaching them.

8. *Isn't adolescent literature formula literature?* Yes, sometimes, but not always. *Formula* is a dirty word—*archetype* has more positive connotations. We are impressed to hear someone talk about Dostoyevsky's grand inevitability in *Crime and Punishment.* We are not impressed to hear someone talk about the total predictability of a Nancy Drew mystery. There's nevertheless an uncomfortable similarity between the two comments, if not the two books. Then we must not forget that there is young adult literature and there is young adult literature. Surely a teacher could be justified in using Cormier's *I Am the Cheese* or Paula Fox's *One-Eyed Cat* in a discussion of archetypes.

9. *Isn't it silly and simple-minded stuff about dating and trivia like that?* Sometimes, yes. Most of the time, no. How long has it been since you read Virginia Hamilton, Jill Paton-Walsh, Cynthia Voigt, or Zibby Oneal?

10. *Isn't it mostly about depressing problems—like suicide, death, abortion, pregnancy? Hasn't it been censored a lot?* Yes, it can be serious, and some of it has been censored, but see the thoughtful comments that follow.

Observations by Elaine Simpson and Dorothy Broderick speak more effectively than we can to the last three objections. Simpson addresses her remarks to those librarians and others who for years criticized junior novels for their innocence and their pat answers that instilled false conceptions and failed to deal with fundamental problems.

Then juvenile authors and editors began giving us such books as *Go Ask Alice; Run Softly, Go Fast; Admission to the Feast; Run, Shelley, Run; The Chocolate War.* I could go on and on naming both fiction and nonfiction.

And what happened? All too many of these same people who had been asking for an honest story about serious teenage problems began protesting: language like *that* in a book for young people? Are rape, abortion, homosexuality, unwed mothers, suicide, drugs, unsympathetic portrayals of parents, and violence appropriate for junior novels? Are young people ready for such explicit realism? Would you want your daughter to read one?[2]

Dorothy Broderick focused on the charge most often expressed by ultraconservatives, "namely, that young adult books are not uplifting. Why, oh why, cry these critics, do the authors have to deal with such depressing subjects. Why can't we go back to the good old days?" Broderick's answer:

> As one who has spent six decades on this planet, let me tell you an important fact: *there were no good old days.* Every problem confronted in a young adult novel today not only existed during my childhood and adolescence, but was known to most of us. There were drunks in families, there were wife abusers, there were child molesters, divorce, certainly death and dying, mental illness, pre-marital pregnancy, and, yes, abortions if you were among the elite. In high school, one of my classmates went home one day to find his father had hung himself in the garage; a couple of weeks later he went home to find his mother had done the same thing.[3]

Adolescent literature has a place in the literature program because it appeals to young people. Why? Young adult novels are short or at least shorter than most modern novels or classics studied in schools. It is easy for teachers to dismiss that point, but it is not a point that young people ignore. Young adult books are easier to read (or so they seem at first reading) than most adult or classic novels. They are about young people the age of the readers and concerned with real issues and problems facing adolescents, particularly the readers (and that's often not true of adult books or classics). They look like they might be fun to read. The dust jackets may bother some adults, but they may also appeal to the young. The photos or paintings on young adult paperbacks are calculated to grab readers just as the photos and paintings on adult novels. With young adult books, there is also a blurb showing, for example, that the book is about a kid who has this wonderful brother who's dying of AIDS, or it is about a girl whose grandmother is senile, or it is about a boy and a girl enmeshed in a love affair against their parents' wishes. With such come-ons, who is surprised when young people grab young adult titles. The last reason for their popularity with many young people is that the books are often perceived to be unacceptable to traditional teachers; that is, they're forbidden fruit.

What makes young adult books so unattractive to some teachers? Besides the reasons listed earlier, Robert C. Small, Jr., adds an unpleasant final reason. He writes that the goal of most literature programs is to designate the teacher as literary expert and translator of books to lowly students who seem to have no role at all, other than to be recipients of the largesse of the expert-translator-teacher.[4] When young people read adolescent books, they are the experts, and they may need to serve as translators to adults who wish to understand the adolescent books.

What makes young adult books so attractive to other English teachers is the fact that for an imaginative teacher, young adult books have so many uses. An individual title can be studied by the whole class, although that's comparatively rare. They can be paired with adult books, classics or not as recommended by some of the books in Appendix C. And they work beautifully in free reading and thematic units. Their possibilities extend as far as the teachers' imaginations because they provide what other good novels do along with an almost guaranteed adolescent interest. Richard Jackson, when he was editor-in-chief at Bradbury Press, explained

YA literature should illuminate rather than educate, raise questions rather than trot out answers. And it should entertain. Though society changes from one generation to another, its rites of passage remain quite fixed. Literature for young adults will endure because the impulse to record and reconsider those rites strikes us all. We can't resist it—and though they may not admit the fact, adolescents do hear us.[5]

Using Short Stories in English Class

One kind of adolescent literature that has grown increasingly popular over the last decade is short stories (see Tim Wynne-Jones's statement on p. 364). Although they fit into today's penchant for condensations and instant gratification, short stories are more than *Readers' Digest* versions of a novel. Because from the beginning, they are planned to fit into less space, they work well in classrooms where students can read fifteen short stories in the time it takes to read one or two novels. Through reading the larger number of short stories, they can meet a greater variety of viewpoints and representatives of different ethnic groups and cultures. Because the best of modern American authors have written short stories, students can experience high-quality writing in pieces that are short enough for comfortable reading.

If students are to enjoy and profit from reading short stories (Focus Box 11.1), some preparation is necessary. Kids are not born with genes labeled "How to Read Short Stories Perceptively." Teachers must help students develop the skills to enter imaginative works. Tempting as simple solutions have been to curriculum designers, students should not be required to master a vocabulary list of "Thirty Magic Literary Terms That Will Change Your Life and Make You the Reader You Have Always Longed to Be." There's a place for learning about *verisimilitude, point of view, unreliable narrator, sprung rhythm, synecdoche, foreshadowing, Petrarchan sonnet,* and *carpe diem* if and when the terms enlighten students but never as a series of terms in a pedagogical vacuum.

Finding out about the codes that make one piece of literature succeed while another one fails forces teachers to consider how they went about getting into a short story, for example, and how they get into a story that's new to them. There is no single way of getting at any literary work, and several approaches may need to be tried. Students may come to class already knowing how to listen, to take assiduous notes on what the teacher says is important, and to play all this back at test time, but none of that has much to do with reading. In many ways, a careful reading of a work by student A produces a different work from an equally careful reading by student B or student C. The words in John Updike's "A & P" (in Robert S. Gold's *Point of Departure*) do not change from reader to reader, but the feelings of the readers based on past experience and present morality yield a slightly different story with each reader, and sometimes a greatly different story. These steps may help a class break the code in reading a short story.

1. Read the first sentence carefully (and the first paragraph). What do they tell you about the setting, characters, or tension?
2. Predict from the first paragraph what's likely to follow.
3. Speed-read the story to get some sense of what it's about and who the characters are (probably the only part that can be done outside of class).

TIM WYNNE-JONES
On Short Stories

I am a slow reader. Always was. Some people can read in an evening a novel that would take me a week. That's the first good thing about short stories; they're short. Edgar Allan Poe said it in 1842 and it's still true. You can read a short story all at once with no distractions—the whole picture forming in your head—before your mother tells you to tidy your room or empty the cat box. (Or, in Poe's case, the raven box.)

In one of my favorite reviews of my own work, Margaret Wiley writing in *Hungry Mind* called me "the master of the glimpse." And that's what a short story is: a moment in a life. A thrilling moment perhaps; a tender moment; in any case, a moment of transition.

There's a fabulously funny short story by Dorothy Parker called "The Waltz"; it lasts as long as a dance. Then there's Howard M. Fast's "The Brood," which recounts the terrifying few hours of a wagon train under siege, hours that make for a lifetime of change for the young protagonist, but which are distilled down to a riveting read of twenty minutes, max.

Let's face it; in this first chapter of the twenty-first century, childhood is occupied territory. Short stories are time sensitive material.

In an age when adults, especially teachers, love to remark on the short attention span of "Today's Youth" the short story seems the perfect antidote: a gripping literary experience in a nut shell. A nut shell, mind you *not* a pill. I think a whole generation or two of kids got turned off from short stories by the far from gripping pabulum served up to them in primers and made-for-instruction school anthologies. You know, those short stories that come with a list of questions hanging off the end. Those shorts would give anyone a wedgie!

A good short isn't a lot of things. It isn't long, it isn't preachy, and it certainly isn't a novel wannabe. It isn't a sketch, it's a miniature. Not the whole season, just the big game. Not the whole sunset, just one straggler on the beach. It does not presume to grandeur. It is happy to invoke a gasp of surprise, a belly laugh, a single tear.

In writing, just as in reading, I love to stretch out in a novel, pacing myself for the long haul, juggling sub plots, keeping things moving, the tension mounting. But I also love the invigoration that comes from a compelling short story—a headlong dash, complete with hurdles, and with the finish line always in view.

Tim Wynne-Jones's books include *Some of the Kinder Planets*, Orchard, 1995; *The Book of Changes*, Viking, 1996; *The Maestro*, Orchard, 1995; and *Lord of the Fries*, Dorling Kindersley Ink, 1999.

FOCUS BOX 11.1

Paperback Anthologies of Teachable Short Stories

American Short Story Masterpieces, edited by Raymond Carver and Tom Jenks. Dell, 1987. Included are Flannery O'Connor's "A Good Man Is Hard to Find," Bernard Malamud's "The Magic Barrell," and Joyce Carol Oates's "Where Are You Going, Where Have You Been?"

Do You Like It Here? edited by Robert Benard. Dell, 1989. Included are stories about school by Sue Kaufman, Maureen Daly, John O'Hara, Tobias Wolff, and Gore Vidal.

Fifty Great American Short Stories, edited by Milton Crane. Bantam, 1980. Included are Mary E. Freeman's "A New England Nun," Conrad Aiken's "Silent Snow, Secret Snow," James Agee's "A Mother's Tale," William Carlos Williams's "The Use of Force," Jack London's "To Build a Fire," Ambrose Bierce's "The Damned Thing," and Stephen Vincent Benet's "By the Waters of Babylon." Crane has also done *Fifty Great Short Stories* (Bantam, 1981).

Great American Short Stories, edited by Wallace and Mary Stegner. Dell, 1957. This fine and safe collection includes William Daniel Steele's "The Man Who Saw Through Heaven," Henry James's "The Real Thing," and Walter Van Tilburg Clark's "The Wind and the Snow of Winter."

Leaving Home: 15 Distinguished Authors Explore Personal Journeys, selected by Hazel Rochman and Darlene Z. McCampbell. HarperCollins, 1997. Allan Sherman, Tim O'Brien, David St. John, Norma Fox Mazer, Gary Soto, and Toni Morrison are among the authors represented.

Mid-Century: An Anthology of Distinguished Contemporary American Short Stories, edited by Orville Prescott. Pocket Books, 1958. Included are Frank Rooney's "Cyclists' Raid," Shirley Jackson's "The Lottery," and Joseph Whitehill's "The Day of the Last Rock Fight."

Point of Departure: 19 Stories of Youth and Discovery, edited by Robert S. Gold. Dell, 1967. Included are John Updike's "A & P" and "Tomorrow and Tomorrow and So Forth," Bernard Malamud's "A Summer's Reading," William Saroyan's "Seventeen," John Bell Clayton's "The White Circle," Allan Sillitoe's "The Bike," William Melvin Kelley's "A Good Long Sidewalk," and Nadine Gordimer's "A Company of Laughing Faces."

Points of View, edited by James Moffett and Kenneth R. McElheny. Mentor/NAL, 1965. Included are William Carlos Williams's "The Use of Force," Nikolai Gogol's "The Diary of a Madman," Joseph Conrad's "The Idiots," Daniel Keyes's "Flowers for Algernon," John Updike's "A & P," and Anton Chekhov's "Enemies."

Short Story Masterpieces, edited by Robert Penn Warren and Albert Erskine. Dell, 1954. Included are Joseph Conrad's "An Outpost of Progress," F. Scott Fitzgerald's "Winter Dreams," D. H. Lawrence's "The Horse Dealer's Daughter," Saki's "The Open Window," Somerset Maugham's "The Outstation," Sherwood Anderson's "The Egg," and William Faulkner's "Barn Burning."

4. Isolate the problems in reading the story (e.g., dialect, structure, conflicting characters).
5. Reread the story, doing parts or all of it aloud.

Going through this with students should help them learn how literary codes can be broken through careful reading. What can we safely say to our classes about virtually all short stories? We can tell students that all fiction is based on conflict, and we might begin by exploring with them different kinds of conflict. We can say, with some confidence, that the title of the story usually is significant. One of the problems young readers have with Updike's "A & P," once they're willing to get beyond the usual remark that "nothing happens," is understanding what the title means, because many A & P (the name of the Great Atlantic and Pacific Tea Company) grocery stores seem to have gone the way of all flesh. Students rarely have a clear idea of what this store symbolized in many communities, which was something quite different from a Safeway or a Vons, for example. Students may not be incredibly richer for knowing about the A & P and its place in Updike's fictional community, but it's essential for understanding the community aspects of the story and who the characters are.

We can tell students that first-person narrators are similar to readers in many ways—fallible mortals likely to make mistakes in judging people or letting their emotions get in the way. Students are sometimes puzzled when we raise this point, but it's essential because readers tend to take the narrator's word for almost anything. In "A & P," Sammy quits his cashiering job when his boss (a family friend) tells some young women that they are inappropriately dressed. Sammy makes the grand gesture at least in part to impress the girls, who leave without witnessing Sammy's nobility. He describes the act as "The sad part of the story, at least my family says it's sad, but I don't think it's so sad myself." A few seconds after Sammy's spur-of-the-moment gallantry, the store manager tells Sammy that he (Sammy) doesn't want to do this. Sammy says something presumably profound about himself and other young romantics: "it seems to me that once you begin a gesture it's fatal not to go through with it." The manager tells Sammy, "You'll feel this the rest of your life," and Sammy adds, "I know that's true, too." More mature students who enjoy talking about the story—and it is slow moving and meditative and unlikely to appeal to younger students—see an eternal romantic doomed to gestures all his life. Readers may put different amounts of faith in Sammy's words, concluding that he doesn't lie, but he may not recognize the truth.

We can also tell students how important those first words are in most short stories. It is the author's opportunity to grab the audience, and some readers (at least outside school) may decide to drop the story and the author based on those words. Most students rush through the first lines. In class we can force them to slow down by reading aloud the first lines over and over.

The questions English teachers pose for students should be carefully thought out and played with. Beginning teachers need to develop and practice the questions before class, while more experienced teachers can rely on mental notes of what makes the discussion worthwhile rather than mere chitchat to take up fifty-five minutes of class.

Many teachers ask students to keep journals and to respond to a question or a comment on the board for the first five or ten minutes of class. This activity serves several purposes, including quieting students, turning their attention to the story, and focusing on an issue in the story (probably a key aspect). It allows or forces students to consider what they will say later in class when the question or comment is posed again. Journals also provide an opportunity for students to outline preliminary ideas for papers that may be developed later.

The first few moments of class discussion are often taken up with simple recall questions, reassuring to students and setting up details in the story that may have significance later on. One schema developed and recommended by Edward J. Gordon and Dwight L. Burton[6] suggests how teachers can move from concrete to abstract, as in the following example based on questions our students devised for teaching Nadine Gordimer's "A Company of Laughing Faces" (again in Gold's *Point of Departure*). (Gordimer's short story is set at a beach resort in South Africa. A young girl has been brought there by her demanding mother to spend Christmas holidays with "nice" people. The girl is almost raped, finds the nice people dull and not all that nice, and finds a friend in a little boy who later drowns.)

1. *Questions requiring students to remember facts:*

   (a). Describe the setting of the story.

   (b). Describe the protagonist and the other major characters.

   (c). What new things had Kathy's mother bought for her?

   (d). List the major events in the story.

2. *Questions requiring students to prove or disprove a generalization made by someone else:*

   (a). Although the story is set in a South African resort, I think it could have happened at any resort frequented by the upper middle class. Do you agree or disagree? What differences were there between this holiday and that of American college students going to Florida beaches during spring break? Are these differences crucial to the story?

   (b). Some readers have interpreted this story as saying that Kathy was a conformist. Do you agree? In what ways was she a conformist? In what ways was she different?

   (c). One interpretation is that the nameless young man in the story represents the anonymous crowds of young people at the resort. Do you agree or disagree? On what evidence?

   (d). When Kathy put on her new clothes, the author said that the "disguise worked perfectly." Was Kathy in "disguise" any more than the others? Support your answer with evidence from the story as well as from your own experiences.

3. *Questions requiring students to derive their own generalizations:*

   (a). What kind of relationship did Mrs. Hack and Kathy have?

   (b). What is Kathy's perception of being young? Who has shaped that perception? Do the events in the story change her perception?

   (c). Why doesn't the author give the "young man" a name?

   (d). Why does the author contrast the constant activity of the other young people with Kathy's stillness?

4. *Questions requiring students to generalize about the relation of the total work to human experience:*

   (a). What did Kathy mean when she said that the sight in the lagoon was the "one truth and the one beauty" in her holiday?

(b). Compare Kathy's relationship with the nameless young man to that of the Bute boy. What is the author saying by showing these two different relationships?

(c). Relate the different parts of the story to Kathy's development in life.

(d). What is the significance of the statement "The only need she [Kathy] had these days, it seemed, was to be where the gang was; then the question of what to do and how to feel solved itself." Is Kathy satisfied with the answer the gang provides for her? Why or why not?

5. *Questions requiring students to carry generalizations derived from the work into their own lives:*

(a). Have you been in a situation similar to the one experienced by Kathy? How did it make you feel?

(b). What kinds of security do you get from a group? How hard is it to break away?

(c). Have you seen parents like Kathy's mother? What are some ways that young people defend themselves from well-meaning parents who don't understand the situation?

While teachers should enter their classrooms having thought enough about a story to devise such questions and to have anticipated possible answers, they should not fire off the questions as if they are giving a spelling test, but instead should use them to inspire thinking and comments from the class. Observers of good literary discussions have found that students circle back around to all these levels and that while students seldom pose questions, they frequently make observations that stimulate other students to comment and add their own opinions.

Probably the most important part of a discussion—and unfortunately the most often ignored—is the summing up. In too many classes, the bell rings in the midst of a discussion and students rush away without gathering their thoughts. Such "fly-away" endings cause students to lose respect for class discussions. If they think the teacher is just filling in time until the bell rings, they won't put forth their best efforts. The successful teacher keeps an eye on the clock and saves at least a couple of minutes to draw things together before students are distracted from the topic at hand. Good teachers continually work to develop skill in summarizing throughout a discussion. They draw attention to those points that the class basically agrees on, they praise insightful comments that help the rest of the class see something they might have missed, they search out reasons for disagreement, and they lead students to see connections between the present discussion and previous ones about similar themes or topics.

Determining what short stories (or poems or plays) belong in what grades is one of life's puzzles. Updike's "A & P" has been taught as early as ninth grade, but that seems a bit premature. Gordimer's "A Company of Laughing Faces" has been taught as early as tenth grade and possibly earlier. Both are frequently taught in college, sometimes in the freshmen year, sometimes in graduate school. Some English departments coordinate their offerings so that the same story won't be studied in two or more grades, while others leave it to chance because of the hundreds or even thousands of stories from which teachers can choose. Probably the most important thing to consider is whether the teacher likes the story and wants to teach it. More objective considerations are the age of the protagonist, how quickly the author "grabs" the readers, the complexity of both plot and characterization, and how well the story fits in with what else the class is doing.

Useful reference tools for finding publication information about particular short stories are the *Chicorel Index to Short Stories in Anthologies and Collections,* which includes information on publications up until 1977, and the *Short Story Index,* published at frequent intervals by the H. W. Wilson Company. The Wilson *Index* includes information on magazine publications from 1953 to the present.

Within the last fifteen years, publishers have produced several attractive collections of short stories written by young adult authors (Focus Box 11.2). Many of these are designed for independent reading, but they can also be brought into classrooms for various purposes. At a session on "The Resurgence of the Short Story" at a recent National Council of Teachers of English (NCTE) convention, teacher Bob Seney from Houston, Texas, recommended more than two dozen such collections and showed how they represented realistic fiction, science fiction, fantasy, humor, animal stories, folklore, and myth. Students who are hung up on a particular kind of book can usually be enticed to try at least a short story in another genre. Within the same genre, they can be encouraged to select more challenging books. While warning teachers not to overanalyze short stories, he suggested reading them aloud in class to introduce a topic for discussion or writing, to illustrate a point, fill out a

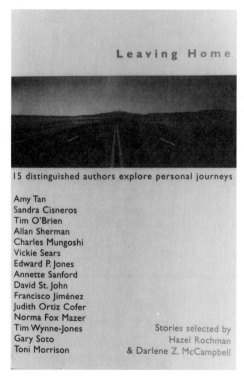

While Focus Box 11.2, p. 370 lists collections we recommend for independent reading and Focus Box 11.1, p. 365 lists collections we recommend for classroom instruction, just how they are used depends, of course, on the students and the teacher in a particular class.

FOCUS BOX 11.2

Short Story Collections by YA Authors

Am I Blue? Coming Out from the Silence, edited by Marion Dane Bauer. HarperCollins, 1994. Several popular writers contributed stories centering on coming to terms with homosexuality.

*Athletic Shorts: Six Short Stories by Chris Crutcher. Greenwillow, 1991. The athletes in these stories may attract readers to Crutcher's sports novels because several of the protagonists are the same.

*Baseball in April and Other Stories by Gary Soto. Harcourt Brace Jovanovich, 1990. These eleven fairly simple stories are about everyday events in lives of Mexican-American kids living in the Fresno, California, neighborhood where Soto grew up.

Doing Time: Notes from the Undergrad by Rob Thomas. Simon & Schuster, 1997. Because of a current emphasis on service-learning, volunteer charity, and community service, Thomas's collection is timely. Ten stories explore the varying motivations and results of a particular community service activity.

Girl Goddess #9 by Francesca Lia Block. HarperCollins, 1996. From reading this collection of nine short stories, readers come away feeling acquainted with some young Los Angeles residents who are a lot more interesting than "the girl next door."

*Heartbeats and Other Stories by Peter D. Sieruta. HarperCollins, 1989. A mix of the romantic and funny, several come from boys' viewpoints.

An Island Like You: Stories of the Barrio by Judith Ortiz Cofer. Orchard, 1995. These twelve stories build on teen preferences for hearing from other teens in that Cofer wrote them in the first person as though they were being told by the young protagonists.

*The Leaving by Budge Wilson. Philomel, 1992. Winner of the 1991 Canadian Young Adult Book Award, these nine coming-of-age stories are written in first person from the point of view of young women. Wilson's 1995 collection, *The Dandelion Garden* (Philomel), was also well received.

Lord of the Fries: And Other Stories by Tim Wynne-Jones. Dorling Kindersley Ink, 1999. Junior high and middle school readers will enjoy meeting the characters in these seven contemporary stories, each with an intriguing plot.

Odder Than Ever by Bruce Coville. Harcourt Brace Jovanovich, 1999. Healthy chunks of humor are included in these nine fantasy or science fiction stories. Readers will also enjoy his earlier collection *Oddly Enough* (Harcourt Brace, 1994).

*Sixteen: Short Stories by Outstanding Writers for Young Adults, edited by Don Gallo. Delacorte, 1984. Gallo's first collection in which he invited YA authors to contribute short stories was followed by several others, all from Delacorte: *Visions* (1987), *Connections* (1989), *Short Circuits* (1992), *Join In: Multiethnic Short Stories* (1993), *Ultimate Sports* (1995), *Within Reach* (1993), and *No Easy Answers* (1997).

*Traveling on into the Light and Other Stories by Martha Brooks. Orchard, 1994. Each story presents a moment that matters, a time that stands out from the "insane jumble" of life experiences.

(*Denotes an Honor List book)

thematic unit, provide material for readers' theater and dramatization, and give students enough experience with literary concepts that they can learn the meanings of literary terms from actual experience rather than from memorizing definitions.

Don Gallo, as much as anyone, deserves credit for promoting short story anthologies designed for teenagers. In 1984, he invited well-known young adult authors to contribute unpublished short stories to a collection that Delacorte published under the title of *Sixteen: Short Stories by Outstanding Writers for Young Adults,* a collection which has found its way onto several cumulative "Best of the Best" booklists.

Using Novels in English Class

Assigning one novel to be read by an entire class is a popular practice with teachers, partly because it is reassuring to know what's on the agenda for the next few days or, in some classes, the next few weeks. After struggling with grammar and composition, in which class members' abilities are obviously at great distances from each other, it should be a treat for teachers and the students all to join in reading the same book, some in class and some at home. For students with reading difficulties, teachers might suggest that they try checking out an audiotape of the novel from a library. A surprisingly large number of books have been recorded. Students can read along with the tape or just listen to the tape. Some are condensations, while others are full readings, but either way the listening experience will be better than resorting to *Cliff's Notes.*

The quality and availability of sound recordings has improved considerably over the past decade. Even though cassette tapes are relatively fragile, teachers and librarians should encourage their use because for some students they are the key that opens the door to a love of literature.

Although many teachers assume that having specific novels read by the entire class has always been a standard part of the English curriculum, the practice is not universally accepted. Some teachers argue that whatever can be learned by studying a common novel can be just as easily learned by studying several short stories. Others say that short stories neither allow for a long-term immersion in a created world nor provide complex character development taking place over a period of a character's lifetime.

One of the problems in using novels is the expense of acquiring a set of novels of your choice (e.g., Bernard Malamud's *The Assistant,* Robin McKinley's *The Hero and the Crown,* or Mary Shelley's *Frankenstein or the Modern Prometheus*) rather than inheriting whatever is left in the English department closet. Another problem is the length of time it takes for students to read the novel (rarely less than a week and more likely two or more). Adults have been known to stop reading when boredom sets in, but no such benediction comes to kids when they're reading a book for a class. More than sixty years ago, Howard Francis Seely wondered about our attraction to novels.

> Just why is it deemed imperative that a whole class read the same novels at the same time, anyway? I haven't heard a sound answer yet. . . . The burden of most of these answers can be recapitulated briefly. A frequent one is that reading one book permits class discussion (which discussion, however, more often than not turns out to be the answering of factual questions chiefly of a trifling nature). . . . A third answer indicates reading this one particular book in this particular class will enlighten the pupils to the structure of the novel as a literary form (which it won't, and which would be of doubtful immediate or ultimate value even if it did). . . . Perhaps the most frequent (and likely the most futile) argument of all is this: If Johnny hasn't read *The Talisman* in the ninth grade with his group, what will happen to him when he comes to *The Spy* in the tenth? That question is generally hurled at me with an air of utter, crushing finality. I can only faintly ask, "Well, just what *would?*" With that I'm given up as hopeless.[7]

A few years later, a teacher from England worried about teaching the novel on other grounds.

> Once the novelty has worn off a book, the child's interest in it can very easily flag. . . . Even the best novel rarely occupies us more than a few evenings. It is curious that teachers . . . should so often expect the restless mind of the child to possess a greater staying power in this respect than they possess themselves.[8]

English teachers who wish to use novels for common reading should choose books they believe will appeal to young people. Never choose something because it is reputedly a classic and, therefore, will somehow be magically good for students. Do not choose a book solely because it has won an award. Some teachers and librarians assume that an award-winning book is quality literature, and generally there's merit in that, but winners are chosen by human beings, not gods, and human beings make mistakes, some of them wondrous to behold. Anyone who has been part of a committee charged with choosing a book award knows that books are removed from final consideration for reasons having nothing to do with literary merit or adolescent appeal. Controversial books, such as those with more than marginal profanity or mild sex, frighten committees, and compromise is inevitable.[9] This is as true of awards for adults as for young people; Pulitzer and Nobel winners have frequently been controversial and debated for years.

Some teachers do not have to worry about selection because choices are established by school or district curricula. Among the most widely used titles are John Steinbeck's *Of Mice and Men*, Harper Lee's *To Kill a Mockingbird*, Mark Twain's *Adventures of Huckleberry Finn*, William Golding's *Lord of the Flies*, and Robert Cormier's *The Chocolate War*. All five are understandably popular with teachers and students, and all five are among the most widely censored books in public schools.

Those interested in finding suggestions on what novels work well in classrooms should skim through back issues of the *English Journal* or their state NCTE affiliate journals, such as New York's *English Record*, the *Arizona English Bulletin*, *California English*, the *Connecticut English Journal*, and the *Virginia English Bulletin*. Successful English teachers understandably love to tell about the ones that didn't get away. Exceptionally helpful questions and ideas about using novels can be found in articles by Geoff Fox[10] and Richard Peck.[11]

A practice that appeals to some English teachers is to divide a class of thirty or forty students into small groups of five to seven people and select five to ten titles with closely related themes. The members of each group read one or more of the books and talk with each other about how the theme was developed in their books. Later in a class discussion each small group presents its theme, why the theme was significant, and what their books had to say about that theme.

An obvious advantage is that while in a class of thirty to forty, students rarely have enough time to get across their ideas, small groups provide time and encouragement even for students fearful of talking in class. Teachers must remember that young people do not automatically know how to take part in a small group. Worthwhile discussions occur only when teachers give guidance and set up specific goals.

Some other advantages of reading in small groups deserve mention. It is often easier to find five or ten copies of a book than thirty copies, and it may be wise to try a novel in a small group before you consider it for an entire class. The procedure also allows students to choose books that match their individual abilities and maturity levels. Books that might cause public relations problems or attempted censorship if they are required reading for an entire class can be examined and studied by small groups whose members can decide for themselves whether or not they wish to read a particular title.

When students have read different books, class members are more interested in hearing about the other books, especially if the teacher encourages a variety of creative activities. Listed below are some of those we have seen some kids enjoy.

1. Do a costumed presentation of your book. Dress either as the author or one of the characters.
2. Write a letter from one character to another character.
3. Outline a sequel.
4. Write a new conclusion or a new beginning.
5. If a journey was involved, draw a map with explanatory notes of significant places.
6. Make a diorama and explain what it shows.

7. Write a book review for a class publication.
8. Make and laminate a new book jacket with an original blurb.
9. Use e-mail to tell a reading pen pal about the book.
10. Participate with three or four classmates in a television talk show about the book.
11. With another student, do a pretend interview with the author or with one of the characters.
12. Use a journalistic style and write a news story about something that happened to one of the characters.
13. For fun, exaggerate either characteristics or events and write a tabloid-style news story related to your book.
14. Cut out magazine pictures to make a collage or a poster illustrating the idea of the book.
15. Draft a letter to a television or movie producer suggesting that your book be considered for a mass-media production. (*Note:* S. E. Hinton's *The Outsiders* was made into a movie as the result of a letter written to Francis Ford Coppola by students at the Lone Star school in Fresno, California.)
16. With two or three other students, do a readers' theater presentation or act out a scene from the book.
17. Lead a small group discussion with other readers of the same book. Focus on a specific topic and report your group's conclusions to the class.
18. Keep a reading journal and record your thoughts at the end of each period of reading.
19. Find a song or a poem that relates to the theme of your book. Explain the similarities.
20. Draw a comic strip about an incident in your book or make a graphic novel by working with the entire book.

Using Young Adult Literature in Creative Writing

In an "Up for Discussion" column in the March 1996 *School Library Journal*, contemporary author and creative writing teacher Jack Gantos told how on the first day of class when he asks his college students about a book they've recently enjoyed, they try to impress him by citing *War and Peace, Crime and Punishment, Wuthering Heights,* and *The Sound and the Fury*. Gantos appreciates and teaches these books in his literature classes, but because not one of his creative writing students "was with Tolstoy when Napoleon retreated from Moscow, or spent part of their youth in a Siberian prison with Dostoyevsky, or wandered the imaginary moors with Emily Brönte while stuck in a parsonage, or sorted mail with Faulkner in Mississippi," he marches his students to the library where he takes them through the stacks and hands them young adult books to read "not for comprehension or analysis, but for inspiration." He wants them to "revel in the juicy details of life" that will help them value their own experiences "with family and friends, in their own communities, observing or participating in the human dramas of the moment."

Language is a social phenomenon, and just as we learned to speak through imitation and trial and error, we learn to write in much the same way. Young adult literature can provide creative teens with inspiration and models to follow because

- The problems in the books are likely to be ones that readers or their friends have experienced or thought about.
- A variety of ethnic backgrounds and settings enlarges the chances of students finding stories with which they can identify.
- Characters' conversations can serve as models for the writing of dialogue because the speech patterns come close to the everyday, spoken language of teenagers and to the *I-wish-I-had-said-that* kind of rejoinder.
- Even in historical fiction or in fantasy or science fiction, the protagonists are young, which means that their intellectual and emotional development is similar to that of teenage readers.
- Most YA authors write in a succinct and straight-forward style so that readers can "get" the story and still have some intellectual energy to expend in looking at the author's techniques.
- The intriguing details that professional writers include in their stories are the same kinds of details that clever and witty teenagers observe and relate to each other, which means they have a head start when it comes to incorporating such details into stories.

See the authors' statements on pp. 376 and 377 for the kinds of inspiration that kids can get from young adult authors. Two YA authors, M. E. Kerr and Marion Dane Bauer, have written books with the specific purpose of encouraging young writers. Kerr entitled hers *Blood on the Forehead: What I Know About Writing* based on the framed quotation that hangs over her desk attributed to Gene Fowler.

> Writing is easy: all you do is sit staring at a blank sheet of paper until the drops of blood form on your forehead.

Bauer's is entitled *Our Stories: A Fiction Workshop for Young Authors*, and in each of the twelve chapters she includes sample stories and essays from young people who are fully identified at the back of the book.

M. Jerry Weiss and Helen S. Weiss put together an anthology *One Experience to Another: Stories About Turning Points* with the intention that creative writing teachers could use the stories as models for students. Among the authors are Joan Bauer, Walter Dean Myers, Richard Peck, Gordon Korman, Avi, Jay Bennett, and Suzanne Fisher Staples. The authors wrote introductory statements tracing the routes their minds took in changing a real life event into a fictional story.

Each of the ten authors in Michael Cart's more fanciful *Tomorrowland: Ten Stories About the Future* also appended comments to their stories. Included among the authors are James Cross Giblin, Ron Koertge, Katherine Paterson, Lois Lowry, and Tor Seidler.

Actually, almost any good collection of contemporary short stories by YA authors could be used for this purpose. One that has worked well for us is Don Gallo's *Sixteen: Short Stories by Outstanding Writers for Young Adults*. Gallo grouped the stories under the categories of friendships, turmoils, loves, decisions, and families, but for creative writing purposes, we regrouped them into types starting with what we judged to be the easiest for students to imitate, then moved on up to the hardest. We started with wish-fulfilling stories so that students could have fun thinking, talking, and then writing about their daydreams and fantasies. We next looked at stories filled with incongruity and surprise, followed by those showing contrasting

JERRY SPINELLI
On the Least-Asked Questions

Q & A sessions. I like them because there's no speech to give, they're chatty and informal, and I could answer questions all day. The most popular questions, as any children's author can tell you, are "How old are you?" "Are you married?" "Where do you get your ideas?" and #1 with my audiences, "How much money do you make?" These questions I have been asked a hundred times. Never have I been asked, "What do you think of alleys?" or "How can you tell if a rock might have a salamander under it?" Or "What about quasars?"

These are the questions I wish I would hear. These are the questions more likely to get out of me what it is that makes me tick.

Take alleys, for example. I love them. Always did. The alleys in my hometown of Norristown, Pennsylvania, were not on the municipal map, they had no names, but they were all the avenue my bike and I needed. Forget streets and front doors—it's from the alleyways that a town reveals itself— and that can give a kid a taste for the edges of things. And so years later, as sports editor of my college newspaper, I wrote my column about the big football game of the year, and I wrote of the mustard on the hot dogs and the smell of peanuts and of tubas tooting and batons cartwheeling in the sky, and only in the very last line did I mention the score.

Ask me about that painting by Pieter Bruegel the Elder, *The Fall of Icarus*. I love it. I love the trick that he plays on me, how he draws my attention to the farmer in the center, dressed in red, plowing his field, dominating the scene. But where's Icarus, the guy in the title? He isn't in the spotlight and he isn't big and he isn't flashy. To find him I have to look all the way over to the right in the picture, then down—and there he is, nothing but his legs showing, ingloriously plunging into the sea while the rest of the world takes no notice.

I wonder if Bruegel knew what I learned in the U.S. Navy, that movement is best detected at the fringes of the eye.

Ask me what part of *National Geographic* I read first. Hint: it's not the big, glossy, glamourous centerbook features. It's the sidebars, the little boxed-in tidbits before and after the headlines. That's what I feast on.

Backstage, offstage, off-center, edgepools, byways, afterthoughts, fillers, peripherals—that's where I look. So much of life is between the parentheses, down in the footnotes. And gutters! Don't get me started on gutters. Suffice this: they're the street's beach. Driftstuff. Curbcomber.

And this: in the summer of my junior year at college, a circus parade came marching up DeKalb Street to the empty lot at Johnson Highway. I followed. I saw them raise the tent and unfold the bleachers and lower the trapeze. I saw the dog trainer share a cigarette with the elephant girl and the band buttoning its red jackets. It was a fascinating several hours, and then the show started. That's when I went home.

Jerry Spinelli's books include *Maniac Magee*, HarperCollins, 1990; *Wringer*, HarperCollins, 1997; and *Knots in My Yo-Yo String*, Knopf, 1998.

DONNA JO NAPOLI
On Writing as an Art and a Need

When you're four and you fingerpaint a snail, your work might well go up on the kitchen wall, perhaps even in a gilded frame, as an object of great admiration. And when you're eight and you write your first cycle of poems, they might go up on the refrigerator door for everyone to read over and over.

But when you're forty and you write a poem, everyone thinks you're deluded. Forty-year-old painters and poets and photographers fare little better.

Somewhere along the way we pick up the idea that art is the result of innate talent or brilliance—and we intimidate ourselves and others out of doing it. This is a pity, and a stupid one—for we deny ourselves a fundamental joy because of a false assumption.

Please believe me. At least some art is the result of neither talent nor brilliance, but of hard work. Fiction writers often spend years on a single story. They often make multiple versions of a story before they dare offer their prose to strangers. They sit down for hour after hour and grapple with issues of character and plot and voice and setting and style, making the piece as good as they can—and then better.

I didn't grow up wanting to be a writer. In fact, I didn't write my first story until I was twenty-eight. But once I did start, I learned very quickly about letters of rejection. I'd write a story, send it to a publisher, wait several weeks, then receive a letter back that said they had no need for my work at this time. These were not delightful letters. They were, in fact, remarkably undelightful. And they were abundant; my husband once said we could wallpaper our house in my letters of rejection, and at the time our house was a big old farmhouse in Michigan. But I kept at it. Almost every day I wrote something, no matter how short. I was bold enough to ask friends to read my stories, and I was brave enough to listen to their reactions. I grew big ears and thick skin so that I could hear criticism without being hurt. With practice and time, I got better. I'm still practicing, and I hope I'm still getting better.

That brings us to my other point—the point about fundamental joy. The privilege of writing is yours for the taking; oh, please, take it. You read, therefore, you should write. Reading without writing is like understanding a language without being able to speak it. It's not satisfying. I'm not urging everyone to become a professional writer. I'm saying everyone should create with words for the pure pleasure of it. When my children were small, my husband and I used to sit in the middle of their bedroom with the lights off and we'd all, parents and children, take turns telling stories. Do that—tell stories to your children and parents and friends. Write letters and e-mails. But don't write only public things—keep a journal, a notebook in which you write whatever you want—things you have no need to share with others—a gift to yourself alone. Perhaps no need is more basic to human beings than self-expression. If we don't create art, that need goes begging, impoverishing our souls.

Be persistent. Be joyful. And be kind to yourself: write.

Donna J. Napoli's books include *Song of the Magdalene*, Scholastic, 1996; *Sirena*, Scholastic, 1998; *Zel*, Dutton, 1996; *Stones in Water*, Dutton, 1997; and *Crazy Jack*, Delacorte, 1999.

points of view. The most sophisticated category of the stories, which we left until last, were the realistic explorations of human emotions.

How much work young writers do depends on their motivation as well as on the setting. Students in a semester- or year-long class probably have more time to put into their writing than those in a six-week unit or in an after-school writing club sponsored by a library or other community organization. Those in extra-curricular writing groups, however, may be more motivated and may be together over several years rather than just for a few months.

While an obvious goal may be the writing of a short story, less ambitious tasks can provide practice as well as feelings of success along the way. For example, students can work in small groups to improvise dialogue for a scene that *might* have occurred in one of the stories, or they can rework a story into a one-act play or a readers' theater production.

Students love to write scenes for movies or television, and now that there are so many teen-centered television shows, they might practice turning a short story into a script for a *Dawson's Creek* or a *Buffy The Vampire Slayer* episode.

Keeping a response journal helps students focus on a story. Prompts to help readers think of themselves as authors include

- The part of this story that comes the closest to something I might write is . . .
- If I had written this story I would have . . .
- If I were to write a sequel . . .
- This author is especially skilled at (choose one) developing characters, writing conversations, describing settings, or creating interesting plots as shown by . . .

In anticipation of creating their own story titles, help students examine the titles in a collection. Which are the most intriguing? The most memorable? For example, in Gallo's *Sixteen* collection, what are the extra meanings in Brancato's "Fourth of July" and Lipsyte's "Future Tense"? Which titles help establish setting by hinting at time and place? Which establish a light tone? How about a dark or serious tone? What is the effect of an author asking a question? Does Cormier's "In the Heat" remind readers of the oxymoronic "In the heat of the night," while Major's "Three People and Two Seats" reminds them of the cliché "Two's company, three's a crowd"?

As part of talking about the individual stories, lead students to devise alternate titles and to discuss the effects. The point in relation to students' own writing is to illustrate how much thought authors put into creating titles that honestly convey the sense of their stories while arousing a reader's interest.

In examining characters' names, talk about what Rosa Guy reveals in her story, "She", when the girl refuses to call her stepmother by her name. In "Midnight Snack," what does it signal when Jerry quits calling his friend *Frogface, Froggy, Froggo,* and *Frog* and calls her *Beth*? What is Richard Peck communicating when he has characters call the bully, Monk Klutter, *Mighty Monk,* and when Monk's gang wears the name *Klutter's Kobras* in silver nailheads on their black, plastic windbreakers?

In "I, Hungry Hannah Cassandra Glen," Glen calls David *Crow,* and he calls her *Hanny,* but at the funeral they sign the condolence book as *David James Alpern* and *Hannah C. Glen.* Students probably won't know about Cassandra, the Greek goddess who makes prophecies that no one will believe, but they might be intrigued by the connection between the mythical Cassandra and Hannah Cassandra's extravagant promises of food with which she entices the reluctant David to crash the family gathering after the funeral.

To give students practice in choosing or creating names that serve multiple purposes, write out two or three obvious plot lines and let students work in small groups to come up with names that are memorable because of alliteration, rhyme, assonance, or a special meaning. It is fine if they exaggerate and have fun while creating puns like the name of cartoon character *Wile E. Coyote* or connotative pseudonyms such as those of performers *Ice-T, Madonna,* and *Magic Johnson.* Once students get the idea that names do more than identify people, teachers can talk about subtlety and how the best writers create names that influence readers at an almost subconscious level.

Picking out figurative language from contemporary short stories is less intimidating than doing the same thing from Elizabethan drama or early American literature. For example, after the funeral hungry Hannah Cassandra describes the widow and her sister as looking "like two swollen black balloons," and in Sebestyen's "Welcome," Tina says when her aunt revealed her reaction to learning that her retarded son "was never going to be right," the effect on Tina's emotions was like taking "the bottom piece of fruit out of the pyramid at the market and everything began to tumble."

Free verse poetry is an inviting genre because pieces do not have to be very long. See Focus Box 9.5, p. 299 for examples, and Focus Box 11.3, Books to Help Students Read and Write Poetry. When encouraging students to write, we should not forget that nonfiction writing also takes creativity and skill. In Focus Box 3.2 Teen Voices, p. 81, much of the writing is personal narrative. Thanks to the World Wide Web, there are more opportunities for students to publish their work; for example, sending in their book reviews to Amazon.com or to a local library Web page. Some English departments or even individual teachers are establishing literary magazines on the Web (Microsoft Front Page software makes this fairly easy). More commercial magazines are also devoting themselves to publishing works by teen writers. The ones in the photo on p. 381 are

> *Teen Ink* (formerly *The 21st Century*)
> P. O. Box 30, Newton, MA 02461
> Web site: www.TeenInk.com
> e-mail: editor@teenInk.com
>
> *Merlyn's Pen: Fiction, Essays, and Poems by America's Teens*
> P. O. Box 910, East Greenwich, RI 02818
> Web site: www.merlynspen.com/home.html
> e-mail: merlynspen@aol.com
>
> *Teen Voices*
> P. O. Box 116, Boston, MA 02123-0116
> Web site: www.teenvoices.com
> e-mail: womenexp@teenvoices.com

Besides the magazines, both *Teen Ink* and *Merlyn's Pen* print a yearly collection of teen writing marketed through book stores.

FOCUS BOX 11.3

Books to Help Students Read and Write Poetry

Getting the Knack: 20 Poetry Writing Exercises by Stephen Dunning and William Stafford. National Council of Teachers of English, 1992. The book does exactly what it sets out to do, which is to give young writers specific details about different ways to write poems.

How to Write Poetry by Paul B. Janeczko. Scholastic, 1999. Part of the Scholastic Guides series, this is an appealing and clearly written book for kids in junior high or middle school. Such essentials as looking for ideas and reading lots of other people's poetry are talked about before specific ideas or suggestions are given. Two of Janeczko's earlier collections, *The Place My Words Are Looking For* (Bradbury, 1990) and *Poetspeak: In Their Work, About Their Work* (Bradbury, 1983) include statements from the poets about the background of the poems in the collection.

I Am Writing a Poem About . . . A Game of Poetry, edited by Myra Cohn Livingston. Simon & Schuster, 1997. Livingston had so much fun with a gift of magnetic strips of words designed for poets in a hurry, that she designed this book to pass the fun onto others. An earlier Livingston book, *Poem-Making: Ways to Begin Writing Poetry* (HarperCollins, 1991) may also be useful.

The List Poem: A Guide to Teaching and Writing Catalog Verse by Larry Fagin. Teachers & Writers Collaborative, 1991. Fagin ex- plains the concept and the history of creating poetry that begins with making lists. A thirty- minute audiocassette comes with the book that includes 200 examples of list poems.

Listening to the Bells: Learning to Read Poetry by Writing Poetry by Florence Grossman. Boynton/Cook, 1991. Aimed at middle school kids, Grossman's book explores honesty in reading and writing poetry.

Patterns: The How-to-Write-a-Poem Program by Jesse Hise. Interaction Publishers, 1995. In spiral ring format, Hise tells young poets and teachers how to go about writing all sorts of poems with particular patterns. It's one of the most effective and readable books on the market.

Teaching Poetry Writing to Adolescents by Joseph I. Tsujimoto. National Council of Teachers of English, 1988. Excellent examples of student poetry are included in this book about getting kids to write better poetry and become better readers of poetry.

Wishes, Lies, and Dreams: Teaching Children to Write Poetry, second edition, by Kenneth Koch. Chelsea House, 1980. In this book, and in *Rose, Where Did You Get That Red?* (Random House, 1974), Koch presents poetry ideas and patterns along with samples of poems written by students in the New York Public Schools, where Koch has been a poet in residence.

Teaching Film in the English Class

In 1913, Robert W. Neal wrote a three-page note in the *English Journal* about a medium that was already controversial.[12] Movies had been damned from the pulpit, and librarians were understandably opposed to them, as they had been to another major time-waster, the dime novel. But Neal did not come to attack. He announced that movies were "here to stay and we shall have to make the best of them." He added that if the teacher were "to turn the moving picture to his own purposes, the teacher of course must be reasonably familiar with it." Neal suggested that teachers should read a book on the technique of the "photo-play" and read a periodical on the medium. So much for the image of the stuffy English teacher in 1913.

However, English teachers proved standoffish about the movies if Samuel Rosenkranz's 1931 comment is to be believed.

Commercial publishers, as well as the Internet, are providing opportunities for teens to publish their own fiction, nonfiction, and poetry.

> We continue to teach our standards of evaluation in the drama and to ignore the cinema, and our pupils continue to patronize the cinema and to ignore the drama. We refuse to recognize the fact that they are going to the picture shows, and that we must adapt our literature and composition courses in such a manner that adequate recognition is given to the fact that there are some genuine needs to be met.[13]

Some teachers must have listened because eight years later, Hardy Finch could brag that English teachers kept up with the times, for "Over two hundred schools throughout the United States are now engaged in the production of films."[14]

The heyday of short and feature-length films in English classes came during the revolutionary 1960s and 1970s, when the most popular reading of many English teachers was not the *English Journal* but *Media and Methods*. Under the direction of Anthony Prete and Frank McLaughlin, *M & M* was possibly the most exciting professional magazine in our history. During those glorious days of yore, English teachers prided themselves on knowing and using short and long films.

In "A Revolution Reshapes Movies," an article about videocassette recorders (VCRs) in the January 7, 1990, *New York Times*, Vincent Canby wrote;

> Nothing that happened in the 1980s compares to the Video Cassette Revolution, sometimes known as the VCR, a term also used to designate the appliance on which cassettes are played. The VCR is turning the business of movies upside down and even affecting the kinds of movies we see. Movies will never be the same.

Doubtless Canby is right, but he missed how the VCR is changing the English classroom in many schools. Teachers can now have at their fingertips most of the great movies of the world to use with the original source, a novel or a play, or with other materials in a thematic unit. See Film Boxes 11.1 and 11.2 for examples. The VCR allows teachers to use films in ways not even foreseen in the happy, teaching-film world of the 1960s and 1970s. For example, in teaching about the subtleties and the power of expectations in communication, a teacher can show the 1979 *Being There*, taken from Jerzy Kosinki's novel about a simple-minded gardener becoming a guru for national politicians. In teaching about connections between politics and the media, a teacher can bring in the 1976 *All the Presidents' Men* showing the role of two reporters played by Robert Redford and Dustin Hoffman.

See Appendix D for a bibliography of materials on films and on transformations from print to film, as well as for the coding to the Film Boxes presented throughout this text. In the meantime, here are a few warnings or comments about using films in classrooms.

1. As with books, especially paperback books, films have a depressingly speedy ability to disappear from catalogues and stores. Don't count on using a film until you have it in your hands.

FILM BOX 11.1

Films from Widely Anthologized Short Stories

(Available from Filmic Archives, Cinema Center, Botsford, CT 06404)

Almos' a Man, (color, 51 min., Lavar Burton) Richard Wright's tale of a young man showing off and killing his immediate future.

Any Friend of Nicholas Nickleby Is a Friend of Mine, (60 min., Fred Gwynne) A lovely little Ray Bradbury Story.

Barn Burning, (42 min., Tommy Lee Jones) William Faulkner's story about revenge and retribution.

The Blue Hotel, (55 min., David Warner and James Keach) Stephen Crane's story of a man who believed everything he'd heard about the Wild West and died for it.

I'm a Fool, (38 min., Ron Howard and Amy Irving) Sherwood Anderson's extraordinarily teachable story about the mistakes of youth.

The Greatest Man in the World, (51 min., Brad Davis and Carol Kane) James Thurber's most pessimistic and funniest story.

The Jilting of Granny Weatherall, (51 min., Geraldine Fitzgerald) Katherine Anne Porter's most widely taught story about love and what becomes of it.

The Man Who Corrupted Hadleyburg, (color, 40 min.) Mark Twain is at his most cynical in this fine short story about avarice.

An Occurrence at Owl Creek Bridge, (French, black and white, 29 min.) Ambrose Bierce's short story, which won a major award at the Cannes Film Festival. It is the only film not of his own making that Rod Serling showed on *The Twilight Zone*.

The Portable Phonograph, (24 min.) Walter van Tilburg Clark's melancholy story set near the end of the world. It's not as well known as it deserves.

The Ransome of Red Chief, (22 min., Jack Elam and Strother Martin) A good reminder of just how funny O. Henry could be.

A Rose for Emily, (27 min., Anjelica Huston) Faulkner's most popular story, delicious and nasty.

Who Am I This Time, (60 min., color, Christopher Walken and Susan Sarandon) One of Kurt Vonnegut's best.

FILM BOX 11.2

Novels into Films—Same Story, Different Medium (see Appendix D)

The Christmas Carol (1951, black and white, 86 min., NR; Director: Brian Desmond Hurst; with Alistair Sim and Marvyn Johns) The best *Carol* around, and one of the best films ever made.

The Gambler (1999, color, 97 min., NR; Director: Karoly Makk; with Michael Gambon and Luise Rainer) Dostoyevsky's autobiographical novel.

Great Expectations (1946, black and white, 118 min., NR; Director: David Lean; with John Mills, Alec Guinness, Jean Simmons, and Martita Hunt) A marvelous cast in Charles Dickens's second best short novel (next only to **Hard Times**).

A Handful of Dust (1988, color, 118 min., PG; Director: Charles Sturridge; with James Wilby, Kirstin Scott Thomas, and Alec Guinness) Evelyn Waugh's moral tale, with a weird ending, of what happens when a marriage goes sour.

I Heard the Owl Call My Name (1973, color, 74 min., made for TV; Director: Daryl Duke; with Tom Courtenay and Dean Jagger) Margaret Craven's novel about a dying priest sent to live among Canadian natives.

The Last Picture Show (1971, black and white, 114 min., R; Director: Peter Bogdanovich; with Timothy Bottoms, Ben Johnson, and Cloris Leachman) Larry McMurtry's story of a dying small town in Texas.

The Loved One (1965, black and white, 116 min., NR; Director: Tony Richardson; with Robert Morse, Jonathan Winters, and Rod Steiger) Another film of an Evelyn Waugh novel, this a satire of burial customs in Los Angeles.

Madame Bovary (1949, black and white, 115 min., NR; Director: Vincente Minnelli; with Van Heflin and Jennifer Jones) Flaubert's moral lesson about sexual honesty.

One Flew Over the Cuckoo's Nest (1975, color, 129 min., R; Director: Milos Forman; with Jack Nicholson and Louise Fletcher) Ken Kesey's account of crazy people who are inmates and crazy people who are in charge of an institution.

Persuasion (1995, color, 107 min., NR; Director: Roger Mitchell; with Amanda Root and Ciaran Hinds) Jane Austen's greatest novel about love the second-time around

The Piano (1993, color, 121 min., R; Director: Jane Campion; with Holly Hunter, Sam Neill, Harvey Keitel, and Anna Raquin) Campion's story of a mute woman who comes to New Zealand to marry.

Sense and Sensibility (1995, color, 135 min., PG; Director: Ang Lee; with Emma Thompson, Kate Winslet, Hugh Grant, and Alan Rickman) Austen's third finest novel sumptuously filmed.

Tess (1980, color, 180 min., PG; Director: Roman Polanski; with Natassja Kinski, Peter Firth, and Leigh Lawson) A young girl's tragedy from Hardy's *Tess of the D'Urbervilles*.

2. Even if you've seen the film years ago or on TV, see it again before you consider using it in class. Films on TV are often edited for time and content and your memory may be faulty. There's little so embarrassing—or potentially so dangerous to your career—as watching an orgy of sex or drugs on screen, which you do not recall but which your students are pleasantly surprised to see in your class.

3. Ratings are, as George Gershwin's song would have it, a sometime thing, and how they are applied or misapplied to a film may defy logic. An R-rated and sensitive film may seem incorrectly rated, and a PG-13 you take your son to see may seem gross and phony and worse. A scene included or cut often makes all the difference. Unhappily, some administrators and school boards make a

nice, if silly, distinction between PG-13 (allowed in school) and R (not allowed). The distinction ignores the worth of films like *Glory* or *The Red Violin*, but the distinction usually ends the discussion. So it goes.

4. Films deserve to be taken as seriously as the literature you use in class. At the least that means you should think through why you're considering a film for class use. What do you think the film will bring to the class? Are there problems you need to work through? How will you present the film and tie it to what you've been doing in class and what you'll be doing next? Are your students mature and sophisticated enough to enjoy the film and get something important from it? Questions posed before the film begins can intrigue students, questions about significant details or themes that run through the movie.

5. Students sometimes argue that films are meant to be fun and nothing more, but most films aren't that simple, certainly not ones we're likely to use in class. Jim Carrey's *The Truman Show* was intended to be fun, but it was meant to be far more. In addition to the fun, the film's director and cast gently—and not so gently—satirized the contemporary world and particularly our TV mania and our unwillingness (or inability) to respect the privacy of others. A large part of some young people's certainty that films should be fluff intended solely for enjoyment stems from film distributors. A report on NBC *Dateline* (July 12, 1999) revealed that while young people make up only 16 percent of the U.S. population, they buy 37 percent of movie tickets. No wonder that Hollywood loves young people and wants to do all it can to please them—or, possibly more accurately—to lower the quality of films to attract the current interests and fleeting passions of young adults. How else can we explain films like *Big Daddy* and *I Know What You Did Last Summer*? There's much to be gained from using a movie that's fun, but films in class ought to be more than a temporary diversion or a reward for a class that's been good for a few days.

6. The entertainment argument is in part a way of staving the claim of teachers that films are worth studying. To study implies work, unlike being entertained—one active, one passive. Seeing *The Grapes of Wrath* and considering what it has to say demands at a minimum that students watch the film rather than looking its way occasionally. The notion that film is only intended to be fun and fun alone takes care of the likelihood of showing challenging work like Orson Welles's greatest (and worst edited) film, *The Magnificent Ambersons*, or one of Meryl Streep's best but often forgotten films, *Sophie's Choice*, or Peter Bogdanovich's finest work, *The Last Picture Show*.

7. Never use a film in place of a book for students who cannot or will not read a book. Never pretend that a book is a film or a film is a book. When filming, scenes or setting or characters may be changed from the original story. If students cannot understand a book, do not recommend they see the film in place of reading it. Recommend another book, perhaps simpler or shorter. If students are not able to read Hardy or Dickens or Waugh, find them other books they can read and possibly enjoy. The world will almost certainly survive the blow to its culture.

8. Perhaps the most irritating student term to describe something not easily understood, certainly not enjoyed, is *boring*, which has apparently replaced *dumb* as the ultimate term of disparagement. *Boring* can easily be applied to *Walden*, most of Shakespeare, almost all black and white films or any film made before

1996, and all world culture and history before 1990. "Boring" means it (whatever *it* is) and you (whoever *you* are) are "not with it," and you cannot "relate" to your students or their world. There are boring movies and boring teachers and boring adults and even boring students. Do not be surprised if students find demanding films difficult or boring. People raised on the comic subtleties of *Police Academy* or *There's Something About Mary* may find much of the world boring.

9. It may be difficult to accept, but many of the greatest films and filmmakers are unlikely to make it into your room, even if your students are brilliant, mature, sophisticated, and more, and that's tough for anyone who loves great film. A glance at the list of 100 greatest films chosen by the American Film Institute—headlined in most newspapers in June, 1998—reveals some (or many) titles not likely to be shown in secondary schools. Most Ingmar Bergman films are unlikely to be enjoyed or appreciated by young people. Bergman's world and his people presuppose life that's been partly lived, not just anticipated. That is equally true of the usually fine (and occasionally pretentious) work of James Ivory. Specifically, it's true of magnificent films like the recent *Mrs. Dalloway* (1998) and *Central Station* (1998) and the memorable *The Garden of the Fintzi-Continis* (1971) and D. W. Griffith's greatest film, *Intolerance* (1916).

10. If you're curious how other teachers use and/or teach film, the books in Appendix D may help. Better yet, dig out old copies of *Media and Methods* magazine, and read anything you find on film. Yes, the early copies are thirty years and more back, but many of the ideas are still worth thinking about. Yes, there is another magazine with the same title being published now. Ignore it.

Using Thematic Units in the English Class

Part of the reason that thematic units have become popular in English classes is that they provide a way to bind together a number of apparently dissimilar elements, including literature, language, media, and popular culture. First, however, we need to distinguish the *thematic unit* from two other kinds of units. The *project unit* has a clear end product, with all the steps that lead up to that end. For example, the production of a class play ends when the play is put on, a class-published slang dictionary ends when the booklet is put together and handed out, and reading and talking about a novel ends with the last discussion and the test. A *subject-centered* unit consists of a body of information the teacher feels is important for the class. For example, units on the history of the language, the rise of drama to Shakespeare's time, or "Our Friend, the Introductory Adverbial Clause" (the last is not made up—we saw it in action, if that's the right word). These units have no clear-cut ending, barring a test, but they do have generally clear limits of what is to be included.

The *thematic unit* is different in that it binds together many elements of English while centering on a theme or motif that runs through a body of literature. For example, a question most of us have asked ourselves is, "Why do some people want to manipulate others?" This question is also asked in Aldous Huxley's *Brave New World*, George Orwell's *1984*, Shakespeare's *Othello* and *King Lear*, F. Scott Fitzgerald's *The Great Gatsby*, Henrik Ibsen's *An Enemy of the People*, Robert Cormier's *Fade*, M. E. Kerr's *If I Love You, Am I Trapped Forever?* and Sophocles's *Antigone*. Is this a theme deserving the four or five weeks' time that the usual thematic unit takes? Here are four criteria against which to stack such a question:

1. The theme needs to appeal to kids. If it is too easy or too hard or too boring, the teacher will lose the students' interest and attention.
2. The theme needs to be worth doing—in other words, intellectually and emotionally respectable for these particular kids at this particular time of their development and at this particular time of the year.
3. There must be lots of easily located literature on the theme.
4. The theme needs to appeal to the teacher; if the teacher is not excited about it, the kids won't be either.

Assuming that the theme meets these four requirements, the teacher must begin a search for literature on the theme that will challenge the students and that they will enjoy, composition topics (written and spoken) worth using and related to the theme, films (short and feature-length) related to the theme and worth viewing, and spelling and vocabulary lists related to the theme. That means the teacher must determine the following:

1. A list of sensible objectives (or learning outcomes, if you prefer) for this *specific* unit (not English classwork in general) that both kids and their parents can understand.
2. A work of some length (usually a short novel or a play) to open the unit and make clear to students at what the unit aims. Such a work is not essential, but it's customary and usually helpful.
3. A body of short works (poetry and short stories and essays) to be used throughout the unit because they are related to the theme.
4. A series of composition assignments (usually two or three written assignments and two or three oral assignments) on the theme.
5. A list of vocabulary words related to the unit topic, perhaps twenty to thirty or so, to be talked about and tested five at a time.
6. A list of spelling words related to the unit topic, perhaps twenty to thirty or so, to be talked about and tested about five at a time.
7. A way of beginning the unit that grabs students' attention and interest while focusing on the theme. Obviously, teachers can (and do) begin thematic units with a "Hey, kids, how would you like to talk about _____?" or a "Hey, kids, we're going to turn to something entirely different now, a unit on _____," but surely there's a slightly more fascinating way. A short film or the teacher reading aloud a short story (or a recent news clipping) might work.
8. A way of wrapping up the unit that ties all the strands together. Tests, the all-American way to wrap anything up, are always possible. Some classes find panel discussions useful, some might profit from a student evaluation of the unit and the literature read, and others might benefit from some creative art project or a dramatization.
9. The problems that the unit—and students—may encounter and how the teacher works through them. Perhaps it's time to incorporate peer editing into the class, and if this unit is as good a time as any other to introduce kids to peer evaluation and editing, the teacher needs to plan on preparing class mem-

bers to work in small groups. Perhaps the short book chosen to get the unit started (e.g., Monica Hughes's *Hunter in the Dark*) has some vocabulary problems, or Nathaniel Hawthorne's short story "Young Goodman Brown" may present problems getting the kids to understand colonial life and religion. These and similar problems need to be worked through and solutions found.

Two exceptionally helpful articles on developing thematic units are Richard S. Alm's "What Is a Good Unit?"[15] and John H. Bushman and Sandra K. Jones's "Getting It All Together . . . Thematically."[16] Thematic units can range from complex and sophisticated topics for college-bound kids to simple topics that are appropriate for junior high. For example, a thematic unit on "Our Ability to Endure," which centers on the theme of survival and power, is a topic of immediate interest to eighth- and ninth-graders. It could open with words from William Faulkner's much-anthologized Nobel Award speech and move to one of these as common reading and the remainder as supplementary reading: Avi's *The True Confessions of Charlotte Doyle,* Alice Childress's *Rainbow Jordan,* Robert Cormier's *After the First Death,* James Forman's *Ceremony of Innocence,* Anne Frank's *The Diary of a Young Girl,* Harry Mazer's *The Last Mission,* or Robb White's *Deathwatch.*

A more intellectually and emotionally complex thematic unit on "Redemption" might begin with reading and discussing Katherine Mansfield's "The Garden Party" in Crane's *Fifty Great Short Stories* or Nadine Gordimer's "A Company of Laughing Faces" in Gold's *Point of Departure* (see Focus Box 11.1 p. 365). This might be followed by the class reading Bernard Malamud's *The Assistant,* and sometime during the unit each student might be asked to read at least one supplementary work on some phase of redemption, for example, classics such as Dante's *The Divine Comedy,* Dostoevsky's *Crime and Punishment,* Goethe's *Faust,* Shakespeare's *King Lear* or *Hamlet,* Sophocles's *Oedipus Rex* or *Antigone,* and almost any other Greek drama or major work of Joseph Conrad, Thomas Hardy, Nathaniel Hawthorne, and Herman Melville. Modern fiction applicable to the same theme includes Hal Borland's *When the Legends Die,* F. Scott Fitzgerald's *The Great Gatsby,* Ursula K. Le Guin's *A Wizard of Earthsea,* Peter Matthiessen's *At Play in the Fields of the Lord,* John Steinbeck's *Of Mice and Men,* Frank Waters's *The Man Who Killed the Deer,* and major works of Arthur Miller, Graham Greene, and Thornton Wilder. Young adult fiction that could fit into the unit includes Fran Arrick's *Tunnel Vision,* Judy Blume's *Tiger Eyes,* Robert Cormier's *After the First Death,* Robert Lipsyte's *The Contender,* Margaret Mahy's *Memory,* Paul Zindel's *The Pigman,* and the novels of S. E. Hinton.

We once had a student come to our office and announce that he wanted to learn everything that a good high school English teacher needed to know. He wondered where he should begin, and we suggested he start with literature. He agreed and wondered yet again where he should begin. We mentioned that good English teachers know the classics. After we cleared up the confusion that we weren't talking about Steinbeck, not yet, we turned to Aeschylus, Sophocles, Euripedes, and Aristophanes, none of whom he knew. Because he begged that we move on to the eighteenth century, where he claimed he knew the novel, we moved onward and upward only to hear his complaint when we brought up writers like John Gay, William Blake, or Richard Brinsley Sheridan. A day or so later, we pointed out that good English teachers not only know English and American literature, of course, but also know Third World literature and German, Japanese, Norwegian, and Russian literature, and more.

Somewhere as we rounded Russian literature, our earnest student gave up. After this catalogue of what he needed to know, he asked one last question before he disappeared from the office, "How can anyone learn all that?"

The answer, which he obviously did not want to hear, was that thousands of good people do it all the time, not in a few hasty weeks but in a lifetime. They are called English teachers.

Notes

1. Louise M. Rosenblatt. *Literature As Exploration,* 4th ed. (Modern Language Association, 1983), pp. 278–279.

2. Elaine Simpson, "Reason, Not Emotion," *Top of the News* 31 (April 1975): 302.

3. Dorothy Broderick, "Serving Young Adults: Why We Do What We Do," *Voice of Youth Advocates* 12 (October 1989): 204.

4. Robert C. Small, "Teaching the Junior Novel," *English Journal* 61 (February 1972): 222.

5. Richard W. Jackson, *CBC Features* 39 (October 1984–July 1985): 5. A publication of the Children's Book Council.

6. Edward J. Gordon, "Levels of Teaching and Testing," *English Journal* 44 (September 1955): 330–334; Dwight L. Burton, "Well, Where Are We in Teaching Literature?" *English Journal* 63 (February 1974): 28–33.

7. Howard Francis Seely, "Our Novel Stock-in-Trade," *English Journal* 18 (November 1929): 724–725.

8. G. F. Lamb, "The Reading Habit," *Tomorrow* (England) 2 (July 1934): 10.

9. Three informative articles that comment on books that did not win awards (or were not nominated), although the books are popular today and deserve careful attention: Joni Bodart's "The Also-Rans; or 'What Happened to the Ones That Didn't Get Eight Votes?'" *Top of the News* 38 (Fall 1981): 70–73; and Pam Spencer's "Winners in Their Own Right," *School Library Journal* 36 (July 1990): 23–27, and "Part II," *School Library Journal* 38 (March 1992): 163–167.

10. Geoff Fox, "Twenty-four Things to Do with a Book," in Anthony Adams, ed., *New Directions in English Teaching* (Palmer Press, 1982), pp. 219–222.

11. Richard Peck, "Ten Questions to Ask About a Novel," ALAN *Newsletter* 5 (Spring 1978): 1, 7.

12. Robert W. Neal, "Making the Devil Useful," *English Journal* 2 (December 1913): 658–660.

13. Samuel Rosenkranz, "English at the Cinema," *English Journal* 20 (May 1931): 365.

14. Hardy R. Finch, "Film Production in the School—A Survey," *English Journal* 28 (May 1939): 365.

15. Richard S. Alm, "What Is a Good Unit in English?" *English Journal* 49 (September 1960): 395–399.

16. John H. Bushman and Sandra K. Jones, "Getting It All Together . . . Thematically," *English Journal* 64 (May 1975): 54–60.

Titles Mentioned in the Text of Chapter Eleven

Alcott, Louisa May. *Little Women.* 1868.

Arrick, Fran. *Tunnel Vision.* Bradbury, 1980.

Avi. *The True Confessions of Charlotte Doyle.* Orchard, 1990.

Bauer, Marion Dane. *Our Stories: A Fictions Workshop for Young Authors.* Clarion, 1996

Beckman, Gunnel. *Admission to the Feast.* Holt, 1972.

Blume, Judy. *Tiger Eyes.* Bradbury, 1981.

Borland, Hal. *When the Legends Die.* Lippincott, 1963.

Cart, Michael, ed. *Tomorrowland: Ten Stories About the Future.* Scholastic, 1999.

Childress, Alice. *A Hero Ain't Nothin' But a Sandwich.* Coward, McCann, 1973.

Childress, Alice. *Rainbow Jordan.* Putnam, 1981.

Cormier, Robert. *After the First Death.* Pantheon, 1979.

Cormier, Robert. *The Chocolate War.* Pantheon, 1974.

Cormier, Robert. *Fade.* Delacorte, 1988.

Cormier, Robert. *I Am the Cheese.* Knopf, 1977.

Dostoyevsky, Fyodor. *Crime and Punishment.* 1866.

Eliot, George. *Silas Marner.* 1861.

Fitzgerald, F. Scott. *The Great Gatsby.* Scribner, 1925.

Forman, James. *Ceremony of Innocence.* Hawthorn, 1970.

Fox, Paula. *One-Eyed Cat.* Bradbury, 1984.

Frank, Anne. *The Diary of a Young Girl.* Doubleday, 1952.

Fugard, Athol. *"Master Harold" . . . and the Boys.* Knopf, 1982.

Gallo, Donald R., ed., *Sixteen: Short Stories by Outstanding Writers for Young Adults.* Delacorte, 1984.

Garner, Alan. *The Owl Service.* William Collins, 1967.

Go Ask Alice. Prentice-Hall, 1971.

Goethe, Johann Wolfgang von. *Faust.* 1808, 1832.

Gold, Robert S., ed., *Point of Departure: 19 Stories of Youth and Discovery.* Dell, 1967.

Golding, William. *Lord of the Flies.* Coward, McCann, 1954.

Hemingway, Ernest. *The Old Man and the Sea.* Scribner, 1952.

Hinton, S. E. *The Outsiders.* Viking, 1967.

Hughes, Monica. *Hunter in the Dark.* Atheneum, 1982.

Huxley, Aldous. *Brave New World.* HarperCollins, 1932.

Ibsen, Henrik. *An Enemy of the People.* 1882.

Kerr, M. E. *Blood on the Forehead: What I Know About Writing.* HarperCollins, 1998.

Kerr, M. E. *If I Love You, Am I Trapped Forever?* HarperCollins, 1973.

Kozinsky, Jerzy. *Being There.* Harcourt Brace, 1970.

Lee, Harper. *To Kill a Mockingbird.* Lippincott, 1960.

LeGuin, Ursula K. *Wizard of Earthsea.* Parnassus, 1968.

Lipsyte, Robert. *The Contender.* HarperCollins, 1967.

Lowry, Lois. *The Giver.* Houghton Mifflin, 1992.

Mahy, Margaret. *Memory.* McElderry, 1988.

Malamud, Bernard. *The Assistant.* Farrar, Straus & Giroux, 1957.

Matthiessen, Peter. *At Play in the Fields of the Lord.* Random House, 1965.

Mazer, Harry. *The Last Mission.* Delacorte, 1979.

McKinley, Robin. *The Hero and the Crown.* Greenwil-low, 1984.

Orwell, George. *1984.* Harcourt Brace Jovanovich, 1940.

Samuels, Gertrude. *Run, Shelley, Run!* Crowell, 1974.

Shakespeare, William. *Hamlet.* c. 1601.

Shakespeare, William. *King Lear.* c. 1605.

Shelley, Mary. *Frankenstein or the Modern Prometheus.* 1818.

Sophocles. *Antigone.* Fifth century B.C.

Sophocles. *Oedipus Rex.* Fifth century B.C.

Steinbeck, John. *The Pearl.* Viking, 1948.

Steinbeck, John. *Of Mice and Men.* Viking, 1937.

Thoreau, Henry David. *Walden.* 1854.

Twain, Mark. *Adventures of Huckleberry Finn.* 1884.

Voigt, Cynthia. *Homecoming.* Macmillan, 1981.

Waters, Frank. *The Man Who Killed the Deer.* Farrar, Straus & Giroux, 1942.

Weiss, M. Jerry and Helen S. Weiss, eds. *From One Experience to Another: Stories About Turning Points.* Forge, 1997.

White, Robb. *Deathwatch.* Doubleday, 1972.

Zindel, Paul. *The Pigman.* HarperCollins, 1968.

Information on the availability of paperback editions of these titles is available online from such book sellers as Barnes & Noble and Amazon.com, and through *Books in Print* compiled by R. R. Bowker Company and available either in person or online from major libraries.

Censorship
Of Worrying and Wondering

Most teachers and librarians are aware that stories about censorship pervade newspapers and magazines. They know that only a few months after publication of *The Satanic Verses* in late 1989, Salman Rushdie's book had been banned in many countries, and that because the Ayatollah Khomeini had determined that the book was blasphemous, Rushdie's life was to be forfeited. At about the same time, Senator Jesse Helms, a politician slightly less powerful than Khomeini, decided that Robert Mapplethorpe's homoerotic art was deeply offensive, particularly because government funds had paid for the Mapplethorpe exhibition. Thereafter, Helms was out to change guidelines for grants from the National Endowment for the Arts to prevent similar horrors.

Occasionally, although not as often as most of us would like, the attacks were so silly that newspaper reports made censorship sound foolish and gave readers an easy chuckle. In Mesa, Arizona, in late July 1990, a mother of two looked closely at the cover of Disney's videocassette of *The Little Mermaid* and found a castle tower that was clearly a phallic symbol. She called a local grocery chain, which pulled the video from its stores. Sanity returned when Disney executives admitted they were upset by the furor but refused to change the cover and the grocery stores went back to selling foodstuffs.

A bill that would have required people to speak kindly about fruits and vegetables in Colorado died after the governor refused to sign it. An apple grower who had noticed the bad press given to Washington apple growers over their use of chemicals to make the fruit look more attractive argued that the bill was needed to keep people from bad-mouthing produce. More people were amused than convinced by his arguments. Recently in Arizona, however, the governor signed an equally silly bill providing relief for families whose crops were criticized.

Far more common than tidbits of humor about censors are grim stories about censors and their fights to purify us all. School texts are rarely safe, as attacks across the United States on the Holt, Rinehart and Winston elementary series *Impressions* prove. Conservative parents in northern California, sometimes representing groups

As these headlines show, censorship crosses a variety of media and a variety of issues.

such as Citizens for Excellence in Education or the Traditional Values Coalition, maintained that the series (1) did not sufficiently emphasize good, old-fashioned American culture and values; (2) focused on occult and Satanic materials; and (3) removed traditional and classic stories in favor of the new and ephemeral. Other parents across the United States attended school board meetings and lambasted the series, maintaining the stories were violent, scary, Satanic, and generally inappropriate for children. Although the series was retained in almost all the several dozen attacks, opposing parents vowed to keep up the fight.

In late 1999, two incidents made the news, one national, one in the Phoenix area. Mayor Rudolph W. Giuliani of New York City announced that he hoped to cut off all city subsidies (seven million dollars for operating costs) to the Brooklyn Museum of Art. Why? Because he was offended by three works to be exhibited, particularly a portrait of the Virgin Mary stained with elephant dung. The question, as in most censorship matters, was whether one person, usually in power, should be able to stop other people from deciding whether they are—or are not—offended by a painting or a book or a film or whatever.

The Arizona case may seem minor compared to the painting issue. It is also much more typical of what happens in schools. On September 3, 1999, a story in the *Arizona Republic* revealed that at Carson Junior High School in Mesa, AZ, a few parents had decided that a musical production of *Tom Sawyer* should be closed before it opened; and the powers-that-be in Mesa agreed. Why? Because as one parent said the script was culturally insensitive. *Tom* was clearly a product of another time and place, and it simply did not fit into our politically correct time. An obvious example, Injun Joe was a slam at American Indians. Critics noted that three female characters were described as "extremely feminine," "an outrageous flirt," and "A large, homey, woman." Equally offensive, the constable is referred to as "a typical redneck." And references to religion were unkind comments on "hellfire," "communion," and "Kingdom of Fire."

Four Mesa school board members apparently supported the ban though none had received a complaint from parents. Worse yet, the District's associate superintendent was quoted as saying,

> A play in which the content and characterization becomes the focus steals the spotlight from the students. A play is entertainment. It's not in an instructional setting.

Obviously, that's not quite what Aristotle said in the *Poetics*. Eugene O'Neill and Tennessee Williams got it wrong. Maybe Arthur Miller and Tom Stoppard can do better by offering only entertainment.

Teachers and librarians know that attacks on books and book banning are here to stay and are deadly serious, increasingly so in the last decade. Colin Campbell's words still ring true:

> A censorial spirit is at work in the United States, and for the past year or so it has focused more and more on books. Efforts to remove certain titles from school and public libraries, from paperback racks and bookstores, from the eyes of adults as well as children, have increased measurably.[1]

Obviously, not everyone who questions or objects to a book is a censor. Most parents are concerned about the welfare of their children but being forced to go to school to make a complaint may make them resentful or nervous or angry. If taking time from work were not enough reason to feel irritated, many parents have a built-in love-hate ambivalence toward schools. They may not have fond memories of English teachers when they were young. They may worry about being talked down to by a much younger teacher or librarian. They may wonder if anyone will take them or their complaint seriously. When parents arrive at the school or the library, it is hardly surprising that they may feel hostile. That's easily misread by equally nervous teachers, who may see aggressive censors where there are only concerned parents.

Keeping this possibility of mistaken identity in mind, educators need to be considerate and reasonable and to listen more than they talk, at least for the first few minutes. Once objectors calm down and recognize that the teacher or librarian might possibly be human, then the educator will learn what is really troubling the parents. Everyone may learn, sometimes to the listener's surprise, that no one wants to ban anything, but parents do wonder *why* the teacher is using the book or *why* the librarian recommended it to their child. They may want their child to read something else but agree that they have no wish to control the reading of anyone else. The problem is easier to handle (not always easy, but certainly *easier*).

In such cases, teachers and librarians should remember that the announced objection may not always be the real objection. Censors might attack Huxley's

Brave New World or Orwell's *1984* for their sexual references when the real objection is to the frightening political attitudes the authors displayed (or were thought to display). It is human nature to fear things we do not understand; hence the discomfort that many parents feel over the recent popularity of scary, supernatural books. An attack on the language in John Howard Griffin's *Black Like Me* may be only a subterfuge for a censor's hatred of African-Americans (and any minority group), whereas an attack on an oblique reference to masturbation in Judy Blume's *Deenie* may in reality be a protest against the liberal attitudes that parents sometimes believe pervade her books.

The underlying reasons for objections to particular books often are more significant than teachers or librarians may suspect. Sometimes the complaining parents do not even realize why a particular author or book makes them feel uncomfortable. This is why it's so important for parents to talk and for educators to listen. Parents who are worried about the moral climate facing their children are painfully aware that they have little power to change the material on television, and they cannot successfully fight the movies offered by local theaters or do away with local "adult" bookstores. Whom, then, can they fight? What can they change? An easy answer is to go to school and protect at least that little corner of their children's lives.

Thoughts of inflation and recession, fears of sexually transmitted diseases, threats of global warming and the depletion of the earth's resources, and faltering communication and affection among family members depress many of us most of the time, and sometimes these parental fears and worries are exploited for political gain. Parents are courted and brought into political action groups advocating censorship. The selling point of such groups is that there is little we can do to attack the gigantic problems spurred on by who knows what or whom. Either we give up or, in the case of censors, we strike back at the only vulnerable element in most communities, the schools. And why not attack schools, what with the rising militancy of teachers and the massive public criticism of schools' performances on SAT or ACT tests? And so the censors attack. (See the statements by highly respected authors on pp. 394, 402, and 416.)

These individuals and groups—as opposed to sincere parents wanting what's best for their own children—are the objectors we define as censors. Their desire is not to talk and reason but to condemn, and as educators we feel a strong obligation to uncover their motives and to counter their claims.

The American Library Association has been on record against censorship since the 1920s, but its strongest statement first appeared in 1939 as the Library Bill of Rights. The document has periodically been tightened and strengthened, and the latest version can be found in the *Intellectual Freedom Manual*, 5th ed. The entire *Intellectual Freedom Manual* is filled with provocative ideas and helpful suggestions and should be required reading for librarians and English teachers alike.

In 1962, the National Council of Teachers of English (NCTE) published the first edition of *The Students' Right to Read* setting forth NCTE's position and containing a widely used form for complaints, "Citizen's Request for Reconsideration of a Book." The 1972 edition expanded and updated the earlier edition, while in 1982, the complaint form was amended to apply to more than books. A complementary publication, *The Students' Right to Know* by Lee Burress and Edward B. Jenkinson, elaborated on NCTE's position toward education and censorship.

JOHN MARSDEN
On Where Adults Get It Wrong

When it comes to dealing with young people, adults still seem to have little idea.

I think this is partly because their attitudes are based on false assumptions.

One of these assumptions is that children are innocent. Lots of adults cling to the myth that childhood is a beautiful place, where sweet children play beautiful games together, and think beautiful thoughts about fairies, butterflies and ice cream.

The truth is that all children can be kind, generous, loving, imaginative, honest, trusting, and brave. Some of these qualities may be related to innocence. But children can also be manipulative, dishonest, violent, selfish, and jealous.

The mistake many adults make is to confuse innocence with ignorance. All children are ignorant, compared to most adults anyway. But time and time again when children display their ignorance, adults confuse this with innocence. For example, if a child says, "I know where babies come from; angels bring them down from the clouds," adults exclaim happily over the "innocence" of the child.

Of couse the child is trying to make sense of something he or she does not understand. The child wants to understand, but doesn't yet have the knowledge.

By pretending that children are innocent, adults are able to justify building walls around them, to protect them from the big bad world. Adults who build such walls are not doing children any favors. In fact they are doing terrible damage to the child, because in protecting them from the "big bad world" they are denying the priceless opportunity to explore life at close quarters, in its beauty and ugliness.

Adults who behave in this way are scared of life. They are people with no insight, no imagination, no understanding. They believe that ignorance is bliss, that children will be happy in their ignorance, despite their awareness that powerful secrets are being kept from them.

Another false assumption that adults make about young people is that they are all impressionable. They seriously believe that reading one book, or watching one movie, or listening to one CD may permanently cripple a young person.

The truth is that we are all impressionable, and children, adolescents and adults can all be powerfully affected by an experience that comes along at a critical moment. How much we are affected, and how strongly, will depend on factors like our upbringing, our personality, our strength of character.

Adults who seek to keep strong material from young people on the grounds that young people are impressionable are taking an extraordinary power upon themselves. There is great arrogance at work here.

Their job is made even harder by the fact that it is impossible to tell what will affect different individuals. One person can watch *Clockwork Orange* and dismiss it from their mind; another is changed for life by *Bambi*. There's no formula to predict how humans will react to different events and experiences.

Many of the books I write are controversial. I don't intend them to be, but it doesn't bother me that they are. I write these books for one main reason, and that is because I want to understand things that are mysterious to me. So if I meet someone who is so depressed and withdrawn that she hasn't spoken for eight months, I want to understand what that is like. If I have a pen friend [pen pal] who lies to me, I want to understand why she might do that. If I meet someone who's violent and negative, who trusts nobody and appears to have no faith or strong values, I want to understand how such a thing can come about.

In exploring these situations through novels I do gain some understanding for myself. Perhaps the greatest pleasure for me in writing is that it appears that some people might have gained greater understanding of life by reading my books. I could ask for no greater reward.

John Marsden's books include *So Much to Tell You*, Little Brown, 1987; *Letters from the Inside*, Houghton Mifflin, 1994; *Tomorrow, When the War Began*, Houghton Mifflin, 1995; and *Darkness Be My Friend*, Houghton Mifflin, 1999.

A Brief History of Censorship

Some English teachers and librarians apparently believe the censorship of young adult reading began with the publication of J. D. Salinger's *The Catcher in the Rye*. But censorship goes far back in history, at least to Plato's 5th century B.C. masterpiece, *The Republic*. Plato argued that banishing poets and dramatists from his perfect state was essential for the moral good of the young. Writers often told lies about the gods, he maintained, but even when their stories were true, writers sometimes made the gods appear responsible for the evils and misfortunes of mortals. Plato reasoned that fiction was potentially emotionally disturbing to the young. Plato's call for moral censorship to protect the young is echoed by many censors today.

In *The Leviathan* in 1615, Thomas Hobbes justified the other basic case for censorship. Humanity was, in Hobbes's view, inherently selfish, venal, brutish, and contentious. Strife was inevitably humanity's fate unless the state established and enforced order. Hobbes acknowledged the right of subjects to refuse to obey a ruler's orders if he did not protect his people, but in all cases the sovereign had not merely the right but the duty to censor anything for the good of the state.

Between Plato and Hobbes and thereafter, history offers a multitude of examples of censorship for moral or political good: The Emperor Chi Huang Ti burned Confucius's *Analects* in 211 B.C.; Julius Caesar burned much of the Library of Alexandria in 48–47 B.C.; English officials publicly burned copies of William Tyndale's translation of the Bible in 1525; the Catholic Index of Forbidden Works was published in 1555; Prime Minister Walpole forced passage of a Licensing Act in 1737, which required that every English play be examined and approved before production.

America's premier censor, although hardly its last, appeared in the early 1870s. Anthony Comstock came from a religious family and before he was 18 had raided a saloon to drive out the devil and the drinkers. In June 1871, Comstock was so outraged by repeated violations of Sunday Closing Laws by saloons in his neighborhood that he reported them to the police. They ignored him, which taught him a good lesson about the futility of fighting city hall alone. Armed with the Lord's help and his own determination, Comstock secured the help of three prominent men and founded the Society for the Suppression of Vice in New York in 1872, and he was off and running. The following year he went to Washington, D.C., to urge passage of a federal statute against obscenity and abortion and contraceptive devices. That same year, he was commissioned a Special Agent of the Postmaster General, all without salary until 1906.

With the new law and Comstock's zeal and energy, he confiscated and destroyed "bad" literature and imprisoned evil authors and publishers almost beyond belief. By 1914, he had caused the arraignment of 3697 people with 2740 convicted or pleading guilty, total fines of $237,134.30, and prison sentences totaling 565 years, 11 months, and 20 days. In his last year of life, 1915, Comstock added another 176 arrests and 140 convictions. He also caused 15 suicides.[2]

Traps for the Young (1883) was Comstock's most famous work. By traps, Comstock meant the devil's work for young people—light literature, newspaper advertisements, saloons, literature obtained through the mail, quack medicine, contraceptives, gambling, playing pool, free love and anyone who advocated it, and artistic works (fine arts, classics of literature, photographic reproductions of art). Comstock was convinced that any young person who shot pool or smoked or chewed tobacco or drank alcohol or read dime novels or did anything else he disapproved of (and that catalogue was long indeed) was doomed to hell and to a life of crime and degradation.

Early librarians, as may be seen in "Fiction and Libraries" in Chapter Two (pp. 52-53), were more likely pro-censorship than anti-censorship. As Arthur E. Bostwick wrote in 1910:

In the exercise of his duties in book selection it is unavoidable that the librarian should act in some degree as a censor of literature. It has been pointed out that no library can buy every title that is published, and that we should discriminate by picking out what is best instead of by excluding what is bad.[3]

Mark Twain came under widespread attack for his ungenteel characters, but he was hardly the only writer to be critized for impropriety or immorality. Stephen Crane's *The Red Badge of Courage* was accused of lacking integrity and being inaccurate. At the sixth session of the American Library Association in 1896, a discussion of *The Red Badge of Courage* and whether it should be included in a list of ALA-recommended books brought forth comments that revealed more about the critics than about the book:

MR. LARNED: "What of Crane's *Red Badge of Courage?*"
A. L. PECK: "It abounds in profanity. I never could see why it should be given into the hands of a boy."
G. M. JONES: "This *Red Badge of Courage* is a very good illustration of the weakness of the criticism of our literary papers. The critics in our literary papers are praising this book as being a true picture of war. The fact is, I imagine, that the criticisms are written by young men who know nothing about war, just as Mr. Crane himself knows nothing about war. Gen. McClurg, of Chicago, and Col. Nourse, of Massachusetts, both say that the story is not true to the life of the soldier. An article in the *Independent,* or perhaps the *Outlook,* says that no such

profanity as given in the book was common in the army among the soldiers. Mr. Crane has since published two other books on New York life which are simply vulgar books. I consider the *Red Badge of Courage* a vulgar book, and nothing but vulgar."[4]

It is more difficult to know how much censorship occurred in English classes of the nineteenth century because the major journal for English teachers, the *English Journal*, did not begin until 1912, but a few items may suggest that some English teachers endured or even encouraged censorship. Until 1864, Oberlin College would not allow Shakespeare to be studied in mixed classes. That Shakespeare was apparently of questionable value can be seen by an editorial in 1893 lauding students of Oakland High School who objected to using an unexpurgated edition of *Hamlet:*

> All honor to the modest and sensible youths and maidens of the Oakland High School who revolted against studying an unexpurgated edition of *Hamlet!* The indecencies of Shakespeare in the complete edition are brutal. They are more than indelicacies, they are indecencies. They are no part of Shakespeare's thought, have no connection with the play, and can be eliminated with as little jar as could the oaths of a modern slugger. Indeed, Shakespeare's vulgarity was, to all intents and purposes, profanity, scattered promiscuously through the lines with no more meaning than so many oaths.[5]

An editorial writer in 1890 quoted from a contemporary account in the *Congregationalist* about books some young people had been reading:

> In this series of papers we purposely avoid all mention of some thoroughly bad books chosen by our young friends. We remember hearing the principal of a young ladies' seminary, in trying to express her strong disapproval of a certain book, say impulsively to the pupils, "I think I should expel a girl if I found her reading such a work." Before the week closed no less than three copies were in surreptitious circulation. There is something in human nature which craves that which is prohibited. Just so surely as we gave the titles of books worthy of condemnation, some youth would thirst instantly for a knowledge of their contents.[6]

Would that present-day censors could recognize what this critic obviously recognized, that merely mentioning an objectionable title creates new readers.

One last incident a few years later: An English teacher reported on her use of *Treasure Island* with a junior high school class. Of the students who were enthusiastic, one student well on her way to becoming a literary snob wrote:

> *Treasure Island* should be read, firstly, because it is by a famous author, secondly, most people like it and, thirdly, because it is considered a classic.

Two other students objected. A boy wrote:

> I like a cleaner story. In this story there is too much bloodshed, drinking, and swearing.

A girl, however, pointed out the evil nature of the story and the nefarious and inevitable consequences of reading Stevenson's awful book:

> This story full of murder, fighting, and wiping blood off of knives is not suitable for boys and girls to read and if these kinds of books were not written there would not be so many boys go wrong. I don't think there should be any more books written like it, because it don't learn you anything and nowadays we should read books that do us some good.[7]

A modern censor might have said it more elegantly but hardly any better.

The State of Classroom and Library Censorship Today

Censorship was hardly a major concern of English teachers or school librarians (although it certainly was for public librarians) before the 1960s. Before World War II, it rarely surfaced in schools, although John Steinbeck's *The Grapes of Wrath* and *Of Mice and Men* caused furor in newspapers, especially in Oklahoma and California, and when students began to read the books, the furor reached the schools. After World War II, Norman Mailer's *The Naked and the Dead* and J. D. Salinger's *The Catcher in the Rye* and other books "indicative of a permissive, lax, immoral society," as one censor noted, caught the eyes of adults and young adults alike. Granted, most objections were aimed at the writers and bookstores that stocked them, but teachers were now aware that they needed to be more careful about books they allowed students to read for extra credit or book reports. Two things changed the mild worry into genuine concern.

Paperback books seemed to offer little of intellectual or pedagogical value to teachers before World War II. Even after the war, many teachers blithely assumed paperbacks had not changed, and given the often lurid covers, teachers seemed to have a point, although it was more superficial than real. Administrators and parents continued to object even after the Bible, Plato's *Dialogues*, and *Four Tragedies of Shakespeare* proved to teachers and librarians that paperbacks had merit. Students discovered even earlier that paperbacks were handy to stick in a purse or back pocket, and paperback titles were appealing, not stodgy, as were most textbooks. So paperbacks came to schools, censors notwithstanding, and these cheap and ubiquitous books created problems galore for teachers.

Perhaps almost as important, young adult books before the late 1960s were generally safe, pure, and simplistic, devoid of the reality that younger people daily faced. Sports and going to the prom and getting the car for the big Friday night date loomed large as the major problems of young adult life in too many of these novels. Young people read them for fun, knowing that they were nothing more than escape reading with little relationship to reality or to anything of significance. Then in 1967, Ann Head's *Mr. and Mrs. Bo Jo Jones* and S. E. Hinton's *The Outsiders* appeared, and young adult literature changed and rarely returned to the good old days. Paul Zindel's *The Pigman* followed in 1968, and although all young adult books that followed were hardly great or honest, a surprising number were. English teachers and librarians who had accepted the possibility of censorship with adult authors popular with the young—Steinbeck, Fitzgerald, Heller, Hemingway, for example—now learned that the once safe young adult novel was no longer safe, and censorship attacks soon began. Head's and Hinton's and Zindel's books were denounced but so were young adult novels as good as Robert Lipsyte's *The Contender* (1967), A. E. Johnson's *A Blues I Can Whistle* (1969), John Donovan's *I'll Get There. It Better Be Worth the Trip* (1969), and Jean Renvoize's *A Wild Thing* (1971)—and that was only the beginning.

Surveys of the state of censorship since 1963 reveal that censorship is either getting worse or fewer teachers and librarians are willing to lie quietly while the censor walks over them. Lee Burress's pioneer study "How Censorship Affects the School," in October 1963, was only the first of these surveys. Nyla H. Ahrens's doctoral study in 1965 was the first national survey. State surveys of Arizona censorship conditions appeared in the February 1969 and February 1975 *Arizona English Bulletin*. National studies appeared ever more often: L. B. Woods's "The Most Censored Materials in the U.S.," in the November 1, 1978, *Library Journal*; Burress's "A Brief Report of the 1977 NCTE Survey," in James Davis's *Dealing with Censorship*; and the much anticipated but disappointing *Limiting What Students Shall Read* (ALA, ASCD), in 1981. The 1982 survey of high school librarians by Burress found that 34 percent of the librarians reported a challenge to at least one book compared to 30 percent in his 1977 survey. A survey of Canadian censorship by David Jenkinson published in the February 1986 *Canadian Library Journal* provided no optimism about censors. Two surveys by Donelson—one in the March 1985 *School Library Journal* of censorship for the previous thirteen years and comparing conclusions from six previous surveys and another in the October–November 1990 *High School Journal* summarizing the censorship incidents in the *Newsletter on Intellectual Freedom* from 1952 through 1989—provide little comfort to teachers or librarians. Don Melichar's comparative study of surveys of Arizona classroom censorship in 1985 and 1994 is the most recent state or national survey that we know of.

Surveys make for dull reading and convey all too little about the individual teacher or librarians besieged by censors. The following reports of a few incidents, quite old or contemporary, suggest some of the emotional and pedagogical dilemmas faced by real people who are too often without allies, not even their supposed fellow professionals.

1. 1877. William Kite, librarian at the Friend Free Library in Germantown, PA, worried about the influence of novels. "I could tell of one young woman of my acquaintance, of fine education, who gratified a vitiated taste for novel-reading till her reason was overthrown, and she has, in consequence, been for several years an inmate of an insane asylum. . . . Instances could be furnished by the records of such institutions in too sad frequency, but we need not seek them. Have we the moral right to expose the young to such cancer?"[8]
2. February, 1903. At the first Library Institute of the State of New Jersey, Father McMahoon, director of the Catholic library, spoke of "the idea of children browsing among books as an educational fad, susceptible of nothing but evil."[9]
3. 1932. At a library meeting in Michigan, Mary Silverthorn recommended ten criteria for fiction allowed in a library. Among them, "1. It was written in good English. . . . 3. It depicted experiences of life worthwhile for others to enter in vicariously. . . . 5. It was stimulating to right thinking and action. . . . 6. It satisfied natural desires and curiosities in a normal, wholesome way. . . . 10. The line between right and wrong was clear-cut and distinct, or there was called forth a judgment on the part of the reader when the issues were blurred."[10]

4. 1982. "I was in Minnesota last November, and two librarians said to me, you know, we decided—and you're not going to like this—but we have to deal with this and you don't. We decided that we're not going to order any more Judy Blume books. Doesn't matter what the reviews are, doesn't matter whether the kids like them or not. Judy Blume is too much trouble. Her very name is going to bring trouble if we order the books and we're not going to do it."[11]

5. 1985. In Lassen County, CA, parents objected to a production of Hellman's *The Children's Hour.* One parent announced, "If something isn't fit for my five-year-old to watch, it's not fit for me."[12]

6. 1987. In Florida, County School Superintendent Leonard Hall announced a three-tier classification to determine what books would or wouldn't be allowed in high school classes. The first category consisted of works that had no vulgarity or explicit sex. The second included books with a "sprinkling" of vulgarity. The sixty-four books in the third group, deemed to have "a lot of vulgarity" and the curse "goddamn," were placed off limits for class discussion. Works in the third group included Shakespeare's *Twelfth Night* and *The Merchant of Venice* and the novels *The Old Man and the Sea, Mister Roberts, The Great Gatsby, Fahrenheit 451, The Red Badge of Courage,* and dozens of other highly regarded works of literature.[13]

7. April, 1990. In Idaho, a teacher assigned *My Name Is Asher Lev* to her twelfth-grade class. A day later, a student returned the book. The student explained, "My family and I don't believe in Israel and we hate Jews. My family wants me to read something else."[14]

8. May, 1990. Culver City and Empire, CA. Two school districts banned a new edition of "Little Red Riding Hood" in which Red carried a bottle of wine for Granny. An assistant superintendent said, "It gave the younger ones the wrong impression about alcohol."[15]

9. September, 1991. In San Ramon, CA, two novels about homosexuality (Nancy Garden's *Annie on My Mind* and Frank Mosca's *All American Boys*) were donated to high school libraries by the Bay Area Network on Gay and Lesbian Educators. The vice-principals at two schools removed the books to "examine them," and that was the end of those books.[16]

10. August, 1991. In Tempe, AZ, after a few parents objected to using the R-rated film, *Glory,* in the classrooms, the school board voted not to allow the use of R films in the classroom. One board member tried to justify his vote. "The time we have with students is precious. We should use that time to expose them to only the best and the brightest things. We don't have time for R-rated films."[17]

11. 1993. In Simi Valley, CA, an objector to Theodore Taylor's *The Cay* said, "I have no qualms about book banning. Any book that offends any group should be taken out of the public libraries and schools."[18]

12. May, 1994. In Tavares, FL, the Lake County School Board ordered teachers to teach young people that American culture is superior to any other. One man said the board acted in response to multiculturalism "being rammed down our throats." Another said, "We need someone to look out for the Christian view" in our schools.[19]

13. May, 1998. In Wisconsin Rapids, WI, Chris Crutcher's *Chinese Handcuffs* was challenged by a parent who complained about the book's "depiction of incest, rape, animal torture, teen drug use, breaking and entering, illegal use of a video camera, profanity directed to a school principal, and graphic sexual references."[20]

If those incidents frighten us, they also perplex us because we sometimes cannot fathom the reasoning underlying the censorship. Note the logic of the censor in these next three incidents.

1. In May, 1993, the Oskaloosa, KS, school board voted 4–3 to enact a new policy requiring teachers to examine their required material for profanities. They are expected to list each profanity and the number of times it's used in the book. They will forward this count to parents who will give permission for children to read the material. Alternate materials must be available for parents who choose not to allow their child to read the required material.[21]

2. In July, 1996, the East Stroudsburg, PA, school board approved, 8–0, to drop Robert Cormier's *The Chocolate War* and several other books from a new English curriculum. The assistant superintendent for curriculum announced that the book was eliminated because of scheduling conflicts, not because of the furor it had caused the previous school year.[22]

3. In 1997, in Marysville, CA, the superintendent removed Salinger's *The Catcher in the Rye* from the required reading list of the district. He announced, "This is not an issue of book banning. Rather, it is an opportunity for parents with varied viewpoints to come together, listen to each other, and define common values. I have taken the book out of the curriculum simply to get that out of the way so we didn't have that polarization over a book."[23]

Some Assumptions About Censorship and Censors

Given the censorship attacks of the last twenty-plus years, we can safely make the following assumptions about censorship.

First, any work is potentially censorable by someone, someplace, sometime, for some reason. Nothing is permanently safe from censorship, not even books most teachers and librarians would regard as far removed from censorial eyes—not *Hamlet* or *Julius Caesar* or *Silas Marner* or *Treasure Island,* or anything else.

Second, the newer the work, the more likely it is to come under attack.

Third, censorship is capricious and arbitrary. Two teachers bearing much the same reputation and credentials and years of experience and using the same work will not necessarily be equally free from attack (or equally likely to be attacked). Some schools in conservative areas go free from censorship problems even though teachers may use controversial books. Other schools in relatively liberal areas may come under the censor's gun.

Fourth, censorship spreads a ripple of fear. The closer the censorship, the greater the likelihood of its effect on other teachers. If the newspaper coverage of the incident has been extensive, the greater the likelihood that schools many miles away will feel the effect. Administrators may gently (or loudly) let their teachers know it is time to be traditional or safe in whatever the teachers choose for the coming year.

Fifth, censorship does not come only from people outside the school. Administrators, other teachers or librarians, or the school board may initiate an incident. That often surprises some English teachers or librarians. It should not.

Sixth, censorship is, for too many educators, like cancer or a highway accident. It happens only to other people. Most incidents happen to people who know "it couldn't happen to me." It did and it will.

Seventh, schools without clear, established, school board–approved policies and procedures for handling censorship are accidents waiting to happen. Every school should develop a policy and a procedure that helps both educators and objectors when an incident arises. The aim of both policy and procedures should be to ensure that everyone has a fair hearing, not to stall or frustrate anyone.

Eighth, if one book is removed from a classroom or library, no book is safe any longer. If a censor succeeds in getting one book out, every other person in the com-

ANGELA JOHNSON
On What Is Appropriate

I was once asked to speak to a group of elementary age children at a suburban school. I asked the teacher what age group I would be speaking to and she kindly told me I'd be speaking to the little ones under ten because the administration considered my work for older children inappropriate.

Hmmm. I was told that it was a private school and their kids were sheltered. I guess they considered my subject matter of a non-graphic flashback of a lynching and mental illness in adolescence to be disturbing.

At first, I was astounded, then angry. I have never thought my subjects disturbing and if they were, so be it. I wanted discussion and I wondered at a small pocket of adult overreaction. I canceled with the school and began asking the people who the books were meant for, anyway, what they thought about difficult subject matter.

On my next school visit, one sixth grader told me she loved how independent all my characters were. The kids talked about imagery and how they were transported to the characters' place and time. One kid did tell me that there was a swear word that his mom had found.

Finally I got an answer from a quiet girl who timidly put up her hand when I asked my endless question. She said,

> How can anything that happens to people in real life not be appropriate. I think if it's dealt with honestly nothing is unsuitable to talk about. Although some adults are pretty scared about so much.

Of course she had hit on it. Some adults were scared for varying reasons of their own and always would be about what their children read. They found even discussion of these books impossible.

Why I didn't see it this way in the beginning made me feel clueless. I preferred to think of all these people as censorship fascists (which of course some may very well be.)

The young woman finally said, "But you shouldn't let any of that bother you. Keep on writing what you like and making a few people uncomfortable about it."

I thanked her and said I would. And I do.

Angela Johnson's books include *Toning the Sweep*, Orchard, 1993; *Gone from Home*, Dorling Kindersley Ink, 1998; and *Heaven*, Simon & Schuster, 1998.

munity who objects to another book should, in courtesy, be granted the same privilege. When everyone has walked out of the library carrying all those objectionable
books, nothing of any consequence will be left no matter how many books remain.
Some books are certain to offend some people and be ardently defended by others.
Indeed, every library has books offensive to someone, maybe everyone. After all,
ideas do offend many people.

Ninth, educators and parents should, ideally, coexist to help each other for the
good of the young, but the clash of parents with some educators appears to be sadly
inevitable. Some people would prefer to see young adults *educated,* which means allowing them to think and wonder about ideas and to consider the consequences of
those ideas. Others would prefer to see young people *indoctrinated* into certain
community or family values or beliefs or traditions and to eschew anything controversial. With so little in common between these two philosophies of schooling, disagreement is not only natural but certain.

Censors seem unwilling to accept the fact that the more they attack a book, the
greater the publicity and likelihood that more young adults will read the offensive
book. In their drive to eliminate a book, censors create a wider circle of readers. In
some cases with older or more obscure works, they revive something that has been
virtually dead for years.

Censors do not believe that in trying desperately to keep young people pure
and innocent they often expose those young people to the very thing the censors
abhor. Several years ago, in the Phoenix area, a group violently objected to a scholarly dictionary that contained some "offensive" words. Worried that others might
not believe all those degrading, evil, pernicious words could be so easily found in
one work, censors compiled a sort of digest of "The Best Dirty Words in _____,"
duplicated the list, and disseminated it to anyone curious, including the very students censors claimed to be protecting. More than one censor has read parts of a
book that would "warp any young person's mind" aloud at a school board meeting
to prove the point while young students raptly listened.

Censors often have a simplistic belief that there is an easily established and absolute relationship between books and deeds. A bad book, however defined, produces bad actions. What one reads, one immediately imitates. To read profane language automatically leads young people to swear. Presumably, nonreading
youngsters who swear must eagerly await more literate fellows to instruct them in
the art of the profane. To read about seduction is to wish to seduce or to be seduced
(although it is possible the wish may precede the book). To read about crime is to
wish to commit that crime or at least something vaguely antisocial. Anthony Comstock loved to visit boys in jail because when he asked what led them into the world
of crime, they told him exactly what he wanted to hear (as they knew full well),
that dime novels and drinking and shooting pool were *the* sources of all their present misery.

Censors seem to have limited faith in the ability of young adults to read and
think. Censors wonder if young people can handle controversial books such as
Huxley's *Brave New World* or Salinger's *The Catcher in the Rye* because the young are
so innocent and pure and untainted by contact with reality. That may have been
what caused one censor who objected to Ann Head's *Mr. and Mrs. Bo Jo Jones* and
Paul Zindel's *The Pigman* to announce to an audience, "Teenagers are too young to
learn about pregnancy."

Censors alternately love and hate English teachers and librarians. Censors
would appear to hate what educators use, but censors would also appear to approve

of great literature, particularly the classics. Being essentially nonreaders, they know little about literature but that it must be uplifting and noble and fine. They may claim to have read the uplifting when they were young, "back when schools knew what they were doing," but they often cannot remember titles; when they do their comments suggest the book was read in an emasculated child's edition. Censors assume that classics have no objectionable words or actions or ideas. So much for *Crime and Punishment, Oedipus Rex, Hamlet, Madame Bovary, Anna Karenina,* and most other classics. For censors, the real virtue of great literature is that it is old, dusty, and hard to read, in other words, good for young people.

Censors care little what others believe. Censors sometimes seem to believe that they are ordained by God to root out evil, and they are divinely inspired to know the truth. Where teachers and librarians may flounder in searching for the truth, censors need not fumble, for they *know.* They are sincerely unable to understand that others may regard the censors' arrogance as sacrilegious, and they rarely worry because they claim to represent the side of morality. One censor counts for any number of other parents. When Judy Blume's *Deenie* was removed from an elementary library in the Cotati-Rohnert Park School District, California, in October 1982, a trustee said that a number of parents from a nearby college wanted the book retained, but "the down-to-earth parents who have lived in the district for quite awhile didn't want it,"[24] and that was clearly that. No one counted the votes, but no one needed to. Orwell was right when he wrote, "All animals are equal but some are more equal than others."

Censors would agree with Orwell's comment if not his ironic intention.

Finally, censors use language carelessly or sloppily. Sometimes they cannot possibly mean what they say. The administrator who said, "We don't wish to have any controversial books in the bookstore or the library," either did not understand what the word *controversial* meant or was speaking gibberish (the native tongue of embarrassed administrators talking to reporters).

Three adjectives are likely to pop up in the censor's description of objectionable works—*filthy, obscene,* and *vulgar*—along with favored intensifiers such as *unbelievably, unquestionably,* and *hopelessly,* although a few censors favor oxymoronic expressions like *pure garbage* or *pure evil.* Not one of the adjectives is likely to be defined operationally by censors who assume that *filth* is *unquestionably filth,* and everyone shares their definition. Talking with censors is, thus, often difficult, which may disturb others, although it is often a matter of sublime indifference to the censors. If talking is difficult, communicating with them is usually nigh unto impossible.

Attacks on Materials

Who Are the Censors?

There are three reasonably distinct kinds of censors and pressure groups: (1) those from the right, the conservatives; (2) those from the left, the liberals; and (3) an amorphous band of educators and publishers and editors and distributors who we might assume would be opposed to censorship. The first two groups operate from different guiding principles, or so one would assume. But it is sometimes easy for educators to be confused; whether the attack stems from the right or the left, the coercive methods, the censorial rhetoric, and the messianic fervor seem so similar.

The third group is unorganized and functions on a personal, ad hoc, case-by-case approach, although people in the group are more likely than not to feel sympathetic to the conservative case for censorship.

An incredible number of tiny censorship or pressure groups on the right continue to *worry* educators (worry in the sense of alarm *and* harass). Many are better known for their acronyms, which often sound folksy or clever—for example, Save Our Schools (SOS); People of America Responding to Educational Needs of Today's Society (PARENTS); Citizens United for Responsible Education (CURE); Let's Improve Today's Education (LITE); American Christians in Education (ACE); and everyone's favorite, Let Our Values Emerge (LOVE). Chapter 9 in Ed Jenkinson's *Censors in the Classroom: The Mind Benders* summarizes quite well the major groups, big or small.

With few exceptions, these groups seem united in wishing to protect young people from insidious forces that threaten the schools, to remove any vestiges of sex education and secular humanism from classes or libraries, to put God back into public schools, and to restore traditional values to education. Few announce openly that they favor censorship of books or teaching materials, although individual members of the groups may so proclaim. Indeed, what is particularly heartening about the groups is that many of them maintain that they are anticensorship, although occasionally a public slip occurs. The president of the Utah chapter of Citizens for Decency was quoted as saying:

> I am opposed to censorship. We are not a censorship organization. But there are limits to the First Amendment. People have the right to see what they want on television, but that has nothing to do with the right to exhibit pornography on television. We're not stopping anyone from buying books and magazines or going to the movies they want. They just can't do it in Utah. Let them go to Nevada. Nobody there cares.[25]

Whether anyone from Nevada with a similar anticensorial attitude responded with a suggestion that people from Nevada seeking cheap thrills should go to Utah is unknown. Something similar to the preceding comment came from the Rev. Ricky Pfeil. Wheeler, Texas, apparently has its moral problems with objectionable movies like *Porky's* and *Flashdance* and *E.T.* (Pfeil's argument against the last-mentioned film was, "The film's an attempt to show something supernatural and it's not God. There's only one other power that's supernatural and that's Satan.") The good minister also is against censorship, as he said:

> You know, I am not for censorship. People have a right to see what they want or read what they want, but I'd just as soon they go to Los Angeles to get a copy of *Playboy* magazine. I'm responsible for here. Evil left unchecked will go rampant. God tells me what to do.[26]

Given the doublespeak of the Utah president and the Rev. Pfeil, readers will admire the honest and the original constitutional interpretation of the Rev. Vincent Strigas, co-leader of the Mesa (Arizona) Decency Coalition. Slashing merrily away at magazines that threatened the "moral fiber" of residents, the Rev. Strigas answered complaints about his approach:

> Some people are saying that we are in violation of First Amendment rights. I do not think that the First Amendment protects people [who sell] pornographic materials. The Constitution protects only the freedom to do what's right.[27]

Surely there is no ambiguity in that message.

Whatever else conservative groups may agree or disagree on, they seem united in opposing secular humanism and the New Age Movement and the teaching of evolution. Secular humanism is both too large and too fuzzy to handle adequately in a few paragraphs (or even a short chapter). Briefly, if inexactly, conservatives appear to define secular humanism as any teaching material that denies the existence of (or ridicules the worth of) absolute values of right and wrong. Secular humanism is said to be negative, anti-God, anti-American, anti-phonics, and anti-afterlife and pro-permissive, pro–sexual freedom, pro–situation ethics, pro-socialism, and pro–one worldism. Conservatives hopelessly intolerant about secular humanism often have problems explaining what the term means to outsiders, or even insiders, usually defining the presumably philosophical term operationally and offering little more than additional examples of the horror that secular humanism implies. Such was the case when secular humanism reared its ugly head at a meeting of the Utah Association of Women:

> One woman says with disgust that two recent school board members didn't know what secular humanism was; thus they weren't qualified to run for office. Lots of "tsks" run through the group until a young woman visitor apologizes for her ignorance and asks, Just what is secular humanism? There is an awkward silence. No one gives a definition, but finally they urge her to attend a UAW workshop on the subject. Later in the meeting, during a discussion of unemployment a vice-president says, "Our young people are only taught to do things that give them pleasure. That's secular humanism."[28]

Fortunately, for educators already concerned about the many pressure groups from the right, only one pressure group from the left need concern them, but that one group was once very worrisome. The Council on Interracial Books for Children was formed in 1965 to change the all-white world of children's books and to promote literature that more accurately portrayed minorities or reflected the goals of a multiracial, multiethnic society. They offer meetings and publications to expedite their goals, but for most teachers, the CIBC was best known for its often excellent *Bulletin.*

No humane person would disagree with the CIBC's goals. As it has maintained over the years, the CIBC does not censor teaching or library materials. It had, however, perhaps inadvertently, perhaps arrogantly, been guilty of coercing educators into not purchasing or stocking or using books offensive to the CIBC or its reviewers. Its printed articles have attacked Paula Fox's *The Slave Dancer,* Ouida Sebestyen's *Words by Heart,* and Harper Lee's *To Kill a Mockingbird.*

Noble as the CIBC was and well-intended as its goals, it appeared to be, inadvertently, censorious in action if not in theory. With the death of its founder and the suspension of the *Bulletin,* its influence seems muted.

The case for the racist-free classroom and library is carried to its absurd conclusion by Bettye I. Latimer in "Telegraphing Messages to Children about Minorities." After defining censorship as the "actual destruction of a book through banning, exiling, or burning it, so that no one has access to it," Latimer proclaims that she is "strongly opposed to censorship for adult readers, since adults are responsible for their own values," but that apparently does not hold true for young people:

> I am *not* suggesting censorship for books that are racist-oriented. I *am* suggesting that we remove these books to archives. This will permit scholars and researchers to have access to them. Since old racist books have no use in constructing healthy images for today's children, they need to be put in cold storage. As for contemporary racist books, educational institutions ought to stop purchasing and thereby stop subsidizing publishers for being racist.
>
> Finally, I would like to see librarians, teachers, and reading coordinators reeducate themselves to the social values which books pass on to children. I invite them to learn to use antiracist criteria in evaluating and assessing books.[29]

Amidst all the noble sentiments in these words, some people may sense a hint of liberal censorship or pressure at work. All censors, whatever their religious or sociological biases, *know* what is good and bad in books and are only too willing to *help* the rest of us fumbling mortals learn what to keep and what to exile (or put in the archives).

The third kind of censorship or pressure group comes from within the schools, teachers or librarians or school officials who either censor materials themselves or support others who do. Sometimes these educators do so fearing reprisals if they do not. Sometimes they do so because they fear being noticed, preferring anonymity at all costs. Sometimes they are fearful of dealing with reality in literature. Sometimes they regard themselves as highly moral and opposed to whatever they label immoral in literature. Sometimes they prize (or so claim) literary merit and the classics above all other literature and refuse to consider teaching or recommending anything recent or second-rate, however they define those terms. Fear permeates many of these people. A survey of late 1960s Arizona censorship conditions among teachers uncovered three marvelous specimens:

> I would not recommend any book any parent might object to.
>
> The Board of Education knows what parents in our area want their children to read. If teachers don't feel they can teach what the parents approve, they should move on.
>
> The English teacher is hired by the school board, which represents the public. The public, therefore, has the right to ask any English teacher to avoid using any material repugnant to any parent or student.[30]

Lest readers assume that Arizona is unique in certifying these nonprofessionals, note these two Connecticut English Department Chairs quoted in Diane Shugert's "Censorship in Connecticut" in the Spring 1978 *Connecticut English Journal:*

> At this level, I don't feel it's [censorship] a problem. We don't deal with controversial material, at least not in English class.
>
> We have no problems at all in my department. The teachers order books directly and don't clear them with me or with a committee. But *I* receive the

shipments. Copies of books that I think to be inappropriate simply disappear from the book room.[31]

So much for the good old days.

And at least one book distributor was only too willing to help librarians pre-censor books. The Follett Library Book Company of Crystal Lake, Illinois (not to be confused with Follett Publishing Company in Chicago), has for several years marked titles with a pink card *if* three or more customers had objected to the vocabulary or illustrations or subject matter of a book. The cards read:

> Some of our customers have informed us of their opinion that the content or vocabulary of this book is inappropriate for young readers. Before distributing this book, you may wish to examine it to assure yourself that the subject matter and vocabulary meet your standards.[32]

Publishers, too, have been guilty of rewriting texts or asking authors to delete certain words to make books or texts more palatable to highly moral librarians or communities. "Expurgation Practices of School Book Clubs" in the December 1983 *Voice of Youth Advocates* and Gayle Keresey's "School Book Club Expurgation Practices" in the Winter 1984 *Top of the News* uncovered censorship practices in Scholastic Book Club selections, as titles were changed and deletions of offensive words or ideas occurred between the hardback edition and its publication in a paperback club edition.

What Do the Censors Censor?

The answer to the question of what censors censor is easy—almost anything. Books, films,[33] magazines, anything that might be enjoyed by someone is likely to feel some censor's scorn and moral wrath.

Some works, however, are more likely to be attacked.

A nearly ten-year survey of books listed as under attack in the *Newsletter on Intellectual Freedom* between May 1986 and September 1995 revealed that several books were repeatedly questioned. The most obvious was John Steinbeck's *Of Mice and Men*, but a few others were also frequently listed. Mark Twain's *Adventures of Huckleberry Finn*, J. D. Salinger's *The Catcher in the Rye*, Maya Angelou's *I Know Why the Caged Bird Sings*, Judy Blume's *Forever*, and Robert Cormier's *The Chocolate War* were all listed at least ten times. Nancy Garden's *Annie on My Mind*, Alice Walker's *The Color Purple*, Kurt Vonnegut's *Slaughterhouse-Five*, Robert Newton Peck's *A Day No Pigs Would Die*, John Gardner's *Grendel*, and the anonymous *Go Ask Alice* followed soon thereafter.

Don Melichar's "Objections to Books in Arizona High School Classes" in the Fall 1994 *Arizona English Bulletin* revealed that the most widely attacked book was *Huck Finn*, but Steinbeck's *Of Mice and Men* and Harper Lee's *To Kill a Mockingbird* were also popular with the censors.

The most frequently challenged books in People for the American Way's *Attacks on the Freedom to Learn, 1994–1995* were these: Alvin Schwartz's *Scary Stories to Tell in the Dark*, *More Scary Stories to Tell in the Dark*, and *Scary Stories 3: More Tales to Chill your Bones*; Angelou's *I Know Why the Caged Bird Sings*; Lowry's *The Giver*; Eve Merriam's *Halloween ABC*; Katherine Paterson's *Bridge to Terabithia*;

Cormier's *The Chocolate War*; Christopher and James Lincoln Collier's *My Brother Sam Is Dead*; and Steinbeck's *Of Mice and Men*.

While there's no guarantee that any one of these golden-goodies on the censor's hit list will come under attack soon, clearly some books are beloved of censors. There was a time when Salinger's *The Catcher in the Rye* led every list of censored books. *Go Ask Alice* occasionally threatened *Catcher*, but more and more *Of Mice and Men* and *Adventures of Huckleberry Finn* lead almost every list of censored works.

Racism raises its ugly head on censorship lists, with titles such as Claude Brown's *Manchild in the Promised Land* and Gordon Parks's *The Learning Tree* and Harper Lee's *To Kill A Mockingbird* appearing with nauseating regularity. There are the usual suspects on every list of censored books—Joseph Heller's *Catch-22*, Aldous Huxley's *Brave New World*, George Orwell's *Animal Farm* and *Nineteen Eighty-Four*, and William Golding's *Lord of the Flies*.

There are a few inevitable censorial favorites such as *The American Heritage Dictionary* or the much-hated story by Shirley Jackson, "The Lottery." Or modern plays such as Tennessee Williams's *The Glass Menagerie* or *Summer and Smoke* or Arthur Miller's *All My Sons* or *Death of a Salesman*.

Readers curious why a commonly censored title is not listed here should feel free to add whatever they wish. Anyone who wishes to expand the list could glance casually through any issue of the *Newsletter on Intellectual Freedom*.

Although most of the titles on these lists were published for adults, today's censors seem quite happy to attack books published for adolescents. Titles such as these now frequently are on lists of censored books, rarely near the top but still disturbingly present:

Judy Blume's *Deenie, Forever*

Bruce Brooks's *The Moves Make the Man*

Alice Childress's *A Hero Ain't Nothin' But a Sandwich*

Brock Cole's *The Goats*

Robert Cormier's *After the First Death, The Chocolate War, Fade, I Am the Cheese*

Chris Crutcher's *Athletic Shorts, Running Loose*

Lois Duncan's *Killing Mr. Griffin*

Paula Fox's *The Slave Dancer*

Rosa Guy's *Ruby*

Nat Hentoff's *The Day They Came to Arrest the Book*

S. E. Hinton's *The Outsiders, Rumble Fish, That Was Then, This Is Now*

Ron Koertge's *The Arizona Kid*

Ursula K. LeGuin's *A Wizard of Earthsea*

Robert Lipsyte's *The Contender*

Lois Lowry's *The Giver*

Harry Mazer's *The Last Mission*

Walter Dean Myers's *Fallen Angels*

Katherine Paterson's *Bridge to Terabithia*

Robert Newton Peck's *A Day No Pigs Would Die*

Jerry Spinelli's *Space Station Seventh Grade*

Todd Stasser's *Angel Dust Blues*

Mildred Taylor's *Roll of Thunder, Hear My Cry*

Paul Zindel's *My Darling, My Hamburger; The Pigman*

Why Do the Censors Censor What They Do?

Why censors censor what they do is far more important and far more complex than what they censor. Unfortunately, for readers who want simple answers and an easy-to-remember list of reasons, the next paragraphs may be disappointing.

In "Censorship in the 1970s: Some Ways to Handle It When It Comes (and It Will)" in early 1974, Donelson listed eight different kinds of materials that get censored. Those that censors:

1. Deem offensive because of sex (usually calling it "filth" or "risqué" or "indecent").
2. See as an attack on the American dream or the country ("un-America" or "pro-commie").
3. Label peacenik or pacifistic (remember the Vietnam War had not yet become unpopular with the masses).
4. Consider irreligious or against religion or, specifically, un-Christian.
5. Believe promote racial harmony or stress civil rights or the civil rights movement ("biased on social issues" or "do young people have to see all that ugliness?").
6. Regard as offensive in language ("profane" or "unfit for human ears").
7. Identify as drug books, pro or con ("kids wouldn't hear about or use drugs if it weren't for these books").
8. Regard as presenting inappropriate adolescent behavior and, therefore, likely to cause other young people to act inappropriately.[34]

In an article entitled "Dirty Dictionaries, Obscene Nursery Rhymes and Burned Books," published in James E. Davis's 1979 *Dealing with Censorship,* Ed Jenkinson added fourteen more likely targets, including young adult novels, works of "questionable" writers, literature about or by homosexuals, role playing, texts using improper grammar, sexist stereotypes, and sex education. In a *Publishers Weekly* article the same year,[35] Jenkinson listed forty targets, with new ones being sociology, anthropology, the humanities generally (if secular humanism is bad, so then must be humanism or anything that sounds like humanism, and that easily extends to humanities), ecology, world government, world history that mentions the United Nations, basal readers lacking phonics, basal readers with many pictures or drawings, situation ethics, violence, and books that do not promote the Protestant ethic or do not promote patriotism.

A year later, Jenkinson had expanded his list to sixty-seven, with additions including "Soviet propaganda," citizenship classes, African-American dialects, uncaptioned pictures in history texts, concrete poetry, magazines that have ads for alcohol or contraceptives, songs and cartoons in textbooks, and "depressing thoughts."[36] The last of the objections is truly depressing, apparently for censors and educators alike.

Some Court Decisions Worth Knowing

Legal battles and court decisions often seem abstract and dull and irrelevant to practical matters for too many educators, but several court decisions have been significant and have affected thousands of educators who hardly knew the battles had taken place, much less their disposition. A brief run-through of two kinds of decisions, those involving attempts to define obscenity and its supposed influence on readers and viewers and those directly involving schools and school libraries, may be helpful to readers.

Court Decisions About Obscenity and Attempting to Define Obscenity

Because censors frequently bandy the word *obscene* in attacking books, teachers and librarians should know something about the history of courts vainly attempting to define the term.

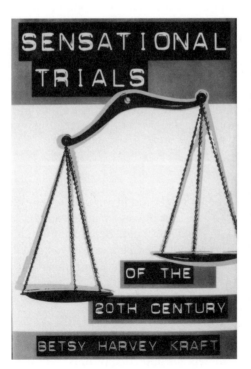

School censorship cases often serve to increase students' interest in legal matters. The general public's interest has already been piqued through the O.J. Simpson trial, the Clinton impeachment hearings, and such television shows as *Court TV*. (See Film Box 12.1 on p. 412).

FILM BOX 12.1

The Drama of the Courtroom (see Appendix D)

Amistad (1997, color 152 min., R; Director: Steven Spielberg; with Morgan Freeman and Anthony Hopkins) In 1839, a Spanish slaveship founders off the American coast, and the slaves are taken into custody. Should they be treated as cargo or free men is the question John Adams raises before the U.S. Supreme Court.

Gideon's Trumpet (1980, color, 104 min., made for TV; Director: Robert Collins; with Henry Fonda and Jose Ferrer) In this true story, an old and stubborn Florida convict feels he's not been fairly treated in court so he appeals to the U.S. Supreme Court.

Inherit the Wind (1960, black and white, 127 min., Director: Stanley Kramer; with Spencer Tracy and Fredric March) A replay of the 1925 Scopes "Monkey" trial.

Judgment at Nuremberg (1961, black and white, 178 min., NR; Director: Stanley Kramer; with Spencer Tracy, Burt Lancaster, Maximilian Schell, and Judy Garland) The president of the court in these German war-crimes trials is pressured to go easy on those being tried to improve relations between a post–World War II Germany and the United States.

The Rainmaker (1997, color, 135 min., PG-13; Director: Francis Ford Coppola; with Matt Damon, Danny De Vito, and Mary Kay Place) From John Grisham's novel, this is the story of a freshly minted lawyer who fights an insurance company refusing to pay a claim.

Separate but Equal (1991, color, 200 min., made for TV; Director: George Stevens; with Sidney Poitier, Burt Lancaster, and Richard Kiley) Thurgood Marshall argues *Brown v. Board of Education* before the U.S. Supreme Court.

Twelve Angry Men (1957, black and white, 95 min., NR; Director: Sidney Lumet; with Henry Fonda, Lee J. Cobb, and E. G. Marshall) One juryman, unsure of the evidence, faces eleven other jurors who want to go home.

The Winslow Boy (1999, color, 110 min., G; Director: David Mamet; with Nigel Hawthorne and Jeremy Northam) Terrence Rattigan's play is about a young man accused of stealing a pittance from his school. He goes to court to save his name. Also filmed in 1948.

Witness for the Prosecution (1957, black and white, 114 min., NR; Director: Billy Wilder; with Charles Laughton, Marlene Dietrich, and Tyrone Power) A handsome ne'er-do-well is charged with murder. His wife must give testimony if he is to be saved, and she refuses.

Young Mr. Lincoln (1939, black and white, 100 min., NR; Director: John Ford; with Henry Fonda and Alice Brady) Lincoln defends a man (who the town knows is guilty) in court. Was there ever a better film actor than Henry Fonda? No, there wasn't.

Although it was hardly the first decision involving obscenity, the first decision announcing a definition of and a test for obscenity came about in an English case in 1868. *The Queen v. Hicklin* (L.R. 3Q.B. 360) concerned an ironmonger who was also an ardent antipapist. He sold copies of *The Confessional Unmasked: Showing the Depravity of the Romish Priesthood, the Iniquity of the Confessional and the Questions Put to Females in Confession,* and although the Court agreed that his heart was pure, his publication was not. Judge Cockburn announced a test of obscenity that was to persist in British law for nearly a century and in American law until the 1930s:

I think the test of obscenity is this, whether the tendency of the matter charged as obscenity is to deprave and corrupt those whose minds are open to such immoral influences, and into whose hands a publication of this sort may fall.

Clearly, but not exclusively, Cockburn was attempting to protect young people.

In 1913 in *United States v. Kennerly* (209 F. 119), Judge Learned Hand ruled against the defendant because his publication clearly fell under the limits of the Hicklin test, but he added:

> I hope it is not improper for me to say that the rule as laid down, however consonant it may be with mid-Victorian morals, does not seem to me to answer to the understanding and morality of the present time, as conveyed by the words, "obscene, lewd, or lascivious." I question whether in the end men will regard that as obscene which is honestly relevant to the adequate expression of innocent ideas, and whether they will not believe that truth and beauty are too precious to society at large to be mutilated in the interest of those most likely to pervert them to base uses.

Then in 1933 and 1934, two decisions (5 F. supp. 182 and 72 F. 2d 705) overturned much of the Hicklin test. James Joyce's *Ulysses* had been regarded as obscene by most legal authorities since its publication, largely for Molly Bloom's soliloquy. The novel was stopped by Customs officials and tried before Judge John M. Woolsey of the Federal District Court for Southern New York. Woolsey found the book "sincere and honest" and "not dirt for dirt's sake" and ruled that in matters determining what is obscene, the work *must* be judged as a whole, not on the basis of its parts. An appeal to the Federal Circuit Court of Appeals in 1934 led to Judge Learned Hand's upholding Woolsey's decision.

In 1957 in *Butler v. Michigan* (352 U.S. 380), Butler challenged a Michigan statute that tested obscenity in terms of its effect on young people, arguing that this restricted adult reading to that fit only for children. Justice Felix Frankfurter agreed, and wrote:

> The State insists that, by thus quarantining the general reading public against books not too rugged for grown men and women in order to shield juvenile innocence, it is exercising its power to promote the general welfare. Surely, this is to burn the house to roast the pig. . . . The incidence of this enactment [the Michigan statute] is to reduce the adult population of Michigan to reading only what is fit for children.

Frankfurter agreed with Butler and declared the Michigan statute unconstitutional.

Later in 1957, in *Roth v. United States* (354 U.S. 476), the U.S. Supreme Court announced that obscenity was not protected by the Constitution, for "implicit in the history of the First Amendment is the rejection of obscenity as utterly without redeeming social importance." (That phrase, "without redeeming social importance" was to cause problems for several years thereafter.) Reading for the majority, Justice Brennan added a new definition of obscenity:

> Obscene material is material which deals with sex in a manner appealing to prurient interest.

And a new test:

> Whether to the average person, applying contemporary community standards, the dominant theme of the material taken as a whole appeals to prurient interest.

Roth rejected the Hicklin test (already in patches) as "unconstitutionally restrictive of the freedoms of speech and press."

Jacobellis v. Ohio (84 S. Ct. 1676) in 1964 further refined the *Roth* test when Justice Brennan announced that the "contemporary community" standard referred to national standards, not local standards although Chief Justice Warren angrily dissented, arguing that community standards meant local and nothing more.

In 1966, in *Memoirs v. Attorney General of Massachusetts* (86 S. Ct. 975), Justice Brennan further elaborated on the *Roth* test:

> Under this definition, as elaborated in subsequent cases, three elements must coalesce: it must be established that (a) the dominant theme of the material taken as a whole appeals to prurient interest in sex; (b) the material is patently offensive because it affronts contemporary community standards relating to the description or representation of sexual matters; and (c) the material is utterly without redeeming social value.

The *Ginsberg v. New York* (390 U.S. 692) decision in 1968 did not develop or alter the definition of obscenity, but it did introduce the concepts of variable obscenity and caused some concern for librarians and English teachers. Ginsberg, who operated a stationery store and luncheonette, had sold "girlie" magazines to a 16-year-old boy in violation of a New York statute that declared illegal the sale of anything "which depicts nudity" and "was harmful" to anyone under 17 years of age. Ginsberg maintained that New York State was without power to draw the line at the age of 17. The Court dismissed his argument, sustained the New York statute, and wrote:

> The well-being of its children is of course a subject within the State's constitutional power to regulate.

The Court further noted, in lines that proved worrisome to anyone dealing in literature, classic, or modern or what-have-you:

> To be sure, there is no lack of "studies" which purport to demonstrate that obscenity is or is not "a basic factor in impairing the ethical and moral development of . . . youth and a clear and present danger to the people of the state." But the growing consensus of commentators is that "while these studies all agree that a causal link has not been demonstrated, they are equally agreed that a causal link has not been disproved either."

Those words were lovingly quoted by censors across the United States, although few of them bothered to read the citations in the decision that suggested the dangers of assuming too much either way about the matter.

Five U.S. Supreme Court decisions in 1973 brought forth a new test of obscenity. The most important, *Miller v. California* (413 U.S. 15) and *Paris Adult Theatre II v. Slaton* (413 U.S. 49), contained the refined test, one presumably designed to remove all ambiguities from past tests. That the test proved as ambiguous and as difficult to enforce and understand as previous tests should come as no surprise to readers. After attacking the 1957 *Roth* test, the majority decision read by Chief Justice Burger in *Miller* provided this three-pronged test of obscenity:

> The basic guidelines for the trier of fact must be: (a) whether "the average person, applying contemporary community standards" would find that the work, taken as a whole, appeals to the prurient interest; (b) whether the work depicts or describes in a patently offensive way, sexual conduct specifically defined by the applicable state law; and (c) whether the work taken as a whole lacks serious literary, artistic, political or scientific value.

To guide state legislatures with "a few plain examples of what a state statute could define for regulation under the second part (b) of the standard announced in this opinion," the Court provided these:

> (a) Patently offensive representations or descriptions of ultimate sexual acts, normal or perverted, actual or simulated.
> (b) Patently offensive representations or descriptions of masturbation, excretory functions, and lewd exhibition of the genitals.

After this so-called Miller catalogue, Burger announced that "contemporary community standards" meant state standards, not national standards.

Paris Adult Theatre II underscored *Miller* and added more worrisome words about the dangers of obscenity and what it can lead to. Chief Justice Burger, again, for the majority:

> But, it is argued, there is no scientific data which conclusively demonstrated that exposure to obscene material adversely affects men and women or their society. It is urged on behalf of the petitioner that, absent such a demonstration, any kind of state regulation is "impermissible." We reject this argument. It is not for us to resolve empirical uncertainties underlying state legislation, save in the exceptional case where that legislation plainly impinges upon rights protected by the Constitution itself. . . . Although there is no conclusive proof of any connection between antisocial behavior and obscene material, the legislature of Georgia could quite reasonably determine that such a connection does or might exist.

In other words, no proof exists that obscenity does (or does not) lead to antisocial actions (or nonactions), yet state legislatures can assume or guess that such a relationship may exist and pass legislation to that effect.

Justice Brennan dissented, noting that the dangers to "protected speech are very grave" and added that the decision would not halt further cases before the Court:

> The problem is that one cannot say with certainty that material is obscene until at least five members of this Court, applying inevitably obscure standards, have pronounced it so.

JUDY BLUME
On Censorship

When I began to write more than twenty years ago, I didn't know if anyone would publish my books, but I wasn't afraid to write them. I was lucky. I found an editor and publisher who were willing to take a chance. They encouraged me. I was never told what I couldn't write. I felt only that I had to write the most honest books I could. Books that came from deep down inside—books about real people, real families, real feelings—books that left the reader hopeful (because I am basically an optimist), without tying up all the loose ends. It never occurred to me, at the time, that what I was writing was controversial. Much of it grew out of my own feelings and concerns when I was young.

There were few challenges to my books then, although I remember the night a woman phoned, asking if I had written *Are You There God? It's Me, Margaret*. When I replied that I had, she called me a Communist and slammed down the phone. I never did figure out if she equated Communism with menstruation or religion.

But in 1980, following the presidential election, everything changed. The censors crawled out of the woodwork, seemingly overnight, organized and determined. Not only would they decide what their children could read, but what all children could read. Challenges to books quadrupled within months. And we'll never know how many teachers, school librarians, and principals quietly removed books to avoid trouble.

I believe that censorship grows out of fear, and because fear is contagious, some parents are easily swayed. Book banning satisfied their need to feel in control of their children's lives. This fear is often disguised as moral outrage. They want to believe that if their children don't read about it, their children won't know about it. And if they don't know about it, it won't happen.

Today, it's not only language and sexuality (the usual reasons for banning my books) that will land a book on the censors' hit list. It's Satanism, New Age-ism, and a hundred other *isms*, some of which would make you laugh if the implications weren't so serious.

Books that make kids laugh often come under suspicion; so do books that encourage kids to think, or question authority: books that don't hit the reader over the head with moral lessons are considered dangerous. (My book, *Blubber*, was banned in Montgomery County, Maryland, for lack of *moral tone*, but in New Zealand it is used in teacher-training classes to help explain classroom dynamics.)

Censors don't want children exposed to ideas different from their own. If every individual with an agenda had his or her way, the shelves in the school library would be close to empty. I wish the censors could read the letters kids write.

> *Dear Judy,*
> *I don't know where I stand in the world.*
> *I don't know who I am. That's why I read, to find myself.*
> *Elizabeth, age 13*

But it's not just the books under fire now that worry me. It is the books that will never be written. The books that will never be read. And all due to the fear of censorship. As always, young readers will be the real losers.

But I am encouraged by a new awareness. This year I've received a number of letters from young people who are studying censorship in their classes. And in many communities across the country, students from elementary through high school are becoming active (along with caring adults) in the fight to maintain their right to read and their right to choose books. *They* are speaking before school boards, and more often than not, when they do, the books in question are returned to the shelves.

Only when readers of all ages become active, only when *readers* are willing to stand up to the censors, will the censors get the message that they can't frighten us!

Judy's Blume's books include *Are You There God? It's Me, Margaret*, 1970; *Just As Long As We're Together*, 1987; and *Forever*, 1975, all now published by Simon & Schuster. *Summer Sisters*, 1998, is published by Delacorte, while her edited collection *Places I Never Meant to Be, Original Stories By Censored Writers*, in which she shares her personal experiences with censorship, is published by Simon & Schuster, 1999. Royalties are going to the National Coalition Against Censorship.

To few observers' surprise, Brennan's prophecy proved correct. On January 13, 1972, police in Albany, Georgia, seized the film *Carnal Knowledge* (starring Jack Nicholson) and charged the manager with violating a state statute against distributing obscene material. He was convicted in the Superior Court, and the decision was affirmed by a divided vote in the Georgia State Supreme Court. In 1974, the U.S. Supreme Court announced its decision in *Jenkins v. the State of Georgia* (94 S. Ct. 2750), Justice Rehnquist reading the unanimous decision to reverse the Georgia Supreme Court opinion. Although *Carnal Knowledge* had been declared obscene by state standards and although it had a scene showing simulated masturbation, Rehnquist stated that "juries do not have unbridled discretion" in determining obscenity and that *Carnal Knowledge* had nothing that fell "within either of the two examples given in *Miller.*"

The history of litigation and court decisions about obscenity and its definition are hardly models of clarity or consistency. Anyone interested in more details of this frustrating but fascinating story should read that marvelous book by Felice Flanery Lewis, *Literature, Obscenity and Law*.

Court Decisions About Teaching and School Libraries

If the implications of court decisions about obscenity are a bit vague, decisions about teaching and school libraries are not notably better. Courts are notoriously leery of decisions involving schools and libraries, lest they be regarded as a national school board, but a few decisions, not unsurprisingly ambiguous, are worth noting about school libraries.

The U.S. Supreme Court had ruled in *Tinker v. the Des Moines (Iowa) School District* (393 U.S. 503) in 1969:

> First Amendment rights, applied in light of the special characteristics of the school environment, are available to teachers and students. It can hardly be argued that either students or teachers shed their constitutional rights to freedom of speech or expression at the schoolhouse gate.

But Courts, federal or state, seemed unwilling to extend those rights to the school library in *Presidents Council, District 25 v. Community School Board No. 25* (457 F. 2d 289) in 1972. A New York City school board voted 5–3 in 1971 to remove all copies of Piri Thomas's *Down These Mean Streets* from junior high libraries because of its offensive nature and language. The U.S. Court of Appeals, Second Circuit, held for the school board. The book, so the Court decided, had dubious literary or educational merit, and because the state had delegated the selection of school materials to local school boards and there was no evidence of basic constitutional impingement by the board, the Court saw no merit in the opposing view.

Presidents Council was cited for several years thereafter as the definitive decision, but because it was not a Supreme Court decision, it served as precedent only for judges so inclined.

A different decision prevailed in *Minarcini v. Strongsville (Ohio) City School District* (541 F. 2d 577) in 1977. The school board refused to allow a teacher to use Heller's *Catch-22* or Vonnegut's *God Bless You, Mr. Rosewater,* ordered Vonnegut's *Cat's Cradle* and Heller's novel removed from the library, and proclaimed that students and teachers were not to discuss these books in class. The U.S. District Court found for the school board, but on appeal to the U.S. Circuit Court of Appeals, the three-member panel reversed the lower court. Judge Edwards focused on the main issues of the case in eloquent words widely quoted and much admired by school librarians:

> A library is a storehouse of knowledge. When created for a public school it is an important privilege created by the state for the benefit of the students in the school. That privilege is not subject to being withdrawn by succeeding school boards whose members might desire to "winnow" the library for books the content of which occasioned their displeasure or disapproval. Of course, a copy of a book may wear out. Some books may become obsolete. Shelf space alone may at some point require some selection of books to be retained and books to be disposed of. No such rationale is involved in this case.

The opinion of the Court that library books gained a tenure of sorts and could not easily be culled by a school board was at odds with the parallel U.S. Circuit Court in *Presidents Council,* but again, the Ohio decision served as precedent only if judges in other Federal District Courts (or Federal Appeals Courts) wished to so use it.

A year later in *Right to Read Defense Committee of Chelsea (Massachusetts) v. School Committee of the City of Chelsea* (454 F. Supp. 703) in the U.S. District Court for Massachusetts, another decision supported the rights of students and libraries. The librarian of Chelsea High School ordered and made available a paperback anthology, *Male and Female under Eighteen,* containing a poem by a student, "The City to the Young Girl," which had, as the judge wrote, "street language." A parent felt the language was "offensive" and called the board chairman, who was also the editor of the local paper. The chair-editor concluded that the poem was "filthy" and contained "offensive" language and should be removed from the library. He scheduled an emergency meeting of the school committee to consider the subject of "objectionable, salacious and obscene material being made available in books in the High School Library" and wrote an article for his newspaper about the matter, concluding with these words:

> Quite frankly, I want a complete review of how it was possible for such garbage to even get on bookshelves where 14-year-old high school ninth graders could obtain them.

The superintendent urged caution and noted that the book could not be removed from the library without a formal review, but the chair was adamant. When the librarian argued that the poem was not obscene, the chair-editor wrote in his newspaper:

> [I am] shocked and extremely disappointed to have our high school librarian claim there is nothing lewd, lascivious, filthy, suggestive, licentious, pornographic or obscene about this particular poem in this book of many poems.

The school committee claimed "an unconstrained authority to remove books from the shelves of the school library." Although the judge agreed that "local authorities are, and must continue to be, the principal policymakers in the public schools," he was more swayed by the reasoning in *Minarcini* than in *Presidents Council.* He wrote:

> The Committee was under no obligation to purchase *Male and Female* for the High School Library, but it did. . . . The Committee claims an absolute right to remove *City* from the shelves of the school library. It has no such right, and compelling policy considerations argue against any public authority having such an unreviewable power of censorship. There is more at issue here than the poem *City.* If this work may be removed by a committee hostile to its language and theme, then the precedent is set for removal of any other work. The prospect of successive school committees "sanitizing" the school library of views divergent from its own is alarming, whether they do it book by book or one page at a time.
>
> What is at stake here is the right to read and be exposed to controversial thoughts and language—a valuable right subject to First Amendment protection.

What may yet prove the most significant decision about school libraries began in September 1975 when three members of the Island Trees (New York) School Board attended a conference sponsored by the conservative Parents of New York—United (PONY-U). After examining lists of books deemed "objectionable" by PONY-U, the three returned home, checked their district's school libraries, and found several suspect works—Bernard Malamud's *The Fixer,* Vonnegut's *Slaughterhouse-Five,* Desmond Morris's *The Naked Ape,* Piri Thomas's *Down These Mean Streets,* Langston Hughes's edition of *Best Short Stories of Negro Writers,* Oliver La-Farge's *Laughing Boy,* Richard Wright's *Black Boy,* Alice Childress's *A Hero Ain't Nothin' But a Sandwich,* Eldridge Cleaver's *Soul on Ice,* and *Go Ask Alice.* In February

1976, the board gave "unofficial direction" that the books be removed from the library and delivered to the board for their reading.

Once the word was out, the board issued a press release attempting to justify its actions, calling the books "anti-American, anti-Christian, anti-Semitic, and just plain filthy" and argued:

> It is our duty, our moral obligation, to protect the children in our schools from this moral danger as surely as from physical or medical dangers.

When the board appointed a review committee—four members of the school staff and four parents—the board politely listened to the report suggesting that five books should be returned to the shelves and that two should be removed (*The Naked Ape* and *Down These Mean Streets*) and then ignored their own chosen committee. (The board did return one book to the shelves, *Laughing Boy,* and placed *Black Boy* on a restricted shelf available only with parental permission.) Stephen Pico, a student, and others brought suit against the board, claiming that their rights under the First Amendment had been denied by the board.

The U.S. District Court heard the case in 1979 and granted a summary judgment to the board. The court held that the state had vested school boards with broad discretion to formulate educational policy, and the selection or rejection of books was clearly within their power. The court found no merit in the First Amendment claims of Pico, et al. A three-judge panel of the U.S. Court of Appeals for the Second Circuit (638 F. 2d 404) reversed the District Court's decision 2–1 and remanded the case for trial. The case then, although not directly, wended its way to the U.S. Supreme Court, the first such case ever to be heard at that level.

In a strange and badly fragmented decision—and for that reason it is unclear how certainly it will serve as precedent—Justice Brennan delivered the plurality (*not* majority) opinion in *Board of Education, Island Trees Union Free School District v. Pico* (102 S. Ct. 2799). He immediately emphasized the "limited nature" of the question before the court, for "precedents have long recognized certain constitutional limits upon the power of the State to control even the curriculum and classroom," and he further noted that *Island Trees* did not involve textbooks "or indeed any books that Island Trees students would be required to read." The case concerned only the removal, not the acquisition, of library books. He concluded the first section of his opinion by pointing out that the case concerned two questions:

> First, does the First Amendment impose *any* limitations upon the discretion of petitioners to remove library books from the Island Trees High School and Junior High School? Second, if so, do the affidavits and other evidential materials before the District Court, construed most favorably to respondents, raise a genuine issue of fact whether petitioners might have exceeded those limitations?

Brennan proceeded to find for *Pico* (and ultimately for the library and the books):

> . . . we think that the First Amendment rights of students may be directly and sharply implicated by the removal of books from the shelves of a school library.
>   Petitioners emphasized the inculcative function of secondary education, and argue that they must be allowed *unfettered* discretion "to transmit commu-

nity values" through the Island Trees schools. But that sweeping claim overlooks the unique role of the school library. . . . Petitioners might well defend their claim of absolute discretion in matters of *curriculum* by reliance upon their duty to inculcate community values. But we think that petitioners' reliance upon that duty is misplaced where, as here, they attempt to extend their claim of absolute discretion beyond the compulsory environment of the classroom, into the school library and the regime of voluntary inquiry that there holds sway.

Petitioners rightly possess significant discretion to determine the content of their school libraries. But that discretion may not be exercised in a narrowly partisan or political manner. . . . Our Constitution does not permit the official suppression of ideas. Thus whether petitioners' removal of books from their school libraries denied respondents their First Amendment rights depends upon the motivation behind petitioners' actions. If petitioners *intended* by their removal decision to deny respondents access to ideas with which petitioners disagreed, and if this intent was the decisive factor in petitioners' decision, then petitioners have exercised their discretion in violation of the Constitution.

Four pages follow before Justice Blackmun's generally concurring opinion and Justices Burger, Rehnquist, Powell, and O'Connor offered their stinging dissents, but it is clear that school librarians won something, although precisely what and how much will need to be resolved by future court decisions.

It is equally clear that secondary teachers lost something in *Island Trees*. In an understandable ploy, the American Library Association, the New York Library Association, and the Freedom to Read Foundation submitted an *Amicus Curiae* brief, which sought to distinguish between the functions of the school classroom and the school library, a distinction that worked to the advantage of the school librarian but certainly not to that of the classroom teacher. Apparently, Brennan bought the argument as readers can see, comparing Brennan's words with those from the following brief:

This case, however, is about a library, not a school's curriculum. This is an extremely important distinction for the evaluation of the First Amendment interests at stake here.

The school board below banned books from a library. Thus, this case does not present an issue concerning the board's control of curriculum, i.e., what is taught in the classroom. We freely concede that the school board has the right and duty to supervise the general content of the school's course of study.

Whether these words will cause serious disagreements between teachers and librarians remains to be seen. Certainly, that phrase, "we freely concede," has rankled a number of English teachers who recognized that *Island Trees* was a serious setback for intellectual freedom in the classroom, a point that was taken up in *Hazelwood* (108 S. Ct. 562, 1988) and later in *Virgil* (862 F. 2d 1517, 11th Cir., 1989).

Anyone who assumed that *Pico* quieted the waters of school censorship must have been surprised by five court decisions from 1986 through 1989. These decisions might have been expected to clear up the censorial waters; instead, they made the waters murkier.

On July 7, 1986, the U.S. Supreme Court announced its decision in *Bethel School District v. Fraser* (106 S. Ct. 3159, 1986) upholding school officials in Spanaway, Washington, who had suspended a student for using sexual metaphors in describing the political potency of a candidate for student government. Writing the majority opinion in the 7–2 decision, Chief Justice Burger said, "Surely it is a highly appropriate function of public school education to prohibit the use of vulgar and offensive terms in public discourse. . . . schools must teach by example the shared values of a civilized social order." To some people's surprise, Justice Brennan agreed with Justice Burger that the student's speech had been disruptive, although Brennan refused to label the speech indecent or obscene.

That decision worried many educators, but a lower court decision on October 24, 1986, frightened more teachers. *Mozert v. Hawkins County (Tennessee) Public Schools* (579 F. Supp. 1051, 1984) began in September 1983 when the school board of Hawkins County refused a request by parents to remove three books in the Holt, Rinehart and Winston reading series from the sixth-, seventh-, and eighth-grade program. The parents formed Citizens Organized for Better Schools and ultimately brought suit against the school board. U.S. District Judge Thomas Hull dismissed the lawsuit, but on appeal before the Sixth Circuit of the Court of Appeals, a panel of three judges remanded the case back to Judge Hull.

Not all the testimony in the trial during the summer of 1986 concerned humanism, particularly secular humanism, but so it seemed at times. Vicki Frost, one of the parents who initiated the suit, said that the Holt series taught "satanism, feminism, evolution, telepathy, internationalism, and other beliefs that come under the heading of secular humanism." Later she explained why parents objected to any mention of the Renaissance by saying that "a central idea of the Renaissance was a belief in the dignity and worth of human beings," presumably establishing that teaching the Renaissance was little more than teaching secular humanism.

Judge Hull ruled in favor of the parents on October 24, 1986, but the U.S. Sixth Circuit Court of Appeals overturned Hull's decision. Worse yet for the fundamentalist parents, the U.S. Supreme Court refused to hear an appeal of the Court of Appeals' ruling in February 1988. Beverly LaHaye, leader of the Concerned Women for America, who had filed the original suit in 1983 and whose group had helped finance the legal fees for the parents, said, "School boards now have the authority to trample the religious freedom of all children." Other people, notably educators, were grateful to the court for giving them the right to teach.

While *Mozert* worked its way through the courts, an even more troublesome and considerably louder suit was heard in Alabama. Judge Brevard W. Hand had earlier helped devise a suit defending the right of Alabama to permit a moment of silence for prayer in the public schools. The U.S. Supreme Court overturned Judge Hand's decision, so he devised another suit, *Smith v. School Commissioners of Mobile County, Alabama* (655 F. Supp. 939, 1987), alleging that social studies, history, and home economics textbooks in the Mobile public schools unconstitutionally promoted the "religious belief system" of secular humanism, as Judge Hand wrote in his March 4, 1987, decision maintaining that forty-four texts violated the rights of parents.

The decision was both silly and certain, but those who feared the bogeyman of secular humanism celebrated for a few weeks. Then, late in August 1987, the Eleventh U.S. Circuit Court of Appeals reversed Judge Hand's decision. The Court of Appeals did not address the question of whether secular humanism was a religion, but it did agree that the forty-four texts did not promote secular humanism. Phyllis Schlafly said she was not surprised by the ruling, but it mattered little because the decision would be appealed to the U.S. Supreme Court. Oddly enough for a case that began so loudly, the plaintiffs were mute, the date for the appeal quietly passed, and all was silence.

The fourth case, *Hazelwood School District v. Kuhlmeier* (108 S. Ct. 562, 1988), will trouble many educators, although nominally the case was concerned with school journalism and the publication of a school newspaper. The case began in 1983 when the principal of a high school in Hazelwood, Missouri, objected to two stories in the school newspaper dealing with teenage pregnancy and divorce's effects on young people.

Associate Justice Byron White wrote the majority opinion in the 5–3 decision announcing that educators (i.e., administrators) are entitled to exercise great control over student expression. Although the case presumably dealt only with a school newspaper, White's words—inadvertently or not—went further. White wrote:

> The policy of school officials toward [the school newspaper] was reflected in Hazelwood School Board Policy 348.51 and the Hazelwood East Curriculum Guide. Board Policy 348.51 provided that "school-sponsored publications are developed within the adopted curriculum and its educational activities."

After commenting on needed school standards and the right of administrators to set standards, White added:

> This standard is consistent with our oft-expressed view that the education of the nation's youth is primarily the responsibility of parents, teachers, and state and local school officials, and not of federal judges.

Kirsten Goldberg warned only a month later that the consequences of *Hazelwood* would likely extend beyond school newspapers and be far more serious than most teachers had thought:

> Less than a month after the U.S. Supreme Court's decision expanding the power of school officials to regulate student speech, lower courts in three widely differing cases have cited the ruling in upholding the actions of school administrators.

The court decisions, which came less than a week apart, support a Florida school board's banning of a humanities textbook, a California principal's seizure of an "April Fool's" edition of a school newspaper, and a Nebraska school district's decision not to provide meeting space to a student Bible Club.

The Florida decision was particularly troubling and hinted that parallel decisions citing *Hazelwood* as precedent might be on the way. *Virgil v. School Board of Columbia County, Florida* (862 F. 2d 1517, 11th Cir., 1989) concerned a challenge to a school board's decision to stop using a humanities text in a high school class because it contained Chaucer's "The Miller's Tale" and Aristophanes's *Lysistrata*, two works to which parents had objected. After a formal complaint had been filed in April 1986, the school board appointed an advisory committee and then ignored that committee when it recommended keeping the text. Parents filed an action against the school board.

In the district court decision in January 1988, Judge Black agreed with the parents that the school board had overestimated the potential harm to students of Chaucer or Aristophanes, but she concluded that the board had the power as announced in *Hazelwood* to decide as it had.

The parents appealed to the Eleventh Circuit Court of Appeals, which, as in the district court, fell back on *Hazelwood* for precedent for curricular decisions, not merely those concerned with school newspapers. As Judge Anderson wrote in his decision of January 1989:

> In applying the *Hazelwood* standard to the instant case, two considerations are particularly significant. First, we conclude that the Board decisions at issue were curricular decisions. The materials removed were part of the textbook used in a regularly scheduled course of study in the school. . . . The second consideration that is significant in applying the *Hazelwood* standard to this case is that the motivation for the Board's removal of the readings has been stipulated to be related to the explicit sexuality and excessively vulgar language in the selections. It is clear from *Hazelwood* and other cases that this is a legitimate concern.

Judge Anderson found that the school board had acted appropriately, although in the last paragraph he and the court distanced themselves from the folly of the board's decision to ban two classics.

> We decide today only that the Board's removal of these works from the curriculum did not violate the Constitution. Of course, we do not endorse the Board's decision. Like the district court, we seriously question how young persons just below the age of majority can be harmed by these masterpieces of Western literature. However, having concluded that there is no constitutional violation, our role is not to second-guess the wisdom of the Board's action.

Florida teachers must have been touched by those words.

Joan DelFattore's *What Johnny Shouldn't Read: Textbook Censorship in America* is a recent scholarly and readable work that admirably covers major court decisions involving teachers and librarians.

Extralegal Decisions

Most censorship episodes do not result in legal hearings and court decisions. Teachers or librarians come under attack and unofficial rumor-mongering charges are lodged because someone objects and labels the offending work "obscene" or "filthy" or "pornographic." The case is heard in the court of public opinion, sometimes before the school board, with few legal niceties prevailing. The censors (and too often the school board) almost never operate under any definitions of obscenity that a court would recognize, but their interpretations of the issues are opera-

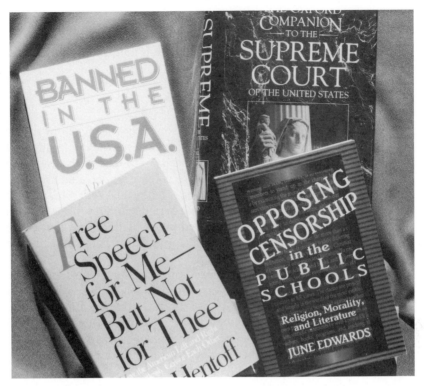

See the "Starter Bibliography" at the end of this chapter for sources to help mitigate the negative effects of censorship.

tionally effective for their purposes. The book may not always be judged as a whole book (although individual parts may be juicily analyzed), and the entire procedure may be arbitrary and capricious. The decision, once announced, rapidly disposes of the offending book and frequently the teacher or librarian to boot, a variation of old-fashioned Western justice at work. Extralegal trials need not be cluttered with trivia such as accuracy or reasoning or fairness or justice. Many of the eighteen censorship incidents described earlier in this chapter were handled extralegally.

Why would librarians or teachers allow their books and teaching materials to be so treated? Court cases cost a great deal of money, and unless a particular case is likely to create precedent, many lawyers discourage educators from going to the courts. Court cases, even more important, cause friction within the community and—surprising to many neophyte teachers and librarians—cause almost equal friction among a school's faculty. A teacher or librarian who assumes that all fellow teachers will automatically support a case for academic freedom or intellectual freedom is a fool. Many educators, to misuse the word, have little sympathy for troublemakers or their causes. Others are frightened at the prospect of possibly antagonizing their superiors. Others "know their place" in the universe. Others are morally offended by anything stronger than *darn* and may regard most of modern literature (and old literature) as inherently immoral and therefore objectionable to high school students' use. Others find additional or different reasons aplenty for staying out of the fray. And that, more likely than not, is the reason most censorship episodes do not turn into court cases.

What to Do Before and After the Censors Arrive

Certain steps should be taken by librarians and teachers, preferably acting in concert, to prepare for censorship.

Before the Censors Arrive

Teachers and librarians should have some knowledge about the history of censorship and why citizens would wish to censor (see the books and articles listed at the end of the chapter). They should keep up-to-date with censorship problems and court decisions and what books are coming under attack for what reason. That means they should read the *Newsletter on Intellectual Freedom, School Library Journal, English Journal, Journal of Youth Services in Libraries,* and *Voice of Youth Advocates,* along with other articles cited in the bibliography that concludes each issue of the *Newsletter.* A lot of work? Of course, but better than facing a censor totally ignorant of the world of censorship.

They should develop clear and succinct statements, devoid of any educational or library or literary jargon, on why they teach literature or stock books. These statements ought to be made easily available to the public, partly to demonstrate educators' literacy—always an impressive beginning for an argument—and to make parents feel that someone intelligent works in the school, partly because teachers and librarians have a duty to communicate to the public what is going on and why it goes on.

They need to develop and publicize procedures for book selection in the library or the classroom. Most parents have not the foggiest notion how educators go about selecting books, more or less assuming it comes about through sticking pins in a book catalogue. It might be wise to consider asking some parents to assist teachers and librarians in selection, partly to let parents learn how difficult the matter is, partly to use their ideas (which might prove surprisingly helpful).

They need to develop procedures for handling censorship, should it occur. The National Council of Teachers of English monographs *The Students' Right to Read* and *The Students' Right to Know* should prove helpful, as should the American Library Association's *Intellectual Freedom Manual,* both for general principles and for specific suggestions. Whether adopted from any of these sources or created afresh, the procedure should include a form to be completed by anyone who objects to any teaching material or library book and a clearly defined way in which the matter will be handled after completion of the form. (Will it go to a committee? How many are on the committee? Are people outside the school on the committee? How many teachers? How many administrators?) The procedural rules must be openly available for anyone to consult, the procedures must apply to everyone (no exceptions should be allowed, no matter whether the complainant is the local drunk or the school board president), every complainant must be treated courteously and promptly, and the procedures must be approved by the school board. If the board does not approve the procedures, they have no legal standing. If the school board is not periodically reminded of the procedures—say, every couple of years—it may forget its obligation. Given the fact that many school boards change membership slightly in three or four years and may change their entire composition within five or six years, teachers and librarians should take it upon themselves to remind the board. Otherwise, an entirely new board may wonder why it should support something it neither created nor particularly approves of.

Teachers who assign long works (other than texts) for common reading should write rationales, statements aimed at parents but open to anyone, explaining why the teacher chose *1984* or *Silas Marner* or *Manchild in the Promised Land* or *Hamlet* for class reading and discussion. Rationales should answer the following, although they should be written as informal essays, devoid of any educational jargon, not answers to essay tests: (1) Why would the teacher use this book with this class at this time? (2) What specific objectives—not couched in behavioral terms unless the teachers are anxious to alienate parents—literary or pedagogical, is the teacher aiming at? (3) How will this book meet those objectives? (4) What problems of style, tone, theme, or subject matter exist, and how will the teacher face them? Answering those questions should force teachers to take a fresh look at the book and think more carefully about the possibilities and problems inherent in the book. Rationales are *not* designed to protect the teacher by showing careful advance preparation before teaching, although clearly such rationales would be valuable should censorship strike. Rather, rationales should be written for public information easily available to anyone interested as part of the professional responsibility of teachers. Diane Shugert offers a number of sample rationales in the fall 1983 *Connecticut English Journal* and in "How to Write a Rationale in Defense of a Book" in James Davis's *Dealing with Censorship*.

Educators should woo the public to gain support for intellectual and academic freedom. Any community has its readers and former teachers interested in students' freedom to read. Finding them ahead of time is part of teachers' and librarians' jobs. Waiting until censorship strikes is too late. Pat Scales's ideas about working with parents in the November 1983 *Calendar* (distributed by the Children's Book Council) are most helpful. Scales was talking to a parent who helped in Scales's school library and who had picked up copies of Maureen Daly's *Seventeenth Summer* and Ann Head's *Mr. and Mrs. Bo Jo Jones* and wondered about students reading books with such provocative covers. Scales asked the mother to read the books before forming an opinion. From that experience came a program called "Communicate Through Literature" with monthly meetings to discuss with parents the reading that young adults do. Also, we should not forget about discussing the topic of censorship with our current students (Focus Box 12.1). They could easily be the parents who in a few years will be on the school board or on the library's board of trustees.

Educators should be prepared to take on the usual arguments of censors—for example, that educators are playing word games when we insist that we select and some parents try to censor. There is a distinction between *selection* and *censorship*, no matter how many people deliberately or inadvertently misuse or confuse the two. The classic distinction was drawn by Lester Asheim in 1952:

> Selection begins with a presumption in favor of liberty of thought; censorship with a presumption in favor of thought control. Selection's approach to the book is positive, seeking its values in the book as a book, and in the book as a whole. Censorship's approach is negative, seeking for vulnerable characteristics wherever they can be found anywhere in the book, or even outside it. Selection seeks to promote the right of the reader to read; censorship seeks to protect not the right—but the reader himself from the fancied effects of his reading. The selector has faith in the intelligence of the reader; the censor has faith only in his own.

FOCUS BOX 12.1

Censorship, Court Cases, and Young Adults

Be the Judge. Be the Jury: The Sacco-Vanzetti Trial by Doreen Rappaport. HarperCollins, 1992. In May of 1920, two Italian immigrants were accused of murder in the midst of a robbery. The result was one of the most misguided trials on record and a lesson for all of us.

Be the Judge. Be the Jury: Tinker vs. Des Moines by Doreen Rappaport. HarperCollins, 1993. This trial is probably the single most influential U.S. Supreme Court decision on students' First Amendment rights.

The Day They Came to Arrest the Book by Nat Hentoff. Delacorte, 1982. Parents object to *Adventures of Huckleberry Finn* because the book is, according to them, racist and sexist. Hentoff advances the cases for both sides.

The Last Safe Place on Earth by Richard Peck. Delacorte, 1995. Walden Woods seems like the perfect place to live until a group dedicated to protecting young people from evil books decides to raid libraries.

Maudie and Me and the Dirty Book by Betty Miles. Knopf, 1980. In this remarkable children's book, two girls read stories to first grade children, but then one story about a dog giving birth offends many parents.

Sensational Trials of the 20th Century by Betsy Harvey Kraft. Scholastic, 1998. Kraft presents the best of the most sensational trials in the twentieth century ranging from Sacco and Vanzetti to O. J. Simpson with stopovers at the Scopes trial, *Brown v. Board of Education*, and Watergate.

Strike by Barbara Corcoran. Atheneum, 1983. Corcoran adds two counter melodies to the basic tune of a father-son debate about the boy's life and plans—a strike by teachers and a group anxious to go through libraries looking for filth.

The Year They Burned the Book by Nancy Garden. Farrar, Straus & Giroux, 1999. Jamie is editor of the school newspaper and a supporter of sex education in schools. Her editorial touches some raw nerves and the fight is on.

In other words, selection is democratic while censorship is authoritarian, and in our democracy we have traditionally tended to put our trust in the selector rather than in the censor.[37]

Finally, teachers and librarians should know the organizations that are most helpful if censorship does strike. Diane Shugert's "A Body of Well-Instructed Men and Women: Organizations Active for Intellectual Freedom," in James Davis's *Dealing with Censorship,* has a long list of such groups. Following are six national groups every educator ought to know:

The American Civil Liberties Union, 132 W. 43rd St., New York, NY 10036

The Freedom to Read Foundation, 50 E. Huron St., Chicago, IL 60611

The National Coalition Against Censorship, 2 W. 64th St., New York, NY 10023

People for the American Way, 2000 M St., N.W., Washington, DC 20036

SLATE (Support for the Learning and Teaching of English), National Council of Teachers of English, 1111 Kenyon Road, Urbana, IL 61801

The Standing Committee on Censorship, c/o National Council of Teachers of English, 1111 Kenyon Road, Urbana, IL 61801

After the Censors Arrive

Teachers and librarians should begin by refusing to panic—easier said than done but essential. Censors always have one advantage. They can determine the time and the place for the attack. No matter how well prepared the teacher or the librarian, only the censor can say *when*.

Educators should not be too surprised or appalled to discover that not all their fellow teachers or librarians rush in with immediate support. If teachers and librarians assume they represent the entire cause by themselves, they are far better off and considerably less likely to be instantly disillusioned.

Educators ought to urge (or even require that) potential censors talk first to the teacher or librarian in question before completing the complaint form, not to stall the objectors but to assure everyone of fair play all around. Teachers or librarians may discover what others have before, that objectors sometimes simply want to be heard and their complaints treated with dignity and dispatch. Sometimes, teachers and librarians may even be able to talk calmly—once the need to battle has died down—with the objectors and to reason with them, which is not exactly the same as convincing them that the teachers or librarians are necessarily right. The objectors may even see why the offending work was assigned or recommended, sometimes even seeing the difficulty in choosing a book for a class or an individual. Many teachers and librarians, although by no means all, agree that if parents ask that their child not be required to read a certain book, educators must agree to find a substitute book. If a substitute book is to be found and if it is to meet a different fate than the first book, parents must help in selecting the new book. Most objectors deeply care about their children's education, and they understand why the substitute book should not be easier or shorter (thus rewarding the student) or harder and longer (thus unduly punishing the student). Finding another book approximately as long and as difficult as the original choice is no easy matter, but parents who demand substitutes must help, lest the teacher offend once more.

Librarians and teachers must treat objectors with every possible courtesy. Objectors should be expected to complete the school's forms detailing the objection, but the forms should be easily accessible and politely distributed. The complaint form should *never* be used to stall objectors. If it is so long that objectors get discouraged, the school may win one battle, but it will have produced one more disgruntled citizen, and at school bond time one irritated citizen and friends are quite enough to harm the cause of education.

Last, a committee (spelled out in detail before the censorship) meets to look at and discuss the complaint. After considering the problem but before arriving at a decision, the committee must meet with the teacher or librarian in question *and* the objectors to hear their cases. The committee then makes its decision and forwards it to the highest administrator in the school, who forwards it to the superintendent, who then forwards it to the school board. That body, already aware of the policy and procedures much earlier adopted to handle such matters, considers this objection and makes its decision, probably after at least one open meeting.

In no case and at no level should the actions of the educators or administrators or the school be viewed as pro forma. They should be considered as thoughtful actions to resolve a problem, not as an attempt to create newer and bigger ones. Objectors should feel that they have been listened to and courtesy has been extended them at all levels and all stages.

We believe that the school—classroom or library—must be a center of intellectual ferment in the community. This implies not that schools should be radical, but that they should be one place where freedom to think and inquire is protected, where ideas of all sorts can be considered, analyzed, investigated, and discussed, and their consequences thought through. We believe librarians and English teachers must protect these freedoms, not merely in the abstract but in the practical, day-by-day world of the school and library. To protect those freedoms, we must fight censorship, for without them no education worthy of the name is possible.

Notes

[1]Colin Campbell, "Book Banning in America," *New York Times Book Review,* December 20, 1981, p. 1.

[2]Comstock's life and work have been the subject of many books and articles. Heywood Broun and Margaret Leech's *Anthony Comstock: Roundsman of the Lord* (Albert and Charles Boni, 1927) is amusing and nasty and still worth reading. A brief overview of Comstock's life can be found in Robert Bremner's introduction to the reprinting of *Traps for the Young* (Harvard University Press, 1967), pp. vii–xxxi. See also Paul S. Boyer's *Purity in Print: The Vice-Society Movement and Book Censorship in America* (Scribner, 1968) and Robert W. Haney's *Comstockery in America: Patterns of Censorship and Control* (Beacon Press, 1960).

[3]Arthur E. Bostwick, *The American Public Library* (Appleton, 1910), pp. 130–131.

[4]*Library Journal* 21 (December 1896): 144.

[5]"Unexpurgated Shakespeare," *Journal of Education* 37 (April 13, 1883): 232.

[6]"What Books Do They Read?" *Common School Education* 4 (April 1890): 146–147.

[7]Evaline Harrington, "Why Treasure Island?" *English Journal* 9 (May 1920): 267–268.

[8]"Fiction in Public Libraries." *American Library Journal* 1 (March 1877): 278.

[9]*Public Libraries* 8 (March 1903): 114–115.

[10]"Standards in Selecting Fiction." *Library Journal* 67 (March 1932): 243.

[11]Nat Hentoff, *Newsletter on Intellectual Freedom* 41 (September 1982): 185.

[12]*Newsletter on Intellectual Freedom* 35 (July 1985): 119.

[13]AP dispatch, *New York Times,* May 15, 1987, p. 47.

[14]*Idaho Language Arts News,* April 1990, p. 1.

[15]*Newsletter on Intellectual Freedom* 39 (July 1990): 128.

[16]*Newsletter on Intellectual Freedom* 41 (January 1992): 5–6.

[17]*Tempe* (AZ) *Daily News,* August 1991, p. B-1.

[18]*Attacks on the Freedom to Learn 1992–1993 Report.* (People for the American Way, 1993) p. 48.

[19]*Phoenix Gazette.* May 25, 1994. p. A-1.

[20]*Newsletter on Intellectual Freedom* 47 (May 1998) : 89.

[21]*Newsletter on Intellectual Freedom* 42 (July 1993): 105–106.

[22]*Newsletter on Intellectual Freedom* 45 (November 1996): 198.

[23]*Newsletter on Intellectual Freedom* 46 (July 1997): 96.

[24]*San Francisco Examiner,* October 8, 1982, p. B-4.

[25]Louise Kingsbury and Lance Gurewell, "The Sin Fighters: Grappling with Gomorrah at the Grass Roots," *Utah Holiday* 12 (April 1983): 46.

[26]Lee Grant, "Shoot-Out in Texas," Calendar section, *Los Angeles Times,* December 25, 1983, p. 21.

[27]*Phoenix Gazette,* June 10, 1981, p. SE-6.

[28]Kingsbury and Gurewell, p. 52.

[29]Bettye I. Latimer, "Telegraphing Messages to Children About Minorities," *Reading Teacher* 30 (November 1976): 155.

[30]*Arizona English Bulletin* 11 (February 1969): 37.

[31]Diane Shugert, "Censorship in Connecticut," *Connecticut English Journal* 9 (Spring 1978): 59–61.

[32]*Publishers Weekly* 215 (April 30, 1979): 24.

[33]Kathleen Beck, "Censorship and Celluloid." *Voice of Youth Advocates* 18 (June 1995): 73–76.

[34]Ken Donelson, "Censorship in the 1970s: Some Ways to Handle It When It Comes (and It Will)," *English Journal* 63 (February 1974): 47–51.

[35]"Protest Groups Exert Strong Impact," *Publishers Weekly* 216 (October 29, 1979): 42–44.

[36]"Sixty-seven Targets of the Textbook Protesters," *Missouri English Bulletin* 38 (May 1980): 27– 32.

[37]Lester Asheim, "Not Censorship but Selection," *Wilson Library Bulletin* 28 (September 1953): 67. See also Asheim's later article, "Selection and Censorship: A Reappraisal," *Wilson Library Bulletin* 58 (November 1983): 180–184. Julia Turnquist Bradley's "Censoring the School Library: Do Students Have the Right to Read?" *Connecticut Law Review* 10 (Spring 1978): 747–775, also draws a distinction between *selection* and *censorship.*

A Starter Bibliography on Censorship

Bibliographical Sources

McCoy, Ralph E. *Freedom of the Press: An Annotated Bibliography.* Carbondale, IL: Southern Illinois University Press, 1968.

McCoy, Ralph E. *Freedom of the Press: A Bibliocyclopedia Ten-Year Supplement.* Carbondale, IL: Southern Illinois University Press, 1979.

Newsletter on Intellectual Freedom. A bimonthly edited by Judith Krug with a sizable bibliography concluding each issue. Available from the American Library Association, 50 East Huron Street, Chicago, IL 60611.

Three Basic Policy Statements and Recommended Procedures

Burress, Lee and Edward B. Jenkinson. *The Students' Right to Know,* Urbana, IL: National Council of Teachers of English, 1982.

Burress, Lee and Edward B. Jenkinson. *The Students' Right to Read,* 3rd ed. Urbana, IL: National Council of Teachers of English (NCTE), 1982. NCTE's official statement on censors and fighting the censors.

Intellectual Freedom Manual, 5th ed. Chicago: American Library Association (ALA), 1996. ALA's official policy statement along with a mass of helpful material.

Court Cases

Bosmajian, Haig A., ed. *Censorship: Libraries and the Law.* New York: Neal-Schuman, 1983. Censorship cases involving secondary schools.

Bosmajian, Haig A., ed. *The First Amendment in the Classroom,* 5 volumes. New York: Neal-Schuman.
No. 1, *The Freedom to Read,* 1987.
No. 2. *Freedom of Religion,* 1987.
No. 3. *Freedom of Expression,* 1988.
No. 4. *Academic Freedom,* 1989.
No. 5. *The Freedom to Publish,* 1989.

de Grazia, Edward, ed. *Censorship Landmarks,* New York: R. R. Bowker, 1969.

Hall, Kermit L., ed. *The Oxford Companion to the Supreme Court.* New York: Oxford University Press, 1992. An encyclopedia of court cases and legal terms and Supreme Court Justices. Invaluable.

Schwartz, Bernard. *A History of the Supreme Court.* New York: Oxford University Press, 1993. Probably the best of the single-volume histories of the Court.

Summaries of Censorship Incidents

Wachsberger, Ken. General editor of *Banned Books,* four volumes, each with its own editor, all from New York: Facts on File, 1998. Each volume summarizes the attempted censorship of an incredible number of books and attempts to discover why various books have come under attack.

Nicholas Karolides, *Literature Suppressed on Political Grounds.*

Dawn B. Sova, *Literature Suppressed on Social Grounds.*

Dawn B. Sova, *Literature Suppressed on Sexual Grounds.*

Margaret Bald, *Literature Suppressed on Religious Grounds.*

Books

Ahrens, Nyla H. *Censorship and the Teaching of English: A Questionnaire Survey of a Selected Sample of Secondary Teachers of English.* Dissertation, Teachers College, Columbia University, 1965. The first national study of school censorship and what it does to teachers and kids and the freedom to read.

Ayers, Stephen Michael. *The Selection Process of the National Endowment for the Arts Theatre Program.* New York: Peter Lang, 1992.

Beahm, George, ed. *War of Words: The Censorship Debate.* New York: Andrews and McMeel, 1993.

Beale, Howard K. *Are American Teachers Free? An Analysis of Restraints upon the Freedom of Teaching in American Schools.* New York: Scribner, 1936.

Black, Gregory D. *The Catholic Crusade Against the Movies, 1940–1975.* New York: Cambridge University Press, 1998.

Bolton, Richard. *Culture Wars.* New York: New Press, 1992. On the National Endowment for the Arts and all its problems, current and not so current.

Boyer, Paul S. *Purity in Print: The Vice-Society and Book Censorship in America.* New York: Scribner's, 1968.

Brown, Jean, ed. *Preserving Intellectual Freedom: Fighting Censorship in Our Schools.* Urbana, IL: National Council of Teachers of English, 1994. A rich collection of articles.

Bryson, Joseph E. and Elizabeth W. Detty. *The Legal Aspects of Censorship of Public School Library and Instructional Materials.* Charlottesville, VA: Michie, 1982.

Burt, Richard. *The Administration of Aesthetics: Censorship, Political Criticism, and the Public Sphere.* Minneapolis: University of Minnesota Press, 1994.

Carmilly-Weinberger, Moshe. *Fear of Art: Censorship and Freedom of Expression in Art.* New York: R. R. Bowker, 1986.

Carrier, Esther. *Fiction in Public Libraries, 1876–1900.* New York: Scarecrow, 1965.

Carrie, Esther. *Fiction in Public Libraries, 1900–1950.* Littleton, CO: Libraries Unlimited, 1985.

Censorship Litigation and the Schools. Chicago: American Library Association, 1983.

Cline, Victor B., ed. *Where Do You Draw the Line?* Provo, UT: Brigham Young University Press, 1974. Conservative points of view on the topic.

Conolly, L. W. *The Censorship of English Drama, 1737–1824.* San Marino, CA: Huntington Library, 1976.

Craig, Alec. *Suppressed Books: A History of the Conception of Literary Obscenity,* Cleveland: World, 1963.

Curry, Ann. *The Limits of Tolerance: Censorship and Intellectual Freedom in Public Libraries.* Lanham, MD: Scarecrow, 1997.

Davis, James E., ed. *Dealing with Censorship.* Urbana, IL: National Council of Teachers of English, 1979. More or less liberal articles on the subject.

DelFattore, Joan. *What Johnny Shouldn't Read: Textbook Censorship in America.* New Haven, CT: Yale University Press, 1992. Court cases involving textbooks. Basic to any study of school censorship and wonderfully readable.

de Grazia, Edward. *Girls Lean Backward Everywhere: The Law of Obscenity and the Assault on Genius.* New York: Random House, 1992. On movie censorship.

de Grazia, Edward and Roger K. Newman. *Banned Films: Movies, Censors, and the First Amendment.* New York: Bowker, 1982.

Donnerstein, Edward, Daniel Linz, and Steven Penrod. *The Question of Pornography: Research Findings and Policy Implications.* New York: Free Press, 1987. Sometimes tough going but rewarding on a topic that's frequently misunderstood and often misused.

Edwards, June. *Opposing Censorship in the Public Schools: Religion, Morality, and Literature.* Mahwah, NJ: Erlbaum, 1998.

Eldridge, Larry D. *A Distant Heritage: The Growth of Free Speech in Early America.* New York: New York University Press, 1993.

Ernst, Morris L., and Alan U. Schwartz. *Censorship: The Search for the Obscene.* New York: Macmillan, 1964.

Fiske, Marjorie. *Book Selection and Censorship: A Study of School and Public Libraries in California.* Berkeley: University of California Press, 1968.

Foerstel, Herbert N. *Banned in the U.S.A.: A Reference Guide to Book Censorship in Schools and Public Libraries.* Westport, CT: Greenwood Press, 1994.

Foerstel, Herbert N. *Banned in the Media: A Reference Guide to Censorship in the Press, Motion Pictures, Broadcasting, and the Internet.* Westport, CT: Greenwood Press, 1998.

Fryer, Peter. *Mrs. Grundy: Studies in English Prudery.* New York: London House and Maxwell, 1964.

Gardiner, Harold C. *Catholic Viewpoint on Censorship,* rev. ed. New York: Image, 1961.

Garrison, Dee. *Apostles of Culture: The Public Librarian and American Society.* New York: Free Press, 1979.

Garry, Patrick. *An American Paradox: Censorship in a Nation of Free Speech.* Westport, CT: Praeger, 1993.

Geller, Evelyn. *Forbidden Books in American Public Libraries, 1876–1939: A Study in Cultural Change.* Westport, CT: Greenwood Press, 1984.

Glasser, Ira. *Visions of Liberty: The Bill of Rights for All Americans.* Boston: Little, Brown, 1991.

Haight, Anne Lyons. *Banned Books,* 4th ed. New York: R. R. Bowker, 1978.

Haney, Robert W. *Comstockery in America: Patterns of Censorship and Control.* Boston: Beacon, 1960.

Heins, Marjorie. *Sex, Sin, and Blasphemy: A Guide to America's Censorship Wars.* New York: New Press, 1993.

Hefley, James C. *Textbooks on Trial.* Wheaton, IL: Victor Books, 1976. A defense of Mel and Norma Gabler's work.

Hentoff, Nat. *The First Freedom: The Tumultuous History of Free Speech in America.* New York: Delacorte, 1980.

Hentoff, Nat. *Free Speech for Me—But Not for Thee: How the American Left and Right Relentlessly Censor Each Other.* New York: HarperCollins, 1992.

Hentoff, Nat. *Living the Bill of Rights: How to Be an Authentic American.* New York: HarperCollins, 1998.

Hofstadter, Richard. *Anti-Intellectualism in American Life.* New York: Knopf, 1963.

Homstad, Wayne. *Anatomy of a Book Controversy.* Bloomington, IN: Phi Delta Kappa Educational Foundation, 1995.

Jenkinson, Edward B. *Censors in the Classroom: The Mind Benders.* Carbondale, IL: Southern Illinois University Press, 1979.

Jenkinson, Edward B. *The Schoolbook Protest Movement: 40 Questions and Answers.* Indianapolis IN: Phi Delta Kappa Educational Foundation, 1986.

Karolides, Nicholas, Lee Burress, and John Kean, eds. *Censored Books: Critical Viewpoints.* Metuchen, NJ: Scarecrow Press, 1993. Essays and rationales on books under attack and ways of justifying using the books.

Kendrick, Walter. *The Secret Museum: Pornography in Modern Culture.* New York: Viking, 1987.

Kronhausen, Eberhard and Phyllis Kronhausen. *Pornography and the Law: The Psychology Of Erotic Realism and Hard Core Pornography,* rev. ed. New York: Ballantine, 1964.

Lehr, Susan, ed. *Battling Dragons: Issues and Controversy in Children's Literature.* Portsmouth, NH: Heinemann, 1995.

Levy, Leonard W. *Blasphemy: Verbal Offense Against the Sacred—From Moses to Salman Rushdie.* New York: Knopf, 1993.

Lewis, Felice Flanery. *Literature, Obscenity and Law.* Carbondale, IL: Southern Illinois University Press, 1976. The best book on legal battles about obscenity and censorship.

Lyons, Charles. *The New Censors and the Culture Wars.* Philadelphia: Temple University Press, 1997.

Martin, Olga J. *Hollywood's Movie Commandments: A*

Handbook for Motion Picture Writers and Reviewers. New York: Wilson, 1937.

McCormick, John and Mairi, eds. *Versions of Censorship.* Garden City: Doubleday Anchor, 1962. A superb anthology of classic documents.

McDonald, Frances Beck. *Censorship and Intellectual Freedom: A Survey of School Librarians' Attitudes and Moral Reasoning.* Metuchen, NJ: Scarecrow, 1993.

Mill, John Stuart. "On Liberty." 1859.

Milton, John. *Areopagitica.* 1644.

Moffett, James. *Storm in the Mountains: A Case Study of Censorship, Conflict, and Consciousness.* Carbondale, IL: Southern Illinois University Press, 1988. The aftermath of the Kanawha County, WV, textbook bannings.

Nilsen, Alleen Pace, ed. *Censorship in Children's Literature,* special issue of *Para*Doxa: Studies in World Literary Genres* 2:3–4 (Fall, 1996), Vashon Island, WA 98070. The writers of the articles include specialists in literature for young people from Japan, Australia, New Zealand, Germany, Spain, Greece, and the former Soviet republic, as well as Canada and the United States.

Noble, William. *Bookbanning in America. Who Bans Books?—And Why?* Middlebury, VT: Paul S. Eriksson, 1990.

Oboler, Eli, ed. *Censorship and Education.* New York: H. W. Wilson, 1981.

Ochoa, Anna S., ed. *Academic Freedom to Teach and to Learn: Every Teacher's Issue.* Washington, DC: National Education Association, 1990.

Ochoa, Anna S. *The Fear of the Word: Censorship and Sex.* Metuchen, NJ: Scarecrow Press, 1974.

O'Neil, Robert M. *Classrooms in the Crossfire: The Rights and Interests of Students, Parents, Teachers, Administrators, Librarians, and the Community.* Bloomington, IN: Indiana University Press, 1981.

Perrin, Noel. *Dr. Bowdler's Legacy: A History of Expurgated Books in England and America.* New York: Atheneum, 1969. Scholarly and great fun. Read anything by Perrin, no matter what the subject.

Pope, Michael. *Sex and the Undecided Librarian: A Study of Librarians' Opinions on Sexually Oriented Literature.* Metuchen, NJ: Scarecrow, 1974.

Rabban, David M. *Free Speech in Its Forgotten Years.* New York: Cambridge University Press, 1997. Free speech between the Civil War and World War II.

Rauch, Jonathan. *Kindly Inquisitors: The New Attacks on Free Speech.* Chicago: University of Chicago Press, 1993.

Rehnquist, William H. *The Supreme Court: How It Was, How It Is.* New York: Morrow, 1987.

Reichman, Henry. *Censorship and Selection: Issues and Answers for Schools,* rev. ed. Chicago: American Library Association, 1993.

Rembar, Charles. *The End of Obscenity: The Trials of Lady Chatterley, Tropic of Cancer, and Fanny Hill.* New York: Random House, 1968. Proof that lawyers can write.

Riley, Gail Blasser. *Censorship.* New York: Facts on File, 1998.

Robbins, Jan C. *Student Press and the Hazelwood Decision.* Indianapolis: Phi Delta Kappa Educational Foundation, 1988.

Robbins, Louise S. *Censorship and the American Library: The American Library Association's Response to Threats to Intellectual Freedom.* Westport, CT: Greenwood, 1996.

Robins, Natalie. *Alien Ink: The FBI's War on Freedom of Expression.* New York: Morrow, 1992.

Schumach, Murray. *The Face on the Cutting Room Floor: The Story of Movie and Television Censorship.* New York: Morrow, 1964.

Selth, Jefferson P. *Ambition, Discrimination, and Censorship in Libraries.* Jefferson, NC: McFarland, 1993.

Simmons, John S., ed. *Censorship: A Threat to Reading, Learning, Thinking.* Newark, DE: International Reading Association, 1994. Fine collection.

Skinner, James M. *The Cross and the Cinema: The Legion of Decency and the National Catholic Office for Motion Pictures, 1933–1970.* Westport, CT: Praeger, 1993.

Smolla, Rodney A. *Free Speech in an Open Society.* New York: Knopf, 1992.

Strossen, Nadine. *Defending Pornography: Free Speech, Sex, and the Fight for Women's Rights.* New York: Scribner, 1995.

Taylor, John Tinnon. *Early Opposition to the English Novel: The Popular Reaction from 1760 to 1830.* New York: King's Crown Press, 1943.

Theiner, George, ed. *They Shoot Writers, Don't They?* London: Faber and Faber, 1984.

Theoharis, Athan G. *A Culture of Secrecy: The Government Versus the People's Right To Know.* Lawrence: University of Kansas Press, 1998.

Thomas, Donald. *A Long Time Burning: The History of Literary Censorship in England.* New York: Praeger, 1969.

Thompson, Anthony Hugh. *Censorship in Public Libraries in the United Kingdom During the Twentieth Century.* New York: R. R. Bowker, 1975.

Wallace, Jonathan and Mark Mangan. *Sex, Laws, and Cyberspace: Freedom and Censorship on the Frontiers of the Online.* New York: Holt, 1996.

Walsh, Frank. *Sin and Censorship: The Catholic Church and the Motion Picture Industry.* New Haven: Yale University Press, 1996.

West, Mark. *Children, Culture, and Controversy.* Hamden, CT: Archon, 1988.

West, Mark. *Trust Your Children: Voices Against Censorship in Children's Literature.* New York: Neal-Schuman, 1988. YA authors speak on censorship.

Westin, Alan E. *The Miracle Case: The Supreme Court and the Movies.* University, AL: University of Alabama Press, 1961.

Wiegand, Wayne A., ed. "The Library Bill of Rights," entire Summer 1996 issue of *Library Trends.*

Zeigler, Joseph Wesley. *Arts in Crisis: The National Endowment for the Arts Versus America.* New York: A Cappella Books, 1994.

Articles

"Are Libraries Fair: Pre-Selection Censorship in a Time of Resurgent Conservatism." *Newsletter on Intellectual Freedom* 31 (September 1982): 151, 181–188. Comments by Cal Thomas, conservative syndicated columnist, and Nat Hentoff, *Village Voice* columnist. Seventeen years old but still worth anyone's time.

Aronson, Marc. "It Starts with a Word." *School Library Journal* 43 (August 1997): 30–32.

Asheim, Lester. "Not Censorship, but Selection." *Wilson Library Bulletin* 28 (September 1953): 63–67. The most widely quoted statement distinguishing between selection and censorship.

Asheim, Lester. "Selection and Censorship: A Reappraisal." *Wilson Library Bulletin* 58 (November 1983): 180–184.

Avery, Kay Beth and Robert J. Simpson. "The Constitution and Student Publications: A Comprehensive Approach." *Journal of Law and Education* 16 (Winter 1987): 1–61.

Baker, Mary Gordon. "A Teacher's Need to Know Versus the Student's Right to Privacy." *Journal of Law and Education* 16 (Winter 1987): 71–91.

Bassett, John. "Huck and Tom in School: Conflicting Freedoms and Values." *Free Speech Yearbook* 27 (1989): 48–54.

Beck, Kathleen. "Censorship and Celluloid." *VOYA* 18 (June 1995): 73–76.

Benjamin, Beth and Linda Irwin-DeVitis. "Censoring Girls; Choices: Continued Gender Bias in English Language Arts Classrooms." *English Journal* 87: (February 1998): 64–71.

Bernays, Anne. "I Don't Want to Read a Novel Passed by a Board of Good Taste." *Chronicle of Higher Education* 37 (March 6, 1991): B-1, B-3.

Bogdan, Deanne. "Reading as Seduction: The Censorship Problem and the Educational Value of Literature." *ADE Bulletin,* (Fall 1992): 11–16.

Booth, Wayne C. "Censorship and the Values of Fiction." *English Journal* 53 (March 1964): 155–164. More than 30 years old and still not dated. Must reading.

Bradley, Julia Turnquist. "Censoring the School Library: Do Students Have a Right to Read?" *Connecticut Law Review* 10 (Spring 1978): 747–775.

Briley, Dorothy. "Are the Editors Guilty of Precensorship?" *School Library Journal* 29 (October 1982): 114–115.

Brinkley, Ellen H. "Faith in the Word: Examining Religious Right Attitudes about Texts." *English Journal* 84 (September 1995): 91–98.

Broderick, Dorothy. "Are There Any Sane School Districts in the U.S.A.?" *Voice of Youth Advocates* 20 (February 1997): 310–311.

Broderick, Dorothy. "Censorship—Reevaluated." *School Library Journal* 18 (November 1971): 30–32.

Broderick, Dorothy. "Serendipity at Work." *Show-Me Libraries* 35 (February 1984): 13–14.

Brudder, Carolyn R. "The Trickle-Up Effect of Censorship in the High School Classroom and Library." *CEA Critic* 56 (Winter 1994): 1–7.

Bryant, Gene. "The New Right and Intellectual Freedom." *Tennessee Librarian* 33 (Summer 1981): 19–24.

Burger, Robert H. "The Kanawha County Textbook Controversies: A Study of Communication and Power." *Library Quarterly* 48 (April 1982): 584–589.

Burress, Lee A. "How Censorship Affects the School." Wisconsin Council of Teachers of English, *Special Bulletin No. 8* (October 1963): 1–23. The first significant study of state censorship conditions.

Campbell, Colin. "Book Banning in America." *New York Times Book Review* (December 20, 1981): pp. 1, 16–18.

Campbell, Patty. "Mainstreaming the Last Taboo." *Horn Book Magazine* 74 (May/June 1998): 379–383. On religion in YA books.

Carey-Webb, Allen. "Racism and *Huckleberry Finn:* Censorship, Dialogue, and Change." *English Journal* 2 (November 1993): 22–34.

Cart, Michael. "Winning One for the First Amendment." *Booklist* (April 15, 1996): 1431.

Clark, Todd, ed. "The Question of Academic Freedom." *Social Education* 39 (April 1975): 202–252.

Click, J. William and Lillian Lodge Kopenhaver. "Few Changes Since *Hazelwood.*" *School Press Review* 65 (Winter 1990): 12–27.

Cockett, Lynn. "Entering the Mainstream: Fiction about Gay and Lesbian Teens." *School Library Journal* 41 (February, 1995): 32–33.

Cornog, Martha. "Is Sex Safe in Your Library? How To Fight Censorship." *Library Journal* 118 (August 1993): 43–46.

Cox, Harvey. "The Warring Visions of the Religious Right." *Atlantic Monthly* 276 (November 1995): 59–69.

Curry, Ann. "Intellectual Freedom and Censorship: A Teaching Challenge." *Education Libraries* 19 (Spring 1995): 5–12.

Davis, James E. "What Principals and Other Administrators Have Done and Can Do in Defending Intellectual Freedom." *ALAN Review* 20 (Winter 1993): 11–13.

Delp, Vaughn N. "The Far Right and Me: It's Not So Far Away and It's Not So Right." *Arizona English Bulletin* 37 (Fall 1994): 71–76.

Donelson, Kenneth L. "Almost 13 Years of Book Protests . . . Now What?" *School Library Journal* 3 (March 1985): 93–98

Donelson, Kenneth L. " 'Filth' and 'Pure Filth' in Our Schools—Censorship of Classroom Books in the

Last Ten Years." *English Journal* 86 (February 1997): 21–25.

Donelson, Kenneth L. "Shoddy and Pernicious Books and Youthful Piety: Literary and Moral Censorship, Then and Now." *Library Quarterly* 51 (January 1981): 4–19.

Donelson, Kenneth L. "Six Statements/Questions from the Censors." *Phi Delta Kappan* 69 (November 1987): 208–214.

Donelson, Kenneth L. "Steps Towards the Freedom to Read." *ALAN Review* 20 (Winter 1993): 14–19.

Donelson, Kenneth L. "You Can't Have That Book in My Kid's School Library: Books Under Attack in the *Newsletter on Intellectual Freedom*, 1952–1989." *High School Journal* 74 (October–November 1990): 1–7.

Dunstan, Angus. "On Not Disturbing Our Students." *California English* 1 (Fall 1995): 16–17.

Edwards, June. "Censorship in the Schools: What's Moral about *The Catcher in the Rye?*" *English Journal* 72 (April 1983): 39–42.

Ellenbogen, Charles M. "Introducing Censorship: One Teacher's Approach." *English Journal* 86 (February 1997): 65–66.

Ellison, Kerry Leigh. "Satan in the Library: Are Children in Danger?" *School Library Journal* 40 (October 1994): 46–47.

Eveslage, Thomas. "10 Court Decisions: First Amendment and High Schools." *Media History Digest* 10 (Fall–Winter 1990): 21–25, 44.

"Expurgation Practices of School Book Clubs." *Voice of Youth Advocates* 6 (Fall 1981): 97–101.

Faaborg, Karen Kramer. "High School Play Censorship: Are Students' First Amendment Rights Violated When Officials Cancel Theatrical Productions?" *Journal of Law and Education* 14 (October 1985): 575–594.

Farrell, Edmund J. "Literature in Crisis." *English Journal* 70 (January 1981): 13–18.

Feiwell, Jean. "Killing Books Softly: Reviewers as Censors." *School Library Journal* 36 (September 1990): 155–162.

Fine, Sara. "How the Mind of the Censor Works: The Psychology of Censorship." *School Library Journal* 42 (January 1996): 23–27.

FitzGerald, Frances. "A Disagreement in Baileyville." *New Yorker* 59 (January 16, 1984): 47–90.

Gagnon, Paul. "What Should Children Learn?" *Atlantic Monthly* 276 (December 1995): 65–78.

Garden, Nancy. "*Annie* on Trial: How It Feels To Be the Author of a Challenged Book." *VOYA* 19 (June 1996): 79–82, 84.

Gardner, Robert. "A New Fashioned Book Burning." *English Journal* 85 (February 1997): 63–64.

Gerhardt, Lillian N. "Access Points." *School Library Journal* 42 (January 1996): 6.

Gerhardt, Lillian N. "Gagging Toward 2000." *School Library Journal* 43 (January 1997): 5.

Gerhardt, Lillian N. "Polishing Policies." *School Library Journal* 42 (February 1996): 4.

Glatthorn, Allan A. "Censorship and the Classroom Teacher." *English Journal* 66 (February 1977): 12–15.

Golderg, Beverly. "On the Line for the First Amendment: An Interview with Judy Krug." *American Libraries* 26 (September 1995): 774–778.

Goldwasser, Marion McAdoo. "Censorship: It Happened to Me in Southwest Virginia—It Could Happen to You." *English Journal* 86 (February 1997): 34–42.

Grant, Cynthia. "Tales from a YA Author: Slightly Uneasy." *School Library Journal* 41 (October 1995): 48, 50.

Greenbaum, Vicky. "Censorship and the Myth of Appropriateness: Reflections on Teaching Reading." *English Journal* 86 (February 1997): 16–20.

Greenlee, Edwin D. "Recommended Adolescent Literature: Avoiding Those 'Hidden Secrets.'" *English Journal* 81 (April 1992): 23–24. See also the responses to Greenlee in the same issue, pp. 25–30, and see Terry Davis' "The Author of *Vision Quest:* Responds to 'Hidden Secrets.'" *English Journal* 81 (September 1992): 87–89.

Griffin, William. "Religious Conservatives and Public Schools: Understanding the Religious Right." *English Journal* 84 (September 1995): 84–90.

Groves, Cy. "Book Censorship: Six Misunderstandings." *Alberta English '71* 11 (Fall 1971): 5–7. Reprinted in the *Arizona English Bulletin* 37 (Fall 1994): 19–20.

Hale, F. Dennis. "Free Expression: The First Five Years of the Rehnquist Court." *Journalism Quarterly* 69 (Spring 1992): 89–104.

Hengstbeck, Marylee. "*Huck Finn,* Slavery, and Me." *English Journal* 82 (November 1993): 32.

Hentoff, Nat. "Any Writer Who Follows Anyone Else's Guidelines Ought to Be in Advertising." *School Library Journal* 24 (November 1977): 27–29.

Hentoff, Nat. "School Newspapers and the Supreme Court." *School Library Journal* 34 (March 1988): 114–116.

Hentoff, Nat. "When Nice People Burn Books." *Progressive* 47 (February 1983): 42–44.

Hielsberg, Amy. "Self-Censorship Starts Early." *American Libraries* 25 (September 1994): 768, 770.

Hildebrand, Janet. "Is Privacy Reserved for Adults? Children's Rights at the Public Library." *School Library Journal* 37 (January 1991): 21–25.

Hillocks, George, Jr. "Books and Bombs: Ideological Conflicts and the School—A Case Study of the Kanawha County Book Protest." *School Review* 86 (August 1978): 632–654.

Hirschoff, Mary-Michelle Upson. "Parents and the Public School Curriculum: Is There a Right to Have One's Child Excused from Objectionable Instruction?" *Southern California Law Review* 50 (1977): 871–959.

Holderer, Robert W. "The Religious Right: Who Are They and Why Are We the Enemy?" *English Journal* 84 (September 1995): 74–83.

Janeczko, Paul. "How Students Can Help Educate the Censors." *Arizona English Bulletin* 37 (February 1975): 78–80.

Jenkinson, David. "Censorship Iceberg: Results of a Survey of Challenges in Public and School Libraries." *Canadian Library Journal* 43 (February 1986): 7–21.

Jenkinson, Edward B. "Protecting Holden Caulfield and His Friends from the Censors." *English Journal* 74 (January 1985): 26–33.

Jones, Janet L. "Targets of the Right." *American School Board Journal* 180 (April 1993): 22–29. See also the responses in the July 1993 issue, pp. 4–9.

Kamhi, Michelle Marder. "Censorship vs. Selection— Choosing the Books Our Children Shall Read." *Educational Leadership* 39 (December 1981): 211–215.

Kearns, Edward A. "Words Worth 1,000 Pictures: Confronting Film Censorship." *English Journal* 86 (February 1997): 51–54.

Keresey, Gayle. "School Book Club Expurgation Practices." *Top of the New* 40 (Winter 1984): 131–138.

Kingsbury, Louise and Lance Gurwell. "The Sin Fighters: Grappling with Gomorrah at the Grass Roots." *Utah Holiday* 12 (April 1983): 42–61.

Klein, Norma. "Being Banned." *Top of The News* 41 (Spring 1985): 248–255.

Klein, Norma. "What Is Fit for Children?" *New York Times Book Review*, August 24, 1986, p. 20.

Kochman, Susan M. "What Happens When a High School Censors." *English Journal* 86 (February 1997): 58–62.

Koertge, Ron. "Sex and the Single Kid." *Los Angeles Times Book Review*, March 21, 1993, pp. 1, 11.

Kopenhaver, Lillian Lodge, David L. Martinson, and Peter Habermann. "First Amendment Rights in South Florida: View of Advisors and Administrators in Light of *Hazelwood*." *School Press Review* 65 (Fall 1989): 11–17.

Lacks, Cissy. "The Teacher's Nightmare: Getting Fired for Good Teaching." *English Journal* 86 (February 1997): 29–33.

Lew, Ann. "Teaching *Huck Finn* in a Multicultural Classroom." *English Journal* 82 (November 1993): 16–21.

MacRae, Cathi Dunn. "Watch Out for 'Don't Read This!' How a Library Youth Participation Group Was Silenced by Schools Yet Made Its Voice Heard." *Voice of Youth Advocates* 18 (June 1995): 80–87.

Manley, Will. "Are We Free To Talk Honestly about Intellectual Freedom?" *American Libraries* 28 (October 1997): 112.

Martin, William. "The Guardians Who Slumbereth Not." *Texas Monthly* 10 (November 1982): 145–150. About Mel and Norma Gabler.

Martinson, David L. "*Hazelwood*: The End of the 'Hidden Curriculum Charade.'" *Clearing House* 75 (February/March 1992): 131–136.

Martinson, David L. "Vulgar, Indecent, and Offensive Student Speech: How Should Public School Administrators Respond?" *Clearing House* 71 (July/August 1998): 345–348.

Maxwell, Marilyn and Marlene Berman. "To Ban or Not To Ban: Confronting the Issue of Censorship in the English Class." *Journal of Adolescent and Adult Literacy* 41 (October 1997): 92–96.

Mazer, Norma Fox. "Silent Censorship." *School Library Journal* 42 (August 1966): 42.

Mazer, Norma Fox. "Young Adult Literature: An Interview." *Voice of Youth Advocates* 12 (October 1989): 147–148.

McFerran, Warren L. "They All Lived Unhappily Ever After: Contemporary Young Fiction Is Corrupting the Innocence of Our Children." *New American* (John Birch Society) 3 (June 1987): 43–44.

McGraw, William Corbin. "Pollyanna Rides Again." *Saturday Review* 41 (March 22, 1958): 37–38. One of the classic statements (and funny, to boot).

Meeks, Lynn Langer. "Who Are the Censors, Why Do They Censor, and What Can We Do About It?" *Idaho Language Arts Newsletter,* April 1990, pp. 1–4.

Melich, Nancy. "Censorship on the Stage," *Salt Lake Tribune,* May 22, 1994, pp. D-1, D-4. Reprinted in Spring 1994 *Arizona English Bulletin,* pp. 35–39.

Melichar, Don. "Objections to Books in Arizona High School English Classes: Nothing Changes but the Changes." *Arizona English Bulletin* 37 (Spring 1994): 3–13.

Merrill, Martha. "Authors Fight Back: One Community's Experience." *Library Journal* 112 (September 1985): 55–56.

Meyer, Randy. "Annie's Day in Court: The Decision from the Bench." *School Library Journal* 42 (April 1996): 22–25. The U.S. District Court decision about the censorship of Nancy Garden's *Annie on My Mind* in Olathe, KS.

Moe, Mary Sheehy. "Selection and Retention of Instructional Materials—What the Courts Have Said." *SLATE.* Entire issue for August 1995.

Moffett, James. "Hidden Impediments to Improving English Teaching." *Phi Delta Kappan* 67 (September 1985): 50–56.

Nagle, Terry Lynn. "The Case of the Offensive Nancy Drew." *Catholic Library World* 50 (September 1978): 79–81.

Nelson, Jack L. and Anna S. Ochoa. "Academic Freedom, Censorship, and the Social Studies." *Social Education* 51 (October 1987): 424–427.

Niccolai, F. R. "Right to Read and School Library Censorship." *Journal of Law and Education* 10 (January 1981): 23–26.

Noll, Elizabeth. "The Ripple Effect of Censorship: Silencing the Classroom." *English Journal* 83 (December 1994): 59–64.

O'Brien, Mrs. Dermod. "The Pernicious Habit of Reading." *Parent's Review* 38 (March 1927): 151–157.

Olson, René. "Editorial: Pleasantville Redux." *School Library Journal* 44 (December 1998): 5.

O'Malley, William J. (S. J.), "How to Teach 'Dirty' Books in High School." *Media and Methods* 4 (November 1967): 6–11.

Orleans, Jeffrey H. "What Johnny Can't Read: 'First Amendment Rights' in the Classroom." *Journal of Law and Education* 10 (January 1981): 1–15.

Parker, Donald. "Freedom of Expression for Students: An Idea Whose Time Has Come—and Gone." *High School Journal* 75 (December–January 1992): 75–76.

Peck, Richard. "From Strawberry Statements to Censorship." School *Library Journal* 43 (January 1997): 28–29.

Peck, Richard. "The Genteel Unshelving of a Book." *School Library Journal* 32 (May 1986): 37–39.

Peck, Richard. "The Great Library-Shelf Witch Hunt." *Booklist* 88 (January 1, 1992): 816–817.

Perini, Flory. "Censorship Redefined." *Arizona English Bulletin* 37 (Fall 1994): 68–70.

Pico, Steven. "An Introduction to Censorship." *School Library Media Quarterly* 18 (Winter 1990): 84–87. Pico was the plaintiff in *Pico v. Island Trees*.

Pincus, Jonathan. "Censorship in the Public Schools: Who Should Decide What Students Should Learn?" *Free Speech Yearbook* 24 (1985): 67–84.

Pipkin, Gloria. "Challenging the Conventional Wisdom on Censorship." *ALAN Review* 20 (Winter 1993) 35–37.

Pipkin, Gloria. "Confessions of an Accused Pornographer." *Arizona English Bulletin* 37 (Fall 1995): 14–18.

"Rationales for Commonly Challenged Taught Books." *Connecticut English Journal* 15 (Fall 1983). Entire issue.

Reed, Michael. "What Johnny Can't Read: School Boards and the First Amendment." *University of Pittsburgh Law Review* 42 (Spring 1981): 653–657.

Robinson, Stephen. "Freedom, Censorship, Schools, and Libraries." *English Journal* 70 (January 1980): 58–59.

Rossi, John et al., eds. "The Growing Controversy over Book Censorship." *Social Education* 46 (April 1982): 254–279.

Rossuck, Jennifer. "Banned Books: A Study of Censorship." *English Journal* 86 (February 1997): 67–70.

Russo, Elaine M. "Prior Restraint and the High School 'Free Press': The Implications of *Hazelwood School District v. Kuhlmeier*." *Journal of Law and Education* 18 (Winter 1989): 1–21.

Salvner, Gary M. "A War of Words: Lessons from a Censorship Case." *ALAN Review* 25 (Winter 1998): 45–49.

Schrader, Alvin M. "A Study of Community Censorship Pressures on Canadian Public Libraries." *Canadian Library Journal* 49 (February 1992): 29–38.

Shafer, Robert. "Censorship in Tucson's Flowing Wells School District Makes for a Nationally Publicized 'Non-Event.'" *Arizona English Bulletin* 37 (Fall 1994): 51–57.

Siegel, Paul. "*Tinkering* with *Stare Decisis* in the *Hazelwood* Case." *Free Speech Yearbook* 27 (1989): 97–103.

Simmons, John. "By Their Names, Ye Shall Know Them." *Arizona English Bulletin* 37 (Fall 1994): 64–67.

Simmons, John. "Censorship and the YA Book." *ALAN Review* 16 (Spring 1989): 14–19.

Simmons, John. "Proactive Censorship: The New Wave." *English Journal* 70 (December 1981): 18–20.

Simmons, John. "What Teachers Under Fire Need from Their Principals." *ALAN Review* 20 (Winter 1993): 22–25.

Small, Robert C., Jr. "Censorship and English: Some Things We Don't Think About Very Often (but Should)." *Focus* 3 (Fall 1976) 18–24.

Small, Robert C., Jr. and M. Jerry Weiss. "What Do I Do Now? Where To Turn When You Face a Censor" in Jean E. Brown, ed., *Preserving Intellectual Freedom: Fighting Censorship in Our Schools.* Urbana, IL: National Council of Teachers of English, 1994, pp. 151–163.

"Some Thoughts on Censorship: An Author Symposium." *Top of the News* 39 (Winter 1983): 137–153. Comments by Norma Klein, Judy Blume, Betty Miles, and others.

Staten, Clifford L. "Teaching the First Amendment to 7th and 8th Graders." *Social Education* 57 (January 1993): 43–44.

Stielow, Frederick J. "Censorship in the Early Professionalization of American Libraries, 1876 to 1929." *Journal of Library History* 18 (Winter 1983): 37–54.

Strike, Kenneth A. "A Field Guide of Censors: Toward a Concept of Censorship in Public Schools." *Teachers College Record* 87 (Winter 1985): 239–258.

Suhor, Charles. "Daddy's Roommate, Satanism, and Other Outrages: An Interview with Judy Krug." *SLATE Newsletter* 19 (September 1994): 1–3.

Suhor, Charles. "Censorship—When Things Get Hazy." *English Journal* 86 (February 1997): 26–28.

Sutton, Roger. "An Interview with Judy Blume: Forever Yours." *School Library Journal* 42 (June 1996): 24–27.

Sutton, Roger. "What Mean We, White Man?" *Voice of Youth Advocates* 15 (August 1992): 155–158.

Thomas, Charles Swain. "Sex—and the Younger Readers of Literature." *Harvard Educational Review* 7 (March 1937): 243–253.

Tollefson, Alan M. "Censored and Censured: Racine Unified School District vs. Wisconsin Library Association." *School Library Journal* 33 (March 1987): 108–112.

Tyack, David B. and Thomas James. "Moral Majorities and the School Curriculum: Historical Perspectives on the Legalization of Virtue." *Teachers College Record* 86 (Summer 1985): 513–537.

Valgardson, W. D. "Being a Target." *Canadian Library Journal* 48 (February 1991): 17–18, 20.

Vonnegut, Kurt. "Why Are You Banning My Book?" *American School Board Journal* 168 (October 1981): 35.

Vrabel, Terri Boucher. "How Books Get Banned—or

Not—in Schools." *Texas Library Journal* 73 (Fall 1997): 132–135.

Watson, Jerry J. and Bill C. Snider. "Educating the Potential Self-Censor." *School Media Quarterly* 9 (Summer 1981): 272–276.

West, Celeste. "The Secret Garden of Censorship: Ourselves." *Library Journal* 108 (September 1983): 1651–1653.

West, Mark. "Censorship in Children's Books." *Publishers Weekly* 232 (July 24, 1987): 108–111.

Whaley, Elizabeth Gates. "What Happens When You Put the Manchild in the Promised Land? An Experiment with Censorship." *English Journal* 63 (May 1974): 61–65.

Whitson, James Anthony. "After *Hazelwood:* The Roles of School Officials in Conflicts Over the Curriculum." *ALAN Review* 20 (Winter 1993): 3–6.

Wickenden, Dorothy. "Bowdlerizing the Bard." *New Republic* 192 (June 3, 1985): 18–19.

Wilson, Robert J. "Censorship, Anti-Semitism, and *The Merchant of Venice.*" *English Journal* 86 (February 1887): 43–45.

Yates, Jessica. "Censorship in Children's Paperbacks." *Children's Literature in Education* 11 (Winter 1980): 180–191.

Zeeman, Kenneth L. "Grappling with Grendel or What We Did When the Censors Came." *English Journal* 86 (February 1997): 46–49.

Glossary of Literary Terms Illustrated by YA Literature

Allegories are extended comparisons or metaphors. They can be enjoyed on a surface level as well as on a second or deeper level. For example, William Golding's *Lord of the Flies* is on the surface an adventure story, while on the allegorical level it is a warning against lawlessness and how easy it is for people to be corrupted by power.

Allusions are an efficient way to communicate because one reference may trigger readers' minds to think of a whole story or extended idea. Robert Cormier's title *I Am the Cheese* alludes to the old nursery song and game, "The Farmer in the Dell." Readers who will get the most from Cormier's writing are those who will connect the family's name of *Farmer* to the nursery song and its closing lines of "The cheese stands alone" and "The rat takes the cheese."

Characterization is what an author does to help readers know and identify with the characters in a story. Among the techniques that authors use are providing physical descriptions, letting readers know what the characters say and what others say to and about them, showing the characters in action, showing how others relate to them, and revealing what they are thinking. **Dynamic** characters are those who undergo some change during the story, while **static** characters remain basically the same. The main characters in a story are more likely to be dynamic than are supporting characters because the author has more space in which to show how the character changes. Not all main characters change, however, especially if the focus is outside the character as with some high-action adventure stories or mysteries.

Dénouements come at the ends of stories; their purpose is to wrap up loose ends and to let the reader down after the excitement of the climax. Orson Scott Card uses a family's nicknames to soften the ending of *The Lost Boys: A Novel* by alluding to an afterlife. The Fletcher family members all have nicknames that started with Step and his wife, Deanne, calling each other *Junkman* and *Fishlady*. The children were Stevie known as *Doorman*, Robbie known as *Robot* or *Roadbug*, Elizabeth known as *Betsy* or sometimes *Betsy Wetsy*, and the new baby Jeremy known as *Zap*. After Stevie's abduction and murder is discovered on a traumatic Christmas Eve,

Card concludes the story by saying that one other thing was lost on that Christmas Eve: their nicknames. No one made a conscious decision, it was just that they were part of a set, and it didn't seem right to use only some of them. "But someday they would use all those names when *Doorman* met them on the other side."

Dialect is an effective device for setting characters apart from mainstream speakers, but difficulties in spelling, printing, and reading mean that most authors use it sparingly. It might be in the wording as when Hal Borland wrote in *When the Legends Die,* "The Ute people have lived many generations, many grandmothers, in that land," or it might be in grammar and pronunciation as when such African-American writers as Ntozake Shange, Maya Angelou, Virginia Hamilton, Toni Morrison, and Walter Dean Myers use black dialect for a variety of purposes including the communication of pride in their ethnic heritage.

Didacticism occurs when writers tack an obvious moral or a lesson onto a story. Actually, most people who write for young readers want to teach lessons or impart some kind of wisdom or understanding. When something is described as being didactic, it means that the lesson was so obvious that it detracted from the story.

Escape Literature is that which requires a minimum of intellectual energy so that readers can relax and enjoy the story with little or no intention of gaining insights or learning new information. Many **formula** mysteries, romances, and even horror stories can be read as escape literature.

Euphemisms are circumlocutions. The word is cognate with *euphonious* meaning "pleasing to the ear." Modern writers usually prefer direct speech, but Margaret Craven's title *I Heard the Owl Call My Name* is more intriguing than a bald statement such as "I knew I was going to die," while Hemingway's title *For Whom the Bell Tolls* is both more euphemistic and euphonious than "the one who has died."

Figurative language is that which has additional meanings to the ones given in standard usage. **Metaphors** are a kind of figurative language based on meaning, while **alliteration** (the repetition of consonants), **assonance** (the repetition of vowels), **rhyme** (the repeating of sounds), and **rhythm** and **cadence** (the patterning of sounds) are examples of figurative language made interesting because of their phonetic qualities.

Foreshadowing is the dropping of hints to prepare readers for what is ahead. Its purpose is not give away the ending but to increase excitement and suspense and to keep readers from feeling manipulated. For example, readers would feel cheated if the problems in a realistic novel are suddenly solved by a group of aliens and there has been no foreshadowing that the story is science fiction.

Formula literature is almost entirely predictable because it consists of variations on a limited number of plots and themes. While to some extent this could be said of most literature, the difference is a matter of degree. Many of the situation comedies, crime shows, and adventure shows on television are formula pieces, as are many of the books that young people—and adults—enjoy reading.

In media res is Latin for "in the midst of things." It names the technique of bringing the reader directly into the middle of a story, usually followed by **flashbacks** to fill in the missing details.

Literature with a Capital L is set apart from, or has a degree of excellence not found in, the masses of printed material that every day roll from the presses. Such literature rewards study not only because of its content but also because of its style, universality, permanence, and the congeniality of the ideas expressed.

Metaphors are among the most common kinds of figurative language. With metaphors, basically dissimilar things are likened to each other. A metaphor can consist of only a word or a phrase (a *head* of lettuce or the *outskirts* of a city), or it can be a series of interwoven ideas running through an entire book as when Walter Dean Myers in *Fallen Angels* compares the Vietnam war to various aspects of movies or television. While some people distinguish between metaphors and **similes** (the use of *like* or *as* makes similes literally true), similes, along with **symbols**, and **allegories**, are in a general sense particular kinds of metaphors.

Mode is sometimes divided into comedy, romance, irony and satire, and tragedy. Together these make up the story of everyone's life, and in literature as in life, they are interrelated, flowing one into the other.

Narrative hooks are the techniques that authors use to entice readers into a story. It might be a catchy title as in Douglas Adams's *The Hitchhiker's Guide to the Galaxy*, a question as in Richard Peck's *Are You in the House Alone?*, or an intriguing first couple of paragraphs as in Paul Zindel's *The Pigman*.

> Now Lorraine can blame all the other things on me, but she was the one who picked out the Pigman's phone number. If you ask me, I think he would have died anyway. Maybe we speeded things up a little, but you really can't say we murdered him.
>
> Not murdered him.

Open endings are those that leave readers not knowing what happens to the characters. For example Alice Childress in *A Hero Ain't Nothin' But a Sandwich* did not want to predict either that Benjie would become a confirmed drug addict or that he would go straight because she wanted readers to think about the fact that boys in his situation turn both ways. Books with open endings are good for group discussions because they inspire involved readers to consider the options.

Personification is the giving of human characteristics to something that is not human. For example, in Maya Angelou's *All God's Children Need Traveling Shoes*, she writes, "July and August of 1962 stretched out like fat men yawning after a sumptuous dinner. They had every right to gloat, for they had eaten me up. Gobbled me down. Consumed my spirit, not in a wild rush, but slowly, with the obscene patience of certain victors."

Plots are the skeletons on which the other aspects of a story hang. They are the conflicts and the problems faced by the main characters. The most exciting plots are the ones in which the action is continually rising, building suspense, and finally leading to some sort of **climax**. In contrast to plots with rising actions are those that are defined as **episodic** because they are accounts of a series of events as with such memoirs as James Herriot's *All Creatures Great and Small* and Maya Angelou's *I Know Why the Caged Bird Sings*.

Point of view determines how far away from the story and from what direction the author stands. The point of view that gives the author the most freedom is the one called **omniscient** or "all knowing." Authors can plant themselves anywhere in the story, including inside characters' minds, to make their observations. With **first person point of view**, the author speaks through the voice of a particular character. While this has the advantage of sounding authentic and personal, only one character's thoughts and observations can be given. Some authors get around this limitation by writing different chapters through the voices of different characters as did

Paul Zindel in *The Pigman* and Alice Childress in *A Hero Ain't Nothin' But a Sandwich*. **Third person point-of-view** is more objective and is used for nonfiction as well as for many fictional stories. In YA books, the third person narrator is often a character in the story who is writing about another "more interesting" or "more extreme" character.

Protagonists are the main characters in stories, the ones with which readers identify. Novels for young readers usually include only one or two protagonists because the stories are shorter and less complex than something like Leo Tolstoy's *War and Peace*.

Protagonist against another is the kind of plot in which two people are in conflict with each other as are Louise and Caroline in Katherine Paterson's *Jacob Have I Loved* and Rambo and the sheriff in David Morrell's *First Blood*. The character who opposes the protagonist is called the **antagonist**.

Protagonist against nature stories are often accounts of true adventures such as Piers Paul Read's *Alive: The Story of the Andes Survivors*, Thor Heyerdahl's *The "RA" Expeditions*, Steve Callahan's *Adrift: Seventy-Six Days Lost at Sea*, and Robin Graham's *Dove*.

Protagonist against self is a common plot in young adult literature because so many stories recount rites-of-passage in which the protagonist comes to a new understanding or level of maturity. In Paula Fox's *One-Eyed Cat*, the conflict takes place inside the mind and heart of 11-year-old Ned who has to come to terms with the fact that when he "tried out" his new gun, he partially blinded his neighbor's cat.

Protagonist against society stories often feature members of minority groups whose personal struggles relate to tensions between their ethnic groups and the larger society. Examples include the Hasidic Jews in Chaim Potok's *My Name Is Asher Lev* and *The Chosen*, the Hispanic characters in Gary Soto's *Baseball in April* and *Jesse*, the Native American characters in Louise Erdrich's *Love Medicine*, and the Korean-American characters in Marie Lee's *Finding My Voice*.

Setting—the context of time and place—is more important in some genres than in others. Fantasies are usually set in the far past or in some place where people have never been, while most science fiction stories are set in the future or in outer space. **Integral** settings are those in which the plot or the problem is tied to the setting as in a protagonist-against-nature story, a historical fiction piece, or a regional story in which characters' searches for their identity cannot be separated from the regions in which they grew up. **Backdrop** settings are like stage sets. They give a general indication of time and place, but do not play an essential or unique part in the plot. The most common backdrop setting is that of a high school because school is the everyday business of teenagers. The fact that there are only so many ways to describe stairways, rest rooms, lockers, cafeterias, classrooms, and parking lots is one of the things that gives a sameness to books for this age group.

Stereotypes are named after a printing process through which an image is created over and over again. When reviewers say that an author's characters are stereotypes, they are probably making a negative criticism. However, at least some characters must be stereotyped because stories would fall of their own weight if authors had to start from scratch in developing each character. For the sake of efficiency, many background characters are stereotypes. To solve the problem of always having the same people stereotyped, contemporary authors are making an effort to feature as main characters many of those who have previously been ignored or relegated to stereotypes.

Stock characters are stereotypes. Authors use them in the way that shoppers pluck items from the well-stocked shelves of grocery stores. While a laughingstock is an object of ridicule, other stock characters include villains, tramps, mothers-in-law, bad boys, and little princesses.

Style is the way a story is written in contrast to what it is about. No two authors have exactly the same style because with writing, just as with appearance, behavior, and personal belongings, style consists of the unique blending of all the choices each individual makes. From situation to situation, these choices may differ, but they are enough alike that the styles of particular authors, such as Kurt Vonnegut, Jr., Richard Brautigan, and E. L. Doctorow are recognizable from book to book. Style is also influenced by the nature of the story being told. For example, Ursula K. LeGuin used a different style when she wrote the realistic *Very Far Away From Anywhere Else* from the one she used when she wrote her fantasy *A Wizard of Earthsea*. Nevertheless, in both books she relied on the particular writing techniques that she likes and is skilled at using. J. D. Salinger's *The Catcher in the Rye* has had such an influence on the style of writing about young protagonists that every year promotional materials or reviews compare two or three new books to *Catcher*.

Theme is what ties a story together and answers such questions as what the story means and what there is to think about when it's all over. Some authors are explicit in developing a theme, even expressing part of it in the title as did Maya Angelou with *All God's Children Need Traveling Shoes* and Virginia Euwer Wolff with *Make Lemonade*. Books may have more than one theme, but usually the secondary themes are less important to the story.

Tone is determined by the author's attitude toward subject, characters, and readers. Biblical language may lend weight and dignity to a book as with James Herriot's title *All Creatures Great and Small* or Claude Brown's *Manchild in the Promised Land*. **Exaggeration** or **hyperbole** may communicate a flip tone as in Ellen Conford's title of *If This Is Love, I'll Take Spaghetti* and Ron Koertge's *Where the Kissing Never Stops*. Because most television shows are aimed at general adult audiences, even though they are viewed by all ages, young people have come to expect the same straight-forward tone that is used with adults. They generally interpret both **didactic** (overly preachy) and **nostalgic** tones as condescending.

APPENDIX

B

Book Selection Guides

The following sources are designed to aid professionals in the selection and evaluation of books and other materials for young adults. We attempted to include sources with widely varying emphases, but, in addition to these sources—most of which appear at regular intervals—many specialized lists are prepared by committees and individuals in response to current and/or local needs. Readers are advised to check on the availability of such lists with librarians and teachers. Also, publications for adults such as *The New York Times Book Review*, give attention to books for children and teenagers, especially in the weeks prior to Christmas when people are looking for gift ideas.

The ALAN Review (Assembly on Literature for Adolescents). National Council of Teachers of English. Order from NCTE, 1111 W. Kenyon Road, Urbana, IL 61801. Subscribers need not be members of NCTE.

> Since 1973, this publication, which is devoted entirely to adolescent literature, has appeared three times a year. Current editor is Pamela S. Carroll, 209 MCH, Florida State University, Tallahassee, FL 32306–4490. Each issue contains approximately fifty "Clip and File" reviews written by ALAN members who are mostly secondary school teachers or librarians. Also included are feature articles, news announcements, and occasional reviews of professional books.

Booklist. American Library Association, 50 E. Huron St., Chicago, IL 60611. Web site: http://www.ala.org

> Reviews, which constitute a recommendation for library purchase, are written by professional staff members, who also attach a *YA* designation to selected adult titles. Hazel Rochman is the current YA editor, while Michael Cart writes a "Carte Blanche" column. The "Books for Youth" section is divided for older, middle, and young readers. Exceptional books are given starred reviews and sometimes special features. For example, the starred review of Sonya Sones' *Stop Pretending: What Happened When My Big Sister Went Crazy* (HarperCollins, 1999) was accompanied by a "Read-alikes" box on "Mental Illness and the Sibling Connection," which gave annotations for seven other recommended books. An end-of-the-year "Editors' Choice" issue is especially useful as are the lists of "Best Books" com-

piled by various committees affiliated with the American Library Association. Check the Web site for several lists related to young adults.

Books for the Teen Age. Published annually by Office of Young Adult Services, New York Public Library. Order from Office of Branch Libraries: New York Public Library, 455 Fifth Avenue, New York, NY 10016.

> The over 1,000 recommendations in this booklet come from the young adult librarians in the eighty branches of the New York Public Library. Annotations are minimal, grouping is by subject with titles and authors indexed.

Books for You: An Annotated Booklist for Senior High, Your Reading: An Annotated Booklist for Middle School Junior High, and *High Interest—Easy Reading: An Annotated Booklist for Middle School and Senior High School.* National Council of Teachers of English.

> Committees of English teachers put these books together every few years. They are written for direct use by students and contain concise annotations for between 200 and a thousand recommended books organized under such categories as "Growing Up," "Issues of Our Time," and "Sports."

Bulletin of the Center for Children's Books. University of Illinois Press, 1324 S. Oak Street, Champaign, IL 61820. Web site:

> http://edfu.lis.uiuc.edu/puboff/bccb

> This is the journal founded by Zena Sutherland and published by the University of Chicago Press. When Chicago's Graduate Library School closed, the *Bulletin* moved to the University of Illinois where Janice M. Del Negro became the editor. In each issue, staff members review approximately sixty new books, with approximately twenty being identified as appropriate for grades 9–12. Reviews are coded with *R* standing for "recommended," *Ad* for "additional title if topic is needed," *M* for "marginal" and *NR* for "not recommended." The Web site reprints starred reviews and each month features a theme-based list of a dozen recommended titles.

Children's Literature in Education: An International Quarterly Kluwer Academic/Human Sciences Press, 233 Spring St., New York, NY 10013–1578.

> This British/American cooperative effort is edited by Margaret Mackey from the University of Alberta, Edmonton, Alberta, Canada, and Geoff Fox from the University of Exeter, Devon, England. The editors show a preference for substantive analysis rather than pedagogical advice or quick once-overs. A good proportion of the articles are about YA authors and their works; for example, the editors plan to include a series of occasional articles about recent controversial titles. The first such article published in June, 1999, was by David Rudd, "A Young Person's Guide to the Fictions of *Junk,*" Melvin Burgess's book which in the United States was titled *Smack* instead of *Junk.*

English Journal. National Council of Teachers of English. 1111 Kenyon Rd., Urbana, Illinois 61801. Editorial correspondence to Virginia Monseau, 309 Tod Hall, Youngstown State University, One University Plaza, Youngstown, OH 44555–0001.

> This is the largest journal published by NCTE with its audience being mainly high school English teachers. It appears six times a year and frequently has articles about young adult literature. Chris Crowe edits a regular column.

Horn Book Magazine. Horn Book, Inc. 11 Beacon St., Suite 1000, Boston, MA 02108. Web site: http://www.hbook.com

> Since 1924, the *Horn Book Magazine* has been devoted to the critical analysis of children's literature. Many of the articles are written by noted authors, while the book reviews are staff

written. In the November/December, 1999 issue, ten of the fifty-four books that were reviewed were for young adults. Editor Roger Sutton wrote about the possible effects of HarperCollins purchasing Morrow Junior Books and closing the Lothrop, Lee, and Shepard line, while Patty Campbell in her "Sand in the Oyster" column devoted five pages to a discussion of Walter Dean Myers's *Monster*. Both Sutton and Campbell have been young adult librarians, which has served to increase the attention given to YA books. *Horn Book* co-sponsors the Boston Globe/Horn Book Awards and also prints a yearly "Fanfare" list of best books.

Journal of Adolescent and Adult Literacy. International Reading Association, 800 Barksdale Rd., Box 8139, Newark, DE 19711–8139.

The audience is high school reading teachers. Although most of the articles are reports on research in the teaching of reading, some articles focus on reading interests and literature and reviews of new young adult books are often included.

Journal of Youth Services in Libraries. American Library Association, 50 E. Huron St., Chicago, IL 60611. Web site: http://www.ala.org

Before 1987, this journal was named *Top of the News*. It covers both children's and YA literature as well as research and developments of interest to librarians.

Junior High School Library Catalog and *Senior High School Library Catalog*. H. W. Wilson Company, 950 University Avenue, Bronx, NY 10452.

These reference sources are designed to assist librarians in building basic collections. They are divided into two parts. First comes an annotated listing by Dewey Decimal Number for nonfiction, author's last name for fiction, and author's or editor's last name for story collections. The second part relists all books alphabetically by author, title, and subject. This outstanding reference tool is revised approximately every five years, with yearly supplements in between.

Kirkus Reviews. Kirkus Service, Inc., 200 Park Avenue South, New York, NY 10003.

Kirkus reviews are approximately 200 words long and are relied on throughout the publishing industry. The big advantage is timeliness and completeness made possible by twice-a-month issues.

The New Advocate. Christopher-Gordon Publishers Inc., 480 Washington St., Norwood MA 02062.

Published five times a year, the purpose of this new journal is to encourage teachers to work with literature. Editors are Kathy Short and Dana Fox from the University of Arizona.

Publishers Weekly. 245 W. 17th St., New York, NY 10011. Web site: http://www.publishers weekly.com

While the focus is on the general world of adult book publishing, much of the information is relevant to anyone working with books; for example, what will company mergers mean to readers, what are the current best sellers, and who are the prize winners. The November 22, 1999 issue included a feature article on Beverly Cleary, Kevin Henkes, David Wiesner, and Susan Cooper under the title "New Books by Old Pros." In the "Authors Series," eleven pages were devoted to Michael Crichton, and there was also information on Peter Jennings and Todd Brewster's new book *The Century for Young People*. Staff members write the reviews, which include some for children ages 12-up.

School Library Journal. Editorial correspondence to *SLJ* Editor-in-Chief Renée Olson, 245 W. 17th St., New York, NY 10011; subscription correspondence to P.O. Box 16388 North Hollywood, CA 80322–7559.

SLJ is the most comprehensive of the review media trying in monthly installments to review all books published for young people. Advertisements and feature articles provide good information along with the reviews, which are written by a panel of 400 librarians. A starred review and/or inclusion on the December best books list signifies an exceptional book. Web site: http://www.slj.com

TALL (Teaching and Learning Literature with Children and Young Adults). Essmont Publishing, P.O. Box 186, Brandon, Vermont 05733–0186.

Aimed at teachers, this journal is published five times during the school year. Its goal is "to promote the reading of literature and engagement in the genuine literary experience." It reviews books and has articles about teaching and literature.

VOYA (Voice of Youth Advocates). Scarecrow Press, Inc. 4720A Boston Way, Lanham, MD 20706.

Published every other month, this is a journal prepared mainly for librarians who work with teenagers. It was founded in 1978 by Mary K. Chelton and Dorothy Broderick and is now edited by Cathi Dunn MacRae. Besides reviewing new books, it consistently has good articles on current trends in literature and youth services in libraries. The editors and contributors do an especially good job with fantasy and science fiction.

APPENDIX C

Some Outstanding Books and Articles About Young Adult Literature

The upcoming list represents our personal choices. We followed our ground rules of the first edition. That may explain, if not justify, why some works were included or excluded. Brief explanations are given where titles are not self-explanatory.

1. Books or articles were primarily about young adult literature, not on the psychology of the young, cultural milieu, literary history, or literary criticism.
2. Books or articles had to cover more than one author. No matter how good articles were on Cynthia Voigt or Leon Garfield or Robert Cormier, we ignored them in favor of articles with broader implications.
3. Books and articles had to excite us.
4. No books and articles were chosen to balance out the list. We chose what we did because we believe in them.
5. Readers will, again, find no books or articles by Nilsen or Donelson. Those desperate to see our work included will search in vain. Readers may continue to assume that we believe none of our work belongs in a list of "outstanding" works, that we long for professional oblivion, or that we are modest to a fault.

Books

Histories of Young Adult Literature

Avery, Gillian. *Behold the Child: American Children and Their Books, 1621–1922*. London: Bodley Head, 1994.

Avery, Gillian. *Childhood's Pattern: A Study of the Heroes and Heroines of Children's Fiction, 1770-1950*. London: Hodder and Stoughton, 1975.

Billman, Carol. *The Secret of the Stratemeyer Syndicate: Nancy Drew, the Hardy Boys, and the Million Dollar Fiction Factory*. New York: Ungar, 1986.

Bingham, Jane and Grayce Scholt. *Fifteen Centuries of Children's Literature: An Annotated Chronology of British and American Works in Historical Context*. Westport, CT: Greenwood Press, 1980.

Bratton, J. S. *The Impact of Victorian Children's Fiction*. Totowa, NJ: Barnes and Noble Books, 1981.

Cadogan, Mary and Patricia Craig. *You're a Brick, Angela! A New Look at Girls' Fiction from 1839 to 1975*. London: Victor Gollancz, 1976. Still one of the most delightful and wittiest books on girls' reading.

Campbell, Patricia J. *Sex Education Books for Young Adults, 1892–1979*. New York: R. R. Bowker, 1979. Always accurate, often funny.

Cart, Michael. *From Romance to Realism: 50 Years of Growth and Change in Young Adult Literature*. New

York: HarperCollins, 1996. One of the best books in the field in recent years.

Children's Fiction, 1876–1984. 2 vols. New York: R. R. Bowker, 1984.

Crouch, Marcus. *The Nesbit Tradition: The Children's Novel in England, 1945–1970.* London: Ernest Benn, 1972.

Crouch, Marcus. *Treasure Seekers and Borrowers: Children's Books in Britain 1900–1960.* London: Library Association, 1962.

Darling, Richard. *The Rise of Children's Book Reviewing in America: 1865–1881.* New York: R. R. Bowker, 1968. A fascinating study of early children's and YA books, book reviewing, and book reviewers.

Darton, F. J. Harvey. *Children's Books in England: Five Centuries of Social Use.* 2nd ed. Cambridge: Cambridge University Press, 1958. First published in 1932. Informative, if a bit stuffy.

Deane, Paul. *Mirrors of American Culture: Children's Fiction Series in the Twentieth Century.* Metuchen, NJ: Scarecrow Press, 1991.

Demers, Patricia. *A Garland from the Golden Age: An Anthology of Children's Literature from 1850 to 1900.* Toronto: Oxford University Press, 1983.

Dyer, Carolyn Stewart and Nancy Tillman Romalov, eds. *Rediscovering Nancy Drew.* Iowa City: University of Iowa Press, 1995. Papers from the 1993 Nancy Drew conference.

Egoff, Sheila. *The Republic of Childhood: A Critical Guide to Canadian Children's Literature in English.* 2nd ed. Toronto: Oxford University Press, 1975.

Egoff, Sheila. *Worlds Within: Children's Fantasy from the Middle Ages.* Chicago: American Library Association, 1988.

Foster, Shirley, and Judy Simons, eds. *What Katy Read: Feminist Re-Readings of "Classic" Stories for Girls.* Iowa City: University of Iowa Press, 1995.

Girls' Series Books: A Checklist of Hardback Books Published 1900–1975. Minneapolis: Children's Literature Research Collections, University of Minnesota Library, 1978. Basic for any work with girls' series books.

Gorham, Deborah. *The Victorian Girl and the Feminine Ideal.* Bloomington: Indiana University Press, 1982.

Griswold, Jerry. *Audacious Kids: Coming of Age in America's Classic Children's Books.* New York: Oxford University Press, 1992. Audacious indeed, but worth reading.

Howarth, Patrick. *Play Up and Play the Game: The Heroes of Popular Fiction.* London: Eyre Methuen, 1973.

Hudson, Harry K. *A Bibliography of Hard-Cover Boys' Books,* rev. ed. Tampa, FL: Data Print, 1977. Basic for any work with boys' books (and fun to skim through).

Jackson, Mary V. *Engines of Instruction, Mischief, and Magic: Children's Literature in England from Its Beginnings to 1839.* Lincoln. NE: University of Nebraska Press, 1989. Beautifully illustrated background material.

Johnson, Deidre. *Edward Stratemeyer and the Stratemeyer Syndicate.* New York: Twayne, 1993.

Johnson, Deidre, ed. *Stratemeyer Pseudonyms and Series Books: An Annotated Checklist of Stratemeyer and Stratemeyer Syndicate Publications.* Westport, CT: Greenwood, 1982.

Kiefer, Monica. *American Children Through Their Books, 1700–1835.* Philadelphia: University of Pennsylvania Press, 1948.

Kloet, Christine A. *After Alice: A Hundred Years of Children's Reading in Britain.* London: Library Association, 1977. Published for an exhibition at the Victoria and Albert Museum of Childhood, 1977–1978.

MacLeod, Anne Scott. *A Moral Tale: Children's Fiction and American Culture, 1820–1860.* Hamden, CT: Archon Books, 1975.

Mason, Bobbie Ann. *The Girl Sleuth: A Feminist Guide.* Old Westbury, NY: Feminist Press, 1975. Perceptive, chatty, and witty words about series books, especially Nancy Drew.

Meigs, Cornelia, et al. *A Critical History of Children's Literature,* rev. ed. New York: Macmillan, 1969. Encyclopedic history of YA literature (and children's literature, of course) from the beginnings.

Michaels, Carolyn Clugston. *Children's Book Collecting.* Hamden, CT: Shoe String Press, 1993. Marvelously entertaining.

Mitchell, Sally. *The New Girl: Girls' Culture in England 1880–1915.* New York: Columbia University Press, 1995.

Musgrave, P. W. *From Brown to Bunter: The Life and Death of the School Story.* London: Routledge and Kegan Paul, 1985.

Nye, Russel. *The Unembarrassed Muse: The Popular Arts in America.* New York: Dial, 1970. Impressive coverage of almost all popular culture.

Quigly, Isabel. *The Heirs of Tom Brown: The English School Story.* London: Chatto and Windus, 1982.

Reynolds, Kimberley. *Girls Only? Gender and Popular Children's Fiction in Britain, 1880–1910.* Philadelphia: Temple University Press, 1990.

Rowbotham, Judith. *Good Girls Make Good Wives: Guidance for Girls in Victorian England.* Oxford, England: Basil Blackwell, 1989.

Salmon, Edward. *Juvenile Literature as It Is.* London: Drane, 1888. One of the seminal books in the field, the first and still one of the best.

Sloane, William. *Children's Books in England and America in the Seventeenth Century.* New York: Columbia University Press, 1955.

Smith, Elva S. *The History of Children's Literature: A Syllabus with Selected Bibliographies,* revised and edited by Margaret Hodges and Susan Steinfirst. Chicago: American Library Association, 1980.

Townsend, John Rowe. *25 Years of British Children's Books.* London: National Book League, 1977. Not easily found but this sixty-page pamphlet is worth the search.

Townsend, John Rowe. *Written for Children: An Outline*

of *English-Language Children's Literature,* 3rd ed. Philadelphia: Lippincott, 1988.

Criticism of Young Adult Literature

Bauer, Marion Dane. *What's Your Story? A Young Person's Guide to Writing Fiction.* New York: Clarion, 1992.

Broderick, Dorothy M. *Images of the Black in Children's Fiction.* New York: R. R. Bowker, 1973. Racism in YA literature.

Cameron, Eleanor. *The Green and Burning Tree: On the Writing and Enjoyment of Children's Books.* New York: Dutton, 1993.

Carter, Betty and Richard Abrahamson. *Nonfiction for Young Adults: From Delight to Wisdom.* Phoenix: Oryx Press, 1990.

Chambers, Aidan. *Reluctant Reader.* London: Pergamon Press, 1969. This reads better the older it gets. Sympathetic and practical ideas about getting hard-to-reach readers to read.

Children's Literature Review. Detroit: Gale Resesarch Co., 1976–. A continuing series and a helpful source of material on YA books.

Christian-Smith, Linda K. *Becoming a Woman Through Romance.* New York: Routledge, 1990.

Contemporary Literary Criticism. Detroit: Gale Research, 1973–.

Dixon, Bob. *Catching Them Young: Political Ideas in Children's Fiction.* London: Pluto Press, 1977.

Dixon, Bob. *Catching Them Young: Sex, Race and Class in Children's Fiction.* London: Pluto Press, 1977.

Dresang, Eliza T. *Radical Change: Books for Youth in a Digital Age.* New York: H. W. Wilson, 1999.

Egoff, Sheila A. *Thursday's Child: Trends and Patterns in Contemporary Children's Literature.* Chicago: American Library Association, 1981. One of the great books in the field.

Ettinger, John R. and Diana L. Spirit, eds. *Choosing Books for Young People, Volume 2: A Guide to Criticism and Bibliography, 1976–1984.* Chicago: American Library Association, 1982.

Fisher, Margery. *The Bright Face of Danger.* London: Hodder and Hodder, 1986.

Fox, Geoff, et al., eds. *Writers, Critics, and Children.* New York: Agathon Press, 1976. Articles from *Children's Literature In Education.*

Harrison, Barbara and Gregory Maguire, eds. *Innocence and Experience: Essays and Conversations on Children's Literature.* New York: Lothrop, Lee and Shepard, 1987.

Hazard, Paul. *Books, Children and Men,* translated by Marguerite Mitchell. Boston: Horn Book, 1944. A seminal book impossible to overrate.

Hearne, Betsy and Marilyn Kaye, eds. *Celebrating Children's Books: Essays on Children's Literature in Honor of Zena Sutherland.* New York: Lothrop, Lee and Shepard, 1981.

Hendrickson, Linnea. *Children's Literature: A Guide to the Criticism.* Boston: G. K. Hall, 1987.

Horning, Kathleen T. *From Cover to Cover: Evaluating and Reviewing Children's Books.* New York: Harper-Collins, 1997.

Howard, Elizabeth F. *America as Story: Historical Fiction for the Secondary Schools.* Chicago: American Library Association, 1988.

Hunt, Peter. *Criticism, Theory, and Children's Literature.* Oxford: Basil Blackwell, 1991.

Hunt, Peter. *An Introduction to Children's Literature.* New York: Oxford University Press, 1994.

Hunter, Mollie. *The Pied Piper Syndrome and Other Essays.* New York: HarperCollins. 1992.

Hunter, Mollie. *Talent Is Not Enough: Mollie Hunter on Writing for Children.* New York: Harper and Row, 1976.

Inglis, Fred. *The Promise of Happiness: Value and Meaning in Children's Fiction.* Cambridge: Cambridge University Press, 1981.

Kelly, Patricia P. and Robert C. Small, Jr., eds., *Two Decades of the ALAN Review.* Urbana, IL: National Council of Teachers of English, 1999. Articles from the *ALAN Review.*

Kohn, Rita, compiler. *Once Upon . . . A Time for Young People and Their Books: An Annotated Resource Guide.* Metuchen, NJ: Scarecrow Press, 1986.

Lesnick-Oberstein, Karin. *Children's Literature: Criticism and the Fictional Child.* Oxford: Clarendon Press, 1994.

Lynn, Ruth Nadelman. *Fantasy Literature for Children and Young Adults.* New York: R. R. Bowker, 1989.

MacCann, Donnarae and Gloria Woodward, eds. *The Black American in Books for Children: Readings on Racism.* Metuchen, NJ: 1972.

Peck, Richard. *Love and Death at the Mall: Teaching and Writing for the Literate Young.* New York: Delacorte, 1994.

Shields, Nancy E. *Index to Literary Criticism for Young Adults.* Metuchen, NJ: Scarecrow Press, 1988.

Sloan, Glenna. *The Child as Critic.* New York: Teachers College Press, 1975. Northrop Frye's theories applied to children's and YA literature.

Soter, Anna. *Young Adult Literature and New Literary Theory.* New York: Teachers College Press, 1999. Likely *the* book in the field for years to come.

Street, Douglas, ed. *Children's Novels and the Movies.* New York: Ungar, 1984.

Sutherland, Zena. *The Arbuthnot Lectures: 1970–1979.* Chicago: American Library Association, 1980.

Tucker, Nicholas, ed. *Suitable for Children? Controversies in Children's Literature.* Berkeley: University of California Press, 1976.

Yolen, Jane. *Touch Magic: Fantasy, Faerie, and Folklore in the Literature of Childhood.* New York: Philomel, 1981.

Libraries and Young Adult Literature

Bodart, Joni. *Booktalking and School Visiting for Young Adult Audiences.* New York: H. W. Wilson, 1980.

Bodart, Joni. *Booktalk 2: Booktalking for All Ages and Audiences*. New York: H. W. Wilson, 1985.

Books for the Teen Age. New York: New York Public Library. Published annually.

Carr, Jo, ed. *Beyond Fact: Nonfiction for Children and Young People*. Chicago: American Librarian Association, 1982.

Edwards, Margaret A. *The Fair Garden and the Swarm of Beasts: The Library and the Young Adult*, rev. ed. New York: Hawthorn, 1974. Some of the problems but mostly the joys of working with YAs.

Eiss, Harry, ed. *Literature for Young People on War and Peace: An Annotated Bibliography*. New York: Greenwood, 1989.

Field, Carolyn W., ed. *Special Collections in Children's Literature*. Chicago: American Library Association, 1982.

Gillespie, John T. *More Juniorplots: A Guide for Teachers and Librarians*. New York: R. R. Bowker, 1977.

Gillespie, John T. and Diana L. Lembo. *Juniorplots: A Book Talk Manual for Teachers and Librarians*. New York: R. R. Bowker, 1967.

Gillespie, John T. and Corinne Naden. *Juniorplots 3: A Book Talk Guide for Use with Readers Ages 12–16*. New York: R. R. Bowker, 1987.

Gillespie, John T. and Corinne Naden. *Seniorplots: A Book Talk Guide for Use with Readers Ages 15–18*. New York: R. R. Bowker, 1989.

Hinckley, Karen and Barbara Hinckley. *America's Best Sellers: A Reader's Guide to Popular Fiction*. Bloomington: Indiana University Press, 1989.

Marshall, Margaret R. *Libraries and Literature for Teenagers*. London: Andre Deutsch, 1975.

Rochman, Hazel. *Tales of Love and Terror: Booktalking the Classics, Old and New*. Chicago: American Library Association, 1987.

Roe, Ernest. *Teachers, Librarians, and Children: A Study of Librarians in Education*. Hamden, CT: Archon Books, 1965. Superb, maybe the best of the lot. First published in Australia.

Rosenberg, Betty. *Genreflecting: A Guide to Reading Interests in Genre Fiction*. 2nd ed. Littleton, CO: Libraries Unlimited, 1987.

Spencer, Pam. *What Do Young Adults Read Next? A Reader's Guide to Fiction for Young Adults*. Detroit: Gale Research, 1994. Invaluable for finding almost anything kids might like.

Taylor, Desmond. *The Juvenile Novels of World War II: An Annotated Bibliography*. Westport, CT: Greenwood, 1994.

English Classrooms and Young Adult Literature

Beach, Richard. *A Teacher's Introduction to Reader-Response Theories*. Urbana, IL: National Council of Teachers of English, 1993.

Beach, Richard and James Marshall. *Teaching Literature in the Secondary School*. San Diego, CA: Harcourt Brace Jovanovich, 1991.

Brown, Jean A. and Elaine C. Stephens. *Teaching Young Adult Literature: Sharing the Connection*. Belmont, CA: Wadsworth, 1995.

Burton, Dwight L. *Literature Study in the High Schools*, 3rd ed. New York: Holt, 1970. For many teachers and librarians, *the* book that introduced them to YA books.

Carlsen, G. Robert. *Books and the Teen-Age Reader*, 2nd ed. New York: Harper and Row, 1980.

Corcoran, Bill and Emrys Evans, eds. *Readers, Texts, Teachers*. Upper Monclair, NJ: Boynton/Cook, 1987. A fine collection of criticism and pedagogy.

Crowley, Sharon. *A Teacher's Introduction to Deconstruction*, Urbana, IL: National Council of Teachers of English, 1989.

Evans, Tricia. *Teaching English*. London: Croom Helm, 1982.

Fader, Daniel. *The New Hooked on Books*. New York: Berkley, 1976. First published in 1966 and revised in 1968, Fader's book made English teachers take YA books seriously. The booklists are dated, but Fader's enthusiasm and caring are not.

Farrell, Edmund J. and James R. Squire, eds. *Transactions With Literature: A Fifty-Year Perspective*. Urbana, IL: National Council of Teachers of English, 1990. Essays honoring Louise M. Rosenblatt.

Hertz, Sarah K., and Donald R. Gallo. *From Hinton to Hamlet: Building Bridges Between Young Adult Literature and the Classics*. Westport, CT: Greenwood, 1996.

Marshall, James D., Peter Smagorinsky, and Michael W. Smith. *The Language of Interpretation: Patterns of Discourse in Discussions of Literature*. NCTE Research Report No. 27. Urbana, IL: National Council of Teachers of English, 1995.

Monseau, Virginia R. and Gary M. Salvner, eds. *Reading Their World: The Young Adult Novel in the Classroom*. Portsmouth, NH: Boynton/Cook, 1992.

Moran, Charles and Elizabeth F. Penfield, eds. *Conversations: Contemporary Critical Theory and the Teaching of Literature*. Urbana, IL: National Council of Teachers of English, 1990.

Ohanian, Susan. *Who's in Charge? A Teacher Speaks Her Mind*. Portsmouth, NH: Boynton/Cook, 1994. Brilliant, witty, and profound.

Peck, David. *Novels of Initiation: A Guidebook for Teaching Literature to Adolescents*. New York: Teachers College, 1989.

Probst, Robert E. *Response and Analysis: Teaching Literature in Junior and Senior High School*. Portsmouth, NH: Boynton/Cook, Heinemann, 1988. A rarity; brilliant pedagogy with understandable and usable material on literary criticism.

Protherough, Robert, Judith Atkinson, and John Fawcett. *The Effective Teaching of English*. London: Longman, 1989. The best text today on teaching English.

Purves, Alan C., Theresa Rogers, and Anna O. Soter. *How Porcupines Make Love II: Teaching a Response-Centered Literature Curriculum*. New York: Longman, 1990.

Richter, David H., ed. *The Critical Tradition: Classic Texts and Contemporary Trends.* New York: Bedford Books, St. Martin's Press, 1989. Plato to Wordsworth to Eliot to Langer on standard texts along with selections from contemporary critical schools: Marxist, psychological, formalism, structuralism and semiotics, feminist, and reader-response. An unwieldy set of texts but generally helpful.

Rosenblatt, Louise M. *Literature as Exploration.* 4th ed. New York: Modern Language Association, 1983.

Sample, Hazel. *Pitfalls for Readers of Fiction.* Chicago: National Council of Teachers of English, 1940. Too little known and appreciated, many insights into reading popular fiction.

Scholes, Robert. *Textual Power: Literary Theory and the Teaching of English.* New Haven, CT: Yale University Press, 1985.

Smagorinsky, Peter and Melissa E. Whiting. *How English Teachers Get Taught: Methods of Teaching the Methods Class.* Urbana, IL: National Council of Teachers of English, 1995.

Somers, Albert B. and Janet Evans Worthington. *Candles and Mirrors: Response Guides for Teaching Novels and Plays in Grades Six Through Twelve.* Littleton, CO: Libraries Unlimited, 1984.

Thomson, Jack. *Understanding Teenagers' Reading: Reading Processes and the Teaching of Literature.* Norwood, Australia: Australian Association for the Teaching of English, 1987.

Authors of Young Adult Literature

Bodart, Joni Richards. *100 World-Class Thin Books, or What to Read When Your Book Report Is Due Tomorrow,* Englewood, CO; Libraries Unlimited, 1993.

Cech, John, ed. *American Writers for Children, 1900-1960. Dictionary of Literary Biography.* Vol. 22. Detroit: Gale Research, 1983.

Chevalier, Tracy. *Twentieth Century Children's Writers,* 3rd ed. New York: St. Martin's Press, 1989.

Commire, Anne, ed. *Something About the Author.* Detroit: Gale Research, 1971. A continuing series about authors and books.

Commire, Anne, ed. *Yesterday's Authors of Books for Children.* Detroit: Gale Research, 1977. Lives of authors who died before 1961.

de Montreville, Doris and Elizabeth D. Crawford, eds. *Fourth Book for Junior Authors and Illustrators.* New York: H.W. Wilson, 1978.

de Montreville, Doris and Donna Hill, eds. *Third Book of Junior Authors.* New York: H. W. Wilson, 1972.

Drew, Bernards A. *The 100 Most Popular Young Adult Authors: Biographical Sketches and Bibliographies.* Englewood, CO: Libraries Unlimited, 1996.

Estes, Glenn E., ed. *American Writers for Children Before 1900. Dictionary of Literary Biography.* Vol. 42. Detroit: Gale Research, 1985.

Estes, Glenn E., ed. *American Writers for Children Since 1960: Fiction. Dictionary of Literary Biography.* Vol. 52. Detroit: Gale Research, 1986.

Estes, Glenn E., ed. *American Writers for Children Since 1960: Poets, Illustrators, and Nonfiction Authors. Dictionary of Literary Biography.* Vol. 6l. Detroit: Gale Research, 1987.

Fuller, Muriel, ed. *More Junior Authors.* New York: H. W. Wilson, 1963.

Gallo, Donald R., ed. *Authors' Insights: Turning Teenagers Into Readers and Writers.* Portsmouth, NH: Boynton/Cook, Heinemann, 1992.

Gallo, Donald R., ed. *Speaking for Ourselves: Autobiographical Sketches by Notable Authors of Books for Young Adults.* Urbana, IL: National Council of Teachers of English, 1990. In this and a 1993 sequel, nearly 200 YA authors introduce themselves.

Haviland, Virginia, ed. *The Openhearted Audience: Ten Authors Talk About Writing for Children.* Washington, DC: Library of Congress, 1980.

Helbig, Alethea K. and Agnes Regan Perkins. *Dictionary of American Children's Fiction, 1859–1959.* Westport, CT: Greenwood, 1985.

Helbig, Alethea K. and Agnes Regan Perkins. *Dictionary of American Children's Fiction, 1960–1984.* Westport, CT: Greenwood, 1986.

Helbig, Alethea K. and Agnes Regan Perkins. *Dictionary of British Children's Fiction.* Westport, CT: Greenwood, 1989.

Hipple, Ted, ed. *Writers for Young Adults.* Three volumes. New York; Scribner, 1997, Volume 4, 2000.

Holtze, Sally Holmes, ed. *Fifth Book of Junior Authors and Illustrators.* New York: H. W. Wilson, 1987.

Holtze, Sally Holmes, ed. *Sixth Book of Junior Authors and Illustrators.* New York: H. W. Wilson, 1989.

Hopkins, Lee Bennett. *Pauses: Autobiographical Reflections of 101 Creators of Children's Books.* New York: HarperCollins, 1995.

Huffman, Miriam and Eva Samuels, eds. *Authors and Artists for Young Adults.* Detroit: Gale Research, 1989.

Jones, Cornelia and Olivia R. Way. *British Children's Authors: Interviews at Home.* Chicago: American Library Association, 1976.

Kirkpatrick, D. L., ed. *Twentieth-Century Children's Writers,* 3rd ed. New York: Macmillan, 1990.

Kunitz, Stanley J. and Howard Haycraft, eds. *The Junior Books of Authors,* 2nd ed. rev. New York: H. W. Wilson, 1951.

Pendergast, Tom and Sara Pendergast, eds. *The St. James Guide to Young Adult Writers.* Detroit: St. James, 1999.

Rees, David. *The Marble in the Water: Essays on Contemporary Writers of Fiction for Children and Young Adults.* Boston: Horn Book, 1980.

Rees, David. *Painted Desert, Green Shade: Essays on Contemporary Writers of Fiction for Children and Young Adults.* Boston: Horn Book, 1984.

Rees, David. *What Do Draculas Do? Essays on Contem-*

porary *Writers of Fiction for Children and Young Adults*. Metuchen, NJ: Scarecrow Press, 1990.

Roginski, Jim. *Behind the Covers: Interviews with Authors and Illustrators of Books for Children and Young Adults*. Littleton, CO: Libraries Unlimited, 1985.

Roginski, Jim. *Behind the Covers: Interviews with Authors and Illustrators of Books for Children and Young Adults*. Vol. 2. Littleton, CO: Libraries Unlimited, 1989.

Samuels, Barbara G. and C. Kylene Beers, eds. *Your Reading: An Annotated Booklist for Middle School and Junior High*. Urbana, IL: National Council of Teachers of English, 1996.

Sarkissian, Adele, ed. *Writers for Young Adults: Biographies Master Index*. Detroit: Gale Research, 1984.

Stover, Lois T. and Stephanie F. Zenker, eds. *Books for You: An Annotated Booklist for Senior High*. Urbana, IL: National Council of Teachers of English, 1997.

Townsend, John Rowe. *A Sense of Story: Essays on Contemporary Writers for Children*. Philadelphia: Lippincott, 1971.

Ward, Martha E. and Dorothy A. Marquardt, eds. *Authors of Books for Young People*, 3rd ed. Metuchen, NJ: Scarecrow Press, 1990.

Weiss, M. Jerry, ed. *From Writers to Students: The Pleasures and Pains of Writing*. Newark, DE: International Reading Association, 1979.

Wintle, Justin and Emma Fisher, eds. *The Pied Pipers: Interviews with the Influential Creators of Children's Literature*. New York: Paddington Press, 1974.

Books of Readings About Young Adult Literature

Broderick, Dorothy M., ed. *The VOYA Reader*. Metuchen, NJ: Scarecrow Press, 1990. Articles from the *Voice of Youth Advocates*.

Egoff, Sheila, G. T. Stubbs, and L. F. Ashley, eds. *Only Connect: Readings in Children's Literature*, 2nd ed. New York: Oxford University Press, 1980.

Fox, Geoff, et al., eds. *Writers, Critics, and Children: Articles from Children's Literature in Education*. New York: Agathon Press, 1976.

Haviland, Virginia, ed. *Children and Literature: Views and Reviews*. Glenview, IL: Scott, Foresman, 1973.

Salway, Lance, ed. *A Peculiar Gift: Nineteenth Century Writings on Books for Children*. London: Kestrel, 1976.

Varlejs, Jana, ed. *Young Adult Literature in the Seventies: A Selection of Readings*. Metuchen, NJ: Scarecrow Press, 1978.

Articles in Periodicals

History and Young Adult Literature

Ashford, Richard K. "Tomboys and Saints: Girls' Stories of the Late Nineteenth Century." *School Library Journal* 26 (January 1980): 23–28.

Cantwell, Robert. "A Sneering Laugh with the Bases Loaded." *Sports Illustrated* 16 (April 23, 1962): 67–70, 73–76. Baseball novels for boys, particularly by Barbour and Heyliger.

Carlsen, G. Robert. "Forty Years with Books and Teen-Age Readers." *Arizona English Bulletin* 18 (April 1976): 1–5. From 1939 to 1976 in YA literature.

Crandall, John C. "Patriotism and Humanitarian Reform in Children's Literature, 1825–1860." *American Quarterly* 21 (Spring 1969): 3–22.

Edwards, Margaret A. "The Rise of Teen-Age Reading." *Saturday Review of Literature* 37 (November 13, 1954): 88–89, 95. The state of YA literature in the 1930s and 1940s and what led to it.

Evans, Walter. "The All-American Boys: A Study of Boys' Sports Fiction." *Journal of Popular Culture* 6 (Summer 1972): 104–121. Formulas underlying boys' school sports books, especially Barbour and series books.

"For It Was Indeed He." *Fortune* 9 (April 1934): 86–89, 193–194, 204, 206, 208–209. An important, influential, and biased article on Stratemeyer's Literary Syndicate.

Geller, Evelyn. "The Librarian as Censor." *Library Journal* 101 (June 1, 1976): 1255–1258. Social control as censorship in late nineteenth century library selection.

Geller, Evelyn. "Tom Sawyer, Tom Bailey, and the Bad-Boy Genre." *Wilson Library Bulletin* 52 (November 1976): 245–250.

Hutchinson, Margaret. "Fifty Years of Young Adult Reading, 1921–1971." *Top of the News* 29 (November 1973): 24–53. The subtitle reads, "A survey of the field (of) young adult reading for the past fifty years by examining articles indexed in *Library Literature* from its inception in 1921."

Kelly, R. Gordon. "American Children's Literature: An Historiographical Review." *American Literary Realism, 1870–1910* 6 (Spring 1973): 89–107.

Lapides, Linda F. "A Decade of Teen-Age Reading in Baltimore, 1960–1970." *Top of the News* 27 (Spring 1971): 278–291.

MacLeod, Anne. "For the Good of the Country: Cultural Values in American Juvenile Fiction, 1825–1860." *Children's Literature In Education* 5 (1976): 40–51.

Morrison, Lillian. "Fifty Years of 'Books for the Teen Age.'" *School Library Journal* 26 (December 1979): 44–50.

Radnor, Rebecca. "You're Being Paged Loudly in the Kitchen: Teen-Age Literature of the Forties and Fifties." *Journal of Popular Culture* 11 (Spring 1978): 789–799. Ways in which YA writers for girls influenced young women.

Repplier, Agnes. "Little Pharisees in Fiction." *Scribner's Magazine* 20 (December 1896): 718–724. The didactic and joyless goody-goody school of YA fiction in the last half of the nineteenth century.

Trensky, Anne. "The Bad Boy in Nineteenth-Century American Fiction." *Georgia Review* 27 (Winter 1973): 503–517.

Vostrovsky, Clara. "A Study of Children's Reading Tastes." *Pedagogical Seminary* 6 (December 1899): 523–535. A pioneer account of the kinds of books young people read.

Criticism and Young Adult Literature

Abrahamson, Jane. "Still Playing It Safe: Restricted Realism in Teen Novels." *School Library Journal* 22 (May 1976): 38–39.

Alexander, Lloyd. "Fools, Heroes, and Jackasses." *School Library Journal* 42 (March 1996): 114–116.

Aronson, Marc. "The Betrayal of Teenagers: How Book Awards Fail America's Most Important Readers." *School Library Journal* 42 (May 1996): 23–25.

Aronson, Marc. "Teenagers and Reading: A Generational Neurosis." *Journal of Youth Services in Libraries* 12 (Winter 1997): 29–30.

Brewbaker, James M. "'Are You There, Margaret? It's Me, God.' Religious Contexts in Recent Adolescent Fiction." *English Journal* 72 (September 1983): 82–86.

Broderick, Dorothy. "How to Write a Fiction Annotation." *Voice of Youth Advocates* 15 (February 1993): 333.

Broderick, Dorothy. "Reviewing Young Adult Books: The *VOYA* Editor Speaks Out." *Publishing Research Quarterly* 8 (Spring 1992): 34–40.

Bushman, John H. "Young Adult Literature in the Classroom—Or Is It?' *English Journal* 86 (March 1997): 35–40.

Campbell, Patty. "Perplexing Young Adult Books: A Retrospective." *Wilson Library Bulletin* 62 (April 1988): 20, 22, 24, 26. Campbell looks back on ten years of her YA column.

Campbell, Patty. "The Sand in the Oyster: YA and OP." *Horn Book Magazine* 73 (September/October 1997): 543–548.

Carlsen, G. Robert. "For Everything There Is a Season." *Top of the News* 21 (January 1965): 103–110. Stages in reading growth.

Carlsen, G. Robert. "The Interest Rate Is Rising." *English Journal* 59 (May 1970): 655–659.

Cart, Michael. "Of Risk and Revelation: The Current State of Young Adult Literature." *Journal of Youth Services in Libraries* 8 (Winter 1995): 151–164.

Carver, Nancy Lynn. "Stereotypes of American Indians in Adolescent Literature." *English Journal* 77 (September 1988): 25–32.

Chambers, Aidan. "All of a Tremble to See His Danger." *Top of the News* 42 (Summer 1986): 405–422. The 1986 May Hill Arbuthnot Lecture.

Chamber, Aidan. "The Difference of Literature: Writing Now for the Future of Young Readers." *Children's Literature in Education* 24 (March 1993): 1–18.

Chelton, Mary K. "Unrestricted Body Parts and Predictable Bliss." *Library Journal* 116 (July 1991): 44–49.

Early, Margaret J. "Stages of Growth in Literary Appreciation." *English Journal* 49 (March 1960): 161–167. A seminal article.

Edwards, Margaret A. "A Time When It's Best To Read and Let Read." *Wilson Library Bulletin* 35 (September 1960): 43–47. Myths of buying books for young adults demolished.

Endicott, Alba. "Females Also Come of Age." *English Journal* 81 (April 1992): 42–47.

Engdahl, Sylvia. "Do Teenage Novels Fill a Need?" *English Journal* 64 (February 1975): 48–52.

Evans, Dilys. "The YA Cover Story." *Publishers Weekly* 232 (July 24, 1987): 112–115. Differences between hardcover and paperback covers on YA books.

Evans, W. D. Emrys. "The Welsh *Mabinogion*: Tellings and Retellings." *Children's Literature in Education* 9 (Spring 1978): 17–33.

Fox, Paula. "On Language." *School Library Journal* 41 (March 1995): 122–126.

Freedman, Russell. "Bring 'em Back Alive: Writing History and Biography for Young People." *School Library Journal* 40 (March 1994): 139–141.

Gale, David. "The Business of Books." *School Library Journal* 42 (July 1996): 18–21. How publishers take a YA manuscript and make it into a book.

Garfield, Leon. "Historical Fiction for Our Global Times." *Horn Book Magazine* 64 (November/December 1988): 736–742.

Gauch, Patricia. "'Good Stuff' in Adolescent Fiction." *Top of the News* 40 (Winter 1984): 125–129.

Gebhard, Ann O. "The Emerging Self: Young-Adult and Class Novels of The Black Experience." *English Journal* 82 (September 1993): 50–54.

Green, Samuel S. "Sensational Fiction in Public Libraries." *Library Journal* 4 (September–October 1879): 345–355. Extraordinarily forward-looking intelligent comments about young adults and their books. The entire issue is worth reading, particularly papers by T. W. Higginson (pp. 357–359), William Atkinson (pp. 359–362), and Mellen Chamberlain (pp. 362–366).

Greenlee, Edwin D. "Recommended Adolescent Literature: Avoiding Those Hidden 'Secrets.'" *English Journal* 81 (April 1992): 23–24. See also responses to Greenlee, same issue, pp. 25–30.

Hamilton, Virginia. "Everything of Value: Moral Realism in the Literature of Children." *Journal of Youth Services in Libraries* 6 (Summer 1993): 363–377.

Hanckel, Frances and John Cunningham. "Can Young Gays Find Happiness in YA Books?" *Wilson Library Bulletin* 50 (March 1976): 528–534.

Head, Patricia. "Robert Cormier and the Postmodernist Possibilities of Young Adult Fiction." *Children's Literature Association Quarterly* 21 (Spring 1996): 28–33.

Hentoff, Nat. "Fiction for Teen-Agers." *Wilson Library Bulletin* 43 (November 1968): 261–264. The shortcomings of YA fiction.

Hentoff, Nat. "Tell It as It Is." *New York Times Book Review*, May 7, 1967, p. 3, 51.

Hinton, Susan. "Teen-Agers Are for Real." *New York Times Book Review,* August 27, 1967, pp. 26–29. Brief and excellent.

Hipps, G. Melvin. "Adolescent Literature: Once More to the Defense." *Virginia English Bulletin* 23 (Spring 1973): 44–50. Nearly thirty years old and still one of the best rationales for adolescent literature.

Hollindale, Peter. "The Adolescent Novel of Ideas." *Children's Literature in Education* 26 (March 1995): 83–95.

Hunt, Caroline. "Young Adult Literature Evades the Theorists." *Children's Literature Association Quarterly* 21 (Spring 1996): 4–11.

Huntwork, Mary M. "Why Girls Flock to Sweet Valley High." *School Library Journal* 36 (March 1990): 137–140.

"Is Adolescent Literature Worth Studying?" *Connecticut English Journal* 10 (Fall 1978). Two opposing positions—Robert P. Scaramella, "Con: At the Risk of Seeming Stuffy," pp. 57–58; Robert C. Small, Jr. "Pro: Means and Ends," pp. 59–63.

Janeczko, Paul B. "Seven Myths About Adolescent Literature." *Arizona English Bulletin* 18 (April 1976): 11–12.

Kaye, Marilyn. "In Defense of Formula Fiction: or, They Don't Write Schlock the Way They Used to." *Top of the News* 37 (Fall 1980): 87–90.

Kraus, W. Keith. "Cinderella in Trouble: Still Dreaming and Losing." *School Library Journal* 21 (January 1975): 18–22. Pregnancy in YA novels from Felsen's *Two and the Town* (1952) to Neufeld's *For All the Wrong Reasons* (1973).

Kraus, W. Keith. "From Steppin' Stebbins to Soul Brothers: Racial Strife in Adolescent Literature." *Arizona English Bulletin* 18 (April 1976): 154–160.

LeMieux, A. C. "The Problem Novel in a Conservative Age." *ALAN Review* 25 (Spring 1998): 4–6.

Louie, Belinda and Douglas Louie. "Empowerment Through Young Adult Literature." *English Journal* 81 (April 1992): 53–56.

Martinec, Barbara. "Popular—But Not Just a Part of the Crowd: Implications of Formula Fiction for Teenagers." *English Journal* 60 (March 1971): 339–344. Formulaic elements in six YA novelists.

Matthews, Dorothy. "An Adolescent's Glimpse of the Faces of Eve: A Study of the Images of Women in Selected Popular Junior Novels." *Illinois English Bulletin* 60 (May 1973): 1–14.

Matthews, Dorothy. "Writing About Adolescent Literature: Current Approaches and Future Directions." *Arizona English Bulletin* 18 (April 1976): 216–219.

McDowell, Myles. "Fiction for Children and Adults: Some Essential Differences." *Children's Literature in Education* 4 (March 1973): 48–63.

Meek, Margaret. "Prologomena for a Study of Children's Literature, or Guess What's in My Head" in Michael Benton, ed., *Approaches to Research in Children's Literature*, Southhampton: University of Southhampton, 1980, pp. 29–39.

Meltzer, Milton. "Where Do All the Prizes Go? The Case for Nonfiction." *Horn Book Magazine* 52 (February 1976): 17–23.

Merla, Patrick. " 'What Is Real?' Asked the Rabbit One Day." *Saturday Review* 55 (November 4, 1972): 43–49. The rise of YA realism and adult fantasy, twenty years old and still valid.

Mertz, Maia Pank and David A. England. "The Legitimacy of American Adolescent Fiction." *School Library Journal* 30 (October 1983): 119–123.

Nicholson, George M. "The Young Adult Novel History and Development." *CBC Features* 47 (Fall–Winter 1994). While not the easiest article to find, it's worth the search. An adaptation was printed in the fifth edition of *Literature for Today's Young Adults,* 1997, pp. 8–9.

Peck, Richard. "Huck Finns of Both Sexes: Protagonists and Peer Leaders in Young-Adult Books." *Horn Book Magazine* 69 (September/October 1993): 554–558.

Peck, Richard. "In the Country of Teenage Fiction." *American Libraries* 4 (April 1973): 204–207.

Peck, Richard. "Some Thoughts on Adolescent Literature." *News from ALAN* 3 (September–October 1975): 4–7.

Peck, Richard. "Young Adult Books." *Horn Book Magazine* 62 (September/October 1986): 618–621.

Peck, Richard and Patsy H. Perritt. "British Publishers Enter the Young Adult Age." *Journal of Youth Services in Libraries* 1 (Spring 1988): 292–304. Useful survey of British YA publishers.

Pierce, Tamora. "Fantasy: Why Kids Read It, Why Kids Need It." *School Library Journal* 39 (October 1993): 50–51.

Poe, Elizabeth Ann, Barbara G. Samuels, and Betty Carter. "Twenty-Five Years of Research in Young Adult Literature: Past Perspectives and Future Directives." *Journal of Youth Services In Libraries* 28 (November 1981): 25–28.

Pollack, Pamela D. "The Business of Popularity: The Surge of Teenage Paperbacks." *School Library Journal* 28 (November 1981): 25–28.

Popkin, Zelda F. "The Finer Things in Life." *Harpers* 164 (April 1932): 602–611. Contrasts between what young adults like to read and what parents and other adults want kids to read.

Probst, Robert. "Reader Response Theory and the Problem of Meaning." *Publishing Research Quarterly* 8 (Spring 1992): 64–73.

Root, Sheldon L. "The New Realism—Some Personal Reflections." *Language Arts* 54 (January 1977): 19–24.

Ross, Catherine Sheldrick. "Young Adult Realism: Conventions, Narrators, and Readers." *Library Quarterly* 55 (April 1985): 174–191.

Silver, Linda R. "Criticism, Reviewing, and the Library Review Media." *Top of the News* 35 (Winter 1979): 123–130. The entire issue on reviewing YA books is fine, particularly "What Makes a Good Review? Ten Experts Speak" (pp. 146–152) and Patty Campbell's "Only Puddings Like the Kiss of Death: Reviewing the YA Book" (pp. 161–162).

Small, Robert. "The Literary Value of the Young Adult Novel." *Journal of Youth Services in Libraries* 5 (Spring 1992): 277–285.

Spencer, Pam. "Winners in Their Own Right." *School Library Journal* 36 (July 1990): 23–27.

Sutton, Roger. "Forever Yours: An Interview with Judy Blume." *School Library Journal* 42 (June 1996): 24–27.

Sutton, Roger. "The Critical Myth: Realistic YA Novels." *School Library Journal* 29 (November 1982): 33–35.

Townsend, John Rowe. "Didacticism in Modern Dress." *Horn Book Magazine* 43 (April 1967): 159–164. Townsend argues that nineteenth century didacticism is remarkably like didacticism in modern YA novels.

Townsend, John Rowe. "Standards of Criticism for Children's Literature." *Top of the News* 27 (June 1971): 373–387.

Unsworth, Robert. "Holden Caulfield, Where Are You?" *School Library Journal* 23 (January 1977): 40–41. A plea for more books about males by males.

Wigutoff, Sharon. "Junior Fiction: A Feminist Critique." *The Lion and the Unicorn* 5 (1981): 4–18.

Wilson, David E. "The Open Library: YA Books for Gay Teens." *English Journal* 73 (November 1984): 60–63.

Using Young Adult Literature in Classrooms and Libraries

Abrahamson, Dick and Eleanor Tyson. "What Every English Teacher Should Know about Free Reading." *ALAN Review* 14 (Fall 1986): 54–58, 69.

Broderick, Dorothy M. "Serving Young Adults: Why We Do What We Do." *Voice of Youth Advocates* 12 (October 1989): 203–206.

Chelton, Mary K. "Booktalking: You Can Do It." *School Library Journal* 22 (April 1976): 39–43. Practical and fun to read and do.

Greenlee, Edwin D. "Recommended Adolescent Literature: Avoiding Those Hidden 'Secrets.'" *English Journal* 81 (April 1992): 23–24. Responses to Greenlee are in the same issue, pp. 25–30.

Hopkins, Dianne McAfee. "Challenges to Materials in Secondary School Library Media Centers: Results of a National Study." *Journal of Youth Services in Libraries* 4 (Winter 1991): 131–140.

Janeczko, Paul B. "Seven Myths About Teaching Poetry, or, How I Stopped Chasing Foul Balls." *ALAN Review* 14 (Spring 1987): 13–16.

Johannessen, Larry. "Young Adult Literature and the Vietnam War." *English Journal* 82 (September 1993): 43–49.

Lesesne, Teri S. "Developing Lifetime Readers: Suggestions from Fifty Years of Research." *English Journal* 80 (October 1991): 61–64.

McGee, Tim. "The Adolescent Novel in AP English: A Response to Patricia Spencer." *English Journal* 81 (April 1992): 57–58.

Mearns, Hughes. "Bo Peep, Old Woman, and Slow Mandy: Being Three Theories of Reading." *New Republic* 48 (November 10, 1926): 344–346.

Nelms, Ben F. "Reading for Pleasure in Junior High School." *English Journal* 55 (September 1966): 676–681.

Peck, Richard. "Ten Questions to Ask about a Novel." *ALAN Newsletter* 5 (Spring 1978): 1.

Probst, Robert E. "Adolescent Literature and the English Curriculum." *English Journal* 76 (March 1987): 26–30.

Probst, Robert E. "Mom, Wolfgang, and Me: Adolescent Literature, Critical Theory, and the English Classroom." *English Journal* 75 (October 1986): 33–39.

Probst, Robert E. "Three Relationships in the Teaching of Literature." *English Journal* 75 (January 1986): 60–68.

Rakow, Susan R. "Young-Adult Literature for Honors Students." *English Journal* 80 (January 1991): 48–51.

Robertson, Sandra L. "Text Rendering: Beginning Literary Response." *English Journal* 79 (January 1990): 80–84.

Scharf, Peter. "Moral Development and Literature for Adolescents." *Top of the News* 33 (Winter 1977): 131–136. Lawrence Kohlberg's six stages of moral judgment applied to YA books.

Scoggin, Margaret C. "Do Young People Want Books?" *Wilson Bulletin For Librarians* 11 (September 1936): 17–20, 24.

Schontz, Marilyn Louise. "Selected Research Related to Children's and Young Adult Services in Public Libraries." *Top of the News* 38 (Winter 1982): 125–142. An excellent list of sources.

Small, Robert C., Jr. "The Junior Novel and the Art of Literature." *English Journal* 66 (October 1977): 56–59.

Small, Robert C., Jr. "Teaching the Junior Novel." *English Journal* 61 (February 1972): 222–229.

Stotsky, Sandra. "Is the Holocaust the Chief Contribution of the Jewish People to World Civilization and History? A Survey of Leading Literature Anthologies and Reading Instructional Textbooks." *English Journal* 85 (February 1996): 52–59.

Stover, Lois T. "What's New in Young Adult Literature for High School Students." *English Journal* 86 (March 1997): 55–62.

Thurber, Samuel. "An Address to Teachers of English." *Education* 18 (May 1898): 515–526. The best writer of his time, and one of the best English teachers of any time, on getting young people excited about literature.

Tuccillo, Diane P. "Leading Them to Books—for Life." *Publishing Research Quarterly* 8 (Spring 1992): 14–22.

Vogel, Mark and Anna Creadick. "Family Values and the New Adolescent Novel." *English Journal* 82 (September 1993): 37–42.

Vogel, Mark and Don Zancanella. "The Story World of Adolescents in *and* out of the Classroom." *English Journal* 80 (October 1991): 54–60.

A Brief Bibliography on Films Generally and on Transformations of Print into Film

Burmester, David. "Mainstreaming Media: 101 Ways to Use Media in the English Classroom." *English Journal* 72 (February 1983): 109–111. Practical suggestions on using film and other media in class.

Costanzo, William V. *Reading the Movies: Twelve Great Films and How to Teach Them.* Urbana, IL: National Council of Teachers of English, 1992. Good throughout, but particularly good on copyright.

Gilmore, Hugh. "What Film Teaching Is Not." *Media and Methods* 7 (September 1970): 41. Succinct and still accurate.

Johnson, Ron and Jan Bone. *Understanding the Film.* Skokie, IL: National Textbook, 1976.

Knight, Arthur. *The Liveliest Art: A Panoramic History of the Movies.* New York: Macmillan, 1957. The easiest place to begin understanding the history of movies.

Kuhns, William. *Movies in America.* Dayton, OH: Pflaum, 1972.

Langman, Larry. *Cinema and the School.* Dayton, OH: Pflaum, 1976.

Maltin, Leonard. *2000 Movie and Video Guide.* Signet annually. Ubiquitous and always helpful, Maltin's 1641-page paperback is loaded with all kinds of information, and the list of mail order sources early in the book is the best of its kind. It's also a great browsing book.

Maynard, Richard. *The Celluloid Curriculum: How to Use Movies in the Classroom.* New York: Hayden, 1971.

Murch, Walter. "Restoring the Touch of Genius to a Classic." *New York Times* ("Art and Leisure" section), September 9, 1999, pp. 1, 16–17.

Murray, Edward. *Ten Film Classics: A Re-Viewing.* New York: Ungar, 1995.

Ross, Lillian. *Picture.* New York: Rinehart, 1952. The making of John Huston's *The Red Badge of Courage.*

Sarris, Andrew. *"You Ain't Heard Nothin' Yet"; The American Talking Film.* New York: Oxford University Press, 1998.

Selby, Stuart Alan. *The Study of Film as an Art Form in American Secondary Schools.* New York: Arno, 1978. First published in 1963.

Street, Douglas, ed. *Children's Novels and the Movies.* New York: Unger, 1983.

Teasler, Alan B. and Ann Wilder. *Reel Conversations: Reading Films with Young Adults.* Portsmouth, NH: Boynton/Cook, 1996.

Wallace, Amy. "How Does the Panel That Judges U.S. Films Rate?" *Los Angeles Times,* July 18, 1999, pp. A–1, 28–30. Valuable information on what kind of people are on the rating board and how they go about determining ratings.

Transforming Print into Film

Bluestone, George. *Novels into Film.* Baltimore: Johns Hopkins University Press, 1957. The pioneer study.

Boyum, Joy Gould. *Double Exposure: Fiction into Film.* New York: Universe, 1985.

Butler, Teri Payne. "Books to Film." *Horn Book Magazine* 71 (May/June 1995): 305–313.

Culkin, John. "4 Voyages of the Caine." *Media and Methods* 3 (October 1966): 21–28. One of the great early discussions books into print—Herman Wouk's novel, *The Caine Mutiny* (1951); Wouk's play, *The Caine Mutiny Court* (1954); the movie, *The Caine Mutiny* (1954); and The TV play, *The Caine Mutiny Court Martial* (1955).

Giddings, Robert, Keith Selby, and Chris Wensley. *Screening the Novel: The Theory and Practice of Literary Dramatization.* Barnstable, England: Macmillan, 1990.

Lupack, Barbara, ed. *Vision/Re-Vision: Adapting Contemporary American Fiction by Women to Film.* Bowling Green: OH: Bowling Green State University Popular Press, 1996.

Marlin, Janet. "If It's in the Book, It Doesn't Mean It's in the Movie." *New York Times,* February 28, 1992; p. B-1.

McDougal, Stuart Y. *Made into Movies: From Literature to Film.* New York: Holt, Rinehart, and Winston, 1985.

McFarlane, Brian. *Novel to Film: An Introduction to the Theory of Adaptation.* Oxford: Clarendon Press, 1996.

Suhor, Charles. "Film/Literature Comparison." *Media and Methods* 12 (December 1975): 56–59.

ACKNOWLEDGMENTS

(p. 1) Jacket cover from *Holes* by Louis Sachar, © 1998, reprinted by permission of Farrar, Straus & Giroux.

(p. 1) Jacket cover from *Missing Angel Juan* by Francesca Lia Block, © 1993, reprinted by permission of HarperCollins.

(p. 1) Jacket cover from *Buried Onions* by Gary Soto, © 1997, reprinted by permission of Harcourt Brace & Company.

(p. 1) Jacket cover from *Dancing on the Edge* by Han Nolan, © 1997, reprinted by permission of Harcourt Brace & Company.

(p. 4) Photo taken by A. P. Nilsen, reprinted courtesy of Mesa, Arizona, Public Library.

(p. 9) Photo courtesy of Will Weaver.

(p. 15) Jacket cover from *The Abracadabra Kid: A Writer's Life* by Sid Fleischman, © 1996, reprinted by permission of Greenwillow Books.

(p. 15) Jacket cover from *Me Me Me Me Me: Not a Novel* by M. E. Kerr, © 1983, reprinted by permission of HarperCollins.

(p. 28) Photo courtesy of Anne Fine.

(p. 35) Photo taken by A. P. Nilsen, reprinted courtesy of Jim Wickman.

(p. 39) Photo courtesy of Robert Lipsyte.

(p. 44) Photo courtesy of Karen Hesse.

(p. 48) Jacket cover from *Ella Enchanted* by Gail Carson Levine, © 1997, reprinted by permission of HarperCollins.

(p. 48) Jacket cover from *Othello: A Novel* by Julius Lester, © 1995, reprinted by permission of Scholastic.

(p. 57) Photo courtesy of Arizona Historical Foundation.

(p. 67) Photo courtesy of Gary Soto.

(p. 84) Jacket cover from *What Are You? Voices of Mixed-Race Young People* by Pearl Fuyo Gaskins, © 1999, reprinted by permission of Henry Holt.

(p. 84) Jacket cover from *Quiet Storm: Voices of Young Black Poets* selected by Lydia Omolola Okutoro, © 1999, reprinted by permission of Hyperion.

(p. 86) Jacket cover from *P. S. Longer Letter Later* by Paula Danziger and Ann M. Martin, © 1998, reprinted by permission of Scholastic.

(p. 86) Jacket cover from *Monster* by Walter Dean Myers, © 1999, reprinted by permission of Scholastic.

(p. 94) Photo taken by Brian Nolan, reprinted courtesy of Han Nolan.

(p. 100) Photo courtesy of Lois Duncan.

(p. 111) Jacket cover from *Smack* by Melvin Burgess, © 1996, reprinted by permission of Avon.

(p. 111) Jacket cover from *War and the Pity of War* ed. by Neil Philip, © 1998, reprinted by permission of Clarion.

(p. 111) Jacket cover from *Shadow of the Red Moon* by Walter Dean Myers, © 1995, reprinted by permission of Scholastic.

(p. 111) Jacket cover from *Name Me Nobody* by Lois-Ann Yamanaka, © 1999, reprinted by permission of Hyperion.

(p. 116) Photo taken by Beth Bergman, reprinted courtesy of Robert Cormier.

(p. 123) Jacket cover from *When She Hollers* by Cynthia Voigt, © 1994, reprinted by permission of Scholastic.

(p. 123) Jacket cover from *When She Was Good* by Norma Fox Mazer, © 1997, reprinted by permission of Scholastic.

(p. 128) Photo taken by Ray Warren, reprinted courtesy of Graham Salisbury.

(p. 132) Jacket cover from *Seedfolks* by Paul Fleischman, © 1997, reprinted by permission of HarperCollins.

(p. 135) Photo taken by A. P. Nilsen, reprinted courtesy of Jamalee Pace.

(p. 145) Jacket cover of *Max the Mighty* by Rodman Philbrick, © 1998, reprinted by permission of Scholastic.

(p. 149) Photo courtesy of Sharon Creech.

(p. 155) Jacket cover of *Winning Ways: A Photohistory of American Women in Sports* by Sue Macy, © 1996, reprinted by permission of Henry Holt and Co.

(p. 159) Photo taken by Dave Thomas, reprinted courtesy of Michael Cadnum.

(p. 179) Jacket cover of *The Pirate's Son* by Geraldine McCaughrean © 1996, reprinted by permission of Scholastic.

(p. 180) Photo taken by C. E. Mitchell, reprinted courtesy of Gary Paulsen.

(p. 193) Photo taken by A. P. Nilsen.

(p. 199) Photo courtesy of Joan Bauer.

(p. 203) Photo courtesy of Louis Sachar.

(p. 217) Photo courtesy of Phillip Pullman.

(p. 218) Jacket cover of *Harry Potter and the Sorcerer's Stone* by J. K. Rowling, © 1998, reprinted by permission of Scholastic.

(p. 223) Photo taken by A. P. Nilsen, reprinted courtesy of Mesa, Arizona Public Library.

(p. 241) Photo courtesy of Geraldine McCaughrean.

(p. 245) Jacket cover of *The Birchbark House* by Louise Erdrich, © 1999, reprinted by permission of Hyperion.

(p. 245) Jacket cover of *Nowhere to Call Home* by Cynthia DeFelice © 1999, reprinted by permission of Farrar, Straus & Giroux.

(p. 252) Jacket cover of *Red Scarf Girl* by Ji Li Jiang, © 1997, reprinted by permission of HarperCollins.

(p. 262) Jacket cover of *With Heroic Truth: The Life of Edward R. Murrow* by Norman H. Finkelstein, © 1997, reprinted by permission of Clarion.

(p. 262) Jacket cover of *Martha Graham: A Dancer's Life* by Russell Freedman, © 1998, reprinted by permission of Clarion.

(p. 263) Photo courtesy of Ellen Levine.

(p. 281) Photo taken by John Craig, reprinted courtesy of Walter Dean Myers.

(p. 286) Photo taken by A. P. Nilsen, reprinted courtesy of Britton Nilsen and Taryn Nilsen.

(p. 288) Jacket cover of *Art Attack: A Short Cultural History of the Avant-Garde* by Marc Aronson, © 1998, reprinted by permission of Clarion.

(p. 292) Photo courtesy of M. E. Kerr.

(p. 302) Jacket cover of *Step Lightly: Poems for the Journey* collected by Nancy Willard, © 1998, reprinted by permission of Harcourt Brace.

(p. 302) Jacket cover of *I, Too, Sing America: Three Centuries of African American Poetry* ed. by Catherine Clinton, © 1998, reprinted by permission from Houghton Mifflin.

(p. 302) Jacket cover of *Pierced by a Ray of Sun* sel. by Ruth Gordon, © 1995, reprinted by permission of HarperCollins.

(p. 332) Photo courtesy of Robin McKinley.

(p. 342) Photos taken by A. P. Nilsen.

(p. 343) Photos taken by A. P. Nilsen; Chess photo reprinted courtesy of Mesa, Arizona Public Library.

(p. 349) Photo courtesy of Ann M. Martin.

(p. 364) Photo courtesy of Tim Wynne-Jones.

(p. 369) Jacket cover of *Leaving Home: Short Stories Selected* by Hazel Rochman and Darlene Z. McCampbell, © 1997, reprinted by permission of HarperCollins.

(p. 369) Jacket cover of *Odder Than Ever* by Bruce Coville, © 1999, reprinted by permission of Harcourt Brace.

(p. 376) Photo courtesy of Jerry Spinelli.

(p. 377) Photo courtesy of Donna Jo Napoli.

(p. 394) Photo courtesy of John Marsden.

(p. 402) Photo courtesy of Angela Johnson.

(p. 411) Jacket cover of *Sensational Trials of the 20th Century* by Betsy Harvey Kraft, © 1998, reprinted by permission of Scholastic.

(p. 411) Jacket cover of *Tinker vs. Des Moines: Student Rights on Trial* by Doreen Rappaport, © 1993, reprinted by permission of HarperCollins.

(p. 416) Photo taken by Peter Simon, reprinted courtesy of Judy Blume.

SUBJECT INDEX

CRITICS AND COMMENTATORS INDEX

Author and Title Index

Helter Skelter: The True Story of the Manson Murders, 268
Hemingway, Ernest, 40, 324, 398
Hendry, Frances Mary, 242
Henry V (movie), 70
Henry, O., 382
Henry, Sue, 184
Hentoff, Nat, 72, 409, 428
Her Stories: African American Folktales, Fairy Tales, and True Tales, 329
Herbert, Frank, 226
Herbert, Janis, 261
Here Is Your War, 71
Here There Be Angels, 192
Here There Be Dragons, 192
Here There Be Ghosts, 192
Here There Be Unicorns, 192
Here There Be Witches, 192
Hernandez, Arturo, 326
A Hero Ain't Nothin' But a Sandwich, 23, 27, 29, 30, 131, 361, 409, 419
The Hero and the Crown, 333, 372
Heroes, 117, 351
Heron, Ann, 81
Herriman, George, 103
Herriot, James, 275, 289
Hersch, Patricia, 34
Herstory: Women Who Changed the World, 264
He's in the Signal Corps Now, 71
Hess, Elizabeth, 160
Hesse, Karen, 13, 29, 44, 299
Hewett, Lorri, 121
Hey Dollface, 140
Heyliger, William, 63
Hickman, Janet, 231, 242
Hide and Seek, 254
Hiding to Survive: Stories of Jewish Children Rescued from the Holocaust, 254, 255
The High King, 220
Highwater, Jamake, 132
Hilgartner, Beth, 242
Hillerman, Tony, 186
Hillesum, Etty, 255
Hilton, James, 214
Him She Loves?, 202
Hinton, S.E., 6, 10, 21, 22, 25, 26, 29, 31, 74, 80, 96, 97, 126, 130, 158, 322, 346, 360, 361, 374, 387, 398, 399, 409
Hiroshima: A Novella, 246
Hiroshima No Pika, 85
Hirschfelder, Arlene, 288
Hirschhorn, Joel, 178
Hise, Jesse, 380
History of Patriarchs, 45
The Hitchhiker's Guide to the Galaxy, 21, 26, 205, 228, 314

Hitler, 296
Hobbes, Thomas, 395
The Hobbit, or There and Back Again, 213
Hobbs, Will, 7, 40, 158, 180, 182
Hogan, William, 139
"Hogan's Alley," 103
Holes, 12, 27, 86, 201–207
Holiday House, 349
Holland, Isabelle, 23, 30, 74, 138, 139, 164
The Holocaust Lady, 256
Holt, Kimberly Willis, 12, 115
Holzol, Tom, 178
Home Before Dark, 22
"Home Improvement," 92, 93
Homecoming, 319, 361
Homeless Bird, 138
Homes, A. M., 127
Hoobler, Dorothy, 187, 237
Hoobler, Thomas, 187, 237
Hoop Dreams, 153
Hoopes, Ned E., 306
Hoops, 157
The Horsemen of the Plains, 63
Hot Rod, 65, 66, 68
Hotshot, 69
The Hound of the Baskervilles, 54
House of Stairs, 23, 30, 227
The House on Mango Street, 11, 20, 26, 328, 330
Houston, James D., 256
Houston, Jeanne Wakatsuki, 256
How Sex Works, 290
How TV Changed America's Mind, 284
How to Be Funny (manual), 196
How to Write Poetry, 380
Howard, Elizabeth, 231
Howe, Norma, 79, 165
Howell, William Dean, 231
Hubert Lee, or How a Child May Do Good, 45
Hughes, Dean, 165
Hughes, Langston, 81, 419
Hughes, Monica, 387
Humming Whispers, 114
The Hundred Days, 179
Hungry Mind, 364
Hunt, Irene, 244
The Hunted, 250
Hunter, Evan. *See* Ed McBain.
Hunter in the Dark, 387
Hunter, Mollie, 18, 31, 32
Hunter's Moon, 184
Hunting a Detroit Tiger, 184
Hustle: The Myth, Life, and Lies of Pete Rose, 153
Huxley, Aldous, 231, 385, 392, 403, 409

Hwang, David Henry, 306, 324
Hyde, Margaret O., 294

I

I Am Mordred, 220
I Am Somebody! A Biography of Jesse Jackson, 296
I Am the Cheese, 22, 83, 116, 117, 351, 361, 409
I Am the Darker Brother: An Anthology of Modern Poems by African Americans, 301
I Am Third, 257
I Am Writing a Poem About . . . A Game of Poetry, 380
I Feel a Little Jumpy Around You: A Book of Her Poems and His Poems Collected in Pairs, 301
I Had a Hammer: The Hank Aaron Story, 153
I Have a Dream: The Life and Words of Martin Luther King, Jr., 296
I Have Words to Spend: Reflections of a Small-Town Editor, 286
I Heard the Owl Call My Name, 165, 383
I Heard the Owl Call My Name (movie), 383
I Know What the Red Clay Looks Like: The Voice and Vision of Black Women Writers, 265
I Know What You Did Last Summer, 99, 100
I Know What You Did Last Summer (movie), 97, 98, 100, 384
I Know Why the Caged Bird Sings, 8, 131, 259, 275, 303, 408
I Love You, I Hate You, Get Lost: A Collection of Short Stories, 170
I Love You, Stupid!, 169
I Miss You, I Miss You, 138
I Never Meant to Tell You This, 114
I Never Promised You a Rose Garden, 145–146
I Never Sang for My Father, 126
I Never Saw Another Butterfly: Children's Drawings and Poems from Terezin Concentration Camp, 1941–1944, 255
I Remember Balanchine: Recollections of the Ballet Master by Those Who Knew Him, 261
I, Too, Sing America: Three Centuries of African American Poetry, 301
I Want to Grow Hair, I Want to Grow Up, I Want to Go to Boise: Children Surviving Cancer, 257
I Was There, 254
I Will Call it Georgie's Blues, 165